LIBERAL CRIMINAL THEORY

This book celebrates Andreas (Andrew) von Hirsch's pioneering contributions to liberal criminal theory. He is particularly noted for reinvigorating desert-based theories of punishment, for his development of principled normative constraints on the enactment of criminal laws, and for helping to bridge the gap between Anglo-American and German criminal law scholarship. Underpinning his work is a deep commitment to a liberal vision of the state. This collection brings together a distinguished group of international authors, who pay tribute to von Hirsch by engaging with topics on which he himself has focused. The essays range across sentencing theory, questions of criminalisation, and the relation between criminal law and the authority of the state. Together, they articulate and defend the ideal of a liberal criminal justice system, and present a fitting accolade to Andreas von Hirsch's scholarly life.

Liberal Criminal Theory

Essays for Andreas von Hirsch

Edited by
AP Simester
Antje du Bois-Pedain
and
Ulfrid Neumann

With translations by
Antje du Bois-Pedain

·H A R T·
PUBLISHING
OXFORD AND PORTLAND, OREGON
2014

Published in the United Kingdom by Hart Publishing Ltd
16C Worcester Place, Oxford, OX1 2JW
Telephone: +44 (0)1865 517530
Fax: +44 (0)1865 510710
E-mail: mail@hartpub.co.uk
Website: http://www.hartpub.co.uk

Published in North America (US and Canada) by
Hart Publishing
c/o International Specialized Book Services
920 NE 58th Avenue, Suite 300
Portland, OR 97213-3786
USA
Tel: +1 503 287 3093 or toll-free: (1) 800 944 6190
Fax: +1 503 280 8832
E-mail: orders@isbs.com
Website: http://www.isbs.com

British Library Cataloguing in Publication Data
Data Available

ISBN: 978-1-84946-514-4

Typeset by Hope Services, Abingdon
Printed and bound in Great Britain by
CPI Group (UK) Ltd, Croydon CR0 4YY

CONTENTS

* Translated by A du Bois-Pedain

LIST OF CONTRIBUTORS

Andrew Ashworth, Vinerian Professor of English Law Emeritus at the University of Oxford and Emeritus Fellow of All Souls College.

Antje du Bois-Pedain, University Senior Lecturer at the University of Cambridge and Fellow of Magdalene College.

Antony Duff, Professor Emeritus in Philosophy at the University of Stirling; Russell M and Elizabeth M Bennett Chair in Excellence at the University of Minnesota Law School.

James Edwards, CUF Lecturer at the University of Oxford and Tutorial Fellow of Worcester College.

Klaus Günther, Professor of Criminal Justice and Legal Theory and Co-Director of the 'Formation of Normative Orders' National Excellence Cluster, Goethe University, Frankfurt.

Winfried Hassemer, late former Vice-President of the German Constitutional Court; late Professor of Criminal Justice Emeritus, Goethe University, Frankfurt.

Tatjana Hörnle, Professor of Criminal Justice, Humboldt University, Berlin.

John Kleinig, Professor of Philosophy at the John Jay College of Criminal Justice and at the Graduate School and University Center, City University of New York; Professorial Fellow at the Centre for Applied Philosophy and Public Ethics, Charles Stewart University, Canberra.

Sandra Marshall, Professor Emeritus in Philosophy at the University of Stirling; Visiting Research Scholar at the University of Minnesota Law School.

Hannah Maslen, Post-doctoral Research Fellow in Ethics at the University of Oxford and Junior Research Fellow of New College.

Ulfrid Neumann, Professor of Criminal Law, Criminal Procedure, Legal Theory and Sociology of Law, Goethe University, Frankfurt.

Nina Peršak, Professor of Criminology and Sociology of Law, University of Ghent.

Paul Roberts, Professor of Criminal Jurisprudence, University of Nottingham; Adjunct Professor, University of New South Wales Faculty of Law.

Julian Roberts, Professor of Criminology at the University of Oxford and Supernumerary Fellow of Worcester College.

Claus Roxin, Professor of Criminal Justice Emeritus, Ludwig Maximilian University, Munich.

Bernd Schünemann, Professor of Criminal Justice and Legal Theory Emeritus, Ludwig Maximilian University, Munich.

Kurt Seelmann, Professor of Criminal Law and Legal Theory, Basel University.

Andrew Simester, Professor and Provost's Chair in Law, National University of Singapore; Honorary Professor, University of Uppsala; Honorary Research Fellow, University of Cambridge.

Michael Tonry, Professor of Law and Public Policy, University of Minnesota.

Wolfgang Wohlers, Professor of Criminal Law and Criminal Procedure, Zurich University.

Lucia Zedner, Professor of Criminal Justice at the University of Oxford and Fellow of Corpus Christi College; Conjoint Professor in the Law Faculty at the University of New South Wales.

EDITORS' INTRODUCTION

How can a liberal state justify the use of penal sanctions? What scope may its criminal laws have? When do such laws treat and respect legal subjects as citizens and as persons, and when do they not? Such questions have animated Andreas von Hirsch throughout his scholarly career. They are also the kinds of questions addressed in this *festschrift*, prepared for the occasion of Andreas's 80th birthday in celebration of him and his work.

The Honorand and his Work

Andreas von Hirsch was born in Zurich in 1934. He grew up in England and the United States of America, studying at Oxford and Harvard. Following on from his first professorial appointment at Rutgers University, he moved in 1994 to the University of Cambridge as Honorary Professor of Penal Theory and Penal Law, where he created the Centre for Penal Theory and Penal Ethics at the Institute of Criminology. In 2007 he founded the *Forschungsstelle für Strafrechtstheorie und Strafrechtsethik* at the Goethe University in Frankfurt – now his main academic home. Von Hirsch was awarded an honorary doctorate from the University of Uppsala in 1988, an LL.D. by the University of Cambridge in 1999, and an honorary professorship at the Goethe University in Frankfurt in 2008. Until 2008, he published most of his work under his anglicised name, 'Andrew von Hirsch'. Since then he has written under his given name, Andreas.

Today von Hirsch is one of the leading figures in penal theory, and perhaps the only scholar in this field to have effectively crossed the divide between common and civilian legal systems. Best known for his work on desert-based sentencing, his approach to proportionate sentencing has been influential within and outside the academy. Indeed, his academic career began with a political brief: to lead a publicly-funded study committee on incarceration chaired by a former US senator. It was in this context that von Hirsch first developed the main elements of his theory of just deserts, which he published in 1976 as *Doing Justice: The Choice of Punishments*. The book laid the foundation for much of his future, more detailed work on parole, proportionate sentencing, the sentencing of juveniles and similar themes. Its desert-oriented perspective gained support from liberal reformers and has influenced sentencing reforms in Finland, Sweden, England (in the early 1990s), Oregon and Minnesota.

Von Hirsch is rightly credited with moving desert-based theories of punishment out of classical retributivism and into a mainstream field that is attractive to political reformers interested in moderate sentencing outcomes. Just as importantly, his theoretical approach provides a counterpoint to the risks of rehabilitative over-zealousness present in much reformist thinking about punishment. From the very start, he proceeded from the liberal view that the state's exercise of power over the individual is neither justified nor unbounded by benevolent intent. Punishment's general justification and the modalities of its exercise are bound up with its public setting, with the citizen–state relationship. Punishment must respect the rights of those punished.

Neither has von Hirsch shied away from the hard work involved in making desert theory fit for practice. His 'micro-jurisprudence of sentence proportionality' addresses the questions of how to gauge the seriousness of different crimes in terms of their harmfulness and the offender's culpability, and of how to use proportionality as a determining rather than a merely limiting principle for the deserved measure of punishment. In works such as *Proportionate Sentencing: Exploring the Principles*[1] and 'Gauging criminal harm: A living standard analysis',[2] von Hirsch has put forward suggested solutions to both of these questions. His views have consequently been debated not just by legal theorists and philosophers but also by criminologists and those involved in formulating and applying sentencing legislation.

On the Continent and specifically in Germany, von Hirsch was first noticed for his explication of the general justification for punishment. For him, state punishment is a blaming institution, rooted in notions of responsibility, culpability and desert; yet it is also an exercise of state power that, like all such practices, must be shown to be rationally oriented toward the achievement of legitimate objectives of state governance. This way of thinking will not strike an Anglo-American philosopher as particularly revolutionary. In Germany, however, it drove a spear into a debate that had become ossified and trapped into classifying all theories of punishment as either 'absolute' (broadly, deontological) or 'relative' (broadly, purpose-oriented and mainly utilitarian). By defying classification under this scheme, von Hirsch's writings are credited with liberating the German discussion from those unhelpful and self-limiting strictures. Indirectly, they have opened German scholars up to rethinking their dominant theory of sentencing (the *Spielraumtheorie*), which allows the sentencing judge to give (within a broad range of 'not disproportionate' punishments) decisive weight to deterrent or rehabilitative purposes in sentencing. Von Hirsch's work on proportionate sentencing is increasingly influential in concretising the boundaries of legitimate sentencing discretion.

The project of legitimating punishment as a state practice has also taken von Hirsch deeper into the question of when the state may deploy the criminal law as a

---

[1] A von Hirsch and A Ashworth, *Proportionate Sentencing: Exploring the Principles* (Oxford, Oxford University Press, 2005).

[2] A von Hirsch and N Jareborg, 'Gauging Criminal Harm: A living standard analysis' (1991) 11 *Oxford Journal of Legal Studies* 1.

regulatory tool. A number of edited collections address questions of criminalisation,[3] as does his recent co-authored monograph on *Crimes, Harms and Wrongs: On the Principles of Criminalisation*.[4] Much of his work in this area builds upon the writings of Anglo-American philosophers such as Joel Feinberg and John Stuart Mill, but nuances it with insights from the civilian legal tradition. The work on criminalisation of offence, in particular, seems to us genuinely to bridge continental European and common law perspectives regarding what individuals owe to each other. Fundamentally and old-fashionedly liberal, von Hirsch also understood well continental ideas of community and solidarity.

This same bridging project is continued, here, by those who honour his work and explore liberal criminal theory across theoretical and jurisdictional divides. Part of our project in this volume is to continue the Anglo-American dialogue that Andreas has done so much to advance, both personally and through research published by the Cambridge and Frankfurt Centres. We are delighted that this volume contains, for the first time, conceptually sophisticated translations (and not mere transliterations) of original essays written especially for the occasion by many of the most eminent German criminal theorists. For monolingual Anglo-American thinkers, this *festschrift* offers an unprecedented insight into the thinking of leading German academics, an opportunity to access and understand the nature and presuppositions of a debate – about fundamentally similar issues – that is structured quite differently from its English-language counterpart. At the same time, German readers will note that there are relatively few essays: just 17; which by Anglo-American expectations is unusually numerous. The task of the English editor differs from that for a *festschrift* prepared in the German tradition. In striving to bring together friends whose individual contributions would speak, not only to Andreas von Hirsch's work, but also to each other (and thus hopefully come together as a coherent whole), we hope that this *festschrift* will constitute another step in the cross-jurisdictional exchange between penal theorists. It is in this spirit that we offer it to Andreas, in admiration and gratitude for the many contributions he has made to our own lives and thought.

---

[3] R Hefendehl, A von Hirsch and W Wohlers (eds), *Die Rechtsgutstheorie: Legitimationsbasis des Strafrechts oder dogmatisches Glasperlenspiel?* (Baden-Baden, Nomos, 2003); A von Hirsch, K Seelmann and W Wohlers (eds), *Mediating Principles: Begrenzungsprinzipien bei der Strafbegründung* (Baden-Baden, Nomos, 2006); A von Hirsch and AP Simester (eds), *Incivilities: Regulating Offensive Behaviour* (Oxford, Hart Publishing, 2006); A von Hirsch, U Neumann and K Seelmann (eds), *Paternalismus im Strafrecht: Die Kriminalisierung von selbstschädigendem Verhalten* (Baden-Baden, Nomos, 2010).

[4] AP Simester and A von Hirsch, *Crimes, Harms, and Wrongs: On the Principles of Criminalisation* (Oxford, Hart Publishing, 2011).

The *Festschrift* Collection

Punishment and prevention

A perennial problem for penal theorists, including Andreas, is the tension between censure and deterrence in the criminal law. As Andrew Ashworth and Lucia Zedner recognise, for example, proportionate sentences may quite commonly prove inadequate deterrents.[5] Drawing on some of von Hirsch's own meta-analyses of the available empirical evidence,[6] they conclude that 'while prevention is central to von Hirsch's justificatory account, its subordinate place as a prudential supplement, taken together with the parsimony constraint, may operate as a significant brake on its efficacy.' Yet, if we grant that the place of prevention within punishment is therefore limited, nonetheless Ashworth and Zedner observe that a fundamental duty lies upon the state to prevent harm and protect security. This duty is a more general one that is not specific to the criminal law, and which stretches beyond acts of state punishment in various ways that they explore.

But is the place of deterrence in punishment really so limited? Claus Roxin points out that justification of criminal punishment as a purely retributive device has nowadays been rejected in Germany;[7] although, as James Edwards and Andrew Simester note, this view still has some Anglo-American supporters.[8] Even there, however, few would argue that criminal punishment is an end in itself.[9] Morally loaded it may be, but the criminal law is *also* a regulatory tool, which offers prudential disincentives to offend. It does not merely utter verdicts of censure but expresses them in terms of harsh treatment.

Different approaches to the problem may be seen in this volume. For Ulfrid Neumann, this is a conceptual matter. Acknowledging that desert and deterrence cannot be reconciled as *justifications* of punishment,[10] he defends the concurrence of censure and hard treatment as *conceptual* components of the institution of punishment. Criminal punishments may thus be *legally* just,[11] but on this, institution-dependent view, 'it is impossible to provide an ultimate basis for the retributive

---

[5] A Ashworth and L Zedner, 'Punishment Paradigms and the Role of the Preventive State', this volume.

[6] A von Hirsch et al, *Criminal Deterrence and Sentence Severity: An Analysis of Recent Research* (Oxford, Hart Publishing, 1999); cited by Ashworth and Zedner, this volume, fn 59.

[7] C Roxin, 'Prevention, Censure and Responsibility: The Recent Debate on the Purposes of Punishment', this volume, section II.A.

[8] JR Edwards and AP Simester, 'Prevention with a Moral Voice', this volume, section I: discussing in particular the work of Michael Moore.

[9] But note Hörnle's quotation of Thorburn: 'legal moralism has become the new orthodoxy in English-language criminal law theory' – a diagnosis that should be opposed. See Hörnle, this volume, text at fn 29.

[10] U Neumann, 'The "Deserved" Punishment', this volume, section III.A: 'If, for the reasons set out above, retributive theories taken by themselves cannot justify punishment, then they cannot make *any* contribution to the justification of punishment – whether alone or in combination with other theories.'

[11] Ibid, section VI.C(iii).

response to conduct that violates central social norms'.[12] By contrast, Edwards and Simester agree that desert and deterrence cannot be reconciled as justifications of *punishment*, but argue that they can nonetheless be reconciled within the criminal law: criminalisation can be motivated by deterrence considerations, while the moral voice of the criminal law requires that punishment be imposed according to desert. This temporal separation, between the ex ante and ex post dimensions of the criminal law, creates room for a defence of punishment that is sympathetic to von Hirsch's account.

Roxin's response to the challenge of combining censure and prevention within punishment is, however, different again. For Roxin, censure limits the quantum of punishment, but taking account of instrumental aims depends on there being a secondary duty of *restoration* owed by wrongdoers:[13]

> [I]t is a general principle of not just the criminal law, but all law, that a person who brings about harm culpably is responsible for restoring the damage he has done. If someone disturbs the civil peace by committing a crime, he must take responsibility for re-stabilising the socio-legal order. Therefore he must, with a view to individual prevention, accept that a sanction is imposed on him to teach him a painful lesson.

Thus Roxin sees the need for preventive measures as being 'triggered by a criminal act';[14] the 'preventive' measures are thus responses. This contrasts strikingly with Edwards and Simester's vision, which sees the preventive measures as residing in the criminal law's ex ante *prohibitions*. In this respect, their account of the relationship between prevention and censure in criminal law has some (limited) resemblances to Feuerbach's notion of threat-based general prevention, taken up by Bernd Schünemann in his contribution to this volume;[15] although Edwards and Simester would surely take issue with Feuerbach's contention that being able to give a deontological justification for the *threat* of punishment also provides a full justification for inflicting the punishment so as to avoid unmasking the threat as an empty one. As Schünemann observes, making room for prevention in the manner contemplated by Feuerbach[16]

> changes the role of the culpability principle, which is transformed from a principle that justifies punishment, with a retributive conception of the criminal law (where it is a nec-essary and sufficient condition of just punishment), into a limiting principle in a preven-tive conception of criminal law (where it is an additional necessary condition).

Yet, if one does not abandon a prevention-based approach to punishment (say, in the way Edwards and Simester propose), how can the culpability principle fit within it? We have noted Neumann's argument that the culpability principle is implicit in the reactive nature of punishment. Von Hirsch's explanation is compat-ible with this view, but also more complex. For von Hirsch, a prevention-based

[12] Ibid, 84.
[13] Roxin, this volume, 36f.
[14] Ibid, text at fn 77.
[15] Schünemann, 'Can Punishment Be Just?', this volume, text at fns 14–20.
[16] Ibid, text at fn 20.

penal system engages with citizens as moral agents by (ex ante) through its penal laws offering citizens additional prudential reasons for desisting from conduct properly criminalised as wrong, and by (ex post) imposing a censuring response to past criminal wrongdoing – a response that presupposes a criminal act that was in itself an expression of the moral agency of the citizen, of his culpable action and choice. It is because the penal sanction responds to the moral agency of citizens as a censuring response that it can only be imposed on culpable wrongdoers.

Punishment, desert and communication

One could say, then, that on Andreas's view the culpability principle is implicit in a practice of censure, and that a practice of censure is implicit in the recognition of persons as moral agents. This, as Kurt Seelmann observes, suggests that 'punishment, compared to alternatives such as culpability-independent measures of re-education or incapacitation, contains a positive positioning of some sort towards the offender'[17] – an interesting parallel to the notion in German idealist philosophy that punishment 'honours the offender'. Von Hirsch's argument, which takes up Peter Strawson's conception of a reactive attitude by which we address another person as a fellow participant in the moral practices of a community, differs from German idealist thought in that those writers – especially Hegel – see punishment as an act that necessarily manifests recognition of the moral personality of the offender, in that it treats the criminal as someone who, through his action as a rational being, has set up the law which may therefore be applied to him as a matter of *his* right.[18] Both views, however, share common roots in the link first made by Locke between the concept of a person and the imputation of responsibility to human agents. In Seelmann's words, 'Imputation of responsibility signifies, for Locke, the identity and continuity of the person; for Hegel, the rationality of the person; and, for Strawson, the inclusion of the person in a moral community.'[19]

Seelmann stresses that, to the extent that punishment is justified as a reaction to crime that takes the offender seriously as a moral agent, the Hegelian and the Strawsonian understandings of the connection between punishment and recognition of the offender's personhood both allow for an alternative response to censure: a 'certain form of forgiveness', granted in the awareness of one's own fallibility, that takes the offender just as seriously as any censuring imputation of responsibility would do. Yet on von Hirsch's view, we may have reason to insist that this recognition should, within the context of a criminal justice system, be accorded through a *censuring response*. This is so because the state's response to criminal wrongdoing must be such that it *also* serves a supplementary, preventive function – a function

---

[17] K Seelmann, 'Does Punishment Honour the Offender?', this volume, text at fn 3.

[18] Klaus Günther suggests a way in which communicative theory can help us make sense of this notion of self-legislation – of implicit normative assertions contained in law-breaking action – upon which Hegel and other Idealist writers rely. See K Günther, 'Criminal Law, Crime and Punishment as Communication', this volume, text at fns 13–20, 41.

[19] Seelmann, this volume, 118–19.

that is bound up with, and runs through, censure. As Anthony Bottoms has observed, von Hirsch's account of human nature requires an account of punishment in which 'censure and prevention are co-equal and interactive.'[20] In von Hirsch's own words:[21]

> If the sanction conveys blame, it may also supply the prudential disincentive [that] an agent who has accepted the sanction's message that he ought not to offend, and who recognizes his susceptibility to temptation, could favour the existence of.

Penal hard treatment, on von Hirsch's view, cannot be split off from the censuring imputation of responsibility because 'it is the penal deprivation, not just the defendant's conviction, that expresses the censure as well as serving as the prudential disincentive.'[22] This interlinking of censuring and preventive functions places von Hirsch's justification for penal sanctions on firmer ground than positions which strive to justify penal hard treatment only through an argument that penal hardship is needed to get the communicative message of disapprobation of the criminal conduct across. In this way, and despite his explication of the point of censure in terms of Strawsonian reactive attitudes, von Hirsch's theory avoids the problems of a purely communicative justification of punishment. Pure communicative theories, as Klaus Günther's contribution illustrates,[23] face great difficulties in generating any justification for penal hard treatment. One challenge, according to Günther, is that certain types of sanctions – particularly, imprisonment – typically restrict the communicative opportunities of the incarcerated individual; which generates a 'paradox', in that it turns punishment into 'a communicative action of non-communication'.[24] Beyond that, moreover, all practices of hard treatment potentially become unnecessary if 'expressing the moral message of censure' constitutes 'a kind of action in itself, and as such, itself a *treatment* of the offender ... embedded in a communicative relationship among offender, victim and society';[25] such that we may be able to 'think of the history of punishment as a development where hard treatment becomes more and more unnecessary for the conveyance of the message.'[26]

Von Hirsch's understanding of the penal sanction, as an expression of censure that also provides a prudential disincentive to crime, can however ground a defence of proportionate sentencing without having to maintain that censure can *only* be communicated through hard treatment. Rather, the argument is that, in so far as the preventive function of penal sanctions is bound up with their nature as censuring responses, the censuring dimension imposes its own logic – in that the severity

[20] AE Bottoms, 'Five Puzzles in von Hirsch's Theory of Punishment' in A Ashworth and M Wasik (eds), *Fundamentals of Sentencing Theory* (Oxford, Oxford University Press, 1998) 82, 89.
[21] A von Hirsch, *Censure and Sanctions* (Oxford, Oxford University Press, 1993) 13.
[22] A von Hirsch and A Ashworth, *Proportionate Sentencing: Exploring the Principles* (Oxford, Oxford University Press, 2005) 26–27.
[23] Günther, this volume.
[24] Ibid, 134.
[25] Ibid, 135.
[26] Ibid, 136.

of the sanction is taken to, and therefore should, reflect the gravity of the crime. Censure, in von Hirsch's theory, thus grounds not only the culpability principle, but also the requirement that punishment be proportionate to the seriousness of the offending behaviour.

But what are the criteria by which we can determine the seriousness of any particular instance of criminal offending? Julian Roberts and Hannah Maslen explore this question further in their discussion of the proper weight to be given, within a desert-theoretical framework, to commendable post-offending conduct of the perpetrator. If harm and culpability are the determinants of a proportionate sentence, can we make room for commendable behaviour that occurs after the crime has been completed? In Roberts and Maslen's account, there is no need for desert theorists to 'construct a "firewall" between the offender's conduct before and during the crime, and his behaviour thereafter.'[27] Provided one restricts mitigation to post-offence conduct that relates to the crime, the offender's efforts may (retrospectively) 'mitigate the harm of the crime, reduce or contextualise the culpability of the offender for the offence, or facilitate the state response to the crime.'[28] As such, Roberts and Maslen argue, these responses to the crime legitimately register as mitigating factors in calculating the deserved sentence. Their argument to this effect is two-pronged. First, they say, determinations of offence-seriousness can legitimately operate within an extended temporal frame, such that much post-offence conduct quite straightforwardly reduces harm or suggests reduced levels of culpability. Secondly, on an expansive account, it may be possible to argue that the post-offence conduct which could not be considered as 'mitigating' on their narrower argument could still give rise to normative grounds for mitigation of punishment. To the extent that[29]

> [p]enal censure communicates a message about the wrongfulness of the offence, while the hard treatment authorised by the sentence both reinforces that message and provides the prudential disincentive to re-offend ... [t]he general level of censure applicable to all offenders – including the impenitent – is unnecessary in the case of the penitent.

Their expansive argument also draws on the communicative justification of punishment:[30]

> Communication gains greater legitimacy when it is tailored to its recipient. If it is not also listening, the state's sentencing process becomes an asymmetric exercise in penal communication: the state broadcasts its censure and the offender passively absorbs the consequent punishment.

This may be an indication that the expansive argument sits less well with von Hirsch's approach to penal desert than the narrower case for an extended time-frame for the determination of offence-seriousness.

---

[27] J Roberts and H Maslen, 'After the Crime: Post-Offence Conduct and Penal Censure', text at fn 12.
[28] Ibid, text at fn 30.
[29] Ibid, text at fn 49.
[30] Ibid, text at fn 52.

Michael Tonry's contribution, by contrast, looks at pre-offence factors. He reminds us that desert-based sentencing only makes moral sense if certain wider institutional and social preconditions are met. As to the former, the imposition of 'just deserts' is not an aim that can be pursued in isolation at the sentencing stage of criminal trials. The equal (and therefore fair) treatment of offenders that proportionate sentencing practices want to achieve is undermined in a system where prosecutorial discretion is unaccountable and unbound, and where the selection of charges in cases of multiple offending is not also subject to guidance ensuring that the charge fairly reflects the gravamen of the alleged criminal conduct. As to the latter, where social injustice reigns, desert-based sentencing may in any event be indefensible unless it takes account of criminogenic impoverished life-circumstances as limiting culpability and calling for mitigation simply in virtue of the offender's disadvantageous social circumstances. Tonry argues that the punishment of cases involving 'deeply disadvantaged defendants' should take account of their deprived backgrounds, and thus that the act-specific features of their crime should set no independent 'lower boundary' for the deserved sanction.[31]

Rechtsgüter, harm and offence in criminalisation

One issue in punishment theory with which Andreas became more preoccupied over time is the role of the state in imposing criminal sanctions. Punishment is not like sending one's child to her bedroom. The state's interest in punishing miscreants is not like that of a parent, or indeed an abbot.[32] Its authority exists for the sake of others, including victims and fellow citizens as well as the wrongdoer. Of course, much the same might be said of the referee who shows a red card in a football game. But that analogy is imperfect, because in the criminal law *the state makes the rules*. It does not merely arbitrate.

So it is natural for an interest in the theory of criminal sanctions to extend into the proscriptions that underlie them. Von Hirsch's earliest significant foray into this area, in the 1996 collection *Harm and Culpability*,[33] foreshadowed a substantial line of writing that has explored, in particular, the justification of proscriptions on grounds of harm or offence, and the legitimate boundaries of paternalism. These issues remain controversial, and a number of our authors make significant contributions to the debate surrounding what kinds of protection the criminal law should offer.

German and Anglo-American criminal theories diverge in their approach to the core principles of criminalisation. In Germany, proscriptions are traditionally justified in terms of the protection of legal goods (*Rechtsgüterschutz*).[34] As Winfried

---

[31] M Tonry, 'Can Deserts Be Just in an Unjust World?', text at fn 77.

[32] Cf von Hirsch, *Censure and Sanctions*, above n 21 at 72–77.

[33] 'Extending the Harm Principle: "Remote" Harms and Fair Imputation' in AP Simester and ATH Smith (eds), *Harm and Culpability* (Oxford, Clarendon Press, 1996) 259.

[34] *Rechtsgut* is a technical term with no clear equivalent in the English language, and there is no generally recognised translation for it. The strategy chosen in this book is generally to opt for a literal

Hassemer observes in this volume, the complexity of modern society has led to increasing pressure being placed on the concept itself: alongside health and property, legal goods may be said to include honour, 'the creditors of a debtor, considered as a group, in respect of the risk or partial loss of their chances of repayment',[35] or 'the good reputation of a financial marketplace' – an example supplied by Wolfgang Wohlers.[36] Both Hassemer and Wohlers lament the amorphousness of the 'legal good' concept, its lack of critical edge; which allows its invocation even to protect morals and traditions.[37] The result is a tendency, Hassemer suggests, for postulated legal goods to 'shoot up like mushrooms.'[38] This may be an area where the Anglo-American approach has some advantage, in as much as it separates the core putative grounds of criminalisation into harm, offence, (perhaps) paternalism, and (even more controversially) moralism. Doing so allows the internal structure of each principle to vary and its legitimacy to be interrogated separately from that of the other putative principles. Indeed, for Wohlers, 'The biggest obstacle to the change of perspective advocated here is probably the strong desire among German scholars to develop a comprehensive theoretical construct that, ideally, derives from one foundational principle.'[39] Provided it is adequately qualified by a criterion of wrongfulness,[40] Wohlers suggests, a distinct offence principle is likely to better equip us (and legislators) to assess the moral case for prohibiting conduct

translation as 'legal good', occasionally using 'legally protected value or interest' when this involves no loss of meaning. However, as a preliminary note, we would like to draw attention to two features that the latter translation does not convey. The first is the distance that the *Rechtsgut* puts between the 'legal good' and the individual and his interest. The object of concern or protection, for the *Rechtsgutslehre* (the 'doctrine of legal goods'), is not simply and straightforwardly a particular interest-holder. Even where the legal good is a 'personal legal good', like the inviolability of the body, the protected entity is the abstraction, the legal good, and not directly the individual person in whom that legal good is present in a particular case. The notion of the *Rechtsgut* is thus much more impersonal or abstract than what most readers would associate with legally recognised or protected interests, which are naturally thought to be the interests of a *person*. When the *Rechtsgutslehre* refers to an affected party, it does so by calling that party not a 'right-holder' but a *Rechtsgutsträger*, a 'carrier of the legally protected good': the latter is essentially a passive object of protection, in whom the abstract legal good is manifested in a particular case; whereas being a right-holder denotes a more active status and agential role, and makes the interest *of that person* the law's concern.

Secondly, even the most uncritical understanding of the *Rechtsgut* carries with it a certain normative undercurrent of meaning, suggesting that legal protection may indeed be warranted or appropriate as a matter of sound political-ethical judgement. If, say, a newly made law set out to protect 'the wellbeing of stones', 'the happiness of the stars', or 'the tears of heaven', and built some prohibition or prescription of conduct on this premise, one would not simply say that such supposed legal goods are foolish. Rather, one would deny them the status of legal goods. *Rechtsgüter* are created and embedded in a system of rational use of legal authority for the promotion of ultimately human needs and interests. For further discussion and explication of the *Rechtsgutslehre*, see K Nuotio, 'Theories of Criminalization and the Limits of Criminal Law: A Legal Cultural Approach' in RA Duff et al (eds), *The Boundaries of the Criminal Law* (Oxford, Oxford University Press, 2010) 238, 244–52.

[35] W Hassemer, 'The Harm Principle and the Protection of "Legal Goods" (*Rechtsgüterschutz*): a German Perspective', this volume, text at fn 38.

[36] W Wohlers, 'Criminal Liability for Offensive Behaviour in Public Spaces', this volume, text at fn 39.

[37] Hassemer, this volume, text at fn 50.

[38] Ibid, text at fn 52.

[39] Wohlers, this volume, text at fn 113.

[40] Ibid, text at fn 95.

such as 'naked rambling', recently held to be a 'gross violation of decency and morals', and as such punishable, by the Swiss Federal Court.[41] If, as von Hirsch and others have argued, offence is a communicative and experiential phenomenon, its role as a positive ground for criminalisation is likely to be structurally different from harm. Indeed, the significance of harm may also vary, depending (amongst other things) on whether the harm is done by the actor to herself or to others.

None of which is to say that the Anglo-American approach is unproblematic. Antony Duff and Sandra Marshall point out that there is an important distinction between harms that may result from an action and harms that are avoided when that action is not done.[42] 'The' harm principle is, in reality, not unitary. Directly harmful conduct may be pro tanto wrongful, and a legitimate candidate for proscription, in virtue of the harm it causes; but criminalisation on the basis of what von Hirsch calls 'remote harms' is quite a different matter. Indeed, it is a misnomer to describe the conduct at issue in such cases as 'remotely harmful', since there is no requirement that such conduct must cause the relevant harm, even indirectly. Extending harm-based criminalisation beyond actions that directly cause or risk harms means that von Hirsch actually subscribes (in Duff and Marshall's terms) to both (i) a *harmful conduct principle* and (ii) a more complex, remote *harm prevention principle*.[43] Duff and Marshall advocate a regulation-based approach to the harm prevention principle; the challenge this poses for von Hirsch is whether that approach really does avoid the need, originally seen by von Hirsch, to grapple with problems of imputation. Certainly, the two (sub-)principles need to be distinguished: not only because they work differently but also because remote harm cases are themselves subject to a direct proscription constraint – which is based on the standard, harmful conduct analysis.[44]

Further debate on the issue of remote harms, and on the birfurcated nature of the harm principle, seems assured. The same holds for Tatjana Hörnle's challenge, which looks to substitute the language of harm with that of *rights*. She concurs with von Hirsch in thinking that the criminal law should ultimately be motivated by the need to protect *individuals* rather than, say, society or some other collective object; but she thinks it should focus primarily on rights rather than interests. One can expect these alternatives to converge in typical cases, in as much as the criminal law requires wrongful as well as harmful behaviour to be engaged; and given that one is generally thought to be harmed only by setbacks to interests 'in which one has a stake'.[45] Rights are, of course, closely related to interests in the sense that the former are a standard means of protecting the latter. Indeed, if the law's motivation is to safeguard the *welfare* of individuals, whether through protecting their rights or through protecting their interests, the two positions are more or less coextensive.

---

[41] See the discussion by Wohlers, ibid, text at fn 16.

[42] RA Duff and SE Marshall, ' "Remote Harms" and the Two Harm Principles', this volume.

[43] Ibid, text at fns 3–6.

[44] Cf AP Simester and A von Hirsch, *Crimes, Harms and Wrongs: On the Principles of Criminalisation* (Oxford, Hart Publishing, 2011) 73.

[45] J Feinberg, *Harm to Others* (New York, Oxford University Press, 1984) 34.

The appeal of that thought is enhanced when Hörnle suggests that[46]

> people are entitled to spheres of liberty which they can manage according to their own choices; intrusions into such important spheres of liberty are to be assessed as a violation of a right; rights violations are prima facie reasons for criminalisation.

The scope of that sphere of liberty might, in turn, be justified in terms of the welfare interests it protects – in terms, ultimately, of preventing harm. For Hörnle, however, not always:[47]

> 'Bodily integrity' and 'sexual autonomy' describe important spheres of liberty the value of which is not or not entirely dependent on functional and future-orientated aspects. The more intimate a sphere of liberty is tied to the idea *what it means to be a person*, the more should freedom from others' intrusions be considered intrinsically valuable.

There are hard questions here, which Hörnle is right to raise. Part of the reason why these wrongs are so serious is because of the great harm they typically involve. If we try to imagine rape as a harmless wrong, we seem to lose our sense of it – and of its gravity. To make the case for criminalisation independent of that harm seems at least partly counter-intuitive. And is there any such wrong where harm is not lurking in the background?

The idea of identifying a protected legal good for each offence does, at least, have a less controversial application: as an organising principle, an analytic device for helping to arrange the criminal law systematically according to the relevant type of 'legal good' being protected.[48] Like Hörnle, Nina Peršak draws out an important underlying connection between such legal goods and concern for human welfare. Beginning with – and modifying – von Hirsch and Jareborg's idea of the living standard,[49] she develops a robust concept of *quality of life*, which she offers as a kind of *Grundrechtsgut*, from which other legal goods (physical integrity, privacy, life, etc) might be derived.[50] By differentiating between types of setback (physical, material, psychological, and normative), she generates a framework with the potential to distinguish between types of criminal wrongs, and to help quantify their seriousness by reference to their impact on the conditions of human well-being. This does not, of course, solve all the problems of criminalisation; nor displace the need for structured principles to deal with issues like remote harm. And, as Peršak sees, protecting normative standards – even if limited to social interaction contexts – necessarily imports all the difficulties of the offence principle, including the risks of aesthetic majoritarianism. Quality-of-life criteria can be traduced, made dependent on the quality of *someone's* life. Whose life? Certainly not the homeless person's. As gaps between rich

---

[46] T Hörnle, '"Rights of Others" in Criminalisation Theory', this volume, 184.

[47] Ibid, 185.

[48] Thus Hassemer notes (this volume, section II.A) that the German Criminal Code is 'divided according to legal good, ranging from "offences against the security of the state" to "offences against the safety and liberty of the person" and "offences committed in public office"; and thus some structure is given to the Code.'

[49] Von Hirsch and Jareborg, 'Gauging Criminal Harm', above n 2.

[50] N Peršak, 'Using "Quality of Life" to Legitimate Criminal Law Intervention: Gauging Gravity, Defining Disorder', this volume, text at fn 28.

and poor, between us and them, widen beyond bridge, the requirement of wrongfulness highlighted by Wohlers may become the only bulwark we have against criminalising conduct that does no more than alter the social tone.

Criminal justice in a liberal state

As Ashworth and Zedner point out, the state's obligation to prevent harm, so central to the justification of state punishment, can be traced back to the liberal theory of the state.[51] The last four essays in the collection address broader questions of what it means for a criminal justice system to live up to the ideal of a liberal polity. Bernd Schünemann distinguishes between three levels on which preconditions for just punishment in a liberal state are located. The first level is constituted by the general justification of state punishment: whether the infliction of an evil on a human being by the state, in response to an earlier evil act committed by that individual, can be just. The second and more concrete level addresses what kind of conduct may justifiably be criminalised. Schünemann stresses that 'the definition and demarcation of conduct proscribed by the criminal law is not simply a task that falls within the legislator's discretion, but part of the justice of punishment in a properly constituted state'; as is, on a third level of concretisation, a system of criminal procedure which maximises 'the likelihood that the criteria for just punishment formulated at the abstract level, as well as those contained in the substantive criminal law, have in fact been satisfied.'[52]

For Schünemann, the deep connection between the justice of punishment and the legitimacy of a liberal state means that the answers given by penal theory on these various levels of concretisation acquire 'constitutional status'. But what exactly does such constitutional status entail? Does it make penal theory enforceable as constitutional law? Or is the answer more complicated – as is, in fact, suggested by Schünemann when he refers to criminal law theory as 'a fourth constitutional power of sorts', exercising 'a kind of non-coercive but nevertheless influential intellectual control over the state's use of penal force'?[53] These questions are pursued further in Antje du Bois-Pedain's contribution. Taking as her starting point the 'shadow' cast by constitutional law over 'the normative claims made by penal or criminal-law theory',[54] du Bois-Pedain first addresses why penal theory threatens to be marginalised under constitutional law doctrine. She then explores the difficulties faced by a strategy of constitutional incorporation of penal theory's normative claims. Ultimately, however, she argues that penal theory need not feel threatened by the fact that its standards and guidance cannot be fully translated into constitutional law. Once we understand that[55]

---

[51] Ashworth and Zedner, this volume, text at fn 6.
[52] Schünemann, this volume, 269.
[53] Ibid, text at fns 2–4.
[54] A du Bois-Pedain, 'The Place of Criminal Law Theory in the Constitutional State', this volume, text at fn 3.
[55] Ibid, text at fn 79.

[t]he role of criminal law theory in political and legal discourse is to perform the *ongoing* task of institutions of liberal-democratic states to develop criteria for the appropriateness of responses to certain rights-violations in reaction to the social realities of the time,

we can accept that 'the criminal justice system cannot, and should not, be *constitutionally coerced* into administering any particular penal theory.'[56] On this view, much penal theory operates at the level of a moral-political appeal; but precisely for this reason, it can give more nuanced and meaningful guidance than 'the bare "ultimate constitutional stop" of [a] constitutional guarantee'.[57] Du Bois-Pedain concludes that[58]

in a constitutional state, criminal law theory has continuing normative importance. While it cannot be restated through or incorporated fully within the set of constitutional guarantees without losing much of its functionality as a comprehensive guidance system for the properly motivated liberal legislator, government official, and judge, it retains the normativity that resides in that function even after the constitutionalisation of the state.

John Kleinig extends the purview of liberalism to the state's policing function, exploring the role that police may have in society's punitive activity. Kleinig stresses that 'the "preservation of public tranquility" . . . has become the more controlling end of liberal democratic policing.'[59] In this context, the police should be viewed not (at least, not primarily) as crime-fighters, but more expansively as social peace-keepers; and, he continues, 'There is nothing in the concept of social peacekeeping that excludes a punitive police role.'[60] Kleinig considers that the strongest case for some legitimate punitive function to be exercised by the police pertains to the maintenance of public order, rather than formal responses to *crime*: 'Some public order infractions may be seen as warranting a punitive societal response, though not one that requires the heavier (or unreliable) machinery of the criminal justice system.'[61] But Kleinig also warns that the possibility of abuse is not far off: public order maintenance may be seen as 'maintenance of authority over [the police officer's] *own* territory,'[62] and that attitude may easily breed excess. Even now, many instances of heavy-handed law enforcement mask (or implement) punitive impulses that arise – inappropriately – when citizens' conduct is seen as a challenge to police authority.[63] Such instances illustrate the moral hazards entailed by any formal justification of a practice of police punishment.

Paul Roberts' contribution draws these lines of thought together in a reflective discussion of what the specifically 'liberal' credentials of Anglo-American criminal law theory may be thought to consist in. He develops a version of liberal political morality that, at its heart, is 'concerned with prioritising individual's *liberty*'.[64] This,

---

[56] Ibid.
[57] Ibid, text at fn 80.
[58] Ibid, section IV.
[59] Kleinig, 'Punishment and the Ends of Policing', 289.
[60] Ibid, 295.
[61] Ibid, 296–97.
[62] Ibid, 267.
[63] Ibid, section IV.
[64] P Roberts, 'Criminal Law Theory and the Limits of Liberalism', this volume, text at fn 9.

he observes, positions liberalism as a secular philosophy in which the (socially-situated and interconnected) individual is the primary object of ethical concern.[65] Yet, as Roberts shows, this generates fewer direct consequences for criminal law theory than one might initially suppose. Even though, particularly in relation to criminalisation and culpability matters, 'an impressive amount of contemporary criminal law doctrine can be spun out of the liberty-premiss,'[66] liberal theory also has significant limitations as a 'resource for theorising criminal law'.[67] On many questions, it offers guidance that is incomplete and indeterminate at best and which needs supplementation from richer ethical frameworks (say, theories of agency) that are *compatible* with liberalism without being part of liberal theory as such.[68] Roberts illustrates liberalism's indeterminacy with a discussion of whether criminal defendants should be entitled to wear the *niqab* in court. Eventually, he thinks, the criminal law theorist may have to give decisive weight to the institutionally crucial consideration that 'we expect to see people's faces in court.'[69] For Roberts, however, the fact that most of the substantive insights of liberal criminal theory are 'compatible with' liberalism, rather than grounded in it, is a strength rather than a weakness. In a global setting where 'To characterise a law or policy as "liberal" is not necessarily to recommend it to the . . . constituency of state and non-state actors,' it is perhaps advantageous that the criminal laws endorsed by liberals 'are not necessarily *liberal criminal laws*, in the sense of finding their direct or exclusive normative grounding in liberal political morality.'[70] The payoff is that a broadly 'liberal' (freedom-valuing and freedom-respecting) criminal law can also be grounded in very different philosophical and political traditions.

In Closing

No prefatory remarks are complete without acknowledgements. We are grateful, as so often to Richard Hart and the team at Hart Publishing, especially Mel Hamill, Rachel Turner, and Tom Adams, for their flexibility and unflinching support in the teeth of overdue copy. Special thanks, too, are due to Francois du Bois for superb pre-editing of the translations. Finally, we are grateful to Tony Bottoms, who supplied the front cover illustration of a Welsh prison flying a white flag. The flag signals that the prison currently has no prisoners inside – a reminder that desert-based sentencing need not require harsher, or indeed any punishments. Those who do not deserve punishment should go free; those who have served their punishments should be released. And if no one is in jail, society could yet be a better place.

---

[65] Ibid.
[66] Ibid, 343.
[67] Ibid, 344.
[68] Ibid, section IV.
[69] Ibid, 354–55.
[70] Ibid, 359–60.

I.

PUNISHMENT AND PREVENTION

1

Punishment Paradigms and the Role of the Preventive State

ANDREW ASHWORTH AND LUCIA ZEDNER

One of the most widely accepted propositions in political theory is that the state has an obligation to take steps to prevent harm to others. Andreas von Hirsch has long advanced the view that the state's role in providing conditions of security is vital to understanding and justifying punishment. Indeed, he has observed,[1]

> The very form of criminal prohibitions strongly suggests a preventive design. When the state criminalizes conduct, it issues a legal threat: Such conduct is proscribed and violation will result in the imposition of specified penalties. This threat surely has *something* to do with inducing citizens to refrain from the proscribed conduct.

This leaves open the question of what conduct the state may proscribe through criminalisation. Von Hirsch is keen to ensure that the security obligation is not embraced so enthusiastically that it attributes to the liberal state a larger moralising role. Thus he writes that[2]

> The state, in a liberal society, should not have a generalized mission of upholding the moral order, but rather such more circumscribed functions as the prevention of harm and the fostering and maintenance of the means for citizens to have a good existence.

This indicates two positive obligations of the state, and they both appear in a subsequent articulation:[3]

> The argument begins with the relatively straightforward proposition that helping to prevent persons from mistreating others is an important and legitimate function of the state. The underlying idea is that the state has, as one of its defining roles, that of encouraging peaceable living among citizens and of safeguarding the basic means by which citizens can live good lives.

---

[1] A von Hirsch, 'Proportionality in the Philosophy of Punishment: From "Why Punish?" To "How Much?"' (1990) 1 *Criminal Law Forum* 259. Matravers draws a telling analogy between von Hirsch's position and that of the political theorist John Charvet with regard to the role of criticism, namely that 'it would indeed be meaningless and futile to criticize people for their actions, if such criticism never did or ever could have an effect on their future conduct.' M Matravers, *Justice and Punishment: The Rationale of Coercion* (Oxford, Oxford University Press, 2000) 246 fn 8.
[2] A von Hirsch and A Ashworth, *Proportionate Sentencing: Exploring the Principles* (Oxford, Oxford University Press, 2005) 14.
[3] Ibid, 28.

These twin obligations are central to von Hirsch's account of the justifications for the state's authoritative response to criminal wrongdoing by way of punishment. Our interest in this chapter will be to explore the further implications of the state's preventive function for punishment and to look particularly at the state's obligations in respect of the form and content of punitive measures. But before we begin to develop that line of argument, we must trace the links that von Hirsch has set out between the state's preventive function and its punitive function.

Punishment involves penal censure of a person for an offence: it 'conveys to the actor a certain critical normative message concerning his conduct,' namely, authoritative disapproval for the wrongful act he has done.[4] Part of that wrongfulness should reside in the requirement of fault on the part of the actor, although not all criminal offences comply with this rule-of-law standard. The critical normative message is also constituted by the quantum of punishment: although there are many contestable judgements involved in any calculation of proportionate sentencing, degrees of punishment within a given penal system convey degrees of censure. However, punishment involves hard treatment as well as censure. The justification for inflicting hard treatment on offenders is preventive – without hard treatment, a system of censure alone might not be taken sufficiently seriously. Thus, according to von Hirsch, the hard treatment element in punishment 'supplies a prudential reason for desistance from offending, but one that is tied to the normative reason conveyed by penal censure.'[5] The preventive element operates only 'within the censuring institution'. It is a deterrent rationale, and this is therefore a 'mixed theory' of punishment: the deterrent element must be contained within the proportionate framework of punishments addressed to moral agents. The need for deterrence stems from the fact that, although humans have a capacity for moral reasoning, they are also subject to strong emotions and instincts, and so penalties may help them to control their fallibility. In sum, 'it is the penal deprivation, not just the defendant's conviction, that expresses the censure as well as serving as the prudential disincentive.'[6]

In what follows, we pay particular attention to the state's obligation to prevent harm, tracing the origins and development of this key idea in liberal theories of the state. Thereafter, we examine a particular dilemma for von Hirsch's penal theory: whether appropriately proportionate, parsimonious,[7] and subordinate prudential supplements to censure can achieve preventive efficacy. In the final section, we explore four concrete examples of the exercise of the state's preventive duty in order tease out what this obligation entails for contemporary penal practice.

---

[4] Ibid, 17.
[5] Ibid, 22–23.
[6] Ibid, 26–27.
[7] 'Parsimony' in this context refers to restraint in the use of imprisonment: see text at nn 53–55 below.

I. The Role of Prudential Disincentives

The von Hirsch account of the preventive function of punishment relies upon a twin-faceted conception of human nature. On the one hand, it assumes that people are moral agents who are 'capable of taking seriously the message conveyed through the sanction, that the conduct is reprehensible.'[8] Those to whom the law speaks are not 'brutes' who cannot be appealed to through censure. On the other hand, it recognises that neither are they 'angels' who would require no such appeal.[9] It is this recognition of human capacity for moral reasoning and, importantly, the simultaneous acknowledgement of human fallibility that informs the preventive rationale. Acceptance of human fallibility is important in von Hirsch's theory because it guards against the temptation to conceive of punishment as something that we, the law-abiding, impose on those who offend against us. Instead, in his account, 'the law thus addresses ourselves, not a distinct "criminal" class of those considered incapable of grasping moral appeals.'[10] Although there are strong independent reasons for moderation, this projection of 'ourselves' as the possible subjects of punishment is a powerful source of restraint against excess and a driver towards fairness. This conception of human nature also acknowledges the complex interactive processes that stand behind human decision-making, which involve basic instincts such as aggression, greed, and gratification, but also the capacity for moral reasoning. Bottoms considers von Hirsch's conception of human nature to be 'an extremely important development in his theorization and one that has received insufficient attention from commentators.'[11] Bottoms goes so far as to suggest that this account of human nature is 'potentially revolutionary in the field of punishment theory' because it 'seems to require a fully *interactive account* of censure and prevention as the core grounds for punishment,' and he suggests that von Hirsch's view of personhood therefore requires a general justifying aim in which 'censure and prevention are co-equal and interactive.'[12]

The evolution of the preventive element in von Hirsch's thinking to its present prominence can be traced over the course of his writing. In his early work *Doing Justice* (1976),[13] von Hirsch's theory of retribution rested partially on the idea of 'unfair advantage', according to which the offender obtained an unfair gain by freeing himself of the burden of restraint to desist from crime, while simultaneously benefitting from the self-restraint of others. Von Hirsch later distanced himself

---

[8] A von Hirsch, *Censure and Sanctions* (Oxford, Oxford University Press, 1993) 13.

[9] Ibid.

[10] A von Hirsch, 'Punishment, Penance and the State: A Reply to Duff' in D Matravers and J Pike (eds), *Debates in Contemporary Political Philosophy: An Anthology* (London, Routledge and Open University Press, 2002) 408, 409.

[11] AE Bottoms, 'Five Puzzles in von Hirsch's Theory of Punishment' in A Ashworth and M Wasik (eds), *Fundmentals of Sentencing Theory* (Oxford, Oxford University Press, 1998) 82.

[12] Ibid, 82, 89.

[13] Von Hirsch, *Doing Justice: The Choice of Punishments* (New York, Hill and Wang, 1976).

from this 'benefits and burdens' account of punishment, partly because the idea of reciprocal obligation fails to capture the essential nature of the wrong entailed by much crime – the wrong of murder is not that the murderer has benefitted from others' self-restraint in desisting from murder – and partly because it provides no metric for the quantum of punishment that should follow.[14] Yet, even within this early work, von Hirsch's approach is not purely retributivist: punishment must also be likely to achieve some social good by helping to prevent crime. In his 1985 book, *Past or Future Crimes*,[15] prevention moves to greater prominence to appear along-side censure: together they provide a general justifying aim for punishment. However, his acknowledgement of the place of prevention within his theory remains, in places, somewhat tentative as late as his 1993 book *Censure and Sanctions.* In it, he examines 'why prevention might in principle be a legitimate sup-porting reason for punishment's existence.'[16] And he insists that prevention 'can-not stand alone' but 'operates only within a censuring framework.'[17] Yet, elsewhere in that book, he acknowledges that prevention is so central to the very justification of punishment that his theory 'would permit the abolition of the institution of pun-ishment were it not needed for preventive purposes.'[18] In a society in which crime was sufficiently rare that the criminal justice system was no longer necessary to keep criminal conduct at a tolerable level, while some sort of official censure might be required, there would be no necessity for, or justification of, punishment. As von Hirsch writes, 'with the need for prevention eliminated, there would no longer be a need for so ambitious, intrusive, and burdensome an institution as the criminal sanction.'[19] The acknowledgement that punishment could no longer be justified if it were unnecessary for preventive purposes places prevention much more squarely at the centre of his theory than in his earlier works. Thus, as Tasioulas observes, in von Hirsch's account 'the criminal sanction expresses censure for wrong-doing but the reason for preferring it to any other means of conveying censure is its preventa-tive role.'[20]

By placing prevention at the heart of the rationale of punishment, von Hirsch distances his position from the wholly deontological tenor of Kant's conclusion, in his famous 'island example', that 'punishment would have to be preserved even if it were found to have no preventive utility.'[21] Duff and Garland acknowledge this

[14] See, eg, von Hirsch, *Censure and Sanctions*, above n 8 at 7–8.
[15] *Past or Future Crimes: Deservedness and Dangerousness in the Sentencing of Criminals* (Manchester, Manchester University Press, 1985).
[16] Von Hirsch, *Censure and Sanctions*, above n 8 at 13.
[17] Ibid, 14.
[18] Ibid. Von Hirsch acknowledges his debt here to his collaborator Uma Narayan, who elsewhere argues, 'even if we had a choice between an institution that could effectively convey degrees of censure without a system of graded pains, and an institution that effectively conveys degrees of censure by means of hard treatment, we might have reason to choose the latter in virtue of its collateral crime preventive benefits.' U Narayan, 'Appropriate Responses and Preventative Benefits: Justifying Censure and Hard Treatment in Legal Punishment' (1993) 13 *Oxford Journal of Legal Studies* 166, 179.
[19] Von Hirsch, *Censure and Sanctions*, above n 8.
[20] J Tasioulas, 'Punishment and Repentance' (2006) 81 *Philosophy* 279, 291.
[21] See Bottoms, 'Five Puzzles', above n 11 at 78, citing A von Hirsch, *Past or Future Crimes: Deservedness and Dangerousness in the Sentencing of Criminals* (Manchester, Manchester University Press, 1986) 59.

move as a 'subtle reworking of the idea that hard treatment has a preventive, deterrent function' that would 'do justice to the consequentialist concern that punishment should prevent crime, whilst still respecting offenders (and potential offenders) as autonomous (but fallible) moral agents.'[22] The centrality of prevention to the justification of punishment is even more firmly embedded in von Hirsch's 2005 book with Ashworth, *Proportionate Sentencing*.[23] Indeed, the title of the second chapter places prevention right alongside censure: 'The Justification for Punishment's Existence: Censure and Prevention'.

II. The Scope of the State's Authority to Censure

Thus far we have established that the state has an obligation to take steps to prevent harms and that this obligation informs the justification of punishment. Indeed, in *Proportionate Sentencing*, von Hirsch and Ashworth make clear that their argument is not 'that blaming is in itself an important state mission: it is harm and prevention that do the main explanatory work.'[24] As we have observed, were this preventive function to be fulfilled by other means, a central justification for punishment would fall away. So far so good, but this leaves unanswered important questions about who has standing to determine what constitutes a harm, by what metric, and about what form and level of punishment is then justified. To justify state monopoly over punishment to the exclusion of citizen vigilantes and private organisations is to make a particular claim about the role of the state.

On the issue of standing, questions arise about what grounds the relationship between state and citizen and what this then permits, which cannot be answered without recourse to a larger political theory of the nature and proper functions of the state. MacCormick went to the heart of the issue when he asked, 'Does the State, when it exacts punishment after due process of law, vindicate its own right, or simply stand in for the citizen who has been wronged?'[25] The public character of the criminal wrong is a powerful ground for the claim that the state neither merely stands in the shoes of the victim nor does it appropriate a private quarrel.[26] However, the stronger view is that the state's monopoly of the right to punish derives from a particular conception of its authority that endows it with exclusive jurisdiction. As Thorburn insists, 'The ground of the liberal constitutional state's legitimacy is the

The island example appears in I Kant, *The Metaphysics of Morals* (1797) (Ak 6: 333) in *The Cambridge Edition of the Works of Immanuel Kant: Practical Philosophy*, trans M Gregor, intro A Wood (Cambridge, Cambridge University Press, 1996) 474.

[22] RA Duff and D Garland (eds), *A Reader on Punishment* (Oxford, Oxford University Press, 1994) 112–13.

[23] Von Hirsch and Ashworth, *Proportionate Sentencing*, above n 2.

[24] Ibid, 29.

[25] N MacCormick and D Garland, 'Sovereign States and Vengeful Victims: The Problem of the Right to Punish' in Ashworth and Wasik (eds), *Fundamentals of Sentencing Theory*, above n 11, 16.

[26] N Christie, 'Conflicts as Property' (1977) 17 *British Journal of Criminology* 1.

simple fact that it – and it alone – can provide the conditions of freedom for all.'[27] In order for each to act in a way that is respectful of the freedom of others, the state must set out rules that demarcate the boundaries of conduct consistent with respect for individual autonomy; ensure compliance with those rules; and provide for the sanctioning of those who do not comply. Moreover, the imposition of sanctions is permissible only where there is strict adherence to the rule of law and, in particular, to the precept that there be no punishment without law.[28]

Having established the prima facie authority of the state to punish, the question then arises: what is the scope of that authority and is it consistent with the security of the individual from unwarranted interference by the state? The question is answered rather differently by communitarian and liberal theorists and there are serious tensions between their respective accounts. Communitarian political theories, such as those advanced by Duff and Lacey, identify the offender as a member of a larger political community that is structured around shared values which are expressed in law.[29] This communitarian conception attributes to the state – as the institutional embodiment of that community – a rightful interest not only in the offender's external conduct towards other members of the community, but also 'an interest strong and extensive enough to justify it in trying to improve her moral condition by punitive coercion.'[30] This interest is predicated upon a conception of the state which presumes that relationships between people are rich and close; that they genuinely share many of the same values; and that they have a common language in which effective communication can take place. Duff argues that his account 'presupposes that those involved have a proper interest in the moral character of each other's conduct, *and* a relationship with each other which gives them the moral standing to comment thus forcibly on that conduct.'[31] It follows that for Duff the purpose of censure is not merely to convey a message or solely to seek to modify the external conduct of those who offend, but rather 'to induce an appropriate moral change in their attitudes and dispositions.'[32] Whether such a conception of the role of the state is consistent with liberalism is an open question. While its proponents aver that such a communitarian account can be predicated upon a liberal community that adheres to some of the central values of liberalism, it is difficult to see how it can be fully compatible with a liberalism that is committed to preserving for each citizen a sphere of freedom from intrusion or coercion by the state.

Certainly for a liberal political theorist like von Hirsch, such an extensive role for

[27] M Thorburn, 'Constitutionalism and the Limits of the Criminal Law' in RA Duff et al (eds), *The Structures of the Criminal Law* (Oxford, Oxford University Press, 2011) 85, 88.

[28] A Harel, 'Why Only the State May Inflict Criminal Sanctions: The Case against Privately Inflicted Sanctions' (2008) 14 *Legal Theory* 113; M Thorburn, 'Criminal Law as Public Law' in RA Duff and SP Green (eds), *Philosophical Foundations of Criminal Law* (Oxford, Oxford University Press, 2011) 21, 42–43.

[29] RA Duff, 'Punishment, Communication and Community' in Matravers and Pike (eds), *Debates in Contemporary Political Philosophy*, above n 10, 387, 392–93; N Lacey, *State Punishment: Political Principles and Community Values* (London, Routledge, 1988) ch 8.

[30] Duff, ibid, 393.

[31] Ibid, 394.

[32] Ibid, 396.

the state as punisher is excessively coercive, overly intrusive, and erosive of the security of the individual. Throughout his writings, von Hirsch insists that the state cannot claim a special position of moral or spiritual authority over the offender that would justify its use of coercion to secure the offender's attention or to address his moral condition.[33] Whereas an abbot might claim such authority over the spiritual lives of the members of a monastic community, the state has no standing to engage in such an intrusive endeavour and to do so would constitute 'overreaching'.[34] While a liberal state may properly communicate the censure deserved by wrongdoers, it may not seek to secure their moral improvement or reform by use of coercive measures.[35] It follows that while the state may assert a legitimate interest in the 'external' conduct of one citizen toward another, unlike the abbot, its standing does not extend to a rightful concern with the 'internal' questions of the offender's own good. By contrast with monasteries, modern societies are not communities that one can choose to join or leave and, while their members may share certain core values, these are limited in scope and do not extend to the spiritual welfare of their members. In sum, to the question 'whether administering penances is a proper role for a liberal state,' von Hirsch replies firmly that it is not.[36]

III. The State's Preventive Obligation

What is the nature of the state's preventive obligation? Classical liberal conceptions of the relationship between state and citizen focus upon the obligations owed to the state by citizens and to citizens by the state. The citizen's obligation to obey the law is explained variously by reference to tacit consent to state authority; fair play to other citizens; assent to reciprocal burdens in return for the benefit of state services and protection; or the consequentialist ground that, without obedience to the law, chaos or relapse into a Hobbesian state of nature would result.[37] What the state owes to citizens is less well defined, but seems always to include a duty to provide protection from the hazards and threats that they would otherwise face.[38] Thus, in exchange for the promise of security of their persons and property, citizens agree to renounce the right to self-government and to submit to the state's coercive force. As Hobbes observed in the *Leviathan*, 'The very end for which this renouncing, and transferring of right is introduced, is nothing else but the security of a man's

---

[33] See, eg, von Hirsch, *Censure and Sanctions*, above n 8 at 72–77.
[34] Ibid, 74.
[35] Duff and Garland (eds), *A Reader on Punishment*, above n 22 at 113.
[36] Von Hirsch, 'Punishment, Penance and the State', above n 10 at 409.
[37] For further analysis, see eg D Knowles, *Political Obligation: A Critical Introduction* (Abingdon, Routledge, 2010).
[38] A Ryan, 'Hobbes' Political Philosophy' in T Sorell (ed), *The Cambridge Companion to Hobbes* (Cambridge, Cambridge University Press, 2011) 208, 228–29. See also K Günther, 'Responsibility to Protect and Preventive Justice' in A Ashworth, L Zedner and P Tomlin (eds), *Preventive Justice and the Limits of the Criminal Law* (Oxford, Oxford University Press, 2013) 69.

person.'[39] It follows that the state's primary task and indeed its very raison d'être is to secure for its citizens the conditions of order and security that are prerequisites of freedom. Accordingly, Hobbes characterised the duty of the state as follows: 'The office of the Sovereign, be it a Monarch, or an Assembly, consists in the end, for which he was trusted with Sovereign Power, namely the procuration of the *safety of the people.*'[40] At least two things follow from this characterisation of the state's primary role. First, the protective or preventive function is written into the very fabric of state authority and imposes upon the state a duty to promulgate laws and pursue policies in order to provide security for its citizens. The state's responsibility to ensure good order and security justifies criminalisation in so far as it serves this end and provided that this could not be achieved by less restrictive means. Secondly, citizens owe prima facie duties, to the state and to one another, to abide by law and to accept state coercion as the necessary price of peace and good order. Determining what it is permissible to criminalise and punish in order to attain good order and security is beyond the scope of this chapter, but it is worthy of note that the security function may provide a justification for the criminalisation and punishment of conduct which is not wrongful or not presently harmful but which, if not criminalised, would lead to harm.[41]

The pursuit of security endows the Leviathan state with near limitless powers to secure protection for itself and its people: there is little in Hobbes' account to protect individuals from the threat to their liberty posed by the state itself. Later liberal theorists sought not only to establish the constitutional justifications for state coercion but also to articulate the limits upon legitimate state endeavour and legislative action. Thus Locke insisted on a system of checks and balances based on the separation of legislature, executive and judiciary. In Locke's account of liberalism, the individual's right to self-preservation is limited by law, and the power to punish is transferred to the government so that it may be exercised for the preservation of the lives, liberties and estates of citizens.[42] The powers ceded to the state are justified only insofar as they tend toward the goal of preservation. Locke thus articulated a powerful set of restraints upon legitimate government and a powerful limit against abuse.

The idea that the provision of security is a core function of the modern state has come to be widely accepted within the liberal tradition.[43] While there is broad

[39] T Hobbes, *Leviathan*, ch XIII. In his earlier writings, von Hirsch adopted a Hobbesian turn of phrase, arguing that without the threat of painful consequences, 'it seems likely that victimizing conduct would become so prevalent as to make life nasty and brutish, indeed.' Von Hirsch, *Past or Future Crimes*, above n 15 at 48.

[40] Hobbes, *Leviathan*, ch XXX ('Of the Office of the Sovereign Representative'). (Emphasis added.)

[41] J Gardner and S Shute, 'The Wrongness of Rape' in J Horder (ed), *Oxford Essays in Jurisprudence* (Oxford, Oxford University Press, 2000); cf A Ashworth and L Zedner, *Preventive Justice* (Oxford, Oxford University Press, 2014) ch 5.

[42] J Locke, *Two Treatises of Government*, student edn (Cambridge, Cambridge University Press, 1988) ch IX ('Of the Ends of Political Society and Government') § 124. For an extended discussion, see the chapter by Kleinig in this volume.

[43] JS Mill famously regarded the preventive function of government as 'undisputed' and argued that 'if a public authority ... sees anyone evidently preparing to commit a crime, they are not bound to look on inactive until the crime is committed, but may interfere to prevent it.' Even so, he also questioned 'how far liberty may legitimately be invaded for the prevention of crime': JS Mill, *On Liberty* (Harmondsworth,

agreement that the state has a fundamental duty to prevent harm and ensure security, there remain questions about the nature and implications of that duty. Later libertarians like Nozick argued that the minimal state has a duty to act as 'night-watchman' or provider of security; but that its role should be no more extensive than this core preventive function.[44] On this account, the goal of prevention is not only an authorisation for, and but also a strict limit on, the state's exercise of coercive powers. As Nozick observes, 'the night-watchman state of classical liberal theory [is] limited to the functions of protecting all its citizens against violence, theft, and fraud.'[45] This narrow view of the protective function has been contested by those who adopt a much broader concept of security that extends beyond the prevention of crime to the provision of the basic necessities of human flourishing. Such an expansive conception informed the development of 'social security' which underpinned the development of the welfare state.[46] It has also come to inform the yet more capacious concept of 'human security',[47] which is predicated on the belief that the chief threats to safety derive from poverty, despair, and instability. Human security seeks to promote human flourishing beyond mere survival[48] and to guarantee the personal safety of individuals in their everyday lives. Unsurprisingly, the scope of this more amorphous definition of security, the determination of what obligations it imposes upon the state and, not least, the delineation of what limits should apply, have been hotly contested.[49]

Whatever definition of security one adopts, the state's obligation to prevent harm may be said to rest on its general obligation to protect the basic means whereby citizens can lead their chosen lives in a peaceful setting and without undue risk of harm.[50] It should not be assumed that the preventive function is to be carried out only through criminal justice policy: on the contrary, the state has a range of techniques, from licensing to regulation and to non-penal forms of law, on which it can and should draw. However, as von Hirsch has observed, these alternative strategies are not free from ethical dilemmas of their own and can encroach on fundamental human rights.[51] Indeed, while it is tempting here to reach for the *ultima ratio* principle (that criminal law should only be used as a last resort), Simester and von Hirsch are right to warn against uncritical support for minimal intervention; 'In any civilised society', they observe, 'murder ought to be condemned through the

---

Penguin, 1979) 165. See also J Feinberg (1984), *Harm to Others* (New York, Oxford University Press).

[44] R Nozick, *Anarchy, State and Utopia* (Oxford, Blackwell, 1974) ch 3.

[45] Ibid, 26. Note that Nozick also includes 'the enforcement of contracts' at the end of this list.

[46] L Zedner, *Security* (London, Routledge, 2009) ch 2 ('A Brief History of Security').

[47] UN Commission on Human Security, *Human Security Now* (New York, United Nations, 2003).

[48] Particularly in developing, transitional, and failing states where sectarian and ethnic violence and human rights abuses are endemic.

[49] SN Macfarlane and YF Khong, *Human Security and the UN: A Critical History* (Bloomington IN, Indiana University Press, 2006). On the broader issue of the right to security see also L Lazarus, 'Mapping the Right to Security' in B Goold and L Lazarus (eds), *Security and Human Rights* (Oxford, Hart Publishing, 2007) 325.

[50] See the quotations at nn 1 and 2 above.

[51] A von Hirsch, D Garland and A Wakefield (eds), *Ethical and Social Perspectives on Situational Crime Prevention* (Oxford, Hart Publishing, 2000).

criminal law.'[52] To preserve both elements, recognition of wrongs and minimal intervention, the *ultima ratio* principle should refer to 'the least restrictive *appropriate* alternative', the word 'appropriate' furnishing the normative element.

The principle of penal parsimony belongs to the same family of principles as the principle of the least restrictive appropriate alternative, but it calls for separate discussion.[53] Penal parsimony requires the legislature, and the courts, to adopt the least severe (or least rights-restricting) punishment for the offence. But this harbours an ambiguity. One interpretation is that it requires the reduction of any individual sentence wherever possible; another interpretation is that its emphasis lies upon the reduction of *overall* sentence levels wherever possible. The latter is strongly preferable. The former, adopted by Morris and Tonry,[54] subverts another valued principle – the principle of equality before the law – by allowing, say, a white offender's sentence to be reduced to a community sentence while a black offender (same offence, same criminal record) is sent to prison, on the ground that a local community-based scheme is available in the former's local area but not the latter's. This is an unacceptable sacrifice of equality before the law and it should be opposed. Parsimony should work in the same direction as proportionality, not against it, by militating in favour of overall reductions in penalty levels rather than reductions in individual cases.[55]

It is a matter for debate whether parsimony can be pursued in a way that is consistent with the preventive function. As we observed in our opening remarks, von Hirsch regards the hard treatment element in punishment as supplying a prudential reason for desistance from offending. He is also clear, however, that penal hard treatment should serve as no more than a prudential supplement to law's normative voice and that it should not be permitted to drown out that voice. In von Hirsch's view, to use penal hard treatment purely as prevention, rather than as a supplement to censure, would be merely 'tiger-control' – a 'naked demand' that would not be respectful of the individual's agency.[56] This requirement that hard treatment be subordinate to the moral message of censure is intended to ensure respect for the autonomy of the individual offender.[57] However, it is questionable whether an appropriately parsimonious and subordinate prudential supplement provides an effective disincentive in all cases. Duff suggests that the prudential claim is most plausible in respect of minor crimes, for which a proportionately light punishment may supply a sufficient disincentive to steer us away from offending.[58]

---

[52] AP Simester and A von Hirsch, *Crimes, Harms and Wrongs: On the Principles of Criminalisation* (Oxford, Hart Publishing, 2011) 198.

[53] For elaboration of the principle, see N Morris and M Tonry, *Between Prison and Probation* (New York, Oxford University Press, 1990) 31, and RS Frase, 'Limiting Retributivism' in M Tonry (ed), *The Future of Imprisonment* (New York, Oxford University Press, 2004).

[54] Ibid. See also Tonry's approach in this volume.

[55] Von Hirsch, *Censure and Sanctions*, above n 8 at 111.

[56] Ibid, 14.

[57] Although, as Tasioulas points out, the distinction between the two is not clear cut: censure can entail hard treatment and some penalties (for example fines) may constitute lighter treatment than some forms of condemnation. See Tasioulas, 'Punishment and Repentance', above n 20 at 296.

[58] Duff, 'Punishment, Communication and Community', above n 29 at 394.

But to the extent that this relies upon an empirical claim about efficacy, it would surely be necessary to establish by research that such a deterrent strategy actually works. Von Hirsch and colleagues' sophisticated meta-analysis of the available primary research evidence on deterrence leaves considerable room for doubt about the claims made in its name, particularly in respect of marginal deterrence.[59]

A different problem arises at the other end of the scale. The more serious the offence and proportionately more severe the penalty, the greater the danger that the prudential supplement that is hard treatment will, after all, 'drown out' the moral voice of censure.[60] As Duff observes,[61]

> The prospect of three years' imprisonment might dissuade some potential murderers or rapists from committing such crimes: but if we ask how that prospect could figure in their deliberations or motivations, the only plausible answer is surely that it would replace, rather than supplement, the law's moral appeal to the wrongfulness of that conduct.

If Duff is right – and again his contention can only be proven or disproven by empirical research – then we are, after all, in the territory of 'tiger-control' that von Hirsch rightly abhors. Indeed, von Hirsch is obliged to concede that[62]

> if severer overall penalty levels are thought necessary to prevent crime more effectively, adopting those higher penalty levels would simply constitute a deviation from my model – and *thus not fully justifiable in its terms*. How problematic this would be would depend on how much more severe those overall penalty levels were.

It would seem that while prevention is central to von Hirsch's justificatory account, its subordinate place as a prudential supplement, taken together with the parsimony constraint, may operate as a significant brake on its efficacy. Indeed, von Hirsch makes clear that he does 'not claim that a penal system based on my theory would necessarily deliver as much crime prevention as, say, the tougher penal policies generally prevailing today.'[63] Acknowledging that 'the attractions of this theory are not to be underestimated,'[64] Tasioulas explores some implications of von Hirsch's account. These include whether, where the preventive effects were 'sufficiently low', the case for punishment might be defeated by other countervailing considerations; whether and to what extent prevention can determine questions of relative priority in punishing different offences; and whether considerations of prevention can help determine questions of standing.[65] In the final section, we pursue

---

[59] Von Hirsch et al find some evidence to suggest that the existence of the penal system has some preventive effect (initial deterrence), but little evidence to suggest that increases in punishment (marginal deterrence) do: A von Hirsch et al, *Criminal Deterrence and Sentence Severity: An Analysis of Recent Research* (Oxford, Hart Publishing, 1999).

[60] Cf the doubts expressed by Tasioulas about the 'drowning out' metaphor: 'Punishment and Repentance', above n 20 at 292–93.

[61] Duff, 'Punishment, Communication and Community', above n 29 at 394.

[62] Von Hirsch, 'Punishment, Penance and the State', above n 10 at 410. (Emphasis added.)

[63] Ibid.

[64] Tasioulas 'Punishment and Repentance', above n 20 at 290.

[65] Ibid, 303.

further this last question of standing to ask what the implications of the preventive function are for state agency in four important domains.

IV. Developing the Preventive Obligation

The focus of attention thus far has been on the place of prevention within the justification of state punishment. This leaves open the question of how far the state's obligation to prevent harm fairly stretches. We now explore four possible implications of the state's obligation to protect. First, we consider whether the state can be said to be responsible for failing to prevent crimes. Secondly, we assess the claim that the state has a positive obligation to combat criminogenic conditions. Thirdly, we examine the state's responsibility to those whom it decides to punish. And fourthly, we look into the state's particular responsibilities to those serving preventive sentences. Our intention in this final section is to consider substantive examples of the exercise of the state's preventive function in order to explore more fully what the obligation entails for contemporary penal practice.

A. State responsibility for failing to prevent crimes?

We have already addressed the standing of the state to punish, but further important questions remain to be addressed in relation to the extent and implications of its preventive obligation. A document produced by the Council of Europe on the rights of victims of crime asserts that the state owes a duty towards victims because 'it has failed to prevent the crime by means of effective criminal policy, and it introduced policy measures which failed.'[66] This is put forward as a ground for the obligation to provide a measure of state compensation for the victims of violent crime, and also for an obligation to provide services of support for victims. The extent of those duties gives rise to controversies that will not be tackled here, but is the argument sound? Can a state be expected to prevent all crimes within its jurisdiction? That would seem unrealistic, since there will always be those who succumb to the temptation to make illegal gains and acquisitions, and always those who yield to strong emotions. Unless the state is to have a police officer at everyone's elbow, which would be both objectionable in principle and virtually impossible in practice, this is surely a non-starter. Thus to refer to the 'failure' of crime prevention measures in this context is unconvincing hyperbole. A more realistic proposition is that the compensation of victims of violent crime should be seen as part of an overall state responsibility for responding to people who suffer harm or who have a disability. Most states now accept the obligation to provide support (medical and/ or financial) for people with a disability and their duty to provide compensation for

---

[66] Council of Europe, *Explanatory Report* on the European Convention on the Compensation of Victims of Violent Crime (ETS No 116), Strasbourg, 23 November 1983, (1984) para 9.

victims of violent crime. This is not so much about the prevention of harm as about the prevention of the disadvantageous consequences of harm, whether congenital or criminal. None of this is to deny that there may be instances where it is possible to point to a particular policy of crime prevention that has either been tried and failed or, worse, has not been tried when it ought to have been. But to establish such a causative failure would rarely be easy. The Council of Europe's proposition should be discarded in favour of broader arguments of social policy and social security.

B. A state obligation to combat criminogenic conditions?

Does the state's obligation to prevent harm extend to an obligation to take all reasonable steps to suppress criminogenic social conditions? Must the punishing state come with 'clean hands', such that failure to suppress criminogenic conditions might disqualify it from standing in judgement on those who offend? These questions arise in the context of the state's proper response to citizens whose offending results from gross social or economic inequality. If the state bears some responsibility for failing to alleviate social inequality and economic deprivation, does this have any bearing on the moral standing of the state to punish or on the responsibility of the offender, and, if so, what should the implications be for sentencing the impoverished offender?

It is commonly argued that justice is blind and that a liberal state should treat citizens alike. If the coercive power of the criminal law is to be applied consistently to all in accordance with rule-of-law standards, the pursuit of justice requires some degree of 'blindness' and of uniformity. Yet as Gardner points out, this is to operate 'against a background of assumed, but often entirely fictitious, uniformity' that may lead to 'a remote and sometimes callous disinterest in people's well-being'.[67] Formal equality may, in practice, deal unfairly with those who offend, in part as a consequence of gross social and economic disadvantage. Likewise, the assumption of moral autonomy at the heart of liberalism may fail to take adequate account of the extreme adverse circumstances in which some offenders act. The difficulties entailed in determining how the state might take into account criminogenic conditions that it has failed to prevent are legion and well-rehearsed. They include: the problem of establishing relative deprivation without enquiries that are intrusive and stigmatising; the risk of discriminating between 'deserving' and 'undeserving' poor; and the danger that those identified as particularly disadvantaged may also be regarded as at particularly high risk of future offending.[68] Possible solutions include the introduction of some form of categorical leniency that acknowledges the effect of criminogenic conditions on moral choice; a partial defence of 'rotten social back-

---

[67] J Gardner, 'Crime: In Proportion and Perspective' in Ashworth and Wasik (eds), *Fundamentals of Sentencing Theory*, above n 11, 36.
[68] L Zedner, 'Reflections on Criminal Justice as a Social Institution' in D Downes, D Hobbs and T Newburn (eds), *The Eternal Recurrence of Crime and Control: Essays in Honour of Paul Rock* (Oxford, Oxford University Press, 2010) 69, 85–88.

ground' or 'economic duress'; or mitigation at sentencing for those whose offending derives from the state's failure to prevent criminogenic conditions.[69]

In our view, the answer to the underlying question of the state's responsibility
should follow the same lines as the discussion in the preceding subsection (IV.A),
but this time with a stronger empirical basis. Even if one accepts that the administration of justice requires a measure of consistency that must be blind to criminogenic conditions,[70] the state's preventive obligation has implications beyond the
courtroom, as well as for the institution of punishment as a whole. It may be difficult for a state to eliminate all forms of socio-economic deprivation, but it is
certainly true that most states could choose to devote much more attention and
resources to reducing it. From that point of view, they can fairly be said to bear some
responsibility for the offending to which it leads – assuming that it is right to infer
from the strong association between offending and deprivation that deprivation
may be so severe as to render compliance with the law especially difficult.[71] Von
Hirsch argues that the fact of social deprivation does not affect the harmfulness of
offending conduct: although some forms of criminalisation may be said to serve the
interests of the powerful, the bulk of the criminal law is needed 'to protect ordinary
people's lives, safety and possessions.'[72] He accepts that socio-economic deprivation may reduce the culpability of some offenders, but argues that only in strong
and demonstrable cases should this be a source of significant mitigation.

Von Hirsch therefore argues that the more appropriate course in a liberal state
would be to proceed along two related lines. The first would be to decline to use the
punishment system as a means of combating social ills but rather to pursue more
direct social and economic policies aimed at eliminating inequalities. This approach
is related to the state's obligation to prevent harm, insofar as socio-economic
inequalities are productive of crimes and harms. The state's obligation should be to
reduce criminogenic conditions, whether that means combating socio-economic
inequalities, introducing measures of situational crime prevention (in the design of
public spaces, for example), and/or introducing measures of social crime prevention (by promoting alternative community activities and facilities). The second
approach would be to ensure that the overall levels of punishment are lowered, to
reflect the state's partial responsibility for the conditions in which criminality takes
place. The reasoning here might be linked to the state's authority to punish: the
state ought to bear responsibility for the criminal law and punishment because
those burdens flow from the obligation to prevent harm, and also because the state
can be impartial and authoritative in a way that victims or the local community

---

[69] R Delgado, ' "Rotten Social Background": Should the Criminal Law Recognize a Defence of Severe
Environmental Deprivation?' (1985) 3 *Law and Inequality* 9; B Hudson, 'Mitigation for Socially Deprived
Offenders' in A von Hirsch and A Ashworth (eds), *Principled Sentencing: Readings on Theory and Policy*
(Oxford, Hart Publishing, 1998) 205–8.
[70] See, eg, S Morse, 'Deprivation and Desert' in W Hefferman and J Kleinig (eds), *From Social Justice
to Criminal Justice* (New York, Oxford University Press, 2000) 114.
[71] Von Hirsch, *Censure and Sanctions*, above n 8 at 108n.
[72] Ibid, 107.

might not be able to be.[73] If there were a situation in which the state could be said to be entirely responsible for the crimes committed within its jurisdiction, this would surely undercut its authority to punish. The argument must therefore be that, if the state has a significant level of responsibility for some crimes in its jurisdiction (because it devotes insufficient attention and resources to combating socio-economic deprivation and inequality, and there is a strong association between that and offending rates), the state should acknowledge this by lowering the level of sentences. If it maintains high sanctioning levels despite its failure adequately to tackle socio-economic deprivation and inequality, it undermines its own authority to punish.

C. A state's obligation to offer rehabilitative programmes to those whom it punishes

If we assume that a particular offender has been duly sentenced for an offence, what are the state's obligations towards that person during the sentence? The minimum obligation is to treat the offender with dignity and with respect for her or his rights. A specific example of this would be the provision of appropriate psychiatric care and support for a mentally disordered detainee;[74] the same would apply in the case of a physically disabled detainee.[75] More generally, the judgments of the European Court of Human Rights have insisted that the substantive right in Article 3 of the European Convention – the right not to be subjected to torture and inhuman or degrading treatment – generates a positive obligation on the state to ensure the detention of its prisoners in conditions respectful of human dignity.[76] That merely establishes a minimum threshold, albeit an important one, and that minimum is reinforced by detailed European standards and by the inspectorial work of the European Committee for the Prevention of Torture and Inhuman and Degrading Treatment.[77] The requirement to treat those serving prison sentences and community sanctions with dignity does not stop at the end of the sentence, however. The Federal Constitutional Court in Germany insisted on support for offenders after the end of the sentence, linking this to the *Sozialstaatsprinzip*, and the Court called for 'public care and assistance for those groups in the community who, because of personal weakness or fault, incapacity or social disadvantage, were retarded in their

---

[73] Von Hirsch and Ashworth, *Proportionate Sentencing*, above n 2 at 30–31.

[74] As the European Court of Human Rights held in *Claes v Belgium* (App No 43418/09), 10 January 2013, [88]–[91].

[75] *Price v United Kingdom* (App No 33394/94), 10 July 2001.

[76] See, eg, *Riviere v France* (App No 33834/03), 11 July 2006, [62], and *Cara Damiani v Italy* (App No 2447/05), 7 February 2012, [66].

[77] See the European Prison Rules (1987, revised 2006) and the European Rules on Community Sanctions and Measures (1992, revised 2000). For discussion, see D van Zyl Smit, 'Community Sanctions and European Human Rights Law' in L Zedner and JV Roberts (eds), *Principles and Values in Criminal Law and Criminal Justice: Essays in Honour of Andrew Ashworth* (Oxford, Oxford University Press, 2012) 191.

social development: prisoners and released prisoners also belong to this group.'[78] This mode of reasoning assigns an expansive role to the fundamental right to dignity. It suggests that measures taken in pursuance of the state's obligation to prevent harm, including punishment (whether in prison or in the community), should respect dignity.[79]

Does dignity have further implications for the nature and content of penal measures? The European Court of Human Rights has recently stated that:[80]

> There is now clear support in European and international law for the principle that all prisoners . . . be offered the possibility of rehabilitation and the prospect of release if that rehabilitation is achieved.

Quite apart from the legal recognition of this principle, it can also be supported by reference to the state's obligation to prevent harm. However, its context within a liberal state which respects each person as a moral agent may give rise to conflicts. The precise argument is that rehabilitative programmes should be *made available* during prison sentences and within the framework of community sentences. Many issues arise from this. First of all, there is little point in offering programmes that have no proven significant effect on offenders. This means that different programmes must be targeted towards particular types of offender, not 'one size fits all', and that they should be piloted, evaluated, and then (if shown to be effective, usually in terms of lower re-offending rates) made available more widely. The literature on 'what works' is burgeoning,[81] but there is also a literature on what does not work and what may even be counter-productive.[82] Since the argument stems from the state's obligation to prevent harm and crime, it requires keen scrutiny of the credentials and effectiveness of any programme to be offered. Enthusiasts are often crucial to the establishment of a particular programme, but effectiveness must be judged on objective empirical grounds.

Secondly, the programmes should be voluntary rather than compulsory insofar as they require changes in attitude or personality. The principle of voluntariness is linked to the idea of respect for all subjects, including offenders, as moral agents capable of deliberation.[83] This raises the difficult question of whether the timing of release from custody or supervision should be dependent on the 'successful' completion of a given programme. Similarly, if a programme is part of a community

---

[78] Translated from the judgment in the *Lebach* case (BVerfGE 35, 202 – Judgment of 5 June 1973) and quoted by van Zyl Smit, ibid, 205.

[79] This is also written into the Rules: eg r 23 of the European Rules on Community Sanctions and Measures states that community sanctions shall be organised with respect for the dignity of the offender.

[80] *Vinter, Bamber and Moore v United Kingdom* (App Nos 66069/09, 130/10 and 3896/10), 9 July 2013, [114].

[81] A fairly balanced official publication is G Harper and C Chitty (eds), *The Impact of Corrections on Re-Offending: a Review of 'What Works'* (Home Office Research Study 291, 2005). See also A von Hirsch, A Ashworth and J Roberts (eds), *Principled Sentencing*, 3rd edn (Oxford, Hart Publishing, 2009) ch 1.

[82] See, eg, AE Bottoms and A von Hirsch, 'The Crime-Preventive Impact of Penal Sanctions' in P Cane and HM Kritzer (eds), *Oxford Handbook of Empirical Legal Research* (Oxford, Oxford University Press, 2010).

[83] See further above, text at nn 33–36, on von Hirsch's position.

sentence, the compulsory element should consist of attendance as required, eg for discussions with a probation officer or to perform unpaid work (as directed), and any programme relating to attitudes or habits should be undertaken voluntarily, once the offender's suitability has been assessed.

One aspect of rehabilitation and voluntariness that causes particular controversy in contemporary sentencing is the availability of drug treatment programmes. English courts have occasionally said that the proportionate sentence for the offence would be three years' imprisonment, but that, in view of the role played by drug addiction in the offending behaviour and in view of the offender's willingness to undergo the programme, the court is willing to make a community order coupled with a requirement of drug treatment.[84] The Sentencing Council has now incorporated this into its guidelines.[85] How, if at all, is this compatible with a framework of proportionality within which the state's obligation of crime prevention should lead to the availability of rehabilitative programmes? Arguably it is not. Neither is the converse situation, also seen occasionally, where the court is told that in order to ensure sufficient time for completion of a rehabilitative programme the sentence should be *longer* than would be proportionate. The proper response would be to apply pressure to ensure that a meaningful programme can be completed within the proportionate sentence or – and this is certainly compatible with the view advanced here – that provision is made for some kind of treatment or support to be available after the offender has completed the proportionate sentence. That would underscore the voluntariness of the programme, and ensure that the sentence is not unfairly lengthened. The more difficult case is where the argument is that the proportionate sentence should be shortened in order to facilitate more effective treatment. Even if the enhanced effectiveness is supported by robust evidence, it is not clear why this should affect the imposition of a proportionate sentence. The state's primary duty should be to provide treatment programmes both within custodial institutions and in the community. This is not to endorse long prison sentences, or to suggest that drug addiction should not be capable of operating as a mitigating factor in sentencing. It is simply to state that, in principle, drug treatment programmes should be available both in the community and in prisons; otherwise there is a danger of distortion.

D. A state's obligations to those preventively detained

The use of indeterminate prison sentences is controversial. They give the state and its organs considerable power over the prisoner's future, while the prisoner has no guarantee of release at any particular stage. Most European countries use indefinite sentences sparingly, if at all, but they have become a major part of the English

---

[84] Eg *R v Kelly* [2003] 1 Cr App R (S) 472, [2002] EWCA 2060; *R v Belli* [2004] 1 Cr App R (S) 490.
[85] Sentencing Council, *Burglary Offences: Definitive Guideline* (London, Sentencing Council, 2011) 8; Sentencing Council, *Sexual Offences: Definitive Guideline* (London, Sentencing Council, 2013) 22.

sentencing system for violent and sexual offenders.[86] Given the immense power possessed by the state in these cases, and the weak position of the prisoner, it is hardly surprising that the European Court has held that the state has a duty to provide support and (where necessary) psychiatric care for those serving indeterminate sentences.[87] However, English law introduced in 2003 a new form of indeterminate sentence – imprisonment for public protection (IPP) – which was much more extensive in its application. It was mandatory for qualifying offenders from 2005 to 2008, and available to the courts as a discretionary sentence from 2008 to 2012. The offenders had to serve a minimum term set by the courts (often fairly short) and thereafter can be released if the Parole Board decides that they no longer represent a more than minimal risk.[88] The most persuasive way in which an IPP prisoner could demonstrate to the Parole Board that they had addressed their behavioural problems was to show that a rehabilitative course had been completed successfully. However, there were few such courses available. Some IPP prisoners claimed that this made their continued detention arbitrary, contrary to Article 5 of the European Convention, and the European Court agreed with them:[89]

> Regard must be had to the need to encourage the rehabilitation of these offenders. In the applicants' cases, this meant that they were required to be provided with reasonable opportunities to undertake courses aimed at helping them to address their offending behaviour and the risks they posed.

The Court found that the continued detention of the applicants (and, by implication, some 3,500 other IPP prisoners who have served their minimum terms) was arbitrary and therefore unlawful. This dramatically underlines the state's obligation to provide rehabilitative opportunities to those prisoners who need to persuade others that they are ready for release.[90]

What are the state's obligations when an offender is sentenced to life imprisonment with a minimum term of life (sometimes known as 'life imprisonment without parole')? A preliminary question is whether a minimum term of the whole natural life is a permissible sentence. The European Court of Human Rights has held that the 'life means life' sentence is not incompatible with human dignity, nor arbitrary, nor inhuman or degrading, referring to the state's obligation 'to take measures for the protection of the public from violent crime.' Those serving indeterminate sentences for murder or other serious offences against the person may be

---

[86] See Ashworth and Zedner, *Preventive Justice*, above n 41, ch 7.

[87] *M v Germany* (App No 19359/04), 17 December 2009, [76]–[77] and [129].

[88] Note that in respect of determinate sentenced prisoners, s 125 of the Legal Aid, Sentencing and Punishment of Offenders (LASPO) Act 2012 sets a new test for release that 'the Board is satisfied that it is no longer necessary for the protection of the public that the person should be confined.'

[89] *James, Wells and Lee v United Kingdom* (App Nos 25119/09, 57715/09 and 57877/09), 18 September 2012, [218].

[90] The IPP sentence was abolished and replaced by an Extended Determinate Sentence for dangerous offenders under s 124 of the Legal Aid, Sentencing and Punishment of Offenders Act 2012. The status of existing IPP prisoners is unaffected and as of June 2013 5,620 IPP prisoners remained in prison. See further, A Ashworth and L Zedner, *Preventive Justice*, above n 41, ch 7.

detained 'for as long as they remain dangerous'.[91] However, the Court went on to hold that there must be 'both a prospect of release and a possibility of review',[92] the so-called right to hope. The Court stated that there is an emerging European consensus that reflects a 'commitment to both the rehabilitation of life sentence prisoners and to the prospect of their eventual release.'[93] The conclusion was that the relevant law should provide for a process whereby the need for continued detention can be reviewed, and that English law was defective in making no such provision.[94] The reasoning in this and the other European cases is that states bear the responsibility for providing all prisoners, even those who have been convicted of the most heinous offences, with rehabilitative opportunities and with the possibility of eventual release.

V. Conclusion

The state's duty to provide preventive programmes within the scope of proportionate sentences is an obligation that derives from the basic preventive function of the state as protector – namely, that the liberal state has a duty to provide the means whereby persons can lead their chosen lives in peace, good order, and without fear or risk of harm. These obligations are owed to all, and thus the state owes duties to victims to minimise the adverse consequences of crime; to offenders to combat criminogenic conditions and to take these into account when sentencing; to provide for decent conditions and rehabilitative programmes for those it punishes; and to ensure that preventive penal measures are the least restrictive appropriate alternative and for the shortest period necessary. Only in this way will the important precept established by Andreas von Hirsch that hard treatment remains a prudential *supplement* to the moral voice of censure be maintained, and the risk that the state resorts to 'tiger-control' be averted.

---

[91] *Vinter, Bamber and Moore v United Kingdom* (App Nos 66069/09, 130/10 and 3896/10), 9 July 2013, [108].

[92] Ibid, [110].

[93] Ibid, [117].

[94] The English Court of Appeal has declined to follow this part of the *Vinter* judgment: see *R v Newell; Attorney General's Reference (No. 69 of 2013)* [2014] EWCA Crim 188, with commentary at [2014] Crim LR 471.

2

Prevention, Censure and Responsibility: The Recent Debate on the Purposes of Punishment

CLAUS ROXIN

I. Overcoming the Simple Contrast between Two Strands of Theories?

The centuries-old debate regarding the meaning and purpose of state punishment has recently been revived in Germany with considerable vigour. Tatjana Hörnle and Andreas von Hirsch's joint paper on 'Positive general prevention and censure', first published in 1995,[1] has received much attention and has been reprinted twice.[2] Another foundational contribution by von Hirsch, 'Why should penal sanctions exist? – Censure and prevention as elements in the justification of punishment', has already appeared twice in German.[3] A third paper, on 'Censure and prevention: hard treatment as an element of punishment',[4] joins them.

As one can already tell from the titles of these papers, von Hirsch's central thesis is that punishment cannot be justified either on exclusively preventive grounds or merely as a social-institutional expression of disapproval of the perpetrator's conduct (censure). Rather, both elements are essential to an adequate justification of state punishment. Von Hirsch speaks of his theory as 'a model that ... attempts to combine censure and prevention,'[5] thus providing 'a mixed justification for the penal sanction' which 'contains elements of prevention as well as censure.'[6]

---

[1] T Hörnle and A von Hirsch, 'Positive Generalprävention und Tadel' (1995) 142 *Goltdammer's Archiv für Strafrecht* 261. [Translator's note: Unless otherwise indicated in the relevant footnote, all translations of quotations from German texts in this chapter are the translator's own.]

[2] In B Schünemann, A von Hirsch and N Jareborg (eds), *Positive Generalprävention: Kritische Analysen im deutsch-englischen Dialog* (Heidelberg, CF Müller, 1998) 83 and in A von Hirsch, *Fairness, Verbrechen und Strafe: Strafrechtstheoretische Abhandlungen* (Berlin, Berliner Wissenschaftsverlag, 2005) 19.

[3] 'Warum soll die Strafsanktion existieren? – Tadel und Prävention als Elemente einer Rechtfertigung' in von Hirsch, ibid, 41 and in A von Hirsch, U Neumann and K Seelmann (eds), *Strafe – Warum? Gegenwärtige Strafbegründungen im Lichte von Hegels Straftheorie* (Baden-Baden, Nomos, 2011) 43. [Subsequent citations of this paper refer to the latter publication.]

[4] A von Hirsch, 'Tadel und Prävention: Die Übelszufügung als Element der Strafe' in Schünemann et al (eds), *Positive Generalprävention*, above n 2 at 101.

[5] Von Hirsch, 'Warum soll die Strafsanktion existieren?', above n 3 at 44.

[6] Von Hirsch, 'Tadel und Prävention', above n 4 at 107.

This overcomes the stark opposition between 'absolute' (deontological) and 'relative' (consequentialist) justifications of punishment, which has long dominated the German debate. On von Hirsch's view, punishment is not justified in the manner of an 'absolute' theory, through the idea of a retributive justice independent of punishment's social effects. Neither is punishment justified, as the 'relative' theories would have it, solely with reference to its intended preventive, crime-averting effects on the perpetrator and on members of the public. In the justification of punishment, desert-related and preventive elements must be combined. Von Hirsch makes it clear 'that a convincing theoretical justification of the institution of punishment must leave the dichotomy between abstract and relative positions behind,'[7] and maintains that 'the traditional distinction between absolute and relative theories must be given up.'[8]

Today these ideas place Andreas von Hirsch in the mainstream of debates among penal theorists. His views receive support from both prevention-oriented and retribution-oriented theorists. An example of the first tendency can be found in my own approach, which I first developed in 1966 and have described as a 'dialectical unified theory'.[9] In the most recent edition of my textbook, I highlight that my 'concept of culpability-constrained prevention rests on the insight that neither culpability nor prevention provide, on their own, a full justification of punishment,'[10] and add in a footnote that 'von Hirsch develops a similar conception . . . when he justifies punishment through a combination of censure and prevention.'[11] As regards modern versions of retributive theories, it suffices to quote Pawlik: 'This theory shares with prevention-oriented theories a concern with the maintenance of social order,' and thus 'the gulf between retributive and prevention-oriented theories can be bridged.'[12] The main contemporary proponent of a neoclassical theory of punishment, Köhler, also accepts that 'just punishment is . . . at the same time the foundation of preventive measures.'[13]

There thus appears to be real opportunity for transcending the theoretical divide. But whether we manage to realise this opportunity will depend on whether we succeed in combining culpability- (and thus, censure-) oriented and prevention-oriented elements in a convincing manner. Each classical justification must therefore be able to compensate for the deficiencies of the other. This festschrift for our revered colleague, the influential penal theorist Andreas von Hirsch, provides me with the ideal setting for pursuing these questions a little further.

---

[7] Von Hirsch, 'Warum soll die Strafsanktion existieren?', above n 3 at 44.

[8] Von Hirsch, 'Tadel und Prävention', above n 4 at 107.

[9] C Roxin, 'Sinn und Grenzen staatlicher Strafe' (1966) *Juristische Schulung* 377 (reprinted in C Roxin, *Strafrechtliche Grundlagenprobleme* (Berlin, De Gruyter, 1973) 1).

[10] C Roxin, *Strafrecht: Allgemeiner Teil*, vol I, 4th edn (Munich, CH Beck, 2006) § 3 marginal note 60.

[11] Ibid, § 3 marginal note 60 fn 98.

[12] M Pawlik, '"Der Täter ist um der Gemeinschaft willen verpflichtet, die Strafe auf sich zu nehmen." Überlegungen zur Strafbegründung im Anschluss an Claus Roxin' (2006) 153 *Goltdammer's Archiv für Strafrecht* 345.

[13] M Köhler, *Strafrecht, Allgemeiner Teil* (Berlin, Springer, 1997) 50.

II. The Shortcomings of Traditional 'Absolute' and 'Relative' Theories of Punishment

To find a convincing solution, we first have to identify the weaknesses of the familiar monistic approaches, insofar as these rely exclusively on a deontological justification of punishment that is independent of any social purposes (as the so-called 'absolute' theories of punishment do), or seek to justify the practice of punishment solely with arguments regarding its intended social consequences (as the so-called 'relative' theories of punishment do).

A. The 'absolute' theories: Punishment as 'commensurate desert' (*gerechter Schuldausgleich*), or as (non-empirical, effect-independent) norm-affirmation (*Bestätigung* der *Normgeltung*)

We find the absolute theory in its purest form in Kant's frequently cited postulate that even if a society decided to dissolve itself, 'the last murderer remaining in prison would first have to be executed, so that each has done to him what his deeds deserve.'[14] This turns the idea of justice into an absolute requirement, which, as a categorical imperative, demands compliance irrespective of any social purposes. 'For if justice goes, there is no longer any value in human beings' living on the earth.'[15]

It is unclear whether such a view has any contemporary support. Winfried Hassemer maintains that modern defenders of 'absolute' theories rely increasingly on the argument that[16]

> the realisation of justice through punishment has a concrete, pragmatic point to it: In the longer run, this secures respect for norms essential to our survival. In other words: the 'absolute' theories we encounter these days are wearing preventive cloaks.

On the other hand, EA Wolff, who was particularly influential after the end of the Second World War in reviving absolute theory in the Kantian tradition, wrote that 'The punishment described here is imposed solely in the interests of justice.'[17] Be

---

[14] I Kant, *The Metaphysics of Morals* (1797) (Ak 6: 333) in *The Cambridge Edition of the Works of Immanuel Kant: Practical Philosophy*, transl M Gregor, introd A Wood (Cambridge, Cambridge University Press, 1996) 474. In view of other passages in Kant's work, it is debatable whether Kant really supported an uncompromisingly absolute theory (this is discussed in T Hörnle, 'Gegenwärtige Strafbegründungstheorien: Die herkömmliche deutsche Diskussion' in von Hirsch et al (eds), *Strafe – Warum?*, above n 3 at 17). The point can remain open here, since only those quotations that support an absolute theory have been historically influential. For a discussion of other variants of absolute theories, see T Hörnle, *Straftheorien* (Tübingen, Mohr Siebeck, 2011) 16ff.

[15] Kant, *Metaphysics of Morals* (1797) (Ak 6: 332), above n 14 at 473.

[16] W Hassemer, 'Variationen der positiven Generalprävention' in Schünemann et al (eds), *Positive Generalprävention*, above n 2 at 30.

[17] EA Wolff, 'Das neuere Verständnis von Generalprävention und seine Tauglichkeit für eine Antwort auf Kriminalität' (1985) 97 *Zeitschrift für die gesamte Strafrechtswissenschaft* 786, 826. Wolff points out

that as it may, 'absolute' theories encounter three major objections which render them incapable of justifying punishment on their own.

First, 'absolute' theories cannot explain why *the state* should punish anyone at all, and conversely why, once an institution of state punishment exists, crimes are often deliberately left unpunished. One cannot reasonably think that a state would maintain an expensive criminal justice system merely in order to realise an abstract ideal of justice. Rather, criminal justice is an instrument of social control. It is meant to contribute to the achievement of one of the state's central tasks, namely to ensure that citizens can lead their lives in freedom and security. Only this can explain why the state may refrain from punishing the perpetrators of less serious crimes due to a 'lack of public interest' in their prosecution and punishment (as the German Code of Criminal Procedure allows in §§ 153, 153a StPO). A duty to bring about justice in each case would commit the state to the prosecution and punishment of every criminal act; a position far removed from our actual legal order.

Von Hirsch, too, raises this concern when he imagines a 'hypothetical society', in which 'acts of violence and theft have become rare' and 'informal social sanctions and tort law would be perfectly sufficient to keep such behaviours under control.'[18] He correctly denies a need to punish in these cases. Of course, this point is true not only for hypothetical but also for real, existing societies. Where any interest in prevention is lacking, one need not punish, at least in cases where the crime is not very serious.

The second objection consists in the realisation that it simply cannot be the state's task to bring about 'ideal justice'[19] irrespective of any preventive aims. In my textbook I explain that:[20]

> The metaphysical ideal of justice is not something that the state, as a human institution, is capable of reaching or may appropriately aim for. The will of its citizens obliges the state to safeguard our communal life in peace and freedom, and the state is limited to this role.

This view is not only held by authors who, like me, see the protective function of the state as a basic precondition for the justified imposition of any penal sanction. Pawlik, an author who takes a primarily retributive view, likewise observes that:[21]

> A theory of justice on its own . . . cannot show us why the state should punish at all. That the state holds the right to punish does not bestow on it the role of defender of ideal justice. A retributive theory of punishment must . . . show that state punishment makes a necessary contribution to the goal of securing citizens' freedom.

---

that 'solely in the interests of justice' is to be understood as 'solely for the preservation of each person's external freedom of choice (external freedom).'

[18] Von Hirsch, 'Warum soll die Strafsanktion existieren?' in von Hirsch et al, *Strafe – Warum?*, above n 3 at 58 (and see also at 45).

[19] Translator's note: 'Ideal justice' is used here for the German term *Gerechtigkeit* when the notion invoked is that of a metaphysical or philosophical ideal of justice.

[20] Roxin, *Strafrecht AllgemeinerTeil I*, above n 10, at § 3 marginal note 9.

[21] M Pawlik, 'Kritik der präventionstheoretischen Strafbegründungen' in K Rogall (ed), *Festschrift für Hans-Joachim Rudolphi zum 70. Geburtstag* (Munich, Wolters-Kluwer, 2004) 213, 229.

Thirdly, even if it were the role of the state to bring about 'ideal justice', it cannot plausibly be argued that this is achieved by adding further injury, in the form of punishment, to the harm done by the perpetrator through his crime. This objection can already be found in the works of Hegel and his successor, Gaus.[22] Von Hirsch puts this objection as follows: it 'remains unclear why the wrongful harm done to the victim by the offender ought to be repaid through a violation of the offender's rights.'[23]

For these reasons, 'absolute' theories, which understand punishment solely as a means to bring about justice, fail to provide us with a convincing justification of punishment.

Similar objections can be made against the theory of punishment developed by Jakobs. Admittedly, for Jakobs the purpose of punishment consists in norm-affirmation, and thus in a social function. In substance, though, his is nevertheless an 'absolute' theory.[24] This becomes evident when Jakobs explains that his position only supports sanctions that 'restore equilibrium by balancing out only the harm attributable to a specific norm-violation. The point is therefore not to deter this norm-violator from future crimes . . . or to discourage other potential perpetrators from acting upon their criminal inclinations.'[25] Once the sentence has been executed, 'the purpose of punishment has necessarily been achieved. The normative order of society has been reaffirmed.'[26]

Yet because of its indifference to the actual social effects of punishment, this view fails to explain why we ought to punish. The continuing validity of the norm an offender has violated can be demonstrated in many other ways. In their 1995 article, Hörnle and von Hirsch make the point that[27]

> we can imagine a whole range of other measures capable of stabilising the validity of norms. Objections against the breach of a norm could be registered through pronounce-ments made by special committees, through interruptions of TV programmes for 'min-utes of silence' after a grave offence has been committed, etc.

Kuhlen's reply is even more straightforward: 'If all we need is a declaration that the violation of the norm was wrong and that the norm continues to be valid, why not just declare this and leave it at that?'[28] Kuhlen concludes that in order to justify

---

[22] References in Pawlik, 'Überlegungen', above n 12 at 347.

[23] Von Hirsch, 'Tadel und Prävention', above n 4 at 101.

[24] The appropriate classification of Jakobs' theory of punishment is debated. He was initially seen as a proponent of positive general prevention due to his reliance on the idea that criminal justice trains citizens to be norm-compliant. In light of Jakobs' more recent publications, Hörnle now understands his theory as a normatively-oriented expressive theory (see Hörnle, 'Gegenwärtige Strafbegründungstheorien', above n 14 at 24 and Hörnle, *Straftheorien*, above n 14 at 30). To my mind, given Jakobs' insistence that consequences be disregarded, the absolute element dominates his theory.

[25] G Jakobs, *Norm, Person, Gesellschaft: Vorüberlegungen zu einer Rechtsphilosophie*, 3rd edn (Berlin, Duncker & Humblot, 2008) 114.

[26] G Jakobs, 'Was schützt das Strafrecht: Rechtsgüter oder Normgeltung?' in T Shiibashi (ed), *Strafrechtswissenschaft: Festschrift für Seiji Saito* (Tokyo, Shinzansha, 2003) 780.

[27] Hörnle and von Hirsch, 'Positive Generalprävention', above n 1 at 266.

[28] L Kuhlen, 'Anmerkungen zur positiven Generalprävention' in Schünemann et al (eds), *Positive Generalprävention*, above n 2 at 55, 62.

punishment, 'we therefore have to take into account the contribution that punishment in fact makes to norm-compliance (and not merely its symbolic contribution to norm-validity), in particular the general-preventive effects of punishment.'[29]

One could go even further and argue that the validity of a norm may remain unaffected even though in some cases a crime meets with no response at all, for instance because no-one knows who committed it.

B. 'Relative' theories: Punishment as a preventive element in the control and pre-emption of crime

The critical engagement with absolute theories has shown that the existence of a criminal justice system cannot be explained, let alone justified, without some reference to empirical social purposes. This can today be taken as a generally accepted insight. Hörnle is quite right to say that, 'For a modern constitutional state, it is simply unthinkable to place no reliance whatsoever on [the criminal law's] functions and purposes.'[30] Von Hirsch stresses that 'the institution of state punishment could well be abolished if it no longer made a useful (or only an insufficiently useful) contribution to the prevention of serious rights-violations.'[31] Schünemann, likewise, 'insists that any legitimate state activity in a secular society presupposes an orientation towards the achievement of a useful social purpose.'[32]

The starting point for any justification of the criminal law is, therefore, preventive: the criminal law ought to secure peace and freedom for all citizens. The specific preventive aims set in pursuit of this function are manifold. In the first instance, we can distinguish between 'special prevention', the influence the law has on particular individuals, and 'general prevention', the law's influence on members of the public generally. 'Special prevention' can be achieved through restraints (say, incarceration) imposed upon, and through deterrent messages directed to, an individual. It can also be brought about through the re-socialisation of individuals, and through the interception of their offending behaviour. 'General prevention' can be encountered in a 'negative' and a 'positive' variant. 'Negative general prevention' consists in the deterrent effect that the existence of a criminal justice system exerts on members of the public generally. 'Positive general prevention' is associated with the reinforcement of the public's respect for the law and commitment to law-abiding behaviour. In this regard, I want to distinguish further between three components: first, the 'educational effects' flowing from the perception of the public administration of criminal justice (what Jakobs thinks of as training for citizens to increase their respect for the law[33]); secondly, the increase in public trust resulting from citizens seeing the law vindicated; and, thirdly, the 'pacifying effect' that results when

---

[29]   Ibid.

[30]   Hörnle, 'Gegenwärtige Strafbegründungstheorien', above n 14 at 30.

[31]   Von Hirsch, 'Warum soll die Strafsanktion existieren?', above n 3 at 44.

[32]   B Schünemann, 'Zum Stellenwert der positiven Generalprävention in einer dualistischen Straftheorie' in Schünemann et al (eds), *Positive Generalprävention*, above n 2, 109, 115.

[33]   G Jakobs, *Schuld und Prävention* (Tübingen, Mohr Siebeck, 1976) 10, 31ff.

the public's sense of justice is appeased by the punishment of the perpetrator and sees the conflict with the perpetrator as resolved thereby.[34]

In sum, prevention aims at a range of different effects, each of which could be subjected to critical evaluation. The question I want to focus on here, however, is whether the totality of these intended effects can, in principle, provide a justification for punishment.

Preventive justifications of punishment also give rise to three major concerns, of which at least two have to be recognised as legitimate objections.

The most frequently made objection to prevention-based arguments is the claim that there is no sociological evidence that any of the expected preventive effects obtain in practice. High rates of recidivism raise doubts about any individual-preventive deterrent effects of punishment. The great expectations placed on re-socialisation in the 1970s have been thoroughly dashed.[35] 'Nothing works' is the new catchword phrase, leaving re-socialisation with few supporters in the more recent literature. Similar voices can be heard against general prevention. Bock observes that, in fact, 'next to nothing is known about whether and how positive general prevention actually works.'[36] With regard to negative general prevention, empirical research results are, he says, equally thin on the ground.[37] Hörnle and von Hirsch agree that positive general-preventive effects have not been empirically proven: 'The sparse and feeble attempts to conduct empirical research into these effects do not support any empirically validated claims about the basic assumptions of the theory.'[38]

This objection can nevertheless be overcome. First, any particular criminal trial can and will have different effects on the defendant, relatives, acquaintances, and the public. The effects will also vary along with the type and gravity of the offence, the social context, and its reverberation in the media. Secondly, it will hardly ever be the case that all the intended general-preventive effects flow from a single trial. For these reasons the social sciences are faced with an almost insurmountable problem if they are to trace concrete preventive effects, 'because the complexity of the causal relationships makes a convincing research design nearly impossible.'[39]

This indeterminacy, however, does not change the fact that a functioning system of social control and criminal justice is – taken in the totality of its social effects – certainly capable of helping to maintain the conditions of individual freedom and civil peace for citizens. Some crimes will, of course, still be committed. But whereas in Germany one can walk the streets safely at night, there are other countries in which this is impossibly dangerous and where people hide away in their houses surrounded by high walls. One cannot seriously doubt that such a deplorable state of affairs is due to failures of preventive social management, ranging from police work

[34] Roxin, *Strafrecht Allgemeiner Teil I*, above n 10 at § 3 marginal note 27.

[35] For details see Roxin, ibid, § 3 marginal note 20.

[36] M Bock, 'Ideen und Schimären im Strafrecht. Rechtssoziologische Anmerkungen zur Dogmatik der positiven Generalprävention' (1991) 103 *Zeitschrift für die gesamte Strafrechtswissenschaft* 636, 654.

[37] Ibid.

[38] Hörnle and von Hirsch, 'Positive Generalprävention', above n 1 at 262.

[39] Ibid.

to the operations of the criminal courts and the correctional system. (That these failures are, in turn, a consequence of poverty and other social problems, is a different point.) For this reason I agree with Kuhlen when he says that,[40]

> If we admit general life experience, whether or not it has been validated by the methods of empirical social research, as a source of knowledge, then we can accept that the mechanisms which produce the effects of negative and positive general prevention are perfectly plausible.

This is just as true for individual-preventive effects.

The second main objection to preventive theories of punishment is, however, irrefutable: that they fail to offer principled guidance regarding the measure of punishment, and that their inner logic has a tendency to support indeterminate and harsh sanctions which take insufficient account of the offender's personality rights and of the consequent limits to state intervention.

This is, first and foremost, true for measures of special prevention. Consider imprisonment. Clearly, while an offender remains in prison, society is ordinarily safe from that particular offender. With respect to dangerous offenders, this can easily lead to a climate of public opinion where demands are made that such individuals be locked away forever. This is by no means a rare political aberration, as can be discerned from the ever-growing legislative expansion of 'imprisonment for public protection' (*Sicherungsverwahrung*), which necessitated strong intervention by the European Court of Human Rights in order to bring about reform.[41] Where the individual-preventive aim of punishment is the re-socialisation of the offender, it appears only reasonable to tie the duration of penal measures to the achievement of the aim, which – given that it cannot be known in advance how long it will take to re-socialise the offender – translates into a demand for sentences of indeterminate length. All this is incompatible with rights of civil liberty, to which offenders, too, are entitled.

Setting *limits* to punishment also does not come easily to theories of general prevention. To the extent that such theories would, qua negative general prevention, aim to deter members of the public from committing crimes, the assumption that harsher and stricter sanctions increase the deterrent effect has so much intuitive plausibility to it, that the tendency to punish overly harshly is effectively built into the theory's starting point.

One cannot quite say the same about theories of positive general prevention, and this is one reason why this preventive theory has in recent years gathered more followers than negative general prevention. An argument one often hears is that positive general-preventive effects (such as strengthened respect for the rule of law, etc) are best achieved through punishments that are commensurate with the

---

[40] Kuhlen, 'Anmerkungen', above n 28 at 58. Similar, though more restrained, is Hörnle, *Straftheorien*, above n 14 at 26.

[41] See S Leutheusser-Schnarrenberger, 'Die auch vom Dialog geprägte Beziehung von EGMR und BVerfG' in M Jahn and A Nack (eds), *Gegenwartsfragen des europäischen und deutschen Strafrechts: Referate und Diskussionen auf dem 3. Karlsruher Strafrechtsdialog 2011* (Cologne, Carl Heymanns, 2012) 9.

offender's guilt. But, as Hörnle and von Hirsch correctly point out, this assumption is 'far removed from a claim capable of empirical validation.'[42] Much depends on societal context. In times of political and economic stability when crime rates are comparatively low, a measured penal practice is socially widely accepted. In times of crisis, however, the 'public's sense of justice', as expressed in opinion surveys and in elections, regularly calls for 'toughness on crime', and politicians are tempted to increase their electoral appeal by taking up such demands.[43] What this illustrates is that an approach based on positive general prevention cannot provide us with a binding upper limit to penal interventions by the state.

Prevention-based theories also have to engage with a third argument: while instrumental reasoning may tell us that the aims of prevention constitute useful social goals, this does not, as such, show that we are justified in pursuing those aims.

Consider, first, individual or 'special' prevention. Let us leave aside the fact that aims like social protection against, as well as deterrence or re-socialisation of, the offender become hollow when any risk of future reoffending by this offender can already be ruled out. Leave aside, too, that it is frequently questionable whether incarceration or a fine is more likely to reduce the likelihood of future reoffending. The question of principle remains: what exactly legitimates these infringements of the rights of the offender? Why should a thief be expected to submit to a period of imprisonment, or to participate in programmes of re-socialisation? As the German Constitutional Court once observed, 'It is not the state's task . . . to make its citizens better people.'[44]

Even more in need of justification is the objective of positive general prevention. If it is indeed the case that the perpetrator is punished in order to increase the general public's respect for the law, punishment is not imposed for his, the offender's, sake. His punishment then pursues a goal that has nothing to do with him; it aims rather to influence others. Punishing a lawbreaker for the sake of general prevention thus stands in need of a justification which is not already supplied by this aim. We must be able to offer the offender an ethically convincing reason why he should accept infringements of his liberty aimed at preventing others from committing crimes. Weigend thinks that such a justification is impossible:[45]

> If we really were to tell citizens straightforwardly that we do not punish offenders because of the crime they have committed, but only because we want to make sure that citizens continue to believe in the validity of the criminal prohibition, the criminal justice system would lose all credibility and could hardly expect to have any socially beneficial effect.

The same point applies to negative general prevention. We need a justification specifically for punishing someone in order to deter others from breaking the law. Hörnle and von Hirsch are certainly right to say that the[46]

---

[42] Hörnle and von Hirsch, 'Positive Generalprävention', above n 1 at 264.
[43] Kuhlen, 'Anmerkungen', above n 28 at 59, is to the same effect.
[44] BVerfGE 22, 180 (219) (Judgment of 18 July 1967 – Jugendhilfe).
[45] T Weigend, 'Kommentar zu Tatjana Hörnle, Gegenwärtige Strafbegründungstheorien' in von Hirsch et al (eds), *Strafe – Warum?*, above n 3, 31, 33.
[46] Hörnle and von Hirsch, 'Positive Generalprävention', above n 1 at 269.

objections against the concept of negative general prevention which are based on the concern that this concept reduces the punished individual to an object made to serve some public good, can be raised with equal force against the functionalistic view of positive general prevention.

III.　Principled Limits on Punishment, Guilt and Censure

In Germany, courts and academics are nearly unanimous in their view that state punishment, even if it has preventive aims, is grounded in and limited by the culpability of the offender. Thus an element of the classic absolute theory of punishment – culpability – is used here, not to justify retribution, but as a limiting principle which determines the appropriate amount of punishment. This is one possible way of combining the different theoretical approaches.

This idea lies behind the position I developed in an early paper on the grounds and limits of state punishment.[47] There I propose a prevention-oriented unified theory, arguing that 'the culpability principle, once we detach it from a retributive theory, functions as an essential consideration to limit the penal powers of a state founded on the rule of law.'[48] In a long line of decisions, the German Constitutional Court has accepted the culpability principle as a constitutional requirement.[49] From this constitutional vantage point, any theory of punishment is pressed into a dualistic shape.[50] Greco, in his comprehensive monograph concerning the foundations of punishment, puts it thus:[51]

> Among the preconditions of legitimate punishment we find some which are purpose-oriented or consequentialist, and others which are desert-oriented or deontological. Considerations of the former kind give us the aims of punishment, whereas those of the latter kind represent deontological constraints on punishment, in short: its boundaries.

One such boundary is the culpability principle.

This argument is broadly compatible with the view taken by von Hirsch. However, instead of developing the limits of punishment primarily with reference to the culpability principle, von Hirsch draws on the writings of the English analytic moral philosopher PF Strawson to argue that it is the censuring function of punish-

---

[47] Roxin, 'Sinn und Grenzen' as published in Roxin, *Strafrechtliche Grundlagenprobleme*, above n 9 at 22.

[48] Ibid.

[49] For details, see Roxin, *Strafrecht Allgemeiner Teil I*, above n 10 at § 3 marginal note 51ff; C Roxin, 'Strafe und Strafzwecke in der Rechtsprechung des Bundesverfassungsgerichts' in W Hassemer, E Kempf and S Moccia (eds), *In Dubio Pro Libertate, Festschrift für Klaus Volk zum 65. Geburtstag* (Munich, CH Beck, 2009) 601, 607ff.

[50] Schünemann, 'Zum Stellenwert', above n 32 at 112.

[51] L Greco, *Lebendiges und Totes in Feuerbachs Straftheorie: ein Beitrag zur gegenwärtigen strafrechtlichen Grundlagendiskussion* (Berlin, Duncker & Humblot, 2009) 252.

ment that gives punishment's preventive elements their ethical legitimacy.[52] The need for censure, in von Hirsch's view, does not merely justify the formal finding of guilt, but also the severity of the sanction. In a recent publication, von Hirsch summarises his mixed theoretical approach as follows:[53]

> Censure is conveyed not only through conviction, but also through penal hard treatment, and both these elements of punishment concurrently serve a preventive function. The imposition of a sanction conveys censure, which is only justified if the offender acted culpably ... Similarly, the severity of the sanction expresses the degree of disapproval of the crime, and should therefore reflect the gravity of the offence. This is the reason why the principle of desert-based, proportionate sentencing should be respected.

If one likens censure to a judgement of blameworthiness, and further equates von Hirsch's proportionate sentence[54] – roughly – with punishment that is commensurate with the amount of blame an offender deserves, then von Hirsch's model is very similar indeed to the dualistic theory of punishment that has come to dominate the German literature. Of course, strictly speaking it is not censure as such, but its ground – the perpetrator's guilt – which is essential for the justification of punishment and the determination of its severity. Censure is, as Schünemann points out, 'inherent in the very notion of a punishment legitimated by the offender's guilt.'[55] In the words of Neumann: 'The imposition of punishment necessarily expresses disapproval of the behaviour for which the punishment is imposed. The element of censure is thus part of the concept, the very institution, of punishment.'[56] But these are mere differences in the formulation of the same substantive point.

IV. Why Must the Perpetrator Allow Himself to be Roped in for the Achievement of the State's Preventive Aims?

The above arguments only address the worry that preventive theories are unable to generate any limits to punitive state action. What remains unaddressed is the further question why a lawbreaker – albeit on condition of, and limited by, his guilt – may legitimately be used at all in the pursuit of the criminal law's preventive objectives. This calls for an additional normative justification, because neither guilt nor censure as such necessarily demand penal sanctions; at least when one

---

[52] For details, see Hörnle and von Hirsch, 'Positive Generalprävention', above n 1 at 271ff. See also Seelmann's discussion in this volume.

[53] Von Hirsch, 'Warum soll die Strafsanktion existieren?', above n 3 at 59.

[54] On criteria for proportionate punishment, see A von Hirsch 'Die Kriterien tatproportionaler Strafen' in von Hirsch, *Fairness*, above n 2 at 131.

[55] Schünemann, 'Zum Stellenwert', above n 32 at 113.

[56] U Neumann, 'Institution, Zweck und Funktion staatlicher Strafe' in M Pawlik and R Zaczyk (eds), *Festschrift für Günther Jakobs: zum 70. Geburtstag am 26. Juli 2007* (Cologne, Carl Heymanns, 2007) 435, 438. See also Neumann's contribution to this volume.

maintains that punishment is imposed, not to bring about ideal justice, but to prevent future crimes. And the problem becomes even more acute when punishment
is intended to affect not just the offender's own future behaviour, but that of the
general public.

This legitimacy gap also exists in the case of prevention-oriented theories which
incorporate culpability as a limiting principle. Many theorists simply fail to spot the
difficulty. Those who are aware of it disagree on the best way of closing the gap. For
Hörnle and von Hirsch, the point of hard treatment is[57]

> to give the agent an additional prudential reason, supplementary to the normative
> reasons that censure represents, to resist temptation. A human being who has inwardly
> accepted the normative appeal not to commit crimes but is also aware of his own weak-
> nesses, may even welcome the existence of such an incentive to norm-compliant behav-
> iour, as providing some reinforcement for his own behavioural expectations.

Such a system, they say, is 'sufficiently different from a purely preventive approach
where the element of a moral appeal plays no role at all.'[58]

I believe that this falls short of providing an ethical justification for the preventive
objectives of punishment. Any 'incentive to norm-compliance' provided through
punishment remains, even when thought of in terms of a moral appeal, restricted to
individual-preventive considerations and cannot explain why someone should be
made to undergo punishment as a means for reinforcing the general public's respect
for legal norms. Moreover, an individual who is not at risk of reoffending needs no
additional incentive. Finally, the supposed incentive for future norm compliance
will often remain ineffectual due to the desocialising effects of punishment. In light
of these consequences it is audacious indeed to liken punishments to a form of 'state
support'.

A very different type of argument to show 'that prevention-oriented punishment
does not infringe the dignity of the offender,'[59] based on the social contract, has
some years ago been put forward by Schmidtchen:[60]

> Potential offenders can be taken to have given constitutional consent to their own pun-
> ishment since it would, in a hypothetical social contract negotiation, be rational for them
> to do so. When a person has consented to her punishment she is not instrumentalised in
> a manner that violates her dignity when she is punished.

But this construction is just too far removed from the social reality of any actual
offender. A 'consent' he has never in fact given is ascribed to him on account of
some theoretical model devoid of any empirical foundation. This is hardly likely to
convince him of the acceptability of the very real hardship imposed upon him.[61]

[57] Hörnle and von Hirsch, 'Positive Generalprävention', above n 1 at 279.
[58] Ibid.
[59] D Schmidtchen, 'Prävention und Menschenwürde. Kants Instrumentalisierungsverbot im Lichte
der ökonomischen Theorie der Strafe' in D Dölling (ed), *Jus humanum: Grundlagen des Rechts und
Strafrecht; Festschrift für Ernst-Joachim Lampe zum 70. Geburtstag* (Berlin, Duncker & Humblot, 2003)
245, 274.
[60] Ibid.
[61] See also Hörnle, *Straftheorien*, above n 14 at 48f.

More promising are compensation theories, of which there are several variants. I will discuss the versions developed by Neumann, Hörnle and Pawlik.[62] Neumann argues as follows:[63]

> Someone who does not restrict himself to lawful conduct increases his opportunities to achieve his goals. One can see it as a demand of 'human justice' that the unlawful increase of a person's opportunities to advance her interests is met with the compensatory imposition of risks by which these opportunities are decreased.

Civil compensation will not be able to bring this about, he continues, 'because the civil law only imposes obligations to compensate for damage done, but does not neutralise the unlawful creation of opportunities through the imposition of additional risks.'

But in the end this still appears to be just a different way of stating the retributive principle. If, for instance, a bodily assault is 'compensated' by way of imprisonment, this really amounts to an imposition of commensurate deserts in that a first hardship is followed with a second hardship. Moreover, this kind of argument does not legitimise, or even address, the various preventive objectives that punishment may aim at.

Hörnle tries to account for these preventive purposes by drawing on the notion of fairness present in various Anglo-American theories of punishment:[64]

> Provided that the offender knows that an action is prohibited by law but still decides to go ahead with the commission of the offence, he cannot complain that he is treated unfairly if a sanction is imposed on him in order to affirm the validity of the norm he breached, and to discourage others from committing crimes in the future ... What matters is that everyone, including the offender himself, benefits from the norm-compliant behaviour of others. This is the reason why the offender must accept impositions placed on him as a contribution to the maintenance of high levels of norm-compliance in the community.

Two different ideas are entwined in this kind of argument. The first, that prior knowledge of the prohibition makes punishment imposed for preventive purposes a 'fair' response, is obviously problematic. Apart from the vagueness of the notion of 'fairness', this argument simply assumes that the imposition of punishment would be justified. It merely adds the condition that the perpetrator did not labour under any mistake of law. More plausible is the second idea, that by contributing through his punishment to the security of others, the perpetrator pays for the security that the criminal law bestows also on him. But this argument fails to convince when offenders live in a criminal sub-culture and place no reliance on the norm-compliant behaviour of others, or when they have committed a crime in response to the fact that others have already frequently broken the rules and have committed manifold wrongs against the perpetrator.

---

[62] See further also Hörnle, *Straftheorien*, ibid, 45ff.

[63] Neumann, 'Institution, Zweck und Funktion', above n 56 at 449f. See also the chapter by Neumann in this volume.

[64] T Hörnle, 'Claus Roxins straftheoretischer Ansatz' in M Heinrich, C Jäger and B Schünemann (eds), *Strafrecht als Scientia Universalis: Festschrift für Claus Roxin zum 80. Geburtstag am 15. Mai 2011* (Berlin, De Gruyter, 2011) 3; Hörnle, *Straftheorien*, above n 14 at 53ff.

The most promising argument of this sort has been developed by Pawlik. Pawlik bases an offender's duty to suffer punishment on the obligations of loyalty which citizens owe to the state. These obligations are the 'price' citizens must pay for the peaceful and free living conditions created by the state.[65] A citizen who violates his duty of loyalty 'must put up with the intrinsic connection between liberty and loyalty being reaffirmed at his expense. This reaffirmation occurs . . . by taking away some of his liberty in order to mark his breach of loyalty.'[66] Pawlik continues: 'The offender shares responsibility for upholding the public interest. His punishment marks this shared responsibility. It is in this sense that . . . punishment honours him as a reasonable person.'[67]

This is effectively a retributivist, Hegel-inspired position, but one that is ultimately concerned with the preservation of social order and hence directed at a preventive aim.[68] This is probably the reason why Pawlik explicitly draws on the version of a prevention-oriented theory of punishment I developed in 1966.[69] He cites my argument that the perpetrator is obliged to submit to punishment in the interest of the community:[70]

> The justification for this is not some categorical imperative which obliges him to allow others to inflict hardship upon him, but that he, as a member of the community, must own up to his deeds in a measure that is commensurate to his guilt for the preservation of public order. This does not turn him into a means for the achievement of others' aims; rather, by being made to share the responsibility for the public good, his status as a citizen with equal rights and equal burdens is confirmed.

Pawlik claims that these remarks express with precision a view that he shares.[71]

Indeed there is much agreement between Pawlik and me. But I doubt that we need the construction of a 'breach of loyalty' at all. The duty to refrain from acts harmful to the social order – in other words, the duty to act loyally – follows, just like the duty to undergo punishment, directly from the existence of a criminal law prohibition. Nothing is added by appending 'obligations of loyalty'. Moreover, the notion of a breach of loyalty cannot explain why such a breach should be responded to with preventive measures and not in some other way.

I believe that the duty to subject oneself to the pursuit of punishment's preventive aims – just like the basic grounding of punishment and its limits – can be derived straightforwardly from the offender's culpable performance of a prohibited wrong. This is so because it is a general principle of not just the criminal law, but all law, that a person who brings about harm culpably is responsible for restoring the damage he has done. If someone disturbs the civil peace by committing a crime, he

---

[65] M Pawlik, *Person, Subjekt, Bürger. Zur Legitimation von Strafe* (Berlin, Duncker & Humblot, 2004).

[66] Pawlik, ibid, 90–91.

[67] Ibid.

[68] This was explained above: see the text at note 12.

[69] Roxin, *Strafrecht Allgemeiner Teil I*, above n 10. Pawlik has published a separate paper on this convergence of opinion: 'Überlegungen', above n 12.

[70] Roxin, 'Sinn und Grenzen', above n 9 at 385.

[71] Pawlik, 'Überlegungen', above n 12 at 349.

must take responsibility for re-stabilising the socio-legal order. Therefore he must, with a view to individual prevention, accept that a sanction is imposed on him to teach him a painful lesson. At least, this is so provided that the hardship he is made to undergo also provides him with an opportunity for his social reintegration. In both respects his punishment aims at the restitution of civil peace, to which the offender must contribute by virtue of his responsibility for his blameworthy, wrongful act.

Equally, it is part of the offender's responsibility for his crime that he must, within the confines of his responsibility, put up with penal hardships connected to the pursuit of general-preventive aims through his punishment. He must thus accept that the example set by his punishment is also intended to discourage others from committing crimes; that through his punishment, the public's awareness of the blameworthiness of the incriminated conduct is to be reinforced (general-educational effect); that his punishment serves to reassure the general population that the rule of law is being upheld (general trust-building effect); and that his punishment restores the disturbed civil peace to the extent that it is seen as an appropriate response to his crime (peace-restoring effect). All this is covered by the responsibility of an offender that arises from his commission of the crime. He must undergo everything necessary to restore the status quo ante insofar as this is possible.

Here, my argument meets again with Pawlik's, when he maintains that 'a person who has brought about some harm is obliged . . . to balance out his destructive conduct with constructive behaviour.'[72] Also when he writes that:[73]

> Having to undergo punishment means that one is under an obligation to accept that one's goods are used to demonstrate the liberty-destroying character of one's criminal project. Punishment is therefore to be understood, not merely in negative terms – as the infliction of hurt – but . . . in positive terms: as an act that draws upon the perpetrator to restore the mutuality of legal relations that he violated through his crime.

I find myself – quite independently of any connection with the notion of a breach of loyalty – in full agreement with this, even though it must be said that Pawlik's retributivist, freedom-based starting point leaves the different preventive aims of punishment rather abstract and colourless. That notwithstanding, Pawlik's theory is one of the few that can generate an obligation for the state to re-socialise offenders through punishment.[74] Pawlik's argument in this regard is that, because the offender 'is and remains a citizen', he can demand 'that he is put in a position where . . . he will be able to comply with the primary obligations of active loyalty properly in the future.'[75]

I do not disagree with this. Civil peace is restored most successfully when a re-socialised offender returns to society. The aspect of responsibility which I have

---

[72] Ibid, 347.
[73] Ibid, 348.
[74] Ibid, 349.
[75] Ibid.

stressed adds another consideration. Part of the responsibility for failed socialisation lies not with the perpetrator himself, but with society. To the extent that an optimal restoration of civil peace requires an offender's reintegration into society, the sanctions imposed on him must also further this aim. This, of course, does not permit subjecting offenders to (medical or psychiatric) treatment programmes against their will. Rather, the perpetrator must be provided with opportunities for skills development and the acquisition of social competence. Society's co-responsibility does not detract from the offender's primary responsibility for his conduct. But it does render it illegitimate simply to leave him to his fate.

Justifying the preventive aims of punishment on the basis of the responsibility of the offender also enables us to integrate new developments in criminal policy, such as victim-offender mediation (*Täter-Opfer-Ausgleich*, §§ 155, 155a StPO), into penal theory. An offender who reconciles with his victim and thereby repairs the damage that he has done, faces up to his responsibility. In this way, he makes a significant contribution to the restoration of the socio-legal order, also in the eyes of the public. For this reason it is only consistent and right for the state to take this factor into account and, in view of it, to refrain completely from punishment in less serious cases.[76]

All this, however, cannot be captured through the normative criterion of censure. This is one reason why I prefer the principle of responsibility over censure when it comes to justifying punishment. The notion of responsibility for a wrongful act already contains the element of disapproval of the act – in other words, the element of censure. But the notion of responsibility also encompasses the requirement that the perpetrator must live up to his responsibility by shouldering what is necessary for the restoration of civil peace by way of prevention. This is, in my view, more illuminating than von Hirsch's quantification-of-censure argument, which he puts as follows: 'The severity of punishment reflects the degree of censure, such that a more severe sanction expresses greater censure, and a less severe sanction, less censure.'[77] The notion of censure does not contain within it the necessity of punishment. By contrast, given the need for preventive measures triggered by a criminal act, the justification for imposing such measures on the offender can easily be deduced from his responsibility for the elimination of the disruption of the social order that he has caused.

The difficulties that re-socialisation as a legitimate penal aim poses for the censure theory are evident in Hörnle's discussion. Hörnle initially rejected resocialisation as a penal aim because of its supposed unattainability:[78]

> If one compares the high costs [of rehabilitative programmes in the penal system] with their negligible positive results, one can only conclude that public funds are better invested in improved childcare and childhood education . . . In the context of penal theory, the aim of individual prevention is irrelevant.

---

[76] § 46a StGB. See also the chapter by Roberts and Maslen in this volume.

[77] Von Hirsch, 'Warum soll die Strafsanktion existieren?', above n 3 at 53–54.

[78] Hörnle, 'Roxins straftheoretischer Ansatz', above n 64 at 17 f; Hörnle, *Straftheorien*, above n 14 at 20ff.

Neither can the argument she relies on to legitimate punishment in her later work, that the perpetrator has 'benefited from the law-abiding behaviour of others,'[79] allow her to incorporate re-socialisation into her theory of punishment.

Hörnle is therefore forced to develop an additional theory concerning the implementation of penal sanctions (*Strafvollzugstheorie*), in the context of which 'the state's commitment to social justice (*Sozialstaatsprinzip*) plays a major role', and 'requires support for resocialisation or at least … offers to help offenders cope with daily life better. These considerations, however, only kick in when one has already shown, on other grounds, that a penal sanction is required.'[80]

It is somewhat contradictory to say, as Hörnle does, that money which she considers ill-spent due to the supposed inability of penal programmes to make a positive preventive difference, nevertheless ought to be spent for the sake of social justice. Moreover, punishment cannot be justified without regard to the penal measures actually used in the practice. In a socially just state, the requirements of social justice are part and parcel of the legitimation of punishment. If the implementation of punishment in such a state requires measures of re-socialisation, then such measures are necessary components of the very punishment itself that must be justified vis-à-vis an offender.

V. On the Expressive Function of Punishment

Even though the notion of censure cannot account adequately for the individual-preventive aims of punishment, it offers a good starting point for attempts to incorporate the vindication of interests of the victim into a theory of punishment – as, among German theorists, Hörnle in particular has argued.[81] According to Hörnle, 'victims of significant criminal invasions of their personal integrity … have a legitimate interest in a public confirmation that they have been seriously wronged.' At least in cases where the victim has 'not, in a significant way, breached her own obligations',[82]

> the absence of a conviction would amount to a negative characterisation of the victim ('You don't matter enough for the state to come to the defence of your interests.'). Such a message would violate the personality rights of the victim.

This purpose of punishment – which can, of course, only play a role with regard to offences of which individuals are victims – is relied upon already in the earliest publication by Hörnle and von Hirsch on this subject:[83]

---

[79] Hörnle, 'Roxins straftheoretischer Ansatz', above n 64 at 17f.
[80] Hörnle, ibid, 21.
[81] For the basic exposition, see Hörnle's Bochum Inaugural Lecture, published as 'Die Rolle des Opfers in der Straftheorie und im materiellen Strafrecht' (2006) 61 *Juristenzeitung* 950. This is also dealt with comprehensively in Hörnle, *Straftheorien*, above n 14 at 29ff.
[82] Hörnle, 'Roxins straftheoretischer Ansatz', above n 64 at 16.
[83] Hörnle and von Hirsch, 'Positive Generalprävention', above n 1 at 275.

One reason why censure is an indispensable component of the imposed punishment is that the punishment not only addresses the perpetrator but also the victim, and provides recognition of the fact that the victim's injuries came about through another person's misconduct (and not through an accident, a natural disaster, or the like).

These considerations are certainly important. Hörnle elaborates on this 'expressive' or 'communicative' theory of punishment[84] by drawing on the Reemtsma kidnapping case,[85] on which much helpful literature exists.[86] Apart from cases of this sort, the expressive purpose of punishment has an important field of application with regard to very grave crimes committed a long time ago. If, for instance, suspected perpetrators of Nazi crimes are put on trial today, when they are already more than 90 years old, it is usually quite evident that it will not be possible or appropriate to make these perpetrators, if convicted, actually serve a sentence of imprisonment. But the surviving victims, and their families (as victims in a wider sense), still have a right to see these persons put on trial, and to have their criminal responsibility marked through a conviction. It is widely accepted that this determination of responsibility for many victims fulfils an existential need.

Hörnle has already shown that it is possible to draw certain conclusions for the application of substantive criminal law from the expressive function of punishment.[87] It can also influence the application of procedural law. Currently, the German Code of Criminal Procedure allows the court and the prosecution to discontinue a criminal case upon payment of a small 'voluntary' penalty 'if this disposition of the case is in the public interest' (§ 153a StPO). The interests of the victim or the victim's relatives are not mentioned. These interests can sometimes be taken into account indirectly, in that 'a very high degree of blameworthiness' is an obstacle to the discontinuation of the case. But this criterion does not explicitly or fully pick up on the interest victims have, as such, in a finding that their rights have been violated by the offender.

The legitimate vindicatory interests of victims of crime, and in some cases also their relatives, ought indeed to be incorporated into a modern theory of punishment. I agree with Hörnle when she says that 'it is high time that penal theories recognise the legitimate interests of victims of crime.'[88] She exaggerates, however, when asserting that, 'In respect of the types of offences where these interests matter, they are more important than general-preventive considerations.'[89] Even more

---

[84] Hörnle, 'Roxins straftheoretischer Ansatz', above n 64 at 15.
[85] Hörnle, 'Die Rolle des Opfers', above n 81 at 954.
[86] Jan Philipp Reemtsma, founder-director of the Hamburg Institute for Social Research and a multi-millionaire following the sale of his inherited share in the Reemtsma cigarette company, was kidnapped in 1996 at the age of 43. After 33 days in captivity, he was freed by his captors after payment of a high ransom. One of the kidnappers was caught, sentenced, and in October 2013 released from prison after completing his sentence. Most of the ransom money has never been recovered. Reemtsma published his reflections on the kidnapping in JP Reemtsma, *Das Recht des Opfers auf die Bestrafung des Täters – als Problem* (Munich, CH Beck, 1999); See also W Hassemer and JP Reemtsma, *Verbrechensopfer, Gesetz und Gerechtigkeit* (Munich, CH Beck, 2002).
[87] Hörnle, 'Die Rolle des Opfers', above n 81 at 956ff.
[88] Hörnle, 'Roxins straftheoretischer Ansatz', above n 64 at 16.
[89] Ibid.

exaggerated is the claim made by another proponent of an expressive theory of punishment, Klaus Günther, that 'there is no need for punishment in the sense of a subsequent imposition of penal hardship' in addition to a finding of responsibility through a criminal conviction.[90] Surely there would be a significant increase in criminal activity if offenders had to fear no worse than a public pronouncement of their guilt. It appears also unlikely that public outrage at the crime could be calmed in this way, leaving an important function of criminal punishment unfulfilled. Be that as it may, the expressive function of punishment constitutes, where it is applicable, a legitimate penal aim alongside the preventive goals of punishment.

It is worth highlighting that the notion of responsibility for culpable wrongdoing on which I draw for the normative justification of punishment is quite capable of accounting for this aspect of penal theory. In fact, the principle of responsibility can do so even better than the concept of censure which Hörnle and von Hirsch employ. This is so because the notion of 'censure' can be applied to all sorts of undesirable behaviours, and is thus less specific than a court's finding of an individual's personal responsibility for committing a particular criminal act. Hence Günther is – in this respect – quite correct when he says that punishment ought to consist in a public declaration 'that the injurious act constitutes a wrong for which a particular individual is responsible, and that the public finds the commission of such wrongs unacceptable.'[91]

The theory of punishment I defend thus encompasses the re-socialising aims of punishment (along with punishment's general-preventive goals), as well as punishment's expressive function. By contrast, Pawlik's theory, which is in many respects so close to my own, can through its reliance on the duty of loyalty incorporate the aim of re-socialisation but not the expressive function of punishment. The justification of punishment through censure, on the other hand, makes it possible to account for the public disapproval of the crime, but struggles to do justice to the re-socialising and other preventive purposes of punishment. The criterion of responsibility for culpable wrongdoing can perhaps act as a bridge between the different theoretical approaches and thus ease the way towards a generally accepted theory of punishment.

VI. Conclusion

My conclusion is, therefore, that punishment ought to serve all individual and general, negative and positive preventive purposes that matter in a particular case. The pursuit of these aims through penal sanctions is justified by the perpetrator's responsibility to restore the civil peace disturbed by his crime, a responsibility

---

[90] K Günther, 'Die symbolisch-expressive Bedeutung der Strafe – Eine neue Straftheorie jenseits von Vergeltung und Prävention?' in C Prittwitz et al (eds), *Festschrift für Klaus Lüderssen: zum 70. Geburtstag am 2. Mai 2002* (Baden-Baden, Nomos, 2002) 205, 219.
[91] Ibid.

which arises from his culpable commission of a wrongful act. Thus punishment presupposes guilt or blameworthiness, and is limited by the measure of that guilt. For such a conception of punishment, the contrast between relative and absolute theories is insignificant because the preventive and the deontological approaches converge and offset each other's theoretical deficits.

The conception of punishment summarised in the preceding paragraph shares many points with Andreas von Hirsch's theory and owes, as I hope the text has shown, much to his writings. I offer my discussion as a small contribution to the Anglo-German debate on the purposes of punishment, which no one has influenced as strongly as has he. This chapter is dedicated to him with the warmest congratulations to his 80th birthday, and in grateful recollection of many fruitful encounters over the years. May our revered honorand retain his admirable intellectual productivity for a long time to come!

3

Prevention with a Moral Voice*

JR EDWARDS AND AP SIMESTER

What good is criminal law? It is tempting to think that any adequate answer would mention the criminal law's *effects*. In particular, it would mention the criminal law's *preventive* effects.[1] That the criminal law prevents people from committing wrongs, when it does so, cannot be anything other than a good thing about criminal law. Does this good thing give us reason to create criminal laws? Here is a simple argument to that conclusion:

(1) People ought not to act wrongly;
(2) Things are better in one respect if fewer people do what they ought not to do;
(3) That X will make things better in any respect is a reason to do X;
(4) If we criminalise φing there will be fewer wrongs;
(5) Criminalising φing will make things better in one respect;
(6) There is a reason to criminalise φing.

(6) does not claim that anything *ought* to be criminalised. It says nothing about the strength of the reason it mentions, or about whether that reason defeats those which countervail. All (6) says is that there is *some* reason to criminalise φing when criminalising φing will prevent wrongs.[2] Some would resist this conclusion by denying (3). They would claim that it does not always follow that if X is of value one has reason to do X. For them, some further story must be told connecting X to the particular actor whose reasons for action we are trying to ascertain.[3] But on no plausible view does the state lack the necessary connection to *all* wrongdoing. There must, in other words, be *some* wrongs which give the state reasons for action, be they harmful wrongs, or public wrongs, or wrongs to others.[4] And in respect of *these*

* Thanks to Andrew Ashworth and Doug Husak for very helpful comments on a draft of this chapter, and to the Singapore MoE Tier One Research Grant (number R241000100112) for research travel support.
[1] Our usage here is technical. The criminal law *prevents* actions, as we will use that term, by deterring (rather than, say, incapacitating) those who would otherwise commit them. All subsequent references to prevention should be understood in this way.
[2] Indeed, (6) is a conclusion Joel Feinberg came to accept: see his *Harmless Wrongdoing* (Oxford, Oxford University Press, 1988) 321–22.
[3] For a clear statement of that view, see RA Duff, 'In Response' in Cruft, Kramer and Reiff (eds), *Crime, Punishment and Responsibility: The Jurisprudence of Antony Duff* (Oxford, Oxford University Press, 2011) 351, 357–61.
[4] For different views, see J Feinberg, *Harm to Others* (Oxford, Oxford University Press, 1984) 14–15; RA Duff and S Marshall, 'Public and Private Wrongs' in Chalmers, Leverick and Farmer (eds), *Essays in*

wrongs, surely the argument above goes through: surely preventing these wrongs makes things better in a respect which gives the state reason to prevent them; so if criminalising φing prevents such wrongs, this is reason to criminalise φing.

The above remarks concern *normative* reasons – they concern, that is, those facts which count in favour of criminalisation. They are thus consistent with the thought that such reasons are not reasons for which law-making officials can legitimately act. To put it another way, the argument outlined above is consistent with the thought that the prevention of wrongdoing never figures among the legitimate *aims* of criminalisation. One might think that, if preventing wrongdoing is a normative reason to criminalise, it follows straightforwardly that law-makers may legitimately aim to conform to that reason. But that is not so. The reason in question may be excluded, or it may be outweighed.[5] To take just one example, no doubt states have reason to create employment opportunities for their citizens. But they cannot legitimately legislate to increase criminal sentences *for the reason that* there will then be more jobs for prison officers: this is not a reason for which such law-making powers can legitimately be exercised.

In this paper we consider whether preventing wrongs really is a legitimate aim of criminalisation. We do so primarily by considering some prominent arguments to the effect that it is not. There are, we think, two main lines of argument worth considering. According to the first, preventive aims cannot be reconciled with another aim the criminal law ought to pursue: the aim of giving culpable wrongdoers their just deserts. Because these aims are irreconcilable, so the argument goes, the pursuit of prevention must be banished from the criminal law (and pursued, if at all, in other areas of the law). According to the second line of argument, the preventive aim should be banished for a very different reason: it should be banished because to aim at prevention, at least via the criminal law, is to treat people badly. Among other things, it is to fail to speak to those subject to the law with what some have called a *moral voice*.[6] To preserve the criminal law's moral voice, so the argument goes, we must give up on prevention as an aim in criminal law. Both lines of thought, we will argue, are mistaken. In what follows, we first show that preventive and retributivist aims can be reconciled within the criminal law. Secondly, we show that pursuit of preventive aims via the criminal law need not treat anyone badly. It is possible, we conclude, for the criminal law to aim at prevention, and for it to do so while speaking with a moral voice.

Criminal Law in Honour of Sir Gerald Gordon (Edinburgh, Edinburgh University Press, 2010) 70, 75; G Postema, 'Politics is about the Grievance' (2005) 11 *Legal Theory* 293. See also the chapters by Hörnle, Hassemer, and Wohlers in this volume.

[5] On exclusionary reasons, see J Raz, *Practical Reason and Norms* (Oxford, Oxford University Press, 1975) ch 1.

[6] See, eg, AP Simester and A von Hirsch, *Crimes, Harms and Wrongs: On the Principles of Criminalisation* (Oxford, Hart Publishing, 2011) 10ff. What it is to speak with such a voice, and why it matters, are questions to which we return below.

I. Reconciling Desert and Deterrence

We can begin to explore the first line of argument via a familiar thought about criminal punishment. According to that thought, articulated and defended by writers such as Andreas von Hirsch, criminal punishment is pro tanto justified when and because it communicates the censure offenders deserve for their crimes.[7] One worry about this justification is the so-called problem of hard treatment.[8] There are, it seems, many ways in which censure can be communicated. Yet criminal punishment also involves the imposition of hard treatment – treatment which would ordinarily be thought to be morally wrong. What, if anything, justifies such treatment? According to von Hirsch, part of the answer is that hard treatment adds a prudential disincentive to the moral appeal made by censure. This prudential disincentive, it is hoped, will deter those wrongdoers insufficiently motivated by the moral appeal, and thus better prevent wrongdoing than would the moral appeal alone.

For von Hirsch, this deterrent element supplements, rather than displaces, the censure with which the criminal law responds to wrongdoing.[9] It is clear, however, that the two aspects of this composite justification may pull in different directions: in particular, deterrence will sometimes count in favour of punishments which are greater than deserved. This worry leads Antony Duff to remark that 'there may then be a tension between preserving the communication of censure as the primary aim of punishment and using hard treatment as a prudential supplement that will have some preventive efficacy.'[10] If deterrence is one component of the justification of punishment, won't the value of deterring wrongs sometimes justify us in imposing more punishment than a wrongdoer deserves? And if such punishments are handed out, won't they fail to communicate deserved censure in the way they must to be justified?

Many attempts have been made in the punishment literature to solve this conundrum.[11] Our primary concern here is not with those solutions. It is rather with the broader problem to which the tension between deterrence and desert allegedly gives rise. In Michael Moore's terms, the problem is one of finding *any* place in the criminal law for preventive aims. Moore himself thinks that such a place cannot be found:[12]

---

[7] For discussion of this so-called communicative theory of punishment, see A von Hirsch, *Censure and Sanctions* (Oxford, Oxford University Press, 1993); RA Duff, *Punishment, Communication and Community* (Oxford, Oxford University Press, 2001); J Tasioulas, 'Punishment and Repentance' (2006) 81 *Philosophy* 279.

[8] For insightful discussion of the problem, see A Lee, 'Legal Punishment, Censure and Hard Treatment' (unpublished ms on file with the author).

[9] Von Hirsch, *Censure and Sanctions*, above n 7, ch 2.

[10] Duff, *Punishment, Communication and Community*, above n 7 at 87.

[11] See the sources referred to above at n 7; also the chapters by Neumann and Roxin in this volume.

[12] M Moore, *Placing Blame* (Oxford, Oxford University Press, 1997) 27–28.

[S]hould we say that the criminal law has two functions of equal dignity, crime-prevention and retribution? Many people have said this, and it is not an implausible thing to say. Yet there are two considerations that suggest that the only function of our criminal law is the achievement of retributive justice. One is the tension that exists between crime-prevention and retributive goals. This tension is due to retributivism's inability to share the stage with any other punishment goal. To achieve retributive justice, the punishment must be inflicted because the offender did the offence. To the extent that someone is punished for reasons other than that he deserves to be punished, retributive justice is not achieved.

Moore concludes that preventive aims must be pursued in other areas of the law.

Let us grant that one of the aims of the criminal law ought to be the doing of retributive justice. Let us further grant, as Moore insists in the quoted passage, that doing retributive justice requires punishing offenders *for the reason that* they deserve to be punished. If offenders are not punished for this reason, retributive justice will not be done. Moore's argument against deterrence as an aim of the crim-inal law is thus built upon the logic of retributive punishment. If retributive justice is to be done, retribution must motivate those who punish, and it must be the sole motive. The infliction of punishment for ulterior purposes such as deterrence only corrupts this goal: either those punished will not receive the quantum of punish-ment they deserve, or if they do retributive justice will anyway not be done when they are punished.

Moore may be right about the legitimate aims of criminal punishment.[13] To the extent that ulterior sentencing rationales are incompatible with giving a wrongdoer his just deserts, they are indeed incompatible with the retributive function the criminal law ought, we are assuming, to fulfil. But it is a non-sequitur to conclude that the prevention of wrongdoing is not a legitimate aim of the criminal law. This would follow only if the legitimate aims of criminal punishment were identical to the legitimate aims of those who *create* the criminal laws for which criminal punish-ments are imposed – identical, that is, to the legitimate aims of *criminalisation*. If that were true, and assuming Moore is right about the aims of criminal punish-ment, it would follow that retributive justice is *also* a legitimate aim of criminalisa-tion, and that the prevention of wrongdoing is not. On this view, law-makers should bother about criminalisation (rather than simply about punishing those who deserve it) primarily for reasons of legality – the state ought to give those subject to the law fair warning that they may be punished, and the creation of offence-definitions which satisfy the Fullerian desiderata provides just that.[14] Those offence-definitions may well have preventive effects, and this may even count in their favour. But it is not something at which their creators may legitimately take aim.

---

[13] Note that if he is, it does not follow that prevention is not a (normative) reason for punishment. The fact that punishing wrongdoers will deter wrongdoing may still count in favour of punishing them. What Moore shows is that this is not a reason *for which punishers can permissibly act*. It is, in other words, *excluded* in the hands of judges, who may not take it into account when imposing punishments (which, ex hypothesi, must be handed out on other grounds).

[14] Moore, *Placing Blame*, above n 12 at 186–87. For the Fullerian desiderata, see L Fuller, *The Morality of Law*, rev edn (New Haven CT, Yale University Press, 1969) ch 2.

Is the Moorean picture correct? We think not. There is no reason to think that the legitimate aims of criminalisation and punishment must be identical. We can see this by reminding ourselves that the criminal law operates not at one moment, but across an extended timeline which includes the following points:

t1:   φing is criminalised by the state
t1a: φ occurs
t1b: The φing is investigated
t1c: D is prosecuted
t2:   D is convicted and punished for φing.

This timeline brings out the fact that the act of criminalisation, at t1, is a very different act to the act of punishment at t2. Those actions, occurring at different points in time, can be performed for different reasons.[15] So punishment may be *imposed* on D (by law-applying officials, at t2) for reason R, but D's offence may have been *created* (by law-making officials, at t1) for reason Q. In other words, one can criminalise in order to prevent (at t1), without punishing in order to prevent (at t2). And one can punish in order to hand out just deserts (at t2), without criminalising in order to hand out any deserts at all (at t1). So even if Moore is right about the legitimate aims of criminal punishment – even if these are restricted to the doing of retributive justice – it does not follow that prevention is not a legitimate aim of the criminal law. *That* aim must simply be pursued at other points in time, including (though perhaps not only) at the moment of criminalisation.

A. Two objections

Moore is mistaken, then, to claim that prevention and retribution cannot 'share the stage' as aims of the criminal law. Or is he? Consider the following two objections, both of which may seem to support Moore's claim. The first draws on a point we noted earlier, namely that desert and deterrence will often pull in different directions. If prevention is one of the legitimate aims of criminalisation, that aim will seemingly pull law-makers in the direction of criminalising conduct which is not wrongful, and in respect of which there is thus no retributive justice to be done.[16] When one criminalises φing, one confers powers of arrest, prosecution, conviction and punishment upon various state officials, many of whom have incentives to exercise those powers.[17] If non-wrongful conduct is criminalised and said powers

---

[15] Cf Simester and von Hirsch, *Crimes, Harms, and Wrongs*, above n 6 at 6–10. Notice that, while the timeline helps to make the distinction between criminalisation and punishment more visible, temporal separation is not required. In principle the two acts could be performed simultaneously by the same person: the point is simply that they are different acts.

[16] Recall that step (4) of the argument sketched in the introduction does not presuppose that φing is wrong, but only that if we criminalise φing there will be fewer wrongs. We may, for instance, better prevent terrorist attacks by criminalising preparatory acts many of which are innocuous.

[17] On some of these incentives, see W Stuntz, 'The Pathological Politics of Criminal Law' (2001) 100 *Michigan Law Review* 505.

are exercised, some offenders who did not act wrongly will nonetheless be punished, and this will be to do retributive *injustice* to those offenders. Such injustice is, one might claim, good reason to doubt that prevention is the legitimate aim we have claimed it is.

This first objection fails. It assumes, wrongly, that if prevention is a legitimate aim of criminalisation, then where there are preventive reasons to criminalise, this is what law-makers ought to do. Not so. The existence of a preventive reason to criminalise φing does not necessarily justify its criminalisation *all things considered*. It is true that if the simple argument sketched in the introduction is sound, the state has normative reasons to prevent (at least some) wrongs, and that if enacting criminal laws can prevent those wrongs, this is reason to criminalise.[18] It is also true that in our view law-makers are at least sometimes permitted to act for those reasons. But it does not follow that law-makers should, or are permitted to, ignore all other reasons. And there are important reasons *not* to criminalise conduct that is not wrongful. Not only does the state treat its citizens badly if it portrays as deserving of censure those whose conduct is nothing of the sort, but if it does that too often the criminal law may lose its moral voice. We return to this below. The point here is not to argue for a wrongfulness constraint on the criminal law. It is, rather, that endorsing such a wrongfulness constraint is perfectly compatible with endorsing prevention as a legitimate aim of the criminal law.[19] The first objection therefore fails to bite.

But perhaps this is too quick. Recall that on Moore's view, retributive justice is not done if D is punished 'for reasons other than that he deserves to be punished'.[20] Imagine now that φing was criminalised in order to deter people from φing. If a judge then punishes D for φing, isn't D *really* punished for those preventive reasons? If this is so, it turns out that retributive justice really can't 'share the stage' with deterrence in the criminal law, because the former will not be done in any case where the latter was the aim of those who created an offence.

One might try to reply to this second objection by arguing that there is a general moral obligation to obey the law. If that is so, then all offenders act wrongly when they offend, and punishing them for the reason that they offend *just is* punishing

---

[18] As we have observed, these reasons will be reasons to criminalise not just the wrongs themselves, but other acts too, whenever criminalising those other acts will itself prevent wrongs. See n 16 for one example.

[19] Perhaps some doubt this because they assume that if one thinks there are reasons to use the criminal law to prevent wrongs, one must endorse a consequentialist moral theory. One can only hope that such assumptions are not widespread. No sensible view holds that the fact X will produce bad consequences is *never* of relevance to whether X ought to be done. As Rawls famously put it, 'all ethical doctrines worth our attention take consequences into account in judging rightness. One which did not would simply be irrational, crazy.' What is distinctive of most non-consequentialist moral theories is not that they ignore the consequences. It is that they accept *constraints* on our pursuit of those consequences, which are not *themselves* justified by the consequences of conformity. To claim that there are preventive reasons to criminalise, and that these reasons can legitimately be aimed at by law-makers, is not to reject such constraints, and thus is not to endorse consequentialism. For Rawls' views, see J Rawls, *A Theory of Justice*, rev edn (Oxford, Oxford University Press, 1999) 26. For helpful discussion, see V Tadros, *The Ends of Harm* (Oxford, Oxford University Press, 2011) ch 2.

[20] Moore, *Placing Blame*, above n 12 at 28.

them for committing a moral wrong; imposing such punishments would then be doing retributive justice. Let us grant, however, that no such general obligation exists.[21] It remains the case that there is a moral obligation to conform to *morally justified* laws. To put it another way, if creation of a law is morally justified, it is morally wrongful to violate it. And both *mala in se* and *mala prohibita* offences may be morally justified laws – the legal duties they impose may be morally binding on those to whom they apply.[22] When this is true of *mala prohibita*, albeit the offending behaviour was not wrongful prior to the law, it is *post-legally* wrongful; not simply because it is legally proscribed but because, and in virtue of the reasons for which, the proscription is morally justified.[23] The key point here is that those who commit such offences *will have acted wrongly* (at t1a), and punishing them (at t2) for the reason that they offended will thus be retributively just – by Moore's own lights.

It is true, as we noted earlier, that there will be reasons of prevention to criminalise conduct which would not be post-legally wrongful. On our view, there is thus *something* which counts in favour of creating these offences. Isn't this a good objection to our view? Not at all. Ex hypothesi, to create the offences in question would be to create *unjustified* legal norms. So on our view such offences ought not to be created. The second objection thus fails. It is not true that when criminal offences are created for preventive reasons, those who are punished for committing them must be punished for those same reasons. They may be punished because they violated a morally justified legal norm, and thus for the reason that they have acted wrongly. Retributive justice can then be done when such offenders are punished.

B. Respectful punishment?

Before moving on, it is worth considering a related objection clearly articulated by David Dolinko.[24] Dolinko claims that because it imposes hard treatment, punishment infringes the *rights* of the punished, and that if this is done for deterrent reasons the act of punishing is exposed to familiar non-consequentialist concerns.[25] One such concern is that the punished are used as mere means rather than treated as ends in themselves. Whatever we make of this objection, it is inapplicable to an account of punishment in which preventive reasons are excluded. More precisely, it is inapplicable to an account of the criminal law in which acting for such reasons is unexcluded at the criminalisation stage but excluded at the sentencing stage. On

[21] Moore explicitly denies the existence of such an obligation: see Moore, *Placing Blame*, above n 12 at 72–73.
[22] This is to claim that the law *may* contribute to the creation of moral reasons, not that it necessarily does so. For discussion in the criminal law context, see Simester and von Hirsch, *Crimes, Harms, and Wrongs*, above n 6 at 24–29. For general discussion, see AM Honoré, 'The Dependence of Morality on Law' (1993) 13 *Oxford Journal of Legal Studies* 1.
[23] Duff now concedes this point: see RA Duff and SE Marshall's contribution to this volume, at fn 33.
[24] D Dolinko, 'Punishment' in J Deigh and D Dolinko (eds), *The Oxford Handbook of Philosophy of Criminal Law* (Oxford, Oxford University Press, 2011) 403, esp 409–11.
[25] For extended discussion of the relationship between criminal punishment and individual rights, see D Husak, *Overcriminalization* (Oxford, Oxford University Press, 2008) 92–103.

this account, no sentencer who acts permissibly will act for reasons of deterrence, and no one thus sentenced will be treated as a means. Escaping this kind of objection is therefore a merit of a view which divides the moral labour in the way we have suggested.

Yet that is not the end of the matter. Moore's reconciliation worry may be dissolved, but the concerns raised by Dolinko can be transferred and levelled, *mutatis mutandis*, at the act of criminalisation performed at t1.[26] To the extent that criminal laws are enacted for preventive reasons, does not the enactment of such laws *itself* fail to show respect for persons in some way? Criticisms of this kind have been raised by Antony Duff. It is to these criticisms that we now turn.

II. Respecting Persons: Hegel and the Moral Voice

Suppose that φing is criminalised in order to prevent some wrong. It may then be said that, whatever else one does when one criminalises φing, one threatens potential φers with conviction and punishment if they φ. On the supposition we are making here, one makes that threat *in order to* get potential φers (not) to act in some way. According to what we shall call *the Hegelian objection*, this is itself a form of disrespectful treatment. For A to try to get B do what A wants by conditionally threatening B with some burdensome consequence, is, it may be urged, to treat B like a beast rather than a responsible agent: 'to raise a stick to a dog.'[27] As Antony Duff puts the objection, potential offenders are faced with a criminal law which[28]

> creates a new reason – the threat of punishment – to make it in their interest to obey laws that they would otherwise have no such reason to obey. But this is no longer to address them as autonomous agents in a language to which they will listen. It is to seek to coerce their obedience by threats which treat them like 'dog[s] instead of with the freedom and respect due to [them]' as moral agents.

One way of unpacking this objection is as follows:

(1) The prospect of conviction and punishment for offending is a prudential reason not to offend;

---

[26] This possibility is noted briefly by Hoskins, who responds to the objection that *punishing* offenders for preventive reasons treats them as mere means, by arguing that it is the threat, rather than the act, of punishment which is intended to deter. We take no position here on Hoskins' argument. See Z Hoskins, 'Deterrent Punishment and Respect for Persons' (2011) 8 *Ohio State Journal of Criminal Law* 369, 372–74.

[27] GWF Hegel, *Philosophy of Right* § 99: 'A threat presupposes that a man is not free, and its aim is to coerce him by the idea of an evil. But right and justice must have their seat in freedom and the will, not in the lack of freedom on which a threat turns. To base a justification of punishment on threat is to liken it to the act of a man who lifts his stick to a dog. It is to treat a man like a dog instead of with the freedom and respect due to him as a man. But a threat, which after all may rouse a man to demonstrate his freedom in spite of it, discards justice altogether.' Transl TM Knox (Oxford, Oxford University Press, 1967) 246.

[28] Duff, *Punishment, Communication and Community*, above n 7 at 85, quoting Hegel (ibid).

(2) To criminalise φing is to introduce the prospect of conviction and punishment for φing;

(3) To criminalise φing is to create a prudential reason not to φ;

(4) To criminalise φing *in order to prevent φing* is to create prudential reasons not to φ *because* this will reduce the incidence of φing;

(5) Because φing is wrongful, there are moral reasons not to φ;

(6) To create prudential reasons not to φ *because* this will reduce the incidence of φing, is to assume that potential φers would fail to respond to the moral reasons not to φ;

(7) To make the assumption mentioned in (6) is to treat potential φers with disrespect;

(8) To criminalise φing in order to prevent φing is to treat potential φers with disrespect.

Premise (5) takes account of a point we defended in the previous section. As we argued there, one may consistently believe both (a) that prevention is a legitimate aim of criminalisation and (b) that it is only permissible to criminalise moral wrongs. If the Hegelian objection is sound, a view comprising (a) and (b) remains open to an important objection: whenever law-makers pursue the aim mentioned in (a) by criminalising some wrong, they necessarily treat potential offenders with disrespect.

The crucial premises are (6) and (7). The truth of the latter depends on a thought well expressed by Margalit:[29]

> Even if there are noticeable differences among people in their ability to change, they are deserving of respect for the very possibility of changing. Even the worst criminals are worthy of basic human respect because of the possibility that they may radically re-evaluate their past lives and, if they are given the opportunity, may live the rest of their lives in a worthy manner ... Even though it is likely that she will continue living this way, this likelihood should not be turned into a presumption, because in principle an evildoer has the capacity to change and repent. This capacity implies that she deserves basic respect as a human being who should not be 'given up on', precisely because there is a chance, no matter how small, that she will repent.

As John Tasioulas has observed, Margalit in effect argues for a particular moral entitlement: an entitlement to respectful treatment possessed by each individual, which 'does not vary with one's estimation of how likely someone is to govern themselves in the light of genuine reasons.'[30] To defend (7) is to claim that this entitlement has the following implication: that one should not assume, of any person, whatever their past wrongs, that they will fail to do what they ought morally to do. To make that assumption about a person is to wrongfully show them disrespect.

What remains unclear, of course, is exactly when the offending assumption is made. It surely is not *always* disrespectful to bring the existence of moral reasons to another's attention because one hopes this will prevent them acting wrongly. Duff

---

[29] A Margalit, *The Decent Society* (Cambridge MA, Harvard University Press, 1996) 70–75.

[30] Tasioulas, 'Punishment and Repentance', above n 7 at 295.

himself accepts this when he claims that the criminal law legitimately aims to 'remind citizens (if they need reminding)' that conduct is morally wrong.[31] According to (6), things are different when one creates new *prudential* reasons in order to prevent wrongdoing. To do this, so the objection goes, is to assume potential wrongdoers would fail to respond to the moral reasons not to act wrongly, and thereby to show them disrespect. But (6) can itself be interpreted in two ways. The narrower possibility is that (6) is engaged only when one refrains from offering potential offenders *any* moral reasons for action *at all*. On this interpretation, when we appeal *exclusively* to prudential reasons in our efforts to prevent wrongdoing, we make the assumption mentioned in (6) and, because of (7), we thereby show potential offenders disrespect.

If we interpret (6) in this way, does the Hegelian objection hold against acts of criminalisation? There seems no reason to think it does. For one thing, the creators of criminal laws may engage with potential offenders via other means. They may *already* have offered potential φers moral reasons not to φ – they may have given speeches, put up billboards, or funded educational initiatives, in each of which φing was declared to be morally wrong. Such law-makers could not be accused of assuming that, were moral reasons offered, potential φers would fail to conform to them. That offer has already been made.

But even if this reply fails, we should anyway reject the claim that when we criminalise to prevent wrongs, we do not offer potential offenders moral reasons to refrain from wrongdoing. For in at least some legal systems, one public message sent by criminalising φing is precisely that φing is considered by the state to be morally wrong. To criminalise it is thus to publicly declare that this is so. And law-makers with preventive aims may well intend to further those aims precisely by making such a declaration. As Duff says,[32]

> The criminal law of a liberal polity, and the criminal process of trial and conviction to which offenders are subjected, are communicative enterprises . . . An important aspect of communication in both these contexts is that it aims not merely to secure present understanding and assent but to affect future conduct. In defining certain kinds of conduct as public wrongs, the law seeks to persuade citizens (those who need persuading) to refrain from such conduct.

Like Duff, we think this declaratory function not merely an incidental feature of some systems of criminal law, but part of what makes criminal law morally legitimate. When it is present, the criminal law communicates with potential offenders as moral agents – it offers them moral reasons for compliance to which they are expected to respond. But precisely because of this point, our first interpretation of the Hegelian objection falls away: in systems of criminal law of the kind just described, potential offenders *are* offered moral reasons for compliance, including by those who criminalise in order to prevent wrongs.

---

[31] Duff, *Punishment, Communication and Community*, above n 7 at 59.
[32] Ibid, 80.

(It might be said in reply that if prevention figures among the aims of criminal law, the message of criminalisation cannot be expected to continue to be that φing is *wrongful*; that message becomes merely that φing is forbidden and is not to be done on pain of sanctions. This overlooks a point we made in the previous section, namely that even if prevention is a legitimate aim of criminalisation (at t1) it may not be a legitimate aim of criminal *punishment* (at t2). Let us again assume that law-applying officials only legitimately punish for reasons of desert. For familiar reasons, such officials must make their reasons for punishing public, so when φers are punished, judges will publicly announce that the punishment imposed for φing is imposed because deserved. Such announcements cannot but imply that, in the eyes of the law, offending acts are morally wrongful – one does not deserve punishment for acts that are not morally wrong.[33])

A. Creating prudential reasons respectfully?

So much for the narrower interpretation. The Hegelian objection may yet be given a second, more stringent, reading. Recall that according to (7), one may show others disrespect by assuming they would fail to respond to moral reasons. We have so far considered the possibility that such disrespect is shown by appealing exclusively to prudential reasons to get others not to act wrongly. Antony Duff suggests a second possibility. Perhaps one also shows such disrespect when, *in addition* to appealing to moral reasons, one *creates* new prudential reasons for others not to commit wrongs.[34]

Now we do not deny that when criminalisation aims to prevent wrongs, potential offenders are given prudential reasons not to act wrongly. We do not think, however, that this commits us to accepting the argument's conclusion, namely that such criminalisation shows potential offenders disrespect. To see this requires noting that we can create prudential reasons for others in different ways. Sometimes, we do so by ourselves acting wrongly. If the occupants of a neighbourhood are ready to assault members of an ethnic group spotted in the area, those members have prudential reasons to stay away. Yet we can *also* create such reasons by acting in ways that are morally justified. Indeed, this is a side-effect of many legitimate activities: pedestrians are given reason to step back from the road when cars approach a nearby puddle. Most importantly here, we can create prudential reasons by being ready to *respond* to wrongdoing in morally justified ways.

---

[33] More generally, it seems to us that declaring φing to be morally wrong is compatible with requiring potential φers not to φ. Indeed, if – as Joseph Raz and others have argued – the law claims moral authority for its requirements, it follows that the law claims that legal subjects are morally obligated to do as the law requires. On the assumption that the criminal law requires us not to offend, it also follows that potential offenders are offered (what are claimed to be) legally-created moral reasons not to commit crime. For Raz's argument, see Raz, 'Authority, Law, and Morality' in his *Ethics and the Public Domain* (Oxford, Oxford University Press, 1995).

[34] This is how Duff puts the objection, in the passage quoted in the text to n 28.

To see this, imagine that A exhibits an aggressive intent towards B, an innocent passer-by. Clearly A has moral reasons not to attack B. But if B is ready to engage in morally justified self-defence, A also has a prudential reason not to attack B: A risks being injured by B if she attacks. The existence of this prudential reason depends on B's readiness to defend herself. But this readiness may, of course, be hidden from A. So B may warn A of her readiness to self-defend. And there are good reasons to do so. If warning A will make A less likely to attack, B has a prudential reason of her own to issuing the warning. Because A's attack would be wrongful, B also has a *moral* reason to warn A – if A heeds the warning, B will have averted a wrongful act.

For our purposes, the important features of this example are as follows: first, that B's readiness to act in morally justified self-defence *itself* creates a prudential reason for A not to act wrongly; secondly, that there are moral and prudential reasons for B to warn A of her readiness. If B warns A for these reasons, her aim is to prevent A from attacking her. Does B thereby show A disrespect? Surely not. It seems clear that B's readiness to defend herself does not *itself* show A disrespect, even though it creates a new prudential reason for A. One does not show another disrespect by being willing to act in ways one is morally justified in acting. Does issuing the warning change things? Let us distinguish between *what* B communicates to A, and *why* B communicates it. As to the former, B communicates to A that she will do to A what she is morally justified in doing. Does B thereby treat A like a dog, denying her the basic respect she is due as a person? No. True, B's warning offers A a prudential reason not to attack. But it offers only the reason given by the prospect of a morally justified response. And that response (ie, action in self-defence) will be the morally justified response precisely because it acknowledges and is sensitive to A's own agency. B's prospective response will treat A with the respect due to an autonomous agent behaving as A does.[35] Far from denying A's personhood, B's warning thus confirms it: because A is a person, there are limits to what may justifiably be done to A, and these are limits the warning respects.

Does it become disrespectful, then, if B warns A *in order to prevent the wrong*? Is warning others for these reasons 'no longer to address them as autonomous agents in a language to which they will listen'?[36] Not necessarily. 'Think about the consequences!' can be part of (respectful) persuasion. In the self-defence case, B warns A only because B has good reason to think A is about to *exercise* her autonomy in a wrongful manner. And in choosing to warn A rather than use some other means, B cannot but be assuming that A *is* an autonomous agent who may choose differently once warned. B cannot but be assuming, in other words, that A has the capacity to conform to those reasons to which the warning draws her attention.[37] Were this

---

[35] For discussion, see AP Simester, 'Necessity, Torture and the Rule of Law' in V Ramraj (ed), *Emergencies and the Limits of Legality* (Cambridge, Cambridge University Press, 2008) 289, esp 309: 'In this sense, one person can harm another person respectfully, without denying their shared humanity.'

[36] Duff, *Punishment, Communication and Community*, above n 7 at 85.

[37] Including both pre-existing moral reasons for A not to attack B and the prudential reasons created by B's willingness to defend herself.

assumption not made by B, the warning would not serve her preventive purpose at all.[38]

Of course, we must still ask whether the case of self-defence supplies a good analogy for criminalisation. Recall first premises (1)–(4) of the Hegelian objection, as earlier unpacked:

(1) The prospect of conviction and punishment for offending is a prudential reason not to offend;

(2) To criminalise φing is to introduce the prospect of conviction and punishment for φing;

(3) To criminalise φing is to create a prudential reason not to φ;

(4) To criminalise φing *in order to prevent φing* is to create prudential reasons not to φ *because* this will reduce the incidence of φing.

Let us assume that when we criminalise φing, we introduce the prospect of punishments which judges would be morally justified in imposing. As section I showed, the claim that prevention is a legitimate aim of criminalisation does not commit one to any particular theory of justified punishment. But we can assume again that justified punishments give wrongdoers what they deserve for their wrongdoing. Just as in the self-defence example, by criminalising φ, and creating the prospect of those punishments, we *also* create a prudential reason for potential φers not to φ. Neither is the existence of that reason hidden. When φing is criminalised, potential φers are warned that if they φ they are liable to be punished. So the existence of the prudential reason is communicated to them. If we communicate this *in order to prevent φing*, do we disrespect potential offenders? Just as in the self-defence example, the answer is no. For just as in that example, the prudential reason exists when and because we are prepared to respond in a morally justified way to wrongdoing. Our willingness to so respond cannot *itself* treat anyone badly. Neither, we think, does communicating that the reason exists. Again we can distinguish between what is communicated and why. As to the 'what', we do not usually treat people badly by warning them that if they φ they are likely to suffer harm we are morally justified in imposing on them. To communicate that it is *these* harms (rather than some others) that we are willing to impose, confirms rather than denies that they are persons in our eyes. Does it change things if, when it comes to the 'why', we warn *in order to* get potential φers not to φ? It does not. To warn for these reasons is to *acknowledge*, rather than ignore, the fact that potential offenders are autonomous agents: we warn them because we have reason to believe they will exercise that autonomy in wrongful ways; and warning them serves our purposes only *because* we believe they may still decide, once warned, to choose otherwise.

---

[38] One might add that it is in A's own interest that the attack be prevented. If it is, A will not commit a moral wrong, and will not expose herself to justified defensive harm. So in trying to bring it about that the attack does not occur, B is trying to bring about a state of affairs which is also better for A.

B. Threats and warnings

Perhaps, though, the analogy to self-defence is misplaced. Perhaps the state threatens, not warns, when it enacts a criminal law, and perhaps this feature of the criminal law is crucial to the Hegelian objection. An obvious rejoinder would be to reinforce the analogy: if criminalisation threatens, so too does the pre-emptive self-defender. Still, it is worth exploring an alternative strategy: we may deny that to criminalise is necessarily to threaten.

Conditional threats are statements of the form 'if you φ, then μing will follow', where μing involves something unwelcome for the addressee. But not all statements of this form are conditional threats. To take Gunderson's example:[39]

> If a dancer informs his partner that he will accidentally step on her foot unless she dances in time with the music he is warning her. If, however, he informs her that he will intentionally step on her foot unless she dances in time with the music he is threatening her.

Gunderson takes this example to show that T threatens V if T communicates that she will *intentionally* bring about the unwelcome consequence. We would add that T must also select that consequence both (i) *because* it is unwelcome for V and (ii) *in order* to get V to act as T wants.[40] That is to say, T's motivation must be taken into account. According to Raz,[41]

> Threats differ from ordinary communications of information about undesirable future events conditional on the addressee's action, for it is alleged that the occurrence of the undesirable future event is under the control of the person making the threat, that he has decided to prevent it only if the threatened person will prevent the triggering event, and that this decision was taken in order to try to get the threatened person to prevent the triggering event by threatening him. In the absence of the last condition, the utterance is not a threat but a warning.

Raz's final condition focuses on (ii). It suggests that T only threatens V if T's speech-act is undertaken in order to get V not to φ. Suppose that the law faculty's uncaring computer officer tells us that, if we don't implement some virus safeguard by the end of this week, he will wipe all our files stored on the network server as part of a standard university procedure. The officer does not care whether we implement the safeguard. He is simply following the standard procedure. Though he communicates an intention to bring about a consequence which is unwelcome for us, the computer officer does not threaten us. He merely issues a warning.

We agree with Raz that this motivational element is a feature of all threats. But we doubt that the conditions Raz identifies are sufficient to mark out a threat. The pre-emptive warning in our self-defence case is a helpful example: that warning is made

---

[39] M Gunderson, 'Threats and Coercion' (1979) 9 *Canadian Journal of Philosophy* 247, 257.

[40] These points are noticed by Grant Lamond: see Lamond, 'Coercion, Threats and the Puzzle of Blackmail' in AP Simester and ATH Smith (eds), *Harm and Culpability* (Oxford, Oxford University Press, 1996) 215, 227–28.

[41] J Raz, *The Morality of Freedom* (Oxford, Oxford University Press, 1986).

in order to get the potential attacker not to attack, and the warner clearly has control over whether to defend herself. But there are two reasons why this is not a threat. The first we already mentioned: to make a threat is to select the announced unwelcome consequence *because it is unwelcome for V.* In the self-defence case, this is not what occurs. The self-defender selects defensive action because this will prevent the attack, not because it will harm the attacker. Indeed, the self-defensive action may succeed without causing any harm at all. In some cases, however, T will know that this is not the case. Even if T is motivated purely by her desire to prevent the attack, she may realise that the only way to do so is by harming V, her attacker. In that case, she at least selects the announced unwelcome consequence *because it is harmful*; moreover, the unwelcomeness of that harm is, in turn, part of the warning's persuasive force. Why is that not a threat?

The answer requires appeal to a second feature of T's own reasons for action. As Lamond puts it,[42]

> A coercive threat does not simply involve the communication of an intention to do something unwelcome. The non-performance of a threatened consequence is made *dependent* upon the recipient doing as demanded. The making of a threat thus creates a *commitment* to the carrying out of the intention. This is reflected in the fact that threats can be made by 'promising' to do something to the recipient. Coercive threats belong to the class of undertakings, including promises and vows, which commit the maker to a certain course of action.

To make a threat, in other words, is to commit oneself to μing if V φs. To commit oneself to acting in some way is to purport to create peremptory reasons – reasons, that is, which exclude some countervailing reasons – to act in that way. In the case of a threat, one purports to create such reasons *merely by issuing the threat* – that is, by communicating to V that if V φs one will impose an unwelcome consequence by μing. Whether a threat successfully creates any reasons for the threatener is, of course, a further question. But as Lamond points out, we miss something important about the social function of threats if we ignore the role they play in the practical reasoning of those who make them – if, that is, we ignore the way threats may make it rational for their makers to μ, when it would not otherwise have been rational for them to do so.[43]

While Lamond does not develop his account of commitment fully, it seems to us that the second feature is crucial. It is not just that T deliberately creates a (prudential) reason for V. It is that she does so *by creating a peremptory reason for herself.*[44] It is this manipulative aspect of threats – their subordination of one will to another –

---

[42] Lamond, 'Coercion', above n 40 at 228.

[43] We assume here that what it is rational for A to do depends on the reasons A takes herself to have. Even unjustified threats may thus make it rational for their makers to impose unwelcome consequences, by giving them what they take to be additional reasons to do so if V φs. For defence of this claim about rationality, see D Parfit, *On What Matters* (Oxford, Oxford University Press, 2011) ch 5.

[44] At least, by purporting to create such a reason. T seeks to create a prudential reason for V by communicating that she, T, will treat V's non-φing as a peremptory reason to μ. For such a reason to be valid, the threat would need to be justified. The key point is that T commits herself to *treating* the reason as valid.

that makes them such serious wrongs. Whether or not μing is independently justifiable, T treats V with disrespect because she commits herself to the possibility of *μing just because V φs.* She will μ, in effect, because of V's insubordination.[45]

This helps to explain why T's speech-act is not necessarily a threat even when she communicates a prudential reason in order to influence V's behaviour. Imagine, this time, that we have a caring computer officer. The officer tells us that, if we don't implement some virus safeguard by the end of this week, she will wipe all our files stored on the network server as part of a standard university procedure. This time, the officer is not motivated merely by procedure: she thinks it is in our interests to keep the files; it is in the university's interests (the files are not lost and security is improved); and it is in her interests too (she will not have to spend time wiping our files). Yet she does not seek to create a new reason for herself. If we don't oblige, she will wipe the files simply because the security concerns make that the right thing to do. Again, she merely issues a warning.

This second feature is also lacking in the self-defence case. In that case, a morally justified response to the impending attack is available to B, and B lets A know she will avail herself of this response if necessary. What she tells A is that if A attacks, she will do what she would have reason to do irrespective of her speech-act; *not* that she takes her speech-act to create new reasons for action. B thus does not threaten her potential attacker.

Where does this leave preventive criminalisation? When we criminalise φing we make those who φ liable to criminal punishment. If, as we assumed in section I, justified punishment gives D what he deserves, the range of punishments to which offenders are liable ought to reflect the blameworthiness of φing, and it is what D deserves that ought to be imposed if it is proved that D φed. Do we *threaten* potential φers if we announce that, if it is proved that they φed, we will give them what they deserve? We do not. Crucially, the second feature we identified above is absent. Consider the intentions of a law-maker who makes φers liable to punishments reflecting the blameworthiness of their conduct. Such a law-maker need *not* intend to commit the state peremptorily to imposing those punishments, merely by announcing that offenders are liable to them if they φ. (Nor, in a liberal polity, should this be the law-maker's intention: she would be attempting to commit the state to punishing citizens merely for defiance, a mark of authoritarian rather than liberal governance.) Indeed, if the punishments to which offenders are being made liable really are deserved, imposing those punishments is *already* an intrinsically appropriate response when φing is proved, so there is already good reason to impose them on wrongdoers. This is not, of course, to say that punishing φers is necessarily *permissible* in the absence of criminalisation. Perhaps it is permissible to punish φers only after they have also had adequate warning that φing is a crime. But this is

---

[45] To sum up: paradigmatically, conditional threats are statements made by T to V of the form 'if you φ, then μing will follow', where (i) μing involves something unwelcome for V; (ii) μing will be done (or allowed to occur) because it is unwelcome to V; (iii) the statement is made in order to get V to not-φ; and (iv) as part of the statement, T communicates an intention to treat V's φing as a peremptory reason to cause (or allow) μing to follow.

just to say that there are reasons not to punish which we criminalise partly in order to defeat. It is not to say that we criminalise in order to create new reasons for ourselves to punish.

To criminalise in order to prevent φing thus need not be to threaten potential φers.[46] This does not mean that prevention is a mere side-effect. As we have noted, warnings can be intended to deter too. Our prospective self-defender warns her would-be attacker in the hope that this will cause her to desist, and does not thereby treat the attacker with disrespect. The same, we have argued, can be true of the act of criminalisation.

III. Not Treating People as Means

That, we think, is enough to dispose of the Hegelian objection. If we are right, to criminalise in pursuit of preventive aims need not be to treat potential offenders as beasts rather than human beings. Notice that our argument goes through even if we are wrong in denying that preventive criminalisation necessarily threatens would-be wrongdoers. If the two features we identified are not features of all threats, then pre-emptive self-defence warnings are also threats: they also communicate that unwelcome consequences will be imposed on potential wrongdoers who φ, in order to get them not to φ. But far from reviving the objection, this only shows that, just as potential attackers are not treated badly in the self-defence example, so potential offenders need not be treated badly when threatened by preventive criminalisation.

At this point, however, a second objection may be pressed against our view. It may be objected that the analogy with self-defence breaks down, because the threat (if it is one) made when φing is criminalised is not made *only* against would-be wrongdoers. Because criminal laws are addressed to all citizens, *every* citizen is threatened with conviction and punishment when such a law is created, even those with no inclination to commit any wrong. According to what we shall call the *mere means objection*, this is an objectionable feature of criminalisation with preventive aims. For A to impose some burden on B in order to prevent C from doing wrong, is, the objection goes, for A to treat B as a mere means of achieving A's ends. And when we criminalise in order to deter, we threaten both would-be wrongdoers (C)

---

[46] This analysis refines the handling of the criminalisation archetype in *Crimes, Harms, and Wrongs* (above n 6), where it is suggested (in chapter 1, section 1.1(c)) that because punishment is *threatened* by criminalisation at t1, the threat generates a commitment 'to respond to proved φing with justified punishment.' On reflection, the position is more complex. There are indeed undertakings made by the state: to punish on proof of guilt; to investigate credible allegations of φing; to prosecute where there is evidence and it is in the public interest to do so; and so on. But these undertakings are not embedded in any threat to punish, and neither are they made specifically to potential wrongdoers. Rather, they are made to the wider community and, especially, to potential victims. Those commitments are ancillary to, and not derived from, the warning that the state communicates to would-be miscreants.

and everyone else (B) in order to prevent the former group from wrongdoing. This seems to be to treat the members of B merely as means.[47]

In order to pursue this objection, we will assume a wider definition of threats than was argued for in section II, and assume that to criminalise is, inter alia, to make a threat. The mere means objection can then be unpacked as follows:

(1)   To criminalise φing is to declare publicly that persons will be convicted and punished if they φ;
(2)   Conviction and punishment are unwelcome consequences for those convicted and punished;
(3)   To criminalise φing is to declare publicly that unwelcome consequences will be imposed on persons if they φ [from 1 and 2];
(4)   To criminalise φing *in order to prevent φing* is to declare publicly that unwelcome consequences will be imposed on persons if they φ, in order to get potential φers not to φ [from 3];
(5)   If A tells B he will do something unwelcome to B if B φs, in order to get B not to φ, A threatens B;
(6)   The declaration made in (4) is a threat [from 4 and 5];
(7)   Criminal offences are addressed to *all*, and thus to many who are *not* potential φers;
(8)   To criminalise φing in order to prevent φing is to threaten (inter alios) many who are not potential φers, in order to get potential φers not to φ [from 6 and 7];
(9)   It is wrong to use others merely as a means of achieving one's ends;
(10) To threaten C, in order to get B to act in some way, is to use C as a mere means;
(11) To criminalise φing in order to prevent φing is to use those who are not potential φers merely as a means [from 8 and 10];
(12) It is wrong to criminalise φing in order to prevent wrongs [from 9 and 11].

We argued in section II that (6) is false. But even if we concede that point, we do not think the mere means objection holds. One further reply denies (11). The wrong identified in (9) is the wrong of using someone as a *mere* means, not a wrong of treating another person as a means *in any respect*. This must be so, because often it is not wrong to use people as means. If I take a taxi to my destination, I use the taxi driver as a means of getting where I want to go. Were he not such a means, I would not interact with him at all. Still, I need not treat the taxi driver as a *mere* means. I will not do so if, among other things, I accept that I must pay the fare he sets. This is to acknowledge that there are constraints on my use of the taxi driver, which derive from my respect for the taxi driver's own agency. To interact with the taxi driver

---

[47]   As Holtug puts the objection, 'the state should not coerce a person to prevent others from behaving wrongfully, because this would be to treat an innocent person as a mere means.' See N Holtug, 'The Harm Principle' (2002) 5 *Ethical Theory and Moral Practice* 357, 379. See also A Ashworth and L Zedner, 'Prevention and Criminalization: Justifications and Limits' (2012) 15 *New Criminal Law Review* 542, 551; Duff, *Punishment, Communication and Community*, above n 7 at 13.

while observing such constraints is not to treat him as a mere means, and is thus not to fall foul of (9).

A similar response can be offered when we criminalise with the aim of preventing wrongs. As we argued in section I, those who criminalise with that aim may accept various constraints on criminalisation. Among others, they may accept that it is only permissible to criminalise morally wrongful conduct. To do otherwise would be to expose citizens to the risk of criminal conviction, and thus public censure, for conduct which is not wrongful. To publicly censure those who have done nothing wrong is to publicly defame them: it is to send the message that they acted wrongly when they did nothing of the kind. To refuse to expose citizens to this risk is thus to accept a constraint on one's actions derived from the interests of those citizens. Those who accept such a constraint cannot be accused of treating their citizens as *mere* means of achieving preventive ends.[48]

This reply, however, is not decisive. Let's say I accept that it would be impermissible to throw the taxi driver out of his taxi and drive myself to my destination. Instead, I simply threaten the taxi driver, and thereby get him to reduce his price. It seems clear that I wrongfully use the taxi driver, even though I acknowledge constraints on how I am permitted to treat him. The final premises of the mere means argument might thus be recast:

(9a)   It is wrong to threaten others as a means of achieving one's ends;

(10a)   To criminalise φing in order to prevent φing is to threaten (inter alios) those who are not potential φers as a means of getting potential φers not to φ;

(12)   It is wrong to criminalise φing in order to prevent wrongs.

Is (10a) true? Not obviously. One way to test whether B is being used by A as a means to achieve some end is to ask whether, if B ceased to exist the moment before A acted, A's action would still achieve that end. If it would, B is not being used by A as a means. To see the point, take two variations on the trolley problem. First, imagine the only way to save five people stranded on a track is to turn the approaching trolley onto a branch on which there is just one person. In this case, if the one person ceased to exist, turning the trolley would still save the five. So the one is not used as a means of saving the five. Now imagine the only way to save the five is to push a fat man off a bridge and block the trolley. In this case, if the fat man ceased to exist, the five would not be saved. So the fat man is used as a means of saving the five.

Assume this is the right way to understand what it is to use someone as a means. Are those who are not would-be wrongdoers used as means when we criminalise to prevent wrongs? They are not. Our preventive ends would be no less well achieved if those who are not would-be wrongdoers ceased to exist the moment before we criminalised. Ex hypothesi, these people would not have committed wrongs even if they had remained. Their non-existence thus does not obstruct the achievement of our ends. One might reply to this by pointing out that if potential offenders *also* ceased to exist, this *also* would not obstruct the achievement of our ends. In fact,

---

[48] For related discussion, see Hoskins, 'Deterrent Punishment', above n 26 at 374–76.

their non-existence would guarantee that there would be no wrongs, and thus guarantee that our ends were achieved. But this only shows that potential offenders *also* are not used as means by preventive criminalisation. Preventing their wrongs is the end we are pursuing, not a means to some further end.

Of course, this reply is not decisive either. Even if those who are not would-be wrongdoers are not treated as *means*, it may be objected that the state still fails to treat such persons *as ends*.[49] Let us thus consider a more direct reformulation of the argument:

(9b)　It is wrong to threaten others;
(10b)　To criminalise φing in order to prevent φing is to threaten (inter alios) those who are not potential φers;
(12)　It is wrong to criminalise φing in order to prevent wrongs.

Yet (9b) cannot be right. It is not always wrong to make threats. If you announce that you will steal my car tomorrow, I may threaten to report you to the police.[50] All else being equal, I do not act wrongly in making this threat. Perhaps this reply only works because I am threatening to do what I am morally justified in doing. Perhaps in all other cases, threats are wrongful. So be it. The type of preventive criminalisation we have defended is criminalisation which confers on judges the power to impose morally justified punishments. Threatening to impose such punishments is to threaten to do what is morally justified. So the objection is inapplicable to our argument here.

Consider one final possibility. Imagine the announcement that my car will be stolen is made anonymously. Not knowing who made the announcement, I decide that the best way to prevent my car being stolen is to threaten everyone I meet that I will report them to the police if they steal my car. We can accept that making these threats is wrong. This may, however, have less to do with the fact that they are threats, and more to do with the way the threats are made. It is natural to think that I wrong a stranger if I approach them and say that if they steal my car I will report them to the police. But this is because my act is an invasion of their privacy – even though they are in a public place, strangers can expect to be left alone by me as they go about their business. If, on the other hand, I announce on my website that anyone who steals my car will be reported to the police, it is far less clear that anyone is wronged. People can ignore my website if they wish, so their privacy is not invaded. The important point here is that the threats made by the criminal law are usually of the second type not the first. Policemen do not routinely announce to those manifesting no signs of imminent criminality that they will be arrested if they commit

---

[49]　It is not entirely obvious what this objection would involve. The thought might be that such persons are dealt with as side-effects (rather than means or ends), and without personal reference to them or their conduct. As Cohen observes, 'by contrast with the comparatively clear idea of not treating someone as a means, the idea of treating a person as an end is neither particularly clear nor well-explained by Kant.' GA Cohen, *Self-Ownership, Freedom and Equality* (Cambridge, Cambridge University Press, 1995) 239–40.

[50]　As mentioned earlier, we are working here with a broader account of threats than was argued for in section II. On our narrower definition, this need not be a threat.

crime. Rather, the existence and definition of offences is published in a form which citizens can largely ignore if they wish. Though offences can be found in criminal codes, online databases, statute books and law reports, it is up to me whether I choose to avail myself of any of this. It is far from obvious that those who are not would-be wrongdoers are wronged by threats addressed to them in these places.

Suppose, though, that we are mistaken about this. It remains the case that the wrong in question may be *justified*. In the case of the criminal law, the justification is found in the ideal of equality before the law. While that ideal has several dimensions, one is the demand that legal officials not sort individuals into classes of wrongdoers and rightdoers, in advance of the application of the law to each individual case. If there is to be equality before the law, any sorting must be done precisely by applying the law, including those norms of procedure and evidence which tell us how to determine whether any legal wrong has occurred (and who committed it). As John Gardner puts a similar point,[51]

> the rule of law is not consistent with the police dividing the world up into 'good guys' and 'bad guys', or into 'law-abiding people' and 'criminals', or into 'respectable women' and 'common prostitutes', or into any other classes of people supposedly more or less entitled to the protection of the law and hence of the police as officers of the law. So when vigilantes say that they are merely law-abiding people out to protect themselves against criminals, the police should reply that one is only ever as law-abiding as the last law one abided by, so that it is always an open question, in any situation of potential conflict, who, if anyone, is (going to turn out to be) a criminal, and hence subject to arrest and other legal consequences.

We should add that this is as much an ideal for law-makers as for law-enforcers. It is true that law-makers have the power to decide which types of action ought to be crimes, and thus which actions ought to result in prosecution, conviction and punishment. But who ought to be prosecuted, convicted and punished is a job for those applying and enforcing the law, not a job for those in the process of making it. When this is forgotten and law-makers begin targeting individuals they think are (would-be) wrongdoers, equality before the law is lost. It follows that law-makers cannot address their laws solely to those they think are inclined to commit wrongs. To maintain equality before the law they must address them to all, leaving it to law-applying officials to decide who to prosecute and convict by applying the law to each case. Even if this does treat those who are not would-be wrongdoers badly, their treatment is amply justified. A legal system which upholds legal equality is an important public good. It is thus a good from which all benefit, including those the law inevitably threatens as a result.

---

[51] J Gardner, 'Criminals in Uniform' in RA Duff et al (eds), *The Constitution of the Criminal Law* (Oxford, Oxford University Press, 2013) 97, 111–12.

IV. Conclusion

The criminal law, it has been claimed, should speak with a moral voice. But what is it to speak with a moral voice, and why does it matter? Take the first half of this question first. According to (MV1):

(MV1) A speaks to B in a moral voice in respect of B's φing if A appeals to moral reasons why B ought not to φ.

Should the criminal law speak in a moral voice in the sense given by (MV1)? It is precisely the thought that it should that animates the Hegelian objection. If we criminalise in order to prevent wrongs, don't we disrespectfully appeal to prudential rather than moral reasons to get others to act morally? And even if we do appeal to moral reasons, don't we *also* create prudential reasons, and isn't this just as disrespectful? To both questions we answered no. As to the first, we argued that the criminal law appeals to moral reasons precisely in order to prevent wrongs. This appeal is in part a function of another way in which one may speak with a moral voice. According to (MV2):

(MV2) A speaks to B in a moral voice in respect of A's φing if A appeals to moral reasons for A to φ.

One speaks with a moral voice in the sense given by (MV2) when one offers moral reasons for one's *own* actions. We have taken for granted here that justified punishment is punishment imposed for the reason that it is deserved, and in the amount deserved by the offender. As we argued in section I, there is no conflict between judges' punishing offenders for such reasons, and in such amounts, and law-makers' criminalising in order to prevent wrongs. The point here, however, is that if judges *do* hand out punishments on the grounds of desert, they cannot but appeal to moral reasons to help justify the punishments they impose. Via these punitive acts the criminal law appeals to such reasons not only as reasons for its punishments, but also as reasons not to offend in the first place. That the criminal law speaks with a moral voice in the sense given by (MV2) thus helps explain why it also speaks with a moral voice in the sense given by (MV1).

None of this is to say that the criminal law appeals only to moral reasons. When we criminalise in order to prevent, we also create prudential reasons not to offend. But those who think this objectionable, we have argued, miss an important truth: that prudential reasons can be created by our willingness to respond to wrongdoing as we are morally justified in responding. When we convey to the would-be wrongdoer that such reasons exist we may do so in order to prevent her wrong; but we do not show the wrongdoer disrespect in the process. So we do not disrespect potential offenders when we confer on judges the power to impose morally justified punishments, and bring this to the attention of would-be wrongdoers in order to try to prevent their wrongs. It is true, of course, that the criminal law does not *only* bring the power to punish wrongdoers to the attention of those inclined to commit wrongs. But as we argued in the previous section, law-makers have ample justification for addressing criminal laws to all subject to their jurisdiction. We conclude that when the aim of criminalisation is to prevent wrongs, the law does not speak with only a moral voice. It appeals to moral and prudential reasons alike. And there need be nothing objectionable about that.

4

The 'Deserved' Punishment

ULFRID NEUMANN

Andreas von Hirsch, to whom this chapter is dedicated in appreciation and friend-ship, is well known in Germany as one of the most important representatives of a sentencing theory according to which the measure of punishment ought to respond only to the severity of the accused's offending behaviour. In principle, expected consequences of the offender's punishment ought to play no role when the judge determines the appropriate sentence in an individual case.

This scheme, which has attracted much support in the German literature,[1] but also drawn some criticism,[2] can be viewed as a deontological model of sentencing and, as such, can be contrasted with effect-oriented or consequentialist models. It is in this sense that I distinguish, in this chapter, between the 'deserved' and the 'effective' penal sanction/punishment. Various further distinctions regarding pun-ishment's possible preventive effects and the mechanisms through which these might be brought about (eg, individual-deterrent or re-socialising influences on the perpetrator; deterrence of other potential law-breakers; validation and thus stabilisation of the violated norm) are not particularly important in this context. The question I want to pursue here is whether, and to what extent, a deontological model of sentencing is tied to a deontological justification of punishment – a justi-fication that has found its clearest expression in the idea that punishment ought to provide just retribution for the culpable wrong committed by the perpetrator.

This question matters not only for sentencing models according to which the severity of the sanction is *fully determined* by the seriousness of the culpable crimi-nal wrong committed by the offender. It is just as relevant for approaches where the seriousness of the offending behaviour merely constitutes an upper limit for the sanction that may be imposed. The 'upper limit' view is by far the dominant approach among German penal theorists. According to this *communis opinio*, the culpability principle not only prohibits punishing a person who acts without guilt (the qualitative dimension of the culpability principle), but also requires that the

---

[1] T Hörnle, *Tatproportionale Strafzumessung* (Berlin, Duncker & Humblot, 1999); G Giannoulis, *Studien zur Strafmessung: Ein Betrag zur Dogmatik, Rechtstheorie und Rechtsinformatik mit Vertiefung in den Eigentums- und Vermögensdelikten* (Tübingen, Mohr Siebeck, 2014).

[2] G Ellscheid, 'Tatproportionale Strafzumessung und Strafaussetzung zur Bewährung – Bemerkungen zu einem kategorialen Irrweg' in G Britz et al (eds), *Grundfragen staatlichen Strafens. Festschrift für Heinz Müller-Dietz zum 70. Geburtstag* (Munich, CH Beck, 2001) 201.

punishment imposed on a guilty person not exceed the 'amount' or 'measure' of her guilt (the quantitative dimension of the culpability principle). Thus, whereas the severity of the sentence in a 'just deserts' model is determined entirely with reference to the seriousness of the offending behaviour, the dominant view in the German literature permits the sentencing judge to rely on preventive considerations and objectives, provided that the imposed sanction does not exceed what can be considered 'still adequate' in relation to the defendant's guilt and the gravity of the wrong.

In a model of just deserts, the 'deserved' punishment is therefore the *only* punishment that can justifiably be imposed in a particular case: there is no room for a modification of the severity of this punishment. For the approach that dominates German penal theory, by contrast, the 'deserved' punishment merely constitutes an upper limit of permissible punishment. Yet both models must face up to the question why the 'deserved' punishment should matter at all, given the broadly consequentialist justifications offered for the *institution* of punishment (say, by pointing to its supposed deterrent effects that keep crime levels under control, or by seeing criminal sanctions as norm-applications that 'stabilise' the normative order).[3] Nothing would appear more natural than to let the notion of efficiency, which according to these views legitimates the institution of punishment, also determine the severity of the sentence in particular cases.

These points regarding the relationship between deontological and consequentialist considerations in the sentencing verdict can be carried across from the questions of how to punish and how much, to the question whether to punish at all. In the latter context we then encounter the familiar problem[4] whether consequentialist (preventive) considerations are capable of justifying the punishment of innocent persons in particular situations. That it appears likely that they could do so is illustrated by the following scenario.[5]

I. 'Effective' versus 'Deserved' Punishment: a Hypothetical Scenario

Let us assume the following facts. One day, Mrs Miller is discovered with a broken neck at the bottom of the staircase of the house she shared with Mr Miller. It is an open secret in the neighbourhood that the marriage between Mr and Mrs Miller had long been conflict-ridden. Loud and aggressive arguments were the order of the

---

[3] This apparent puzzle also provides a starting point for the contribution by Edwards and Simester to this volume, although those authors seek to resolve it in quite a different way.

[4] On this point, see K Papageorgiou, *Schaden und Strafe. Auf dem Weg zu einer Theorie der strafrechtlichen Moralität* (Baden-Baden, Nomos, 1994) 58ff with further references to the current discussion.

[5] I restrict myself to an evaluation from an act-utilitarian perspective. The rule-utilitarian perspective is explored in this context by Papageorgiou, ibid, 65ff.

day. People are convinced that Mr Miller must have deliberately pushed his wife down the staircase during one of these rows.

Mr Miller is charged with, and convicted of, the homicide of his wife. He is sentenced to 15 years' imprisonment. (Assume that this is close to the upper limit of the length of sentence permitted by law.) The court reasons that a heavy sentence is warranted because society must be protected against the aggressive behaviour of Mr Miller. Additionally, given Mr Miller's anti-social personality traits, as evidenced by a history of alcohol abuse and a string of prior convictions for violent assault, any measures to re-socialise Mr Miller will need time to take effect. Moreover, the court considers that domestic killings have to be punished particularly harshly in order to deter others from similar crimes, and in order to reinforce social trust in the validity of one of society's central norms, the prohibition on killing.

Let us accept, for the sake of argument, that all of the court's analysis regarding the effectiveness of the sentence is, in substance, correct; 15 years of imprisonment is the right sentence, in that it is optimally capable of achieving the individual- and general-preventive objectives of the sanction imposed. Neither can it be denied that Mr Miller, if he remained free, would be highly likely to commit further serious crimes of violence. There is just one catch: Mr Miller has nothing whatsoever to do with his wife's death. His wife slipped and fell down the stairs when she rushed to the door after the postman had rung the doorbell.

Is Mr Miller's sentence justified? Obviously not. But just as easy as it is to give this answer, so difficult is it to show why it is correct, if one employs the preventive understanding of punishment that dominates German discussions. Viewed from the perspective of prevention, it is difficult to find anything wrong with Mr Miller's detention. So far as individual prevention is concerned, this may well be the last opportunity to counteract Mr Miller's tendency to criminal behaviour. With regard to general prevention, the merely imagined commission of a homicide, which the public is convinced has in fact been committed, has exactly the same significance as a real homicide. This is as true of the deterrence of other potential perpetrators (negative general prevention) as it is of the reaffirmation of the validity of the apparently-violated norm (the prohibition against killing). In both respects, what matters is how an incident is perceived by the general public (as a crime or as a tragic accident), and not whether the incident really was a crime or a tragic accident.[6]

If the proponents of purely preventive theories of punishment nevertheless consider Mr Miller's conviction and sentence unjustified, they most likely do so because of a sense that Mr Miller does not 'deserve' this punishment. He is punished for doing something he did not do. Statements like these, which reflect our everyday moral intuitions, are of course highly imprecise and can at most provide a preliminary basis for scholarly discussion. The crucial question is: how, and at what

---

[6] It is irrelevant in this context that the truth might later become public knowledge. This would, with respect to the preventive effect achieved at the time of conviction and sentence, be no different from a case in which the conviction was for a true crime but a mistaken belief arose later that the conviction was unfounded. In both situations, whatever preventive effects the conviction and sentence had when they were passed are not undone by the subsequent further developments.

juncture, can we integrate this moral intuition into a normatively convincing theory of punishment?

II. The Deserved Punishment: an Essential Component of 'Absolute' (Deontological) Theories of Punishment

The simplest solution consists in recasting this everyday moral intuition as a constitutive element of a normative conception of punishment. Ultimately, this is what the theories we classify as 'absolute' or 'deontological' theories of punishment do. According to these views, the penal sanction is justified as some kind of 'equivalent' to the crime – and, in the strict versions (such as the one supported by Kant), punishment is thereby not merely justified but also required. Such theorists do not rule out the possibility that punishment may have some preventive effects, but these effects play no role in their justification of punishment. Punishment is justified intrinsically as a legitimate (or even morally required) response to crime.

This position, usually labelled 'retributivism', is difficult to defend in a secular state committed to the traditions of the Enlightenment and to the notion that any rights infringements by the state must be rationally grounded. Retributivist theory explicitly declares that the social consequences of punishment are irrelevant to its justification, and necessarily remains unconnected to the social reality in which punishment operates. It is thus, logically speaking, not immanent, but transcendental. This gives bite to the objection that it is a metaphysical conception of punishment.[7] A metaphysical justification of punishment might, in today's 'postmetaphysical age' (as Habermas put it), perhaps still find its way into some personal views and convictions, but it is simply untenable as a justification of state conduct that infringes fundamental rights of citizens (regarding life, liberty, and property).

It is indeed hard to see how one could overcome the epistemic concerns raised by a retributive theory that is based on an assumed ontological connection between crime and punishment. This problem becomes even more troubling if the conception of retribution is informed by religious notions of divine justice which the state is then charged with carrying out. One of the great changes wrought by the Enlightenment is the thoroughgoing 'privatisation' of religion. In consequence, religious beliefs cannot, as such, carry any weight as arguments in political public discourse.

It is a different question whether retributive punishment can be interpreted as a demand of ordinary 'human' justice, whose realisation might well be considered a legitimate state function. We would not doubt, for instance, that it is the task of the state to see to it, by way of corrective intervention, that a thief returns stolen goods

---

[7] C Roxin, *Strafrecht: Allgemeiner Teil*, vol I, 4th edn (Munich, CH Beck, 2006) § 3 marginal note 8: 'The metaphysical ideal of justice is not something that the state, as a human institution, is capable of reaching or may appropriately aim for.'

to the person he stole them from, or at least compensates the victim of his theft. Why should we view the kind of justice served by civil law as ordinary, human, justice, but assume that the justice pursued by the criminal law is of a different, metaphysical, sort?

There is an obvious answer to this question. Civil compensation repairs the damage caused to the victim by the perpetrator's unlawful act. The detriment suffered by the perpetrator, when forced to restore value to the victim, is equivalent to the victim's benefit. The civil remedy is thus a zero-sum move. The amount of goods is constant; compensation merely affects the distribution of these goods. With regard to the latter, it is surely evident that the legal order must shift the loss or 'damage' (back) to the person who initially imposed equivalent losses unlawfully on the other party. In a sense, this conclusion already follows from the fact that the legal order initially allocated the goods in question to the victim. It would be inconsistent for the legal order to recognise the victim's ownership of the goods but not to offer any legal remedies by which violations of the victim's ownership rights could be corrected.

By contrast, the thief's punishment is precisely not a zero-sum move. Here, an additional 'negative good' or harm (the taking away of liberty, property, or even – in case of the death penalty – life) is brought into play; a harm which is, at least prima facie, without any corresponding gain on the part of the victim. Hence this is not a situation where harms are being redistributed as justice demands, by shifting the damage where it belongs. Rather, this is a case where additional harms are artificially 'created', harms which are neither 'neutral' entities, nor add any positive value to the sum total of goods in the world, but which do quite the opposite and bring the overall balance down significantly.[8] A penal sanction responds to a detrimental interference with one good (typically belonging to a victim), by a detrimental interference with another good (belonging to the perpetrator), without there being any recognisable way in which the second interference provides material compensation for the first. (Disregard, for the moment, the thought that a different argument may be possible concerning the interference with non-material interests of the victim.) Any possible 'advantage' that society might gain from the perpetrator's punishment is, in the present justice-based context, not to be taken into account. Of course, in current discussions of the legitimacy of punishment we quite often encounter the thought that the perpetrator is obliged to submit to 'a just punishment' in order to contribute to the re-stabilisation of the norm he violated.[9] But this idea only becomes pertinent after one has already accepted that punishment serves a preventive function – in other words, when one has already made the switch from an 'absolute' to a 'relative' theory of punishment.[10]

---

[8] On this aspect, see further U Neumann, 'Dimensionen der Strafgerechtigkeit' in SI Liu and U Neumann (eds), *Justice – Theory and Practice* (Baden-Baden, Nomos, 2011) 117, 129.

[9] M Pawlik, *Person, Subjekt, Bürger. Zur Legitimation von Strafe* (Berlin, Duncker & Humblot, 2004) 88.

[10] See, for example, Roxin's contribution to this volume.

III. The Deserved Punishment in Complex ('Unified') Theories of Punishment

A. Retribution as a component of a retributive-preventive 'unified' theory

Sometimes the retributive perspective is joined together with preventive considerations in a 'unified theory' which strives to combine aspects of absolute and relative theories of punishment. This kind of multi-dimensional penal theory is very popular in Germany, both in the courts and among academics. The German Constitutional Court has summarised its position on penal justice as follows:[11]

> The Constitutional Court . . . views the function of criminal law in general terms as the protection of the fundamental values of communal life. Commensurate deserts ['*Schuldausgleich*'], prevention, the resocialisation of offenders, atonement and retribution for past wrongs have all been recognised as elements of an appropriate penal sanction . . . Notwithstanding its task to deter and to resocialise, [the criminal sanction is] retribution for past wrongdoing.

The German Federal Court takes a similar position.[12] Various scholars have likewise made attempts to connect elements of absolute and relative theories into some form of unified theory of punishment.[13]

But these unified theories are not very convincing, at least as justifications of punishment. If, for the reasons set out above, retributive theories taken by themselves cannot justify punishment, then they cannot make *any* contribution to the justification of punishment – whether alone or in combination with other theories. This is so because the criticism in section II above of the retributivist justification of punishment is not that it is somehow too *weak* to justify the massive interference with the interests and goods of an offender that penal sanctions usually entail. Rather, our discussion so far suggests that the notion of retribution is utterly *incapable* of legitimating punishment. If this is so, retribution does not provide us with a merely inadequate argument for punishment: it provides us with absolutely no argument. Thus retribution cannot – given the arguments we have encountered so far – contribute to the justification of punishment, even in combination with other considerations.

---

[11] See, for instance, BVerfGE 39, 1 (57); BVerfGE 109, 133 (172ff).

[12] See, for instance, BGHSt 24, 40, 44.

[13] R Maurach and H Zipf, *Strafrecht Allgemeiner Teil,* vol 1, 8th edn (Heidelberg, CF Müller, 1992) § 6.I.D; HW Laufhütte, R Rissing-van Saan and K Tiedemann (eds), *Strafgesetzbuch: Leipziger Kommentar,* vol 1, 12th edn (Berlin, De Gruyter, 2006) Einleitung, marginal note 60 (commentary by T Weigend); K Lackner and K Kühl (eds), *StGB-Kommentar,* 27th edn (Munich, CH Beck, 2011) § 46 marginal note 2 (commentary by K Kühl).

B. Purely preventive unified theories

Some writers conclude at this point that retribution cannot be a function of punishment or contribute to its justification. Consequently, they see punishment as an institution directed solely towards preventive goals. These goals consist in influencing the offender to be law-abiding in the future ('special prevention'), and in bringing about various broader social effects, such as general deterrence ('negative general prevention') and the stabilisation of the legal order. In these 'unified preventive' models, retribution is explicitly excluded from the list of penal aims.[14] The offender's culpability here merely serves a constraining function: no offender may be punished more severely than he deserves to be punished for his crime, and a punishment can only be deserved if its severity is commensurate to the degree of blameworthiness of the offender.[15] This approach then quite naturally arrives at the conclusion that the punishment of an innocent person cannot be justified. The reasoning that leads to this conclusion, however, differs significantly from that followed by theories which recognise the imposition of commensurate deserts as a penal aim in its own right – a point that will be pursued further in the next section.

IV. The Culpability Principle: Ways towards its Recognition within a Theory of Punishment

A. The culpability principle as an internal limit on punishment

If one considers just retribution for the offender's wrongful act to be a constitutive element of punishment, the reason why punishment of an innocent person cannot be justified is simply that there is no wrong for which commensurate punishment could be imposed. This conclusion must necessarily be drawn regardless of whether one views retribution as the main function of punishment, or as one function among others (as many unified theories do). Insofar as unified theories incorporate a retributive aspect, retribution is a constitutive element of punishment within these theories. From the perspective of retributive or preventive-retributive unified theories, the punishment of a person for something they have not done is simply pointless, indeed incoherent. The culpability principle, which allows punishment only for, and commensurate to, the accused's culpable wrongdoing, leads to a retributively oriented criminal law simply through the function that it attributes to punishment. It is woven into the fabric of this understanding of the criminal law, and in this sense is 'internal' to the justification of punishment.

---

[14] Roxin, *Strafrecht Allgemeiner Teil I*, above n 7, § 3 marginal notes 37–47.
[15] Ibid, § 3 marginal note 53.

B. The culpability principle as an external limit on punishment

(i) Counter-productivity of the culpability principle in a preventive criminal law

Matters look very different from the vantage-point of a preventive theory. Recall the example of Mr Miller's punishment: with a view to prevention, Mr Miller's conviction and punishment makes perfect sense. After all, it would (given how the example was constructed) optimally achieve the various preventive aims of a crim-inal sanction. As regards Mr Miller himself and thus the aim of special prevention, Mr Miller's imprisonment would open up opportunities for his longer-term re-socialisation. At the same time, the general-preventive function of deterrence would be activated through his punishment, and the prohibition against killing would be stabilised.

In contrast to retributive theories of punishment, preventive theories thus need to incorporate an additional safeguard to make sure that the theory does not allow the conviction of an innocent person. Retributive theories avoid this danger simply through their inner logic, but preventive theories can only do so by introducing a further, external condition of justified punishment – 'external' in the sense that this condition does not already flow from the functions the theory ascribes to punish-ment.

The culpability principle is also for many preventive theories the source of this external condition. After all, this principle prohibits the punishment of the inno-cent, and it also prohibits penal sanctions that exceed the severity of punishment fairly reflecting the offender's guilt. The central question is how the culpability principle can be argued for in the context of a theory that sees the functions of pun-ishment purely in terms of preventive outcomes. Retributive theories, as we have seen, have it easy here: for those theories, the culpability principle simply follows from the retributive purpose of punishment, and the punishment must naturally be derived from the gravity of the wrong. By contrast, the logic of preventive theories suggests that the expected preventive effects of a person's punishment should determine both whether, and how much, punishment should be imposed. Indeed, this is the classic objection raised against purely preventive theories. Prevention is forward-looking, directing its gaze to the future behaviour of the offender; the cul-pability principle looks backwards, to the gravity of the wrong done and the degree of blameworthiness of the perpetrator. Why this switch of direction? Why should a preventive criminal law also turn its head backwards, instead of consistently look-ing forward into the future?

(ii) The principle of humanity?

Let us first remind ourselves that the principle of humanity, though an acknowl-edged principle of criminal law systems, does not equip us with the resources to develop the culpability principle. The principle of humanity is capable of excluding, as inhumane, certain kinds of punishments from the arsenal of criminal law: for instance, flogging, the death penalty, or life imprisonment without the possibility of parole. But a principle of humanity cannot distinguish between persons according to their individual features, such as gender, ethnicity, or even past conduct. The essential standards of humanity are by definition universal. A punishment that it would be inhumane to impose on an innocent person cannot become humane if it is imposed instead on a guilty person. Put differently: the principle of humanity precisely forbids us to draw the kinds of distinctions between persons which the culpability principle, in its sphere of application, calls upon us to make – the distinction between the guilty and the innocent, as well as distinctions among the guilty according to different degrees of guilt.

(iii) The proportionality principle

Seemingly more promising is the attempt to derive the culpability principle from the principle of proportionality, which has been recognised as a requirement of constitutional law in the jurisprudence of the German Constitutional Court.[16] The appeal lies in the fact that the culpability principle is, *in its logical structure*, a principle of proportionality, in as much as the culpability principle asserts that the imposed sanction must stand in adequate proportion to (or at least not exceed) the gravity of the offence and the blameworthiness of the offender. Insofar as the culpability principle prohibits the punishment of the innocent (the qualitative dimension of the culpability principle), it can also be interpreted as following the logical boundaries of proportionality: where no culpable wrongdoing exists, any punishment would be a logically disproportionate response.

Nevertheless, the attempt within a preventive penal theory to develop the culpability principle entirely out of the constitutionally recognised principle of proportionality cannot, in the end, succeed. This is so because the principle of proportionality is, as such, merely formal. It leaves open what the elements are that must stand in an appropriate relation to each other. It is concretised as a legal, and particularly as a constitutional, principle in that the state may pursue its chosen aims only through using appropriate means. What it calls for is that an aim selected by the state must be appropriately related to the means employed to achieve that aim. In this way, one can for instance consider whether the restriction of the freedom to choose one's profession which results from regulations governing the registration of medical practitioners is justified by the aim of protecting the health of the population.

If one sees the aims of punishment – as the purely preventive theories do – exclusively as the prevention of future crimes, or the stabilisation of social norms, then

---

[16] BVerfGE 45, 187 (260); BVerfGE 70, 297 (311) and BVerfGE 90, 145 (173). The punishment-limiting function of the proportionality principle is discussed further by W Hassemer, 'Der Grundsatz der Verhältnismäßigkeit als Grenze strafrechtlicher Eingriffe' in A von Hirsch, K Seelmann and W Wohlers (eds), *Mediating Principles. Begrenzungsprinzipien bei der Strafbegründung* (Baden-Baden, Nomos, 2006) 121; U Neumann, 'Das Verhältnismäßigkeitsprinzip als strafbegrenzendes Prinzip' in von Hirsch et al, ibid, 128.

one must relate the means ('punishment') to *these* aims. In other words: the proportionality of the punishment is not determined with reference to the past crime, but with regard to the preventive effects the punishment appears capable of achieving. Instead of the question, 'What punishment does this offender deserve for the crime he has committed?', we would need to ask: 'What punishment can be justified in this case in view of the significance of the preventive effects we can reasonably expect to result from it?' The proportionality principle would have to direct itself at the positive consequences of imposing the sanction, as well as the magnitude of the danger which the sanction is meant to prevent (as in fact happens in Germany to some extent, in respect of culpability-independent 'preventive measures').[17] In the context of a purely prevention-oriented criminal legal system, the proportionality principle and the culpability principle pull in different directions. The culpability principle instructs us to look at the past (and to refer to the gravity of the offending behaviour), whereas the proportionality principle enjoins us to look at the future (and refer to the looming dangers and the sanctions necessary to prevent them from materialising).

(iv) The culpability principle as an effective factor within the dynamic of general prevention

An interesting attempt to develop the culpability principle within a purely prevention-oriented conception of punishment has been made by Claus Roxin. He calls the culpability principle 'the most liberal and, in terms of social psychology, best suited means to limit the punitive power of the state that we have found so far.'[18] As it stands, this is a plausible evaluation. But it is not yet an argument for the culpability principle, as the question is precisely whether, and (if so) why, limitations on the state's punitive power should not be derived merely from a principle that punishment must be proportionate to the positive consequences expected from it. The beginnings of a positive argument for the culpability principle can, however, be found in Roxin's suggestion that compliance with the culpability principle is necessary for positive general prevention to work:[19]

> The sense of justice which plays such an important role in stabilising the public's commitment to the normative legal order, requires that nobody is punished more harshly than he deserves to be punished, and only a punishment commensurate with the punished person's guilt can be 'deserved'.

In this way, the culpability principle is not added to a preventive theory as an external principle. Instead, it is developed within the preventive framework as a

---

[17] Existing German law looks both to the severity of the crime and to the size of the future risks. § 62 StGB states that a 'corrective measure' may not be imposed if it 'would be disproportionate to the seriousness of the crimes the offender has committed and is likely to commit in the future, and to the degree of danger that he poses to others.'

[18] Roxin, *Strafrecht Allgemeiner Teil I*, above n 7, § 3 marginal note 49.

[19] Ibid.

necessary component of the social-psychological mechanism of positive general prevention. This is methodologically sound. Nevertheless, it is open to challenge.

To start with: as long as we remain within a purely preventive model, the culpability principle cannot, per se, require 'punishment commensurate with the punished person's guilt' – its point of reference will rather be, a punishment that the general population *considers to be* commensurate with the punished person's guilt. This is so because 'the public's sense of justice' is represented, not by what normative argument shows to be legally required and just, but by what people 'view as just'. The quantitative dimension of the culpability principle would have to be reformulated accordingly, to require that 'a punishment may not be more severe than what the general public's sense of justice considers just.' Likewise, the qualitative dimension of the culpability principle would take the form, 'a punishment may only be imposed when the public's sense of justice considers that a culpable wrong has been committed.' In effect, this approach would make the culpability principle beholden to popular opinion about what punishment certain conduct deserves. At least in some areas to which the culpability principle speaks, such a change would not be without risk. It certainly seems that the culpability principle, interpreted as a normative standard by the courts and in legal scholarship, draws tighter boundaries for legitimate punishment than 'the public's sense of justice' would be likely to do.

The point here is not simply that discrepancies may exist between the normative programme of the legal order, on the one hand, and the views of members of the public about what punishment is deserved, on the other. What is in issue is, also, whether the culpability principle can, in principle, be convincingly grounded in sociological assumptions regarding the psychological mechanisms of positive general prevention. This ought to be denied. As Andreas von Hirsch has convincingly argued, the attempt to derive the culpability principle from the social operating conditions of positive general prevention misunderstands the character of the culpability principle as a normative-ethical principle.[20]

V. The Culpability Principle as an Integral Component of the Institution of Punishment

A. Punishment as a reactive institution

Indeed, a convincing basis for the culpability principle cannot be found in the preventive function of punishment, but only in its institutional structure. As a social institution, punishment is a burdensome reaction towards the perpetrator of some

---

[20] A von Hirsch, 'Die Existenz der Institution Strafe: Tadel und Prävention als Elemente der Rechtfertigung' in his *Fairness, Verbrechen und Strafe: Strafrechtstheoretische Abhandlungen* (Berlin, Berliner Wissenschaftsverlag, 2005) 41, 47.

past deed that is evaluated negatively according to the norms of that society. To that extent punishment necessarily has a retributive structure.

This retributive structure exists prior to any question about the purpose for which punishment may be employed. The institutional link between deed and punishment is reflected at a conceptual level in the requirement that the determination that someone has been punished must be accompanied by identification of the deed he is punished for. The statement 'X was punished' contains incomplete information because it does not tell us the crucial part. A statement of this kind immediately provokes the question: 'What was X punished for?'

In a sense, this institutionally and conceptually necessary connection of punishment to a prior, disapproved of, deed is already reflected in the very possibility of asking what punishment is 'deserved'. We 'deserve' something, either positively (say, a prize) or negatively (a sanction), in virtue of something we have done in the past. By contrast, the connection to future consequences runs through the criterion of necessity. For this reason, we ask, when a person falls sick, not what medical treatment is 'deserved' but what medical treatment is 'needed' for his illness. Inversely, when we punish someone, we are first and foremost concerned with what punishment is 'deserved', and it is very much a secondary question how much punishment is 'needed'. The very question why it should be the 'deserved punishment' that matters already contains the answer. The question 'Why it should matter when deciding whether and how to punish someone, what punishment that person deserves', can only be meaningfully asked because, institutionally, punishment refers to disapproved past conduct with respect to which one can judge whether the perpetrator deserves a particular sanction, or not.

B. The culpability principle as a consequence of the reactive nature of the institution of punishment

Since punishment in reaction to a past offence does not express regret in respect of an event, but disapproval of the conduct of an agent, one must be able to blame the agent subjectively for this conduct. The question whether one may do so is raised as a question concerning the offender's culpability or guilt.[21] The culpability principle – as the principle *nulla poena sine culpa* – thus necessarily follows from the inner logic of the institution of punishment.

The connection between punishment and disapproved past conduct by the punished person, which is necessitated by the inner logic of the institution of punishment, has not only a qualitative but also a quantitative dimension. To be recognisably punishment, the reaction must reflect the severity of the past crime. Life imprisonment in reaction to theft of a piece of cake would not (to modern-day

---

[21] A different view is now taken by Tatjana Hörnle, who wants to keep the precondition of 'personal responsibility of the perpetrator for his conduct' but suggests that the notion of 'guilt' or 'blameworthiness' should be eliminated from the criminal law. See T Hörnle, *Kriminalstrafe ohne Schuldvorwurf. Ein Plädoyer für Änderungen in der strafrechtlichen Verbrechenslehre* (Baden-Baden, Nomos, 2013) 62.

observers) be a punishment for petty theft, but an act of state terror; conversely, the imposition of a moderate fine for murder committed in the course of a robbery would not be a punishment for murder but rather an endorsement. In so far as the culpability principle prohibits the imposition of punishments which do not stand in an adequate relation to the culpability of the offender, this aspect of it also follows already from the institution of punishment.

The question we started with – how and at what point we can incorporate into a convincing normative model of punishment our ordinary moral intuition that only 'deserved' punishment can be justified – can now be answered as follows. The logical place where this intuition enters into our theory of punishment is via the structure of the institution of punishment, which is a given before any purpose can also be attached to the practice. This means that, irrespective of whether one follows deontological (retribution or atonement) or consequentialist (special or general, positive as well as negative, prevention) explanations of the purpose of punishment, as long as one is concerned with a theory of punishment, one remains tied to this institutional structure of punishment. In this sense, the culpability principle, which creates and concretises this link, is likewise already contained within the institution of punishment.[22]

VI. Punishment as Reaction and as Retribution

A. Punishment as censure

The reactive character of the institution of punishment, and its relation to the culpable conduct of a person, are expressed with precision in the model of penal censure that Andreas von Hirsch has suggested and developed across a range of publications.[23] The intrinsic, purpose-independent connection between the criminal deed and some hard treatment imposed on the perpetrator in reaction to his crime implies disapproval of the deed – just like, in a mirror image of this connection, a reward given for some past act necessarily expresses positive appreciation of that act. To deny this is to fail to grasp the inner logic of the institutions of 'punishment' and 'reward'. Institutionally speaking, punishment necessarily involves censure, and a reward always involves praise.

---

[22] See, further, U Neumann, 'Institution, Zweck und Funktion staatlicher Strafe' in M Pawlik and R Zaczyk (eds), *Festschrift für Günther Jakobs: zum 70. Geburtstag am 26. Juli 2007* (Cologne, Carl Heymanns, 2007) 435.

[23] A von Hirsch, *Censure and Sanctions* (Oxford, Clarendon Press, 1993); T Hörnle and A von Hirsch, 'Positive Generalprävention und Tadel' in von Hirsch, *Fairness, Verbrechen und Strafe*, above n 20, 19; AP Simester and A von Hirsch, *Crimes, Harms, and Wrongs: On the Principles of Criminalisation* (Oxford, Hart Publishing, 2011) 10ff.

B. Punishment as hard treatment

However, punishment is, institutionally, not exhausted by censure. This follows from the fact that we can distinguish between conduct meeting with punishment, on the one hand, and conduct meeting with simple disapproval, on the other. To give some examples outside the context of state punishment: a teacher confronted with a pupil who repeatedly disturbs class by using his cell-phone can either punish the pupil, say by giving him extra homework, or let matters rest with a stern telling-off. Parents can respond to their child's misdemeanours with mere criticism, or by imposing sanctions (such as a reduction of pocket money). Of course in both cases the affected person might experience even the disapproval itself as a hardship and, in this sense, as a punishment. But this doesn't change the fact that one can, and must, distinguish between a burden that exhausts itself in disapproval, on the one hand, and a further intentionally imposed burden ('hard treatment') on the other.

The same holds true of judicially imposed responses to past misconduct. Here, it is also possible to imagine a reaction that is limited to expressing official disapproval of the conduct and refrains from interfering further with the interests of the affected person through the imposition of sanctions.[24]

Von Hirsch takes a different road. He sticks to the imposition of hard treatment as a necessary component of state punishment. This position rests on subtle argumentation which combines deontological and consequentialist considerations. First, the severity of the sanction expresses the degree of disapproval of the crime; to that extent, hard treatment is an integral element of censure. Secondly, hard treatment (as well as the threat of it) has a preventive function, in that it discourages potential perpetrators from committing a penalised act. That von Hirsch speaks of 'discouragement', not 'deterrence', lets the sanction appear as a form of communication rather than as an act of control.

This integrative model is superior to both a purely consequentialist and a purely deontological grounding of the hard treatment component in punishment. But as a communicatively oriented model which takes the perpetrator seriously as a morally competent agent, it rests on the precondition that the imposition of hard treatment can be shown to be just vis-à-vis the perpetrator. The arguments summarised thus far do not make it obvious that this condition is fulfilled. Different degrees of disapproval (the censure element) could also be conveyed through differentiated 'virtual' sanctions. And 'discouragement' remains within the realm of a prevention-oriented theory – which may be capable of explaining the instrumental necessity of imposing actual penal sanctions, but cannot establish the normative acceptability (justice) of doing so. We turn now to consider this issue in more detail.

---

[24] On such a model, see further K Günther, 'Die symbolisch-expressive Bedeutung der Strafe – eine neue Straftheorie jenseits von Vergeltung und Prävention?' in C Prittwitz et al (eds), *Festschrift für Klaus Lüderssen: zum 70. Geburtstag am 2. Mai 2002* (Baden-Baden, Nomos, 2002) 205. For criticism, see K Kühl, 'Zum Missbilligungscharakter der Strafe' in J Arnold et al (eds), *Menschengerechtes Strafrecht. Festschrift für Albin Eser zum 70. Geburtstag* (Munich, CH Beck, 2005) 149, 159ff; *Roxin, Strafrecht Allgemeiner Teil I*, above n 7, § 3 marginal note 46.

C. Hard treatment as a component of the institution of punishment

(i) The difference between 'disapproving' and 'punishing'

Regarding the question whether penal sanctions are just we must bear in mind that the normative link between a disapproved of act and the imposition of hard treatment is, in a manner of speaking, 'stored' within the institution of punishment (see the argument made in the previous subsection). Punishment is disapproval *by way of* an intentional setback to the interests of the punished person. Mere disapproval of an act is not punishment. A sentence like, 'The perpetrator was punished for raping the victim through disapproval of the rape,' is internally suspect. The point I am making here is not that the rape victim might well object that such a statement, psychologically and ethically, makes a mockery of her suffering. Rather, I am concerned with the structure of punishment as a social institution. To refrain from the imposition of the sanction is simply *not* to punish someone in the accepted social meaning of 'punishment', and in the linguistic usage that corresponds to that meaning.

This means that the institution of punishment contains an element of retribution beyond the element of censure. Of course it is possible to suggest that the state's reaction to crime should do away with this retributive component and restrict itself to verbal or symbolic disapproval of the act. This, however, would involve not merely a new understanding of criminal law, but an alternative to criminal law as a fairly universal feature of known legal orders. What is in issue here is not a disagreement as to the use of words, but an analysis of institutions. The rules of linguistic usage of the term 'punishment' merely reflect the patterns of the denominated social institution.

(ii) Distinction from retributive theories of punishment

I want to stress that this reconstruction of the reactive and retributive element of punishment is not a return to a retributive theory of punishment. This is so because the retributive theory of punishment, just like the preventive theories against which it competes, gives an answer to the question why (that is, to what end) an offender ought to be punished. The theory is thus concerned with the 'teleology' of punishment. Here, however, I have developed the reactive and retributive element of punishment as part of the inner logic of the institution of punishment, and not as part of the teleology of the activity of punishing. This reconstruction is neutral vis-à-vis alternative theories of punishment, because it starts at an earlier point, with the institutional structure of punishment. This institutional structure is something that all theories of punishment must be faithful to if they want to be taken seriously as theories of *punishment*.[25] The (formal) culpability principle necessarily follows

---

[25] A parallel argument regarding the institutional connection between punishment and a statement of disapproval is made by A von Hirsch and N Jareborg, *Strafmaß und Strafgerechtigkeit. Die deutsche Strafzumessungslehre und das Prinzip der Tatproportionalität* (Bonn, Forum Verlag, 1991) 14ff.

from the structure of the institution of punishment as soon as a society has reached a stage in its development where retribution for disapproved conduct is tied to the condition of personal responsibility of the agent for the conduct. This is the reason why the culpability principle is almost universally accepted amongst the proponents of various different theories of punishment.

(iii) The normativity of the institution

It remains possible to object that the structure of the institution of punishment, as a social fact, cannot allow us to derive from it the culpability principle as a normative principle or desideratum. But this objection misfires. The prohibition against deriving an 'ought' from an 'is' applies only to natural, not to institutional facts.[26] It is the very point of institutional facts (like punishment) that they are established through certain (constitutive) rules of the institution, with further (regulative) rules emerging from them. In all societies, institutions are central points of reference for judgements of justice. When sons or daughters become millionaires through inheritance law, this is considered just because the institution of the family justifies privileging children over the general public in this way. When someone becomes a head of state not by way of election or personal achievement, but through birth, this is considered just in the institutional framework of hereditary monarchy. Likewise it would be just, in the context of a system of the relevant kind, if the holders of public authority were to be identified by drawing lots. Whether public appointments based on patronage are viewed as nepotism or as family loyalty is a question of the institutional structure of society.

The insight that societal judgements of justice are necessarily focused on social (and state) institutions may also shed some light on the current debate regarding whether basing the justification of punishment on the demands of justice is ruled out in a system where only the state and no private person may execute punishment.[27] The problem is this: is the prohibition of private punishment simply a restriction on doing justice for external reasons (the state's monopoly of power in order to preserve social peace), or does this limitation of the right to punish criminal wrongdoing to the state mean that when the state punishes it is concerned only with furthering goals and purposes of the state and not with the pursuit of justice?

Suppose that, according to some particular theory of justice, a world in which the violation of the victim is met with a corresponding violation of the perpetrator, is as such morally a better (a more just) world than a world in which this is not the case. This conclusion could not depend on how and by whom the corresponding violation of the perpetrator is brought about. Consequently one would have to accept, according to this theory of justice, that, where the legal order imposes the death penalty for some crime, the killing of the perpetrator by the victim or his relatives

---

[26] See further, and also more generally on the theory of institutional facts, J Searle, *Speech Acts: An Essay in the Philosophy of Language* (London, Cambridge University Press, 1969); J Searle, *Making the Social World: The Structure of Human Civilization* (Oxford, Oxford University Press, 2010).

[27] On this debate, see recently A Haque, 'The Revolution and the Criminal Law' (2013) 7 *Criminal Law and Philosophy* 231, 236ff.

would be an act of just punishment. Such an argument would, however, overlook the fact that the assessment of an act as 'just' always relates to the institution of criminal punishment in its concrete societal shape. Among the institutionally-given elements of criminal punishment in modern western states is the notion that only a sanction which is imposed on the perpetrator through a neutral, state-constituted institution is recognised as 'punishment'.[28] The 'punishment' (in an extreme case, the killing of the perpetrator by the victim or his relatives) cannot be a just punishment in modern states and societies for the very reason that in the context of the institutions governing the practice it cannot qualify as punishment in the first place.

(iv) Historical relativity of the institution

This relativity of judgements of justice, their relation to social institutions, also means that structural changes to these institutions (in extreme cases, their aboli-tion) change judgements of justice. When the family as a social unit recedes fully behind the social collectivity, the right of children to inherit family wealth appears unjustified[29] – and, indeed, this right was initially abolished in Russia after the Revolution, and reintroduced only step by step.

The same applies to the institution of punishment. Were a future society to react to breaches of its norms never through sanctions but only and exclusively with educational measures, such a society would have given up the reference point for the notion of 'just punishment'. This would also be true if the state were to desist from imposing punishment, and react to violations of the law only with pedagogi-cal measures, thereby replacing 'punishment' (as we understand it today) with 'pedagogy'. Speaking from the perspective of a theory strictly committed to special prevention, von Liszt was, thus, in substance correct to say that 'the just punish-ment is the preventively required punishment.'[30] What is objectionable about this formulation, however, is the choice of terms. This is so because a purely prevention-oriented reaction does not constitute a punishment but a technical-social measure, and its point would be, therefore, not justice but suitability in an instrumental sense.

But of course one can question the institution of punishment from a position of justice as well. One can, for instance, argue that it is unjust to seriously set back the interests of a person (an offender) if, by doing so, one cannot at least prevent other setbacks to human interests of comparable seriousness. In short: social institutions are simultaneously *points of reference* for social judgements of justice and *objects* of social judgements of justice (in the latter case one can speak of second-order judge-ments of justice).

---

[28] See further Neumann, 'Institution', above n 22 at 440.

[29] On the problems of inheritance law from a legal-philosophical prespective, see G Radbruch, 'Rechtsphilosophie' in A Kaufmann (ed), *Gustav-Radbruch-Gesamtausgabe*, vol 2 (Heidelberg, CF Müller, 1987) 206, 391ff.

[30] F von Liszt, 'Der Zweckgedanke im Strafrecht' (1882), reprinted in his *Strafrechtliche Aufsätze und Vorträge*, vol 1 (Berlin, Guttentag, 1905) 126, 162.

In other words, because any assessment of the justice of (a concrete) punishment depends on the structure of the institution of punishment, it is impossible to provide an ultimate basis for the retributive response to conduct that violates central social norms. Institutions can change over time and can come to be replaced by other institutions. In particular, there is no necessary reason why, at all times, a central institution (the state) should respond through retributive measures to serious misconduct by individuals. After all, the state's penal law that we know today is the product of a specific historical development. It is a different question whether alternative institutions would really be preferable. Certainly, neither the institution of the blood feud, nor compulsory state re-education, appear to be particularly appealing alternatives to 'deserved punishment'.

II.

PUNISHMENT, DESERT AND COMMUNICATION

5

After the Crime:
Post-Offence Conduct and Penal Censure*

JULIAN V ROBERTS AND HANNAH MASLEN

Can the actions of the offender *following* the commission of the crime justify imposing more or less punishment? Utilitarians will see obvious reasons to mitigate sentence – for example, if the defendant relieves the state of the expense and burden of
proving the offence, or if she provides valuable information which facilitates the
prosecution of other offenders. Yet is there any room for recognising post-offence
conduct from a censure-based perspective?

The vast literature on retributivism has explored the factors relevant to a proportional sentence. The determinants of seriousness – harm and culpability – have
attracted considerable attention from scholars, and in particular the honorand of
this festschrift volume, Andreas von Hirsch. One issue that has received inadequate
discussion, however, relates to the actions of the offender following commission of
the crime, which we refer to hereafter as Post-Offence Conduct (POC). Two forms
may be distinguished: *commendable* POC encompasses laudable actions relating
to the victim (eg, facilitating medical or other assistance or making voluntary
compensation); the defendant's actions involving the prosecution of the crime (eg,
culpable admissions during interview by the police; entering a guilty plea) or her
responses to penal censure – such as undertaking treatment. *Culpable* POC involves
conduct which enhances the harm of the offence (eg, actions which protract the
harm inflicted by the crime in ways that fall short of constituting a fresh criminal
offence[1]). For reasons of space, in this chapter we shall focus on commendable post-
offence actions which might justify mitigation.

* The authors thank the editors of this volume, Patrick Tomlin, Andrew Ashworth, Ambrose Lee,
Johan Boucht and Jesper Ryberg for their comments on a previous draft of the chapter. We are also
grateful for the feedback from scholars attending a seminar at Oxford in October 2013, and to Gabrielle
Watson for research assistance.

[1] An example of such conduct can be found in a recent English case. An individual awaiting trial on a
series of historical sexual offence charges made public statements denouncing the alleged victims whose
reports had initiated criminal charges. This conduct goes beyond the mere affirmation of innocence,
exacerbates the suffering of the named victims as well as impeding any potential additional prosecutions
by undermining other victims' confidence that they will be believed. Taken together, they constitute
legitimate grounds for enhanced state censure and this was acknowledged by the Court of Appeal: see *R
v Hall* [2013] EWCA Crim 1450.

The chapter begins by noting examples of POC recognised by sentencing statutes and sentencing guidelines in a variety of jurisdictions. The prevalence of the phenomenon itself provides a reason to explore the issue at the level of theory. We then discuss the conventional retributive approach to sentencing, which establishes strict temporal limits on the circumstances relevant to a proportional sanction. The chapter then offers both a narrow and a more expansive account of the mitigating role of POC within desert theory. Additional clarity regarding the nature of, and limits upon, POC is necessary to promote consistency of application – otherwise individual courts will favour or disfavour particular defendants in an unpredictable and unprincipled fashion. The chapter draws upon the writings of Andreas von Hirsch, who has exercised a huge influence on penal theory and the practice of sentencing ever since the publication of *Doing Justice* in 1976,[2] and in particular upon his writings with Andrew Ashworth.

I. Introduction

POC falls within the general rubric of mitigation and aggravation at sentencing. Conceptual frameworks for mitigating and aggravating factors are rare; the issue is clearly under-theorised.[3] The literature focuses almost exclusively on issues relevant to the commission of the offence. Retributivists in particular have generally either rejected or ignored the significance of the defendant's post-offence conduct. For example, Ashworth endorses 'the principled stance that events occurring after the crime are not relevant to sentence';[4] this position suggests that nothing the offender does after the crime can affect crime seriousness or culpability.[5] Less stringently, Manson discusses a range of factors which 'support a claim for mitigation but do not fit neatly into gravity and culpability categories'.[6] Post-offence conduct is included in his list but Manson offers no theoretical justification for taking this conduct into account.[7] Even advocates of a more expansive role for mitigation at sentencing have failed to evince much interest in highlighting the actions of the

[2] A von Hirsch, *Doing Justice: The Choice of Punishments* (Boston MA, Northeastern University Press, 1976).

[3] Jacobson and Hough provide an empirically-derived classification involving categories of factors such as responses to the offence, to the prosecution and the defendant's present and future lifestyle. Our concept of POC does not fit squarely within their scheme. See J Jacobson and M Hough, *Mitigation: The Role of Personal Factors in Sentencing* (London, Prison Reform Trust, 2007) 9–11.

[4] A Ashworth, 'Re-Evaluating the Justifications for Aggravation and Mitigation at Sentencing' in JV Roberts (ed), *Mitigation and Aggravation at Sentencing* (Cambridge, Cambridge University Press, 2011) 21, 34. Ashworth includes 'reparation, remorse and other post-offence matters' under the heading of 'mitigating factors that have no bearing on proportionality' (at 27).

[5] Ashworth acknowledges the utility (if not the desirability) of allowing reductions for a guilty plea, but he regards these as pragmatic rather than principled mitigations.

[6] A Manson, 'The Search for Principles of Mitigation: Integrating Cultural Demands' in JV Roberts (ed), *Mitigation and Aggravation at Sentencing* (Cambridge, Cambridge University Press, 2011) 54.

[7] Manson discusses circumstances such as the collateral consequences of the crime on the offender and justifies these drawing on the culturally-derived concept of 'legitimate sympathy': see Manson, ibid.

offender *after* the offence, preferring to stress factors which mitigate the offender's culpability at the time of the crime.[8]

The principal reason for this lack of theoretical engagement with the offender's post-offence behaviour is that it is seen as being irrelevant to a calibration of the harm inflicted or the offender's level of culpability for the offence. Simply put, no matter how much he may regret or wish to undo the act, the offender cannot change his past mental states (affecting culpability) or, for most forms of offending, fully restore the victim to his (unharmed) state prior to victimisation. What's done cannot be undone, as it were. This position assumes an analysis which works backwards from the commission of the crime. The manner in which the crime was committed may be relevant to a determination of the harm inflicted;[9] moreover, the offender's blameworthiness – determined by his state of mind and relevant conduct prior to the offence (eg, level of planning or premeditation) – are also factors in the retributive sentencing equation. In addition, some retributivists regard prior convictions as justifying an uplift in severity.[10] The retributive analysis closes, however, with the commission of the crime. Nothing the offender does after the offence, it would appear, aggravates or mitigates sentence severity because the elements of a proportional sanction have been exhausted; the calibration of harm and culpability draws exclusively on the circumstances surrounding the commission of the crime and (possibly) certain actions antecedent to the offence.[11]

Most retributivist theories thus construct a 'firewall' between the offender's conduct before[12] and during the crime, and his behaviour thereafter. Yet, while retributive theorists may pay little attention to POC, in practice the offender's conduct after the crime plays an important role in sentencing hearings through advocates'

---

[8] Eg, A Lovegrove, 'The Sentencing Council, the Public's Sense of Justice and Personal Mitigation' (2010) 12 *Criminal Law Review* 906. One exception to this observation is Cooper, who stresses the importance of considering the offender's willingness to engage in restorative justice opportunities and other post-offence actions. See J Cooper, 'Nothing Personal' in A Ashworth and JV Roberts (eds), *Sentencing Guidelines: Exploring the English Model* (Oxford, Oxford University Press, 2013).

[9] Generally in aggravation, offenders who inflict suffering gratuitously or who cause more harm than is necessary to accomplish the offence – of robbery for example – are punished more severely because this bespeaks a higher level of harm and blameworthiness.

[10] Eg, Lee argues that repeat offenders are reasonably adjudged to be more culpable for failing to rectify the causes of their offending: Y Lee, 'Repeat Offenders and the Question of Desert' in JV Roberts and A von Hirsch (eds), *Previous Convictions at Sentencing: Theoretical and Applied Perspectives* (Oxford, Hart Publishing, 2010). Other retributivists take the view that previous convictions simply disentitle the offender to mitigation or should play no role at sentencing. For exposition of the various perspectives and further discussion, see C Tamburrini and J Ryberg (eds), *Recidivist Punishments. The Philosopher's View* (Plymouth MA, Lexington Books, 2012) and Roberts and von Hirsch (eds), ibid.

[11] These factors generally relate to the offender's capacity to act: are there plausible reasons to believe that his capacity to comply with the law was impaired – for example, by extreme provocation by the victim or exceptional social adversity of some kind?

[12] We do not explore the period prior to the offence, but a number of arguments can be made to support the view that the offender's desert is affected by actions prior to the crime. Eg, a number of European jurisdictions allow 'total mitigation' to result when an offender voluntarily desists from completing an offence during an attempt. Offenders who desist prior to completing the offence may thus be deemed less or even not culpable. The offender's suffering before the crime may also affect his deserved sentence; see discussion in J Ryberg, *The Ethics of Proportionate Punishment* (Amsterdam, Kluwer, 2004) 18.

submissions.[13] In addition, as we shall document, sentencing regimes around the world recognise a broad range of circumstances in mitigation, many of which relate to the period after the crime and prior to determination of sentence.

A. POC in sentencing statutes, practices and sentencing guidelines

Post-conviction conduct is currently recognised in sentencing statutes and guideline schemes in many jurisdictions. These include England and Wales,[14] New Zealand, Israel, and Sweden where the legislature has placed proportionality on a statutory footing as the fundamental principle at sentencing. This cross-jurisdictional consistency is itself an indication that there may be some retributive significance to these behaviours.

Three of the most comprehensive sentencing laws which provide detailed 'guidance by words' are found in Sweden, Finland and Israel. All three statutes are based on proportionality and provide lists of circumstances which may justify sentence reductions for post-offence conduct. Section 5 of the Swedish sentencing law provides a diverse collection of factors which may mitigate the sentence, although they are not considered to affect the 'penal value' of the offence. For example, it includes actions by the offender which mitigate harm as well as other issues which invoke the differential impact of the sentence but which are unrelated to the offence or the administration of justice.[15] Two of these factors relate to the offender's conduct after the crime, namely whether he tried to repair or mitigate the harmful consequences of the offence and voluntarily surrendered to the authorities.

The Finnish statute is even more explicit in its recognition of post-offence conduct. Chapter 1, Section 6 of the Criminal Code recognises a number of grounds for reducing the punishment imposed, including: 'attempts by the perpetrator to prevent or remove the effects of the offence, or his or her attempt to further the clearing up of the offence'.[16] The more recent (2012) Sentencing Law in Israel recognises several post-offence actions as being relevant to sentencing, including co-operation with the authorities; efforts by the offender to mitigate the harm caused by the

---

[13] Advocates will highlight important changes in the offender's lifestyle since the crime, citing any efforts he or she has undertaken to mitigate the harm or promote his or her own rehabilitation. This is reflected in professional training publications: eg, M Hannibal and L Mountford, *Criminal Litigation Handbook* (Oxford, Oxford University Press, 2011) 388. One of the most common (and indeed persuasive) appeals in mitigation is that through his recent actions, and since the commission of the crime the offender has 'turned his life around'. This claim is obviously relevant to rehabilitation as a sentencing objective but some of the offender's acts may also justify reduced censure for the reasons we explore in this chapter.

[14] In addition to recognition of post-offence conduct in the English guidelines, the offender's actions after conviction may justify a court in deferring sentence for a period of up to six months: see s 1 of the Power of Criminal Courts (Sentencing) Act 2000.

[15] These include the consequences for the offender of a criminal conviction or imposition of a particular sentence which may trigger state action to have him deported.

[16] Many other examples may be cited. Article 48(d) of the Albanian Criminal Code notes the following mitigating circumstances: 'When the person has compensated for the damage caused by the criminal act or has actively helped to eliminate or decrease its consequences'.

offence; voluntary compensation he has made to the victim and efforts on the part of the offender to become more law-abiding.[17] Finally, sentencing at the international level also recognises the relevance of post-offence conduct. Voluntary surrender, assisting the prosecution and other circumstances have been recognised in judgments of the international tribunals.[18]

Sentencing guidelines often acknowledge the relevance of the offender's actions following the offence. In the English guidelines the following post-offence factors are recognised as 'reducing the seriousness of the offence or reflecting personal mitigation': voluntary reparation to the crime victim; remorse; determination or demonstration of steps to address addictions or offending behaviour.[19] The New Zealand guidelines recognise co-operation with the authorities as a source of mitigation as well as a range of behaviours such as prompt confessions, disclosing the benefits of the offending and helping or compensating the victim, although these latter circumstances are subsumed under the broader heading of remorse.[20] Across the US, many sentencing guidelines recognise post-offence conduct such as making voluntary disclosures relating to the offence or providing 'substantial assistance' to prosecutors.[21] In practice,[22] then, actions of the offender after the crime do affect sentencing. But can they be justified in terms of censure theory or are they simply utilitarian incentives to facilitate the administration of justice?

B. Derogations from proportionality

One way of accommodating POC within the sentencing equation is to classify these actions as justifying utilitarian derogations from a proportional sanction – a necessary impurity in the model in order to achieve wider social goals. This approach both recognises the relevance of POC while protecting the proportional model from corruption. The guilty plea is the classic example: An offender pleads guilty and in turn the state awards a sentence reduction. The plea, it is always asserted, has no retributive value, but the system permits this derogation from a truly

---

[17] Section 40k. See JV Roberts and O Gazal-Ayal, 'Sentencing Reform in Israel: An Analysis of the Statutory Reforms of 2012' (2013) 46 *Israel Law Review* 455.

[18] See S D'Ascoli, *Sentencing in International Criminal Law* (Oxford, Hart Publishing, 2011) 251 and B Hola, *International Sentencing* (Amsterdam, Free University, 2012).

[19] These factors are found at Step Two of the guidelines methodology, where they affect sentence but not to the extent of factors cited at Step One. See Sentencing Council, *Burglary Offences: Definitive Guideline* (London, Sentencing Council of England and Wales, 2011).

[20] New Zealand Law Reform Commission, *Mitigating Factors. Draft Guideline* (Wellington, New Zealand Law Reform Commission, undated). The New Zealand guidelines have yet to be enacted into law.

[21] See US Sentencing Commission, *2009 Sourcebook of Federal Sentencing Statistics* (Washington DC, US Sentencing Commission, 2010).

[22] Empiricists have also overlooked this issue. Eg, while there is a vast and growing literature on public attitudes to mitigating and aggravating factors at sentencing, few post-offence issues have been explored beyond the guilty plea. These studies suggested public support for sentence reductions for post-offence conduct, particularly when it involves reparation to the victim or some form of assistance to the state. See, eg, JV Roberts, M Hough, J Jacobson and N Moon, 'Public Attitudes to Sentencing Purposes and Sentencing Factors: An Empirical Analysis' [2009] *Criminal Law Review* 771.

proportional sanction in order to promote wider aims of criminal justice – conserving court resources to permit the more effective prosecution of other cases and promoting victim welfare.

Is it appropriate, however, to relegate POC to the category of utilitarian intrusions or does the offender's conduct after the offence carry normative significance? Treating these actions as external to the proportional sanction strips them of any potential relevance they may have for the censuring activity of the state; they become administrative counting rules rather than issues addressed within a penal communication. A second potential weakness of this tightly-drawn retrospective analysis is that it may overlook information legitimately affecting the appropriate sanction in ways more straightforwardly connected with harm and culpability. To the extent that POC is relevant to sentencing, retributivist analyses which are temporally restricted to the commission of the crime will result in a less accurate calibration of the offender's true desert.

To summarise, our intention in this chapter is to determine whether a proportional sentencing model should merely tolerate POC (in order to secure utilitarian benefits external to a censure-based model of sentencing) or whether some accommodation for the offender's post-offence actions may be found *within* the model.

C. The Contention

The traditional retributive approach calculates the seriousness of the offence from factors relating to harm and culpability arising from the circumstances surrounding the commission of the crime. For this reason, the factors considered relevant are closely temporally linked to the offence, to the time of the crime. However, the conventional approach also considers relevant actions that are more remotely antecedent to the crime – factors such as premeditation and prior offending are seen to enhance culpability, in part because they demonstrate a deep commitment to the offence.

Our argument is that just as antecedent conduct can legitimately influence sentence, post-offence-related conduct can also be relevant. POC can reduce the harm of the offence, and/or serve to confirm or challenge the offender's commitment to his actions at the time of the offence. As an extension of this symmetrical approach, we further argue that, where POC is deemed too far removed to affect harm or culpability, there may still be censure-based grounds on which to reduce the punishment: where commendable POC has been demonstrated, the need for the full quantum of censure is absent, and the severity of the sanction may be moderated accordingly. Censure involves a communication between the state, the offender and the crime victim. The stringency of that message should be modulated to reflect legitimate distinctions between offenders which relate to their post-offence conduct. We use the qualification 'legitimate' because authorising all manner of commendable conduct after the crime to mitigate sentence will undermine proportionality and indeed other principles such as equity and consistency. We also distinguish between POC and remorse – although theoretically and empirically the two are linked. On our analysis POC is more than simply 'remorse in action'. POC is not just evidence of remorse: other justifications can speak in favour of mitigation even in the *absence* of remorse.

Finally, it is important to acknowledge the multiple versions of retributive theories. Some of these will be (or should be) more amenable[23] to incorporating POC than others. Our concern here is not to provide a thorough taxonomy of different theories and the relevance of POC for each; it is, rather, to explore the significance of post-offence conduct for a generically retributive approach to sentencing – that is, for a scheme which is concerned with deontological rather than utilitarian motives, and which focuses on the censure of the offender rather than the prevention of offences in the future.

II. Defining Post-Offence-related Conduct

The work by von Hirsch which most clearly engages with this issue is *Proportionate Sentencing.*[24] This influential work considers the offender's conduct after the offence, although the discussion is relegated to the volume's Appendix – in recognition perhaps that the arguments are explored 'in tentative and exploratory fashion'.[25] The authors draw upon the Swedish sentencing law to discuss a range of circumstances tangentially relevant to retributive principles. POC falls clearly under the heading of what the Swedish law[26] refers to as 'Equity Factors' or 'Quasi-Retributive' Factors. The factors discussed which are relevant for present purposes include 'significant efforts to alleviate the offence's consequences after the event' – for example, where an offender has made voluntary reparation. With respect to such forms of conduct, von Hirsch and Ashworth adopt an approach which involves the expression of state sympathy: 'we should show some sympathy towards a person who seems already to have taken a message of punishment to heart and to have started to mend his ways.'[27] Below, we argue for a more principled justification than mere sympathy: on our reading, the offender is *entitled* to some mitigation if the criteria for POC as a mitigator have been met. Moreover, we suggest, state recognition of

---

[23] Eg, Nozick takes the view that there is less or no requirement for punishment in the case of an offender who repents his crime, makes amends and returns to a law-abiding lifestyle – all before conviction: see R Nozick, *Philosophical Explanations* (Oxford, The Clarendon Press, 1981) 384. See also the discussion in J de Keijser, *Punishment and Purpose: From Moral Theory to Punishment in Action* (Amsterdam, Thela, 2000) 16–17.

[24] A von Hirsch and A Ashworth, *Proportionate Sentencing: Exploring the Principles* (Oxford, Oxford University Press, 2005).

[25] Ibid, 3.

[26] For discussion of the Swedish statute, see N Jareborg, 'The Swedish Sentencing Reform' in C Clarkson and R Morgan (eds), *The Politics of Sentencing Reform* (Oxford, The Clarendon Press, 1995).

[27] Von Hirsch and Ashworth, *Proportionate Sentencing*, above n 24 at 171.

this form of mitigation should be signalled in advance, through the sentencing statute or sentencing guidelines.[28]

What counts as post-offence-related conduct which is potentially relevant to mitigation? It is important that in recognising POC we do not legitimise a return to the social accounting at sentencing which characterised an earlier period, and vestiges of which remain today.[29] In general terms, legitimate POC encompasses the actions of the offender which mitigate the harm of the crime, reduce or contextualise the culpability of the offender for the offence, or facilitate the state response to the crime.[30] All three grounds justify a less stringent level of state censure.

Some features of POC are common to all three grounds of mitigation. Most importantly, only acts by the defendant *which relate to the crime* are relevant. This limiting criterion excludes all other manner of commendable conduct – exemplary professional work records, volunteer work for charity, acts of individual heroism and so forth.[31] Allowing these actions to affect sentencing would promote a wider social and moral accounting exercise in place of an offence-based analysis. A second limiting criterion involves accessibility of this kind of mitigation. On grounds of equity, POC should potentially be accessible to all defendants. While, in practice, ensuring equal access is likely to be challenging, this restriction would prevent a millionaire reducing his sentencing liability by writing a large cheque for the victim or the state. Finally, we are concerned here with subsequent actions by the defendant. Legitimate claims for post-offence-based mitigation can also be made on the grounds that the offender suffered as a result of the crime, the response of the victim, or indirectly as a result of the criminal proceedings. 'Immanent' or 'extra curial' punishment of this kind is also considered by the courts but results in mitigation for other reasons,[32] and is not included in our analysis.[33]

Beyond their shared features, commendable POC can be divided into three main categories, for which different desert-based justifications for mitigation exist. Some POC will traverse more than one category but all instances of commendable POC

---

[28] This would carry several benefits. It would clarify for the offender, the victim and the community the grounds for any mitigation, and would alert potential and actual offenders to the importance of rectifying their criminal conduct.

[29] Some advocates will make a robust submission in mitigation at sentencing on the basis of the defendant's good character, contributions to society and the like. In addition, as we note, some guideline schemes explicitly acknowledge the relevance of some aspects of the offender's lifestyle that are clearly unrelated to the offence of conviction.

[30] That is, the investigation, prosecution and punishment of the offence.

[31] Sentencing guidelines recognise these kinds of actions as relevant, within the amorphous category 'personal mitigation'. Eg, according to the English guidelines, 'exemplary conduct' and 'good character' are relevant factors (see, eg, the guideline for assault, available at: sentencingcouncil.judiciary.gov.uk/). We exclude such considerations from our category of POC.

[32] It does not justify a reduction in censure, but rather generates a more sympathetic response from the state.

[33] Eg, the offender may be seriously wounded at the hands of the victim, may lose his employment following the laying of a criminal charge or suffer in other ways which a sentencing court might take into account in mitigation of the ultimate, legal punishment: see J Duffy, 'Roll the Dice, Rational Agent: Should Extra-Curial Punishment Mitigate an Offender's Sentence?' (2012) 31 *University of Queensland Law Journal* 115.

will fit into at least one. The categories are: (i) reparative acts, (ii) state-assistive acts, and (iii) reformative acts.

A. Reparative acts

The first category of commendable POC includes any actions that reduce the harm of the offence or otherwise improve the well-being of the victim. Examples of this category of POC include voluntary reparation and providing assistance to the victim either immediately after the offence or at some later period prior to conviction. In these cases the offender's actions mitigate the harm and thereby reduce the 'penal value' of the offence – even though the conduct may occur long after the crime. On all retributive accounts the level of punishment should reflect this fact and mitigate the sentence. Of course, the reparation must constitute a response to the offence; without this causal link the mitigation would lose its principal focus.

B. State-assistive acts

The second category of commendable POC includes any conduct that facilitates the state's criminal justice response to his offence. These acts are justified principally because they reduce the necessary level of censure, but also because they may also mitigate the harm of the offence. Examples include: voluntary surrender to authorities, pleading guilty to the offence, and assisting in the prosecution of the offender's crime[34] by disclosing details of the crime which the state would otherwise have to discover through investigation. This category is more problematic for a number of reasons. In recognising these actions it is vital that they constitute departures from the suspect's or defendant's undeniable right to refuse to participate in the state's prosecution of his offence. The presumption of innocence requires that individuals remain free to deny the allegation without thereby incurring a penalty;[35] as such, assisting the state is an act of supererogation by the offender. At the same time, the need to protect the integrity of the presumption of innocence will have consequences for the magnitude of POC-based reductions:[36] very substantial sentence reductions in return for early admissions of guilt will constitute an unacceptable incentive to plead guilty. For this reason, some limits on the mitigating effect of

---

[34] Assisting the state in the prosecution of other offenders may be commendable, carries clear benefits for the administration of justice, promotes wider social goals and is recognised by courts in mitigation. However, since it is unrelated to the offence with which the offender is charged, it is excluded from our analysis for two reasons. First, the retributive focus must remain on the offender's conduct, and not stray into alleged wrongdoing by others. Secondly, were we to admit this under the heading of POC we would have to include much else besides – eg, making a significant donation to general funds for the benefit of victims.

[35] Thus there is a need to establish a norm: with respect to plea, the norm is a 'not guilty' plea, meaning that a guilty plea mitigates from the norm and that defendants who contest the charge are not disadvantaged. The presumption of innocence requires that a guilty plea is the departure from a norm of requiring the state to prove its case.

[36] Some, but by no means all of the concern over the presumption of innocence is assuaged by the fact that POC-based sentence reductions apply after conviction, when the presumption is no longer in play.

post-offence actions by the offender are needed; we return to this issue later in the chapter.

C. Reformative acts

The third category of POC includes any conduct intended by the offender to reform or rehabilitate herself prior to sentencing. The prototypical examples of this type of POC will be the voluntary undertaking of treatment for criminogenic needs – treatments such as anger management courses or drug or alcohol abuse programmes. The retributive significance of these acts is not immediately apparent, although they will be relevant to rehabilitation. A rehabilitationist will recognise that the steps taken by the offender will lower her risk of re-offending and enhance her rehabilitative prospects; some of the punishment may therefore be curtailed. However, several censure-based accounts of sentencing should also take these steps by the offender into account. Central to a censure-based account such as Duff's, for example, is the desire to recall the offender to a law-abiding lifestyle by awakening his moral conscience.[37] Even a less penitential account of punishment, we shall argue below, is capable of responding to reformative efforts made by the offender.

III. Justifying the Mitigating Role of Commendable POC: An Offence-seriousness Approach

Two models may be used to justify the mitigating effects of POC. One is a relatively narrow one, in which the harm of the offence, or the offender's culpability for it, is affected by post-offence conduct. For this *offence-seriousness* model to be defensible, the retributive analysis simply needs to expand beyond the hitherto strict temporal limits on the offence employed by some penal theorists. Later, we shall come to a more expansive model, which invokes broader considerations related to penal censure. The second model involves more than simply expanding the ambit of analysis; under the expansive model, censure is reduced for reasons unrelated to reduced seriousness.

Let us begin with the offence-seriousness approach. In our view, there are good reasons why some post-offence-related conduct is relevant to an assessment of the seriousness of the offence.[38] Where this is the case, POC can (and should) affect the quantum of punishment the offender deserves, on almost all retributive accounts.

---

[37]   Eg, Duff claims that 'a process of censure or punishment aimed at inducing repentance thus also aims to induce reform: not to re-form the wrongdoer as an object that we must mould to our wishes, but to persuade her of the need to reform herself': RA Duff, *Punishment, Communication, and Community* (Oxford, Oxford University Press, 2001) 108.

[38]   The limits of the analysis of harm or seriousness have yet to be systematically explored, and we agree with Ryberg when he notes that 'when it comes to the harm dimension of crime seriousness there is still much work to be done ... of clarifying what basically matters': *Proportionate Punishment*, above n 12 at 67.

In presenting this argument, we draw attention to two related issues which so far have received little attention from theorists. These are: 1) How tightly-tied the determinants of offence-seriousness should be to the actual time of the offence; 2) Why 'antecedent' conduct (such as provocation, premeditation and relevant previous convictions) should affect the assessment of seriousness but not 'subsequent' conduct (such as assisting the victim or the state in a way related to the offence).

A. Expanding the time-frame

When desert theorists talk of the 'harm of the offence' and the offender's 'culpability for the offence', it is often assumed that what constitutes 'the offence' – the actions and states of mind for assessment – will be uncontroversial. However, there is room for disagreement between theorists (although less so in established practice) about 1) how the offence should be delineated – where it starts and where it stops – and 2) how time-constrained the determinants of its seriousness should be – how far before and after commission of the offence retributivists can look to assess its harm and calibrate the offender's level of culpability. The latter of these two issues is our principal focus.

The following example demonstrates that determinants of culpability – in this example, relevant mental states – do not have to be temporally co-extensive with the commission of the offence. Imagine that two offenders, offender A and offender B, are sentenced for separate burglaries causing the same amount of harm to the respective victims – the burglaries are equally intrusive and result in equal loss. Further, offender A and offender B both had the same state of mind at the point of entry: a clear intention to take as many items of value as they can carry. Both offenders retain this intention throughout their time in the respective victims' houses. Taking the similarities in states of mind and harm caused into account, we might assume that they are both equally culpable. However, at the respective sentencing hearings, evidence indicates that A had been planning the crime for months. Further, one year prior to the offence, he had attempted a burglary but had run away when the house alarm had gone off, resulting in his serving a community order. This antecedent conduct serves to increase his blameworthiness for the offence, even though it is separated in time from the present offence and even though his intentions and actions were the same as offender B's at the time of the offence. Retributivists tend to accept that a thorough assessment of the offender's culpability for the offence incorporates culpable conduct that occurs prior to the actual commission of the offence.[39]

Expanding the time-frame in the other direction, the assessment of the harm of the offence typically takes into consideration the state of the victim weeks or months

[39] Variation across jurisdictions in the definition of crimes complicates the determination of when a crime begins and ends. The general point, however, remains: the duration of the crime cannot be easily or strictly defined for the purposes of establishing the offender's criminal liability; and even where it can, the determinants of harm and culpability might extend before or beyond the time of its commission.

later. Admittedly, and often when it comes to assessing physical harm, this is sometimes because the extent of injury only becomes apparent over time. However, the
inclusion of aggravating factors such as the 'ongoing effect [of the assault] upon the
victim' in English sentencing guidelines demonstrates that, at least in practice, the
assessment of harm considers the victim's welfare far beyond the pain or injury
experienced at the time of the assault.[40] In both directions, then, the temporal
bounds of what is relevant to the seriousness of the offence are sometimes broader
than the temporal limits of the offence itself.

If, as we have shown, the determinants of offence-seriousness are not sharply
delineated, then this raises the question of whether post-offence-related conduct
can be amongst these determinants. The traditional retributive approaches set
important limits on the relevance and effect of conduct not central to the offence,
but the precise boundaries are open to some debate. Limits on what constitutes
relevant premeditation, for example, will in some cases be fairly clear-cut: the
offender who carefully plans to fraudulently extract money from an individual but
instead spontaneously burgles his house cannot have been said to have planned or
organised the burglary – even though the same individual was targeted, and for
similarly acquisitive purposes. However, perhaps more difficult to ascertain would
be whether and at what point an instance of planning 'expires' if the offence is not
committed. If an offender plans a burglary – perhaps in great detail – but then
changes his mind, what consequence does this have for his potential future culpability? What if, five years later, without any additional planning, he commits the
planned or a similar offence? Would desert theorists argue that, having planned it
once, it is from that point bound to be premeditated if it ever occurs?

So, whilst desert theory sets limits on the antecedent factors that can legitimately
affect the assessment of the offender's culpability for his offence, the retributive
estimation of offence seriousness encompasses events occurring before the offence
was committed and more distant consequences for the victim. We argue that post-
offence conduct, when it is related to the offence, can just as legitimately be considered as relevant to the seriousness of the offence.

B. Modifying the culpability assessment

POC might mitigate the seriousness of the offence[41] by either reducing the offender's culpability for it or by reducing the harm caused by the offence (or sometimes
both). One way of conceptualising the offender's culpability is to represent it as the
extent to which the offender is fully committed to the offence – the extent to which
he commits the offence purposefully and without hesitation. For example, the

---

[40] Sentencing Council of England and Wales, *Assault Offences: Definitive Guideline* (London,
Sentencing Council of England and Wales, 2011).

[41] On a practical level, the degree of harm in many cases cannot be determined at the time of or shortly
after the crime has been committed. The victim's injuries or losses may not be clear for weeks or months
– one reason why victim impact statement regimes allow victims to update their impact statements at
any time up to the sentencing hearing.

offender who meticulously plans and organises his offence is prima facie more committed to it than the offender who offends spontaneously. But, in addition to prior conduct providing evidence of the offender's degree of commitment, that level of commitment can also be confirmed or challenged by his subsequent conduct. At one end of the spectrum is the individual who, after offending, boasts of committing a crime and who should therefore be seen as fully committed to the offence. On the other end is the offender who, immediately after the offence, is seized of a sense of shame and self-reproach and who seeks to redress the harm – in such a case the offender's rejection of her offence provides some evidence of a lack of commitment to it at the time of its commission. If she was not fully committed to it, she is accordingly reasonably deemed to be less culpable.[42] In invoking the concept of 'degree of commitment to the offence' we are not alluding to a view according to which the offender's long-term character is more or less instantiated in her conduct. Rather, we simply mean to draw on familiar notions such as deliberate and intentional offending compared with opportunistic and spontaneous offending. Correspondingly, we are here reminded of Duff's comments on 'immediate repentance', in which he argues that:[43]

> [S]ometimes an offender's *immediate* repentance can cast a different light on her crime by showing it to have been a momentary aberration. She attacked another person but at once repents the attack, is horrified by what she has done, and tries to help and apologise to her victim. We can now see the attack itself in a different light – not as a vicious assault to which she was wholeheartedly committed, but as an aberration for which she already condemns herself. Her immediate repentance is then a proper mitigating factor: it mitigates the seriousness of her crime.

This leaves open for discussion the question of how much time can pass before POC cannot demonstrate an offender's weak commitment to her offence at the time of its commission, and the answer to this is unclear. Nonetheless, we argue that POC can, in some cases, provide evidence of weaker commitment just as pre-offence culpable conduct provides evidence of stronger commitment. Of course, neither pre- nor post-offence conduct offers a window into the offender's mind; but both can justifiably aid a judge in the assessment of her culpability.

To recap, culpable conduct which occurs before the offence was committed – for example, extensive planning and careful preparation of the crime – confirms the offender's commitment to the crime at the time of its commission; post-offence conduct can confirm or challenge this relationship. The boastful offender and his

---

[42] We distinguish between POC that indicates something about the offender's state of mind – and hence his culpability – *at the time of the offence*, and POC that is relevant to the censure the offender deserves without it revealing anything about the offender's state of mind at the time of the offence. The timing of the POC is crucial to this distinction: the former, 'evidentiary' POC reveals that the offender deserves mitigation because of a lack of commitment to his offence at the time of its commission. The latter, 'substantive' POC earns the offender mitigation because of its relevance to the appropriate quantum of censure even in cases where evidence suggests the offender was committed to his offence at the time of its commission. We discuss this latter function of POC below.

[43] Duff, *Punishment, Communication, and Community*, above n 37 at 120–21.

offence may be represented as perfectly overlapping circles in a Venn diagram.[44] Relevant post-offence conduct has the potential to provide evidence that the circles were in fact further apart, justifying a less stringent level of state censure when the overlap is minimal. However, we concede that the time-window in which POC can have this effect on seriousness will be limited. The offender's POC would have to have some credibility as a legitimate challenge to his commitment to his offence, and this is an issue to be resolved within an adversarial sentencing hearing.

C. Modifying the harmfulness

Mitigating the offender's culpability is not the only effect of post-offence conduct. POC can also reduce the harm of the offence. If the harm of the offence is reduced, there will be straightforward retributive grounds on which to mitigate sentence. Voluntary reparation for property offences may sometimes be able to achieve this. If an offender has stolen items from the victim but then returns them or offers an equivalent sum of money then much of the harm of the offence has been mitigated, even if the offence of appropriating another's property has been committed.[45] (Of course, there will be instances where no sum of money could 'replace' an item that was of sentimental value or unique; this will be a case-by-case matter.)

Against this, it could be argued that the 'harm of the offence' must necessarily be crystallised at some particular point, after which voluntary reparation would be seen as commendable but not relevant to an assessment of the harm of the offence. As noted above, it is part of our contention to challenge such a restricted time-window for the determination of offence-seriousness. We acknowledge that it is difficult to make a convincing case for accepting one proposed demarcation over another: Is the harm of the offence set at the point that the offender transfers the victim's property into her possession, or slightly later when she returns home with it, or at the point that she engages in a different, unrelated activity? Although we grant that some (perhaps arbitrary) line has to be drawn in order to make an assessment of the harm caused, it is not clear where this should be. However, especially if the line will be arbitrary, we cannot see why an offender's attempts to reduce the harm of his wrongdoing should always fall beyond this cut off point; particularly when the 'ongoing [harmful] effect upon the victim' is sometimes taken into account.

A similar debate about when the harm of the offence is established can arise in the case of facilitating medical or other assistance. An offender who goes to exceptional lengths to facilitate medical assistance for the victim may be deserving of less pun-

---

[44] A classic Venn diagram would consist of two partially overlapping circles; the overlapping portion represents the common interest of the two entities or concepts represented by each circle.

[45] In such circumstances the POC may play a role in the decision to prosecute. Whether a prosecution is in the public interest – one branch of the test for prosecution – may be affected by the offender's actions after the crime. If an offender has undertaken very significant steps towards repairing the harm of the offence, there may be an argument that prosecution is no longer in the public interest.

ishment, especially where this limits the harm of the offence.[46] We might imagine an offender who assaults her victim, leaving him with moderate bleeding. Instead of running away or merely calling an ambulance the offender, seeing the extent of the injuries, immediately attends to the wounds and summons not only an ambulance but friends of the victim to further assist. In such a case, it is likely that the harm of the assault will have been reduced. For the sake of argument, let's say that the offender's actions meant that the victim only needed to spend the afternoon receiving professional medical treatment, rather than the three days that untended injuries would have necessitated. Due to the offender's reparative POC, the victim has sustained less harm than otherwise would have been the case. This assessment of harm therefore extends beyond the time of the assault.[47] The 'harm coefficient' of the crime, in practice at least, is therefore not static in time.

D. Addressing retributive objections to the narrow account

A desert theorist who wants to preserve the relevance of antecedent conduct, whilst denying the relevance of POC, might offer two possible objections.

The first objection is that taking POC into account is unfair, as offenders will have differing lengths of time between committing the offence and the sentencing hearing. This permits some offenders more of an opportunity to engage in commendable POC. This is an argument about fairness in sentencing practice, not about what is theoretically relevant to desert. We regard this objection as weak for two reasons. First, whilst it will be true that a longer time period creates more opportunities for POC (and so those who have longer between offence and sentence are arguably at an advantage), this is not generally considered a problem when antecedent conduct is taken into account by retributivists. Older offenders are not considered to be at a disadvantage because they have had to remain law-abiding for longer. The courts are not concerned that, by taking relevant antecedent conduct into account, they are inadvertently favouring those who have had less time to display such conduct. Secondly, the conduct considered relevant – both before and after the offence – cannot be *too* removed in time from the offence. Most often considerable time passes between the commission of the offence and the sentencing

---

[46] It should be noted that, whilst the harm caused in the counterfactual scenario in which the offender did *not* help will to some extent be uncertain, medically assistive POC might sometimes have the effect of changing the offence: where medical assistance prevents an assault from resulting in death, for example, the offender will in some sense already have reduced the punishment he will receive (relative to the counterfactual in which he did *not* assist) because he will be sentenced for an offence of lesser gravity. In such cases, it is less clear whether assistive POC should then further reduce the punishment (relative to the counterfactual).

[47] There is a clear parallel between harm-restricting actions before and after the crime has been committed. Individuals who withdraw from continuing with a crime even after having caused some but not all the harm of the completed offence are 'allowed' to effectively withdraw from the offence and avoid or minimise their criminal liability. In this sense the cut-off points between an attempted and a completed offence and the completed offence and post-offence conduct are somewhat arbitrary. The offender's reaction to his wrongdoing after it has been committed is as relevant as his response to his own conduct as the offence unfolds.

hearing, even if the exact durations vary. It is our view that all offenders will have sufficient opportunity to demonstrate commendable POC.

The second and more difficult objection is theoretical and taps into the different natures of 'past' conduct and 'future' conduct. The objection is that, whilst all conduct prior to the commission of the offence is 'set', all future conduct – and any effects it can have – is open. This uncertainty means that the offender has to be considered fully responsible for the *likely* harms of the offence, even if these do not in fact materialise or are repaired. The objection is particularly troubling for the argument that reparative or medically- assistive POC can reduce the harm of the offence. Recall the offender who makes great efforts to minimise the harm caused to her assault victim. The objection would be that, whilst the victim is less harmed than he would have been absent the POC, the offender nonetheless *risked the full harm* by her punches: the harm caused or risked was set by the acts (and only the acts) that constituted the assault. Whilst it was commendable that the offender took action to mitigate the actual harm, this does not change the degree of harm risked. At the time of the punches, there was no guarantee that the offender would or could mitigate the harm.

Although this second objection is based on the uncertainty of the eventual degree of *harm*, we think that the concern it embodies is more to do with culpability – the idea that the offender should be considered fully *responsible* for the harm that he risked regardless of how things in fact turn out. We have already noted that the assessment of harm extends to the on-going effects on the victim, which clearly are uncertain at the time of the commission of the offence. Yet, openness of the future does not prevent these effects from being relevant to assessment of the harm caused. The real concern, instead, is that the openness – the uncertainty – of the future means that risking a particular degree of harm is always as *culpable*, regardless of whether that harm eventuates or is prevented, since at the time of the offence there is no guarantee about which way it would go – this concern is thus not about the harm of the offence but about the offender's blameworthiness for it.

When we understand the objection this way, the focus then returns to the relevance of POC to culpability. Whether the openness of the future objection is convincing will depend in large part on whether it is conceded that POC can provide evidence of the offender's culpability at the time of the offence, which is, by definition, not in the future. Where POC serves this function, it is irrelevant that we can have no guarantee about how things will turn out. We have argued that POC allows us to infer something about the offender's state of mind at the time of the offence; it is 'evidentiary' and reveals that the offender was not as culpable as the fully committed offender. In such cases, it is not true that it was left open as to whether the offender would disown his offence – he was never fully committed to it. The 'openness of the future' argument therefore does not work here, as the assessment of culpability – even that which takes POC into account – is not looking to the (open) future. Rather, it infers something about past culpability from what happened subsequently: the POC provides evidence that the Venn circles were never particularly overlapping.

IV. A More Expansive Account of the Normative Value of POC: Censure and Broader Retributive Values

Even if POC does not affect the seriousness of the offence, it may still have normative significance within a retributive framework. Following von Hirsch and Ashworth, we first argue that commendable POC is relevant to the censuring function of punishment – not simply because it justifies sympathy, but because it changes the quantum of censure that is appropriate.[48] Finally, we suggest that even where censure is unaffected by POC, there may be some instances that justify a step-down of punishment to reflect other communicative goals.

A. Censure-based sentencing

Penal censure communicates a message about the wrongfulness of the offence, while the hard treatment authorised by the sentence both reinforces that message and provides the prudential disincentive to re-offend. Yet censuring an individual for acts which he already accepts as wrongful, and for which he has already voluntarily accepted responsibility, seems gratuitous and a violation of the principle of penal restraint. Communicating a message of maximal censure to the truly penitent offender is preaching to the converted. Similarly, von Hirsch's 'prudential disincentive' to re-offend[49] becomes less necessary when the offender has accepted his culpability for the offence. Imposing the full quantum of punishment on the truly reformed individual amounts to punishing in order to prevent a recurrence of a crime which has, to a large extent, already been prevented by the offender.

An offender deserves censure for several reasons. First, there is a public element to the offence and the forum in which censure is expressed. The community has an interest in the offender's wrongdoing, and the sentence is imposed in open court. Failing to censure the offender constitutes a failure to acknowledge that the community's values have been infringed at a level justifying state intervention. From this perspective, the penitent offender deserves no less censure than the impenitent; the public dimensions of his crime call for the same state response. Yet with respect to the relationship between the individual offender and the state, there is some room for accommodation. The general level of censure applicable to all offenders – including the impenitent – is unnecessary in the case of the penitent.

If the purpose, or a purpose, of state censure is to encourage a moral transformation in the offender, the censuring agent needs to be sensitive to signs of moral

---

[48] One of us has developed an argument along these lines in relation to the mitigating effect of remorse. See H Maslen, *Remorse, Penal Theory and Sentencing* (Oxford, Hart Publishing, forthcoming 2014).

[49] A von Hirsch, *Censure and Sanctions* (Oxford, Oxford University Press, 1993) 12.

awakening.[50] Creating, for the purposes of sentencing, a firewall between past and future conduct seems unwise. A rigid position – which considers only conduct during the commission of the offence – deprives the offender of any agency to participate in his own moral evolution. He is deprived both of the incentive to achieve change and the tools to assist in self-reform.

Admittedly, not all desert theorists would go so far as to suggest that the purpose of state censure is to encourage a moral *transformation* in the offender. In fact, von Hirsch explicitly rejects the idea that state censure is an attempt to *encourage* or *elicit* remorse in the offender. His position is the more liberal one that merely identifies remorse (amongst other things) as the *appropriate* response to censure. In collaboration with Andrew Ashworth, he says:[51]

> A response to criminal wrongdoing that conveys disapprobation gives the individual the opportunity to respond in ways that are typically those of an agent capable of moral deliberation: to recognize the wrongfulness of the action; to feel remorse; to express regret; to make efforts to desist in the future.

Yet it seems to us that the state also needs to be sensitive to signs of moral awakening even if its aim is no more than to engage in a moral *communication* with the offender. Communication gains greater legitimacy when it is tailored to its recipient. If it is not also listening, the state's sentencing process becomes an asymmetric exercise in penal communication: the state expresses its censure and the offender passively absorbs the consequent punishment.[52]

A refusal to entertain POC-based mitigation may undermine or compromise the state's moral standing to punish. Prison regimes may constitute a useful analogy. A prison which treated all prisoners alike, which punished regardless of the extent to which inmates engaged in remedial initiatives (such as substance abuse treatments, anger management courses or professional training), would suffer both in terms of its perceived legitimacy and its rehabilitative effectiveness. It would be strange if an institution designed to rehabilitate ignored inmates' efforts in this regard. Indeed, it is a well-known correctional axiom that rehabilitation cannot be *imposed* on offenders, for both practical and moral reasons. Offenders and inmates must choose to participate and for this reason prisons often (and should) modulate the conditions of confinement in response to prisoners' efforts to self-reform.[53]

---

[50] See Duff, *Punishment, Communication, and Community*, above n 37, and his emphasis (at 108) on '*self*-reform': 'A constructive process of censure will ... aim to help the wrongdoer come to see what she must do [to reform] and how she can do it.'

[51] Von Hirsch and Ashworth, *Proportionate Sentencing*, above n 24 at 92.

[52] Further, whilst we have suggested that this argument has force even on a minimally communicative account such as von Hirsch's, it has even greater force where *dialogue* between the state and offender is emphasised. Duff, eg, argues that the offender should not be a 'passive recipient' but should actively participate in the dialogue: RA Duff, 'Penal Communications: Recent Work in the Philosophy of Punishment' (1996) 20 *Crime and Justice* 1. For an account of the communicative dimensions of criminal law, crime and punishment, see also Günther's contribution to this volume.

[53] Another analogy: imagine a hospital which treated patients for coronary or pulmonary disease and yet took no interest in whether post-operative patients continued to smoke, eat or drink to excess or actively participated in exercise regimes.

Considering the first offender sentencing discount reveals further asymmetry in the factors deemed relevant to the appropriate quantum of censure. First offenders attract a more lenient sentence under almost all retributive theories of punishment and in all sentencing regimes.[54] For example, according to the progressive loss of mitigation model propounded by von Hirsch and Ashworth, first offenders should receive a discount to reflect their crime-free lifestyle prior to the offence: They have 'lapsed' into offending, as is only human on occasion, and are yet to hear the message of censure. This claim for mitigation on the basis of lapse creates a paradox: passive compliance with the law before the crime attracts a significant sentence reduction, yet active attempts to co-operate with the state after the crime generate no such benefits for the defendant.

To summarise, our censure-based argument runs as follows: if, as von Hirsch and Ashworth argue, the offender's reflective process is important to the rationale underlying the censuring response, then an offender who independently engages with the reflective process should be censured in light of this. Adopting a limited dialogical model of censure achieves this, making room for input from the offender on the subject of his wrongdoing. Of course, this does not mean that censure is inappropriate in cases where the offender demonstrates commendable POC. The censure still needs to reiterate and confirm the wrongfulness of the offence, but the offender's mind does not need to be drawn to the conclusion. Consequently, the magnitude of the censure required in response is reduced. Failing to moderate the degree of censure would be to address the offender as if she lacked any appreciation of the seriousness of the offence. To address her in this way would demonstrate deficient communication on the part of the state. There is also a need to communicate the reason for the moderated level of censure to the community in general and the crime victim in particular; the communication is addressed to more than simply the offender appearing for sentencing.

This argument explains why commendable POC – even that which does not occur immediately after the offence – is relevant to the quantum of censure that the offender deserves at the time of sentencing. Even if it does not affect the seriousness of the offence (as we have argued it can on our alternative, narrow account), it is nonetheless relevant to the censuring function of punishment: censure should not address the offender whose POC demonstrates understanding of the wrongfulness of his conduct as if he is yet to understand.

It might be pointed out, however, that this argument depends on the commendable POC's revealing something about the offender's renunciation of his offence. We concede that, for POC to alter the censure that is appropriate, there needs to have been some reflection on and understanding of the wrongdoing; otherwise censure still has its full job to do. Are there, then, any additional justifications a desert theorist could give for allowing POC to mitigate, justifications that are not dependent on a renouncing of the offence? We think there are two.

---

[54] See JV Roberts, 'Re-Examining First Offender Discounts at Sentencing' in Roberts and von Hirsch (eds), *Previous Convictions at Sentencing*, above n 10.

B. Broader community values

The offender who demonstrates assistive POC whilst retaining ownership of her offence clearly does not – at that point – accept the particular moral demands that should lead her to renounce her wrongdoing. However, it could be argued that, in performing assistive POC, the offender to some extent demonstrates acceptance of wider community values related to law-abiding society and the criminal process. In so far as this is the case, the offender who performs assistive POC could be seen to have reduced the distance between herself and the community in terms of assent to *these* values. Whilst the offender may not be repentant – may not yet accept that she was at fault – she might nevertheless accept that her criminal conduct is of legitimate public interest, and assist for this reason. She may accept that the prosecuting authority has the right to call her to account for her actions to the community. Comparisons here might be drawn with Duff's discussion of what the law should 'say' to the 'principled dissident' who wants to engage with the community about the (non-mainstream) values to which she is committed. He suggests that, in some such cases, the punishment must embody a more 'complex message' and 'will probably be lighter'.[55] The ambit of relevance is important however; actions which merely demonstrate support for positive social values – exemplary conduct – are excluded from our account as they are unrelated to the offence or the prosecution of the offence.

C. Pre-empting punishment

The third line of justification for mitigating the sentence of the offender who demonstrates commendable POC is that it can, in some cases, pre-empt the punitive measures that the court would have imposed. Whatever the offender's motivation, reparative or reformative POC will sometimes lead to such an outcome. Courts have the power to order the offender to pay compensation to the crime victim. This is not formally part of the sentence, but a sentencing court will clearly calibrate the severity of the penalty in light of the size of the compensation order. If the offender has the means to pay compensation and a fine, a court may impose both, but in the event that a fine is also ordered, it may well be lower to ensure the offender is not disproportionately affected. Requiring the offender who has already paid compensation voluntarily to do so again would be tantamount to ordering compensation without considering any compensatory payments already made.

This justification is based on an extended notion of proportionality, and is analogous to reductions in sentence for time served on remand.[56] Similarly, voluntarily undertaking treatment for criminogenic needs might in some cases pre-empt part

---

[55] See Duff, *Punishment, Communication, and Community*, above n 37 at 122.

[56] Most jurisdictions reduce the time the offender must serve in prison by the amount of time he has already served on remand in detention: this reflects the fact that the offender has already 'settled' some of the penal invoice that is imposed at sentencing.

of the sentence. For the sake of proportionality, we argue in this case too that the pre-empted 'part' of the sentence should not be supplemented with something else just because the treatment was already underway prior to sentencing. It should be noticed that if pre-emption were the only justification operating to reduce the severity of an offender's sentence, it would not change what the offender is seen to deserve, but instead allows that some of what is deserved has already been fulfilled.[57]

V. Some External Objections to POC as a Sentencing Factor

Broadly speaking, we have argued that post-offence-related conduct affects deserved punishment when either the harm or culpability is mitigated, the offender is justifiably regarded as deserving of less state censure, or the offender has pre-empted some of the deserved punishment. Nontheless, the authors of *Proportionate Sentencing* may object to our invocation of examples such as voluntary surrender or culpable statements to the police, in part because their moral significance is obscured. There are, after all, 'so many possible reasons'[58] for such actions other than moral transformation. This observation is particularly telling when applied to the guilty plea – which may reflect a radical change of heart on the part of the offender or simply a desire for a sentence reduction without even a minor shift in moral development. A wealthy CEO donates a large sum of money to charity: is this motivated by pure philanthropy or the desire for a tax credit?

A similar argument is often levelled at remorse: is the offender genuinely remorseful or just mouthing a formula of words suggested by his legal advocate? We are not convinced that the existence of multiple explanations strips an act of all moral significance. Even if we cannot decide with certainty which explanation is correct, ignoring the gesture seems to be a case of losing the baby along with the bathwater. On our reading, we simply have to know that the act was related to the offence or the state's prosecution of the offence, and was open to all offenders to activate. Thereafter, the benefit of the doubt is extended to the offender: although there must be at least an 'air of reality' to the claim of mitigation, and extending the benefit of the doubt to the offender will not continue to apply across repeated convictions.

There are other dangers to opening the door to post-offence-related conduct. Some retributivists will regard this as undermining the retributive focus on the offence and the offender's culpability for that offence. From a practical perspective,

---

[57] A note about sentencing procedure: the offender's claim for POC-based sentence reductions should be subject to scrutiny according to a classic model of adversarial sentencing proceedings. Consistent with sentencing procedure, defence advocates should not be required to prove claims in mitigation to a civil or criminal standard, but there must be at least an 'air of reality' to such claims, and the prosecutor is best placed to raise questions about the claim.

[58] Von Hirsch and Ashworth, *Proportionate Sentencing*, above n 24 at 177.

defence advocates may well oppose a wider analysis in which the offender's actions both before and after the crime come under the scrutiny of the court; there will be fears that including POC will lead to additional punishment being imposed on defendants who fail to act in ways consistent with social expectations of a guilty party. Imposing liability on defendants for failing to acknowledge guilt or co-operate with enforcement authorities will raise clear threats to the presumption of innocence.

To accommodate these concerns, limits are needed on the extent to which severity may be modified. Equal opportunity creates one such restriction. As we have already noted, a wealthy offender who makes a large donation to the victim should not benefit from a sentence reduction; the means by which compensation is achieved are here adventitious. On the other hand, all defendants may avail themselves of the opportunity to co-operate by entering a guilty plea. Crime seriousness represents an internal limit on POC mitigation. As the offence becomes more serious and intrudes more deeply into the victim's living standards, there are two reasons to constrain POC. First, in practical terms the offender cannot hope to rectify fully the harm caused by a very serious personal injury offence. Secondly, the more egregious the wrong, the greater the distance that offenders must travel on the journey to moral transformation, and post-offence actions can only take them a short distance in this respect.

On what basis, then, should the quantum of POC-based reductions be determined? Intuitively it would seem appropriate to limit the impact of POC in a manner similar to the way in which other sentencing factors are limited. For example, for reparative acts the magnitude of the reduction will reflect the degree to which the harm is reduced. Ultimately, with respect to quantum of reduction, we would echo the response of von Hirsch and Ashworth to the question of how many prior convictions are allowed before first-offender mitigation is lost: 'This is a matter of judgment . . . but there are no magic numbers.'[59] In practice we would anticipate that the mitigation would be relatively modest, reflecting the limits on the extent to which the offender can reduce the harm or otherwise minimise the need for state censure.

VI. Conclusions

To summarise, we have argued the following:

(i)   censure-based sentencing should not set its face against taking account of the actions of the defendant after the crime has been committed – conduct we label 'POC';

---

[59] Von Hirsch and Ashworth, ibid, 155.

(ii) although in this chapter we only discuss commendable actions, POC may be negative or positive in valence,[60] with a corresponding aggravating or mitigating impact on the sentence imposed;

(iii) only certain actions are legitimately considered by a sentencing court – they must affect harm, culpability, or deserved censure – to avoid social accounting at sentencing;

(iv) the mitigating role of commendable POC is justified within a desert framework where it either (a) reduces the seriousness of the offence, thus straightforwardly reducing the quantum of punishment deserved, (b) demonstrates that the offender has already taken on board (at least some of) the message that censure intends to communicate, or (c) pre-empts a portion of the sanction that should not be twice imposed. This being the case, visiting the unattenuated censuring power of the state would include a degree of over-punishment – relative to the offender's individual circumstances; and

(v) for external reasons, POC should not alone carry great weight at sentencing – and for internal reasons, it is not likely to do so.

We pose one final question. Since a number of post-offence actions are already recognised in sentencing law and practice, does our proposal represent a mere 're-branding' of this source of mitigation? We think not. Our analysis would modify the practice of granting POC-based reductions in a number of ways. First, the emphasis in guidelines and sentencing statutes would shift towards recognising conduct *directly* related to the offence – and away from the social accounting model of 'good character and exemplary conduct' currently followed. This would mean that personal mitigation would become more proportional in nature, and less of a free-for-all in terms of anything plausible that advocates can employ to elicit sympathy from the court. It would focus attention on the harm created by the offence, and emphasise the importance of actions which mitigate harm. It might also stimulate greater efforts at reparation by offenders. Finally, it would also help to restore some agency to the offender for his own censure and moral development.

---

[60] As noted, limitations on space prevent an exegesis of what may be termed negative POC. The two forms of post-offence conduct will not assume symmetrically opposing functions. Eg, claims for mitigation on the basis of commendable POC will become increasingly implausible with repetition: an offender cannot make the claim repeatedly any more than the first offender can plausibly, repeatedly claim first offender mitigation. As with the progressive loss of mitigation, POC eventually loses plausibility. However, the state may demand a more stringent response if, after every charge the offender engages in conduct which exacerbates the harm of the crime (short of committing a fresh offence).

6

Does Punishment Honour the Offender?

KURT SEELMANN

I. Overview

Hegel's dictum, that through punishment the criminal is 'honoured as a rational being',[1] is legendary. Punishment, then, as an honour? It appears possible to arrive at an equivalent position also from a completely different philosophical direction. Andreas von Hirsch has made a slightly differently formulated, but substantially similar, point with reference to PF Strawson.[2] Through the censure connected to punishment, the perpetrator is 'addressed as a "moral agent", that is, as a person who is capable of acting morally.'[3] Both statements suggest that punishment, compared to alternatives such as culpability-independent measures of re-education or incapacitation, contains a positive positioning of some sort towards the offender. In what follows, I will first address the arguments made by our honorand and their grounding in the philosophy of Strawson (section II). By way of comparison with this view, I will then place alongside it the similar – but also in some respects different – position of the German idealist writers (section III), seeking out both differences (in section IV) and common roots (in section V). The chapter concludes with some reflections on the tenability of such a position and seeks to consider whether it is indeed the case that only a censuring attribution of criminal acts takes the other person seriously (section VI).

---

[1] GWF Hegel, *Elements of the Philosophy of Right*, ed AW Wood, transl HB Nisbet (Cambridge, Cambridge University Press, 1991; orig 1820) § 100 (Anmerkung), 126. [Translator's note: Where the footnote to a translated quotation cites a published translation of the original work as a source, the translation is taken from that publication. Where the footnote to a translated quotation gives the original German source, the translation of the quotation is the translator's own.]

[2] PF Strawson, 'Freedom and Resentment' in his *Freedom and Resentment and other Essays* (London, Routledge, 2008) 1.

[3] A von Hirsch, 'Warum soll die Strafsanktion existieren? Tadel und Prävention als Elemente einer Rechtfertigung' in A von Hirsch, U Neumann and K Seelmann (eds), *Strafe – Warum? Gegenwärtige Strafbegründungen im Lichte von Hegels Straftheorie* (Baden-Baden, Nomos, 2011) 43, 51. See further A von Hirsch, 'Begründung und Bestimmung tatproportionaler Strafen' in W Frisch, A von Hirsch and H-J Albrecht (eds), *Tatproportionalität. Normative und empirische Aspekte einer tatproportionalen Strafzumessung* (Heidelberg, CF Müller, 2003) 47, 52ff.

II. Reprobation and Treatment as a 'Moral Agent', ie as a Participant in Moral Discourse

For our honorand, the first and (given our theme) central feature of punishment is that it is characterised by the expression of censure vis-à-vis the perpetrator. That such censure must take place, and that it may not be foregone, follows, for von Hirsch, from the point, mentioned above, that it is only in this way that the offender is treated as a 'moral agent', that is to say, as a human being who acts responsibly in a moral universe. Censure, according to von Hirsch, constitutes 'a moral communication with the perpetrator'.[4] Neutral sanctions that convey no disapproval 'would . . . not sufficiently recognise the status of the perpetrator as a *person*,' but rather would treat offenders 'much as animals might be treated in a circus, as creatures that have to be intimidated or conditioned into compliance.'[5] By contrast, censure categorises the perpetrator as 'a person capable of moral deliberation'.[6]

The object of the recognition specifically afforded by the expression of censure is, then, the status as a person, understood here not in its legal meaning as bearer of legal rights and duties – ie, as a legal subject – but in its meaning as a participant in moral discourse and, in this sense, as a 'moral agent'. Designation as a 'moral agent' is, apparently, grounded in a *capacity*, namely the capacity to engage in 'moral deliberation'. This is a capacity which a 'moral patient', who is merely the object of morally motivated duties of others, does not necessarily possess. Thus there is here also a clear demarcation from animals, which, notwithstanding debates regarding their status as 'moral patients', uncontroversially lack the status of 'moral agents'. The difference between 'moral agents' and 'moral patients' exists, *not* in the realm of subjective *rights* but in the realm of *duties*. Moral agents inescapably have such duties, whereas moral patients might have moral duties but do not necessarily have them. The traditional characteristic of the 'moral agent' is consequently that he bears responsibility for his actions, whereas in the moral universe a 'moral patient' may (but need not) be limited to being an object of the responsibilities of others.

Von Hirsch explicitly seeks to distinguish his model – in which censure signifies the inclusion of the censured individual in the (active) moral community – from traditional 'absolute' theories of punishment. He claims that his model does not 'suffer from the obscurity of traditional retributive theories'[7] or presuppose any 'unclear metaphors of the restoration of moral equilibrium or of the legal and moral order which characterise traditional retributive positions in the literature.'[8] Since von Hirsch does not elaborate on this, I will return to this point, and hence the contrast he draws between the two positions, in section IV of this chapter.

---

[4] Von Hirsch, 'Warum soll die Strafsanktion existieren?', above n 3 at 50.
[5] Ibid, 51.
[6] Ibid.
[7] Ibid.
[8] Ibid, 52.

Let us now turn our attention to Strawson's philosophy as the basis for this view. While Strawson's work contains the groundwork for von Hirsch's censure-based arguments, Strawson himself does not present his position as a normative one. That is, Strawson draws the distinction von Hirsch utilises but does not argue in favour of censuring or, in his own development of the distinction, express any preference for the *participant's*, as opposed to the *observer's*, perspective. Strawson employs the distinction between observer and participant simply to describe different moral relations. He differentiates between, on the one hand, a position he calls a 'participant attitude', where allegations of misbehaviour can be responded to by putting forward justifications or excuses, and, on the other hand, an 'objective attitude'. The latter attitude we take towards a child or someone incapable of sound judgement. Such an objective attitude merely seeks to explain but does not enter into a moral interaction with the other person.[9] Someone who is merely an object of objectivising observation 'is not seen . . . as a morally responsible agent, as a term of moral relationships, as a member of the moral community.'[10] By contrast, someone whose actions are (from the first person standpoint) justified or excused is someone with whom one jointly participates in a moral communication. Strawson himself does not point to censure as characteristic of such a communication. However, his view necessarily includes the position that someone whom others could potentially consider justified or excused, in respect of whom we therefore look for grounds of justification or excuse, remains an object of a participatory communication rather than of a mere observation even if no justification or excuse is discovered in his specific case – in contrast to children or persons incapable of sound judgement.

III. Punishment as Honouring the Offender in German Idealist Philosophy

In German idealist philosophy we find, at first blush, a similar position which also ascribes a positive status to the individual censured through punishment. This is the notion of punishment as a means of recognising the offender as a reasonable being. The beginnings of this view can be observed in Kant's penal theory. Kant hints at the idea that the criminal, as a reasonable being, passes sentence upon himself. This is suggested by Kant's reference to 'the criminal's own judgment (which must necessarily be ascribed to his *reason*) that he has to forfeit his life.'[11] Here the perpetrator is acknowledged as possessing reason, in a sense that enables a legitimation of punishment through the idea that the offender, in willing his action, sets up

---

[9] Strawson, 'Freedom and Resentment', above n 2 esp at 8, 10.
[10] Ibid, 18.
[11] I Kant, *The Metaphysics of Morals* (1797) (Ak 6: 335) in *The Cambridge Edition of the Works of Immanuel Kant: Practical Philosophy*, ed AW Wood, transl M Gregor (Cambridge, Cambridge University Press, 1996) 476. [das 'eigene Urteil des Verbrechers (das man seiner Vernunft notwendig zutrauen muss) des Lebens verlustig werden zu müssen.']

the law by which he is then punished.[12] It is not said explicitly that it is precisely *through* his punishment that the perpetrator is honoured as a reasonable being. This claim is, however, implicit insofar as the criminal, who as a reasonable being passes judgment upon himself, in being punished undergoes only what he himself (possessing the will of a reasonable being) has willed.

Another source of the idea of recognition as a reasonable being – in this case already through the attribution of responsibility for an act to a subject – can be found in Kant's writings in a different context. This is when he addresses the constitution of the person: 'A *person* is a subject whose actions can be *imputed* to him. *Moral* personality is therefore nothing other than the freedom of a rational being under moral laws.'[13] An action is imputable to a will which, as a reasonable one, is cognisant of the moral law, and only to such a will. This also means that, when imputing an *act* to a person, we assume her to have a reasonable will capable of moral orientation, that is, to be a person in the moral sense.

This thought is subsequently taken up by other writers, including Hegel: implicit in the criminal's action 'as that of a rational being' is 'that it is universal in character'; that, by performing it, the criminal 'has set up a law which he has recognised for himself in his action, und under which he may therefore be subsumed as under *his* right.'[14] The notion that the offender's rational self is honoured through the imposition of punishment is thus explicit in Hegel: 'In so far as the punishment which this entails is seen as embodying *the criminal's own right*, the criminal is *honoured* as a rational being.'[15] Similarly, Hegel says in his lectures two years later that, 'this is the honour one shows to the criminal: that what is imposed on him is his right, the right that he himself has posited and recognised.'[16] In another lecture, again two years later, Hegel stresses: 'This is an important point, that the honour which is shown to human beings is to recognise what a person does as a free human being, that he is not subjected to another's law but to his own.'[17] This honour is denied to the offender 'if he is regarded simply as a harmful animal which must be rendered harmless'[18] – an interesting parallel to the Strawson-inspired argument made by

---

[12] See AS Oersted, *Über die Grundregeln der Strafgesetzgebung* (Kopenhagen, Goldenbarsche Buchhandlung, 1818) 20, arguing that the offender 'must be treated according to the very rule which he made into a law for himself.'

[13] Kant, *Metaphysics*, above n 11 at Ak 6: 223. ['Person ist dasjenige Subjekt, dessen Handlungen einer Zurechnung fähig sind. Die moralische Persönlichkeit ist also nichts anders, als die Freiheit eines vernünftigen Wesens unter moralischen Gesetzen.']

[14] Hegel, *Philosophy of Right*, above n 1 at § 100.

[15] Ibid. ['Dass die Strafe darin als *sein* eignes Recht enthaltend, angesehen wird, darin wird der Verbrecher als Vernünftiges *geehrt*.']

[16] GWF Hegel, *Vorlesungen über Rechtsphilosophie. Philosophie des Rechts. Nach der Vorlesungsnachschrift von HG Hotho 1822/23*, ed K-H Ilting, vol 3 (Stuttgart-Bad Cannstatt, Frommann-Holzboog, 1974) § 100, note 3. ['so ist es die Ehre, die man dem Verbrecher anthut. Am Verbrecher wird sein Recht ausgeübt (dann aber) das von ihm gesetzte, anerkannte Recht.']

[17] GWF Hegel, *Vorlesungen über Rechtsphilosophie. Philosophie des Rechts nach der Vorlesungsnachschrift K.G. v. Griesheims 1824/25*, ed K-H Ilting, vol 4 (Stuttgart-Bad Cannstatt, Frommann-Holzboog, 1974) § 100. ['Es ist diess eine wichtige Bestimmung, es ist die Ehre die dem Menschen widerfährt d.h. dass das anerkannt wird was der Mensch thut als freier, er wird nicht unter ein fremdes Gesetz gestellt, sondern unter sein eigenes.']

[18] Hegel, *Philosophy of Right*, above n 1 at § 100 (Anmerkung).

von Hirsch, where withholding censure is also placed on a par with the treatment meted out to animals.

The honouring of the offender as a reasonable creature thus consists in the fact that one universalises his action under the principle that the perpetrator, qua rational human being, must also have endorsed his punishment in his own will, and therefore cannot now complain when he is treated according to the norm he set up through his acts. It is only by punishing a human being that one really treats him as a responsible agent, as a moral person – in contradistinction to an animal.

IV. What are the Differences between Strawson and the German Idealists with respect to the Function of Penal Censure?

Granted these parallels, let us now ask how Strawson's position, which is taken up by von Hirsch, differs from that of the German idealists. Our honorand himself has made some suggestions in this regard, which I have briefly canvassed above. He considers the classic retributive theories to be 'obscure' and 'unclear', and to be based on (problematic) metaphors of restoration of moral or legal systems.[19] This criticism is quite understandable if one recalls Kant's theory of punishment, which draws on the notion of the 'blood guilt' of the people.[20] But Hegel's case is different. Whether one should subscribe to Hegel's argument is certainly debatable in relation to the legitimation of punishment quoted in section III, that the criminal must be subsumed under a 'law' which he himself has posited.[21] But even if one is sceptical about this, it is hardly far-fetched to maintain, as Hegel does, that punishment must be justified to the perpetrator and that it therefore matters what commitments are implied by his criminal act. And if German idealist thought is not always characterised by obscurity and lack of clarity, it becomes important to ask how a Strawsonian theory of punishment differs from a Hegelian theory of punishment regarding this first aspect of 'censure' as an ultimately positive orientation of the penalising agent towards the offender.[22] After all, there are at first blush significant commonalities: punishment is seen as something which treats the perpetrator in some sense with a high degree of respect and which puts him in a better position than a sanction devoid of any censuring quality – and both Strawson and the idealists think that the advantageous position of the criminal compared to an animal

---

[19] Von Hirsch, 'Warum soll die Strafsanktion existieren?', above n 3 at 51.

[20] Kant, *Metaphysics*, above n 11 at Ak 6: 333. Kant argues here for the death penalty 'so that ... blood guilt does not cling to the people for not having insisted upon this punishment.' ['die Blutschuld nicht auf dem Volke laste, das auf diese Bestrafung nicht gedrungen hat.']

[21] For criticism of Hegel in this respect see K Seelmann, 'Hegels Straftheorien' in von Hirsch et al (eds), *Strafe – Warum?*, above n 3 at 79f.

[22] I discuss the differences between von Hirsch's and Hegel's theories regarding the element of hard treatment in Seelmann, ibid, 82ff.

that is being conditioned consists precisely in the former's 'privileged treatment' through punishment. For both positions, censuring punishment apparently means that someone is treated by the criminal law 'as a human being', as a 'moral creature' or a 'moral agent'.

Let us take another look at Strawson's view, then, and let us attempt to apply it specifically to the criminal law. Klaus Günther describes the core of Strawson's argument as follows: 'We react from the internal perspective of a participant whenever we hold the other person responsible for his conduct and blame him for an act.'[23] By contrast, we treat the other person as a mere object of observation[24]

> when we have reason to believe, either that the act by which he injured us was not one for which he is responsible, or that his mental condition is such that one generally cannot attribute his actions to him, such that it would be senseless to hold him responsible for his actions.

Günther takes this as his starting point for contrasting a discourse-ethical theory of punishment which builds on Strawson with the punishment theories of German idealist philosophers, as follows:[25]

> A discourse-ethical justification of the criminal law takes from the idealist doctrine of 'retributive pay-back' (*Wiedervergeltung*) only this point: that a morally grounded criminal law may not abstract from the participant's perspective. Idealist philosophers from Kant and Hegel to Schelling . . . have obscured this insight by combining it with an individualist conception of subjectivity and a substantialist notion of the public sphere.

What does this mean? With an 'individualist conception of subjectivity' Günther apparently has in mind that the German idealists ascribe reason to an offender *qua individual* (ie, irrespective of his membership in a moral community, and simply in virtue of his being a rational human being); whereas in Strawson's arguments the offender remains embedded in a 'moral community'.[26] The accusation of 'substantialism' with regard to the public sphere appears to be rooted in the thought that Kant and Hegel, in their depiction of the offender, employ a conception of reason that pre-exists the moral communication of the participants, rather than one that emerges from their moral interaction as the intersubjective product of discourse.

These are genuine differences. But two points must be noted. First, as was observed earlier, for Strawson, too, membership in a moral community depends upon an individual's capacity for morally responsible agency, the capacity for moral deliberation.[27] Hence his view also has some individualistic features which parallel

---

[23] K Günther, 'Möglichkeiten einer diskursethischen Begründung des Strafrechts' in H Jung, H Müller-Dietz and U Neumann (eds), *Recht und Moral. Beiträge zu einer Standortbestimmung* (Baden-Baden, Nomos, 1991) 205, 212.

[24] Ibid. Similarly, see K Günther, 'Die symbolisch-expressive Bedeutung der Strafe. Eine neue Straftheorie jenseits von Vergeltung und Prävention?' in C Prittwitz et al (eds), *Festschrift für Klaus Lüderssen: zum 70. Geburtstag am 2. Mai 2002* (Baden-Baden, Nomos, 2002) 205, esp 215ff.

[25] Günther, 'Möglichkeiten', above n 23 at 211. ['Substantialist' is a term used (often with a pejorative connotation) for views that ascribe a material, thing-like nature to some entity.]

[26] Ibid, 214. Compare also the discussion by Günther in his contribution to this volume, section IV.

[27] This point is also made by von Hirsch, 'Warum soll die Strafsanktion existieren?', above n 3 at 51.

the reference to individual reason in idealist thought. Secondly, at least for Hegel, the notion of personhood linked to reason depends on a process of mutual recognition and thus also depends on an intersubjective product in Strawson's sense. It is nevertheless true that the primary entry point of their doctrines of imputation differs: for Strawson, it is the (moral) community, and for the idealists, individual reason – but the difference only pertains to what is primary.

V. Imputation and the Person prior to Idealism: Attribution of Responsibility as a way of Taking Identity Seriously

The proximity to each other of the positions taken by Strawson and by the German idealists is, as we shall soon discover, not really that surprising. It appears that there are common roots for the idea that the censured individual is honoured by the imposition of penal censure. Let us now look for them.

The imputation of responsibility – more specifically, the imputation of responsibility for one's agency – was first explicitly related to a certain relationship to oneself in the early Enlightenment.[28] Only someone who has a certain mental relationship to his self, someone capable of scrutinising himself in reflective thought, can be a responsible agent – and it is only to a being with these qualities that one can impute actions and omissions as their own. In classical modern philosophy, this capacity to develop a mental connection to oneself and thus to reflect critically on and direct one's conduct determines personhood; which is, to that extent, a mark of honour. Conversely, someone is recognised as a person – has this honour bestowed upon him – as soon as an act is imputed to him.

This link between personhood and imputation developed with particular intensity in the century from John Locke to Immanuel Kant. For the early Enlightenment writers, certain relations to the self were already seen as prerequisites for the imputation to an agent of moral and juridical responsibility for his actions (with the term 'imputation' coming into common use in the seventeenth century to denote the attribution of responsibility).

It was John Locke who developed a conception of self-cognition in his famous chapter 27 of *An Essay Concerning Human Understanding*, which appeared in 1694.[29] In this essay Locke connects – in a way that has received much attention ever since – the attribution of actions with the concept of a person and with the question of what makes a human being identical to himself, that is, why we can say about

---

[28] See further K Seelmann, 'Personalität und Zurechnung von der Aufklärung bis zur Philosophie des Idealismus' in M Heer et al (eds), *Toujours agité – jamais abattu: Festschrift für Hans Wiprächtiger* (Basel, Helbing & Lichtenhahn, 2012) 575.

[29] John Locke's *An Essay Concerning Human Understanding* was first published in 1689. Chapter 27, which is discussed here, was however first included in the second edition which appeared in 1694.

someone that he was the same being earlier as he is now. Locke uses the term 'person' to denote that which remains identical about a human being across time. What is remarkable about this, and central to our discussion, is that he does so under the aspect of a 'Forensick Term' (in Locke's spelling), that is, a term of law. 'Person' is, for Locke, a relation to oneself that is tied to the imputation of responsibility for one's own actions:[30]

> Where-ever a Man finds, what he calls *himself*, there I think another may say is the same *Person*. It is a Forensick Term appropriating Actions and their Merit; and so belongs only to intelligent Agents capable of a Law, and Happiness and Misery.

These intelligent agents concerned with their own right, happiness and misery, are the creatures to whom something can be imputed. It is their presence in the individual consciousness of the person concerned that determines for Locke which actions are attributable to a 'person' in the sense of his 'Forensick Term'. Indeed, since we are concerned with past events, one might also speak of the individual recollections of that person.[31] The individual thus performs the act of imputation already inwardly, within himself. Not only the imputation of the act, but also the consequences of this imputation in the shape of punishment and reward, are traced back to personal identity – although what matters in this regard is less consciousness as such and more the emotional reactions of the affected self: 'In this *personal Identity* is founded all the Right and Justice of Reward and Punishment; Happiness and Misery, being that, for which every one is concerned for *himself*.'[32] Our consciousness must operate in a context of concern for ourselves, of pleasure and displeasure – creatures that 'have no concern for their pleasure and displeasure, and hence know neither fear nor hope, are unable to develop a personal identity.'[33] And this, of course, also means that the very imputation of an action to a human being as responsible for the action signals recognition of the personal identity of this human being, encompassing both his consciousness and emotions. One can hardly deny that Locke's description of the relations of the self persistently links the notions of 'consciousness', 'concern' and 'accountability'.

A censuring attribution of responsibility is therefore already, for Locke, constitutive of the person, and German idealist philosophy can pick up this idea just as easily as Strawson and his tradition. The small successive changes are nevertheless interesting. Imputation of responsibility signifies, for Locke, the identity and con-

---

[30] J Locke, *An Essay Concerning Human Understanding* (1689/1694), ed PH Nidditch (Oxford, Clarendon Press, 1975) ch 27, § 26.

[31] Ibid; see also ibid, ch 27, § 9: 'And as far as this consciousness can be extended backwards to any past Action or Thought, so far reaches the Identity of that *Person*; it is the same *self* now it was then; and 'tis by the same *self* with this present one that now reflects on it, that that Action was done.'

[32] Ibid, ch 27, § 18.

[33] R Brandt, 'John Lockes Konzept der persönlichen Identität' in L Kreimendahl (ed), *John Locke. Aspekte seiner theoretischen und praktischen Philosophie* (Hamburg, Felix Meiner, 2006) 37, 42. See also MS Lotter, 'Rechtsprechung im Jenseits' (2006) 92 *Archiv für Rechts- und Sozialphilosophie* 511, pointing out that 'it is hard to see how a mere subject of experiences could arrive at an awareness of a finite self without assuming its difference to other persons.'

tinuity of the person; for Hegel, the rationality of the person; and, for Strawson, the inclusion of the person in a moral community.

VI. Criticising this Tradition with Assistance from Hegel? (The Case of Forgiveness)

In conclusion, however, we must ask whether it is really true – as the German idealists and Andreas von Hirsch assert – that it is (only) through penal censure, through an individual responsibility-imputing judgment of blame, that the offender is taken seriously as a rational being and as a member of the moral community?

In his legal philosophy, Hegel addresses the question – and this might be another difference between von Hirsch and the German idealists – whether refraining from punishment could not also be a requirement of justice. Here he takes up mercy as located at the meta-level of the doctrine of imputation, and he does so with respect to the principle of justice. This orientation is important. If Hegel were to argue here instead from a perspective of expediency for third parties, or for society as a whole, the directly affected person would not necessarily be taken seriously. The only forms of renunciation of punishment that are of interest to our discussion are those which do take the offender seriously – only these are capable of refuting the claim that only a censuring response takes the perpetrator seriously.

In the chapter of his *Elements of the Philosophy of Right* concerning 'civil society', Hegel links imputation to the efficacy of norms, arguing that a society with a stable, effective normative order can react to norm-violations with greater leniency than a society which is still inwardly unstable.[34] When Hegel returns to the theme in his subsequent chapter on the 'state', however, he links his discussion initially to mercy as a response to subjective conflict and then eventually to the achievement of a justice that surpasses mere Right.[35] Hegel is in this context concerned particularly with the sovereign's right of pardon, in that he attributes to the sovereign the function of 'undo[ing]' what has been done and to nullify crime by forgiving and forgetting.'[36] But why should the crime be 'forgiven and forgotten'?[37]

---

[34] See Hegel, *Philosophy of Right*, above n 1 at § 218 (Anmerkung; Addition).

[35] [Translator's note: 'Right' is capitalised here to indicate that it is used in the same sense in which Hegel employs the term in his *Philosophy of Right*: ie, as denoting the ideal set of laws and institutions that actualises human freedom.] (Even this sphere of Right can be surpassed by a higher sphere – that higher sphere being constituted by 'the majesty of the spirit'. Cf Hegel, *Philosophy of Right*, above n 1 at § 282 (Anmerkung): 'The right of pardon is one of the highest acknowledgements of the majesty of the spirit. Furthermore, this right is one of those instances in which a determination from a higher sphere is applied to, or reflected in, a lower one.')

[36] Ibid, § 282.

[37] For elaboration, see K Seelmann, 'Ethische Räume jenseits rechtlicher Institutionen? Gnade, Versöhnung und Verzeihung bei Hegel' in K Seelmann and B Zabel (eds), *Autonomie und Normativität. Zu Hegels Rechtsphilosophie* (Tübingen, Mohr Siebeck, 2014).

This thought is not developed further in the *Philosophy of Right* and can only be understood with reference to Hegel's other work, particularly his writings on theology and the philosophy of religion. We must go back, first, to Hegel's *Early Theological Writings*, in which he opposes the notion of penal justice to the forgiving love of Christ.[38] Similarly, in his *Lectures on the Philosophy of Religion*, he says that 'What has been done can be undone in spirit by spirit itself; the action is still preserved in memory, but spirit casts it off. Imputation hence does not reach into this sphere.'[39]

It is, inter alia, the idea of comparative observation that Hegel is concerned with here. No human being, according to Hegel's starting point, has any right against others to put himself in the place of virtue, to raise himself arrogantly above the antagonisms of life – not even when another's action clearly demands criticism.[40] This means that forgiveness is a waiver of imputation *to a person* and does not relate to the event as such – what has been done in the past can still be criticised, but blame is no longer imputed.[41] But why must this forgiveness take place? Hegel believes that the subjective opinion of any person always constitutes only a particular version of the (morally) good life. To insist, as a human being, on certain rights and justice, and to demand recognition of these rights and this justice from others, betrays a certain one-sidedness; since no human being can be absolutely sure that he is not mistaken when he declares his individual perspective as the general norm – which would be to bring about what Hegel considers per se evil: to declare the particular as the universal truth.[42]

This kind of forgiveness, which takes place in awareness of one's own fallibility, neither denies the perpetrator's responsibility (and, connected to this, his identity as a moral person), nor his rationality, nor his membership in a moral community. Someone who forgives another in consciousness of his own moral fallibility also does not take up the viewpoint of a mere observer, but retains the position of a participant in moral discourse, likewise leaving his opponent in the moral community of responsible agents.

The line between observer status and participant status with respect to shared membership of a moral community therefore does not simply track the difference between an objective explanation devoid of censure and a censuring reaction. Rather, alongside censure there is at least one type of forgiveness that is fully compatible with a joint retention of membership in the moral community. This is the

---

[38] See GWF Hegel, '*Der Geist des Christentums und sein Schicksal*' in E Moldenhauer and KM Michel (eds), *Werkausgabe*, vol 1 (Frankfurt, Suhrkamp, 1971) 274, 317ff, 341ff.

[39] GWF Hegel, *Vorlesung über die Philosophie der Religion*, vol 2 in H Glockner (ed), *Jubiläumsausgabe*, vol 16 (Stuttgart-Bad Cannstadt, Frommann-Holzboog, 1965) 305 ['Der Geist kann das Geschehene ungeschehen machen; die Handlung bleibt wohl in der Erinnerung, aber der Geist streift sie ab. Die Imputation reicht also nicht an diese Sphäre hinan.'] Cf also Hegel *Philosophy of Right*, above n 1 at § 282 Addition (H).

[40] M Kodalle, 'Verzeihung – Hegels Denkanstoss. Wider die Verdrängung eines zentralen philosophischen Themas' in A Arndt, K Bal and H Ottmann (eds), *Phänomenologie des Geistes, Zweiter Teil* (Berlin, Akademie-Verlag, 2002) 88, 92f.

[41] Ibid, 90.

[42] Ibid, 94.

case when forgiveness is triggered by the thought that one is oneself fallible and should therefore exercise great restraint in blaming others. Indeed, it is even possible to say that the most intense form of interaction as a moral community consists in this, and that the practice of forgiveness is therefore a particularly impressive way of taking the other person seriously as a member of the moral community.[43]

To conclude: the theory of penal censure that Andreas von Hirsch develops certainly has many similarities with the philosophies of punishment in German idealist thought regarding the notion that the perpetrator must be 'taken seriously'. Moreover, both perspectives have common roots in the ideas of John Locke and Immanuel Kant. But as we have seen in this final section, the censuring imputation of responsibility to an agent is only one way of taking an offender seriously. It exists alongside a certain form of forgiveness which has the same effect.

---

[43] See further A Schmidt, *Strafe und Versöhnung. Eine moral- und rechtsphilosophische Analyse von Strafe und Täter-Opfer-Ausgleich als Formen unserer Praxis* (Berlin, Duncker & Humblot, 2012) esp 186ff.

7

Criminal Law, Crime and Punishment as Communication

KLAUS GÜNTHER*

I. Punishment:
From Welfare Instrumentalism to Moral Expressivism

When Andreas von Hirsch's conception of punishment as censure was published, quickly getting considerable attention, this was at the peak of a criminal law politics which considered punishment as an instrument for the realisation of political goals. The most important goal was, of course, prevention of crime. Preventive criminal law politics was part of the welfare state reform agenda of most of the wealthier countries in the western world during the Cold War period.[1] It conceived of law as a form of political instrumentalism, wherein punishment was an integral part. Embedded in a broader policy of societal reform, which included measures designed to address economic inequality and to improve the situation of the poor by redistribution of wealth and public support, one of its primary goals was the rehabilitation of the offender and the prevention of offending. Punishment could only be justified as a means to an end, ie, an end which was politically justified by the public good of increasing the welfare of society.[2]

The articulation of *punishment as censure* was intended and widely regarded as part of a general critique of political criminal law instrumentalism, in particular of simple-minded or purely symbolic measures of crime prevention. This critique is founded primarily on moral reasons and assumes a moral conception of criminal law. One of its central objections is that political instrumentalism disregards the status of the perpetrator as an (autonomous) moral person and treats him or her as a mere object of preventive intervention – as an object of rehabilitative treatment or police intervention, or as a tool for public security measures via punishment; and in

* I am very grateful to the editors for their valuable comments and editorial help. Thanks to Rebecca Schmidt for her help and encouragement. All remaining mistakes and ambiguities are mine.
[1] D Garland and RA Duff, 'Preface: A von Hirsch, Censure and Proportionality' in RA Duff and D Garland (eds), *A Reader on Punishment* (Oxford, Oxford University Press, 1994) 112.
[2] For an analysis of this long tradition of welfare and punishment, which began around 1900, see D Garland, *Punishment and Welfare* (Aldershot, Ashgate, 1985).

general as a means for the realisation of political ends in criminal law legislation. Although political criminal law instrumentalism had its merits, notably for abrogating old-fashioned and unjustifiable prohibitions in the realm of offences against public morality, it was at the same time very expansive. There seemed to be no limit to criminalising any behaviour that was regarded as somehow dangerous and socially dysfunctional; no reference to essential moral values, to a moral relationship between victim and offender, or to the offender as a moral agent. Why should, eg, *insider trading* on the financial market be declared a crime (as it was done in Germany 1994), when it serves only a collective good like the efficiency of the stock market, and when there is no real victim in a moral relationship to an offender? As a consequence, a *political* conception and justification of criminal law is either rejected or modified into a conception of political *morality*. It is rejected to the extent that it is equated with an instrumentalist view of the political in general.

Doing justice instead of pursuing political goals with punishment implies that crime is primarily considered as a moral interaction between moral and autonomous persons: the *offender* as a responsible subject, and the *victim* as a moral subject whose autonomy and integrity is denied by the offender. And it involves a *third party*, society: not as a collective agent whose public welfare should be served by punishment but, again, as moral agents who get a moral message by the punishment of the offender, 'providing them with reason for desistence.'[3] Furthermore, punishment has to be a *proportionate* reaction ('just deserts') which expresses moral condemnation to the degree of 'the blameworthiness of the conduct', instead of a reaction which is chosen for instrumentalist reasons as a means to realise the political goal of prevention.[4] Its expressive function is central, because it detaches punishment from any further political purpose which should be realised. As an expression, or manifestation, of moral condemnation of the offender as a responsible agent, at the same time addressed to the victim as a moral person who was wronged by the fault of the offender, and as an expression of moral indignation about and moral disapproval of the crime by third parties or society, punishment can stand on its own feet and does not need any further political justification.

II. The Communicative Turn

The shift from *political instrumentalism* to *moral expressivism* of punishment has of course to do with a general critique of welfare state political instrumentalism which was raised for many different reasons. Although welfare state politics was inaugurated for the benefit of society, for the realisation of social equality and justice, and directed by democratic legislation, there was a strong tendency to treat citizens

---

[3] A von Hirsch, *Censure and Sanctions* (Oxford, Oxford University Press, 1993) 10.
[4] Ibid, 15ff; A von Hirsch, *Doing Justice: The Choice of Punishments* (New York, Hill and Wang, 1976); T Hörnle, *Tatproportionale Strafzumessung* (Berlin, Duncker & Humblot, 1999).

more as objects of intervention than as subjects or participants. Consequently, experts played an important role on all levels from legislative measures to individual cases, and society in general was envisaged as an entity of regulation, steering, and control by the state and the political system. At the end of the Cold War period, the experience of self-empowerment of the civil society came more and more to be regarded as an important resource of social integration. Civil rights movements were one part of this experience of civil solidarity; the struggle of minorities of different kinds for recognition of their identity, and for equal concern and respect in a pluralistic society, was another.[5] As a consequence, citizens discovered the empowering dimension of their rights, actively participating in the self-organisation of society on different levels and in different areas. Demanding reasons and justifications as part of a fair procedure with equal participation became an end in itself, thus transforming the top-down-structure of welfare state politics. Participation could be demanded and organised by increasing communication, among the members of civil society as well as between the state and its citizens. Indeed, social integration can only be realised through communication, wherein the citizen is regarded and treated as a moral person, taking responsibility for himself; this could be achieved by treating him as a communicative actor.

With regard to punishment, the *communicative turn* of modern societies was naturally ambivalent. On the one hand, it lead to a re-discovery of the offender as a communicative agent, as a person who had *to respond to* and had to be treated as *responsible for* the crime he or she had committed. The crime has to be *censured*, because this reaction is appropriate among equal members of a moral community who treat each other as responsible persons. PF Strawson had demonstrated that a *reactive* attitude, expressing resentment or indignation to another person because of a violation of a moral norm, differs from the objectifying attitude which we take from the observer's point of view when the offender obviously lacks the capability of responsibility. On the other hand, the communicative turn also led to a re-discovery of the victim of crime as a moral person with his or her own needs and interests which should be recognised by the reaction to crime. If preventive justice ignored the moral personhood of the offender, it did the same with the victim, who was more or less neutralised and excluded from the public justification of preventive punishment. Recognising the offender as a communicative actor went hand in hand with recognition of the victim as a communicative actor in the penal justice system. According to David Garland, the public rehabilitation of the victim was one of the strongest motives for a critique of welfare state criminal law instrumentalism.[6]

Taking the communicative turn into account, treating offender and victim as moral persons implied treating them as communicative actors who are able to and have an obligation to respond, who have a right to ask for justifications, and an

[5] J Alexander, *The Civil Sphere* (Oxford, Oxford University Press, 2006) part III.
[6] D Garland, *The Culture of Control* (Oxford, Oxford University Press, 2001); also of the role played by criminology experts, whose expertise was rejected because of the different experience of the members of civil society.

obligation to give answers. Consequently, punishment had to change its identity. It turned from being a political measure, from being a means to an end, into a moral message, an expression of censure; which must be conveyed to the offender, to the victim, and to society.

As censure, punishment differs from other kinds of sanctions. It adds a further element to the visible element of hard treatment. As Joel Feinberg has pointed out, without this additional element, punishment would not differ from other kinds of sanctions or taxes.[7] This additional element is communicative. With censure, punishment begins to speak, to say something. It gets a meaning which has to be articulated and can be expressed by a judgment. It does so not by uttering words and sentences, but by the performance of something, by hard treatment. The two constitutive elements of punishment always appear together, and they are always experienced at once, but they can be separated conceptually: 'It is the communicative element of censure which links punishment with the public.'[8] Furthermore, the communicative element has a justification of its own, which also differs from the justification of the hard treatment element: 'The rationale of censure is the conveyance of a message, whereas other communicatively mediated reasons have to be put forward for hard treatment.'[9] As Antony Duff has pointed out, that message has to be conceived as a communicative sequence in which persons are *addressed* as rational agents.[10] But what does it mean for punishment and censure to become communicative?

III. Punishment as Communication

Most studies of punishment as communication start with the communicative meaning of punishment. As mentioned above, punishment addresses the offender as a responsible agent; likewise the victim and the other members of the community. Punishment conveys a message to them too. But it is always part of any standard explanation of punishment that it is also, and perhaps primarily, a response to *a crime*. As an 'answer', it not only addresses the offender, the victim and the community, but it does so because of the crime committed by the offender. This is true independently of any goal or message which is attributed to hard treatment. Even preventive theories of punishment do not deny the fact that a crime was committed as a necessary condition for preventive punishment.

---

[7] J Feinberg, 'The Expressive Function of Punishment', reprinted in Duff and Garland, *A Reader on Punishment*, above n 1 at 73, 80.

[8] T Hörnle and A von Hirsch, 'Positive Generalprävention und Tadel' (1995) 142 *Goltdammer's Archiv für Strafrecht* 261, 266.

[9] Ibid, 267; von Hirsch, *Censure and Sanctions*, above n 3 at 9–10.

[10] RA Duff, *Punishment, Communication, and Community* (Oxford, Oxford University Press, 2001) 79.

But how do communicative theories of punishment refer to the crime? Is it only the cause, the occasion, for conveying the message of censure to the offender and to other persons? It must be more. The concept of a censure which addresses the offender as a responsible agent, sensitive to reason and capable of deliberation, being convinced by normative reasons that her behaviour was wrong, is also committed to the view that what the offender did has a communicative meaning too. To treat the offender and the community as rational and communicative agents who are responsible for their actions, who can respond to censure, leads necessarily to the conclusion that the crime itself, insofar as it was committed by a rational and communicative agent, has a communicative meaning too.[11] Just as punishment addresses the offender and sends a message to her, to the community, and to the victim, the *crime* sends a message to the victim and to society too. Treating the offender as a rational agent and person recognises the crime as a communicative action to which the communicative act of censure (and/or punishment) is the *communicative answer.*

If the crime is communicative in itself, two kinds of reaction are possible. Of course, it would be possible to conceive of a communication about crime without any communicative relationship to the offender or her crime. Society could communicate about them like it communicates about other matters of the objective world. Crime and offender would be external to the communicative relationships among the citizens. They would communicate *about* the crime and the offender, but not *with* the offender as a responsible agent of her crime. There are indeed some cases in which a society does this, and crime is viewed with an objective or propositional attitude from an observer's point of view: for example, if a society or its authorised representative has to decide what to do with a dangerous offender who suffers from severe deficits and therefore has to be detained; or when the crime is considered as an effect of a cause which can be empirically studied and remedied, say as a problem of social regulation, of means–end interventions designed to neutralise the cause. But these examples of a communication about the crime and the offender have no internal relationship to punishment. They lead only to interventions according to observations and scientific hypotheses about cause–effect relations. If punishment is to have any communicative meaning, it must be conceived of as a part of a communicative relationship with the offender – that is, as a communicative response to an offender because of her crime.

IV. What does the Crime Say?

Therefore one should conceive of punishment-as-communication as part of a communicative sequence which starts with the crime itself. As a communicative

---

[11] For an interpretation of the 'crime as an icon', see I Puppe, 'Strafrecht als Kommunikation – Leistungen und Gefahren eines neuen Paradigmas in der Strafrechtsdogmatik' in E Samson et al (eds), *Festschrift für Gerald Grünwald zum siebzigsten Geburtstag* (Baden-Baden, Nomos, 1999) 469, 473ff.

action, punishment says something, because of a crime, to somebody. As an answer, there has to be something prior, to which it is a response. Crime and punishment stand in a communicative relationship. It is the meaning of the crime to which the meaning of punishment is related. One can think of crime and punishment as speech acts which refer to each other.

But what could be the meaning of the crime to which punishment is the answer? Obviously, it must be more than the meaning of the volitional action which is labelled a crime. One might draw an analogy with a simple version of a theory of meaning, according to which the meaning of a sentence is the intention of the speaker. Analogously, the meaning of a crime could be the purpose of the offender, for example the end which an actor wants to realise by moving his body in a certain way, the reason he would give when asked why he did it. But considered as an intentional action only, the movements of the body are neutral towards the question whether the action is a crime or not. If A intentionally kills B, A might pursue some end with the action (eg, getting money), but it is not inherent in that description whether A's action is a crime. As a crime, an action contains an additional meaning; or at least, an additional meaning is attributed to it. As a crime, it is a violation of a norm of criminal law, a violation of legally protected interests or goods, a harm to others which is legally prohibited. Usually, this is not the meaning which was attributed to the action by the offender himself, except in rare cases where the offender aims at the violation of the law *intentione recta*, like civil disobedience (with the additional aim of defending the law in general and protesting against what she considers to be a violation of the law by the political system), or like offenders who act as terrorists. If so, the problem is that such an additional meaning cannot simply be attributed to the offender.[12] The typical crime of theft or killing is not done with the intention of committing *a crime*; rather, that status is attributed to the offender's action by the victim and by society.

One can find conceptions of a crime as communicative action among retributivist theories, including perhaps Kant and Hegel. Although neither of them elaborated on a *communicative* theory of punishment in the strict sense, they conceptualised crime and punishment as a sequence which is structured by a meaning beyond the intention of the offender. For both, the crime is self-negating because of its meaning: 'If you offend him, you offend yourself; if you rob somebody of something, you rob yourself, if you beat him, you beat yourself; if you kill him you kill yourself.'[13] According to the law of retribution, 'What does it mean: "If you rob him of something, you rob yourself?" Whoever shall steal makes the property of all insecure; he robs himself (according to the law of retribution) of security of property.'[14] This sounds as if the law of retribution simply requires us to do to the offender the same as he did to the victim. But the story is more complicated than that. Kant's explanation gives the law of retribution a specific meaning. Retribution

---

[12] Puppe, ibid, 474.

[13] I Kant, 'Metaphysik der Sitten, Rechtslehre' in I Kant, *Schriften zur Ethik und Religionsphilosophie*, K Vorländer (ed) (Darmstadt, Wissenschaftliche Buchgesellschaft, 1975) A 198 (454) [transl by author].

[14] Ibid, 199 (454).

is not a simple *tit-for-tat*. It works by universalisation. If stealing makes property insecure, it means that, by his act of stealing, the offender denies the security of property; similarly, by one act of killing he makes life insecure. Making the individual victim's property insecure means, by universalisation, that the property *of all* is insecure. And because the quantifier 'all' includes the offender as well as the victim and everybody else, the offender's property becomes insecure too. 'Insecure' means that the rights to property and to life lack sufficient protection; as they do in the state of nature, where each individual is responsible for his own security. It characterises not a normative, but a *factual* state of affairs. An act of theft or killing does not deny the right to property or life, but denies its security, its factual protection against violation. Punishment then performs the truth of the descriptive statement that property is insecure with regard to the offender. If the offender denies protection of rights, he will not be protected against any intrusion into his own rights. But why and how can Kant interpret the law of retribution in this way? Because criminal law is public law – it is publicly executed, and those who fail to punish a crime could be considered as participants in the 'public violation of justice'[15] – and because the offender is a person. Punishment articulates the implicit public meaning of the offender's criminal act, which was itself communicative.

Hegel seems to be more precise on this point. For him, it is not that the crime is a normative statement which has to be falsified. Rather, the important argument is that punishment has to deny the crime because, otherwise, 'it would become valid.'[16] By contrast with Kant, it is not the probable factual effect that property would become *insecure* if the violation of the law of property by theft or robbery were unpunished; that nobody would trust in the validity of property law anymore and therefore try to care for his or her own security. For Hegel, insecurity of property is only a side-effect of something different which happens when an act of theft is committed. Whereas for Kant, an individual crime of theft denies the validity of property law and, as a *factual* consequence, makes property insecure for all, Hegel emphasises the *normative* point that by an individual crime of theft a *new norm is asserted*. It is the norm which would become valid if theft were not punished. According to this norm, violation of property by theft is permitted.[17] Of course, this new norm is essentially *defective*, but nevertheless, it is stated by the offender as a norm with a claim to validity.

But why and how can an individual offender, who is by no means an authorised legislator, make new law? Hegel does not say very much about this question. Of course one could presume that in the chapter on crime in his '*Philosophy of Right*' everybody is a legislator, because on this stage there is still no state or sovereign established; nobody who would be legitimately authorised to enact new law. It is like in the state of nature, where, according to Locke, everybody has a right to

[15] Ibid, 199 (455).
[16] GWF Hegel, *Grundlinien der Philosophie des Rechts*, E Moldenhauer and KM Michel (eds), 6th edn (Frankfurt, Suhrkamp, 2000), § 99.
[17] K Seelmann, *Anerkennungsverlust und Selbstsubsumtion. Hegels Straftheorien* (Freiburg and Munich, Alber, 1995) 88.

punish any violation of the natural law. But it seems that for Hegel it is not necessary that the offender could make new law, that he had the authority to enact a statute or to pronounce a rule according to which theft were permitted. It is already sufficient that the offender makes an assertion, performs a speech act, which claims to be recognised as valid – as any other assertion or imperative which claims to be true or morally right. As an assertion which raises a validity claim, it has to be taken seriously: it has to be regarded as a communicative act which is addressed to others with the claim to be based on reasons and the responsibility to commitments which are inferentially entailed in the statement. Hegel links the validity of the implicit statement inherent in the criminal act to its 'subjective imputation' to the will of the offender: 'that the crime is committed without any hesitation . . . that it shall be *valid*'; the offender commits it 'as *something that is valid*'.[18] Because the offender commits a crime as an autonomous person acting wilfully, the act can become a statement about normative validity. This is made clear in § 100 of *Philosophy of Right*, where Hegel says that because the actor acts as a reasoning person, his action is in itself reasoning: it is 'something general', something by which '*a law* is postulated, which he has recognised for himself.'[19]

The normative validity of this postulated law is, of course, a false one, because it contradicts itself or destroys itself. It can only be generalised as a reasonable normative statement, as a law which is valid for an indeterminate number of persons and cases, if a single exception is made for the offender. Theft shall be prohibited to everybody, except the offender; or, to put it the other way round, theft shall be permitted to the offender, but not to anybody else. Killing shall be permitted for the killer, but not for anybody else. As a normative statement with a single exception or privilege, the normative statement implicit in the crime it is also self-destructive for a second and more important reason. The defective norm denies the possibility of legality (justice) as such. As Günther Jakobs has pointed out, such a law would contradict Hegel's definition of legality ('Recht') in § 26: that being a person and respecting others as persons is the (sole) basis for anything as law.[20] Punishment, again, implements the self-destruction of the norm by hard treatment of the offender.

Presumably following Hegel in this respect Jakobs has made the relationship between crime and punishment explicit as a communicative sequence: 'Human behaviour is not only an occurrence with external effects, but insofar as a human being surveys or is able to survey the effects of his behaviour, his behaviour also *means* something, like a spoken sentence means something.'[21] Jakobs also makes clear that this communication is not asserted as such by the offender himself – that the meaning of his behaviour does not necessarily coincide with the meaning of an act as it is represented in the offender's mind, for example as his intention or con-

[18] Hegel, above n 16, § 96 (Addition).
[19] Hegel, above n 16, § 100.
[20] G Jakobs, *Staatliche Strafe: Bedeutung und Zweck* (Paderborn, Schöningh, 2004) 26 fn 135.
[21] G Jakobs, *Strafrecht Allgemeiner Teil: die Grundlagen und die Zurechnungslehre*, 2nd edn (Berlin, De Gruyter, 1993) 9.

sciousness of wrongfulness – but that it is attributed to him by society. As such, the meaning does not depend on the intention of the offender, but only presupposes that he is a responsible agent. What is imputed to him is that 'he considers his behaviour as an authoritative design of the world.' For example, a drunken driver 'expresses by his behaviour that in this specific situation other things are more important to him than dominantly taking seriously into account the lives of others.' This is the opposite of the normative statement of the legal norm prohibiting drunken driving, an objection against the legal norm articulated by behaviour. Criminal behaviour entails a message which cannot be ignored.[22] Punishment, in turn, is an objection against the violation of the norm whose validity is re-affirmed so that the citizens can continue to rely on that norm when planning their lives.

If one takes together Kant's, Hegel's and Jakobs' interpretation of the message which is conveyed by the crime, it turns out that the argument of self-destruction of the implicitly proposed norm, and the self-contradiction of the offender who wants to get the advantages of a law which she denies by her crime, works only because the legitimacy of a general normative order is somehow presupposed. The offender, as well as the victim and society as a whole, inhabit a normative order which is already accepted and intelligible for everyone. But if that's right, the message of the crime can be denied without any real communication. Either punishment takes place *within* the offender because of her self-contradiction – it simply executes the internal communication of the offender with herself about the contradiction of the two norms she wants to propose at once – or it takes place within the society which re-affirms the validity of its normative order and re-integrates its members into it by punishing the offender. Here, society communicates with itself, and the offender is only confronted with the law.[23] *The law doesn't speak.* Yet, if one takes crime and punishment as communication seriously, one has to include the law in the communicative sequence and look more closely at its communicative role within this sequence.

V. What does the Criminal Law Say?

As the explanation of the communicative meaning of punishment by Kant, Hegel and Jakobs has demonstrated, we have to start the communicative sequence not just with the crime, but earlier with the *criminal law* prohibiting a certain human conduct and defining it as a crime. But why and how, and to whom does the criminal law speak? And how is its message related to the message conveyed by punishment? According to Kant and Hegel, the law does not speak, because it is

---

[22] T Hörnle, *Straftheorien* (Tübingen, Mohr Siebeck, 2011) 30, interpreting Jakobs' theory.
[23] A similar objection against 'norm-oriented' communicative theories of punishment is made by Tatjana Hörnle, ibid, 30ff.

already and obviously present as the reasonable and general will. According to Jakobs, it does not speak because it is already there as the normative structure of a functionally differentiated society. By contrast, Antony Duff has made the important point that the communicative sequence begins with the criminal law:[24] 'In claiming authority over the citizens, it claims that there are good reasons, grounded in the community's values for them to eschew such wrongs . . . It speaks to the citizens as members of the normative community.'[25] Duff's emphasis on reasons makes a difference here to the authors just mentioned, because reasons are usually addressed to persons who are able to understand reasons and to deliberate with and about them. Of course, criminal law is an authoritative normative reason and therefore it is exclusionary with regard to other reasons the addressee may have in mind, in particular reasons favouring the prohibited action.[26] But as a legitimate authority, criminal law claims justification with regard to the values and principles of the normative community. The members of a normative community can claim that the legal reasons are justified by the values of the community, and they have a right to contest it when there is no justification at all or a defective one. This is why the criminal law can *speak*; why it can speak *to them*, and not only about them. It takes its addressees seriously as deliberative persons who respond to reasons and who guide their intentions and their behaviour according to reasons.[27] Of course this becomes manifest only in a democratic procedure of legislation where each citizen has a right to participate. The citizens are regarded – and understand themselves – as co-legislators who participate in public deliberation about the justification of their criminal law. Therefore, they have a right to claim that a valid criminal law is justified by reasons – as long as nobody puts forward a new reason against it in the public procedure of legislation.

Tatjana Hörnle has objected to 'norm-oriented expressive theories of punishment' like the one proposed by Jakobs, on the ground that they treat the legal norm and its validity as an end in itself; representing the state or some generalised interest, detached from the individual interests of the citizens and, in particular, from the victim.[28] According to this interpretation, punishment which communicates the validity of the norm has the function merely of stabilising mutual expectations of behaviour, and of enhancing the security of rights and goods *in general*. But this is not the crucial criticism. In a democracy, legal norms are the result of a legitimate process of deliberation and inclusion, where every citizen has the right and the chance to participate via the public sphere of civil society, via the right to freedom of expression and information, and via the right to vote for Members of Parliament

---

[24] Duff, *Punishment, Communication, and Community*, above n 10 at 80ff.

[25] Duff, ibid, 80.

[26] For the role and function of exclusionary reasons see J Raz, *The Authority of Law*, 2nd edn (Oxford, Oxford University Press, 2009) 3ff.

[27] K Günther, *Schuld und kommunikative Freiheit* (Frankfurt, Klostermann, 1995); K Günther, 'Welchen Personenbegriff braucht die Diskurstheorie des Rechts? Überlegungen zum internen Zusammenhang zwischen deliberativer Person, Staatsbürger und Rechtsperson' in H Brunkhorst and P Niesen (eds), *Das Recht der Republik* (Frankfurt, Suhrkamp, 1999) 83.

[28] Hörnle, *Straftheorien*, above n 22 at 30ff.

(in a representative democracy). The legal norm is then a manifestation of political autonomy and represents a republican self-understanding. It is not a generalised will viewed from nowhere, detached from the real interests of individual citizens, but the result of a public deliberation about interests.

When such a justified criminal law is violated, this means that the offender rejects the reasons for the law. But instead of putting her reason against the law forward to the democratic procedure of legislation, she expresses her dissent by committing a crime. Furthermore, the offender denies to the victim her status as a co-legislator – who has to be convinced by reasons in a deliberative procedure, not by doing harm to her. Punishment can then be considered as a manifest rejection of the law-negating reasons of the offender, thereby reinforcing the reasons which justify criminal law in a fair and inclusive democratic procedure of legislation. As such, punishment addresses the offender as a reasonable, responsible person, as well as the victim and the other citizens. On this view, the communicative sequence is extended to criminal law, crime and punishment. Insofar as it is based on justifying reasons, one could even speak of a circle: punishment communicates with the offender, the victim, and society about the justifying reasons of legislation and the unjustified reasons of the offender.

VI. Why Hard Treatment?

If the communicative circle of criminal law, crime and punishment is complete, the obvious question arises why the other element of punishment, hard treatment, is necessary. If the communicative meaning of punishment can be made completely explicit by the communicative circle, why is it necessary to add more, to put the offender in jail or to take her money? What could hard treatment do what cannot be done by the explicit performance of the communicative action? As Duff asks:[29]

> But censure can be expressed by a formal conviction, or by a purely symbolic punishment that burdens the offender only insofar as it takes its message of censure seriously. Why then should we express it through the kinds of hard treatment punishment that our existing penal system impose[s] – punishments that are burdensome or painful independently of their communicative content?

One can distinguish two different answers to this question. The first admits that the meaning of punishment can be made fully explicit and performed by communicative action, and that hard treatment is – at best – a different kind of reaction to the crime and the offender which is independent of the communicative meaning and pursues a different purpose, eg deterrence.[30] The second answer claims that the meaning of punishment cannot be made completely explicit without hard

---

[29] Duff, *Punishment, Communication, and Community*, above n 10 at 82; Puppe, above n 11 at 475.
[30] von Hirsch, *Censure and Sanctions*, above n 3 at 12ff.

treatment, that the performance of the communicative action is incomplete without some extra-linguistic behaviour.

This second, constitutive line of thinking is found in writers such as Jakobs, for whom the communication of the norm's validity through punishment is in need of a 'cognitive safeguard of the norm's validity'.[31] Similarly, Duff has suggested that the communication of censure has to be followed by a 'purposive communication' with the offender who takes a burden upon herself, by which she can make explicit that she understands the communicative message – like a procedure of mediation between victim and offender or different kinds of community services.[32]

Hörnle also claims that the communication of censure is in need of a 'symbolic substantiation' by hard treatment, because otherwise there would be no quantifying scale to capture differences which are proportionate to the degree of injustice.[33] But although the argument for scaling different degrees of unlawfulness and criminal responsibility is convincing, it is not obvious that hard treatment is a necessary medium of scaling; it remains an open question whether hard treatment is the only possible scale to express different degrees of unlawfulness and responsibility. One could imagine a scale, analogous to years of imprisonment or to different sums of money in order to translate the different degrees of unlawfulness and criminal responsibility: for example, 'A is convicted of theft in degree 3 (within a scale of 0.1 to 5).' If such a scale gets recognised and accepted within a community as the measure for expressing different degrees of crime seriousness, we would not need to add further actions like imprisonment or fine for the same purpose.

But the most important problem is that communication and hard treatment – at least as they are practised in most societies today, by imprisonment – are in a certain way mutually exclusive. It sounds awkward to emphasise the communicative meaning of punishment on the one hand and to do exactly the opposite by hard treatment on the other. Whereas communication is inclusive, respecting and treating the offender as a responsible person with a right to justification, hard treatment is always exclusionary. This is manifest in imprisonment. Imprisonment is by definition non-communicative social exclusion of the prisoner, placing the offender in a situation where nobody does communicate with him, and where nobody is allowed to communicate with him – except for residual communications with prison guards and restrained and supervised communication during a limited time with some relatives or by letter; or, again limited, communication with a lawyer. If one takes the communicative message of punishment with regard to the offender seriously, it leads into a paradox. The communicative message is that he or she deserves to be deprived of communication opportunities. Thus punishment is a communicative action of non-communication. It treats the offender as a communicative actor just as long as it is necessary to pass along the communicative

---

[31] G Jakobs, *Rechtszwang und Personalität* (Paderborn, Schöningh, 2008) 33f.
[32] Duff, *Punishment, Communication, and Community*, above n 10 at 82ff.
[33] T Hörnle, *Straftheorien*, above n 22 at 42.

message; after that, the communication ends, together with recognition of the prisoner as a communicative actor.

VII. Communication as an Action

It is quite surprising that most authors who emphasise the communicative meaning of punishment do not consider communication as a kind of action in itself, as something which can stand on its own feet as an action. Typically, either hard treatment is considered as a medium for the transfer of punishment's propositional content – the moral message of censure – or, if hard treatment and the moral message are separated, the pure expression of the message is considered to be something deficient, something which lacks an important element. On the latter view, without hard treatment the pure expression would come down to a simple utterance of words which were not taken seriously, not by the victim, not by society, and primarily not by the offender. This is even true for expressive theories like von Hirsch's, according to which hard treatment can be justified by deterrence, as an addition to the separately justified censure. But is either view really true? What if expressing the moral message of censure were already a kind of action in itself, and as such, itself a *treatment* of the offender, and if it were already embedded in a communicative relationship among offender, victim and society which can be made explicit?

One possible interpretation of communication as an action is provided by speech act theory.[34] As John Searle has stated his central hypothesis, 'speaking a language is engaging in a rule-governed form of behaviour. To put it more briskly, talking is performing acts according to rules.'[35] This interpretation of communication as action does not deny that communicative action is often accompanied by extra-linguistic actions which get their meaning by an interpretive relationship with a speech act. Hörnle is right in stating that praise and recognition are often accompanied by a gift, like money, and that the same is true for blame and censure with regard to hard treatment. But this relationship is contingent and conventional, and one can easily imagine other situations (or other cultures) where praising someone is not accompanied by a gift, where the act of praising someone is in itself enough. It depends, among other things, on the ways and manners of evaluating, viewing, experiencing and receiving an act of praise. It is also true that in law in particular, a speech act with legal significance is often related to a symbolic action. But one can also observe that in many cases a symbolic substantiation becomes more and more unnecessary. For example in contract law, Roman law and Common Law always required a symbolic action for a promise to constitute a contractual obligation. But since Grotius and Savigny, the promise itself was more and more recognised as the

---

[34] J Austin, *How to do Things with Words* (Oxford, Clarendon Press, 1962); J Searle, *Speech Acts: An Essay in the Philosophy of Language* (Cambridge, Cambridge University Press, 1969).
[35] Austin, ibid, 5; Searle, ibid, 22.

source of obligation, because of its performative character. So why not think of the history of punishment as a development where hard treatment becomes more and more unnecessary for the conveyance of the message?

In order to elaborate more on the distinctive communicative aspect of punishment, it may be helpful to take some insights from speech act theories.[36] According to these theories, communicative action can be analysed on three levels. The formal (*locutionary*) act is generally the act of uttering the sentence itself, and communicates the surface propositional content of the utterance. This act should be distinguished from the *illocutionary act*, which refers to the *illocutionary force* of the locutionary act – its real, intended meaning – and from the act's *perlocutionary effect*, which refers to the actual effect of the act (whether or not intended).[37] What is most important for understanding the nature of the speech act as an action is the illocutionary act and its illocutionary force, since this identifies what a speaker intentionally *does* by uttering a sentence with propositional content: it is the purpose inherent in the act and which can be realised by performing the speech act. This is most obvious with explicit illocutionary acts that use performative verbs, like 'I promise [...]'. The illocutionary act fulfils those rules which are constitutive of the promise, so that the speaker intends her utterance to be a promise and the hearer understands it as a promise. As an action it changes the world – specifically, the social (and moral) world of speaker and hearer. By performing a promise the speaker commits herself in her social relationship to the hearer to do what she has promised. This constitutive effect of the illocutionary act of promising is independent of all those additional effects which can also be caused in the social world by the commitment. If the hearer – or third parties – understand the speaker's utterance correctly as a promise, this might generate certain additional effects like emotions of delight, trust, or a motive for other actions of the hearer. These effects – perlocutionary effects – may well be intended by the speaker too, but they are incidental and not inherent in the illocutionary force. A speaker can have various purposes for making a promise, but these (ulterior) purposes are not relevant to the question whether the locutionary act itself *is* (or is not) a promise qua illocutionary act.

In cases such as promising, the illocutionary force of speech acts may depend on the existence of extra-linguistic rules. The utterance of the word 'yes!' as an answer to the celebrant's question whether one will marry one's partner may count toward a valid marriage only when a system of rules about the legal institution of marriage already exists, and when it is inter-subjectively recognised by the collective intention of the members of the group. A marriage is an *institutional* social fact which is constituted by rules; as an institution it consists of a 'system of constitutive rules'.[38]

---

[36] R Hamel, *Strafen als Sprechakt. Die Bedeutung der Strafe für das Opfer* (Berlin, Duncker & Humblot, 2009).
[37] For example, the locutionary act of of saying, 'there's a man behind you with a gun' might have the illocutionary force of a warning not to move, and the perlocutionary effect of making the addressee turn around.
[38] Searle, *Speech Acts*, above n 34 at 51.

Institutional facts can be generated by *declarative speech acts*; with them a speaker can declare that the fact *x counts as y*, within a certain context (which may be constituted by other institutional facts). *Y* is a new status and function of *x*, which consists in a collective attribution and recognition. The social relationship between A and B may count as a *marriage* when the required performative utterances are made by the celebrant and the partners in the celebrant's presence, according to a pre-existing system of (legal) rules. Following a previous suggestion made by Searle, Roman Hamel has suggested analysing the verdict in a criminal law trial as a declarative speech act and considering *this* to be the core communicative meaning of punishment. By its performance, the institutional reality is said by Hamel to be changed in two dimensions: issuing the verdict re-constitutes and re-affirms the validity of the norm which was violated by the offender, and it censures the individual criminal act, as legally adjudicated, from a general and public point of view.[39] In both dimensions, a new institutional reality is created.

But Hamel's picture is incomplete. By performing a speech act, an inter-subjective relationship is established by the illocutionary force between speaker and hearer. This relationship goes beyond the particular normative relationship which is created constitutively by performing a speech act according to specific institutional rules. As Habermas has demonstrated, the illocutionary force of a speech act is related to mutual understanding of speaker and hearer when the illocutionary act is performed sincerely, without any hidden reservations.[40] Certainly, in the case of a (successful) act of promising, that promise is understood and accepted as creating a specific bond between speaker and hearer with regard to the propositional content of the promise. But what is most important to Habermas is that the illocutionary force always generates a wider binding effect, of a different and more general character, among speaker and hearer *because of its purpose that the speech act shall be understood and accepted.*

This general binding effect differs from the specific one of a speech act which is related to institutional facts, like a promise; and it is an essential feature of all kinds of illocutionary speech acts that are performed sincerely. The general binding effect can be revealed on occasion by a rejection or critique of the illocutionary act by the hearer. If there is disagreement, the speaker is obliged to give reasons to support what he said and, on the other side, the hearer is obliged to give reasons for her dissent. In this way an acceptance or consensus can be established between speaker and hearer, emerging from a rational discourse between them. The discourse is itself a sequence of communicative interaction, and the consensus generates further binding effects for speaker and hearer because of its possible inferences and commitments.

One could therefore say that a speaker raises *a claim* by performing a speech act sincerely, a claim which is directed to its acceptance by reasons. The kinds of reasons which are given and demanded by the participants in a discourse depend, in

[39] Hamel, *Strafen als Sprechakt*, above n 36 at 128, 152–53.
[40] J Habermas, *Theorie des kommunikativen Handelns*, vol I (Frankfurt, Suhrkamp, 1981) 391, 395.

turn, on the nature of any ensuing disagreement. Habermas distinguishes *three* different issues of disagreement: the *truth* of the propositional content, as well as of the implicit and presupposed assertions regarding contextual facts of the speech act; the *correctness* of the explicit or contextual normative content of the speech act; and the *sincerity* and authenticity of the speaker's performance of the speech act. Thus, what the speaker claims with her performance of the illocutionary act is that its assertive component is true, that its normative component is correct, and that its subjective component is sincere. These *validity claims* are challenged and confirmed through reasoning, by the speaker, the hearer and – because they are reason-dependent and to that extent general – by any third party. By raising such validity claims with the illocutionary component of her speech act, the speaker is obliged to justify its truth, correctness, and sincerity, should her claim be challenged by the hearer or anybody else.

If one takes this extended interpretation of the illocutionary meaning into account, it becomes obvious that, whether or not it happens to contain performative elements of the kind Hamel envisages, communicative action is always embedded in an inter-subjective context which has a normative structure. The normative structure is made explicit in the case of contestation, when a validity claim is rejected and reasons are demanded by hearer and speaker. Reasons and justifications are always in the background when a speech act is performed sincerely. An important part of this normative structure is that speaker and hearer are obliged to treat each other as *persons* who have a *right* to disagree, to demand reasons; and an *obligation* to give reasons. This normative and social relationship is constituted by the illocutionary force of the speech act.

VIII. Again: Punishment as Communication

This interpretation allows for a new approach to the communicative meaning of punishment, one that does not depend so much on the classification of censure as a declarative act. The important point is that censure as a speech act raises a validity claim which refers to a valid normative order whose legitimacy can be justified by reasons in a rational discourse. It refers to the normative order, the system of legal norms, to the victim, and to the offender.

From this point of view, it can be seen that the crime as well as the response to it must be understood in a communicative fashion. In a democratic and republican setting, where legal norms are legitimised in a public and inclusive process of deliberation and contestation, citizens are primarily regarded and regard themselves as *communicative actors*. Such a setting institutionalises the normative structure of the inter-subjective relationship between speaker and hearer with regard to law and politics. Citizens are regarded, treated and understand themselves as rational beings who raise claims, who give and receive reasons, who interpret their actions as meaningful and self-authored, and who are able to take reasons into account when planning and performing an action. This is the reason why they can be considered as co-legislators, and it grounds the public meaning of crime. And this is the reason why Hegel could claim that, by committing a crime, the offender proposes a new norm. It rests on the concept of a responsible agent: 'Democratic law need[s] to rest on beliefs in the civil qualities of actors; it is centred, in fact, on motives, on cultural assumptions about agency, understanding, and responsibility.'[41]

Furthermore, it is not the act of punishing itself which somehow introduces a new meaning or a message, one that can be made independently explicit, translated and pronounced: the criminal procedure is already a communicative process, and its end, *the verdict*, is an essentially communicative act.[42] It fulfils the requirements of a communicatively integrated society: it is public and reasoned. Of course, the verdict is institutionally related to hard treatment – and hard treatment gets its meaning through an interpretation which refers to the verdict. But this relationship does not mean that both have to be necessarily considered and treated as a unity. They have to be treated separately.[43]

With regard to the *offender*, the communicative message is twofold. As has been suggested by von Hirsch and others who propose a communicative interpretation of punishment, one part of the meaning conveyed to the offender is that what he did is *wrong*. But the pure statement of wrongfulness is not enough. The norm is not presented to the offender as something that he has to take for granted. Because the verdict is, as a speech act, performed in an inter-subjective relationship with a normative structure based on reasons and justifications, the claim of the verdict that the crime is wrong can be justified by reasons. Furthermore, in a democratic society, one can interpret the violation of the norm itself as a normative statement, an expression of dissent against the valid norm.

But here is the crux. The offender's expression of dissent was not articulated through the public deliberative procedures of the public sphere of civil society, even though he had a right – in that forum – to propose an abrogation of the valid norm. As a statement of dissent, the offender's norm-violating act is legitimately rejected as wrong. He did not address the other citizen – the victim – as a communicative actor, as an equal participant in the public discourse, but denied his status. Consequently, the offender is not regarded as a co-legislator. He has to bear the burden of being forced into a legal procedure which treats him as a person, a responsible agent, but only with regard to his role as an addressee of the norm, not as its co-author.

---

[41] Alexander, *The Civil Sphere*, above n 5 at 178.

[42] S Schork, *Ausgesprochen schuldig – Dogmatische und metadogmatische Untersuchungen zum Schuldspruch* (Frankfurt, Peter Lang, 2005).

[43] I consider this to be the mistake of Hamel, *Strafen als Sprechakt*, above n 36, who always speaks of the verdict *and* punishment.

8

Can Deserts Be Just in an Unjust World?

MICHAEL TONRY

No one seems much to have worried about 'just deserts in an unjust world' as a normative problem in the philosophy of punishment, before the retributivist revival exemplified by the early writings of Herbert Morris,[1] Jeffrie Murphy,[2] John Kleinig,[3] and Andreas von Hirsch.[4] This was not because the association between crime and disadvantage went unrecognised. Commission of commonplace property and violent crimes has long, perhaps always, been understood to be probabilistically related to a congeries of socio-economic and other characteristics of individuals. Oliver Wendell Holmes, Jr, observed in *The Common Law* that if punishment[5]

> stood on the moral grounds which are proposed for it, the first thing to be considered would be those limitations in the capacity for choosing rightly which arise from abnormal instincts, want of education, lack of intelligence, and all other defects which are most marked in the criminal classes.

Desperate people like Jean Valjean experience stronger temptations to steal than do comfortable people. Deeply disadvantaged young people in socially disorganised areas are more tempted than are Harvard undergraduates by the attractions of gang membership and street-corner drug dealing. Some women sell sex unlawfully because that appears to be the least worst – or only – way available to them to earn enough money to survive.

Before the 1970s, such cases could be, and occasionally were, dealt with sympathetically by judges and juries, on an ad hoc basis, without flouting prevalent normative ideas about the criminal law or punishment. Juries and, less openly, judges could express compassion by refusing to convict. The jury's capacity to add a measure of human sympathy to the cold application of legal rules was long said by defenders to be its central virtue.[6] Roscoe Pound argued that[7]

---

[1] H Morris, 'Persons and Punishment' (1966) 52 *Monist* 475.
[2] J Murphy, 'Marxism and Retribution' (1973) 2 *Philosophy and Public Affairs* 217.
[3] J Kleinig, *Punishment and Desert* (New York, Springer, 1973).
[4] A von Hirsch, *Doing Justice: The Choice of Punishments* (New York, Hill & Wang, 1976).
[5] OW Holmes, Jr, *The Common Law* (Boston MA, Little, Brown & Co, 1881) 45.
[6] Eg OW Holmes, Jr, 'Law in Science and Science in Law' (1899) 12 *Harvard Law Review* 443; MR Kadish and SH Kadish, 'The Institutionalization of Conflict: Jury Acquittals' (1971) 27 *Journal of Social Issues* 199.
[7] R Pound, 'Law in Books and Law in Action' (1910) 44 *American Law Review* 18.

> [j]ury lawlessness is the great corrective of law in its actual administration. The will of the state at large imposed on a reluctant community, the will of a majority imposed on a vigorous and determined minority, find the same obstacle in the local jury that formerly confronted kings and ministers.

Frank Remington, director of the American Bar Foundation's Survey of the Administration of Criminal Justice in the 1950s, observed that legislative prescription of harsh sentences is often[8]

> likely to result in a reduction in charges at the prosecution stage, or if this is not done, by a refusal of the judge to convict at the adjudication stage. The issue . . . thus is not solely whether certain offenders should be dealt with severely, but also how the criminal justice system will accommodate [statutory directives].

Less conspicuously, judges could take account of sympathetic circumstances by factoring them into individualised consideration of the sentences they imposed.

Prevailing ways of thinking have changed. Both devices – nullification by jury or judge and informal mitigation at sentencing – became harder to justify when retributive ways of thinking became prevalent. Few people now approve or celebrate jury nullification; jury instructions do not acknowledge the inherent power to nullify or, lest it influence consideration of guilt, indicate what sentence might or must be imposed following conviction. Judicial nullification is usually characterised as a breach of the judge's duty to enforce the law. Except for a smattering of law review articles published in the 1970s and 1980s, a 2000 book edited by William C Heffernan and John Kleinig,[9] and a 2011 symposium published in the *Alabama Civil Rights and Civil Liberties Law Review*, few scholars have written about special problems of justice in criminal cases involving deeply disadvantaged offenders. Lawyers usually adopt formalistic positions opposing legal recognition of social adversity considerations. Philosophers, especially more recently, sometimes adopt more sympathetic positions.[10] Andreas von Hirsch, however, has consistently addressed the subject. He discussed sentencing of such defendants in chapter 17 of *Doing Justice*, and revisited the subject regularly in subsequent decades.[11] He has consistently opposed the argument that a defendant's deprived background can, as such, merit the reduction of an otherwise deserved sentence.

In this chapter I argue that juries and judges should have greater leeway to acquit defendants on the basis of deep disadvantage, and that judges should be encouraged to mitigate sentences for that reason when they believe it appropriate to do so. The

---

[8] F Remington, 'Introduction' in R Dawson (ed), *Sentencing* (Boston MA, Little Brown & Co, 1969) xvii.

[9] WC Heffernan and J Kleinig (eds), *From Social Justice to Criminal Justice: Poverty and the Administration of Criminal Law* (New York, Oxford University Press, 2000).

[10] Eg RA Duff, *Punishment, Communication, and Community* (New York, Oxford University Press, 2001) 179; S Green, 'Hard Times, Hard Time: Retributive Justice for Unjustly Disadvantaged Offenders' (2010) *University of Chicago Legal Forum* 43.

[11] von Hirsch, *Doing Justice*, above n 4; von Hirsch, *Past and Future Crimes: Deservedness and Dangerousness in Sentencing Criminals* (New Brunswick NJ, Rutgers University Press, 1985); von Hirsch, *Censure and Sanctions* (Oxford, Oxford University Press, 1993) 106; A von Hirsch and A Ashworth, *Proportionate Sentencing: Exploring the Principles* (Oxford, Oxford University Press, 2005).

arguments for a social adversity defence have not changed since they were vigorously debated by Judge David Bazelon and Stephen Morse in 1976. The arguments for mitigation at sentencing were always strong. However, indeterminate sentencing, and the broad judicial discretion to individualise sentences that it justified, had by 1976 become discredited in the United States. Consequently, the arguments in favour of mitigation were overshadowed. At a time when most sentencing reform advocates wanted to see the scope of sentencing discretion narrowed, proposals to broaden it found little traction.

It seems to me timely to revisit that debate. The main argument against allowing mitigation for an offender's deep disadvantage was that doing so would violate the proportionality norm: that persons convicted of comparable offences should receive comparable punishments. The same conviction should, in principle, yield the same sentence (or the same range of sentences, subject to adjustment for the particular circumstances accompanying commission of the offence). However, because of the ubiquity and diversity of American plea bargaining, that proposition always made unrealistic assumptions about the degree to which sentencing based on *the identity of the offence of which the offender is convicted* – usually referred to as the conviction offence – could be robustly proportionate. In the United States, the use of diverse plea bargaining methods often means that the conviction offence is only weakly related to the offence actually committed. Depending on the method used, defendants who could be proven to have committed an armed robbery might variously be convicted of armed robbery, simple robbery, theft, or a related attempt or conspiracy offence. This makes the pursuit of the goal of proportionate sentencing in relation to the conviction offence largely chimerical. As a result, it is difficult credibly to make the case that individualised justice to deeply disadvantaged defendants must be sacrificed in order to protect an abstract value of proportionality.

An important caveat is that the discussion here is focused on the recent history and distinctive characteristics of American sentencing. The arguments might be somewhat different, say, in England and Wales, where plea negotiation centres on the presence and timing of a guilty plea that triggers a discount on sentence; and not primarily on the availability of mandatory minimum penalties, charge dismissals, and negotiated sentences, all matters in the United States within the control of the prosecutor, not the judge.[12] The arguments might be very different again in many continental European systems where explicit plea negotiation is rare and where prosecutors cannot manipulate charges for tactical reasons; judges have discretion to convict offenders of offences more or less serious than those with which they were charged.[13] Scandinavian asymmetric proportionality doctrine, in which offence severity sets an upper but not a lower limit on sentence, exemplifies another major difference from the American context.[14]

---

[12] A Ashworth and M Redmayne, *The Criminal Process*, 4th edn (Oxford, Oxford University Press, 2010) ch 7.

[13] Eg in Sweden: P Asp, 'The Prosecutor in Swedish Law' in M Tonry (ed), *Prosecutors and Politics: A Comparative Perspective* (Chicago IL, University of Chicago Press, 2012).

[14] T Lappi-Seppälä, 'Sentencing and Punishment in Finland: The Decline of the Repressive Ideal' in M Tonry (ed), *Why Punish? How Much?* (New York, Oxford University Press, 2011).

This chapter consists of five sections. The first sketches the intellectual context in which foundations for thinking about special treatment of deeply disadvantaged defendants were laid in the 1970s. Things are different now. Individualisation is back in vogue. The second section discusses contemporary evidence on the causal effects of individual differences and contextual pressures on offending, anticipating the claim made most vigorously by Stephen Morse that all that is really at issue in cases raising social adversity concerns is culpable failure to resist temptation.[15] The third section briefly discusses the literature on proposals for a 'social adversity'[16] or 'rotten social background'[17] defence, and concludes that no significant harm would result from instructing juries that they may acquit if they believe that under the conditions of the defendant's life he or she should not be held criminally responsible for unlawful acts. The fourth section argues in favour of mitigation at sentencing for disadvantaged offenders. Finally, I conclude with a tip of the hat to Andreas von Hirsch for opening the subject up for consideration four decades ago.

I. Recognition of the 'Unjust World' Problem

Before retributivism began to gain currency in the 1970s, deeply disadvantaged defendants might have presented a trial court with no special problems. If juries or judges chose not to convict, the matter ended there. If there was a conviction, the judge was expected to individualise sentence. The American Law Institute's 1962 Model Penal Code is illustrative.[18] The Code contained a presumption in favour of probation in all cases, and for those sent to prison it created a presumption in favour of release at the first opportunity. In the world of punishment theory, Jeremy Bentham's 'frugality', Norval Morris's 'parsimony', and the Model Sentencing Act's 'least restrictive alternative' prescribed imposition of the least punitive or burdensome sanction that would serve the purposes of sentencing. Judges or parole boards who wanted to reduce penalties for sympathetic defendants could easily justify doing so. The problem arose when the shift to retributivism created a logic according to which offence severity should serve as an exclusive calibrating guide to the severity of sentences. In principle, or in the Eye of God, specification of the severity of an offence would take account of circumstances related to the particular offender's culpability. The difficulty is that in practice American sentencing policies are generally based on the much cruder determinant of the statutory offence of which the defendant is convicted.

---

[15] SJ Morse, 'Deprivation and Desert' in Heffernan and Kleinig (eds), *From Social Justice to Criminal Justice*, above n 9; Morse, 'Severe Environmental Deprivation (aka RSB): A Tragedy, Not a Defense' (2011) 2 *Alabama Civil Rights and Civil Liberties Law Review* 147.

[16] D Bazelon, 'The Morality of the Criminal Law' (1976) 49 *Southern California Law Review* 385.

[17] R Delgado, '"Rotten Social Background": Should the Criminal Law Recognize a Defense of Severe Environmental Deprivation?' (1985) 3 *Law and Inequality* 9.

[18] American Law Institute, *Model Penal Code – Proposed Official Draft* (Philadelphia PA, American Law Institute, 1962).

It is easy to forget, or not to recognise at all, that retributive ideas about punishment only recently became widely influential. To many people in our time they appear to be self-evident.[19] Yet the 1970s' reorientation away from consequentialism was a sea change. As law professor Albert Alschuler put it, bewilderedly, 'That I and many other academics adhered in large part to [a] reformative viewpoint only a decade or so ago seems almost incredible to most of us today.'[20] Prior to that, consequentialist theories of punishment had been ascendant among the theory classes in English-speaking countries for more than a century. In a landmark 1937 article, for example, Jerome Michael and Herbert Wechsler explained that there are 'two competing normative hypotheses which merit serious attention' concerning punishment. In our time, one would expect them to be retributivism and consequentialism. In their time, they were '(1) the so-called classical hypothesis ... that the dominant purpose of treatment should be the deterrence of potential offenders; (2) the positivist hypothesis which dominates contemporary criminological thought, that incapacitation and reformation should be the dominant treatment ends.'[21] Retributivism was relegated to a footnote and discussed there only to defend Bentham and others against the 'improper' allegation that, like Kant and Hegel, they believed that punishment '*should be* retributive' (emphasis added). Michael and philosopher Mortimer Adler had earlier explained that there are two incompatible theories of punishment: the 'punitive' and the 'non-punitive' and that 'it can be shown that the punitive theory is a fallacious analysis and that the non-punitive theory is correct.'[22] That being so, '[t]he infliction of pain is never justified merely on the ground that it visits retributive punishment upon the offender. Punitive retribution is never justifiable in itself.'[23]

HLA Hart, a transitional figure who acknowledged some legitimate role for retributive ideas in thinking about punishment, discussed the problem of deeply disadvantaged people explicitly. In discussing excusing defences in the criminal law, he noted,[24]

> [t]he admission that the excusing condition may be of no value to those who are below a minimum level of economic prosperity may mean, of course, that we should incorporate as a further excusing condition the pressure of gross forms of economic necessity.

To my knowledge he did not develop that reflection further in print and it tiptoes only a short distance away from traditional criminal law doctrine. 'Gross forms of economic necessity' might excuse Jean Valjean. Most analysts of necessity defences would in any case excuse hungry people lost in the woods who fastidiously break

---

[19] PH Robinson, 'Hybrid Principles for the Distribution of Criminal Sanctions' (1987) 82 *Northwestern Law Review* 19; MS Moore, 'Justifying Retributivism' (1993) 27 *Israel Law Review* 15.

[20] A Alschuler, 'Sentencing Reform and Prosecutorial Power' (1978) 126 *University of Pennsylvania Law Review* 552.

[21] J Michael and H Wechsler, 'A Rationale of the Law of Homicide' (1937) 37 *Columbia Law Review* 1262.

[22] J Michael and M Adler, *Crime, Law, and Social Science* (New York, Harcourt Brace, 1933) 341.

[23] Ibid, 344.

[24] HLA Hart, *Punishment and Responsibility: Essays in the Philosophy of Law* (Oxford, Oxford University Press, 1968) 51.

into cabins in order to find food. Whether for Hart it would have exonerated deeply disadvantaged young men who sold drugs on street corners or committed street robberies, or drug-dependent young women who sold drugs or sex, is unknowable.

On a psychological and practical level, too, the problems presented by deeply disadvantaged defendants became harder to accommodate as prevailing thinking about punishment shifted toward retributivism. Most people tend to think in ways that reflect the ethos of their times, especially concerning emotional and moral issues.[25] Not surprisingly, many criminal law scholars became enamoured of a conception of criminal cases as morality plays in which judgements of offenders' mental capacities for moral choice and their exercises of moral responsibility in relation to wrongdoing were seen as the only important questions.[26] Jury or judicial nullification of criminal charges against sympathetic defendants ceased being viewed as a legitimate option. If defendants were mentally competent, satisfied mens rea requirements, and failed to satisfy the requirements of traditional excusing or mitigating defences, that was the end of the matter. The jury or the judge had no choice but to convict; the defendant culpably failed to resist temptation. That it was an especially strong temptation did not signify.

Others among the influential early writers on retributive punishment theory acknowledged the special situations of deeply disadvantaged offenders, but seldom proposed or approved excuses or explicit sentencing discounts. After developing a punishment theory based on a social contract analysis of benefits and burdens, University of Arizona philosopher Jeffrie Murphy rejected it on the grounds that it could not deliver justice until 'we have restructured society in such a way that criminals genuinely do correspond to the only model that will render punishment permissible – ie, make sure that they are autonomous and that they do benefit in the requisite sense.'[27] English philosopher Ted Honderich observed that '[t]here is nothing that can be called the question of [punishment's] moral justification which is left to be considered,' if 'the great question of the distribution of goods in society' is not addressed.[28] Antony Duff developed a communicative theory but then rejected it as a basis for policy in favour of a deterrence-premised system: '[p]unishment is not justifiable within our present legal system; it will not be justifiable unless and until we have brought about deep and far-reaching social, political, legal, and moral changes in ourselves and our society.'[29]

Andreas von Hirsch, too, acknowledged that 'as long as a substantial segment of the population is denied adequate opportunities for a livelihood, any scheme for

---

[25] D Musto, *The American Disease: The Origins of Narcotic Control*, 3rd edn (New York, Oxford University Press, 1999; orig 1973); M Tonry, *Thinking about Crime: Sense and Sensibility in American Penal Culture* (New York, Oxford University Press, 2004).

[26] Eg, SJ Morse, 'The Twilight of Welfare Criminology: A Reply to Judge Bazelon' (1976) 49 *Southern California Law Review* 1247; G Fletcher, *Rethinking Criminal Law* (Boston MA, Little Brown & Co, 1978).

[27] Murphy, 'Marxism and Retribution', above n 2 at 243.

[28] T Honderich, *Punishment: The Supposed Justifications* (Cambridge, Polity Press, 1989) 238.

[29] RA Duff, *Trials and Punishments* (Cambridge, Cambridge University Press, 1986) 194; Duff, *Punishment, Communication, and Community*, above n 10.

punishing must be morally flawed.'[30] Nonetheless, he neither ducked like Murphy, nor sidestepped like Duff. He accepted the implications of his views and argued that a retributive system committed to apportioning punishment to offence seriousness was justifiable even for the deeply disadvantaged because it would do less harm to them. They would be punished no more severely than others as, for incapacitative or invidious reasons, they might well have been under indeterminate sentencing. Because poor employment records, limited educations, and other markers of disadvantage are correlated with offending, incapacitative considerations would often justify harsher treatment of the deeply disadvantaged under individualised, indeterminate sentencing. By contrast, proportionality-based systems would limit their vulnerability to harsher punishment.

Against a backdrop of indeterminate sentencing in which the putatively dangerous could be held for long periods, von Hirsch may have been right at the time. That backdrop was changing, however, even as he wrote. Prevailing ways of thinking and policies were changing. Problems that Andreas sought to address became less acute in many jurisdictions. Statutory determinate sentencing laws and guidelines emerged, some explicitly providing that racial and socio-economic factors should play no role as sentencing criteria. Parole boards' release powers were eliminated or greatly curtailed in many States. Most remaining boards created guidelines systems based primarily on conviction offences and previous convictions. Practically no one since the 1970s has argued that offence seriousness is irrelevant to sentencing or that judges and parole boards should have vast unregulated discretion.

At the time I thought, and today continue to think, von Hirsch's argument unpersuasive for a number of reasons. It was courageous in acknowledging and addressing difficult moral and policy problems that others saw but evaded. However, at least in the US context, its effect was to prioritise formal notions of proportionality at the price of substantive justice. As I noted earlier, conviction offences forming the basis for sentences are often merely artifacts of plea bargaining and provide an inadequate basis for comparative assessments of moral culpability. More importantly, von Hirsch did not refute the proposition that deeply disadvantaged defendants may be less morally culpable than others.

II. Deep Disadvantage and Criminal Behaviour

To justify their proposals, proponents of social disadvantage defences typically provide lists of conditions known to be correlated with offending, together with illustrative citations to supporting sources.[31] Such things as being raised in a single-parent household, experiencing inconsistent parental discipline and poor parenting

---

[30] A von Hirsch, *Doing Justice*, revised edn (Boston MA, Northeastern University Press, 1986) 149.
[31] Eg, most exhaustively, R Delgado, 'The Wretched of the Earth' (2011) 2 *Alabama Civil Rights and Civil Liberties Law Review* 1.

skills, living in socially disorganised areas, suffering from attention deficit disorder, having a low IQ, attending inferior schools, associating with deviant peers, and having deviant parents or siblings are all associated with any number of adverse outcomes including school failure, early pregnancy, early drug use, delinquency, and crime.[32] However, things usually go fuzzy from there, with writers noting that many offenders experience those conditions and effectively inferring that ipso facto the conditions *cause* the behaviour: '[u]nremitting, long-term exposure to conditions of threat, stress, and neglect indelibly mark the minds and bodies of those exposed.'[33]

The evidence that individual characteristics and experiences and contextual factors powerfully shape behaviour is, however, stronger than that. This can be seen by juxtaposing findings by developmental psychologists with those of urban sociologists regarding the causes and correlates of offending.

Developmental psychologists investigate the antecedents and causes of prosocial and anti-social behaviour.[34] Most rely heavily on prospective longitudinal cohort studies that allow examination of causal sequences in individual lives. It has long been recognised, for example, that 'birds of a feather flock together' among school-failing delinquent children. What was for long not known, however, was whether this happens mostly because deviant children or groups recruit otherwise adequately performing students who then fail, or mostly because children who are failing seek other forms of validation and find it among deviant peers. Knowing the answer to this question has important implications for running schools and enhancing children's life chances or, in the terms of the discipline, altering developmental trajectories.[35]

Developmentalists distinguish between 'risk' and 'protective' factors in trying to explain developmental trajectories and design interventions that aim to make positive outcomes more likely. All else being equal, risk factors such as low IQ, impulsivity, attention deficit disorder, inconsistent parenting, and deviant peers increase the likelihood of delinquency, teenage pregnancy, drug abuse, early alcohol consumption, and school dropout. Protective factors such as improved parenting skills, cognitive-skills training, mental health services, improved educational opportunities, and pro-social peers can offset risk factors and reduce the likelihood of negative outcomes.

I discuss developmental psychology to make two points relevant to imputation of personal culpability to deeply disadvantaged people. First, developmental trajectories are established in early childhood, at ages at which no one would impute moral responsibility to young people for the trajectories that will characterise their

---

[32] See, eg, D Farrington, 'Developmental and Life-course Criminology: Key Theoretical and Empirical Issues' (2003) 41 *Criminology* 221; AR Piquero, D Farrington and A Blumstein, 'The Criminal Career Paradigm' in M Tonry (ed), *Crime and Justice: A Review of Research*, vol 30 (Chicago IL, University of Chicago Press, 2003).

[33] Delgado, 'Rotten Social Background', above n 17 at 80.

[34] M Le Blanc and R Loeber, 'Developmental Criminology Updated' in M Tonry (ed), *Crime and Justice: A Review of Research*, vol 23 (Chicago IL, University of Chicago Press, 1998).

[35] M Tonry, LE Ohlin and DP Farrington, *Human Development and Criminal Behavior: New Ways of Advancing Knowledge* (New York, Springer, 1991).

later lives. A celebrated article by Terrie E Moffitt,[36] one of the most cited in developmental criminology,[37] established that two major categories of offenders can be identified in early childhood. She called them 'life-course persisters' and 'adolescence-limited' offenders; the terms describe their patterns of delinquency and criminality.

Moffit's typology rests comfortably with knowledge about offending. 'Age/crime curves' have shown for at least 50 years that sizable majorities of teenagers, especially boys, engage in behaviour which, if coming to police attention, would justify criminal prosecution.[38] Property offending peaks in the mid-teenage years and violent offending one or two years later. There are rapid fall-offs from the peaks. For most people a process of natural desistance occurs as maturity, employment, continuing sexual relationships, and conventional aspirations make the risks of criminality apparent. These are Moffitt's adolescence-limited offenders. Life-course-persistent offenders typically begin offending at younger ages than do others and continue to offend well into adulthood. Those in the latter group can in no credible way be said to have chosen to become members.

Secondly, offending trajectories of young people can often be altered through identification of risk factors and strengthening of protective factors. Whether those analyses are undertaken and acted upon, and whether interventions are competently and appropriately executed by responsible adults, are also matters about which no one would impute moral responsibility to children. As William Wordsworth put it, the child is father of the man. The deeply disadvantaged defendants for whom Judge Bazelon would have made a social adversity defence available, and concerning whom von Hirsch would deny judges authority to mitigate punishments, are often people who were launched when young on grievous trajectories in which no one constructively intervened.

The causal forces of personal and community influences on offending are vividly demonstrated by work that combines developmental psychology and urban sociology. Table 1 is drawn from a classic article by Wikström and Loeber.[39] It shows percentages of various groups of Pittsburgh boys who admitted to committing serious delinquent acts up to age 18. Because of the age cut-off, the percentages are underestimates. The table's purpose is to demonstrate the relative influences of individual differences (the psychologists' turf) and community characteristics (the

---

[36] TE Moffitt, 'Adolescence-Limited and Life-Course-Persistent Antisocial Behavior: a Developmental Taxonomy' (1993) 100 *Psychological Review* 4, 6.

[37] Or in criminology generally: 5700 times by Google Scholar count in early 2014.

[38] D Farrington, 'Age and Crime' in M Tonry and N Morris (eds), Crime and Justice: An Annual Review of Research, vol 7 (Chicago IL, University of Chicago Press, 1986).

[39] P-OH Wikström and R Loeber, 'Do Disadvantaged Neighborhoods Cause Well-Adjusted Children to Become Adolescent Delinquents? A Study of Male Juvenile Serious Offending, Individual Risk and Protective Factors, and Neighborhood Context' (2000) 38 *Criminology* 1109. Rolf Loeber, a leading developmental criminologist, over three decades prospectively followed the lives of three age cohorts of initially young and ultimately middle-aged men in Pittsburgh. Per-Olof H Wikström, an influential urban sociologist, directs the Peterborough Adolescent and Young Adult Development Study, a multi-decade prospective longitudinal study of contextual influences on young people's behaviour.

sociologists'). It illustrates the overwhelming causal influence of deep disadvantage on offending.

The vertical axis divides the boys into three groups on the basis of individual characteristics associated with offending: high protective scores (ie, low offending probability), balanced scores (moderate probability), and high risk scores (high probability). The horizontal axis divides the boys into four groups on the basis of the characteristics of the neighbourhoods in which they lived: above average neighbourhoods, average neighbourhoods, disadvantaged neighbourhoods composed primarily of private sector housing, disadvantaged neighbourhoods composed primarily of public housing.

Table 1. Percentage Committing Serious Offences by Risk Score and Neighbourhood Context

Risk and Protective Score	Housing Type					
	Advantaged	Middle	Disadvantaged (Private Housing)	Disadvantaged (Public Housing)	Gamma	N
High Protective	11.1	5.1	16.7	37.5	0.23	155
Balanced Risk and Protective	27.3	40.1	38.5	60.7	0.23	651
High Risk	77.8	71.3	78.3	70.0	n.s.	222
Gamma	0.70	0.74	0.69	n.s.		
N	142	556	188	142		

Source: Wikström and Loeber, 'Disadvantaged Neighborhoods' (above n 39), table 6.

Two patterns leap out. First, individual differences matter. No matter what the neighbourhood, 70–80 per cent of children with high risk scores engaged in serious delinquency. Secondly, however, for the low- and moderate-risk children, living in a disadvantaged public-housing neighbourhood mattered much more. In particular:

(i) For young people living in above average neighbourhoods, individual differences are strongly associated with offending probabilities: only 11 per cent of low-risk children admitted offences compared with 78 per cent of high-risk children;

(ii) For young people living in disadvantaged public-housing neighbourhoods, neighbourhood effects swamped individual differences: nearly 40 per cent of low-risk, 60 per cent of mid-risk, and 70 per cent of high-risk children admitted offences.

The vast majority of high-risk children admit offences, no matter where they live. Almost irrespective of their individual characteristics, most boys living in highly disorganised urban neighbourhoods admit offences. A few do not, but they are exceptions to the rule. The likely explanations for the exceptions' comparative success are that, despite living in a distressed environment, they were raised in a home with capable, caring parents, were for some reason unrepresentative of neighbourhood demographics (eg, the minister's or school teacher's or doctor's children), or were just lucky.

The study shows clearly that offending patterns are probabilistic and depend in substantial part on the circumstances of people's lives. To insist that the difference between those who do and those who do not offend is simply that some resisted temptation is to celebrate an abstract and idealised conception of personal moral choice. It is to insist on heroic behaviour by people who face overwhelming odds against them and from whom it is unfair to demand heroism.

Individuals do, of course, make moral choices, but the conditions in which they make them vary enormously. Most people understand this without looking at data of the sort presented in table 1. Long-time *Chicago Tribune* columnist Mike Royko made the point much more intuitively in this account of the criminal calculations of two Chicago boys:[40]

> You take some teenager in an affluent suburb. He has just returned from playing tennis or football after school . . . He walks into a seven- or eight-room house in which he has his own room, equipped with a stereo and maybe his own TV set, and a closet full of clothes.
>
> After having dinner with his father, who has a well-paying job, and his mother, who might work but also might be home every day, he goes in his room, looks in the mirror and asks himself: 'What is in my heart? Do I want to join a gang and go out and mug somebody and pursue a life of violence and crime? Or do I want to go to college and become a CPA?' Goodness, thank goodness, usually prevails over evil. So the lad does not go out and join [a street gang].
>
> A similar decision is made by a youth in one of the city's many slum areas. His home is a dismal flat or a congested housing project. Income is his mother's welfare check. School is a place where the most important thing you learn is not to turn your back on strangers. Security and social life are the other kids on the street – the gang.
>
> So he looks in the cracked mirror and asks: 'What is in my heart? Do I want to become a CPA, or a physician, or a lawyer? Do I want to go to Northwestern or Georgetown or maybe Yale? Hell no. I *want* to pursue the life of crime and violence. I *want* to go out and mug somebody. I *want* to wind up doing 10 to 20 in [prison] so I can be with my friends. I want this because it is in my heart and has been there since I was born.'

We know why the inner-city youth does not plan to be an accountant and why the suburban youth is unlikely to participate in a gang fight. We also know a lot about the reasons why the inner-city youth's prospects are so bleak. Contexts in which choices are made matter. It seems odd that criminal law doctrine, sentencing policy, or sentencing decisions would be predicated on any other view. People from deeply disadvantaged backgrounds face vastly harder choices and larger

[40] Reprinted in D Bazelon, *Questioning Authority* (New York, Knopf, 1988).

temptations than do the rest of us. The moral of Royko's examples and the under-pinning of Bazelon's insanity and social disadvantage defences is the belief that deep disadvantage is relevant to assessments of moral culpability. Decisions to commit crimes are not always simply failures to resist temptation. To the contrary, they often result from the regrettable but understandable choices of people whose lives present few positive options and who are subject to extraordinary stress. Drug selling is a wholesale example that has sent hundreds of thousands of disadvantaged Americans to prison in recent decades. It would make little sense for most people who have reasonably good prospects of living a satisfying life to accept the risks of street-level drug dealing. Especially during the American War on Drugs of recent decades, the chances of ruining one's life have been high, and well-known. For young disadvantaged people with little social capital and limited life chances, with substandard educations and few skills that are marketable in the legal economy, however, drug dealing appears to present opportunities that are not otherwise available. Such young people overestimate the benefits and underestimate the risks.[41] This is compounded by peer influences, social pressures, and deviant role models provided by successful dealers who live conspicuously affluent lives and manage to avoid arrest.

This is at once a simple and a complicated problem. 'Do the crime, do the time' appears to offer a simple solution. It is a solution, however, that ignores and lacks empathy for the complex circumstances of the lives of deeply disadvantaged people. Proponents of a social disadvantage defence or of sentence mitigation are respond-ing to that deficiency by searching for a better solution.

III. Deep Disadvantage as an Excuse or Mitigation

Discussion of a social adversity defence is usually linked to the writings of the late federal court of appeals judge David Bazelon. His proposal was prompted by two personal experiences and one empirical assertion. The first experience was his role as draftsman of the Federal Circuit Court for the District of Columbia's 1954 opin-ion in *Durham*,[42] which replaced the *M'Naghten* insanity test in the District of Columbia Circuit with one that asked the jury to decide whether a defendant's behaviour was the 'product' of mental disease or defect. The aim was to permit expert testimony on the defendant's mental condition while allowing the jury to decide the ultimate factual question of whether, because of that condition, the defendant should be regarded as not legally responsible for his or her actions.

---

[41] P Reuter, RJ MacCoun and P Murphy, *Money from Crime: The Economics of Drug Dealing in Washington, DC* (Santa Monica CA, RAND, Drug Policy Research Center, 1990); MAR Kleiman, 'The Problem of Replacement and the Logic of Drug Law Enforcement' (1997) 3 *Drug Policy Analysis Bulletin* 8.

[42] *Durham v United States* 214 F 2d 862 (DC Circuit 1954).

Durham was abandoned in 1972 in *Brawner*[43] because, according to Bazelon, it proved impossible to establish the sought-after division of function between experts, who usually proved unable to resist testifying on the ultimate causal questions, and juries.

Bazelon's second experience was participation in consideration of the appeal in *US v Alexander*,[44] in which a black man responded with violent rage to race-baiting language from the victim. He proposed to introduce evidence on the deeply disadvantaged conditions of his life and his experience as a victim of racial maltreatment to explain and excuse his actions and the two deaths that resulted. The courts refused to allow the defence. Bazelon dissented.

The empirical assertion came from Norval Morris who observed, in arguing for abolition of the insanity defence, that an 'adverse social and subcultural background is statistically *more* criminogenic than is psychosis.'[45] His point was that commission of serious crimes can more accurately be predicted from knowledge of a person's background and circumstances than from knowledge of his or her psychiatric diagnosis. Since the insanity defence is premised on the proposition that people should not be held criminally responsible for actions over which they lack capacity for self-control, Morris contended that the same deterministic insight would equally, or even more plausibly, support recognition of a social disadvantage defence.

Morris took it as given that a deep disadvantage defence would raise insuperable problems; his point was to suggest that there was even less basis for recognition of an insanity defence. Bazelon, who believed there should be an insanity defence, flipped that argument around and drew the opposite conclusion: there should be a social disadvantage defence.

Bazelon proposed that testimony be permitted in appropriate cases concerning the influence of deep disadvantage on behaviour and that the jury be directed 'that a defendant is not responsible if at the time of his unlawful conduct his mental or emotional processes or behavior controls were impaired to such an extent that he cannot justly be held responsible for his act.'[46] The aim was for the jury – 'the traditional representative of our consensual sense of morality' – to be able to decide in each case 'whether, in light of that morality, the defendant can justly be held responsible for his act.'[47] In anticipating the criticism that juries should not be allowed such great discretion, he observed that juries in many areas of law are given comparable or greater discretion to interpret and apply open-textured terms and concepts. The ultimate factual questions in tort, contract, and indeed criminal cases often turn, for example, on evaluative standards such as 'reasonableness'.

---

[43] *United States v Brawner* 471 F 2d 969 (DC Circuit 1972).

[44] *United States v Alexander* 471 F 2d 923 (DC Circuit 1972).

[45] N Morris, 'Psychiatry and the Dangerous Criminal' (1968) 41 *Southern California Law Review* 514.

[46] D Bazelon, 'The Morality of the Criminal Law: A Rejoinder to Professor Morse' (1976) 49 *Southern California Law Review* 1269.

[47] Ibid, 1270.

Bazelon believed that, paralleling experience with the insanity defence, juries would seldom acquit defendants on the basis of deep disadvantage, partly because they would be influenced by their emotional reactions to crimes and their concerns about a defendant's possible dangerousness. And if defendants were occasionally acquitted because of the defence, he argued, it would show that the jurors believed the defendant should be excused and would draw attention to the seriousness of the social problems that underlay the acquittal.

If Bazelon's speculations are right, recognition of a deep disadvantage defence would not often result in acquittals. Assuming some non-trivial number of offenders ought to be acquitted on moral-desert grounds, invoking the defence would comparatively seldom exculpate them. This emphasises the importance of recognising deep disadvantage as a valid basis for mitigation of sentence in cases where judges believe that to be appropriate. Bazelon would say, I have no doubt, that recognition of a formal defence is important on moral grounds, even if it were seldom applied. And, just as incomplete self-defence or subjectively experienced but objectively insufficient provocation are often viewed as valid bases for mitigation in sentencing, recognition of a social adversity defence would lay a comparable foundation.

Bazelon's proposal and arguments elicited an immediate response from Stephen Morse,[48] who offered three main objections. The first is that some individuals exposed to the deepest disadvantage do not become offenders, thereby refuting any claim that the conditions themselves are causal. The second is that a social disadvantage defence would imply that affected offenders lack capacity for moral choice, and no legal system should want to do that, especially when the individuals concerned would often be members of socio-economic or ethnic minority groups. The third, the gravamen of the difference between them, is that Morse argued that situations in which a capacity for moral choice is eliminated are already dealt with adequately by traditional criminal law doctrines such as insanity, necessity, duress, and provocation.

One way of framing this disagreement is as a fundamental difference about the rule of law. When one talks, as lawyers do, about 'justice according to the law', it is an open question which of the two comes first. For Morse, it seems, it is more important that rules be consistently applied than that just results be obtained in individual cases. Thus, at the end of the day, Morse does not want juries to be told that they may apply their collective sense of justice in deciding cases:[49]

> [t]he problem with this view is that although juries are representatives of the moral standards of the community, each jury is not a totally independent 'legislature' free to decide what those moral standards should be. Juries do not create community moral standards; they apply them after being instructed on the law by the judge.

Bazelon, by contrast, was not troubled by the more activist phenomenon of nullification in which juries choose to disregard what they understand the law to be in

---

[48] Morse, 'Reply', above n 26.
[49] Ibid, 1254.

order to achieve a just result: 'I view nullification as an important means of bringing to bear on the judicial process a sense of fairness and particularised justice.'[50]

Sentencing is and always has been a human process. Some people must make weighty decisions about other people's lives. Judges and juries usually take that responsibility seriously and want both to apply the law in what is generally understood to be the appropriate way, and to do justice to the people whose lives are in their hands. When those aspirations conflict, concerns for justice sometimes do, and should, defeat concerns for literal application of legal standards. That is why juries in eighteenth-century England often refused to convict people of property crimes punishable by death and, in twentieth-century America, why judges and prosecutors have often nullified mandatory minimum sentence laws.[51]

Were I a legislator or a judge, I would support Bazelon's proposal. Inevitably there will be cases that present the kinds of sympathetic factual patterns that Bazelon describes. It would be open and honest to authorise acquittals when the fact-finder concludes the defendant's behavioural controls have been impaired by life circumstances to such a degree that they cannot justly be held responsible for their acts. To do so would channel predictable human emotional reactions to difficult cases and allow them to be dealt with justly without requiring nullification.

There are few negatives. As Bazelon believed, human scepticism and emotional reactions to serious crimes (and to seemingly dangerous defendants) would doubtless limit acquittals to a small number of cases. In the parallel situation of insanity defence claims, juries have traditionally been loath to vote in favour of acquittals. They are rare. The explanations usually given for this are that juries disbelieve the factual claims underpinning the defence, they worry that calculating guilty defendants may evade responsibility by means of a false claim, and they worry about the offender's dangerousness. For violent crimes, similar considerations are likely to weigh heavily in deep disadvantage cases. For property and drug crimes, they may weigh less heavily – but so what? If the fact-finder concludes that the offender's life circumstances substantially or completely excuse his or her actions, where is the loss? Human beings will have behaved in a way they believe to be just and acknowledged that that defendant acted under extraordinary pressure for which sympathy is due.

Larger numbers of cases might be affected at the plea bargaining stage by giving defendants something more to be bargained away in exchange for a charge reduction or lesser sentence following a guilty plea. Prosecutors, of course, tend to oppose anything that empowers defendants; but it is hard to explain why a defendant with a plausible hope for acquittal on this basis should not receive concessions that defendants might receive in other cases in which convictions are uncertain, for example when a case presents evidentiary problems.

---

[50] Bazelon, 'The Morality of the Criminal Law', above n 16 at 397.
[51] D Hay, 'Property, Authority, and the Criminal Law' in D Hay, P Linebaugh, and EP Thompson (eds), *Albion's Fatal Tree: Crime and Society in Eighteenth Century England* (New York, Pantheon, 1975); F Remington, 'Introduction' in R Dawson, *Sentencing* (Boston MA, Little, Brown, 1969); M Tonry, 'The Mostly Unintended Effects of Mandatory Penalties: Two Centuries of Consistent Findings' in M Tonry (ed), *Crime and Justice: A Review of Research*, vol 38 (Chicago IL, University of Chicago Press, 2009).

In any case, Bazelon's proposal has won little support from lawyers and has received none from judges or legislators. Morse rightly observed that the discussion has been 'entirely [within] the province of intellectuals engaged in scholarly debate.'[52]

Discussion has percolated through the criminal law literature since 1976 but almost nothing is written that does more than rehash familiar arguments.[53] Stuart Green, in a recent article, however, offered a framework for assessing claims that socially disadvantaged defendants might make. He proposed that three considerations be considered: '(1) the kind of unjust deprivation, if any, to which the offender has been subjected; (2) the kind of unfair advantage or disadvantage to which the victim has been subjected; and (3) the particular offense committed.'[54] This is a substantial advance on earlier work, and could provide useful guidance for juries. In the end, however, the result would be similar to the gestalt calculation that Judge Bazelon proposed.

Even the most ardent opponents of Bazelon's proposal acknowledge the human difficulty of the problem.[55] It is but a small step from that acknowledgment to conclude that, whether or not an excusing defence should be recognised, deep disadvantage should be regarded as a mitigating condition in sentencing.

IV. Social Adversity in Mitigation

The arguments for authorising mitigation of sentences for socially disadvantaged defendants are straightforward. There are at least two retributive justifications for doing so. The first is that deeply disadvantaged offenders are subject to more powerful environmental and subcultural pressures to commit offences than are most other people, especially the privileged, and deserve as a class to be punished less severely when they do. Sentencing codes and guidelines systems often explicitly describe factual patterns that underlay incomplete affirmative defences – for example claims of self-defence, compulsion, necessity, or provocation that appear to be psychologically valid but not to satisfy legal standards – as appropriate bases for mitigation of sentence. The second is that, taken seriously, retributive punishment ideas require that fact-specific culpability always be taken into account and serve as the, or a, principal measure of deserved punishment. Mitigation of penalties for many deeply disadvantaged offenders should occur as a natural application of a fact-specific and subjective assessment of culpability.

There are also consequentialist arguments favouring discounting punishments for deeply disadvantaged offenders. Few theorists or policy analysts in recent years

---

[52] Morse, 'Deprivation and Desert', above n 15 at 170.

[53] A Taslitz, 'The Rule of Criminal Law: Why Courts and Legislatures Ignore Richard Delgado's Rotten Social Background' (2011) 2 *Alabama Civil Rights and Civil Liberties Law Review* 79.

[54] Green, 'Hard Times', above n 10 at 59.

[55] Eg Morse, 'Deprivation and Desert', above n 15.

have offered fleshed-out consequentialist accounts of punishment that address case-level issues, so I shall use Bentham's ideas illustratively. One argument for discounting emerges from Bentham's notion that any intentional infliction of suffering is 'wicked' and its corollary that punishments should be no more severe than is necessary to achieve their preventative goals. This implies inter alia that punishments should inflict no greater suffering on offenders than the suffering of others that their infliction would prevent. The current state of the art of evidence on deterrent and incapacitative effects of imprisonment cautions that few assumptions about their preventative effectiveness should be made.[56] Reinforcing that reason for scepticism, recent research findings show that, all else being equal, sending an offender to prison does not result in lower reoffending rates than if he or she had been sentenced to a community punishment; the best evidence suggests to the contrary that imprisonment increases reoffending.[57] Thus, no strong and perhaps no credible claims can be made that punishment of any particular offender will have significant preventative effects.

A related Benthamite limitation directs that punishment not be imposed if some other non-punitive means would as well or better achieve the same effects. In many or most situations, this limitation undermines arguments in favour of prison sentences. The current evidence on the effects of non-incarcerative punishments shows that many well targeted, resourced, and managed programmes reduce reoffending.[58] Moreover, accumulating research on the effects of imprisonment upon offenders' subsequent labour force participation, life-time earnings, physical and mental health, and family functioning (and upon the education, mental health and delinquency of their children) document substantial unintended consequences and costs that offset preventative gains.[59]

From a preventative perspective, the consequentialist implications of recent research findings are clear. In general, there should be a presumption against the use of imprisonment or other especially stigmatising punishments, and a presumption in favour of mitigation.

The challenge during an era in which, at least among the theory class,[60] retributive ideas are in vogue is to justify those presumptions in retributivist terms. For some retributivist sympathisers, that is easy to do; for others, less so. My effort to do so unfolds in three steps. The first is to show that, at least in the United States, there is no reasonable basis for believing that conviction offences, which are the primary

[56] DS Nagin, 'Deterrence in the Twenty-first Century' in M Tonry (ed), *Crime and Justice in America: 1975–2025* (Chicago IL, University of Chicago Press, 2013); J Travis and B Western (eds), *The Causes and Consequences of High Incarceration Rates in the United States*, Report of the National Academy of Sciences Committee on the Causes and Consequences of High Rates of Incarceration (Washington DC, National Academies Press, 2014) ch 5.

[57] DS Nagin, F Cullen and C Lero-Jonson, 'Imprisonment and Re-offending' in M Tonry (ed), *Crime and Justice: A Review of Research*, vol 38 (Chicago IL, University of Chicago Press, 2009).

[58] DL MacKenzie, *What Works in Corrections: Reducing the Criminal Activities of Offenders and Delinquents* (Cambridge, Cambridge University Press, 2006).

[59] Travis and Western, *Causes and Consequences*, above n 56, chs 6–9.

[60] M Tonry, 'Can Twenty-first Century Punishment Policies Be Justified in Principle?' in M Tonry (ed), *Retributivism Has a Past: Has It a Future?* (New York, Oxford University Press, 2011).

Michael Tonry

determinant of sentencing, provide a reliable basis for imposition of punishments apportioned to offenders' relative blameworthiness. The second is to show that a humane retributivism would in any case be based on subjective assessments of offenders' blameworthiness. The third is to show that sentencing laws and policies have changed radically since the 1970s, so that there is now less risk that judicial discretion to mitigate will instead be used to aggravate. The objective versions of retributivism that gained support in the 1970s were understandable as reactions to the unrestrained individualisation of indeterminate sentencing, but not now.

The principal objections to acknowledging the complexities of disadvantaged peoples' lives by mitigating their punishments come from supporters of positive retributivist views: offenders may and must be punished as much as they deserve, neither more nor less. Andreas von Hirsch's work is illustrative. In *Doing Justice* and since,[61] he has consistently opposed social adversity mitigation, for three reasons. First, he argues that punishment is a blaming institution, and that blameworthiness should be assessed relative to the offence for which punishment is due. As a practical matter, the authoritative assessment of that is the criminal conviction. Secondly, a corollary, punishments should not reflect 'whole life judgements' of the offender's character. Third, punishments should not take account of aspects of offenders' lives that are unrelated to the offence of which they are convicted. Examples of forbidden criteria include education, living arrangements, marital status, and employment, all of which are results of lifestyle choices that are not the law's business.

These three points all make sense in the 1970s context of perceived excesses of indeterminate sentencing. Nominal sentence lengths and times served bore no necessary relation to blameworthiness. Judges and parole boards made whole-life judgements about offenders, and believed it was appropriate to do so. Judges and parole boards by the 1960s sometimes but not always took account of personal characteristics in predicting reoffending as a component of making punishment decisions.[62]

Von Hirsch's three points are also understandable in terms of the broader intellectual climate of the 1970s. Rights-centred political philosophy, left[63] and right,[64] and jurisprudence were taking wing.[65] The due process movement of the 1960s extended newly elaborated constitutional procedural protections into sentencing, probation, prison, and parole processes. The prisoners' and civil rights movements hammered away at abuses of discretionary power, at inconsistencies in decision-making, and at biased and idiosyncratic decision-makers.[66]

---

[61] Von Hirsch, *Doing Justice*, above n 4. For an argument supporting von Hirsch's position, see Ashworth and Zedner's chapter in this volume, section IV.B.

[62] DM Gottfedson, LT Wilkins and PB Hoffman, *Guidelines for Parole and Sentencing* (Lanham MD, Lexington, 1978).

[63] J Rawls, *A Theory of Justice* (Cambridge MA, Harvard University Press, 1971).

[64] R Nozick, *Anarchy, State, and Utopia* (New York, Basic Books, 1977).

[65] R Dworkin, *Taking Rights Seriously* (Cambridge MA, Harvard University Press, 1977).

[66] See, eg, American Friends Service Committee, *Struggle for Justice: A Report on Crime and Punishment in America* (New York, Hill and Wang, 1971).

The ideas that there should be rules for sentencing and parole decision-making, that officials' discretionary powers should be narrowed, and that all decisions affecting liberty should be reviewable were therefore unsurprising themes of the early sentencing reform movement.[67] In retrospect, the shift toward retributive theories of punishment focusing on blameworthiness and abjuring individualisa-tion on the basis of personal characteristics is also no surprise. Lack of consistency, fairness, and transparency were the principal worries about indeterminate sentenc-ing. Policies that called for creation of published rules linking punishments closely to offence seriousness could address all those problems. If individualisation was out, few or no other coherent criteria were available for regularising sentencing decisions. Indeed, some of the retributive writers of the time proposed mechanical, deterministic notions of just punishment that would sacrifice offenders on altars of rigidly proportionate punishments.[68]

That was unimaginative and inhumane.[69] In practice, abolishing altogether any discretion to tailor sentences to the context of the offence is a recipe for injustice. Nonetheless, most of the early American sentencing commissions were influenced by the retributivist ideas and the social movements of the 1970s. Many forbade judges to 'depart' from sentencing guidelines on grounds of the offenders' personal circumstances, partly in the stated hope of lessening differentially *harsher* punish-ment of disadvantaged and minority offenders. The perversity of such policies is that they have operated to treat many disadvantaged offenders unfairly as individu-als. In practice they mostly damaged poor and minority offenders. As Kate Stith and Steve Koh long ago observed, 'denying judges the opportunity to mitigate sentences on the basis of social disadvantage has worked *against* poor and minority defendants.'[70]

Even setting those considerations aside, there is a bigger difficulty for real-world applications of positive retributivist accounts of punishment. Conviction offences, at least in the United States, are the only basis for beginning consideration of sentence. Under mandatory sentencing laws, conviction offences are determina-tive. Under sentencing guidelines systems, they are the starting point; judges must sentence within the authorised range or give reasons to rebut the presumption, and policy statements generally forbid consideration of socio-economic factors.

---

[67] Eg, M Frankel, *Criminal Sentences – Law Without Order* (New York, Hill and Wang, 1973); N Morris, *The Future of Imprisonment* (Chicago IL, University of Chicago Press, 1974); A Dershowitz, *Fair and Certain Punishment* (New York, Twentieth Century Fund, 1976).

[68] Eg, RG Singer, *Just Deserts: Sentencing Based on Equality and Desert* (Lexington MA, Ballinger, 1979); Robinson, 'Hybrid Principles', above n 19.

[69] Kant, by contrast, gives approving examples of individualisation of punishments that vary with the characteristics of the offender. For 'verbal injuries', for example, a fine might ordinarily suffice but not for a wealthy person; the 'humiliation' of a public apology and kissing the hand of a lower social status victim would better serve as the equivalent of a poor man's fine. When a high-status person assaults a social inferior, he must apologise but might also be condemned to 'solitary and painful confinement, because by this means, in addition to the discomfort suffered, the pride of the offender will be painfully affected.' I Kant, 'The Penal Law and the Law of Pardon' in J Ladd (transl), *The Metaphysical Elements of Justice* (Indianapolis IN, Liberal Arts Press/Bobbs-Merrill, 1965; orig 1798) 101.

[70] K Stith and SY Koh, 'The Politics of Sentencing Reform: The Legislative History of the Federal Sentencing Guidelines' (1993) 28 *Wake Forest Law Review* 223.

A punishment system that uses conviction offences in this way as the only or presumptive measure of offenders' blameworthiness for determination of deserved punishments is fundamentally flawed, because conviction offences are an inadequate measure of offence seriousness. There are several related challenges. First, plea negotiation is ubiquitous in the United States. Depending on the jurisdiction, 95–98 per cent of convictions result from guilty pleas, almost all following negotiation. Secondly, prosecutors' choices of charges to file and to dismiss are, for constitutional separation of powers reasons, immune from review by the courts. The conviction offence is determined in bargained cases by the prosecutor and not by the underlying provable conduct. In a strong guidelines system, the prosecutor can determine the sentence by deciding what charges to file or dismiss. The conviction offence is thus at least as much a product of the prosecutor's discretionary choices as it is of the defendant's criminality. That is why the US Sentencing Commission developed its 'relevant conduct' policy under which application of the federal guidelines is based not on the conviction offence but on the facts that the judge finds to have happened on a 'balance of probabilities' standard.

Only the federal system has adopted the relevant conduct approach, but the issues that the US Sentencing Commission sought to address are larger than I've thus far sketched. Sentencing in State courts is determined by State laws. In principle, in Minnesota as in Sweden, the sentence a defendant receives should be the same wherever he or she is sentenced. In practice, prosecutors' practices and policies vary substantially between counties within a State, both substantively and procedurally. Some insist on harsher punishments for particular crimes than others do. Some charge strategically, alleging a more serious crime than is justified, in order to pressure the defendant to plead guilty under a plea bargain in which the overcharged offence will be dismissed. Some charge only some of several possible offences; others charge all. Some use the threat of possible conviction of an offence bearing lengthy mandatory minimum sentences, including life imprisonment, to pressure defendants into pleading guilty.

Even the mechanics of plea bargaining vary substantially in ways that make conviction offences unreliable as an indicator of offence severity. In some places, horizontal charge bargaining involves dismissals of some offences, for example three of five burglary charges, and guilty pleas to the other two. In vertical charge bargains, the prosecutor agrees to dismiss the most serious charge, for example armed robbery, if the defendant pleads guilty to a lesser included offence (simple robbery, grand theft, or assault). In sentence bargaining, the negotiations concern whether the defendant will receive a jail or prison term and, if so, for how long.

In one county, robbery charges may consistently result in guilty pleas to grand theft; in another, to robbery. In one county, robbery defendants may be required to plead guilty to robbery, but with explicit agreements about the sentence. In another, robbery defendants who agree to plead guilty may always be entitled to dismissal of the robbery charge and to plead guilty to a lesser offence.

Lurking in that detail is this reality: conviction offences are artifacts of prosecutors' choices and strategies. There is no reason to assume that the behaviours underlying two convictions for a particular offence are even vaguely similar.

In a perfect system of criminal justice, like cases would be treated alike and different cases differently according to established principles for the distribution of punishment. No real-world system can do that, partly because human beings must operate it, even ignoring distinctive characteristics of American sentencing. Judges vary in personalities, socialisation, beliefs, and life experience. Their assessments of information and normative judgements occur within different cognitive frames. Even if all judges were well meaning, ethical, and intellectually honest, they would sometimes interpret facts and rules differently.

The effects of interpersonal differences can be reduced by making sentencing policies detailed and clear and sentencing processes transparent and mechanical; as the United States Sentencing Commission tried to do in its 'mandatory guidelines' before they were made 'advisory' by the US Supreme Court in *US v Booker*.[71] However, while mechanical decision systems may increase the likelihood of treating relevantly like cases alike, they carry with them increased risk that relevantly different cases will not be treated differently. In the words of Australian lawyer Arie Freiberg, unwarranted disparities may be replaced by unwarranted parities.[72]

Mitigation of punishments of deeply disadvantaged offenders can be justified on retributive grounds. At least in an American context, no credible case can be made for real-world application of a positive retributivist theory of punishment based on conviction offences. Positive retributivists believe that offenders both may and must be punished as severely as they deserve. Negative retributivists believe that offenders may be punished as much as they deserve, but need not be. Because offence seriousness is not reliably indicated by conviction offences, and no other general measure is available, except in ideal theory, a system of positive retributivism is unachievable.

Even if conviction offences were reliable, they would be insufficient. Any genuinely retributive system that took itself seriously would measure the moral desert of offenders subjectively, as a Recording Angel would see it.[73] The mens rea and actus

[71] *United States v Booker* 543 US 220 (2005).

[72] A Freiberg, 'Three Strikes and You're Out – It's Not Cricket: Colonization and Resistance in Australian Sentencing' in M Tonry and RS Frase (eds), *Sentencing and Sanctions in Western Countries* (New York, Oxford University Press, 2001). Freiberg's quip exposes a second fundamental impediment to treating like cases alike in American courts. People differ substantially in their views of what makes cases comparable or, put differently, about what principles should govern the distribution of punishment. During the heyday of indeterminate sentencing in the United States, many informed people including Herbert Wechsler, primary draftsman of the Model Penal Code, believed that punishment decisions should be based on individualised assessments of offenders' rehabilitative prospects and dangerousness. (See J Michael and H Wechsler, *Criminal Law and Its Administration* (Chicago IL, Foundation Press, 1940).) 'Like cases alike' was not an explicit goal under the Code but, if it had been, the criteria of likeness would have been individual characteristics related to past crimes and future dangerousness. Sentencing under the Code was not meant to be based on offence seriousness. There are no mandatory minimum sentences. Probation is the presumptively appropriate sentence in every case, including for people convicted of rape and murder. A similar presumption calls for release on parole at the earliest opportunity irrespective of the offence.

[73] N Walker, *Why Punish?* (Oxford, Oxford University Press, 1991).

reus of crimes are inadequate for that purpose. Offenders' motives, mental capacities, and material circumstances differ widely. Some offenders act impulsively, under the influence of powerful emotion, extreme social pressures, or alcohol or drugs, others deliberately after cold calculation. Some are motivated by want or material need, some from indifference or for thrills. These are things that do not determine convictions but are often germane to judges and others in deciding what punishment is appropriate in a given case. I can see no good reason why, amongst the complex factors and motivations that inform such assessments, we should exclude deep social disadvantage, which so clearly affects offenders' choices in the ways explored in section II.

Mitigation can also be justified on consequentialist grounds, because adequate justifications will seldom exist for the harsher punishment that would otherwise be imposed. Benthamite utilitarian theory explicitly called for the use of proportionality in relation to crime seriousness as an upper limit on punishment; if punishments were not apportioned to offence seriousness, would-be offenders would have no incentive to commit less serious crimes. For Bentham, penalties should be set so that the expected burden of punishment is greater than the benefits of crime. In determining the amount of punishment required, the offender's situation had to be considered. The offender's 'sensibilities', by which in modern vocabulary he meant sensitivities, must be taken into account. People have different sensitivities and are affected in different ways by the same experience, including experiences of punishment. Accordingly, '[t]hat the quantity actually inflicted on an individual offender may correspond to the quantity intended for similar offenders in general, the several circumstances influencing sensibility ought always to be taken into account.'[74] Imposition of the generally applicable punishment on a deeply disadvantaged offender will be more burdensome than on others because in both direct and collateral ways it will deepen his or her disadvantage.

V. A Celebration

It is at least unimaginative to base adjudication and sentencing on a model of like-situated persons who simply do and do not have fortitude to resist temptations. The developmental research on criminal careers, offender typology, age/crime curves, and the influences on offending of individual differences and community context show that many deeply disadvantaged offenders cannot reasonably be described as like-situated with non-disadvantaged people. Assuming that is true, reasonable people, including reasonable writers about punishment, will disagree about whether and to what extent it is relevant to moral culpability in individual cases. Jeffrie Murphy, Ted Honderich, and Antony Duff, in passages quoted above, in

---

[74] J Bentham, 'The Utilitarian Theory of Punishment' in *An Introduction to the Principles of Morals and Legislation*, ed JH Burns and HLA Hart (London, Athlone, 1970; orig 1789) 169.

different ways suggest that deep disadvantage calls into question the legitimacy of any system of criminal punishment.

Three ways of addressing the problem seem to be on offer. The first, represented by the work of David Bazelon, is to recognise a social disadvantage defence and defer to the judge or jury to decide whether it should exculpate in specific cases. If the defence is unsuccessful, it is implicit that the judge should be able to mitigate sentences on the same basis. The second, represented by the work of Stephen Morse, is to acknowledge the difficulty of the problem and accept that it cannot be addressed in the substantive criminal law; in relation to sentencing, Andreas von Hirsch has taken a similar position. The third is to acknowledge the difficulty of the problem, accept that it cannot adequately be addressed by means of a formal defence, and take it into account in sentencing to the extent that it is relevant to assessing the offender's moral culpability in relation to a specific offence.

The third approach in turn offers two options. One is to take deep disadvantage into account in assessing culpability, but in consistent ways that are (or in principle could be) expressed in rules. The concern is achievement of horizontal equity, the aspiration that offenders who are like-situated in relation to their moral culpability should receive the same or equivalent punishments. That concern is implicit in von Hirsch's general theory, which calls for punishment apportioned to individualised culpability.[75] Within that concern, however, on the specific question of social deprivation, he has favoured basing sentences on conviction offences and opposed recognition of disadvantage as a basis for mitigation.[76]

The other option is, as I do, to adopt a limiting or negative retributivist position, and recognise deep disadvantage as a mitigating circumstance in sentencing that acknowledges offenders' lesser moral culpability. Limiting/negative retributivists will differ on precisely how that might be done and the extent to which the discretion recognised might be bounded.[77] Some will take the position that retributivist concerns require that both upper and lower bounds of deserved punishment must be recognised and that deep disadvantage, like other circumstances that mitigate moral culpability, may be taken into account (if at all) in determining punishment only within the established boundaries. Others will take the position that a retributive calculus can set only an upper bound and that there should be no lower bound.

I take the last position and would treat cases involving deeply disadvantaged defendants in parallel with mercy killings. In some cases, for example, when an aged husband administers an overdose of sleeping pills to his terminally ill and profoundly suffering wife, at her request, few people are comfortable with the defendant's being sentenced to prison. Formal mens rea and actus reus requirements for homicide are met but a prison sentence in many factually uncontroverted cases would be widely regarded as unjust. This is an extreme case, of course, but enabling just sentences for a broader category of cases of which this is an extreme example is

---

[75] Eg von Hirsch and Ashworth, *Proportionate Sentencing*, above n 11.

[76] Eg von Hirsch, *Doing Justice*, above n 4; von Hirsch, *Censure and Sanctions*, above n 11.

[77] R Frase, *Just Sentencing: Principles and Procedures for a Workable System* (New York, Oxford University Press, 2013).

why the Model Penal Code's drafters made probation the presumptively applicable sentence for every case.

Much more could and should be said. One question unaddressed, for example, is whether deep disadvantage should be treated as a special mitigation that would justify reduced sentences below generally applicable lower bounds in limiting/negative retributivist models that recognise them. Another is whether typologies of deep disadvantage should be elaborated that would differentiate degrees of moral culpability among such defendants with criteria developed to specify the degrees of mitigation that are warranted. Stuart Green has laid the foundations for such an analysis.[78] Yet another is whether an offender who, despite a deeply disadvantaged background, has achieved conventional success, remains entitled to mitigation or is deemed to have forfeited his claim. I leave these and other issues for another day and another place.

Many of these issues, and others discussed in this chapter, have been recognised and explored primarily because Andreas von Hirsch exposed them to light. Under the consequentialist framework of indeterminate sentencing, they were not germane. In this and in many other ways he has made a unique, distinctive, and invaluable contribution to thinking about punishment in our time.[79] He was among the most influential of the early proponents of contemporary retributive theory. Unlike most writers on the subject,[80] he has stayed the course and continued to concentrate on punishment theory throughout his career. Alone among major retributive writers, he has consistently examined the general justification of punishment as a legal institution, and has also attended to applied questions concerning the punishment of offenders in the real world. Along the way he has offered, elaborated, and examined distinctions and problems that illuminate policy-making and punishment in individual cases – cardinal versus ordinal proportionality, the justification of 'hard treatment', the relevance of prior crimes to current punishments, and the problem of 'just deserts in an unjust world'.

The part of his work focusing on applied questions has been unparalleled. Many writers who have written about punishment in recent decades have confined themselves to questions of general justification.[81] The following from Dan Markel:[82]

> One question is: What might justify the state's creation of legal institutions of punishment? This is what we call the 'justification' question. The second question is: Once the state has determined someone's liability for a crime, how much and what kind of punishment should the state mete out in response? This is the 'sentencing' question. That a retributivist theorist gives a retributive (or, specifically, communicative) answer to the

---

[78] Green, 'Hard Times', above n 10.

[79] Von Hirsch, *Doing Justice*, above n 4; von Hirsch, *Past and Future Crimes*, above n 11; von Hirsch, *Censure and Sanctions*, above n 11; von Hirsch and Ashworth, *Proportionate Sentencing*, above n 11.

[80] Paul Robinson is another rare exception: Robinson, 'Hybrid Principles', above n 19; Robinson, *Distributive Principles of Criminal Law: Who Should be Punished How Much* (New York, Oxford University Press, 2008).

[81] Moore, 'Justifying Retributivism', above n 19.

[82] D Markel, 'Bentham on Stilts: The Bare Relevance of Subjectivity to Retributive Justice' (2010) 98 *California Law Review* 951.

justification question does not require her to offer a precise answer for each sentencing question . . . A retributive conception of proportionality need not have much in the way of precision to say about the particular details of punishment's implementation, consistent with its greater concern with justifying the institution of punishment within and by the liberal state.

For Markel, the only important question is how the institution of punishment is to be justified. Questions of what happens to individual offenders are not especially important unless, objectively considered, the punishment is so excessively lenient or severe that it fails adequately to convey the wrongfulness of the offender's behaviour. This is in effect to define away the problem. If only the general justification question is considered, however, as HLA Hart long ago pointed out, a separate question of justice in the distribution of punishments remains.[83]

For von Hirsch, that separate question has been central. The problem of punishing deeply disadvantaged defendants is one to which he has repeatedly attended. His solution in 1976 was understandable in the context of American sentencing as it then existed. To me it is time to reconsider that response, especially in light both of the accumulation of empirical evidence on the predictive power of individual differences and neighbourhood settings for offending, and of the demise of indeterminate sentencing. Andreas may well disagree. However, we have been disagreeing about this for nearly four decades and well may continue to do so. Others will decide which of us, if either, is right.

---

[83] HLA Hart, 'Prolegomenon to the Principles of Punishment' (1959) 60 *Proceedings of the Aristotelian Society, New Series* 1; Hart, *Punishment and Responsibility*, above n 24.

III.

RECHTSGÜTER, HARM AND OFFENCE IN CRIMINALISATION

9

'Rights of Others' in Criminalisation Theory

TATJANA HÖRNLE

Criminal norms must aim to protect something, and the first step in a theorist's approach consists in clarifying what this 'something' is. At a second stage, considerations turn to the kind of conduct that should be prohibited. This second stage involves decisions about extensions beyond a core offence description (including endangerment offences, inchoate offences and criminal liability for different kinds of participation); furthermore, side constraints and other mediating principles need to be taken into account. My discussion in this chapter will be limited to the *first stage* that regards the entry decision for any theory of criminalisation: the choice of protected objects. Candidates include: '*legal goods*' (*Rechtsgüter*, a popular notion in German criminal law theory[1]); moral values; the legal order as such; collective interests; individuals, to be protected against harm; individuals, to be protected in their rights. These concepts can be divided into two groups: one large group is characterised by a collectivistic focus according to which the protected goods are *not* assigned to specific individuals (legal goods, moral values, the legal order and collective interests belong to this group), while the other approach defines the criminal law's core task[2] as protecting individuals.

With regard to this dividing line, my position falls on the same side as Andreas von Hirsch's position, that is, we both prefer an individualistic approach over a strictly collectivistic choice of protected objects. According to von Hirsch's view, criminalisation theory should start with the premise that criminal prohibitions can

---

[1] See for a defence of the *Rechtsgutsdoktrin*: C Roxin, *Strafrecht Allgemeiner Teil*, vol I, 4th edn (Munich, CH Beck, 2006) 13–29; C Roxin, 'Der gesetzgebungskritische Rechtsgutsbegriff auf dem Prüfstand' (2013) 160 *Goltdammer's Archiv für Strafrecht* 433; B Schünemann, 'Das Rechtsgüterschutzprinzip als Fluchtpunkt der verfassungsrechtlichen Grenzen der Straftatbestände und ihrer Interpretation' in R Hefendehl, A von Hirsch and W Wohlers (eds), *Die Rechtsgutstheorie: Legitimationsbasis des Strafrechts oder dogmatisches Glasperlenspiel?* (Baden-Baden, Nomos, 2003) 133; U Kindhäuser et al (eds), *Nomos Kommentar zum StGB*, vol 1, 4th edn (Baden-Baden, Nomos, 2013), Vor § 1 note 62 (commentary by W Hassemer and U Neumann). For a critical analysis: CF Stuckenberg, 'Grundrechtsdogmatik statt Rechtsgutslehre' (2011) 158 *Goltdammer's Archiv für Strafrecht*, 653, 656–57; G Jakobs, *Rechtsgüterschutz? Zur Legitimation des Strafrechts* (Paderborn, Schöningh, 2012) 16, 21.

[2] Protection of individuals cannot be the exclusive task because individuals depend on natural resources and institutional arrangements, too. On the individualistic approach, however, protecting such resources and institutions will be secondary.

be legitimate if they aim to prevent harm done to individuals (whether they can be ultimately justified depends on the question of wrongdoing and mediating principles). Within the scope of this contribution, I cannot discuss the details of theories that are based on the alternative view, that is, strictly collectivistic premises. Just to mention one example from German criminal law theory: Günther Jakobs expressed his anti-individualistic stance with the unequivocal formulation that the criminal law's task is not to protect 'every Tom, Dick and Harry' ('*Hinz und Kunz*').[3] But this is not a very plausible position if we look at the core of criminal norms that penalise bodily assaults, killings, sexual offences, burglaries, robberies etc. The point of such criminal prohibitions is to deliver communicative messages and to give potential offenders additional pragmatic reasons in form of sanction threats in order to prevent criminal offences.[4] The notion that this is done in order to protect moral values or a collective interest in society's continued existence[5] is much more artificial than the straightforward explanation that criminal norms indeed protect 'every Tom, Dick and Harry'. The individualistic approach has the advantage of 'better fit' with foundational concepts in contemporary constitutional theory. Modern constitutions which have been impregnated by liberal political philosophy are built around individuals' rights. Within these constitutional contexts, moral values and communitarian ideas might figure, too (for instance in a 'balancing of interests'), but they are not of primary normative concern. This characteristic feature of 'normative individualism'[6] ought to be replicated in criminal law and criminalisation theory.

If one agrees with these preliminary thoughts, the following question needs to be answered: *against what* should individuals be protected? It is often assumed that an approach that focuses on individuals' interests must or should lead to a defence of the harm principle and that the only alternative would be to abandon the protection-of-individuals camp and advocate, for instance, for a position of legal moralism. My aim is to challenge this assumption. In the following sections, I will discuss the strengths and weaknesses of the harm principle, and I will ultimately defend a different theory which regards *individuals' rights* as the protected object.

I. Strengths and Weaknesses of the Harm Principle

A common starting point for depicting the 'harm principle' is John Stuart Mill's proposition in 'On Liberty': 'that the only purpose for which power can be right-

---

[3] Jakobs, *Rechtsgüterschutz?*, above n 1 at 28.

[4] A von Hirsch, *Censure and Sanctions* (Oxford, Oxford University Press, 1993) 9–14; A von Hirsch, 'Warum soll die Strafsanktion existieren? Tadel und Prävention als Elemente einer Rechtfertigung' in A von Hirsch, U Neumann and K Seelmann (eds), *Strafe–Warum? Gegenwärtige Strafbegründungen im Lichte von Hegels Straftheorie* (Baden-Baden, Nomos, 2011) 43.

[5] See for the latter explanation Jakobs, *Rechtsgüterschutz?*, above n 1.

[6] See for this term D von der Pfordten, 'Five Elements of Normative Ethics: A General Theory of Normative Individualism' (2012) 15 *Ethical Theory and Moral Practice* 449.

fully exercised over any member of a civilised community, against his will, is to prevent harm to others.'[7] Mill argued in the broader context of political philosophy. The reference to harm serves to limit a community's power to coerce individuals (with legal means or with moral pressure) as well as individuals' interference with the lives of others.[8] Legal theorists adopted this foundational thought for the narrower purpose of criminalisation theory. Joel Feinberg and his seminal four volumes on *The Moral Limits of the Criminal Law*[9] must be mentioned here. Today, the harm principle is widely regarded as a master principle for criminalisation, at least in the English-speaking world.[10] Because the 'harm principle' is taken for granted, Anglo-American writers hardly ever inquire why this way of framing the issues gained such a high degree of popularity. But from a German perspective, considering that the 'harm principle' has hardly been known in our legal culture until rather recently,[11] this question may well be asked.

One strand of explanation points to Mill's commitment to political liberalism, which makes 'On Liberty' and the harm principle an attractive choice for contemporary authors. Political liberalism has shaped our mainstream opinions about the appropriate relationship between individual and communities or the state, both within the general intellectual Zeitgeist and within constitutional theory. Straightforward expressions of normative individualism such as Mill formulated are, thus, obvious starting points for contemporary reflections about the foundations of criminalisation theory. Compared to the German preference for 'legal good' (*Rechtsgut*) as a paraphrase of what the criminal law ought to protect, the clear positioning of the harm principle in political philosophy is an advantage. The political and philosophical roots of *Rechtsgüterschutz* (protection of legal goods) are much more obscure. From a historical perspective, was the emergence of this concept in German criminal law theory part of a liberal movement or not? Is there a conceptual closeness between political liberalism and *Rechtsgüterschutz*? There is an ongoing debate about these questions in the German literature and beyond.[12]

---

[7] JS Mill, 'On Liberty' (1859) in *On Liberty and Other Essays, Oxford World's Classics* (Oxford, Oxford University Press, 2008) 14.

[8] Mill, ibid, 14.

[9] J Feinberg, *The Moral Limits of the Criminal Law* (Oxford, Oxford University Press): vol I *Harm to Others* (1984); vol II *Offense to Others* (1985); vol III *Harm to Self* (1986); vol IV *Harmless Wrongdoing* (1988).

[10] Feinberg, *Harm to Others*, above n 9; J Raz, *The Morality of Freedom* (Oxford, Clarendon Press, 1986) 418–19; A Ashworth, *Principles of Criminal Law*, 5th edn (Oxford, Oxford University Press, 2006) ch 2; D Husak, *Overcriminalization. The Limits of the Criminal Law* (Oxford, Oxford University Press, 2008) 65–72; AP Simester and von Hirsch, *Crimes, Harms, and Wrongs: On the Principles of Criminalisation* (Oxford, Hart Publishing, 2011) 35–88.

[11] See, for introductions of the harm principle into the German discourse, G Seher, *Liberalismus und Strafe. Zur Strafrechtsphilosophie von Joel Feinberg* (Berlin, Dunker & Humblot, 2000); A von Hirsch, 'Der Rechtsgutsbegriff und das "Harm Principle"' (2002) 149 *Golddammer's Archiv für Strafrecht* 2.

[12] See for the discussion about the positioning of the *Rechtsgutsdoktrin* in the history of political ideas K Amelung, *Rechtsgüterschutz und Schutz der Gesellschaft* (Frankfurt, Athenäum, 1972); L Greco, *Lebendiges und Totes in Feuerbachs Straftheorie* (Berlin, Dunker & Humblot, 2009) 316–33; JL Guzmán Dalbora and T Vormbaum (eds), *Johann Michael Franz Birnbaum, Zwei Aufsaetze* (Münster, LIT Verlag, 2011); W Wohlers, 'Die Güterschutzlehre Birnbaums und ihre Bedeutung für die heutige Rechtsgutstheorie' (2012) 159 *Golddammer's Archiv für Strafrecht* 601.

But it is safe to conclude that the notion of *Rechtsgüterschutz* is not nearly as firmly and unequivocally rooted in political liberalism as is the harm principle.

A second strand of explanation for the harm principle's popularity refers to adaptions of Mill's general notion in criminal law theory in the second half of the twentieth century, mainly in Feinberg's ground-breaking work. Feinberg's approach bears testimony to the spirit of this period, which is characterised by a functionalist, consequentialist and anti-metaphysical approach to criminalisation. The harm principle fits perfectly with these premises: it is the product of a down-to-earth, secular, functionalist and consequentialist way of thinking *and* it rests on a liberal basis which values individuals' interests higher than communitarian ideals or the ideals of value ethics or religion. Its central feature is to focus on the *consequences* which an act has for the future lives of those persons who are affected by it. Joseph Raz points to 'making another worse off in a way which affects his future wellbeing',[13] Simester and von Hirsch to 'a diminution of the kind of things that make one's life go well' and to an 'impairment of resources in the sense of longer-term means or capabilities'.[14] Such explanations *why* typical crimes which form the core of criminal codes are objectionable demonstrate sober consequentialist reasoning. They keep complex normative assessments that are highly charged with cultural influences at bay.[15] Of course, it would be naïve to assume that value judgements can be avoided entirely – genuine 'naturalistic' arguments fail in a normative context such as criminal law theory as soon as premises are scrutinised (with the question *why* wellbeing and the availability of 'longer-term means and capabilities' are of high importance). However, answers can be given with modest normative assumptions that should seem reasonable to our contemporaries.

The harm principle cannot stand on its own as a master principle for decisions about criminalisation. A normative second element is needed when criminalisation theory starts with the notion of harm: the element of wrongdoing. Harmful outcomes which significantly impair well-being and resources can be the consequence of events which are of no interest to the criminal law (a thunderstorm, for instance). The point of introducing criminal norms is not to prevent harm as such (that would be factually impossible and beyond the tasks of the law) but to protect persons against other persons' acts, and not against *any* acts but only wrongful acts. Proponents of the harm principle routinely emphasise the requirement of wrongdoing as a second necessary condition.[16] Andreas von Hirsch has recently defended such a 'dual-element account (wrongfulness plus harm)'.[17]

---

[13] Raz, *The Morality of Freedom*, above n 10 at 414.

[14] Simester and von Hirsch, *Crimes, Harms, and Wrongs*, above n 10 at 36–37.

[15] By way of contrast, consider the much more problematic theory of value ethics with its claim that values exist in an objective sense: see M Scheler, *Der Formalismus in der Ethik und die materiale Wertethik* (Halle, Niemeyer, 1916).

[16] Feinberg, *Harm to Others*, above n 10 at 105–6; Husak, *Overcriminalization*, above n 10 at 71; A Duff *Answering for Crime* (Oxford, Hart Publishing, 2007) 126–35; Simester and von Hirsch, *Crimes, Harms, and Wrongs*, above n 10 at 38–40,

[17] 'Harm and Wrongdoing in Criminalisation Theory' (2014) 8 *Criminal Law and Philosophy* 245.

As this dual-element account has reached a remarkable stage of sophistication, are there any reasons *not* to be content with it? This question deserves attention because criticism of the harm principle has become widespread. Two strands of critical analysis should be distinguished. One rather popular view that can be called the 'criminologists' critique of the harm principle' describes contemporary criminal justice discourses and practices. The criminologists' critique concentrates on harm arguments that are used to promote an ever-increasing number of new criminal laws and repressive controlling strategies. The second group of authors who criticise the harm principle does not focus on the factual use and abuse of harm-related criminal policy arguments but on a conceptual analysis.

A criminologist's critique, prominently expressed by Bernard Harcourt, argues that the initially progressive reliance on the harm principle 'opened the door to the proliferation of harm arguments and brought about the collapse of the harm principle'.[18] In assessing his analysis, diagnosis and conclusions should be distinguished. The diagnosis is that arguments about harm in public discourses often refer to remote harms. Proponents of new legislation or law enforcement strategies claim that harmful outcomes might or will occur eventually if the conduct in question is not suppressed. A well-known line of reasoning argues that disorder and neglect (broken windows, graffiti, loitering, etc) promote developments which lead to the rise of serious crimes. Early interventions are, according to this thesis, necessary to prevent remote harms. Other examples are debates about eventual harm caused by media content, for instance, if others imitate what they see on the internet. Harcourt describes a number of cases where criminal policies have been based on notions of remote harm. On a descriptive level, it might be interesting to differentiate more clearly between politicians' honest reliance on remote harm arguments and cases where 'remote harm' serves to rationalise proposals which are driven by resentment against certain groups. But from a theorist's perspective, the more salient point is: what conclusions should be drawn from such descriptions? Does the fact that the harm principle can and has been (ab)used to promote repressive criminal law policies force us to give up on this principle? Is it correct to speak of a 'collapse of the harm principle'? The answer should be: no. Admittedly, Harcourt has a point with his diagnosis that the harm principle does not offer 'further guidance' how to evaluate the relevance of remote harms.[19] But this does not prove that criminal law theory *cannot* make progress at this point. Perhaps we should conclude instead that more efforts are needed to develop criteria which could restrict prima facie arguments in favour of criminalisation. Von Hirsch spelt out this point: we need to pay more attention to problems of fair attribution in order to decide which remote harms can justify prohibitions and which cannot.[20] Judgements about causality and prospective judgements about the likelihood of

---

[18] B Harcourt, 'The Collapse of the Harm Principle' (1999) 90 *Journal of Criminal Law & Criminology* 109, 186.

[19] Harcourt, ibid, 193. See also Duff, *Answering for Crime*, above n 16 at 138.

[20] A von Hirsch, 'Extending the Harm Principle: "Remote" Harms and Fair Imputation' in AP Simester and ATH Smith (eds), *Harm and Culpability* (Oxford, Clarendon Press, 1996) 259.

harm are *necessary, but not sufficient* conditions. Criminal law theory must develop criteria for the fair attribution of outcomes to actors. Even if extended causal links can be established between acts and harm which eventually occurs after a complex sequence of events, this does not suffice for an attribution of personal responsibility. In a complex world with myriads of causally related interactions, attribution of personal responsibility cannot be *the default position* for *everybody* who has made *any* causal contribution.

The criminologists' criticism falls short of effectively dismantling the harm principle. However, critical arguments are also raised from the perspective of criminal law theory. A dual-element analysis which applies the harm principle and, in a second step, the filtering question 'was this also wrongdoing?' will not always lead to adequate results. One major problem is that acts can evidently wrong someone despite the fact that this will not impact any of the victim's resources or capabilities that are needed in the future. In the newer literature, an increasing number of criminal law theorists agree that this is a weak spot for theories which claim that harm must be a *necessary* element.[21] The problem with the harm principle is its consequentialist, future-oriented view of what is blameworthy about a certain act. The notion of harm necessarily has this forward-looking character.[22] If the act in question could not possibly have any adverse effects on the victims' future lives, it will not be covered by the harm principle. And even if there is harm of some sort, a *full* description of the extent to which this act is objectionable often cannot be given by pointing to the harm done.

Von Hirsch does not see this as a major problem. In a recent article, he argues that 'it is not easy to think of an attractive case for criminalising offence where no form of harm is present.'[23] He then discusses insult as an example for wrong without harm. In considering whether harm occurs, von Hirsch distinguishes racial insults from other commonplace cases of insults, arguing that racial insults are harmful because they have 'the potential of restricting victims' opportunities to participate in the community's working and social life'.[24] This invites first the question of a sharp line between racial and 'commonplace' insults. Segregating effects depend on the severity of the insult and the likelihood of repetition, not on specific content (repeated hurtful non-racial insults at one's workplace, for instance, will taint the recipient's willingness to go there, too). Secondly, the issue of fair attribution would need to be addressed. Von Hirsch demands that the present conduct must 'implicitly affirm or underwrite the eventual injurious behaviour'. According to this standard, a racial insult that is part of a 'project' geared towards the exclusion of fellow

---

[21] A Ripstein, 'Beyond the Harm Principle' (2006) 34 *Philosophy & Public Affairs* 215; Duff, *Answering for Crime*, above n 16 at 126–38; A Brudner, *Punishment and Freedom* (Oxford, Oxford University Press, 2009) 9; H Stewart, 'The Limits of the Harm Principle' (2010) 4 *Criminal Law Review* 17; A Spena, 'Harmless Rapes? A False Problem for the Harm Principle' (2010) *Diritto & Questione Publicche* 497, 514–24; D Scoccia, 'In Defense of 'Pure' Legal Moralism' (2013) 7 *Criminal Law and Philosophy* 513, 517–19.

[22] Raz, *The Morality of Freedom*, above n 10 at 414.

[23] 'Harm and Wrongdoing', above n 17, text accompanying fn 22.

[24] Ibid, text accompanying fn 14.

citizens passes the test of fair attribution for remote harm (the remote harm being actual withdrawal from social live). But more often insults are spontaneous expressions of frustration and anger after an interpersonal interaction went wrong. In such situations, the choice of words is guided by the spontaneous evaluation what could hurt this individual opponent most effectively. It is debatable whether such expressions of strong emotions must be understood as affirming a larger project of exclusion. The example of racial insult shows that arguments about remote harm can be quite attenuated.

But this does not imply lack of wrongdoing. If a person fails to deal with anger in an appropriate way and lets off steam at another with abusive words, she wrongs the other person. This judgement stands independent of effects that her conduct might or might not have on the other's future life. Problems which are created by references to remote harm dissolve if one resorts straightforwardly to the concept of rights (see section III below). Speech can violate the rights of others, and this supports a prima facie case for criminalisation (prima facie only because countervailing reasons such as freedom of speech are of high importance).

Besides the case of insult, can one really say that there is no attractive case for criminalisation if no form of harm is present? In the literature, a couple of examples are discussed to demonstrate that this thesis is unconvincing. Arthur Ripstein used the example of unnoticed trespass.[25] A person is wronged if the privacy of her living space has been invaded by an intruder who uses the space for his own purposes. This evaluation holds if this trespass did not leave any tangible traces and the owner of the space never got notice of the incident. The other well-discussed example concerns sexual acts with an unconscious person, ie sexual acts which do not lead to bodily injuries and which are never revealed to the victim,[26] or, one could add, sexual acts with very young children under the same conditions. With a future-oriented, consequentialist concept of harm, it cannot be explained why this kind of conduct should be prohibited. The point of such examples is that the act will not have any negative impact on the victims' future lives. At this point, one might consider emphasising the generality and abstractness of norms which means that they are tailored to typical cases rather than atypical constellations. In many or perhaps most cases, victims *will* get to know about the trespass or sexual abuse which occurred while they were absent or unconscious or babies. Such ex post knowledge, once acquired, can have disturbing effects and thus affect their future lives. But this way of establishing harm is not a promising strategy. It paints a false picture of the wrong done because the objectionable feature is not the ex post information about the incident. Wrong is done at the point in time when the victims' private spheres are invaded.

Another approach relies on harm to *other persons* than the direct victim: we all might feel insecure if we know about the possibility of others invading our homes

---

[25] Ripstein, 'Beyond the Harm Principle', above n 21 at 218.
[26] See J Gardner and S Shute, 'The Wrongness of Rape' in J Horder (ed), *Oxford Essays in Jurisprudence*, Fourth series (Oxford, Oxford University Press, 2000) 193; Ripstein, 'Beyond the Harm Principle', above n 21 at 218.

or bodies while we are absent or unconscious, and therefore one might say that we are all harmed.[27] Similar arguments appear in discussions about racial insults: according to this view, *all* member of the vilified group are harmed. However, such referrals to collective interests exacerbate the problems connected with the issue of 'remote harm' – harm becomes very, very remote. And again, this is not the most plausible way to describe wrongdoing. In the case of insult as well as in the case of sexual abuse the actor targets an individual, and the violated rights of *this individual* should be taken seriously.

It is not the best solution to insist on separate categories of 'harm' and 'wrongdoing' and to stipulate that harm is a necessary condition. First, there are wrongful acts without harm. Secondly, this approach understates the importance of wrongdoing even in those cases when future lives are affected by diminished capabilities or resources. Consider an attack on sexual autonomy or bodily integrity. It is not the most plausible way to describe the blameworthiness of such an act with references to 'harm' and 'wrongdoing' as separate categories. The full degree of an act's reprehensible character cannot be grasped unless the feature of an *attack* figures prominently in the description.[28] The effects that physical and psychological wounds will have for the victims' future lives matter, too. But the main point of reference should be the violation of victims' rights at the time of the act.

II. Legal Moralism as the Only Alternative?

Why would criminal law theorists insist that harm as a future-oriented concept must be retained as one of two central pillars? I presume that Andreas von Hirsch defends a dual-element account because he assumes that the *only alternative* would be legal moralism. His commitment to the harm principle seems to be rooted in the conviction that to give it up would mean to abandon liberal premises. Within the Anglo-American debate about criminalisation, framing the discussion as a choice between *either* harm principle *or* legal moralism is common. However, if one assumes that there are not just these two alternatives, a solution could be to opt *neither* for the harm principle *nor* for legal moralism (see section IV below).

From a German perspective, the diagnosis that 'legal moralism has become the new orthodoxy in English-language criminal law theory'[29] is rather surprising. After all, there is a long tradition of opposition to moralism in criminal law. Theorists who share normative premises regarding the fundamental importance of individuals' liberty worry about the possible anti-liberal consequences of moralistic

---

[27] See Gardner and Shute, 'The Wrongness of Rape', above n 26 at 216; critically, Simester and von Hirsch, *Crimes, Harms, and Wrongs*, above n 10 at 47–48.

[28] RA Duff, 'Harms and Wrongs' (2001) 5 *Buffalo Criminal Law Review* 13, 21–26; Duff, *Answering for Crime*, above n 16 at 149–53.

[29] M Thorburn, 'Constitutionalism and the Limits of the Criminal Law' in RA Duff et al (eds), *The Structures of Criminal Law* (Oxford, Oxford University Press, 2011) 85, 86.

criminal policy discourses. Such a policy approach promotes tendencies towards over-criminalisation and illiberal content of criminal laws. From the perspective of legal theory, the main problem is a conflation of morality and legal concepts. Conflating morality and legality means a failure to pay proper attention to the law's tasks. 'Wrongdoing', in the context of criminalisation theory, must be recognised as a *legal* concept. Speaking of 'moral wrongs' should be avoided if the task is to define the boundaries between legal and illegal conduct.

The lack of distinction between the legal order and the moral world is most pronounced if one turns to simple or intuitionist versions of legal moralism. Simple versions claim that it is always a legitimate reason to prohibit conduct by criminal laws that the conduct is morally wrong.[30] Such views also prevail in public demands for criminalisation. If a broad, intuitionist understanding of moral wrongfulness seeps into criminal law theory, this means that criminal law theory will not be able to carefully evaluate ill-reflected proposals in the area of criminal policy. Accepting arguments about immorality for the entry decision in criminalisation theory widens the scope for criminal prohibitions considerably.[31]

Besides these concerns regarding outcomes in our criminal justice systems, there are numerous counter-arguments from the perspective of criminal law theory. If 'morality' refers to a version of 'true morality' (moral requirements that are defended independently of their actual acceptance in a given society), issues of epistemology and moral authority (who should establish the contents of 'true morality'?) arise. If arguments point to conventional morality, that is, if they suppose that certain rules are in fact broadly accepted as moral norms, problems with validating such claims can also be expected. Another critical question asks why a majority should be able to impose their norms on a minority if there would be nothing to be gained for society as a whole. A standard move in dealing with this question presents conventional morality as beneficial for all, for instance with the argument that it is the glue which holds society together. This might be defensible as a general thesis but for a decision about criminalisation one would need to make the point that a *specific prohibition* is necessary to prevent a weakening of societal cohesion. The speculative nature of such pseudo-empirical statements is obvious. And for both true morality as well as conventional morality, the crucial normative problem is to justify why pursuing moral rightness should be more important than liberty rights. In pre-constitutional periods of legal history, statements about an intimate relation between morality and the criminal law encountered lesser misgivings than nowadays, when normative individualism has gained the victory over competing concepts.

More refined versions of legal moralism, such as Antony Duff's proposal for a 'modest legal moralism',[32] guard more carefully against simple conclusions which follow the logic 'morality forbids it, therefore let's criminalise it'. Duff argues that conduct's being morally wrong can be reason for a criminal prohibition – provided,

[30] See M Moore, *Placing Blame* (Oxford, Oxford University Press, 1997) 69–70.
[31] Von Hirsch, 'Harm and Wrongdoing', above n 17.
[32] RA Duff, 'Towards a Modest Legal Moralism' (2014) 8 *Criminal Law and Philosophy* 217.

however, that the wrong is a *public* wrong, that is, a wrong that concerns the public and that requires a collective response. According to this proposal, it is necessary to single out a *smaller subcategory* of public wrongs from the larger category of morally objectionable conduct in general.[33] This ameliorates the problems with legal moralism because not *any* breach of conventional or true morality counts as prima facie reason for criminalisation.

However, from a German or Continental European perspective, a puzzling aspect of *all* contemporary Anglo-American versions of 'legal moralism' still is the reference to *moral* wrongs. Why should morality be invoked in the context of a legal discourse? The answer to this question probably can be found if we turn to the opposite notion of 'legal'. In the Anglo-American discussion, the underlying premise seems to be that 'legal' necessarily refers to *positive law*, and to positive law *only*. This view assumes that either arguments are based on the content of positive law within a given legal system, or, if not, that *any kind of normative evaluation* automatically falls in the second category of moral evaluations. This way of framing the issues in a dichotomy means to assign the whole area of transnational, pre-positivistic thinking about criminal law theory to the world of morality. But such a large category of 'morality' that encompasses every kind of assessment, from references to conventional morality to all kinds of normative arguments in the context of criminal law theory, is rather broad. A project like Duff's version of 'modest legal moralism' might be more promising if it would avoid the term 'moralism' altogether. It is predictable that criticism against the older school of traditional moralism spills over to an approach which shares the substantive in its label.

The preferable solution would be a *tripartite approach* which distinguishes: first, conventional moral norms and systems of a 'true' morality that are discussed independent of legal concepts; second, legal arguments in a pre-positivistic stage; and third, legal norms belonging to a system of positive law. The underlying assumption is that the distinction between 'legal' and 'moral' must be taken more seriously – and not just as a matter of conceptual clarity but because the tasks assigned to legal norms are different from the tasks assigned to moral norms. For a theory of criminalisation, the relevant one of the three categories is the second: arguments in a pre-positivistic stage that are, however, embedded in the framework of considerations what the law has to achieve.

III. The Tasks of Law

If criminalisation theory is seen as a transnational enterprise, valuable elements can be assembled from the history of ideas in different national streams of tradition. Citations of John Stuart Mill's work pay tribute to his lucid account of liberty as a central cornerstone in political philosophy (and today also in constitutional the-

---

[33] Duff, ibid.

ory). For delineating the tasks of the law, based on the assumption that these tasks are *different* from those assigned to morality, it is worthwhile to consider some passages in the works of Immanuel Kant. Unlike some German colleagues, I do not assume that criminal law theory can be developed more or less exclusively on the basis of interpreting Kant's texts (or any other canonised philosophical text from the late 18th or early 19th century). However, a somewhat sceptical attitude regarding a quasi-theological approach to 'holy scriptures'[34] does, of course, not preclude acknowledging the roots of important ideas in political philosophy.

My point of reference is the concise definition of law in a general sense (carefully distinguished from positive law) in Kant's 'Metaphysics of Morals' (*Metaphysik der Sitten*). The 'Metaphysics of Morals' consists of two different parts, the *Rechtslehre* (which includes a general part of legal theory and more specific considerations about branches of the law) and the *Tugendlehre* (moral theory, also with a general part and detailed descriptions of moral duties). The section titled 'Introduction to Law' summarises what law is: 'the sum of the conditions under which the choice of one can be united with the choice of another in accordance with a universal law of freedom.'[35] This passage describes the core task for all legal regulations, including the criminal law. The central purpose of law is to assign spheres of liberty to persons and to grant that these spheres of liberty are to be defended with legal means against intrusions by other persons.[36] This is a classical liberal, non-communitarian notion: the law should protect individuals' liberty rights and *not be focused* on a defence of public values or collective interests. Admittedly, for our contemporary societies with their historically unknown degrees of social, economic and technological complexity, Kant's vision is somewhat too restrained and too individualistic. Nowadays, persons are even more than in prior centuries dependent on institutions such as efficient and just administrations and courts, a functioning currency system etc. Collective interests regarding such essential institutions can require criminal norms, too. However, the indisputable necessity to protect genuine collective interests does not render the classical liberal definition of law otiose. A core task for the criminal law still consists in protecting individuals' spheres of liberty against intrusions by others.[37]

The point I want to make in this subsection is that criminalisation theory should

---

[34] See T Hörnle, 'Strafrecht und Rechtsphilosophie: Traditionen und Perspektiven' in S Grundmann et al (eds), *Festschrift zum zweihundertjährigen Bestehen der Juristischen Fakultät der Humboldt Universität Berlin* (Berlin, De Gruyter, 2010) 1265.

[35] I Kant, *Metaphysics of Morals*, ed AW Wood, transl M Gregor (Cambridge, Cambridge University Press, 1996; orig 1797), Introduction to the Doctrine of Right, § B. ['Das Recht ist also der Inbegriff der Bedingungen, unter denen die Willkür des einen mit der Willkür des anderen nach einem allgemeinen Gesetze der Freiheit zusammen vereinigt werden kann.'] Cf W Weischedel (ed), *Werkausgabe Band VIII* (Frankfurt, Suhrkamp, 1977) 337.

[36] Thorburn, 'Constitutionalism', above n 29 at 88.

[37] Thorburn, ibid, 100–102 distinguishes between criminal law and civil law and argues (at 100) that 'criminal wrongs are those that demonstrate a willingness . . . to displace the legal rules themselves.' I disagree with him at this point with my assumption that *both* civil law and criminal law protect individuals' rights directly (in my view, the difference between civil law and criminal law has to do with the very limited means of the civil law).

begin with an explicit account of the law's tasks and a clear understanding that the background must be a conception of the *state*. The state enforces legal rules with coercive measures, and the coerciveness of legal measures is a particular prominent feature of criminal law in action. Justifications of punishment and criminalisation which (like Antony Duff's approach) focus on a soft vision of a 'community' which calls members of this community to account[38] do not portray the criminal law adequately. They fail to distinguish between civil society and the state and they pay insufficient attention to the fact that the state acts when criminal laws are enacted and enforced. This blurs distinctions between rather different collectives: moral communities (which can also be religious communities) and their norms; civil society and shared public values; the state and legal norms. Moral communities as rule-giving communities have a wider set of tasks than civil societies: the former are concerned with norms for considerate interpersonal dealings in general, while civil society should only be concerned with rules regarding public morality. Turning to the most powerful of these associations – that is, the state – tasks should be assigned in an even more narrow way. Justifying penal laws and their enforcement with the state's monopoly on violence is a different matter from justifying censure by civil society or by a moral community.[39] It is an appropriate task for civil society to discuss public values in their state of flux and to defend those public values which are widely shared in all kind of public discourses. However, the tasks for the criminal law should be kept narrow, to the core of protecting individuals where they are most vulnerable against attacks by others.

IV. The Concept of 'Rights'

Assuming that law in general and the criminal law in particular should protect individuals' spheres of liberty against intrusions by others leads to the following definition of the protected objects: the rights of others. A first step for criminalisation theory should be the question: Does this kind of conduct violate the right of another person? With this approach, criminalisation theory is tied to the aforementioned classical liberal concept of the law.

Obviously, however, reference to the concept of 'rights' does not answer all our questions. It needs clarification: what is meant when invoking 'rights'? At first view, the obvious choice would be to point to rights as they are granted within a given system of positive law. Within positive law, a human rights catalogue in a constitution could be the relevant point of reference; but so too could be rights established in other parts of the legal system, for instance, property rights or personality rights acknowledged in civil law. This might lead to plausible results if the system of positive law recognises a comprehensive set of subjective (that is, individuals') rights,

---

[38] Duff, *Answering for Crime*, above n 16, ch 2; Duff, 'Towards a Modest Legal Moralism', above n 32.
[39] Thorburn, 'Constitutionalism', above n 29 at 87, 96.

particularly in a modern written constitution with an extensive catalogue of human rights; indeed, I have explored this avenue to criminalisation theory with regard to the German constitution and German constitutional jurisprudence where we can find such a comprehensive set of subjective rights.[40]

Von Hirsch, however, has expressed some scepticism regarding the idea of using the constitution as a starting point. For one thing, he fears that constitutional rights are too strong in the sense that it might become difficult to counter demands for criminalisation with references to mediating principles.[41] However, this worry can be dispelled: almost all constitutional rights are open to a process of weighing against countervailing reasons. Secondly, von Hirsch is concerned that some constitutional references to human rights catalogues might backfire. He argues that constitutional human rights clauses have been invoked for anti-liberal purposes, that is, as reasons to restrict liberty. The example he refers to is a ruling by the German Federal Administrative Court (Bundesverwaltungsgericht) about the prohibition of so-called peep-shows.[42] The court used the human dignity clause in the German Constitution (Artikel 1 I *Grundgesetz* (GG)) to justify prohibitions which ignored the choices of adult women working in such establishments. The problem with this ruling was, however, not a reference to a constitutional right as subjective right. On the contrary, the Court referred to human dignity as an *objective value* in order to argue why the women's autonomous choices, particularly their waiver of their subjective human dignity rights, was deemed irrelevant. This positioning of human dignity as objective value over human dignity as subjective right deserves criticism. A liberal conception of subjective rights must conceptualise them as 'defensive rights' (*Abwehrrechte*) which includes the choice to waive the exercise of any of these defensive rights. If defensive rights are waived, this decision should not be overridden by references to human rights as an 'objective value'.[43] The peep-show decision is problematic for this reason; but it does not demonstrate that references to constitutional subjective rights might lead to illiberal criminal laws.

Von Hirsch also invokes constitutional theory to raise a fundamental objection against references to constitutional human rights catalogues in criminalisation theory. According to a traditional, narrow understanding of human rights, such rights have a single purpose: to assign defensive rights to individuals *against the state* – but not against other individuals.[44] But this is neither state of the art in constitutional theory nor can one develop a plausible portrayal of the state's raison d'être on this basis. Within constitutional theory, the *Drittwirkung* (the third-party effect)

[40] T Hörnle, *Grob anstössiges Verhalten. Strafrechtlicher Schutz von Moral, Gefühlen und Tabus* (Frankfurt, Klostermann, 2005).

[41] A von Hirsch, 'Harm und Offence: Schädigungsprinzip und Belästigungsprinzip als Kriterien für die Kriminalisierung von Verhalten' in H Putzke et al (eds), *Strafrecht zwischen System und Telos. Festschrift für Rolf Dietrich Herzberg zum siebzigsten Geburtstag* (Tübingen, Mohr Siebeck, 2008) 915, 928–29; Simester and von Hirsch, *Crimes, Harms, and Wrongs*, above n 10 at 136.

[42] See BVerwGE 64, 274; von Hirsch, 'Harm und Offence', above n 41 at 927; Simester and von Hirsch, *Crimes, Harms, and Wrongs*, above n 10 at 135.

[43] See T Hörnle, 'Criminalizing Behaviour to Protect Human Dignity' (2012) 6 *Criminal Law and Philosophy* 307.

[44] See for this point Simester and von Hirsch, *Crimes, Harms, and Wrongs*, above n 10 at 134–35.

of human rights is intensively discussed. Starting with the thesis that, within citizen-to-citizen relationships, human rights cannot be *directly* invoked, the conclusion is to stipulate protective duties of the state within the triangle citizen–citizen–state. The state accordingly must protect human rights not only against interferences by state officials but also against interferences by fellow citizens.[45] Within political philosophy, it would be equally unconvincing to deny the foundational importance of such protective efforts. Of course, *once* a state has been formed, it becomes an important function of human rights to protect citizens against abuses of power by state officials. However, for the *antecedent* justification of having a state at all, one does not need to be a fervent supporter of Hobbes' position in all details to acknowledge that protective duties supply at least *one of the state's central functions* (to be supplemented in modern contexts with others tasks).

This leaves us with yet another objection raised by von Hirsch against the idea of anchoring criminalisation theory in constitutional law. How could one, if this must be the starting point, proceed if a legal system does *not* include a written constitution, or a fragmentary constitution without a comprehensive catalogue of human rights?[46] And is not focusing on positive law in general an unsatisfactory solution from the perspective of transnational criminal law theory? Would we not lose important perspectives if discussions about criminalisation were restricted to lawyers who limit their attention to their system of national positive law? Such questions should be taken seriously.

Moreover, even within a given system of positive law, arguments which rely on the identification of rights as acknowledged in positive law will encounter difficulties. It might be difficult to pinpoint a legal rule in constitutional or civil law which clearly affirms a specific right. Or one might find a legal provision somewhere which clearly formulates a right – however, the right might be of a rather trivial nature.

For these reasons, criminalisation theory cannot be anchored in a simple, genuinely positivistic way. This is not to say that the notion of rights as granted in a given legal system should be entirely ignored. If a written constitution *does* list human rights, this should be an *indicator* that individuals might legitimately expect to be protected against acts by others which violate those rights.[47] But beyond such constitutional rights, criminalisation theory needs to work with the concept of 'rights of others' in a wider sense.

If positive law is not the only basis for finding a right, how should we proceed? What should count as a right? The answer might appear simple to some theorists. If one presupposes the existence of natural law and natural rights,[48] it would be an obvious move to point to such natural rights. However, ontological assertions, ie

---

[45] See W Rüfner, 'Grundrechtsadressaten' in J Isensee and P Kirchhof (eds), *Handbuch des Staatsrechts*, Vol IX, 3rd edn (Heidelberg, CF Müller, 2011) § 197.

[46] Von Hirsch, 'Harm und Offence', above n 41 at 926; Simester and von Hirsch, *Crimes, Harms, and Wrongs*, above n 10 at 134.

[47] The emphasis must, of course, be on the word 'indicator': in the end, all things including countervailing rights and other mediating principles considered, the recommendation might be not to criminalise such acts.

[48] J Finnis, *Natural Law and Natural Rights* (Oxford, Clarendon Press, 1980).

assertions that rights *exist as legal rights independent of any legislative process*, are problematic.[49] Talking about 'rights claims' is the more accurate description to distinguish the prescriptive statement, 'should be acknowledged as a right,' from the descriptive statement, 'has been acknowledged as a right in the legislative proceedings'. The point for our purpose is not to 'find' a right. The point is to give reasons which support the claim of a right which ought to be protected against interferences by others with the means of the criminal law.

V. Legal Rights Claims versus Moral Rights

What could be the content of such rights claims? At this point, the discussion should be tied back to the preceding section about the role of the law. If one accepts a narrow, classical liberal understanding of the law's function (to protect spheres of liberty), the consequence is a strict distinction between moral rights on the one hand, legal rights claims on the other hand. Within discussions about criminalisation, it is essential to ask the right kind of questions and to avoid lines of thoughts which are appropriate in the area of morality but not for claims concerning legal rights. For instance: Thomas Scanlon's question 'what do we owe to each other?'[50] is both important and legitimate in the context of moral philosophy but should be avoided in a legal context. For this reason, I would argue against some of Simester's and von Hirsch's considerations regarding the offence principle as one of their prima facie reasons in support of criminalisation. Simester and von Hirsch stipulate that the wrong of offensive behaviour lies in the 'failure to treat others with due consideration and respect'.[51] If the task is to describe moral duties and corresponding moral rights, it makes perfect sense to argue that persons have a right to be treated with due consideration and respect. However, my point is that this is not the right way to approach claims of legal rights in the context of criminalisation theory. The same criticism applies to a proposal made by Kurt Seelmann, based on the idea that we owe each other the protection of conditions that underpin identity.[52] Legal rights which deserve to be protected with the means of the criminal law can only demand from others that they abstain from intruding into an individual's sphere of liberty. More demanding expectations against other individuals[53] should in general[54] be left to the sphere of morality.

[49] See JL Mackie, *Ethics: Inventing Right and Wrong* (London, Penguin Books, 1977) 172–80.
[50] See T Scanlon, *What We Owe to Each Other* (Cambridge MA, Harvard University Press, 1998).
[51] Simester and von Hirsch *Crimes, Harms, and Wrongs*, above n 10 at 100.
[52] K Seelmann, 'Was schützt der liberale Rechtsstaat?' in L Siep et al (eds), *Von der religiösen zur säkularen Begründung staatlicher Normen. Zum Verhältnis von Religion und Politik in der Philosophie der Neuzeit und in rechtssystematischen Fragen der Gegenwart* (Tübingen, Mohr Siebeck, 2012) 171.
[53] Expectations regarding the community's solidarity, for instance financial support, are another matter – but not to be covered in our context because laws based on social solidarity are not criminal laws.
[54] I have to leave open whether exceptionally severe breaches of duties to act (such as: not using one's mobile phone for an emergency call to prevent the imminent death of a fellow citizen might justify a

This way of describing the protected objects as 'rights of others' should not be understood as an argument that moral judgments have no role to play in criminalisation theory. Penal censure must be comprehensible from a moral point of view. This means that the *final evaluation* of certain conduct as being worthy of penal censure must not stand in contradiction to fundamental moral principles of attribution. For instance, because our moral judgements about an act depend on foreseeability of outcomes and the actor's intentions, the penal law must integrate such filtering questions. My plea for a separation between legal rights and moral rights concerns the *entrance decision* of criminalisation theory, the fundamental question for which protective purpose criminal prohibitions may be used. This does not preclude assigning morality a filtering role in further steps on the way to the final decision what to penalise and what not to penalise. Moral principles can be exclusionary rules but they should not be the primary reasons for criminalisation.

Making a 'rights claim' in the sense used here must therefore follow this line of reasoning: regarding important aspects of their lives, people are entitled to spheres of liberty which they can manage according to their own choices; intrusions into such important spheres of liberty are to be assessed as a violation of a right; rights violations are prima facie reasons for criminalisation. This invites the next questions: how should we determine what counts as an important sphere of liberty, what is important, and why so? Answers often will include references to functional aspects and future well-being. Such considerations mirror those which appear in the context of the harm principle. If we ask why bodily integrity is important, an obvious answer is, for instance, that severe injuries have the effect of pre-empting many opportunities to fashion one's life in terms of work, traveling, leisure activities, etc. Similar thoughts apply to property: free disposition over certain items is a condition for leading an autonomous life.

However, functional aspects do not cover the whole terrain.[55] Bodily integrity has meaning *beyond* its functional value. The reason for this is that the modern concept of a person is highly dependent on the physical reality of a body (once the idea of an immortal soul as the true incarnation of a person has lost its standing in the 'western' world). We presume that the body is an important object of one's own designing efforts, and at the same time sacrosanct for other persons' choices. This means that unwanted intrusions into bodily integrity are in themselves taken seriously, independent of broken bones, wounds, and the like. The same reasoning applies, even more forcefully, to sexual autonomy. In contemporary societies, the

departure from the rule. See for the discussion about solidarity: A von Hirsch, U Neumann and K Seelmann (eds), *Solidarität im Strafrecht. Zur Funktion und Legitimation strafrechtlicher Solidaritätspflichten* (Baden-Baden, Nomos, 2013).

[55] In Anglo-American legal theory, the analytical discussion about rights has focused on a dichotomy between what is labelled 'Interest Theory' and 'Will Theory', see MH Kramer, NE Simmonds and H Steiner, *A Debate over Rights* (Oxford, Oxford University Press, 1998). My position with its emphasis on persons' choices is in some ways closer to the latter theory. However, I presume that this also can be related to persons' interests. After all, an explanation *why* bodily integrity and sexual autonomy are important beyond aspects of future well-being points to shared human interests. Persons would describe a vital interest in being left alone if this is what one wants.

right to decide freely about one's sexual preferences and practices goes hand in hand with strong condemnation for unwanted interferences. 'Bodily integrity' and 'sexual autonomy' describe important spheres of liberty the value of which is not or not entirely dependent on functional and future-orientated aspects. The more intimate a sphere of liberty is tied to the idea *what it means to be a person*, the more should freedom from others' intrusions be considered intrinsically valuable.

VI. A Final Remark

Over many years, Andreas von Hirsch has been a wonderful friend and colleague – many thanks to him for stimulating discussions and the insistence on a liberal concept of the criminal law. Sharing his critical views on positions of legal moralism, I hope to have shown that this does not necessarily compel us to base criminalisation theory on the notions of harm and offence. It could be an alternative to develop a restrained, liberal version of criminal law by relying on 'rights of others' in a way that is not tied inescapably to positive law.

10

The Harm Principle and the Protection of 'Legal Goods' (*Rechtsgüterschutz*): a German Perspective

WINFRIED HASSEMER

I. Dedication

Andreas von Hirsch, our friend and colleague, has – to our and, I am convinced, also to his own happiness – some time ago moved the centre of his life and academic activity to Germany, joining the Institute of Criminology and Legal Philosophy at the Goethe University Frankfurt. Those who know his cosmopolitan outlook will not expect this to have resulted in great changes – after all, our honorand has for many decades been part of the fellowship of German criminal law theorists and legal philosophers.

A. Methods

The contribution Andreas has made to our ways of thinking and to the main assumptions and debates seems to me nevertheless to have grown enormously in recent years, in its extent, depth and profile. Monographs[1] and conference papers[2] evidence the distinctiveness of his theoretical contributions: engaging with the foundational concepts of Continental criminal law and legal philosophy, von Hirsch reconstructs these according to the Anglo-American methodology that shaped him intellectually, and enriches them with carefully considered additions, modifications and new perspectives.

This is – at any rate, in German criminal law theory – a noteworthy way of practising legal comparison, and, to my mind, the only sensible one. The application of this method, which leaves both sides of the legal comparison able to speak, presupposes however that the comparative scholar knows his way about on both sides of

---

[1] See, eg, A von Hirsch, *Fairness, Verbrechen und Strafe: Strafrechtstheoretische Abhandlungen* (Berlin, Berliner Wissenschaftsverlag, 2005): hereafter von Hirsch, *Fairness*.

[2] Eg A von Hirsch, K Seelmann and W Wohlers (eds), *Mediating Principles. Begrenzungsprinzipien bei der Strafbegründung* (Baden-Baden, Nomos, 2006).

the legal-cultural ocean, and is therefore not reduced to bean-counting exercises but is able to grasp structures and foundations – abilities that German criminal law scholars tend to lack when it comes to foreign criminal law. The (elsewhere rightly admired) complexity of our doctrinal structures, and the richness of the questions we pose, are diminished by our traditional ignorance of foreign criminal legal systems, including their foundations and critiques.[3]

There are no signs that this is going to change anytime soon. With a few exceptions, our efforts at comparative criminal law scholarship will continue to depend on friendly colleagues from other countries who take the trouble to learn our language, study our system of criminal law and its theoretical foundations, listen carefully and then explain our system back to us afresh from their different and illuminating perspectives.[4]

Von Hirsch works differently. He mentions how things are done 'back home' only when this aids our line of thought. He chooses the subject-matter of his scholarly work according to the relevance of the issue for German criminal law theory. He enters the discussions that are important to us, and contributes facts, questions and ideas from his academic and policy experiences that engage directly with our own understanding of the issue.

B. Objects of inquiry

Three areas in particular have been presented to us by von Hirsch in this scholarly style.[5] These areas encompass both criminal law theory and penal theory, the central building blocks of our Continental-European criminal law scholarship. He treats them in a manner that reveals his Anglo-American scholarly training. The argument does not merely develop as a logical sequence. Each central point is additionally supported by references to insights and experiences which are congenial to the way criminal lawyers think, but are in Germany traditionally not derived from criminal law theory or closely connected thereto. Criminology[6] and ethics[7] in particular are sources from which von Hirsch additionally draws. He also has no principled objection to supporting his arguments with assumptions based on everyday morality or everyday experience. In this way we frequently encounter his thoughts

---

[3] See, for instance, the polite but noticeably critical remarks by G Fletcher, F Munoz Conde and A Zoll in A Eser, W Hassemer and B Burkhardt (eds), *Die deutsche Strafrechtswissenschaft vor der Jahrtausendwende. Rückbesinnung und Ausblick. Dokumentation einer Tagung vom 3. bis 6. Oktober 1999 in der Berlin-Brandenburgischen Akademie der Wissenschaften* (Munich, CH Beck, 2000) 235ff (comments by G Fletcher), 199ff (comments by F Munoz Conde) and 283ff (comments by A Zoll).

[4] A recent example is the well-reasoned and critical discussion of the main problems raised by the doctrine of legal goods in Y-W Kim, 'Verhaltensdelikte versus Rechtsgutsverletzungen – Zur aktuellen Diskussion um einen materiellen Verbrechensbegriff' (2012) 124 *Zeitschrift für die gesamte Strafrechtswissenschaft* 591.

[5] See, on this point, also U Neumann's Introduction to von Hirsch, *Fairness*, 13.

[6] A good example is A von Hirsch and C Shearing, 'Freizügigkeit und Generalprävention. Die Ausschließung aus dem öffentlichen Raum' in von Hirsch, *Fairness*, 243.

[7] See, eg, A von Hirsch, 'Ethische Fragen zur Videoüberwachung des öffentlichen Raums' in von Hirsch, *Fairness*, 221.

concerning our fundamental theoretical concerns wrapped in the cloak of Anglo-American reasoning and rhetoric. This certainly does them no harm.

The three areas are: the justification of state punishment; the consequences of this justification for sentencing theory; and the notion of legally protected interests (*Rechtsgüterschutz* or protection of 'legal goods'). These are well suited for transatlantic legal comparisons, since they are traditionally also of interest in Germany, and at the same time their treatment in the Anglo-American tradition is independent and distinct. For this reason they can serve a bridging function.

As regards the first theme, the German debate concerning the aims and justification of state punishment generally draws a basic distinction which is not central to von Hirsch's theoretical arsenal. We tend to discuss these questions by contrasting consequence-oriented and justice-oriented approaches (prevention and retribution), dividing under these opposing headings issues concerning the justification, criticism, traditionalism and modernity of various theories of punishment; and using this contrast as a point of entry into questions concerning the degree of empirical support for thoughts and judgements about punishment.

For von Hirsch, the argument runs on different tracks.[8] He construes the problem – with reference to the English tradition – through a category that we also recognise as centrally important: 'commensurate deserts' or proportionality, which appears to belong to retributivist thinking. This then gives rise to the difficult comparative question whether and how this line of reasoning can be incorporated into hundreds of years of Continental criminal law theorising which, after all, also has important roots in ethics and in criminology. A central tenet of both theories is, however, clear and convergent: the punished individual should be burdened as little as possible.[9]

In this way, and regarding the second theme, theoretical conclusions regarding the point of state punishment connect effortlessly to the criteria of just sentencing that follow from them. The notion central to von Hirsch's conclusions is 'censure'.[10] This notion is also difficult to fit into our traditional debates. The connection von Hirsch has drawn to a modern variant of preventive theories, positive general prevention, stokes the flames of comparative law fires. After all, German understandings of positive general prevention have tended to conceive of the purpose of punishment in terms of beneficial consequences, while the notion of censure reflects a conception of punishment that is focused on the offender and his criminal acts – a conception that is, to put the point cautiously, not close to consequentialist understandings of punishment. Von Hirsch's work leads, in its further development, to many instructive arguments that culminate in concrete and convincingly grounded conclusions regarding the determination of a just sentence.[11]

---

[8] See, eg, A von Hirsch, 'Tatproportionalität und Sanktionshärte – Führt ein tatproportionales Strafzumessungsmodell zu strengeren Sanktionen?' in von Hirsch, *Fairness*, 175.

[9] I will elaborate on this aspect below.

[10] See, eg, A von Hirsch and T Hörnle, 'Positive Generalprävention und Tadel' in von Hirsch, *Fairness*, 19; A von Hirsch, 'Die Existenz der Institution Strafe: Tadel und Prävention als Elemente einer Rechtfertigung' in von Hirsch, *Fairness*, 41.

[11] Eg A von Hirsch, 'Proportionale Strafen für Jugendliche' in von Hirsch, *Fairness*, 157.

In this chapter, however, I want to focus on the third theme of von Hirsch's work: his use of the harm principle, and its relationship to the protection of legal goods in our criminal law.

II. Harm Orientations through the Doctrine of Legal Goods and the Harm Principle

Mainstream criminal law theory knows more than one way of orienting criminalisation norms about the prevention of harm. Addressing this orientation in his third theme, von Hirsch provides neither a new systematic place nor a new meaning for the German doctrine of the '*Rechtsgut*' (legal good) but a better understanding thereof and a fresh context.[12] It gets a new neighbour, the transatlantic harm principle,[13] with which it can make friends or engage in arguments; for me it is still an open question whether the two will, in the end, turn out to be compatible, whether they will be mutually enriching or whether they will be locked in inconclusive contestation.

Von Hirsch is, with regard to this third topic, noticeably more guarded than in his other work. Having compared the harm principle and the doctrine of 'legal goods', he asks modestly 'to what extent the result can make a useful contribution to ongoing debates about the German concept of the "Rechtsgut".'[14]

My answer is that it certainly can. All in all, Anglo-American and German approaches to criminal law theory can connect better and more effectively in the chapter entitled 'harm principle and the doctrine of legal goods' than in the areas concerning the justification of punishment, and in sentencing theory.[15] Closer examination shows a number of inspirations, confirmations, queries and lessons which our doctrine of legal goods may expect to receive from Anglo-American legal circles. I will not list all of these, but concentrate on those which are sufficiently fundamental to cast our debates in a fresh light. If one were to gather these, with a little force, under one roof, one could say that they concern the harm orientation of the criminal law in theory and practice; under this roof, it seems to me, the harm principle and the doctrine of legal goods can stand together and understand each other.

A. Divisions

As far as the concept and structure of the theory of legal goods are concerned, von Hirsch starts his essay about the harm principle and the doctrine of legal goods with

---

[12] For me, von Hirsch's central publication in this context is A von Hirsch, 'Der Rechtsgutbegriff und das "Harm Principle"' in von Hirsch, *Fairness*, 69.

[13] Ibid, 73ff.

[14] Ibid, 70.

[15] See especially section I.B above.

the familiar distinction between the ('immanent') internal-systemic function and the ('transcendental') critical function of the doctrine of legal goods.[16] The – limited – value of this distinction becomes evident in von Hirsch's treatment. After all, the distinction is just an analytical device to split off one already clearly defined (internal) function of the concept of a legal good, with the aim of separating it from the area that really requires further thought, thus narrowing the latter down in order to identify it more precisely. The internal-systemic functioning of the doctrine of legal goods is obvious, and we benefit from it when dealing with analytical questions; but it cannot be of any help when the aim is to provide criminal law theory with arguments of a substantive kind that would enable criminal law policy to be more transparent, principled and controllable. The internal-systemic aspect can thus safely be left to the textbooks; it helps them to present the special part of the criminal law as an ordered system, arranged according to the relevant 'legal good' or legally protected interest or value. Correspondingly, the sections of the German Criminal Code are divided according to legal good, ranging from 'offences against the security of the state' to 'offences against the safety and liberty of the person' and 'offences committed in public office'; and thus some structure is given to the Code.

Yet, if one wants to know whether the offences contained in such a section reflect good criminal law policy, the internal-systemic perspective can only give an internal-systemic answer. It can, for instance, establish that the legislator introduced a systemic flaw by bundling different legal goods together in the same section of the Code.[17] But it cannot tell us more. This is, of course, not insignificant, and at least one can reach some definite results here; but it is – on this side of the Atlantic just as on the other – not a substantive, let alone a critical, argument.

Now, one should not – at least in our system of codified law – brush such internal-systemic insights aside too quickly with legal-theoretical considerations. From a legal-sociological perspective it is certainly noteworthy that the notion of the legal good has stood the test of time as an ordering principle for new criminal legislation, that it has proven itself to be practically sensible and effective. The concept of legal goods is in use both analytically and doctrinally and shapes the daily discourse of criminal lawyers. And it probably suggests, if one looks carefully, something else too: that the legislator, throughout countless legislative reforms and modifications of the German Criminal Code, has seen fit to leave unchanged the historical order of the different sections of the Code – which starts with treason[18] and resisting public officials and only subsequently moves to offences against the person, with offences of environmental damage slotted in towards the end. This may be considered a signalling of their hierarchy and significance that is not exactly congenial to

---

[16] Von Hirsch, 'Rechtsgutbegriff' above n 12 at 69. See also my book *Theorie und Soziologie des Verbrechens. Ansätze zu einer praxisorientierten Rechtsgutslehre* (Frankfurt, Athenäum, 1973) 19ff.

[17] This is what the legislator has done in Chapter 30 of the German Criminal Code; compare the criticism and references in H Matt and J Renzikowski (eds), *StGB-Kommentar* (Munich, Franz Vahlen, 2013) § 331 marginal note 5f (commentary by S Sinner).

[18] For an instructive review of the legislative reform process in particular cases, see U Kindhäuser, U Neumann and H-U Paeffgen (eds), *Nomos-Kommentar zum StGB*, 3rd edn (Baden-Baden, Nomos, 2013) Vor § 80 f marginal notes 2ff and 15ff (commentary by H-U Paeffgen).

the constitutional order instituted by the German Basic Law.[19] Such issues are important. But von Hirsch's concern is with the transcendental: with the critical function of harm-orientation doctrines and with the substantive critique they promise for the criminal law.

III. Aims of the Harm-Orientation Doctrines

The level of critique is only reached when one asks what principles of harm orientation – the harm principle, and the doctrine of legal goods – are meant to do: what are their objectives?[20] This is the critical function level with which the legal goods doctrine is concerned.[21] At this central juncture the harm principle and the doctrine of legal goods show themselves again to be closely related. Both have the same objectives, and both employ similar means to reach these objectives. In what follows, I consider some central objectives – freedom, transparency, consistency, and social morality – and assess how the two doctrines, German and Anglo-American, help us to secure them.

A. Freedom

If one looks at the harm principle in respect of its origins[22] and aims,[23] its proximity to the doctrine of legal goods is evident. This proximity concerns the historical reasons for which, and in the context of which, these two concepts have been developed.

(i) Orientation towards human beings

For both doctrines, the central aim is to preserve citizens' freedom vis-à-vis a punitive state that wields the powers to prosecute and punish and can use those powers to achieve its own aims (faster, cheaper, more fully, more effectively). Both the doctrine of legal goods and the harm principle are instruments put into service to limit the legitimate use of state punishment – an aim that has been the hallmark of liberal criminal law theories for centuries. In both cases, the concern is to have external, clear and concrete criteria to delimit the area within which the state can legitimately criminalise and punish behaviour. Those criteria are, respectively, the

[19] The German Constitution (*Grundgesetz*) begins with the protection of personal legal goods and only then moves to the institutional framework of the state.
[20] For a discussion of the general systemic aims not focusing specifically on a comparison with the harm principle, see additionally U Kindhäuser, U Neumann and H-U Paeffgen (eds), *Nomos-Kommentar zum StGB*, 3rd edn (Baden-Baden, Nomos, 2013) Vor § 1 marginal note 110ff (commentary by W Hassemer) with further references.
[21] I start to develop such an approach in Hassemer, *Theorie und Soziologie*, above n 16 at 61ff.
[22] I am thinking here of the writings of John Stuart Mill and Joel Feinberg.
[23] See the references in von Hirsch, 'Rechtsgutbegriff', above n 12 at 73ff.

violation of a legal good (legally protected interest or value), or the imposition of harm on another person (harmfulness to others).

In both doctrines we find a perspective that has left the legitimating culture of natural law reasoning behind.[24] This discourse is no longer concerned, as natural law theory was, with the faithful determination of rights and permissions which are given to human society from outside or from above; the issue now is to discover and to ground these rights and permissions as such.[25] From there it is only a small step to the discovery that the criterion for legitimate criminal law legislation (that is, the criterion for legitimate threats of punishment, prosecution and sanctioning of breaches as the sharpest instruments of state regulation) can only be the protection of human beings from other human beings – and not as such the wish of the state to pursue a certain kind of policy or to put an end to, bring about, or secure, a certain state of affairs.[26] The infringement of a legal good is, just like the infringement of a human interest,[27] the core requirement which legitimates criminalisation, prosecution and enforcement of punishment; this core is human-oriented. The right to punish arises from the violation of a concrete human interest, and it ends there. Beyond this area one must be free from punitive intervention. Leviathan is bound by these conditions.[28] The existence of a legitimate interest on the part of one citizen (that is, of a legal good), and the violation of that interest by another citizen, lies at the heart of the state's right to punish.

This is, of course, only the core. It needs manifold additions, concretisations and also practical adjustments, before it can provide a blueprint for liberal criminal legislation and criminal justice. Thus we must, for example, ask and answer what counts when as an 'interest', whether this interest has to be a 'legitimate' one, and what that means concretely: say, whether 'the health of the population' can be a 'legal good' (for instance, in the area of drugs offences) even though this is not just a many-faceted but also an ever-changing notion, an ephemeral state of affairs subject to constant technical, medical and cultural changes. In states that adhere to the Rule of Law, criminal law theory and doctrine as well as the criminal courts have over a long period of time developed – and then put into practice, actualised and

---

[24] On what follows, see also W Hassemer, *Warum Strafe sein muss. Ein Plädoyer*, 2nd edn (Berlin, Ullstein, 2009) 149ff.

[25] From the perspective of the harm principle, von Hirsch says in 'Rechtsgutbegriff', above n 12 at 71: 'If we draw the boundaries between citizens' spheres of individual freedom according to the harm principle, then every citizen has the freedom to pursue his own aims and wishes so long as he does not thereby harm others, that is, set back their legitimate interests.' ['Grenzt man die Freiheitssphären der Bürger nach dem Harm Principle voneinander ab, dann hat jeder Bürger die Freiheit, seine eigenen Wünsche und Ziele zu verfolgen, solange er dadurch anderen nicht schadet, d.h. ihre legitimen Interessen nicht beeinträchtigt.']

[26] The central importance of the protection of freedom for the conception of the harm principle von Hirsch develops is also evident in his strong criticisms of paternalistic arguments for criminal prohibitions, which runs like a red line through his work. See, eg, *Fairness*, 79ff and 85ff.

[27] See, for this conception of the harm principle, with reference to Feinberg, von Hirsch, 'Rechtsgutbegriff', above n 12 at 73f; 'harmful conduct' is defined there as 'interference with a resource to whose unaffected existence another person has a normative claim.' ['Beeinträchtigung einer Ressource, auf deren unbeeinträchtigte Existenz ein anderer einen Anspruch hat.']

[28] E Denninger, *Der gebändigte Leviathan* (Baden-Baden, Nomos, 1990) esp 51ff.

adapted – systems that have given shape and content to the notions of legal goods and harm orientation, concretising them and adjusting them to the times. These systems are themselves in need of application and interpretation; they are subject to change, and such changes keep them relevant on an ongoing basis in the world in which and to which they are intended to apply.

(ii) Personal legal goods

To these systems of thought belongs, for instance, the question whether human interests only qualify as legal goods or whether institutional interests are also (or even mostly or exclusively) eligible.[29] After all, it is said that human beings don't live by their own efforts alone, but also thanks to, say, the smooth operation of energy supply systems and the functioning of the Constitutional Court; indeed that humans depend so strongly on institutions of this kind that the protection of legal goods is, first and foremost, a matter of protecting institutions. The protection of legal goods is thus connected not merely to freedom but to security and welfare.

These are, I think, confusing and confused lines of reasoning; they flourish more easily in our country than in the province of the harm principle (which, with its simple focus on human actors standing opposed to each other, stays out of this line of fire and asserts the freedom-protecting aspect of its harm orientation effectively by itself and without much further thought). Nobody would deny that we need not only our health but also public transport systems; and no court would consider a punch-up among youths more deserving of punishment than, say, the destruction of central data processing equipment, or a poisonous leakage into groundwater, merely because the first case concerns direct injury to personal legal goods. For the practical implementation of harm-oriented considerations in criminal law policy decisions, the stark either-or opposition between 'persons' and 'institutions' is a dead end. As long as people live in societies, we are necessarily concerned with both, and the institutions criminal law sensibly protects will always be those that concern human beings. Criminal law policy, engaged in concretising and protecting both person and institution, faces the task of determining the weight of the different legal goods in question and of bringing these into a reasonable relation to each other.[30]

Many of these disputes are quotidian, and can be pitched at concrete or more abstract levels.[31] These are the insignia of all substantive basic concepts, not only in

---

[29] See further on the discussion of the doctrine of personal legal goods U Neumann, ' "Alternativen: keine". Zur neueren Kritik an der personalen Rechtsgutslehre' in U Neumann and C Prittwitz (eds), *Personale Rechtsgutslehre und Opferorientierung im Strafrecht* (Frankfurt, Peter Lang, 2007).

[30] We will encounter another such task in section III.C(ii) below, when we are concerned with the weighting of violations and with degrees of exposure to risk of legal goods.

[31] At a more abstract level, the conviction has grown that the German Constitution, and the worth and dignity it attributes to the human person, mean that one should not start with the institutions when approaching such questions; quite the opposite. The Constitution bestows no original value on the institutions but only a derivative one, and it realises this, for example, in the balancing of person-oriented and institution-oriented interests. I elaborate my arguments concerning the doctrine of personal legal goods in W Hassemer, *Strafen im Rechtsstaat* (Berlin, Berliner Wissenschaftsverlag, 2000) 160ff, to which Andreas von Hirsch contributed a Foreword (ibid, 7ff).

criminal law theory and practice. That these concepts remain permanently challenged, also among us, is not evidence for any systemic impotence, but rather of their fundamental nature and their connectedness with a changing world. Moreover, the open texture of these concepts does not distract from their orientation towards civic freedom; in fact this is what makes this orientation concrete. Anyone considering the doctrines of harm orientation to be too vague ought to recall concepts like conduct, causality, and culpability: these have always and constantly occupied us. All concepts which are fundamental and linked to life are also open to the influence of social change.

B. Transparency

Criminal law theories should be transparent – indeed, transparency is a self-evident goal for any academic discipline. Transparency, clarity and comprehensibility are, moreover, also aims of the system of criminal law itself, which is the object of criminal law theory. Hence their importance is especially strongly grounded in this context. Criminal law theory is not an abstract system. Transparency of the system of criminal law is a precondition for its proximity to, and its control by, the citizenry; without transparency, criminal law is necessarily unable to fulfil its task of (positive) general prevention[32] because citizens lack a proper grasp of what happens in this system and why.

Obscure criminal law concepts also prevent the law from achieving its aims of certainty, predictability and control, which are precisely what the constitution expects of the criminal law.[33] Clarity and transparency of criminal law interventions, from legislation through to the implementation of sanctions, are not decorative features of some artful and complex system; they are instruments of freedom. They are meant to give people direction, to provide them with an opportunity to gauge their situation, form a judgement and, if necessary, to resist. They are therefore, ultimately, also a component of the central Rule of Law principle of the public administration of justice.[34] In this regard, both the harm principle and the doctrine of legal goods are satisfactory. Both attend to these tasks and fulfil them, if everything goes well, in their own way and with their own means. They aim at transparency, and they do this through the notions of 'legal goods' and 'harm'.

(i) 'Core' criminal law

The legal goods of core criminal law (life, health, property, clean water, freedom, reliability of monetary transactions, and possibly also honour) are part of our ordinary lives. Their importance for human beings, their value and their purpose are

---

[32] See on this point already W Hassemer, *Einführung in die Grundlagen des Strafrechts*, 2nd edn (Munich, CH Beck, 1990) 309ff and 324ff.

[33] See Article 103 and Article 104 of the German Constitution (*Grundgesetz*).

[34] See my recent comment 'Über die Öffentlichkeit gerichtlicher Verfahren – heute' (2013) 46 *Zeitschrift für Rechtspolitik* 149.

self-evident; we all know them well and are concerned about their preservation. In order to understand what they mean and when they are violated, no theoretical work is necessary, unlike other legal concepts; it is enough simply to look at them.

The harm principle achieves the same objectives of visibility and transparency via a different – and theoretically shorter – path. The mutuality of interests and protection against harm postulated by this principle places the injuring and the injured party in an irrevocable, clearly structured, experience-based relation to each other, which neither leaves open the question of what is at stake nor clouds the answer to this question. Those who consider the concept of core criminal law to be primitive or simplistic have not understood the point of the constitutional requirement of legal certainty in respect of criminal law. This point is not a linguistic one, but one concerned with practical action and protection. The concept of a core criminal law rests on, and realises itself in particular through, the number and texture of those legal goods and interests which may count as legitimate and protected in a given system of criminal law. Core criminal law wants to keep the number of legitimate legal goods and interests low and their determinations concrete; this is its raison d'être. With the modernisation of criminal law, however,[35] notions have found their way into the criminal law system which have not only enriched that system but also made it more complicated, thus reducing its transparency. In the first line of attack stands the doctrine of the legal good, which has become a victim of efforts to adapt the legal system to the social changes of modernity. This is because it is particularly in the area of legitimate legal goods that new objects of attack, modes of attack, and also protective techniques are conceived.[36]

The chain of new legal goods outside the core criminal law is, by now, long; its links are comparatively abstract, complex, vague, and thin in content. To give some examples: 'the domestic justice system with respect to its task of counteracting the effects of crimes,'[37] 'the creditors of a debtor, considered as a group, in respect of the risk or partial loss of their chances of repayment,'[38] or 'the general interest in the reliable operation of the data processing systems used in industry and administration.'[39]

These are, to start with, when compared to our traditions, substantive and linguistic abnormalities in the special part of our criminal law. They are of a very different kind from honour, health, or clean water. Together with the much discussed tendency of modern criminal law legislation to criminalise conduct in the very early stages of preparation,[40] long before any legal good is violated or even endangered,

---

[35] That the concept of 'core criminal law' has been coined at all reflects the increasing speed of social change in the last decades and the legitimate need – even duty – of the criminal law system to react appropriately to this change. See, eg, W Naucke, *Über die Zerbrechlichkeit des rechtsstaatlichen Strafrechts. Materialien zur neueren Strafrechtsgeschichte* (Baden-Baden, Nomos, 2000) 97ff and 307ff.

[36] On the protective techniques of modern criminal law, see my *Theorie und Soziologie*, above n 16 at 194ff; also my remarks in U Kindhäuser, U Neumann and H-U Paeffgen (eds), *Nomos-Kommentar zum StGB*, 3rd edn (Baden-Baden, Nomos, 2013) Vor § 1 marginal note 170ff (commentary by W Hassemer).

[37] See, in the German Criminal Code, § 261(i) StGB (money laundering).

[38] See, in the German Criminal Code, § 283 StGB (criminal bankruptcy).

[39] See, in the German Criminal Code, § 263 a StGB (computer fraud).

[40] See, eg, U Kindhäuser, U Neumann and H-U Paeffgen (eds), *Nomos-Kommentar zum StGB*, 3rd edn (Baden-Baden, Nomos, 2013) Vor § 1 marginal note 116ff (commentary by W Hassemer).

and to construe crimes of 'abstract endangerment' where no concrete risk to a legally protected interest exists,[41] this results in a picture of modern criminal law where we can hardly speak of transparency any longer. Instead we find across-the-board criminalisation based on maximal semantic stretching of the protected legal good.

The reasons for and against this have been debated thoroughly in recent years; they extend in their significance much further than the principle of transparency in the determination of the legally protected good – they reach across to the very image of modern criminal law.[42] I am concerned here only with a side issue, which is the insight that a theoretical doctrine of legal goods cannot confine itself to drawing the boundaries of criminalisation by the state, including its reasons and lines, but must also concern itself with the ways and means by which these boundaries are drawn. This is so because whether the criminal law can communicate effectively with citizens depends on these ways and means.[43] A woolly determination of the legally protected good, a misshapen outline of its contours, is not merely regrettable; in a state committed to the Rule of Law it is a manifest violation of right. It obscures the commands of the criminal law, it neglects the constitutional criminal law obligation of legal certainty, and it thereby withholds from the citizen essential – and possible[44] – direction. This is something that criminal law theorists – their understandable fascination with the modernisation of their object of study, and its nomenclature, notwithstanding – should not simply accept.

C. Consistency

Consistency, too, is a tenet not only of criminal law theory but also of the criminal justice system.[45] The theory as well as the practice of a liberal criminal law are both very much in need of the consistency of conceptual organisation offered by the doctrine of legal goods or the harm principle. A concept which fails to provide consistent answers to similar questions not only fails to systematise, but also endangers consistency in the practice which strives to follow it. The doctrine of the legal good is also in respect of this desideratum less than perfect (although it does somewhat better here than in respect of transparency).

The doctrine of the legal good – and the harm principle too – must provide a consistent answer to the question: is the use of state punishment legitimate in this or that situation? If they provide different answers to the same question (rendering

---

[41] We will address this tendency, and its consequences, further in section III.C(ii) below.

[42] On the notion and the forms of 'modern' criminal law, see W Hassemer, *Produktverantwortung im modernen Strafrecht*, 2nd edn (Heidelberg, CF Müller, 1996) 3ff.

[43] Von Hirsch appears to offer a somewhat different perspective in 'Rechtsgutbegriff', above n 12 at 75.

[44] That it is possible, within the theoretical framework of the doctrine of legal goods, to avoid such voluminous and inflated constructions is shown by K Kühl in his discussion of the legal good protected by the offence of computer fraud: see K Lackner and K Kühl (eds), *StGB-Kommentar*, 27th edn (Munich, CH Beck, 2011) § 263a, marginal note 1 with further references (commentary by K Kühl).

[45] See already section III.B above on this point and the causes, in the context of the discussion on transparency.

them seriously deficient as criterial theories), they would fatally undermine the clear and principled guidance expected of them by the criminal law system,[46] thus failing in their task of securing human freedom.[47]

This problem is particularly acute for the doctrine of the legal good. It has different aspects. I address two typical instances which have received considerable academic and practical attention.

(i) Modern legal goods

Well before the development of a 'modern' criminal law concerned to safeguard every relevant object of protection through criminal law,[48] the criminal law system has been put under pressure by an expansive criminal policy seeking to bestow the label 'legal good' generously in order to turn criminal law into a modern, flexible and all-encompassing protective instrument which leaves no actual challenges unanswered. This is, for instance, the case today in respect of phenomena such as cybercrime,[49] and here lies the main problem; it is also true of long-standing attitudes to criminal policy which fail to see anything wrong with treating morals and traditions as 'legal goods' and protecting them through criminal law prohibitions.[50] Again and again, criminal law policy disputes concerning the criminal character of conduct focus on whether the conduct counts as a violation of a legal good. If it does, this assists the aim of criminalisation and facilitates the protection of an interest through the criminal law.[51]

The consequences of this state of affairs are obvious. In times when a strong belief in the ability of criminal law to resolve actual social conflict holds sway,[52] 'legal goods' shoot up like mushrooms; after all, they open the portals of the Criminal Code. Ultimately, this is, of course, not really a problem concerning the coherence of the concept of the legal good. Its coherence is, indeed, preserved when everything that can just about be fitted under this heading is subsumed under it; almost anything can then be a 'legal good'. The problem lies, rather, as has been argued here, with the transparency of the concept of the legal good[53] and with the protection of freedom that it is supposed to secure.[54] This is where the burdens of an overextended concept of the legal good come to rest: criminal prohibitions of conduct grow surreptitiously, and the concept of the legal good accompanies and hides that growth.

---

[46] See section III.B above.

[47] See section III.A above.

[48] See section III.B above.

[49] See, in the German Criminal Code, § 263a StGB (computer fraud).

[50] Instructive in this regard is the minority opinion of the decision of the German Constitutional Court (Bundesverfassungsgericht) regarding the constitutionality of the criminal prohibition of incest (§ 173(ii)(2) StGB): see decision of 26 February 2008, BVerfGE 120, 224 (255).

[51] This mechanism, of course, also shows that the doctrine of legal goods has a good reputation with policy-makers in our region.

[52] I am critical of such an aim in Hassemer, *Einführung*, above n 32, at 279ff.

[53] See section III.B above.

[54] See section III.A above.

(ii) Early stage criminalisation

On the other hand, another problem of consistency is discussed by von Hirsch[55] when he identifies the problems that undoubtedly arise[56] from the criminalisation of abstract endangerments, and of conduct that precedes actual crime, as problems of imputation and seeks to resolve them within this framework.

If this were the correct approach, these two theories of harm orientation would give different answers to the same question concerning the legitimate criminalisation of conduct which merely endangers a legal good (the answers would, on the one hand, rely on the criterion of proximity of harm and, on the other hand, rely on the criteria of intent and recklessness). That would indeed be problematic. But it appears to me – along with Feinberg – that the solution via imputation is a false path: the concepts of harm orientation are in themselves and by their own means capable of giving a complete and convincing answer to the question of penalising endangerments; imputation doctrines are, in this context, unnecessary.

Two steps suffice to make this clear. The first is as follows. That the legitimating force of a harm orientation approach in the criminal law is not restricted to actual injuries and factual harms, needs – for a conception of harm – no further argument. In our world, there are *threats* to legal goods (the drunken bus driver, the person playing with matches on commercial premises full of highly flammable goods) which far outweigh in seriousness some *actual* violations (eg, a mere bruise) and, from the perspective of a conception of harm, there is no good reason to regard only the latter as harm on the ground that only the latter supposedly involves the 'violation' of a legally protected good. There has always been good reason – all the more so in our highly technological world – to consider the risk of harm as an object for inclusion within the scope of the concept of harm. Someone who refuses to entertain the possibility of a violation of a legal good unless a legal good has been literally 'violated' has fallen victim to the laziness of ordinary language. The 'violation' of a legal good in the criminal law sense can, in our shared understanding of the notion, be constituted by a threat to that legal good. There are venerable offences of early stage criminalisation, whose relationship to a legal good is uncontroversial for the simple reason that if one were to wait until the legal good has already been violated, the very state of affairs which the threat of a legal sanction was meant to prevent would have been brought about.[57]

The second step is this. A problem of early stage criminalisation, if there is indeed such a problem, begins only on the next level up. This level enquires critically into the systemic and substantive appropriateness of including early stage conduct and abstract endangerment offences in a criminal law based on the protection of legal goods (or on the harm principle) – given that these types of conduct have not (yet)

---

[55] Von Hirsch, *Fairness,* 78f and 85ff.

[56] See already my remarks on this point in section III.B above.

[57] See, eg, the offences in §§ 81ff StGB (high treason). The protected legal good is the territorial and constitutional integrity of the German state. See further U Kindhäuser, U Neumann and H-U Paeffgen (eds), *Nomos-Kommentar zum StGB,* 3rd edn (Baden-Baden, Nomos, 2013) § 81 marginal note 5 with further references (commentary by H-U Paeffgen).

brought about actual harm. I consider this a false problem which does not give us cause either to discard the notion of harm orientation[58] or even just to make corrective adjustments to the harm principle or the concept of legal goods:

If, as explained above in the first step, the reasoning based on harm and the violation of a legal good is compatible with the realisation that manifest threats of damage to a legally protected value or interest can constitute a violation of that legal good, the only question that remains is what criminal law consequences should follow from the fact that the conduct of the offender did not cause any actual damage to the legal good in question but merely endangered it.

This question is unavoidable in our constitutional legal system. It is the inevitable consequence of the Rule of Law principles of proportionality and appropriateness of state punishment: it acknowledges that abstract endangerment is a 'normative minus' compared to a concrete violation or even damage. It is normatively of a lower order because both the harm principle and the doctrine of legal goods assess the weight of a punishable infringement of the goods and interests of others according to two criteria: the significance of the interest and the intensity of its infringement. (A criminal law system determining the degree of desert of punishment of human conduct according to the seriousness of the duty violation involved, or according to the distance of the conduct to accepted socio-moral standards of decency, would come to very different results.)

This does not completely solve the difficulties of practical application when it comes to the appropriate treatment of the endangerment of legal goods. It remains the task of the penalising state to concretise this problem and its consequences and, in the course of doing this, to decide two things: first, what is the threshold above which mere endangerment can be considered deserving of punishment, and secondly, which mitigation reflects appropriately the circumstance that we are dealing here with a 'normative minus'.

This decision must be made according to the concept of harm orientation we follow, for instance the normative weight of the threatened legal good, the proximity of the risk-creating conduct to the occurrence of harm, and the factual and legal possibilities of preventing that harm effectively by other means. And this process of inquiry makes clear that early stage criminalisation does not lead harm-oriented doctrines of criminalisation into trouble. Rather, it provides them with the opportunity to be applied in a manner that is in tune with the Rule of Law as well as practically reasonable.

D. Social morality

Perhaps we now live in a period when it has become necessary to point out that the long-term goals of the criminal law's orientation towards the concept of harm[59] include the objective of furthering the social morality of the population through

---

[58] See section II above.
[59] See section II above.

this very means: that is, via a reserved, consistent and appropriate criminal law policy and criminal adjudication, based on concepts such as the harm principle and legal goods. In other words, the notions of legal good and harm are aimed at no less than the achievement of a legitimate criminal justice system as such.

The reason for this remark is not any claim by criminal law scholars that the protection of legal goods and the harm principle, on the one hand, and social morality, on the other hand, have nothing to do with each other – this claim is, as far as I know, not made by anyone. The reason is, rather, that a complete theory of criminal law must address the question of legal goods and social morality – whatever result it reaches. Maintaining silence on this issue tends to conduce towards the conclusion that the concept of harm orientation ought to stay away from the discussion of the aims of punishment – be it because of an exaggerated critique of paternalism, or on account of too narrow a conception of liberalism. I certainly cannot see any good reason for such silence.

If one looks for an instructive example characterised by our three elements (ie, high appreciation for the doctrine of legal goods, openness towards the legal value of social morality, and careful restraint in face of the temptation to connect legal goods and social morality too easily), one can find one in Hans Welzel's textbook,[60] which has pointed the way for addressing the problem that concerns us here. Welzel addresses, in a prominent place,[61] the 'socio-ethical function of criminal law',[62] and he leaves no doubt that it is the central 'task of the criminal law' to 'protect the fundamental values of communal life.'[63] Moreover he does not hesitate to bring the protection of legal goods into this circle of guiding principles,[64] and he ultimately intertwines the protection of the fundamental socio-ethical values of practical actions in an intricate manner with the protection of legal goods.[65] This is a far-reaching and at the same time complex understanding of the relationship between the protection of legal goods and social morality.

Admittedly, this model hails from a time in which criminal law theorists spoke and reasoned differently from today, and the possible affinity between Welzel's notion of 'the attitudes to legal values manifested in behaviour' (*rechtliche*

---

[60] H Welzel, *Das Deutsche Strafrecht. Eine systematische Darstellung*, 11th edn (reprinted: Berlin, De Gruyter, 2010; orig 1969).

[61] Ibid, § 1 ('Sinn und Aufgabe des Strafrechts').

[62] Ibid. In § 1.II we find the discussion of the preventive functions of criminal law.

[63] Ibid, § 1.I, especially the 'First guiding maxim' stated there.

[64] Ibid, § 1.I: 'By penalising conduct indicative of a real defection away from attitudes of respect for legally protected values, the criminal law automatically protects the legal goods which refer to the values of these actions.' ['Indem das Strafrecht so den wirklichen Abfall von den rechtlichen Gesinnungswerten bestraft, schützt es zugleich die Rechtsgüter, auf die jene Aktwerte bezogen sind.']

[65] Ibid, § 1 (Second guiding maxim): 'The task of criminal law is the protection of the fundamental socio-ethical value of attitudes and actions and only contained therein is the protection of particular legal goods.' ['Aufgabe des Strafrechts ist der Schutz der elementaren sozialethischen Gesinnungs-(Handlungs-)werte und erst darin eingeschlossen der Schutz der einzelnen Rechtsgüter.'] Also the Third guiding maxim: 'The task of criminal law is the protection of legal goods through the protection of the fundamental socio-ethical value of actions.' ['Aufgabe des Strafrechts ist der Rechtsgüterschutz durch den Schutz der elementaren sozialethischen Handlungswerte.']

Gesinnungswerte) and 'social morality' deserves critical investigation.[66] However, it seems to me beyond doubt that, for Welzel, the protection of legal goods and 'the attitude of respect for legally protected values' (*rechtliche Gesinnung*) go together as central elements of a theory of criminal law, and relate to each other in the following way:[67] the 'values of practical actions' as the basis of attitudes of respect for legally protected values are strengthened by the reliable and constant protection of legal goods and, in turn, contribute to the successful protection of legal goods. In his words,[68]

> More important than the protection of concrete individual legal goods is the task of securing the actual validity of (compliance with) the values of practical actions manifest-ing respect for legally protected values; these are the strongest foundation for the state and the community.

At least in its outcome, this perspective sits well with the message of positive gen-eral prevention that, when it comes to the long-term preservation of social morality as a precondition of loyalty to the legal order and respect for law, the criminal law ought not to rely on fear but on acceptance.[69] In doing so, it should be careful not to confuse acceptance with subjection to manipulation. General prevention is 'posi-tive' only when it takes citizens seriously through democratically based participa-tion in 'our law' and its application in practice.[70]

This demand of positivity is, of course, difficult to fulfil, particularly for the crim-inal law which must in the foreseeable future continue to rely on punishment and its threat. But in a democratic community there is no way that leads past this demand. In my view, acceptance is most likely to be brought about through an approach to prevention that does not merely flash before citizens' eyes the array of instruments designed to force their compliance: ie, the special part of the criminal law with its threats of punishment, and the procedural law with its authorisations to enforcement agencies. Such an approach is nothing but a remnant of deterrence-based or negative general prevention. 'Our criminal law', which in a democratic state can claim to be the criminal law 'of us all', encompasses also the safeguards provided by constitutional criminal law and the general part of the criminal law with its inherent limitations of liability.

---

[66] The examples of these values given by Welzel (loyalty, obedience, respect for the person: see Welzel, ibid, § 1.I) suggest, however, that he means 'social morality' in a somewhat different packaging from what we are used to today.

[67] Keeping criminal law restricted to a 'core area' belongs here. See Welzel, ibid, § 1.I.2: 'By restricting itself to the fundamental duties, the criminal law is able to fulfil an important social character-building function in order to better protect legal goods.' See also the discussion in section III.B(ii) above.

[68] Ibid, § 1.I. ['Wesentlicher als der Schutz der konkreten einzelnen Rechtsgüter ist die Aufgabe, die reale Geltung (Befolgung) der Aktwerte rechtlicher Gesinnung sicherzustellen; sie sind das stärkste Fundament, das den Staat und die Gemeinschaft trägt.']

[69] For a more extensive discussion, see Hassemer, *Warum Strafe*, above n 24 at 107ff ('our criminal law').

[70] This consideration touches closely on von Hirsch's urgent appeal for a legal order that as far as possible refrains from paternalistic intervention: see, eg, von Hirsch, *Fairness*, 85ff.

This is the context in which reasoning in terms of legal goods and the harm principle can find its way to social morality. (And based on what I have just said, it is clear that it is accompanied on this path by many other criminal law guarantees: from the culpability principle, and the principle of legal certainty, to the principle of *in dubio pro reo*.) Regular adherence to these in the processes of criminal legislation and adjudication, and their constant application in public criminal trials, constitute the model of legality and reliability which turns the criminal law of a Rule of Law state into an ideal blueprint of everyday social control.[71]

A conception of harm[72] – which rests on, and serves, the guarantee of liberty,[73] whose instructions are transparent[74] and give consistent[75] answers to the problems connected with crime and punishment – may join the ranks of the principles of a legitimate criminal law which can count as 'our criminal law' and which contributes to the emergence of social morality through consistency, appropriateness, publicity and proportionality.

IV. Limits

In exploring the instruments of harm orientation and their aims we have, at the same time, investigated their limitations: without an understanding of its limits, an object of cognition cannot be understood. The red line directing our inquiry – 'What ought, and what can, the doctrine of the legal good do?' – always carried the black line with it: 'And what ought, and can, this doctrine not do?' For this reason all that now remains is to provide a few reminders and underlinings.

We have seen that conceptions of harm are not principles capable of derivation, but argumentative principles: they are an – admittedly strong – argument in the debate concerning the features of a legitimate criminal law, but no more. Moreover, the concept of harm orientation is not capable of standing alone. It belongs in the context of other fundamental principles of constitutional criminal law which strive to provide clarity (like the principle of legal certainty) and to prevent excessiveness (like the principle of proportionality), and it needs this environment in order to bring about its effects.

We have also seen that the implementation of the goals of transparency and consistency of the concept of a legal good runs up, as a matter of fact, against the modern desire to construct modern legal goods. Yet, in the final analysis, reasoning on the basis of legal goods cannot itself determine where the limits of its application lie. Someone who subscribes to this mode of reasoning cannot know, simply on the basis of this commitment, whether there exist any 'reasons for criminalisation

---

[71] For details, see Hassemer, *Einführung*, above n 32 at 323ff.
[72] See section II above.
[73] See section III.A above.
[74] See section III.B above.
[75] See section III.C above.

outside the harm principle',[76] or what a harm-oriented criminal law should do about 'offensive behaviour'[77] that falls short of the threshold of wrongdoing deserving of criminal punishment. In both cases, implementation through criminal policy is essential in order to determine, for instance, whether they should meet with an administrative or preventive policing response, or perhaps be treated as 'quasi-criminal' regulatory offences; or receive no official response at all. But what such a person will know is the importance, when making such implementing decisions, of bearing in mind the core features of reasoning when thinking in terms of legal goods – such as the principle of freedom,[78] the concern for clarity,[79] and the principle of the 'normative minus'.[80]

---

[76] Von Hirsch, *Fairness*, 79ff.
[77] Ibid, 109 ff.
[78] See section III.A above.
[79] See section III.B above.
[80] See section III.C(ii) above.

11

'Remote Harms' and the Two Harm Principles

RA DUFF AND SE MARSHALL

It is often said that philosophers show respect for another's work not by uncritical expressions of admiration, but by engaging with it critically; that is the spirit in which we will discuss Andreas von Hirsch's work on 'remote harms'. We will focus on the paper in which he first identified the problem of 'remote harms', and sketched some ideas for dealing with it – a paper that deservedly became a reference point for subsequent discussions of the viability of the Harm Principle as a guide to (or constraint on) criminalisation;[1] and on the further development of those ideas in his recent book with Andrew Simester.[2] We will argue that, although he identifies a real problem, a failure to distinguish between two Harm Principles leads to a mis-characterisation of the problem, and thus to proposed solutions that are needlessly overcomplicated. The failure to distinguish the two Harm Principles, however, is not just his: it pervades debates about 'the Harm Principle'. By getting clearer about the difference between the two principles, about their different logics, we can clarify some central issues in those debates, including the issue that von Hirsch has done so much to illuminate – that of 'remote harms'.

I. The Two Harm Principles

Von Hirsch and Simester begin their chapter on the Harm Principle by noting a 'familiar tenet of liberalism': 'the state is justified in intervening coercively to regulate conduct only when that conduct causes or risks *harm to others*.' This tenet was '[f]irst articulated' in Mill's dictum: 'the only purpose for which power can rightfully be exercised over any member of a civilised community against his will is to prevent harm to others.' They also quote Feinberg's version: 'it is always a good

---

[1] A von Hirsch, 'Extending the Harm Principle: "Remote" Harms and Fair Imputation' in AP Simester and ATH Smith (eds), *Harm and Culpability* (Oxford, Oxford University Press, 1996) 259. (Cited hereafter as 'Remote Harms'.)

[2] AP Simester and A von Hirsch, *Crimes, Harms, and Wrongs: On the Principles of Criminalisation* (Oxford, Hart Publishing, 2011), especially chs 4–5. (Cited hereafter as *Crimes, Harms, and Wrongs*.)

reason in support of penal legislation that it would be effective in preventing . . . harm to persons other than the actor.' These are, it seems, meant to be three ways of articulating the same principle: 'the Harm Principle'.[3] What we actually have, however, are two different principles.

The first principle, which we can call the Harm Prevention Principle, is the one classically formulated (in slightly, but crucially, different ways) by Mill and by Feinberg:

> We have good reason to criminalise a type of conduct if [and only if] doing so will efficiently prevent harm to others.

Two brief clarifications (which will also apply to the second principle) are in order. First, it talks (as Mill and Feinberg talk) not of what justifies criminalisation, but of what gives us good reason to criminalise. Several hurdles lie between 'we have good reason to criminalise Φing' and 'we ought all things considered to criminalise Φing,' including countervailing reasons of principle not to criminalise Φing, the costs (material, social, and moral) of criminalising Φing, and the possible availability of other and better ways of preventing the harm in question;[4] the most that a Harm Principle should aim to specify is what gives us good reason, in principle, to criminalise a type of conduct. Secondly, the '[and only if]' distinguishes Millian from Feinbergian versions of the Principle: for Millians, harm prevention is the only good reason for criminalisation (or any other kind of collective coercion); for Feinbergians it is one among other sources of good reasons to criminalise.[5]

The second principle, which we can call the Harmful Conduct Principle, is what von Hirsch and Simester identify as a 'familiar tenet of liberalism':

> We have good reason to criminalise a type of conduct if [and only if] it is harmful to others.

The points noted above about 'good reason' and '[and only if]' apply to this principle as well; we will say more about 'harmful' shortly.

Theorists discussing 'the Harm Principle' often begin by quoting or citing Mill's version, the Harm Prevention Principle, but then go on to discuss and apply the Harmful Conduct Principle. Indeed, Mill himself makes this move: in explaining the meaning and implications of the Harm Principle in its classic formulation (quoted above), he says that to 'justify [any kind of coercion], the conduct from which it is desired to deter him must be calculated to produce evil to someone else.'[6]

---

[3] Ibid, 35; see JS Mill, *On Liberty* (London, Parker, 1859) ch 1, para 9; J Feinberg, *Harm to Others* (New York, Oxford University Press, 1984) 26.

[4] See *Crimes, Harms, and Wrongs*, chs 11–12.

[5] Which is why Feinberg devoted three further volumes (*Offense to Others*; *Harm to Self*; *Harmless Wrongdoing* (New York, Oxford University Press, 1985; 1986; 1988)) to other possible reasons; see also *Crimes, Harms, and Wrongs*, chs 6–8 (on offence) and 9–10 (on paternalism).

[6] *On Liberty*, above n 3, ch 1, para 9. See also ch 4, para 3, for a clear statement of the 'only if' version of the Harmful Conduct Principle: 'As soon as any part of a person's conduct affects prejudicially the interests of others, society has jurisdiction over it, and the question whether the general welfare will or will not be promoted by interfering with it, becomes open to discussion.' Feinberg makes a similar move in *Harm to Others*.

This is, we will argue, a mistake, and a source of needless confusion – confusion that is avoided if we distinguish the two principles. It is of course a mistake, or a significant mistake, only if these two principles generate different results: if they do not, if the Harm Prevention Principle gives us good reason to criminalise all and only the types of conduct that the Harmful Conduct Principle gives us good reason to criminalise, we might reasonably say that these are not two distinct and separate principles, but two versions of what is in substance the same principle. However, they do generate different results, especially in relation to 'remote harms'; the mistake is not trivial.

If we assume that the aims of a system of criminal law are at least in part preventive, and that a system of criminal law can have some preventive efficacy, it is true that whatever the Harmful Conduct Principle gives us good reason to criminalise is also, in principle, criminalisable under the Harm Prevention Principle: for by criminalising, and thus reducing the incidence of, harmful types of conduct we reduce the incidence of the harms that such conduct causes; if our aim is to prevent harm, one effective way to do so is to reduce the incidence of kinds of conduct that cause harm. However, the Harm Prevention Principle reaches further than the Harmful Conduct Principle: it can, we will see, give us good reason to criminalise types of conduct that are not themselves harmful. That might suggest that we still really only have one principle, the Harm Prevention Principle: that the Harmful Conduct Principle is not a separate principle, but a more specific implication or application of the Harm Prevention Principle. It is still useful to distinguish the two principles, however, for two reasons. First, while the Harm Prevention Principle implies a Harmful Conduct Principle, one can espouse a Harmful Conduct Principle for reasons quite unrelated to the Harm Prevention Principle: we need not think that the sole or primary reason for criminalising harmful conduct is to prevent the harms that it causes; we could instead hold that the primary reason for criminalising such conduct is that it constitutes the kind of wrongdoing that should be censured by the criminal law, for which its perpetrators should be called to public account in a criminal court. Secondly, the two Principles identify two different routes towards criminalisation – two different ways in which we can come to see good reason to criminalise a type of conduct.

We will begin our examination of the two principles with the Harmful Conduct Principle. It is this version that is most often actually applied in discussions of criminalisation, and that brings the problem of 'remote harms' to light.

II. Remote Harms and the Harmful Conduct Principle

We can see how the problem of 'remote' harms arises by noting two necessary amendments to, or clarifications of, the Harmful Conduct Principle. One has the effect of narrowing its scope, while the other expands it; the problem emerges from the tension between this contraction and this expansion.

The contraction arises from the need to build in a wrongfulness constraint. Since the criminal law is a punitive, censuring institution, it is properly mobilised only against wrongful conduct; so while the Harmful Conduct Principle, as simply expressed above, allows for the criminalisation of any harmful conduct, it should be interpreted to permit the criminalisation only of wrongful conduct.[7] One way to do this is to build the constraint into the Principle's own specification of 'harm'. Thus Feinberg specifies the 'sense of "harm" as that term is used in the harm principle': 'only setbacks of interests that are wrongs ... are to count as harms in the appropriate sense.'[8] Or we could specify a wrongfulness constraint distinct from the Harmful Conduct Principle: conduct that is to be criminalised must be both harmful and wrongful.[9] However, even if we do specify a distinct wrongfulness constraint, it seems plausible to say that the wrongfulness of the conduct must be grounded in, or closely related to, its harmfulness: it would be odd, and a radical version of the *versanti in re illicita* doctrine, to hold that we may criminalise wrongful conduct so long as it has harmful consequences, even if those harmful consequences are unrelated to the respects in which it is wrongful. That is not to say that the wrongfulness of criminalisable conduct must be grounded *solely* in its harmfulness;[10] but it must be at least in part a matter of its harmfulness.

The expansion of the potential scope of the Harmful Conduct Principle flows from a closer examination of what it is for conduct to be, in the relevant sense, 'harmful'. Conduct is of course harmful if it directly causes harm (or would directly cause harm if it was committed), but no one thinks that the Harmful Conduct Principle permits us to criminalise only actually harm-causing conduct.[11] If we have good reason to criminalise conduct that actually causes harm, we have just as good reason, of the same kind, to criminalise conduct that creates a direct risk of the relevant kind of harm – conduct that would, were that risk actualised, directly cause that harm.[12] Whether our interest is in harm-prevention or in the formal censure of wrongfully harmful conduct, and whether or not we think that 'resulting harm' properly makes a difference to the character or the seriousness of the wrong, the reasons we have to criminalise actually harm-causing conduct also apply to conduct that creates a direct risk of harm. That remains true even if we cannot point to a determinate person whose interests are actually put at risk: the driver who speeds

---

[7] See *Crimes, Harms, and Wrongs*, ch 2.

[8] *Harm to Others*, 36. See also DN Husak, *Overcriminalization: The Limits of the Criminal Law* (Oxford, Oxford University Press, 2007) 71; and *Crimes, Harms, and Wrongs*, 38–39 (the 'Harm Principle provides for protection against only those setbacks that D was not entitled to inflict on V').

[9] See Husak, *Overcriminalization*, 72–76, on the 'wrongfulness constraint'; *Crimes, Harms, and Wrongs*, 22–24, on the 'Necessity Thesis' (that Φing is wrongful is necessary to justify its criminalisation).

[10] See *Crimes, Harms, and Wrongs*, 51.

[11] Though see C Finkelstein, 'Is Risk a Harm?' (2003) 151 *University of Pennsylvania Law Review* 963, whose argument that risk *is* a harm seems in part (but unnecessarily) intended to render the criminalisation of risky conduct consistent with the Harm Principle.

[12] By 'directly' we mean that the harm would flow from the conduct without mediation by further human actions or unforeseeable events: but nothing significant for present purposes hangs on the precise meaning of 'directly'. Compare H Gross, *A Theory of Criminal Justice* (New York, Oxford University Press, 1979) 428–36.

round a blind bend creates a direct risk of harm even if in fact no car is coming the other way and no one apart from himself is actually put in danger.[13]

However, once we extend the scope of the Harmful Conduct Principle beyond the categories of actually harm-causing conduct to those of conduct that creates direct risks of harm, it becomes notoriously difficult to draw a firm line: it is tempting (especially for governments that believe in the efficacy of criminal law as a means of preventing harm, or as an easy way to be seen to take harm seriously) to extend the criminal law to cover kinds of conduct only remotely connected to the harms that ultimately justify criminalisation; that is one way in which, notoriously, the Harm Principle has been undermined as a constraint on criminal law.[14] This is the problem of 'remote' harms or risks, which 'are remote in the sense that they involve certain kinds of contingencies.'[15] Von Hirsch describes three kinds of remote harm: the first point to note is that they are 'remote' from the conduct whose criminalisation is at issue in quite different ways.

The most straightforward case is that of 'intervening choices':[16] the conduct at issue makes possible, or easier, or more likely, further actions by the agent himself or by others, which more directly cause the relevant harm or create an immediate risk of harm. The conduct plays a role in the occurrence of the harm (or would have played a role if the harm had ensued), and might be a 'but for' cause of that harm; indeed, had it been committed with the intention of bringing about, or of assisting the bringing about of, that harm, it would have been criminalisable as incitement, or aiding and abetting: but suppose there was no such intention, even if the agent realised that what she did might contribute to such eventual results? I leave a gun, with its ammunition, in my unlocked car, realising that someone might break into the car, steal the gun, and use it to cause harm; or, even more remotely, I have a gun at home, in a locked cabinet, realising that someone might break in and steal the gun, and use it to cause harm. Do we have good or legitimate reason to criminalise such conduct on the grounds that it is a source of possible harm? We would, of course, as with any application of a Harm Principle, need to weigh the likelihood and gravity of the ultimate harm against the value of the activity to be criminalised, and the burdens involved in having to refrain from it: if the activity is valuable enough, or the burdens of refraining from it onerous enough, it might be worth permitting it even if it increases the risk of moderately serious ultimate harm; that is why we do not criminalise driving per se.[17] But should we even go that far towards considering its criminalisation, when the ultimate harm would be directly caused by others?[18]

---

[13] And so German theory counts this as a case of 'concrete' rather than 'abstract' endangerment (see 'Remote Harms', 263); but we will argue later that this schema of 'concrete' and 'abstract' endangerment is misleading.

[14] See, famously, B Harcourt, 'The Collapse of the Harm Principle' (1999) 90 *Journal of Criminal Law and Criminology* 109.

[15] 'Remote Harms', 263.

[16] 'Remote Harms', 264–65; see *Crimes, Harms, and Wrongs*, 58, on 'mediating interventions'.

[17] See 'Remote Harms', 261 and *Crimes, Harms, and Wrongs*, 55, on the 'Standard Harm Analysis'.

[18] We can leave aside here the distinct question of whether the risk that the agent himself will go on to cause harm can give us good reason to criminalise the conduct.

This is where the wrongfulness constraint is relevant: to show that we have good reason to criminalise the conduct, we must show not merely that it might lead to harm (even to wrongful harm, as when my gun is used in a robbery), but that it is wrongful in virtue of its relationship to that potential harm; which means, von Hirsch argues, that we must show that that eventual harm (or the risk of it) can be fairly imputed to the agent.[19] Imputation need not depend on causation: we can impute the eventual harm to the agent without claiming or showing that he caused it. But imputation is legitimate, von Hirsch and Simester go on to argue, if (and only if) the agent has 'some form of normative involvement' in the further actions that will cause the harm: if, for instance, the agent advocates, encourages, assists or advises those further actions.[20] To require a 'normative involvement' of these kinds in the subsequent harmful conduct would indeed quite radically restrict the scope of the criminal law;[21] whilst many would argue that that is a merit of, not a flaw in, their account, we might wonder whether so drastic a constraint on the law's scope can be so easily justified. It seems, for instance, to bar (in principle) the criminalisation of such conduct as carelessly leaving a gun and ammunition in full view in one's unlocked car, since one cannot be said to be thereby 'affirming' or 'endorsing' the wrongs that one realises others might be motivated or enabled to commit; but surely we have some good reason to criminalise that.[22] Von Hirsch allows that we might have reason to do so – but only at the expense of justice: if the prospective harm is grave enough, the fair-imputation 'constraints of justice' can be 'overridden' if 'the countervailing concerns about preventing harm are of extraordinary urgency,' which he thinks might be true in the case of gun control legislation.[23] Now it is far from obvious that restrictions on the ownership and use of guns can be justified only as an admittedly unjust measure to meet an urgent need for harm-prevention – and we will see that von Hirsch and Simester do indeed have the resources to offer a better solution. The point to notice here, however, is that if we rely on the Harmful Conduct Principle, and even if we supplement it with a doctrine of imputation, many such restrictions will be problematic: for we will have to show that the conduct that is to be criminalised is both 'harmful' (classifiable, that is, as a potential source of harm, either directly or by imputation), and also wrongful in virtue of that (potential) harmfulness. We will find a better route towards the legitimate criminalisation of some of these kinds of conduct by working not with the Harmful Conduct Principle, but with the Harm Prevention Principle.

Another example of remote harms is that of 'accumulative' harm, when the prospective harm will be significant enough to warrant the criminal law's attention, or

---

[19] See *Crimes, Harms, and Wrongs*, 80 fn 27: 'our concern is with how the prospect that P might Φ can possibly make S's act of Σing wrongful and eligible for prohibition.'

[20] *Crimes, Harms, and Wrongs*, 81–85.

[21] Especially if 'assistance' is interpreted as narrowly as von Hirsch and Simester interpret it: *Crimes, Harms, and Wrongs*, 84.

[22] And, we might say, we can recognise such reason without abandoning this version of the Harm Principle, if we avoid the extreme individualism that informs von Hirsch and Simester's account of 'normative involvement'; but that is not something we can discuss here.

[23] 'Remote Harms', 271.

(in cases of threshold harm) will ensue at all, only if many people engage in the relevant conduct: if enough people dispose of their garbage in the river, there will be a threat to health; but if only I do it, there will be no such threat.[24] Here too, the actual occurrence of the relevant harm would depend on a 'contingency' to do with the conduct of others: but this case differs from that of 'intervening choices', first, in that their conduct does not depend on what I do; and secondly, in that if the harm or risk does ensue, I will have made a direct and immediate causal contribution (albeit a very modest one) to it. If we ask whether, in such a case, my conduct is wrongfully harmful, we find ourselves in the territory of 'Suppose everyone did the same?': why should the fact that if enough others Φ as I am Φing, harm will ensue, give me reason not to Φ? I might be tempted to argue as follows:

(a) The chances that my Φing will tip the balance towards harm are vanishingly small;
(b) If others are not Φing in significant enough numbers for the harm to ensue, my Φing will not be harmful;
(c) If others are Φing in significant enough numbers, then (to [mis]quote Yossarian[25]) I'd be a damn fool not to;
(d) So either way round, my Φing will not be wrongfully harmful.

We do not suggest that this is a good argument; only that it is a kind of argument that it is hard to rebut on the basis only of the Harmful Conduct Principle, since it is hard to show of any instance of the conduct in question that it is wrongfully harmful. It is true that any instance of dumping garbage in the river is of a type that is harmful if generally practised: but to justify punishing my particular example of garbage dumping by appeal to the Harmful Conduct Principle, we must show that that particular action was wrongfully harmful or risky; and the argument above suggests that that will be hard to show. What is wrong with my conduct is that it is, if not harmful, then unfair, as taking advantage of the self-restraint of others who do not throw their garbage in the river – I am being a free-rider; but unfairness is not a species of harmfulness (unless, perhaps, it involves the kind of visible unfairness that is likely to provoke harmful reactions).

Or could we argue that my conduct either contributes, to a tiny but nonetheless real extent, to the harm that ensues, if it does ensue; or at least contributes to bringing us closer to the point at which the harm will ensue; that in either case the eventual harm would be fairly imputable to me, if it occurred (not of course only to me, but to me along with all those others who behaved in the same way as I am behaving); and that therefore my conduct is wrongfully harmful? Perhaps we could – that would depend on the details of how the harm would come about in particular cases; but it is still quite challenging to show that the criminalisation of such conduct fits the Harmful Conduct Principle; and if the challenge can be met, it is by showing

---

[24] 'Remote Harms', 265; see *Crimes, Harms, and Wrongs*, 59, on 'conjunctive' harms.
[25] Captain J Yossarian, *Catch 22*, Joseph Heller (Simon & Schuster, 1961): 'Then I'd certainly be a damned fool to think any other way.'

that such conduct does, after all, fall within the scope of the Standard Harms Analysis.[26]

The third kind of remote harm that von Hirsch describes is that of 'abstract endangerment'.[27] The simplest example of this is drink-driving.[28] If we define the drink-driving offence in terms of being 'unfit to drive through drink or drugs',[29] we meet the requirements of the Harmful Conduct Principle: one who drives while unfit to drive thereby creates an unacceptably higher risk that he will cause serious harm to others; his conduct is wrongfully harmful. But if we instead define it in terms of driving 'after consuming so much alcohol that the proportion of it in his breath, blood or urine exceeds the prescribed limit,'[30] the matter is less straightforward. A rational legislature will of course set the 'prescribed limit' at a level above which many drivers would indeed suffer significant impairment of their fitness to drive – although depending upon our assessment of the harms in prospect, and of the extent to which a strict limit infringes individual liberty, we might not insist that the level must be such that *most* of those with a higher proportion of alcohol would have their fitness impaired.[31] There will thus be many who, in committing the offence, do act in a wrongfully harmful (risky) way that is in principle apt for criminalisation. There will be others who do not actually suffer any impairment of their fitness to drive by consuming enough alcohol to put them over the limit, whose driving therefore does not actually create a unjustifiable risk of harm, but who do not know that this is true: like one who drives round a blind bend on the wrong side of the road, they too can be said to take an unjustified risk of causing the relevant harm. The point is not that they actually *create* such a risk (any more than driving round the bend when no car is in fact coming the other way creates a risk); but they *take* a risk – that by drinking that much they will have impaired their fitness to drive – that they should not take.[32] There will, however, be some who *know* that drinking that much alcohol does not impair their fitness – their capacities and their willingness to drive safely (perhaps they have even taken tests that show them to be thus immune to the effects of alcohol). How can we justify criminalising their conduct on the basis of the Harmful Conduct Principle?[33]

---

[26] See n 17 above.

[27] 'Remote Harms', 263–64; see *Crimes, Harms, and Wrongs*, 57–58.

[28] This is a simpler example than speeding: with speeding we may need to attend to the effect of D's speeding on others of seeing it, and to the way we rely on drivers not to speed (see *Crimes, Harms, and Wrongs*, 78–79).

[29] Road Traffic Act 1988, s 4(1).

[30] Road Traffic Act 1988, s 5(1).

[31] Contrast 'Remote Harms', 264 (*Crimes, Harms, and Wrongs*, 57–58) on the Swedish limit of 0.2 as compared to the English limit of 0.8; see Husak, *Overcriminalization*, above n 8 at 110–11, on 'the majoritarian condition' that more than half of those who commit such an offence must actually cause harm or create an unjustified risk.

[32] Their conduct 'places or may place another person in danger': Model Penal Code, § 211.2.

[33] See Husak, *Overcriminalization*, above n 8 at 106–12; RA Duff, *Answering for Crime* (Oxford, Hart Publishing, 2007) 166–72. As von Hirsch and Simester point out (*Crimes, Harms, and Wrongs*, 26), Duff needlessly complicates the issue; our argument in this paper is thus (on Duff's part) an exercise in self-criticism and self-correction.

The problem is concealed by talking of 'abstract endangerment', since that suggests that the conduct of a driver who knows that she is unimpaired still endangers others – albeit 'abstractly' rather than 'concretely'.[34] But she does not endanger anyone; she neither takes nor creates an unreasonable risk of harming others. Her conduct might, as we will see, be wrongful; but it is not wrongfully harmful. Harm might ensue from the impaired driving of other less competent drivers whose fitness is impaired by the alcohol they have drunk; but such harm cannot be fairly imputed to her even if she is over the limit (unless her example encouraged others to drink more). Harm might indeed ensue from her driving, if she has an accident; but we could fairly impute it to her, and count her conduct as wrongfully harmful, only if she acted wrongfully in driving as she did – which is just what we have so far failed to show.

We are not assuming that the creation of such drink-driving offences is justifiable; for all we have shown so far, we might conclude that they are not. Legislatures might perhaps (though even this would be controversial) define the drink-driving offence as one of driving with more than a specified alcohol level, so long as most people with that much alcohol in their blood suffer some impairment of their capacity to drive safely;[35] or as driving when 'unfit to drive through drink', but creating a legal presumption that anyone with more than the specified level of alcohol is unfit to drive.[36] If they were to stay true to the Harmful Conduct Principle, however, they would need to provide a defence for a driver who can adduce evidence that in her case alcohol does not have that effect, or make the presumption rebuttable by such evidence.[37] Or it might be argued that we can justify our existing drink-driving offences, but only by overriding 'the constraints of justice' to meet the urgent need to prevent the harms that flow from drink-impaired driving:[38] to convict a driver who knows that her fitness is not impaired by drinking (somewhat) more than the legal limit does her an injustice – but a necessary injustice. All we have argued so far, however, is that if we ground criminalisation in the Harmful Conduct Principle, we cannot yet see good reason to create drink-driving offences

---

[34] This is nonetheless a common way of using the notion of 'abstract endangerment', for instance in connection with environmental offences: see, for just one example, S Mandiberg and M Faure, 'A Graduated Punishment Approach to Environmental Crimes: Beyond Vindication of Administrative Authority in the United States and Europe' (2009) 34 *Columbia Journal of Environmental Law* 447, 453–54. A similar criticism applies to Duff's use of the idea of 'implicit endangerment' (*Answering for Crime*, above n 33 at 166–68).

[35] Compare, eg, Terrorism Act 2000, s 57(1): the offence of 'possess[ing] an article in circumstances which give rise to a reasonable suspicion that [the] possession is for a purpose connected with . . . terrorism.'

[36] Compare Prevention of Corruption Act 1916, s 2: if it is proved that a government contractor gave a gift to a civil servant, it must be presumed that the gift was 'given and received corruptly'.

[37] Compare Prevention of Corruption Act 1916, s 2; Terrorism Act 2000, s 57(1) (as read in the light of s 118's definition of 'prove'). We leave aside here the further problem that it might be hard for drivers to know whether they are over the limit: a legislature that is to respect the requirements of fair notice must either enable drivers to find out, or argue that the law really says 'Don't drink and drive', and that those who drive after drinking must therefore know that they are driving 'on thin ice' (see Duff, *Answering for Crime*, above n 33 at 167, 255–57).

[38] See at n 23 above.

of the kind we now have, since they criminalise kinds of conduct that cannot be described as wrongfully harmful. As we will see, the Harm Prevention Principle provides a more plausible route to the legitimate creation of such offences.

Our discussion so far might seem somewhat disingenuous, and clearly unfair to von Hirsch and Simester: it has ignored much of what they say about the ways in which 'the Harm Principle' can justify criminalisation in the context of 'remote harms' – in particular about duties 'to co-operate in safety-promoting scheme[s]';[39] and about the ways in which the state can 'contribute to the *creation* of moral reasons', and thus to making conduct relevantly wrongful, by creating regulations that serve a legitimate harm-preventive purpose, and whose breach then constitutes a 'post-legal wrong'.[40] But we have been postponing, rather than ignoring, those aspects of their discussions: for to make clear what force they have, and how they can clarify the different routes by which we can be led to criminalisation, we must turn from the Harmful Conduct Principle to the Harm Prevention Principle; and we will see that, when we ground criminalisation in that principle, the issue of wrongfulness arises in a quite different way, that of imputation is much less significant, and we will not need to talk about 'remote' harms as problematic. Sometimes von Hirsch and Simester note the difference between Harm Prevention and Harmful Conduct – between grounding criminalisation in the harmfulness of the conduct in question, and grounding it in the harm-preventive efficacy of criminalisation[41] – but they persist in talking about 'the Harm Principle', as if these are just two aspects of a single principle; the result is a lack of clarity about the different grounds for, the different possible routes to, criminalisation.

III. The Harm Prevention Principle and Regulatory Offences

The Harm Prevention Principle is, as we noted above, the principle classically formulated by Mill and by Feinberg:[42]

> We have good reason to criminalise a type of conduct if [and only if] doing so will efficiently prevent harm to others.

One point that will be important in what follows is that whilst Feinberg's principle is concerned only with criminalisation, Mill's is concerned with any kind of coercion by the state, or indeed by one's fellow citizens: it precludes any 'compulsion and control, whether the means used be physical force in the form of legal penalties, or the moral coercion of public opinion,' unless the purpose is to prevent harm to

---

[39] See 'Remote Harms', 268, 272–73; *Crimes, Harms, and Wrongs*, 62–63, 86–87.
[40] *Crimes, Harms, and Wrongs*, 24–30.
[41] See, eg, *Crimes, Harms, and Wrongs*, 47–48.
[42] See at nn 4–5 above.

others.[43] Now if we are to use the Harm Prevention Principle as a basis for crimi-nalisation in particular, as distinct from other modes of 'compulsion and control', we will of course need to add in a wrongfulness constraint, as we did for the Harmful Conduct Principle: but that constraint will now figure in a rather different way, since we will not need to focus only on wrongful harms, or on conduct that is wrongful because it is harmful.

First, as to wrongful harm, some of the harms that we will see reason to use the criminal law to prevent will of course be wrongful harms, and that wrongfulness will be part of what gives us reason to seek to prevent them: it is a state's proper task to protect its citizens against wrongful attacks that are intended to injure them, and wrongful endangerments that directly expose them to unreasonable risks of harm. But if our starting point is harm prevention, as a justification for coercive interven-tion by the state, we will not attend only to wrongful harms. We will see reason, in principle, to use the law (as well as other kinds of social pressure) to protect our-selves against a wide range of harms that can be averted, or be rendered less threat-ening, by kinds of conduct that the law can require, including natural or accidental harms. It is a state's proper task to help to protect us against threats to our lives or health, as well as to our property and other resources, whether those threats arise from natural causes, from non-wrongful accidents, or from wrongful human conduct;[44] and we cannot rule out in advance the possibility that the criminal law can play a proper role in such protection.

Secondly, as to wrongfully harmful conduct, conduct that is to be criminalised must certainly be wrongful, given the criminal law's censorial character; and it must be wrongful in a way that has some connection to the reasons for criminalising it. Now the reason that the Harmful Conduct Principle gives us for criminalising a type of conduct is precisely its harmfulness: if that is why we criminalise it, its wrongfulness must therefore also consist, at least in part, in that harmfulness.[45] However, under the Harm Prevention Principle the connection between harm and the conduct's wrongfulness may be less straightforward, since the reason for crimi-nalising it is now that doing so will prevent harm: whilst one way to prevent harm is indeed to criminalise harmful conduct, we cannot rule out in advance the possibil-ity that we can sometimes also contribute to the efficient prevention of harm by criminalising conduct that is not itself harmful – in which case its wrongfulness will not need to consist in its harmfulness; indeed, we will now show how that possibil-ity is an actuality.

The pattern of argument that leads from the Harm Prevention Principle to the criminalisation of (or to the recognition of good reason to criminalise) conduct that is not itself harmful is roughly this. We take it as a collective aim, one which the

[43] Mill, *On Liberty*, above n 3, ch 1, para 9.

[44] Of course, if the state has a duty to protect us against a certain kind of harm, and fails to do so, that becomes a wrongful harm – a harm that we are wronged in suffering; but our concern here is with whether a harm must be wrongful if it is to justify coercive state intervention, not with whether it would become wrongful if such state intervention was obligatory but not forthcoming.

[45] See at nn 9–10 above.

state should pursue, to reduce the incidence of a certain kind of harm. We realise that one means towards that end is to regulate certain kinds of human conduct – kinds of conduct that are liable to cause such harm, or kinds of conduct whose appropriate regulation can help to prevent it. Such regulations will sometimes, of course, prohibit conduct that is harmful or dangerous: conduct that is already harmful prior to and independently of the regulation, or conduct that becomes harmful once the regulation is in place (as driving on the right hand side of the road is typically harmful once we have in place, and generally obeyed, a requirement to drive on the left). But they will also sometimes prohibit conduct that is not itself harmful: for instance, regulations aimed at harmful conduct can be over-inclusive in that the type of conduct that they prohibit is known to include many non-harmful examples; other regulations are concerned with what is needed to ensure the efficient working of the regulatory system, and may be such that breaches of them are far removed from any eventual harm. Such regulations are not yet, as far as the logic of their introduction is concerned, a matter of criminal law (not all regulatory law is criminal law); but we might then see reason to criminalise, when we ask how we should respond to breaches of the regulations. We have reason to criminalise such breaches if they are wrongful in a relevant way; but surely they are thus wrongful. For if those regulations have been legitimately passed, as a means to the legitimate goal of harm prevention, they are regulations that we ought to obey as citizens of the polity whose law this is and whose aims we should share.[46] We thus do wrong in breaching them – a wrong that is indeed a public wrong, as a breach of our public regulations, and that thus merits a formal, public, censuring response. Such breaches are thus, in principle, candidates for criminalisation: this is not to say that we should criminalise them, since other ways of dealing with them might be more efficient or appropriate; but it is to say (which is all that the Harm Prevention Principle says) that we have good reason to criminalise them.

This pattern of deliberation towards criminalisation can be discerned in a number of areas – for instance in matters to do with health and safety at work; with financial transactions; with the systems of taxation and social security; with environmental safety and pollution. It can be simply illustrated, however, by looking again at the case of driving.

Driving is an activity which creates significant risks of serious harms, but in which we think it beneficial for individuals to be able to engage – and to engage not only if they are highly trained experts acting in a professional capacity, but as (as it were) amateurs. We also think it beneficial for them to be able to engage in it in ways that are very far from maximally safe: for instance, to drive at speeds at which collisions are likely to cause serious harm, in vehicles that do not have the kinds of

---

[46] Two glosses should be noted here. First, many such regulations are of course also binding on non-citizens who are within the jurisdiction of the polity's law: the normative description relevant to them is not citizen but guest (see RA Duff, 'Responsibility, Citizenship and Criminal Law' in RA Duff and SP Green (eds), *Philosophical Foundations of Criminal Law* (Oxford, Oxford University Press, 2010) 125, 141–43). Secondly, matters might be less straightforward when the regulations are not well-suited to their purported aim; we comment on this in section IV below.

protective build and equipment that would make such harm very unlikely. Of course, such judgements are controversial: people will have different views about the extent to which, for instance, private motoring should be allowed or encouraged, about eligibility to drive, and about speed limits and car safety requirements. But if we are to allow driving at all, we must engage in a process of weighing harms and benefits: what kinds of risk should we collectively accept for the sake of the benefits that flow from the conduct that creates those risks?

If we think about how we can minimise the risks of harm, without reducing the benefits too far, we might begin (naïvely) by simply declaring that those who are going to drive should make sure that they are competent to handle the kind of vehicle they plan to drive, that the vehicle is in safe and roadworthy condition, that they are fit to drive, that they exercise appropriate care and attention in driving, and that they are able to ensure payment for any harms that they cause. Such declarations are, in part, reminders of duties that we already have independently of any system of formal regulations, and we have good reason, under the aegis of the Harmful Conduct Principle, to criminalise conduct that is inconsistent with them: someone who drives when incompetent or unfit to do so (at least if he knows that this is or might be the case), or drives what he knows is or might be an unsafe vehicle, or drives without due care and attention, or fails to make sure that he can meet any liabilities he might incur for damage he causes, risks causing harm to others, and acts as he should not act; he is a harmful wrongdoer. For a range of familiar reasons, however, such a simple approach will be predictably ineffectual in reducing the incidence of harm. There will be coordination problems that are not easily solved if each driver is acting on the basis of her own judgement; even drivers who are well-intentioned might not be sure what counts as safe conduct – what kinds of check it is appropriate to make on one's own and one's vehicle's fitness; drivers who are rather stupid, or not well-intentioned, will behave dangerously (encouraged, in the latter case, by the thought that it might be hard to prove what would need to be proved to convict them). We thus have reason to introduce various kinds of formal regulation to deal with these problems.

For instance, we will see reason to create regulations to solve straightforward coordination problems – regulations about which side of the road to drive on, about who has right of way at junctions (which might include regulatory traffic lights), and so on. We will see reason to create regulations requiring kinds of conduct that generally conduce to safety, or prohibiting kinds that generally create unreasonable levels of risk – regulations imposing speed limits, and about when it is permissible to overtake. We will see reason to create regulations concerning competence to drive and vehicle roadworthiness – including regulations requiring would-be drivers to take a test to demonstrate their competence, and requiring cars to be tested for safety at regular intervals.[47] We will see reason to create regulations concerning fitness to drive safely, including prohibitions on, for instance, driving

---

[47] We will also see reason to create regulations for those who manufacture and sell cars, and special regulations for drivers engaged in particularly demanding or potentially dangerous kinds of driving (bus drivers, lorry drivers . . .); but our focus here is on the regulations we might create for ordinary drivers.

when one's fitness is likely to be impaired by alcohol or other drugs. If we maintain a system of tort law to allocate the costs of wrongfully caused harm (rather than, for instance, dealing with such costs under a general scheme of state insurance), we will see reason to create regulations aimed at ensuring that those who cause harm by bad driving will be able to pay for it, for instance through a scheme of car insurance.

In all these cases, we might also see reason to make the regulations peremptory, rather than merely advisory (to make them regulations, rather than guidelines); and to limit or eliminate the discretion they allow to drivers, although this will make them over-inclusive. We know that there are drivers who – although not so authorised – are competent (and who know that they are competent) to exercise discretion as to whether to stop at traffic lights or conform to other road signs, speed limits, or even drink-driving limits – to treat the regulations as advisory, rather than peremptory. But we also know that some, probably dangerously many, would misuse such discretion through incompetence, lack of care, or misjudgement; and we know that safe coordination is made easier if everyone can be seen to be following the same rules. We know that some people are (and know that they are) competent to drive without having undergone a formal test, and that some keep their vehicles in roadworthy condition without any formal guidance or testing. But we also know that too many are not like that: that we and they can know that they are competent, and their vehicles safe, only through a system of driving tests and vehicle inspections. We know that some drivers are rich enough to be able to pay for any harm that they cause from their own pockets, but that many are not, and will need insurance if they are to ensure that such harm can be paid for.

In the light of such considerations as these, we can consider which of a spectrum of possible modes of guidance or regulation we should adopt, a spectrum ranging from the kind of general declarations of norms noted above to the kind of strict prescriptions that we actually have:

(a) Regulations requiring drivers to drive safely, to ensure that they are competent and fit to drive, to ensure that their vehicles are safe, and so on.

(b) Guidelines containing advice about how to ensure that one meets the kinds of requirement noted in (a): recommendations about such matters as driver training, vehicle testing, speed limits, drink-driving limits, taking out insurance, and so on.

(c) Regulations of a more peremptory but exception-allowing kind: would-be drivers must pass a driving test, unless they know that they are competent; drivers must observe speed limits, and drink-driving limits, and traffic signs, unless they know that they can safely diverge from them; drivers must carry third-party insurance, unless they know that they can cover from their own resources the cost of any harm for which they might be held liable.

(d) Regulations that are peremptory and exceptionless: anyone who wishes to drive must pass a driving test; all vehicles (over a certain age) must be tested for safety; all drivers must obey speed limits and other kinds of traffic signal; no one may drive with more than the specified proportion of alcohol in their blood; all drivers must carry at least third-party insurance. Even a true claim to know that one can safely breach such regulations does not constitute a defence.

The familiar points noted above give us good reason, in at least some cases, to opt for (d), rather than a milder regime of the kind that (a)–(c) offer. The greater the discretion we allow drivers to decide for themselves on such matters, the greater the danger that such discretion will be abused by those who are incompetent, or careless, or who think that they will be able to get away with it; the requirements will be harder to enforce, since breaches will be harder to prove; we will lose such benefits as would accrue from a system in which everyone can be seen to be obeying the same set of regulations (versions of these points will apply differentially to different matters). It is of course true that a regulatory system of type (d) imposes burdens. Any regulations impose burdens on those bound by them, but (d)-type regulations are in particular burdensome on those for whom they are, individually, unnecessary – those who would be entitled to claim exceptions for themselves under a (c)-type regime. For what we must say to such drivers is not, as we could say to others, 'You must obey the regulations in order to make sure that you are driving safely,' since we know and they know that that is not true; but 'You must obey the regulations because we need to enforce such a regime in order to make sure that others drive safely.' That we would be imposing such a burden is certainly a consideration to which we must attend, as a good reason against type-(d) regulations and in favour at least of type-(c) regulations; but if the burden is not unduly burdensome, if it does not impose unreasonable restrictions on their liberty, it might be one that we can say they ought to accept, for the sake of the common good that such regulations efficiently serve.[48]

There is one further kind of regulation that we would see reason to create in order to improve the system's efficiency: regulations to do with verifying that other regulations are being obeyed. Would-be drivers must not only pass a test, but must also obtain a licence, and be ready to produce it upon reasonable demand. They must not only have their cars checked and licensed, but have the documentation to prove it; and so on. Regulations of this kind do not directly serve the aims of harm prevention; conduct that violates them does not create a direct risk of harm: but they make the regulatory system easier to manage, and the regulations easier to enforce; thus, so long as they do not impose unreasonable burdens on those subject to them, we may reasonably create them. More generally, while we should be reluctant to weaken the conditions of criminal liability for the sake merely of administrative convenience,[49] considerations of efficiency in administration and enforcement are

[48] Although we have talked so far (since we are talking about the Harm Prevention Principle) of regulations that aim ultimately to prevent harm, we need not suppose that all systems of legal regulation have that as their sole or primary aim; some might serve other aspects of the polity's common good, which cannot without distortion be brought under a Harm Principle. That, however, is not a debate on which we can embark here.

[49] A point often made in discussions of strict liability (at least for 'real' crimes): the fact that making liability strict would ease the prosecutor's burden or improve cost-effectiveness is not a good enough reason to do so.

not so clearly out of place in designing regulations: although we must still attend to the burdens that a proposed regulation would place on those subject to it, and should not readily allow the convenience of officials to weigh more heavily than citizens' freedom from regulatory burdens, there is still balancing to be done: we can still ask whether it is reasonable to ask citizens to accept this kind of regulatory burden for the sake of the efficient and economical administration of a system from which all benefit.

A crucial point to note is that we are not yet talking about criminal law or criminalisation: all we are discussing so far is the creation of regulations. Any suggestions about criminalisation will arise only when we ask how the regulations should be enforced: how should we treat breaches of them? As we saw above, we have obvious, and pre-regulatory, reason to criminalise the kinds of conduct covered by type-(a) regulations, since such conduct is already wrongfully harmful in a way that gives us reason to criminalise it under either Harm Principle. Type-(b) 'regulations' are not really regulations, but advisory guidelines: so the most that 'violations' of them would justify would be more forceful advice. With type-(c) regulations, we can still bring violations under the Harmful Conduct Principle: so long as they are sensibly created, someone who infringes them without knowing that he is entitled to an exception is like someone driving round a blind bend on the wrong side of the road; even if he is not actually creating a risk, he is taking an unjustified risk that his conduct is harmful. With type-(d) regulations, however (and regulations concerned with the administration of the system and with checking whether other regulations are obeyed), the Harmful Conduct Principle cannot help us: for we know that they prohibit some conduct that is not harmful, and that does not create or take an unjustified risk of harm or danger. But we can still see reason to criminalise breaches of them, on the basis of the Harm Prevention Principle, and consistently with the wrongfulness constraint: for if the regulations are justified as being efficient and not unduly burdensome ways of preventing harm, they are regulations that citizens ought to obey, breach of which is then wrongful – wrongful in a way that properly concerns the polity whose safety these regulations serve, and that thus merits formal, public censure.

This is a key difference between the Harmful Conduct Principle and the Harm Prevention Principle: that the latter can justify, as the former cannot, criminalising breaches of regulations which serve the ultimate aim of preventing harm, but which do so in part by prohibiting conduct that might not itself be harmful or dangerous. These are also offences which consist in conduct whose wrongfulness is post- rather than pre-legal: what makes the conduct wrongful is precisely the fact that it violates a legitimate regulation. However, we should note that this is *not* to say that what makes the conduct wrongful is even in part its criminalisation:[50] criminalisation, if

---

[50] See further RA Duff, 'Towards a Modest Legal Moralism' (2014) 8 *Criminal Law and Philosophy* 217, 219–21. Contrast *Crimes, Harms, and Wrongs*, 20: 'Sometimes, the very act of criminalisation plays a constitutive role in marking conduct out as wrongful' (see also at 72). It is true that a legislature might in fact combine regulation and criminalisation in the same statute: one might then say that 'the very act of criminalization [of passing the statute] plays a constitutive role in marking . . . out as wrongful'

it is to be legitimate, must still presuppose wrongfulness, and thus cannot without vicious circularity be said to create it. What helps to constitute the wrongfulness is the legal regulation, prior to which the conduct in question might not have been wrongful. Four points should be noted here.

First, we say only that the conduct '*might* not have been wrongful' prior to its regulation, not that it *would* not have been: for sometimes regulations prohibit types of conduct many examples of which are already wrongful because harmful, and prohibits them for just that reason. This is true of such familiar offences as speeding, and driving with excess alcohol. A defendant convicted for breaking the regulation, however, is convicted precisely for that breach, not for acting harmfully or dangerously: one whose fitness to drive was impaired by the amount of alcohol he had drunk is convicted of the same offence as someone who drove with the same level of alcohol but knew that it did not impair his fitness. He committed two wrongs, breaking the regulation and driving when unfit through drink, and if our laws include the latter offence as well as the former he could in principle be convicted of both; but his sentence for breaking the regulation should not reflect a judgment about whether his fitness was actually impaired, unless that has been proved.

Secondly, this provides part of the answer to the suggestion that, even if the regulation should be strict, allowing no exceptions for those who know that they can safely break it, once we move to criminalise breaches of the regulation we should also allow one who breaks it a defence if she can 'prove' that she knew that she could do so safely:[51] the primarily pragmatic reasons that can justify making regulations strict cannot justify making criminal liability strict. Now there are indeed questions about whether liability *for breaking the regulation* can legitimately be strict, as it often is under current law; but that is not the issue here. The case for allowing such a defence would be strong if the convicted defendant were being held liable for an offence of endangerment, since then she could properly argue that she should be allowed to offer evidence that her conduct was not dangerous; but that is not what she is being held liable for. If we can justify making the regulation strict, we can justifiably claim that drivers ought to obey it even if they know that they would not be creating or taking an unreasonable risk of causing harm if they broke it; and if that claim is justified, a driver who breaks the regulation commits a wrong – the wrong for which she is convicted.[52]

Thirdly, not only is the conduct that violates the regulation often not harmful, or dangerous, or wrongful independently of the regulation: it is often not even possible prior to the regulation. I can drive dangerously whether or not there are legal speed limits, but cannot break a speed limit unless there is one; I can fail to check whether my vehicle is in roadworthy condition whether or not there are formal

---

the conduct that is prohibited by the regulation and then criminalised in the same statute. But that would be misleading, since what makes the conduct wrongful is not the act of criminalisation qua act of criminalisation; it is made wrongful by the (logically pre-criminal) regulation.

[51] See n 37 above, and accompanying text.

[52] This is another reason why it is misleading to call these offences of (abstract, implicit) endangerment.

regulations on the matter, but cannot fail to obtain a MOT Test Certificate until there is a regulatory regime for such testing.

Fourthly, we have argued that such offences are post-legal, but not post-criminal: what makes the conduct relevantly wrongful is not that it constitutes a criminal offence (rather, it is made into a criminal offence because it is wrongful), but that it violates a legal regulation that we ought to obey. This distinction between 'post-legal' and 'post-criminal', however, is logical, rather than necessarily chrono-logical. That is, a legislature might simultaneously create the regulation, and crimi-nalise breaches of it, in the same statute. This does not undermine our argument, which is about the logic of criminalisation – about the logical structure of the kind of practical reasoning whose conclusion could be 'And therefore we should crimi-nalise Φing.' Within that structure, we have argued, a justification of regulation must be logically prior to criminalisation.

The materials for this kind of account, indeed its essential elements, are to be found in what von Hirsch and Simester say about 'remote harms';[53] indeed, a signal merit of their discussion is the way in which it brings these elements to light. However, the account becomes very much clearer once we distinguish, as they fail to distinguish clearly enough, the two Harm Principles in play in their discussion; once we realise that, under the Harm Prevention Principle, we need not worry about whether the ultimate harm to be prevented can be 'imputed' to the agents who are subject to the regulatory prohibition; and once we distinguish, as they fail to distinguish clearly enough, the question of regulation from that of criminalisa-tion. We have talked here in particular about what they call offences of 'abstract endangerment', but similar points apply (though not in quite the same way) to the other two kinds of 'remote harm' offences.[54]

IV. Why Should We Obey?

The argument of the previous section depended crucially on a claim about our duty to obey the regulations whose breach is to constitute a criminal offence. Such a claim raises two familiar questions: what grounds this duty to obey; and what is its scope? We cannot do more than note two points about these questions here.

First, the character, grounding and extent of any such duty of obedience clearly depend on a political theory – and we do not offer one here. However, if we ground the duty in an account of the associative duties that belong with citizenship in a

---

[53] See especially 'Remote Harms', 268 (on the 'obligation to co-operate in a safety-promoting scheme'), 272 (on 'duties of co-operation which each person owes in his capacity as citizen,' and more demanding, role-based 'responsibilit[ies] for co-operating to prevent remote harms'), 276 (on 'why ... those "safe" drivers should have an obligation to co-operate in such a scheme of driving safety'); *Crimes, Harms and Wrongs*, 73 (on the wrong done in breaches of harm-preventive regulations), 77–78 (on 'obligations of cooperation').

[54] See text at nn 16–26 above.

republican polity, we can see how there is room for talk of the 'civic arrogance' displayed by one who breaks the regulations.[55] The point is not that the criminalisable wrong consists in civic arrogance, or that that is what the rule-breaker should be convicted for; it is rather that one who flouts such rules, which serve the common good so long as they are obeyed by most people, might be accused of arrogantly setting himself above his law-abiding fellows. But the more relevant general point is that the duty to obey will take on a different character in relation to different rules; for we should expect a responsible citizen to obey, not blindly, but because she sees the point of the rule and of obeying it.[56] We might say that it is a matter of solidarity with one's fellow citizens to share in this way in the legal burdens that are imposed for the sake of some aspect of the common good (even, or especially, if the reasons for imposing the regulations have to do with the harms that others might cause but that I myself would not cause); we might talk of a duty to reassure others that we respect and obey the rules; but we might also have to talk of the particular ways in which particular kinds of regulation serve particular aspects of the common good.

Secondly, we have talked so far of the simple kind of case in which the regulations can be seen to be well-suited to their legitimate aims: in obeying them, we assist in a regulatory regime that serves the common good. But regulations are not always like that: they can mark reasonable but misguided attempts to serve the common good; they can be aimed as much at political advantage as at the common good; they can be incompetently, or corruptly, created. This problem is not peculiar to this context or to our account: any account of the law's authority (and this is a matter of the law's authority, not of the criminal law's authority; it concerns the duty whose violation is then a candidate for criminalisation) must have something to say about what obligations, if any, we have to obey legal regulations that we reasonably take to be in some way misguided, inapt, or improper; but that is not something we can discuss further here.[57] Since we have not suggested that citizens have a general duty to obey the law come what may, we need not say that they ought to obey, or may be convicted for disobeying, any and every kind of regulation that a government might create. We have appealed only to the more plausible idea that citizens have obligations to obey regulations that are well-designed to prevent kinds of harm that are the proper business of the polity, and that do not impose unreasonable burdens or limits on those required to obey them: such obligations can be generated by applying the Harm Prevention Principle (but not always by applying the Harmful Conduct Principle), and we have reason to criminalise failures to fulfil them.

---

[55] See n 33 above.

[56] Compare WA Edmundson, 'The Virtue of Law-Abidance' (2006) 6 *Philosophers' Imprint* 1.

[57] For useful discussion, see D Markel, 'Retributive Justice and the Demands of Democratic Citizenship' (2012) 1 *Virginia Journal of Criminal Law* 1, on 'dumb but not illiberal' laws.

12

Using 'Quality of Life' to Legitimate Criminal Law Intervention: Gauging Gravity, Defining Disorder

NINA PERŠAK

So far, the concept of the quality of life has not received much theoretical examination in substantive[1] criminal law. This has partly to do with the criminal law being more immediately focused upon the criminal infringements or offences than on the value (ie quality of life) which the prohibitions supposedly protect, and partly with the notion of the quality of life itself, its medical and environmental connotations. Even where the underlying protected values have been given more consideration, this has happened under their more 'legal' name, eg legal goods (*Rechtsgüter*) or legally protected interests, which have been examined without much further attempt to connect them to even more basic underlying notions, such as the notion of the quality of life.

One writer who has explicitly examined the normative prospects of quality of life is Andreas von Hirsch, in his work on the seriousness of crime and particularly in his and Nils Jareborg's article on the gauging of crime seriousness through the conception of a 'living standard'. It is von Hirsch's account that has particularly inspired this chapter. Criminalisation of incivilities progressively expanded across the last decade in several European countries, bringing new challenges to the measuring of the seriousness of 'crime', broadly conceived. Challenges arise, first, because incivilities are not always criminalised as a crime proper, ie as a criminal offence in the strict sense, but often are instead regulated through the law of violations,[2] civil law (eg ASBO orders), or administrative law. Secondly, challenges also lie in the fact that while some anti-social behaviour decidedly involves harm, some other types of

---

[1] In procedural criminal law, the term quality of life has been occasionally linked with the benefits of the existence of criminal procedure or proceedings. For example, a day in court has been said to have advantages over other possible methods of crime control in that 'private enterprise vengeance and control through executive action would avoid the drama and procedural messiness of a criminal trial, but would vastly diminish the quality of life': D Lanham, B Bartal, R Evans and D Wood, *Criminal Laws in Australia* (Sydney, The Federation Press, 2006) 1 (ch 1.B).

[2] Violations (*Ordnungswidrigkeiten* in German, *prekrški* in Slovenian) are minor offences, somewhat similar to regulatory offences save for the fact that violations are considered part of the criminal law, not of the administrative law. Together with the criminal law in the strict sense (criminal offences encapsulated in the Criminal Code) they form part of the so-called criminal law in the broad sense.

uncivil behaviour involve no setback to an individual's interest (ie harm), but are merely (or at most) offensive and sometimes nothing more than just annoying.

This chapter will first reflect on the possibility and importance of using quality of life standards in assessing the harmfulness of prohibited conduct. Then, we shall assess how the 'quality of life' concept can be used to legitimate criminal law interventions in two ways. Primarily, we shall examine how it can be used to define and categorise harm, partly drawing on von Hirsch and Jareborg's model (as expounded in the 2005 updated and amended version of their article),[3] and partly developing, or rather outlining, an amended account (by making some changes to the proposed model). Lastly, we shall inspect the role and usefulness of this concept in the definition or criminalisation of disorder ('incivilities').

I. Assessing Harm

The importance of gauging the seriousness, particularly the harmfulness, of crime – in absolute and comparative terms – cannot be over-emphasised. The notion of harm paves the way for a large proportion of criminalisation. Several authors who have attempted to flesh out principles of legitimate criminalisation[4] as well as some countries (eg Finland and Sweden) have extensively engaged with it. Similar efforts can recently be observed at EU level with main EU institutions publishing their own views on the strategy for future EU criminal law development. In all of these attempts, harm-based criminalisation takes centrestage.[5] In modern criminalisation theory, harm to others constitutes one (and the most widely-accepted)[6] of the 'good reasons' or legitimate grounds for criminalisation.

[3] A von Hirsch and N Jareborg, 'Gauging crime seriousness: A "Living Standard" conception of criminal harm' in A von Hirsch and A Ashworth, *Proportionate Sentencing: Exploring the Principles* (Oxford, Oxford University Press, 2005) 187.

[4] See, eg, J Feinberg, *Harm to Others: The Moral Limits of the Criminal Law* (New York, Oxford University Press, 1984), N Peršak, *Criminalising Harmful Conduct: The Harm Principle, its Limits and Continental Counterparts* (New York, Springer, 2007), AP Simester and A von Hirsch, *Crimes, Harms and Wrongs: On the Principles of Criminalisation* (Oxford, Hart Publishing, 2011).

[5] The Council of the EU (2009) has thus on 30 November 2009 issued its *Conclusions on model provisions, guiding the Council's criminal law negotiations* (2979th Justice and Home Affairs Council meeting, Brussels, 30 November 2009), suggesting the model on which the future proposals in the area of criminal law should be based. In September 2011, the European Commission, followed with a landmark Communication *Towards an EU Criminal Policy: Ensuring the effective implementation of EU policies through criminal law* (COM(2011) 573 final of 20 September 2011), wherein it stressed, for example, that seriousness and character of the breach of law must be taken into account when choosing among different types of regulation. The European Parliament issued its own document on the topic in May 2012, emphasising (inter alia) 'that the necessity of new substantive criminal law provisions must be demonstrated by the necessary factual evidence making it clear . . .that the criminal provisions focus on conduct causing significant pecuniary or non-pecuniary damage to society, individuals or a group of individuals' (*European Parliament resolution of 22 May 2012 on an EU approach to criminal law,* 2010/2310(INI) of 22 May 2012).

[6] Despite its wide acceptance, the harm principle's underlying cultural or political assumptions should be acknowledged. The harm principle, and more concretely its articulation (what should

The notion of harm, as 'the fulcrum between criminal conduct and the punitive sanction',[7] does not pave the way merely for the justification for criminalisation, but also for the sentencing process. The principle of proportionality demands that the sentence be proportionate to the seriousness of crime, which means that assessments of harm have important criminal policy as well as penological relevance. Moreover, they are also of central importance in various restorative justice initiatives, which are primarily oriented towards doing justice by restoring the harm resulting from the criminal offence.[8]

The seriousness of crime has two main dimensions: the (wrongful) harmfulness of the act (or omission) and the culpability of the offender.[9] While the latter has received some doctrinal itemisation into different categories (ie intent, negligence, etc), the ranking of the former has received no such or similar theoretical attention, which is surprising considering its pivotal role in determining crime seriousness and providing a yardstick for criminal law policy. Furthermore, in today's times, marked by the proliferation of criminalisation of less-than-seriously harmful (or even harmless) conduct – as reflected, for example, in the criminalisation of incivilities – an assessment of the harm involved is particularly needed to pin that which is worthy of criminalisation to a set of objective, justifiable criteria.

A. Different types of harm assessments

The harm that is the object of assessment in this chapter is the general, standard harm that regularly or ordinarily results from a particular type of harmful conduct, not the post facto harm that actually results in a concrete case. In this respect, harm – and our enterprise – differs from harm as usually examined within mainstream criminology. Harm-based approaches in criminology are mostly concerned with harm that can be empirically measured, harm that has resulted from some criminal activity (such as drug trafficking), and often include harm very broadly conceived (including self-harm, remote harms and harm not limited to setback of interests). The first steps towards the measuring of harm were done by Sellin and Wolfgang's

---

count as harm), rests on a certain political-normative vision of society, a concretely liberal democratic society, which exposes it to challenges of cultural or political diversity between states, which may have implications for criminal law and criminal policy. Diversity and cultural particularities may, for instance, influence the decision regarding the selection of legitimate principles for criminalisation. More in N Peršak, 'Norms, harms and disorder at the border: the legitimacy of criminal law intervention through the lens of criminalisation theory' in N Peršak (ed), *Legitimacy and Trust in Criminal Law, Policy and Justice: Norms, Procedures, Outcomes* (Farnham, Ashgate, 2014).

[7] J Hall, *General Principles of Criminal Law*, 2nd edn (Clark, Lawbook Exchange, 2008; orig 1960) 213.

[8] G Bazemore and L Walgrave, 'In search of fundamentals and an outline for systemic reform' in G Bazemore and L Walgrave (eds), *Restorative Juvenile Justice: Repairing the Harm by Youth Crime* (Monsey, Criminal Justice Press, 1999) 45.

[9] Not only doctrinally, but also in people's assessments, it seems: 'intentionality and victim harm were the two primary dimensions represented in the offences sorted by the respondents' (DA Parton, M Hansel and JR Straton, 'Measuring crime seriousness: Lessons from the National Survey of Crime Severity' (1991) 31 *British Journal of Criminology* 72, 75.

influential work *The Measurement of Delinquency*,[10] which led to the development of the National Survey of Crime Severity (NSCS) in the United States. Subsequent research on crime seriousness has mostly focused on traditional street crimes such as murder and burglary, with occasional examinations of white-collar crimes.[11] However, measuring perceived or actually resulting harm is not the same as using harm as a criminalisation yardstick. The concept of harm in our enterprise is a general, standard, regularly occurring wrongful harm that is typical for a given (paradigmatic) criminal offence. Whereas such criminological initiatives aim predominantly at measuring the impact of criminal victimisation or at calculating the costs of crime, and are conducted for prevention purposes (to make criminal policy recommendations directed toward reducing aggregate harm in the future), our task here is to find normative justification for state penal intervention in cases of certain wrongful harms, to explain why they justify prima facie criminalisation.

The concept of criminal harm, ie wrongful harm to others, as used here is also different from the concept of social harm, advocated by the social harm approach. The latter is primarily concerned with the harm that is caused to society in general, not necessarily individualised and not limited to criminal harm, ie harm caused by a crime. For this reason, social harm analysis also aims to inform or influence broader social policy decisions, extending beyond criminal policy.[12]

Another type of measuring of harm, or rather measuring of perceived harm, is through public opinion surveys (sometimes also using focus groups, vignettes, etc). Such empirical studies are clearly important since, amongst other things, having criminalised offences and their penalties broadly in line with people's expectations is important for trust in the criminal justice institutions and consequently for the perceived legitimacy of criminal law.[13] Regular testing of people's assessment of harm and comparison with the actual black-letter law is therefore valuable, as it provides a litmus test for the public support of criminal law and affects compliance therewith. Empirical studies, such as the one by Sellin and Wolfgang, are important also because they indicate that persons from different backgrounds and walks of life tend to rank some common offences similarly.[14] This may suggest that certain gradations of harm are intuitive or perhaps socialised, acquired quite early on in our

---

[10] T Sellin and M Wolfgang, *The Measurement of Delinquency* (New York, John Wiley, 1964).

[11] T O'Connor Shelley, T Chiricos and M Gertz, 'What about the environment? Assessing the perceived seriousness of environmental crime' (2011) 35 *International Journal of Comparative and Applied Criminal Justice* 307.

[12] P Hillyard, Ch Pantazis, S Tombs and D Gordon (eds), *Beyond Criminology: Taking Harm Seriously* (London, Pluto Press, 2004).

[13] See eg T Tyler, 'Legitimacy and criminal justice: the benefits of self-regulation' (2009) 7 *Ohio State Journal of Criminal Law* 307 and Peršak, 'Norms', above n 6.

[14] A certain consensus has been noted since the early days of assessing perceived crime seriousness. O'Connor, Shelley, Chiricos and Gertz ('What about the environment?', above n 11) mention several studies which have found a general consensus on crime seriousness across class, gender, age, and racial or ethnic categories. For example, studies by T Sellin and M Wolfgang, *The measurement of delinquency* (Montclair, Patterson Smith, 1964); PH Rossi, R Waite, CE Bose and RE Berk, 'The seriousness of crimes: A normative structure and individual differences' (1974) 39 *American Sociological Review* 224; ME Wolfgang, RM Figlio, PE Tracy and SI Singer, *The national survey of crime severity* (Washington DC, Government Printing Office, 1985).

lives; or at least that consensus on the ranking of harms is not as difficult to achieve as one might think.

However, such public opinion-based or factual assessment of harm is not appropriate for our purposes. Our exercise is normative and strives to formulate some objective criteria for distinguishing between different types of harms. As von Hirsch and Jareborg emphasise, developing a conceptual basis for notions of crime seriousness requires a normative grading of the important human interests that are violated or harmed by legitimate proscribed offences. People's subjective assessments may be grounded on such rational notions, albeit not reflected upon; they may, alternatively, stem from their own personal experiences, past victimisations, current insecurities, their subjective valorisation of certain interests as more important than they ordinarily are (in an average person in normally peaceful times and so forth). They may be too subjective and biased. Either way, even if people's assessments are based on unarticulated yet objective, rational criteria, these moral judgements need to be clearly articulated. In short, although empirical studies on public views of harmfulness may provide a welcome evidence base for future criminal policy (particularly relevant if the gap between the existing legal rankings and people's expressed rankings is very wide), they should not in themselves represent a basis for the legal–rational ranking of harms.

B. Conceptions of harm

Kleinig[15] was one of the first writers to tackle the underdeveloped concept of harm, noting four traditions in the historical development of the concept. In the first tradition, harm (from Old English 'hearm') denoted grief or sorrow and was thus a psychological phenomenon, which was experienced or sensed. In the second tradition, harm came to be associated also with the loss that occasioned the grief or sorrow. Harm could now occur without being felt, without the 'hurt'. A subsequent tradition narrowed the notion to a moral concept ('only acts are harmful; only people do harm') and, it seems, linked it with wrongfulness, for 'who harms me wrongs me.' The fourth tradition, which is a legal one, defines harm as a violation of a legally protected interest. Kleinig further distinguishes three uses of the ambiguous concept of 'interest', only one of which – based on the notion of welfare – he believes to be of central importance for an understanding of harm.[16] Harm is ultimately to be understood as 'the impairment of a being's welfare interests.'

Similarly, Feinberg conceived of 'harm' as an invaded interest or as any thwarting, setting back or defeating of an interest,[17] and defined one category of

---

[15] J Kleinig, 'Crime and the concept of harm' (1978) 15 *American Philosophical Quarterly* 27.

[16] The other two uses of 'interest', according to Kleinig, are: (a) interest as a more psychological phenomenon ('X is interested in Y'), and (b) stake-related interest ('X has an interest in Y').

[17] See J Feinberg, *Social Philosophy* (Englewood Cliffs, Prentice-Hall, 1973) and Feinberg, *Harm to Others*, above n 4. Harm as defeating of an interest is used when the harm is conceived in a non-normative way. However, in several places, Feinberg also defines harm as a 'wrongful setback of interests'. See H Stewart, 'Harms, wrongs, and set-backs in Feinberg's 'Moral Limits of the Criminal Law' (2001) 5 *Buffalo Criminal Law Review* 47, on discussion of Feinberg's dual use of the notion of harm.

particularly serious harms as harms thwarting 'basic welfare interests'. Feinberg's welfare interests are those that provide 'the generalised means to the advancement of ulterior interests' of a person.[18] This seems very future-choice-oriented and not sufficiently present-oriented: a welfare interest is, on this account, set back only if it reduces or limits our *future* decisions, options, life plans or advancement of our ulterior interests, not because it hurts us now. Causing pain, as von Hirsch and Jareborg note,[19] is harmful not (or not only) because it reduces our future options but because 'avoidance of pain is in itself essential to the quality of a person's life.'

Some progress can be made by connecting basic welfare interests with human needs. Ward, for example, links Feinberg's basic welfare interests with basic human needs and describes them as interests in 'those elements of freedom and wellbeing that are necessary for human beings to function effectively as purposive agents.' Such basic interests include 'such things as life, physical and mental health, freedom from severe pain, freedom from confinement or coercion, and sufficient education and financial resources to enable one to play a part in the life of one's society.'[20] A similarly significant overlap of human needs with the existing schemes of basic interests can be found in Kleinig's account of human welfare interests. These provide 'preconditions for the pursuit or fulfilment of whatever specific projects we have', tend to be 'fairly uniform' and clearly include 'bodily and mental health, normal intellectual development, adequate material security, stable and non-superficial interpersonal relationships, and a fair degree of liberty'.[21] The account of criminal harm that ties interests with human needs is promising and appealing not only because basic human needs are fairly universal and well explored (albeit not within the law), but also because it accords with the *ultima ratio* principle or minimalist orientation towards criminal law. For this reason, it will be advocated here and further elaborated below. First, however, we turn to von Hirsch and Jareborg's account of harm, based on the notion of a living standard.

C. The 'living standard' conception

The grading of criminal harms through a living standard analysis, proposed by von Hirsch and Jareborg, includes several elements. First, certain assumptions have to be made regarding an average person's resources, in order to be able to gauge standard harms. The assumptions include that the average person has a variety of interests, ranging from subsistence interests to higher wellbeing interests. Secondly, a middle-term perspective of about one year is proposed as a time frame for assessing the quality of someone's life. Thirdly, the four-level grading scheme, which describes the categories of one's living standard or wellbeing, is composed of: sub-

---

[18] Feinberg, *Harm to Others*, above n 4 at 42.
[19] von Hirsch and Jareborg, 'Gauging crime seriousness', above n 3 at 192.
[20] T Ward, 'State harms' in P Hillyard, Ch Pantazis, S Tombs and D Gordon (eds), *Beyond Criminology: Taking Harm Seriously* (London, Pluto Press, 2004) 84, 85.
[21] Kleinig, 'Crime and the Concept of Harm', above n 15 at 31.

sistence (survival, maintenance of merely elementary human capacities to function), minimal wellbeing (maintenance of minimal level of comfort and dignity), adequate wellbeing (maintenance of adequate level of comfort and dignity), and standard wellbeing (maintenance of full life quality). These levels correspond to the degree to which a given intrusion affects a victim's living standard. These four gradations have been proposed because the differences among them are reasonably apparent, although the authors acknowledge that the reality is to be found on a continuum. Fourthly, the suggested generic interest dimensions that harmful conduct can infringe upon are three: physical integrity, material support and amenity, and privacy/freedom from humiliation. This list is based on the authors' impressions of the main kinds of concerns that seem typically involved in 'victimising crimes', and is not claimed to be exhaustive.

Later, the authors present their harming scale, ranging from very grave (death), grave, serious, upper-intermediate, lower-intermediate to lesser harmful consequences (living standard not affected or only marginally so) and apply their analysis to some cases of harms. The proposed assessment or grading of harms should start with identifying the interest dimensions involved in an offence, followed by an application of the living standard gradation criteria to each dimension in a successive order. In the case of a simple burglary (stolen TV set), for example, the interests identified would thus be material amenity and privacy, and the living standard impact (regarding the material amenity) would usually be quite limited.

II. Developing a Quality of Life Conception of Harm

The model proposed by von Hirsch and Jareborg presents a pioneering work in terms of examining harm theoretically and assessing philosophically how to rank 'harms'. It provides us with a well-substantiated conception of harm and ways to differentiate between various types of harm as well as conceptualised different degrees of harm, ie degrees of intrusion or violation of our legally protected interests. Moreover, the model allows further elaboration, some of which will be outlined next.

Some may take issue with the living standard conception as such and find it, at least *qua* name, inadequate, as 'standard of living' is essentially an economic term. It focuses on economic standing, economic standard of living or the 'level of wealth, comfort, material goods and necessities available to a certain socioeconomic class in a certain geographic area'.[22] Elsewhere it is described as a 'level of material comfort as measured by the goods, services, and luxuries available to an individual, group, or nation',[23] 'a level of subsistence or material welfare of a community, class, or person' or 'the degree of wealth and material comfort available to a person or

---

[22] en.wikipedia.org/wiki/Standard_of_living.
[23] www.thefreedictionary.com/standard+of+living.

community',[24] and 'the amount of money and comfort people have in a particular society'.[25] Economic indicators, however, do not provide sufficient information on the quality of life of an individual. In fact, the standard of living is precisely for this reason often contrasted with the quality of life: it is commonly said that the latter 'takes into account not only the material standard of living, but also other more intangible aspects that make up human life, such as leisure, safety, cultural resources, social life, physical health, environmental quality issues, etc.'[26] Von Hirsch and Jareborg explicitly state that they use Amartya Sen's broad conception of the living standard, which includes economic as well as non-economic interests;[27] however, it seems that this broad notion has not penetrated into the usual, everyday discourse on the living standard. The latter still evokes a predominant economic vision of human wellbeing, while 'quality of life' itself is understood in a broader sense even in ordinary language. It may therefore be preferable to use the notion of 'quality of life' and develop a model based on 'quality of life' standards, even though this is by no means an easy task.

A. What is 'Quality of Life'?

Quality of life is a multi-dimensional notion that shies away from precise definition. Its meaning changes across time and place. Furthermore, different people understand it differently. Some understand the notion to primarily require a clean environment without litter and nasty smells; others understand it as having (at least) a job that allows bills to be paid regularly; some see it as having a clean bill of health; others again as having enough money to have (at least occasional) access to luxury. How should we then define the quality of life? And more concretely, how should it be defined for legal purposes?

Is it possible to understand quality of life as a legal good (*Rechtsgut*) or even as a criminal law good, whose infringement should be prohibited by criminal law? In its complexity, it is perhaps more suitable for what the German legal theory describes as *Grundrechtsgut*, ie the most fundamental legal good, from which other legal goods/values, such as inviolability, privacy, life, etc, can be derived. Is it thus already protected in the existing black-letter law – albeit largely indirectly, through protecting the values that concretise this 'ultimate' value? Perhaps the quality of life is comprised of Finnis' seven basic objective goods that are good in themselves, ie whose worthiness is evident and objective, independent from our experience (or lack thereof) of pleasure while pursuing them?[28] Or Rawls' 'primary goods' that

---

[24] www.oxforddictionaries.com/definition/english/standard-of-living.

[25] www.dictionary.cambridge.org/dictionary/british/standard-of-living.

[26] en.wikipedia.org/wiki/Standard_of_living.

[27] Von Hirsch and Jareborg, 'Gauging crime seriousness', above n 3 at 191.

[28] See J Finnis, *Natural Law and Natural Rights* (Oxford, Oxford University Press, 1997; orig 1980). According to Finnis, seven self-evident goods are: life, knowledge, play, aesthetic experience, friendship (sociability), religion and practical reasonableness. The first five may truly be self-evident to the majority of people, while religion may be self-evident only to religious people, although he defines it broadly as

every rational person is presumed to want 'whatever a person's rational plan of life',[29] such as basic liberties, self-respect, opportunity and minimum of wealth (primary social goods)?

A sufficiently useful account of the requirements of quality of life for legal purposes must clearly include all preconditions for a healthy and successful life of an individual in a society, which first and foremost means the fulfilment of basic human needs. As such, a useful conception should incorporate not just basic goods but also capabilities of pursuing these goods. The preconditions for healthy, successful living should therefore include resources, capabilities, opportunities, choices, mental and physical capacities to make choices and a sufficient autonomy and freedom to do so. Preconditions also include access to those resources that grant or enhance these capabilities and freedoms, ie to education and employment.[30] A good quality of life must therefore include interests as basic as health, food, sleep (which, according to Maslow, satisfy lowest-level 'physiological needs'), shelter, safety or freedom from danger and freedom from pain, as well as 'ulterior interests' catering to higher needs and desires, such as friendship, cooperation, having stable and meaningful interpersonal relationships (Kleinig), belonging, esteem, self-esteem and possibility for personal growth, self-betterment or self-actualisation. As such, it fully covers Maslow's structure of basic needs.[31] It also corresponds to Doyal and Gough's ordering of needs, which includes 'health needs', 'autonomous needs' and 'intermediate needs' as well as material and procedural preconditions.[32] Autonomous needs, closely linked to esteem, allow us to make informed choices to achieve conscious goals and contain mental health, cognitive skills and opportunities to engage in social participation. Intermediate needs, which are essential for basic needs and for enabling the satisfaction of autonomous needs are: adequate nutritional food and water, adequate protective housing, non-hazardous work environment, non-hazardous physical environment, appropriate health care, security in childhood, significant primary relationships with others,

---

'all those beliefs that can be called matters of ultimate concern; questions about the point of human existence'. Practical reasonableness, on the other hand, is not entirely clearly defined and remains somewhat controversial: see S Buckle, 'Natural Law' in P Singer (ed), *A Companion to Ethics* (Oxford, Blackwell Publishers, 1997) 161.

[29] J Rawls, *A Theory of Justice* (Cambridge MA, The Belknap Press of Harvard University Press, 1995; orig 1971) 62.

[30] Due to the employment's role in reducing poverty, it constitutes a very pervasive component of the individual's self-concept: see P Kelvin and JE Jarrett, *Unemployment: Its Social Psychological Effects* (Cambridge, Cambridge University Press; Paris, Editions de la Maison des Sciences de l'Homme, 1985) 58. Employment links with (social) security against unemployment as well as health security. It is a well-known fact that unemployment has negative social psychological impacts on people's health. From the1930s onwards, there is ample research (eg M Jahoda, PF Lazarsfeld and H Zeisel, *Marienthal: The Sociography of an Unemployed Community* (New York, Aldine-Atherton, 1971; orig 1933); D Fryer and R Fagan, 'Coping with unemployment' (1993) 23 *International Journal of Political Economy* 95) showing that unemployment is producing a series of unwelcome psychological consequences, ranging from anxiety, depression, reduced self-esteem to social isolation and reduced levels of activity.

[31] AH Maslow, 'A Theory of Human Motivation' (1943) 50 *Psychological Review* 370 and AH Maslow, *Motivation and Personality* (New York, Harper & Row, 1970).

[32] L Doyal and I Gough, *A Theory of Human Need* (Basingstoke, Macmillan, 1991).

physical security, economic security, safe birth control and child-bearing, and appropriate basic and cross-cultural education. Procedural preconditions relate to our ability to identify needs and ways how to satisfy them, while material ones refer to the capacity to produce those things that can satisfy the needs.

This does not necessarily mean, however, that all interests within the concept of quality of life (that can be realised in different degrees) are necessarily relevant for the notion of 'criminal harm' or that all intrusions on the protected interests count equally. As a matter of principle, criminalisation should include only sufficiently serious harm (in the sense of serious encroachment upon significant interests). One could argue that if certain interests, despite their importance, are not significant enough, or if infringement of significant interests is not of a sufficiently high degree, criminalisation should be avoided. For example, although privacy is an important interest, even need, and a violation of it therefore potentially relevant harm, minor intrusions (eg taking a photo of someone standing on their balcony or other less-than-public place) may not be deemed sufficiently intrusive or significantly harmful to justify invoking the criminal law.

B. Outlining an amended framework: the Quality of Life model

Based on human needs as conceptualised above, we may try to derive 'quality of life' interests, and consequently harm (derived from the infringements thereof), in the following way:

- Physical: fulfilled physiological needs, food, physical (including sexual) integrity, safety, etc;
- Material: including shelter, economic or financial resources, access to education, a healthy and unpolluted environment, etc;[33]
- Psychological: mental health needs, self-esteem, belonging, etc;
- Normative: (living conditions that respect) widely acknowledged normative standards and values, which allow the individual to pursue his life choices, express himself and engage in meaningful social interactions (eg privacy, autonomy, individuality, fairness, equal treatment, being treated with respect/dignity, etc).

The first two categories are quite straightforward or self-explanatory, included also in von Hirsch and Jareborg's model. The latter two categories, which are not present or are differently conceptualised on their model, need some further explanation.

Regarding the third, psychological category, von Hirsch and Jareborg expressly refuse to include it in their generic interest dimensions, arguing that it is 'too much

---

[33] Adequate environment is also a legal right. For the discussion on this, see MJ Azurmendi and I Olaizola, 'Sustainable Quality of Life: Cultural Diversity, Environmental Law and Building Citizenship' (2003) 4 *Medio Ambiente y Comportamiento Humano* 127.

of a catch-all to be of help'.[34] This criticism could be avoided, however, if the category is sufficiently narrowly defined. Having a separate category of psychological harm is, additionally, more in line with victimological categorisation of harms, which would be important in the context of victimising harms (and these are the ones von Hirsch and Jareborg, and myself are concerned with).[35] To make the category useful, however, psychological harm should not be defined as any negative emotional state or unpleasant psychological impact (this danger, it seems, is also the main reason why von Hirsch and Jareborg prefer to disregard it). The latter could arise for entirely subjective reasons in the mind of the 'victim', without being explicable in a way that says anything about the wrongfulness or harmfulness of conduct that stimulated it. For this reason, conduct amounting to psychological harm (or violation of the psychological quality of life) has to be limited to proper harm, meaning that there should be a setback of interest, making the victim 'worse-off'.[36] Temporary offendedness will not do.[37] Psychological harm would therefore include such harms as lingering (longer-term) adverse psychological consequences caused by physical harm (torture) or emotional manipulation (in kidnapping or in domestic violence), effects of stalking, harms arising out of harmful psychological treatments,[38] trauma (Post Traumatic Stress Disorder), defamation (a setback to the interest of good reputation) and other similar harms to the psychological quality of life.

The fourth category comprises widely accepted normative standards and values (or living conditions that respect those values), which allow the individual to pursue his life choices, express himself and engage in meaningful social interactions. These values or interests are often constitutionalised (such as privacy) or elevated to the status of rights or freedoms (eg freedom from humiliation, or dignity). This category hosts normative elements that individually or collectively make our lives in a certain time and place more 'valuable'. Self-direction and autonomy[39] are, for example, values or interests that allow us to construct and follow our own life plans. Individuality may be important for its contribution to one's personal identity.[40]

---

[34] von Hirsch and Jareborg, 'Gauging crime seriousness', above n 3 at 207.

[35] Eg B Spalek, *Crime Victims: Theory, Policy and Practice* (Basingstoke, Palgrave Macmillan, 2006).

[36] Feinberg, *Harm to Others*, above n 4; Peršak, *Criminalising Harmful Conduct*, above n 4.

[37] Simester and von Hirsch, *Crimes, Harms, and Wrongs*, above n 4 at 112–14, when discussing psychological harm versus offence, stress that for a person to be psychologically harmed their personal resources or coping abilities need to be impaired in various ways (as examples, they mention trauma, having difficulty concentrating on one's work or having difficulty conducting normal social relations), which are 'not the standard effects of offensive behaviour'.

[38] See, eg, SO Lilienfeld, 'Psychological treatments that cause harm' (2007) 1 *Perspectives on Psychological Science* 53.

[39] L Tay and E Diener, 'Needs and Subjective Well-Being around the World' (2011) 101 *Journal of Personality and Social Psychology* 354.

[40] John Stuart Mill (*On Liberty and Other Essays* (Oxford, Oxford University Press, 1991; orig 1859)), who built upon the Aristotelian and Humboldtian account of happiness (expounded in chapter 3 of his book), considered a person's individuality as being one of the elements of wellbeing. Drawing upon this, he viewed all interference with the liberty of action of the individual as prima facie wrong. See more in DG Brown, 'Mill on liberty and morality' in CL Ten (ed), *Mill's moral, political and legal philosophy* (Aldershot, Ashgate, 1999) 137.

Many of the interests or values pertaining to this group, eg individuality and privacy, are, however, culturally specific or culturally determined, which allows some variance between countries.

Some values included in our fourth category overlap with von Hirsch and Jareborg's third interest dimension, which is named 'privacy/freedom from humiliation' – one dimension with two elements. Our category of widely acknowledged values includes privacy, while freedom from humiliation is, at least on the account proposed here, tantamount to dignity, ie to treating people in a way that respects their dignity. Von Hirsch and Jareborg find freedom from humiliation more appropriate than dignity, which they claim is too broad, as it depends in part on one's own self-conceptions. It is unclear how the notion of 'humiliation' in itself escapes this subjectivity. An individual who has an inflated conception of their dignity, on account of which any negative opinion against their person or another member of their family is seen as an affront to their personal dignity, would define 'humiliation' in terms just as broad as is their conception of dignity. What is required, rather, is to narrow it down, objectify and standardise the notion of dignity, so that it is pertinent for the ranking of criminal harms and allows minimal variation among people.

Since violations or infringements of values, interests and rights included in the fourth category can cause negative psychological reactions, one may ask, however, whether there is an overlap with the third category of psychological quality of life/ harms. Some of these values – particularly when (repeatedly) attacked or violated – may trigger negative emotions in us (make us angry, sad, fearful, etc). One may be therefore inclined to categorise such harms prima facie as psychological harm, arguing that some psychological harm does not necessarily arise from, say, factual trauma but rather may arise from an affront to these well-accepted societal values, particularly when they are internalised (merging the normative and the factual).

I would argue that harms arising out of humiliation or privacy violation, or violation of other important socially recognised values/rights (eg autonomy, respect, self-direction[41]), should be assessed separately, on their own merits. Such harms should be placed in a separate category of violations of widely accepted values to bring out the fact that, both in our ordinary language and in our ordinary moral judgements we differentiate between what we see as psychological harms, and what we object to as violations of privacy. We may get angry when our privacy is violated (eg someone takes a close-up picture of us without asking for permission or sits too closely, puts down a towel at the beach too close to ours) but we rarely see that as a psychological harm.

This does not mean, however, that such violations – when repetitive – cannot involve psychological harm. If or when violations of these values regularly (on average) trigger reactions that may be considered psychological harm, one might conclude that they should be accounted for (primarily) in that category. The question then arises as to whether it should be accounted for only in the third category or in

---

[41] Tay and Diener, 'Needs and Subjective Well-Being', above n 39 at 355.

both. As a rule, we ought to avoid double counting, which would happen if we penalised twice for the same harm. However, if a harmful conduct contains several different violations of quality of life categories, ie several different kinds of harm (or a composite harm, composed of several types of harm), then it could be accounted for in both – to the extent or degree the relevant type of harm intrudes upon a certain category of interests. A severe, repetitive violation of privacy or dignity that results in anxiety or distress that persists for a longer period of time may, for example, violate severely the fourth quality of life category and (only) moderately the third.

To sum up, the Quality of Life model involves the following substantive differences as compared to the 'living standard model' put forward by von Hirsch and Jareborg. First, this model builds on established schemes of human needs and consequently conceptualises 'harm' as a violation or a setback of those interests, capabilities or resources that are used to fulfil those needs. Secondly, the model's primary goal is not to inform sentencing decisions (as is the aim of von Hirsch and Jareborg's exercise), but to use it in order to justify criminalisation of harms and ascription of appropriate/proportionate sanction to the criminal offence in the process of criminalisation. Therefore, harm used for my purposes is less personalised than the concrete harm that needs to be taken into account when sentencing. Yet, even criminalisation does not fully avoid personalisation. At the criminalisation level, offences are also personalised to a certain extent (eg when an act is only a crime when committed against a certain group of people, such as presidents or policemen); however, the personalisation here is more group-based than individual-based. General mitigating or aggravating circumstances are only personalised at the stage of sentencing. However, certain offences, which are only aggravated (more harmful) versions of the basic offence, may already gain independent status at the criminalisation level. Aggravated theft is, for example, a graver version of the offence of theft and yet a criminal code may define it separately as an independent offence.[42] Thirdly, the new model includes the psychological dimension, thereby expanding the categories of harm/quality of life, drawing on the victimological categorisation of harm (or of victimisation), making the categories perhaps more coherent and more in line with how we typically see harm. Fourthly, groups of important interests are somewhat differently conceptualised: physical, material, psychological and normative.

On the other hand, a lot remains the same: harm within the terms of this new model remains a standardised harm, ie harm to an average person that ordinarily arises from the relevant conduct. It is also individualised, ie individual or victimising harm (harm to identifiable victims), not collective or aggregate harm and, similarly, includes interests that are only self-regarding. Moreover, I fully accept the grading of the degrees of intrusion. The ultimate ranking of harm must accommodate the fact that these interests may be harmed to a different degree by a given type

---

[42] As it is, for example, in Slovenia. Theft is criminalised in Art 204, while Grand Theft (*velika tatvina*) is a separate offence, criminalised in Art 205 of the Slovene Criminal Code (KZ-1-UPB2, Official Journal no 50/2012 from 29 June 2012).

of harmful conduct. On the basis of differential interference with one's quality of life, the four groups or degrees of intrusion, as developed by von Hirsch and Jareborg, continue to be useful; as does the proposed procedure of ranking of harms. As regards the types of intrusions or gradations of the seriousness of the violation, I propose a somewhat simpler nomenclature, eg mild, moderate, serious, and grave/severe.[43] Content-wise, these categories are not very different from the six gradations proposed by von Hirsch and Jareborg;[44] they may be, however, more useful for the legislator. The legislator, contemplating criminalisation – in opposition to the judge, contemplating sentencing – has to address abstract harms, ie harms that have not yet materialised, which are therefore more prototypical harms (arising out of a specific type of human conduct), harms that are less shaped by the particular details of the case. For this reason, the legislator could use a less nuanced approach.

The legislative exercise of assessing conduct on the Quality of Life model proposed above would therefore look very similar. Since von Hirsch and Jareborg already provide several illustrations of the ranking exercise for paradigmatic crimes, I will sketch one involving also psychological harm, as it is not included in their account: a case of domestic violence. Turning first to the sorts of considerations that a liberal-democratic legislator might engage in, his or her reasoning could look something like the following. Categories of quality of life/harm that are relevant in this case are the physical (violations of physical integrity and safety), psychological (a setback to mental health) and normative (violation of privacy, autonomy, dignity, etc) harm. Next, based also on empirical evidence, the regular (usual) degree of intrusion in these life-quality categories should be established; for example, moderate to serious intrusions in category 1 (physical), severe in category 3 (psychological) and serious in category 4 (normative). Assuming (as may be obvious), there is enough here to warrant criminalisation, this should be then compared to other similar offences, ie offences involving violations of similar interests (and their regular levels of intrusion in these interests) before deciding on an appropriate, proportionate sentence interval.

---

[43] Perhaps three main gradations (mild, moderate, severe) would initially suffice for the legislator, ie pre-criminalisation. Within each main gradation, however, there may be several other shades (of mildness, moderateness and severity), allowing for a more nuanced approach – particularly relevant for a judge in a concrete case.

[44] Von Hirsch and Jareborg ('Gauging crime seriousness', above n 3 at 213) list the following gradations, corresponding to the affected level of the living standard: I = very grave, II = grave, III = serious, IV = upper-intermediate, V = lower-intermediate, VI = lesser. 'Mild' intrusion on our proposed account could encompass their harm gradations V and VI, moderate could correspond to IV, serious to III and grave to their II and I.

III. Application of the Model in Different Cultural Settings

It may be, however, that in certain cultures (eg nomadic) the proposed four-partite structure of harms outlined above would not fully work – because, for example, a certain culture may not recognise or value private property or financial resources. There may therefore be some variations of the quality of life conception of harm in different cultural settings. Within the European context, however, it is difficult to find a country to which the proposed structure of harms (and implicitly protected legitimate interests) would not apply. Even so, there may still be time- and place-specific differences in the weight given to each individual interest (and consequently in valuing the graveness of a harm). Sweden may, for example, consider violations of individual interests that are tied to the individual's participation in the community to be more serious than would the United Kingdom. And the same country (eg the United States) may, for example, consider white-collar crime to be more serious because of its fuller comprehension of the extent of its harmful consequences now than it did 30 years ago.

Within the European culture(s), greater differentiation across time and place would probably be found in categories of material and psychological harm than in physical harm, as a physical pain (from eg a broken arm) is a rather stable indicator of harm, has identifiable objective or physical characteristics, relies little on symbolic interpretation, and is felt similarly unpleasant irrespective of whether one is Greek or Swedish, British or Bulgarian. In our European context, some variation may also arise with respect to the 'normative harm' (harm arising from the violation of the fourth quality of life interests category, as expounded above), despite the fact that certain fundamental values are considered to be shared among Member States. Regarding shared European standards, the Preamble to the Charter of Fundamental Rights refers to the shared values of human dignity, freedom, equality and solidarity, and the Preamble of the Treaty on European Union confirms Member States' attachment to the principles of liberty, democracy, respect for human rights and fundamental freedoms, to the rule of law and fundamental social rights. In Article 2, it states further that the Union is founded on the values of respect for human dignity, freedom, democracy, equality, the rule of law and respect for human rights, including the rights of persons belonging to minorities, and claims that these values are common to the Member States in a society in which pluralism, non-discrimination, tolerance, justice, solidarity and equality between women and men prevail.[45] Psychological harm, although more stable than mere offendedness, may be more contingent on the socialisation that shapes our sensibilities. It may be shaped by contexts that can transform the moral status of events.[46] Yet, even here,

---

[45] Treaty on European Union (TEU, Consolidated version), [2010] OJ C83/13, 30 March 2010.
[46] See CC Helwig, C Hildebrandt and E Turiel, 'Children's Judgments about Psychological Harm in Social Context' (1995) 66 *Child Development* 1680.

recent research suggests that there is not a great deal of difference. Tay and Diener thus note that 'the ordering of need fulfilment for psychosocial needs was fairly consistent across country conditions';[47] it was, rather, the fulfilment of basic and safety needs that was country-dependent.

IV. Quality of Life in Defining and Regulating Disorder? Distinction from Security Discourses

The concept of the quality of life that has been proposed in this chapter – offered as a measuring stick for all harms – differs markedly from references to quality of life in security-based discourses on 'disorder', or incivilities. This section will first outline the rather different concept of the quality of life that forms part of current rhetoric on disorder or 'quality of life crimes', before turning to consider the possible application of our new model of the quality of life in the area of incivilities, which is often regulated through the law of violations (rather than through criminal law in the strict sense).

Recent developments in security-based discourse owe much to the processes of gentrification in the metropolis, which have raised the quality of life of a certain class of people, while diminishing it for others.[48] The building of parks with benches which are built in such a way that no one can lie down on them may raise the quality of life of those who use the park for walks and benches for a short stop and rest, while at the same time they exclude certain other social groups (eg the homeless, who may use benches for sleep). The rhetoric of maintaining the quality of life is, furthermore, often used in existing immigration politics. The proponents of criminalisation of irregular migration often draw from the quality of life rhetoric by equating the very presence of immigrants with crime and subsequent devaluation of living environment, and through security discourse legitimate the growing number of surveillance techniques over immigrants.

The discourse of the quality of life has also been heard in the area of public order or incivilities. Incivilities include various infractions from writing graffiti and vandalism to littering, begging and making noise and so forth. This category comprises different socially undesirable behaviours (ranging from truly harmful to only minor or harmless) that are deemed to reduce the quality of people's lives in the community in some way, eg by disorderly conduct, by visible disorder in the neighbourhood, and so on. Zero tolerance that is exhibited towards such transgressions is often translated, directly or indirectly, into criminal prohibitions, which are often very vague and yet may attach quite severe and disproportionate penalties to the

---

[47] Tay and Diener, 'Needs and Subjective Well-Being', above n 39.
[48] S Sassen, *The Global City: New York, London and Tokyo* (Princeton NJ, Princeton University Press, 1991).

violation.[49] In the United Kingdom this type of human conduct is regulated under the term 'anti-social behaviour',[50] in the Netherlands and Belgium they are treated as incivilities, in Slovenia as public order offences and so forth.

In the United States, incivilities have not only been linked but also effectively renamed, in line with the desired rhetoric, as 'quality of life crime'.[51] The name in itself is interesting. If we see all crime as diminishing the victim's quality of life – as it effectively does – then why attach the notion only to a subcategory of crime? Does only littering or graffiti 'attack' one's 'quality of life' (if it does, at all), while much more serious crimes such as murder, rape, and burglary do not? These offences seem to relate purely or mostly to the top layers of Maslow's needs pyramid (aesthetics,[52] belonging, etc) while the bottom layers (shelter, etc) are left intact by such incivilities. When it is only or primarily aesthetically challenging acts (eg graffiti), or acts that offend our gaze due to their visibility or 'unsightliness', that are named quality of life offences, what conclusions can be drawn from this? That quality of life is reserved only for higher tastes? That mere attack on physical needs is not (yet) a quality of life issue?

To understand the (very limited) concept or definition of the quality of life within this existing discourse, one has to look at the political and criminal policy context of criminalising incivilities. The idea behind the more recent criminalisation of anti-social behaviour draws on the 'broken windows thesis',[53] which claims that even the slightest violation of social norms, first signs of disorder (such as broken windows) should be taken seriously and properly dealt with, as they will – if left unattended – escalate into more serious crime. This controversial hypothesis has been made a cornerstone of many an electoral campaign, often leading to punitive regulation of socially undesirable behaviour and unusual lifestyles; not necessarily via criminal law proper but, for example, through the law of violations[54] or through administrative sanctions (as in Belgium).

---

[49] See N Peršak, 'Norms', above n 6.

[50] See T Budd and L Sims, *Antisocial behaviour and disorder: findings from the 2000 British Crime Survey*, Findings 145 (London, Home Office, 2001); E Burney, *Making People Behave: Anti-Social Behaviour, Politics and Policy* (Cullompton, Willan Publishing, 2005); A von Hirsch and AP Simester, 'Penalising offensive behaviour: Constitutive and mediating principles' in A von Hirsch and AP Simester (eds), *Incivilities: Regulating Offensive Behaviour* (Oxford, Hart Publishing, 2006) 115.

[51] D Husak, 'Disgust: Metaphysical and Empirical Speculations' in von Hirsch and Simester (eds), *Incivilities*, ibid, 91.

[52] Millie observed that what people see as anti-social behaviour depends on situational (temporal and spacial) circumstances and that aesthetics are very important in determining the behavioural acceptability. See A Millie, *Anti-Social Behaviour* (Maidenhead, McGraw Hill/Open University Press, 2009).

[53] J Wilson and G Kelling, 'Broken windows: the police and neighbourhood safety' (1982) March, *The Atlantic Monthly* 29.

[54] Although violations are minor offences, they belong to the realm of criminal law in the broad sense (*lato sensu*) and considering they (at least some of them) may carry censure similar to those in criminal offences *stricto sensu* (see N Peršak, 'In den Nebengebieten des Strafrechts: Paternalistische Interventionen im Recht der Ordnungswidrigkeiten' in A von Hirsch, U Neumann and K Seelmann (eds), *Paternalismus im Strafrecht: die Kriminalisierung von selbstschädigendem Verhalten* (Baden-Baden, Nomos, 2010) 173), they, too, need to be based on the legitimate grounds for criminalisation and adhere to the fairness constraints, such as proportionality between the offence and its sanction.

This criminological trend reflects a wider social problem – that of increasing disparities between different segments of society, of progressive physical segregation and social exclusion of whole parts of society, and of crucial lack of communication between different social groups, which fuels distrust, inflames fear of 'the other' and exacerbates further social misunderstandings. The security discourse that often accompanies such phenomena tends to legitimise state actions aimed at reducing the individual's liberty in order to, allegedly, raise security, the by-product being the erosion of the *Rechtsstaat* and its liberal foundations from the inside. When the quality of life discourse amounts to nothing more than a species of this security discourse, especially in the context of defining incivilities, the use of the concept of quality of life to legitimise state punitive intervention becomes problematic indeed.

However, the concept of the quality of life proposed in this chapter is clearly different from the one used in security discourse. Although usages in the latter discourse are skewed, this does not mean that we have to give up on using *our* notion in relation to incivilities altogether. Indeed, in terms of research implications and future prospects, it would be valuable to apply our quality of life notion to incivilities. There would of course be several limitations and challenges with extending the proposed scheme to an area that is traditionally governed by the law of violations. Limitations would be necessary because the legal regime of violations is likely to overlap with but extend beyond paradigmatic 'criminal harm'. Additionally, many violations (even incivility violations) do not target 'identifiable victims'. Many such offences are against 'public order' or against such abstract notions such as public health or cleanliness of public places.

It is therefore unlikely that the above structure of grading harms could be imposed on all incivilities; nonetheless, the structure could be of use in assessing the harms of those incivilities that are harmful and which target identifiable victims. Certain incivilities can be harmful, which is reflected also in the fact that many anti-social acts have already been criminalised as crimes proper.[55] Ashworth recognises that violations or regulatory offences often involve 'harm' (albeit minor harm).[56] In cases of harmful incivilities, the model proposed in this chapter above would be relevant. On the other hand, applying the model to (merely) offensive incivilities would require further elaboration.

Von Hirsch and Jareborg expressly state that their living standard may not be applicable in cases of offensive conduct, as offence 'does not necessarily involve being made worse off in the sense of having one's personal resources diminished' and that gauging the gravity of offensive conduct may thus require 'a standard other than one that refers to reduction in the offended person's living standard'.[57]

---

[55] Burney, *Making People Behave*, above n 50.

[56] Although it may not be merely minor. Ashworth emphasises that 'all regulatory offences are minor' would be a wrong assumption and mentions several Acts, such as the Food Safety Act 1999, that contain offences which may have much more serious consequences than a minor theft, a traditional criminal offence. See A Ashworth, *Principles of Criminal Law*, 5th edn (Oxford, Oxford University Press, 2006) § 2.8.

[57] Von Hirsch and Jareborg, 'Gauging crime seriousness', above n 3 at 195 fn c.

Although it is true that offensive incivilities rarely diminish one's resources, I am hesitant to dismiss the quality of life model prematurely in the penal regulatory context. Even the law of violations, albeit not considered as criminal law proper (ie in the strict sense), still needs some limitations, some gauging of when the (bad) quality of conduct is such that the conduct is legitimately criminalised; and conversely, delimiting boundaries beyond which it is illegitimate to criminalise. Such boundaries should normally exclude conduct that may be unpleasant to some, but otherwise does not contain significant 'penal value',[58] from proscription and sanction, whether as criminal offences or violations. Yet, although von Hirsch and Jareborg shy away from applying their model to offensive conduct for the above-mentioned reasons, they acknowledge that 'the evil' of offensive conduct 'resides [simply] in being dealt with without consideration or respect.'[59] Lack of respect, if serious or acute enough, may – on our quality of life-based account – qualify as such an intrusion on another person's quality of life that it may prima facie warrant a state intervention.[60]

The quality of life model, if and when applied to violations that address incivilities, could be extended by including other elements. Examples of further extension could be: extension to include even minor harms or minor intrusions (intrusions to a lesser degree, which, for example, would otherwise not qualify as a sufficiently serious harm to be criminalised in criminal law proper); inclusion of conduct that is not harmful but significantly offensive or unpleasant – possibly limited to only significant, objective, other-regarding conduct that is deemed unpleasant enough by all (or by the vast majority, and different segments, of the community); inclusion of some social harms and offences (conduct that is not aimed at identifiable victims but more collective agents); inclusion of more variable cultural-regional considerations of harm or offence (particularly applicable where administrative offences are in the hands of municipal authorities, such as in Belgium or Italy); inclusion of certain remote harms, etc. The arguments advocating desirability of any such extension should be, however, additionally supported by good reasons, taking into account also the proportionality between the infringement and the sanction, and

---

[58] N Jareborg, 'Criminalization as last resort (ultima ratio)' (2005) 2 *Ohio State Journal of Criminal Law* 521.

[59] Von Hirsch and Jareborg, 'Gauging crime seriousness', above n 3 at 195 fn c.

[60] A serious type of disrespect, which may prima facie justify state punitive intervention, would be, for example, one having long-term harmful effects. Moreover, the social convention, underpinning the finding of disrespect as an offensive wrong, would have to be justified (see Simester and von Hirsch, *Crimes, Harms and Wrongs*, above n 4 at 102–3). However, to really warrant criminalisation, other mediating and criminalisation-limiting factors should also be taken into account. According to Schonsheck's 'filtering approach' to criminalisation, the legislator should at the first level (Principles Filter) determine whether the action in question falls within the moral authority of the state. At the second level (Presumptions Filter), the legislator should look into other possible means, less coercive and intrusive than the criminal statute, which could perform satisfactorily enough, that is, reduce the occurrence of the negative conduct to an acceptable level. Finally, the third filter (Pragmatics Filter) contains cost/benefit analysis, where the legislator should inspect the consequences of enacting and enforcing a prohibition. A particular piece of proposed legislation has legitimately criminalised an action if it has 'successfully and successfully' passed through all of these filters. See J Schonsheck, *On criminalization: An essay in the philosophy of the criminal law* (Dordrecht, Kluwer, 1994) 25.

the amount (or lack of) censure present in the sanction, in addition to other crim-inalisation-limiting factors and mediating principles.[61]

V. Concluding Thoughts

Law in itself – as a system of legal norms that shapes human life[62] and binds all mem-bers of society – is deeply connected to the notion of the quality of life. It may be argued that the birth of the state and consequently of law itself raised the quality of life of the population. The imposition of rules has eliminated 'the war of all against all',[63] where life was filled with constant fear of violence. However, the erosion of the state of law (*Rechtsstaat*), which can materially be observed in the shape of, eg walled cities, protected by armies, to keep away the 'threatening "hordes" of the impover-ished and dispossessed',[64] the proliferation of gated communities and the privatisa-tion of security, often comes at the expense of the rest of the population. Widening of the gap between the rich and the poor, as Durkheim observed, results in those groups starting to see each other as a threat.[65] The powerful then go for more radical methods of crime prevention, including the 'widening of the net',[66] stretching of the definition of a 'crime' and treating minor infringements – incivilities – as serious harms that need to be criminalised.

With respect to the current trends in disorder regulation, particular attention has to be paid to the security discourse, which is known to have legitimated a number of crime-control mechanisms – sometimes also in the name of the quality of life – based on reported insecurities, which have often more to do with the lack of social trust than with actual crime. Founding criminalisation of disorder or incivilities on the notion of the quality of life has to proceed carefully, disassociating itself from those zero tolerance discourses. However, this does not mean that the quality of life concept should be abandoned altogether. Abuses, which may always happen, do not in themselves disqualify a concept (although they can weigh against its adop-tion), and there is a lot to be said for grounding harms on such a universal notion of human welfare. Having said this, while the notion is certainly applicable to harms – be they part of the criminal code or law of violations – it may not be equally appli-cable to conduct that merely offends.

In the realm of harm, however, what is defined as harm does matter, for it changes our perspective and legitimises (more serious) state punitive intervention. Although there are other dimensions of crime seriousness, such as intent or culpability, which

---

   [61] Peršak, *Criminalising Harmful Conduct*, above n 4 at 91–94; Simester and von Hirsch, *Crimes, Harms and Wrongs*, above n 4 at 123–38.
   [62] N Luhmann, *A Sociological Theory of Law* (London, Routledge & Kegan Paul, 1985).
   [63] T Hobbes, *Leviathan*, ed CB Macpherson (Harmondsworth, Penguin, 1968).
   [64] S Castles and A Davidson, *Citizenship and Migration: Globalization and the Politics of Belonging* (Basingstoke, Macmillan Press, 2000) 230.
   [65] E Durkheim, *The Rules of the Sociological Method* (New York, Simon & Schuster, 1982; orig 1895).
   [66] S Cohen, *Visions of Social Control* (Cambridge, Polity Press, 1985).

may also affect the grading of crimes, seriousness is also responsive to the external effects of one's act. Harm matters in our everyday life, our everyday moral reasoning, so it should matter in law as well. However, harm differs in the value or interest it sets back and in the intensity of that setback. Different harms require different treatments. (Distributive) justice requires that sanctions be proportionate to harm, which implies that harms need to be ranked according to some acceptable criterion.

Choices involved in the ranking of harm are ultimately normative choices and, while empirical reality may inform about the regularity and average levels of impact for some type of harmful activity, empirically measured or calculated costs in themselves do not necessarily satisfy the criminalisation test. Such conduct also has to be wrongful and this is where many incivility criminalisations fail. Lumping together harm that results as a natural by-product of urban environment (eg occasional rubbish bags being left behind or not being put out on the right day but a day before, as owners are leaving on a holiday) and harm that results from intentional polluting acts (such as throwing cigarette packs and other litter on the pavement) and fining both the same, affronts our sense of justice as the wrongfulness of these two types of conduct is not the same. Treating alike what is different, be it in terms of harm or in terms of wrongfulness, delegitimates such legislation. Moreover, in addition to harm and wrongfulness, there may be other countervailing objections to criminalisation (such as social importance of the conduct, the principle of last resort, rule of law objections, enforceability problems, costs of enforcement, and so forth). The latter can defeat the case for criminalisation, even if the conduct itself is deemed sufficiently detrimental to various dimensions of the quality of life.

13

Criminal Liability for Offensive Behaviour in Public Spaces

WOLFGANG WOHLERS

According to the leading German texts, the criminal law should, and may, only be used for the protection of particularly important social norms and thus only for the protection of fundamental rules of social interaction.[1] It is considered to be a central feature of an enlightened criminal law that criminal prohibitions may not (any longer) seek to protect moral and/or conventional ethical convictions for their own sake.[2] Moreover, when a fundamental norm is being protected, criminal sanctions are supposed to be threatened and imposed only as the last resort (*ultima ratio*); that is, the criminal law should be deployed only if the societal problem in question cannot be solved by other, less intrusive, means.[3] However, if one notes that the initial reaction of the media as well as the legislature to almost any societal problem is to call for a criminal law response, it becomes clear that the subsidiarity principle is, at the end of the day, nothing more than an ideal with little grounding in social reality.[4] In our social reality, the criminal law is not *ultima ratio* but rather, as

---

[1] H Welzel, *Das Deutsche Strafrecht. Eine systematische Darstellung*, 11th edn (reprinted: Berlin, De Gruyter, 2010; orig 1969) 4f; F Riklin, *Schweizerisches Strafrecht, Allgemeiner Teil I – Verbrechenslehre*, 3rd edn (Zürich/Basel/Genf, Schulthess, 2007) § 4 marginal note 4; see also C Roxin, *Strafrecht: Allgemeiner Teil*, vol I, 4th edn (Munich, CH Beck, 2006) § 2 marginal note 7; J Wolter (ed), *Systematischer Kommentar zum Strafgesetzbuch* (Cologne, Carl Heymanns, 1997), Vor § 1 marginal notes 1, 10 (commentary by H-J Rudolphi) (here cited after the 8th edn, looseleaf addition No 26). Critical in respect of the ability of this maxim to contain the reach of criminal law is K Seelmann, *Strafrecht, Allgemeiner Teil*, 5th edn (Basel, Helbing & Lichtenhahn, 2012) 6f.

[2] Roxin, *Strafrecht: Allgemeiner Teil I*, above n 1, § 2 marginal note 17ff; Wolter, *Systematischer Kommentar*, above n 1, Vor § 1 marginal notes 1, 10 (commentary by H-J Rudolphi).

[3] Wolter, *Systematischer Kommentar*, above n 1, Vor § 1 marginal note 14 (commentary by H-J Rudolphi); A Donatsch and B Tag, *Strafrecht I: Verbrechenslehre*, 8th edn (Zürich/Basel/Genf, Schulthess, 2006) 5; see further G Stratenwerth, *Schweizerisches Strafrecht, Allgemeiner Teil I: Die Straftat*, 4th edn (Bern, Stämpfli, 2011) § 3 marginal note 14; very sceptical of the subsidiarity principle's usefulness is W Wohlers, 'Strafrecht als ultima ratio – tragender Grundsatz eines rechtsstaatlichen Strafrechts oder Prinzip ohne eigenen Aussagegehalt?' in A von Hirsch, K Seelmann and W Wohlers (eds), *Mediating Principles. Begrenzungsprinzipien bei der Strafbegründung* (Baden-Baden, Nomos, 2006) 54; see also G Seher, 'Kann Strafrecht "subsidiär" sein? Aporien eines "unbestrittenen" Rechtsgrundsatzes' in von Hirsch et al, ibid, 70; Seelmann, *Strafrecht*, above n 1, 7f.

[4] See Riklin, *Strafrecht*, above n 1, § 4 marginal note 8; Stratenwerth, *Strafrecht Allgemeiner Teil I*, above n 3, § 3 marginal note 14; W Wohlers, *Deliktstypen des Präventionsstrafrechts – zur Dogmatik 'moderner' Gefährdungsdelikte* (Berlin, Duncker & Humblot, 2000) 36ff.

Hassemer put it,[5] *prima ratio* and sometimes, unfortunately, also *sola ratio* – regardless of the fact that everything we know about this indicates that the criminal law is a particularly unsuitable tool if the aim is not merely to suppress but genuinely to solve societal problems.[6]

The fact that the legislature almost instinctively responds to virtually any problem by creating new criminal laws challenges not only the notion of criminal law as *ultima ratio*. It also raises the question whether the very idea that criminal law serves to protect fundamental behavioural norms is nothing more than an ideal conception that exists only in the minds of criminal law scholars. A glimpse into the German and Swiss criminal codes reminds us that our existing criminal law contains many prohibitions that are hardly compatible with the ideal – perhaps one should say, idealised – picture of the criminal law of an enlightened and secular society. Take the crime of incest (§ 173 StGB in Germany; Article 213 StGB in Switzerland). In light of current scientific knowledge, this prohibition cannot be justified by a risk of genetic damage,[7] and thus turns out to be a norm that responds to age-old taboos according to which sexual relations between blood relatives are considered inappropriate.[8] This raises the further question whether and, if so, under what circumstances the existence of a taboo, and/or of strong aversions to certain conduct, can be a legitimate reason for designating that conduct as an offence.[9] The question is whether there are plausible reasons for protecting certain moral values or beliefs as such through the criminal law – and, if so, which values or beliefs – or whether such criminal law prohibitions must be abolished.[10] The thesis

---

[5] W Hassemer, 'Kennzeichen und Krise des modernen Strafrechts' (1992) 25 *Zeitschrift für Rechtspolitik* 378, 381; W Hassemer, 'Rauschgiftbekämpfung durch Rauschgift? – BGH, NJW 1991, 2359' (1992) 32 *Juristische Schulung* 110, 113.

[6] W Wohlers, 'Zwangsehen in strafrechtlicher Sicht' (2007) 8 *Die Praxis des Familienrechts* 752, 753.

[7] This could in any event not justify the scope of the provision, since it also applies to conduct where the risk of pregnancy is absent. See W Joecks and K Miebach (eds), *Münchener Kommentar zum Strafgesetzbuch*, vol 3, 2nd edn (Munich, CH Beck, 2012) § 173 marginal note 3 (commentary by C Ritscher). But compare the German Constitutional Court, BVerfGE 124, 224 (247–48).

[8] T Hörnle, *Grob anstössiges Verhalten. Strafrechtlicher Schutz von Moral, Gefühlen und Tabus* (Frankfurt, Klostermann, 2005) 455f; Roxin, *Strafrecht Allgemeiner Teil I*, above n 1, § 2 marginal note 43; C Roxin, 'Zur Strafbarkeit der Geschwisterinzests – Zur verfassungsrechtlichen Überprüfung materiellrechtlicher Strafvorschriften' (2009) 29 *Strafverteidiger* 545, 548; Joecks and Miebach, *Münchener Kommentar*, above n 7, Art 173 marginal note 7 (commentary by C Ritscher).

[9] For various views, see W Wohlers and FH Went, 'Die Bedeutung der Straftheorie Hegels für die aktuelle strafrechtstheoretische Diskussion' in A von Hirsch, U Neumann and K Seelmann (eds), *Strafe – Warum? Gegenwärtige Strafbegründungen im Lichte von Hegels Straftheorie* (Baden-Baden, Nomos, 2011) 173, 193–94; T Hörnle, 'Das Verbot des Geschwisterinzests – Verfassungsgerichtliche Bestätigung und verfassungsrechtliche Kritik' (2008) 61 *Neue Juristische Wochenschrift* 2085, 2087f; Hörnle, *Grob anstössiges Verhalten*, above n 8 at 457; G Stratenwerth and F Bommer, *Schweizerisches Strafrecht, Besonderer Teil II: Straftaten gegen Gemeininteressen*, 6th edn (Bern, Stämpfli, 2008) § 26 marginal note 2f; G Jakobs, *Rechtsgüterschutz? Zur Legitimation des Strafrechts* (Paderborn, Schöningh, 2012) 24; M Kubiciel, 'Das deutsche Inzestverbot vor den Schranken des EGMR: Die Entscheidung und ihre Folgen für die strafrechtswissenschaftliche Debatte' (2012) 7 *Zeitschrift für internationale Strafrechtsdogmatik* 282, 289 (arguing that while incest certainly reflects a deep-seated cultural taboo, this taboo and its concretisation in a criminal law prohibition are less irrational than is often assumed).

[10] W Wohlers, 'Verhaltensdelikte: Standard, Ausnahme- oder Unfall der Strafrechtsdogmatik' in M Böse and D Sternberg-Lieben (eds), *Grundlagen des Straf- und Strafverfahrensrechts: Festschrift für Knut Amelung zum 70. Geburtstag* (Berlin, Duncker & Humblot, 2009) 129, 132.

that the criminal laws in question are relics of a bygone era is refuted by the fact that criminal laws of much more recent provenance, for instance laws addressing denials of genocide, such as the offence of holocaust denial (in § 130(3) StGB in Germany and Article 261bis(4) StGB in Switzerland), on closer inspection turn out to be norms which are intended not to protect any traditional legal goods, but to protect beliefs and value judgements.[11]

The gap between scholarly ideal and legal reality becomes drastic if one extends the analysis beyond the confines of the core criminal law and considers also what might be called 'ancillary' criminal law; that is, criminal prohibitions contained in enactments other than the Criminal Code itself. If one does this, one must acknowledge that, according to both the German law of violations (*Ordnungswidrigkeiten* (OwiG))[12] and cantonal Swiss ancillary criminal law, the 'gross violation of decency and morals through conduct performed in public' constitutes an offence.[13] The question whether behaviour can be penalised for the sole reason that it is considered 'grossly indecent' has been put on the table in Switzerland recently by a phenomenon that, in connection with the trend to regulate 'uncivil behaviour' through the criminal law,[14] has also played a certain role in the United Kingdom. The behaviour in question is naked rambling; the question posed is whether one can, should, or even must, impose criminal sanctions on those who wander around naked.[15]

The Swiss Federal Court decided in a judgment of 17 November 2011 that naked rambling in a public space fulfils the preconditions of the offence of a 'gross violation of decency and morals' according to Article 19 of the cantonal criminal law of the Canton Appenzell/Ausserrhoden, and that it can lawfully be punished on this basis.[16] The Court considered at length, and answered in the affirmative, the question whether cantons have the legislative competence for penalising indecent conduct.[17] Furthermore, the Court found that the pertinent provisions of cantonal

[11] See C Bernhard, *Das Rechtsgüter-Trilemma. Von der Legitimität staatlichen Strafens am Beispiel der Völkermordleugnung* (Basel, Helbing & Lichtenhahn, 2011) 107ff; see further Jakobs, *Rechtsgüterschutz*, above n 9 at 30–31 (what is in issue is the prohibition of speech acts which question the self-image of a society); similarly G Stratenwerth, 'Zum Begriff des "Rechtsguts"' in A Eser, U Schittenhelm and H Schumann (eds), *Festschrift für Theodor Lenckner zum 70. Geburtstag* (Munich, CH Beck, 1998) 377, 388f.
[12] See § 118(1) OwiG. The text of the provision is: 'Anyone who performs an act which grossly violates common decency and which is capable of causing serious offence or risk to members of the public or to disturb the peace, is liable for a violation.' ['Ordnungswidrig handelt, wer eine grob ungehörige Handlung vornimmt, die geeignet ist, die Allgemeinheit zu belästigen oder zu gefährden und die öffentliche Ordnung zu beeinträchtigen.']
[13] Art 19 al 2 of the Statute of the Canton Appenzell/Ausserrhoden concerning the Cantonal Criminal Law (dated 25 April 1982) covers persons who 'grossly violate common morality and decency in public.' Other Swiss cantons have similar provisions; see the examples given by the Bundesgericht in BGE 138 IV 13 (21).
[14] See A von Hirsch and AP Simester, 'Penalising Offensive Behaviour: Constitutive and Mediating Principles' in A von Hirsch and AP Simester (eds), *Incivilities: Regulating Offensive Behaviour* (Oxford, Hart Publishing, 2006) 115.
[15] See also the brief reference given in AP Simester and A von Hirsch, *Crimes, Harms, and Wrongs: On the Principles of Criminalisation* (Oxford, Hart Publishing, 2011) 125 fn 5.
[16] BGer, Judgment of 17 November 2011, 6B_345/2011 (published in the official collection at BGE 138 IV 13 (21ff).
[17] BGE 138 IV 13 (165ff).

criminal law of the Canton Appenzell/Ausserrhoden satisfied the requirement that criminal prohibitions must be precise,[18] which flows from the principle of *nulla poena sine lege (stricta)*.[19] The Court also held that the complainant's argument, 'that public decency is today no longer in itself a legitimate object of protection through (cantonal) criminal law,'[20] 'misses the point.' Rather, the issue is[21]

> the interpretation and application of a criminal law enacted by a competent legislator, that is, of a legal norm according to which someone who grossly violates public decency and morals is to be punished. Such a provision is, contrary to what the complainant argues, not to be considered impermissible and inapplicable because 'public decency' is no longer in itself a legitimate object of legal protection. In principle, the legislator is free to enact such a criminal prohibition. The judge for his part does not – subject to fundamental rights protection – have to determine whether the criminal prohibition as such, or its application in an individual case, is in the public interest, or whether such an interest arises with respect to 'public safety'. Nor does he have to consider whether the prohibition contained in the criminal norm, and the imposition of a sanction for the breach of this norm generally or in the case at hand, is necessary for the peaceful communal life of a pluralistic society. The judge in a criminal case has to concern himself – in the course of his deliberations – with questions of the public interest and its determination only in so far as he has to review whether the criminal law in question or its application in the individual case constrains fundamental rights, since this, according to Art. 36 (2) of the Swiss Constitution, must be justified either in the public interest or by the protection of the fundamental rights of others.

One certainly has to agree with the Swiss Federal Court that in a modern democratic state governed by the Rule of Law, only the legislator can legitimately decide whether grossly indecent conduct should be penalised or not.[22] But when the Federal Court

---

[18] BGE 138 IV 13 (19).
[19] This principle is codified in Art 1 StGB/CH: 'A sanction or measure may only be imposed for conduct which has been explicitly criminalised by law.' ['Eine Strafe oder Massnahme darf nur wegen einer Tat verhängt werden, die das Gesetz ausdrücklich unter Strafe stellt.']
[20] BGE 138 IV 13 (18).
[21] BGE 138 IV 13 (19).
[22] See the positions taken by the German Constitutional Court in BVerfGE 120, 224 (241f, 250); see also W Hassemer's minority opinion in BVerfGE 124, 224 (256); F Saliger, 'Was schützt der liberale Rechtsstaat?' in L Siep et al (eds), *Von der religiösen zur säkularen Begründung staatlicher Normen. Zum Verhältnis von Religion und Politik in der Philosophie der Neuzeit und in rechtssystematischen Fragen der Gegenwart* (Tübingen, Mohr Siebeck, 2012) 184; D Willisegger, 'Strafrechtswissenschaft und Rechtsprechung des Bundesgerichts – zwei fremde Welten?' (2013) 6 *Forumpoenale* 104, 111. On constitutional standards binding the legislator, see I Appel, *Verfassung und Strafe: zu den verfassungsrechtlichen Grenzen staatlichen Strafens* (Berlin, Duncker & Humblot, 1998); T Hörnle, *Grob anstössiges Verhalten*, above n 8 at 22ff; O Lagodny, *Strafrecht vor den Schranken der Grundrechte: die Ermächtigung zum strafrechtlichen Vorwurf im Lichte der Grundrechtsdogmatik dargestellt am Beispiel der Vorfeldkriminalisierung* (Tübingen, Mohr Siebeck, 1996); C Roxin, 'Zur neueren Entwicklung der Rechtsgutsdebatte' in F Herzog and U Neumann (eds), *Festschrift für Winfried Hassemer zum 70. Geburtstag am 17. Februar 2010* (Heidelberg, CF Müller, 2010) 581; G Stächelin, *Strafgesetzgebung im Verfassungsstaat: Normative und empirische, materielle und prozedurale Aspekte der Legitimation unter Berücksichtigung neuerer Strafgesetzgebungspraxis* (Berlin, Duncker & Humblot, 1998); CF Stuckenberg 'Grundrechtsdogmatik statt Rechtsgutslehre' (2011) 158 *Goltdammer's Archiv für Strafrecht* 653; see further M Bunzel, 'Die Potenz des verfassungsrechtlichen Verhältnismäßigkeitsprinzips als Grenze des Rechtsgüterschutzes in der Informationsgesellschaft' in R Hefendehl, A von Hirsch and W Wohlers

then states that the legislature is 'in principle free' in its choice whether 'to enact such a criminal law provision,' one should still ask whether the legislature is, in this regard, completely free or whether there are standards by which it has to orientate itself. Connected to this is the further question whether such standards are justiciable; that is, whether the decision of the legislator to criminalise a certain behaviour can be challenged in the courts. In Swiss law, this question cannot arise with respect to *federal* criminal law: Article 190 of the Swiss Constitution (*Bundesverfassung* (BV))[23] stipulates that the courts must apply federal criminal laws even if they consider those laws to be unconstitutional.[24] An exception might exist (based on the so-called Schubert-practice) with respect to laws that violate the European Convention on Human Rights (ECHR).[25] *Cantonal* criminal laws are, however, subject to more extensive judicial control. These norms (including Article 19 of the cantonal criminal law of the Canton Appenzell/Ausserrhoden) can be judicially reviewed with respect to their compatibility with Swiss federal law.[26]

Such control, however, only has a point to it if there is a standard which binds the legislator and against which his decisions can therefore legitimately be measured. The dominant view among German criminal law scholars is that the limits of legitimate criminal law are, and can be, determined with the aid of the doctrine of legal goods.[27] The critical power of the concept of legal goods is, however, not just challenged in scholarly discourse,[28] but also put in question by the fact that, for instance, the German Constitutional Court in its decision concerning incest between adult siblings explicitly rejected the argument that the doctrine of legal goods generates binding standards for the legislature,[29] whereas the Swiss Federal Court did not

---

(eds), *Die Rechtsgutstheorie. Legitimationsbasis des Strafrechts oder dogmatisches Glasperlenspiel?* (Baden-Baden, Nomos, 2003) 65; O Lagodny, 'Das materielle Strafrecht als Prüfstein der Verfassungsdogmatik' in ibid, 83; D Sternberg-Lieben, 'Rechtsgut, Verhältnismäßigkeit und die Freiheit des Strafgesetzgebers' in ibid, 96. Sceptical regarding the limitations thus determined is Wohlers, *Deliktstypen*, above n 4 at 241ff.

[23] 'Federal laws and international law must be applied by the Federal Court and by all other law-applying agencies.' ['Bundesgesetze und Völkerrecht sind für das Bundesgericht und die anderen rechtsanwendenden Behörden massgebend.']

[24] BGE 136 I 65 (70); G Biaggini, T Gächter and R Kiener (eds), *Staatsrecht* (Zürich and St Gallen, Dike Verlag, 2011) § 27 marginal notes 89, 91 (entry by A Griffel); B Ehrenzeller et al (eds), *Die schweizerische Bundesverfassung. Kommentar*, 2nd edn (Zürich and St Gallen, Dike Verlag, 2008) Art 190 nn 26, 33 (commentary by Y Hangartner).

[25] BGE 125 II 417 (424); BGE 128 III 113 (116); BGE 128 IV 201 (205); Biaggini et al, *Staatsrecht*, above n 24, § 9 marginal notes 30ff (entry by G Biaggini); Biaggini et al, ibid, § 27 marginal note 95 (entry by A Griffel); U Häfelin, W Haller and H Keller, *Schweizerisches Bundesstaatsrecht: Die neue Bundesverfassung*, 8th edn (Zürich/Basel/Genf, Schulthess, 2012) marginal notes 19, 25ff; Ehrenzeller et al, *Die schweizerische Bundesverfassung*, above n 24, Art 190 marginal note 32 (commentary by Y Hangartner).

[26] BGE 138 IV 13 (15); Biaggini et al, *Staatsrecht*, above n 24, § 27 marginal notes 47, 50, 90, 103 (entry by A Griffel).

[27] See Roxin, *Strafrecht Allgemeiner Teil I*, above n 1, § 2; Wolter, *Systematischer Kommentar*, above n 1, Vor § 1 marginal notes 1ff (commentary by H-J Rudolphi).

[28] Stratenwerth, 'Zum Begriff des "Rechtsguts"', above n 11 at 377ff; G Jakobs, *Strafrecht, Allgemeiner Teil: die Grundlagen und die Zurechnungslehre*, 2nd edn (Berlin and New York, De Gruyter, 1993) section 2/7ff; Jakobs, *Rechtsgüterschutz*, above n 9.

[29] BVerfGE 120, 224 (241f), and commentary by T Hörnle, 'Das Verbot des Geschwisterinzests', above n 9; L Greco, 'Was lässt das Bundesverfassungsgericht von der Rechtsgutslehre übrig? Gedanken

even mention the doctrine in its decision on naked rambling. This has to be seen against a background of indefatigable insistence by the champions of the doctrine of legal goods that one of its most important achievements is to show that the protection of moral convictions for their own sake has no place in a modern criminal law, and why.[30] We must ask, therefore, are these decisions right, or are they wrong in law? Winfried Hassemer, who as the then vice-president of the German Constitutional Court voted against the Court's incest decision and recorded his diametrically opposed position in his minority opinion,[31] had already, some time before that decision, taken the view that 'if a prohibition of conduct cannot be backed up with the need to protect a legal good, it amounts to an act of state terror.'[32]

In what follows, I will first address the question whether the doctrine of legal goods indeed provides any authoritative and substantively useful standards for the legislator (section I.A). The rather pessimistic answer I give to this question then raises the further question whether there are alternatives capable of replacing or supplementing the doctrine of legal goods. As a second step, I therefore analyse the alternative conception of 'behavioural crimes' (*Verhaltensdelikte*) developed in the German legal literature (section I.B), before turning to the notion which Andreas von Hirsch proposed some time ago as a necessary and sensible addition to the 'harm principle' for responses to annoying or irritating behaviours: the 'offence principle' (section I.C).

---

anlässlich der Inzestentscheidung des Bundesverfassungsgerichts' (2008) 3 *Zeitschrift für internationale Strafrechtsdogmatik* 234; C Roxin, 'Zur Strafbarkeit des Geschwisterinzests – Zur verfassungsrechtlichen Überprüfung materiellrechtlicher Strafvorschriften' (2009) 29 *Strafverteidiger* 545; B Zabel, 'Die Grenzen des Tabuschutzes im Strafrecht' (2008) 11 *Juristische Rundschau* 453; J Ziethen, 'Anmerkung zu BVerfG, Beschluss vom 26.2.2008 – 2 BvR 392/07' (2008) 28 *Neue Zeitschrift für Strafrecht* 614. See further NK Androulakis, 'Abschied vom Rechtsgut – Einzug der Moralität? Das "Erschütterungsprinzip" (zu der Entscheidung BVerfGE 120, 224–73)' in Herzog and Neumann, *Festschrift für Winfried Hassemer*, above n 22 at 271; W Bottke, 'Roma locuta causa finita? Abschied vom Gebot des Rechtsgüterschutzes?' in W Hassemer, E Kempf and S Moccia (eds), *In Dubio Pro Libertate, Festschrift für Klaus Volk zum 65. Geburtstag* (Munich, CH Beck, 2009) 93; D Krauß, 'Rechtsgut und kein Ende' in Herzog and Neumann, *Festschrift für Winfried Hassemer*, above n 22 at 423ff; K Kühl, 'Von der gerechten Strafe zum legitimen Bereich des Strafbaren' in R Bloy et al (eds), *Gerechte Strafe und legitimes Strafrecht: Festschrift für Manfred Maiwald zum 75. Geburtstag* (Berlin, Duncker & Humblot, 2010) 433, 447; Roxin, 'Zur neueren Entwicklung der Rechtsgutsdebatte', above n 22 at 581; Wohlers and Went, 'Die Bedeutung der Straftheorie Hegels', above n 9 at 192ff. On the decision on the European Court of Human Rights in the incest case (*Stübing v Germany*, judgment of 12 April 2012), in which the complaint against the decision by the German Constitutional Court was rejected, see Kubiciel, 'Das deutsche Inzestverbot vor den Schranken des EGMR', above n 9 at 382ff.

[30] See the references in n 2 above.
[31] See BVerfGE 120, 224 (255ff).
[32] W Hassemer, 'Darf es Straftaten geben, die ein strafrechtliches Rechtsgut nicht in Mitleidenschaft ziehen?' in Hefendehl et al (eds), *Die Rechtsgutstheorie*, above n 22 at 64.

I. Searching for Standards of Legitimate Criminal Legislation

A. The doctrine of legal goods

According to a view widely accepted among German criminal law scholars, criminal prohibitions are only legitimate if they serve to protect a legal good.[33] The significance of the doctrine of legal goods consists, first, in the fact that reference to the legal good protected by a criminal law norm is a central theme in the (particularly, teleological) interpretation of criminal laws when the aim is to determine the reach of a criminal prohibition. Alongside this 'immanent' function of the doctrine as an aid to legal interpretation, scholars frequently also ascribe to it a critical function. The doctrine of the legal good is thus[34]

> intended to provide the legislator with a plausible and usable criterion for his decisions, as well as to supply an external standard against which the justice of these decisions can be judged.

This ambition is one that the doctrine has, thus far, been unable to fulfil because no one has yet managed to develop a substantive conception of the notion of the legal good that commands widespread, let alone universal, agreement.[35] Indeed, despite many sustained efforts, it has[36]

> not been possible to reach any consensus regarding the criteria and standards according to which it could be determined what sorts of entities 'legal goods' are, and when conduct that interferes with or endangers a legal good, deserves to be penalised. Certain is only that the 'legal good' must not be seen as identical to the interest that has motivated the legislator to create a penal norm. The legal good is, rather, the 'something' to which the interest recognised by the legislator refers. What exactly this 'something' is, however, has been and remains utterly controversial.

---

[33] Cp U Kindhäuser, U Neumann and H-U Paeffgen (eds), *Nomos-Kommentar zum StGB*, vol 1 (§§ 1–79 StGB), 4th edn (Baden-Baden, Nomos, 2013) Vor § 1 marginal note 108 (commentary by W Hassemer and U Neumann); Wolter, *Systematischer Kommentar*, above n 1, Vor § 1 marginal notes 1ff (commentary by H-J Rudolphi); Roxin, *Strafrecht Allgemeiner Teil I*, above n 1, § 2 marginal notes 1ff. Sceptical regarding the usefulness of the doctrine of legal goods is Stratenwerth, *Strafrecht AT I*, above n 3, § 3 marginal notes 6ff; also Jakobs, *Strafrecht AT*, above n 28, section 2/7ff.

[34] See Kindhäuser et al, *Nomos-Kommentar*, above n 33, Vor § 1 marginal note 115 (commentary by W Hassemer and U Neumann).

[35] K Amelung, 'Der Begriff des Rechtsguts in der Lehre vom strafrechtlichen Rechtsgüterschutz' in Hefendehl et al (eds), *Die Rechtsgutstheorie*, above n 22, 155, 160; Stratenwerth, 'Zum Begriff des "Rechtsguts"', above n 11 at 379; Wohlers, *Deliktstypen*, above n 4 at 219–20; Wohlers, 'Verhaltensdelikte', above n 10 at 129–30; Saliger, 'Was schützt der liberale Rechtsstaat?', above n 22 at 187; W Joecks and K Miebach (eds), *Münchener Kommentar zum Strafgesetzbuch*, vol 1, 2nd edn (Munich, CH Beck, 2011) Introduction, marginal notes 34 and 36 (commentary by W Joecks).

[36] Wohlers, 'Verhaltensdelikte', above n 10 at 129; Wohlers and Went, 'Die Bedeutung der Straftheorie Hegels', above n 9 at 189–90.

(i) The internal-systemic function of the doctrine of legal goods

Problems with the application of the doctrine of legal goods already begin when one turns one's attention to the so-called 'immanent' or internal function of the doctrine within the system of criminal law. The generally undisputed, internal-systemic function of the doctrine of legal goods[37] finds its most obvious expression in the systematic ordering of criminal norms according to the legal good protected by these norms; an order evident from the contents pages of the Criminal Codes of various German-speaking jurisdictions. In practically all commentaries and textbooks, explanations of particular criminal prohibitions start by identifying, at lesser or greater length, the legal good(s) that the norm seeks to protect. This identification of the protective aim of the norm is viewed as fundamental to the identification of the legislative purpose, and this in turn is considered central to the proper interpretation of the provision concerned.[38]

Precisely at this point, however, various difficulties arise in the concrete application of the doctrine. So long as it remains unclear what can constitute a legal good, the doctrine imposes practically no limits on the determination of the legislative purpose. For instance, can 'the good reputation of a financial marketplace' constitute the legal good protected by various offences of financial market manipulation, as was recently suggested in Switzerland?[39] And how should one deal with the situation where the legislator connects a certain prohibition with a range of different legal goods? For instance, both the Swiss Federal Court and the dominant view in the Swiss legal literature agree that the prohibition against insider trading in its original form aims to safeguard 'not primarily economic interests but the loyalty of the insider towards the affected company, as well as the integrity and the smooth operation of capital markets, including equality of opportunity of investors.'[40] When considerations of the protected legal good turn into attempts to unite a potpourri of divergent legal purposes, one must ask how much guidance the notion of the legal good can then provide. Must we, for example, exclude conduct from the scope of a legal prohibition when it affects only some of the legal goods protected by the norm, or does it suffice if just one such good would be protected more effectively by the proposed interpretation? Again using insider trading as an example, assuming that one of the protected legal goods is the loyalty of the insider towards the affected company, ought one to restrict the application of the norm to persons

---

[37] HH Jescheck and T Weigend, *Lehrbuch des Strafrechts, Allgemeiner Teil*, 5th edn (Berlin, Duncker & Humblot, 1996) 259.

[38] W Hassemer, *Theorie und Soziologie des Verbrechens. Ansätze zu einer praxisorientierten Rechtsgutslehre* (Frankfurt, Athenäum, 1973) 57ff; Jescheck and Weigend, *Lehrbuch*, above n 37 at 259; Roxin, 'Zur neueren Entwicklung der Rechtsgutsdebatte', above n 22 at 586; G Stratenwerth, 'Zur Legitimation von "Verhaltensdelikten"' in von Hirsch et al (eds), *Mediating Principles*, above n 3, 157, 163.

[39] See the communique in the Swiss legislative bulletin, 'Botschaft über die Änderung des Schweizerischen Strafgesetzbuches (Insidergeschäfte)', 1 May 1985, BBl 1985, Vol II, at 69, 71, 78, 84, 86. For critical comment, see J Hurtado Pozo, *Droit pénal, Partie spéciale* (Genf/Zürich/Basel, Schulthess, 2009) fn 1614.

[40] Bger, judgment of 26 November 2002, 1a110/2002, E 4.4; compare also BGE 118 Ib 448 (456–57); BGE 118 Ib 547 (558).

who owe a fiduciary duty to the company,[41] or can one argue that the application of the provision is not thus restricted since some of its other protective purposes can be affected by persons who are under no such obligation?[42] Even if we manage to resolve problems like these, it is important not to overlook the fact that the *ratio legis* or purpose of a criminal law norm must not be identified simplistically with the optimal protection of a particular legal good.[43] One must also pay attention to other maxims, such as the need for clarity of penal laws[44] and the liberty interests of potential perpetrators.[45]

(ii) The critical function of the doctrine of legal goods

The proponents of the doctrine of legal goods contend that one of the most important and lasting achievements of their theory is that it has served to demonstrate the illegitimacy of criminal laws which merely protect shared moral beliefs or values. As evidence, they point to the reform of the law of sexual offences, particularly the abolition of provisions criminalising homosexual intercourse and sexual intercourse with animals.[46] One must, however, ask the question whether it does not amount to a *petitio principii*, or an inversion of cause and effect, to view the abolition of these criminal prohibitions as a consequence of the rise of the doctrine of legal goods. It was, after all, not criminal law scholars but legislatures which abolished these crimes. And legislatures are quite evidently not guided by criminal law theory and doctrine, but by considerations of criminal policy. Against this background, it appears rather more likely that criminal prohibitions of homosexual intercourse and sexual intercourse with animals were abolished because social attitudes and beliefs had changed to such an extent that these practices were no longer viewed as unacceptable or as deserving of penal sanctions.[47]

Indeed, much supports the hypothesis that the concept of the legal good is nothing more than the linking element between criminal law doctrine and criminal law policy.[48] In other words, the notion of the legal good serves to identify the purposes pursued by the legislature in creating a criminal law norm. The criteria which can tell us whether certain conduct is sufficiently socially harmful to be considered as requiring a penal sanction cannot be derived from the concept of the legal good itself[49] but must be brought to the doctrine of legal goods from

---

[41] So C Peter, *Aspekte der Insiderstrafnorm* (Chur/Zürich, Rüeger, 1991) 12ff.

[42] See M Jean-Richard-dit-Bressel, *Der Aktionär als Insider am Tatort Börse?* (Zürich/Basel/Genf, Schulthess, 2003) 28ff.

[43] W Wohlers, *Fallbearbeitung im Strafrecht*, 3rd edn (Zürich/Basel/Genf, Schulthess, 2009) 101–2.

[44] See Art 1 StGB/CH (Swiss Criminal Code); Art 103 (2) GG (German Constitution), read in conjunction with § 1 StGB/D (German Criminal Code).

[45] Jakobs, *Rechtsgüterschutz*, above n 9 at 20.

[46] Roxin, *Strafrecht Allgemeiner Teil I*, above n 1, § 2 marginal notes 17ff; Roxin, 'Zur neueren Entwicklung der Rechtsgutsdebatte', above n 22 at 579–80.

[47] See already Wohlers, *Deliktstypen*, above n 4 at 227–28.

[48] Amelung, 'Der Begriff des Rechtsguts', above n 35 at 159; Wohlers, *Deliktstypen*, above n 4 at 229.

[49] See further Jakobs, *Rechtsgüterschutz*, above n 9 at 16 (suggesting that the doctrine of legal goods owes its success to its 'chameleon-like qualities').

outside.[50] Legal goods are constituted through a societal process of communication and collective self-affirmation, and this process is one in which the legislative organs play a leading role. Two things follow from this. First, the content of criminal law norms is time-bound, in that it responds to the societal context in which they are created.[51] Secondly, this means that one cannot even argue that the rejection of the idea that criminal laws should protect moral beliefs is a true consequence of thinking in terms of legal goods. This is so because whenever a society regards certain moral values as being central to societal interaction, it will have no difficulty in considering the integrity of these values to be a legal good deserving of protection by the criminal law. Doubts about the validity of such classification will only arise when – due to the passage of time, or cultural change – the belief or value as such is questioned. To see this, one only needs to think of the once near-ubiquitous criminal laws against sorcery and witchcraft which were abolished in Europe only slowly with the advent of modernity.[52]

With regard to the protection of moral beliefs and values through the criminal law, one must also not forget that, in practice, the issue is rarely if ever one of legal moralism in its purest form. The point is usually not to protect these beliefs and values for their own sake, but to prevent certain socially damaging consequences of the violation of these values: an 'impure' legal moralism that is concerned with the preservation of certain social sub-systems or (in rare cases) with the prevention of widespread social disintegration.[53] Consider, for example, laws against the consumption of certain drugs. The practical objective of these laws is to penalise and thereby stigmatise non-conformist lifestyles.[54] Analysed in terms of the categories of the doctrine of legal goods, however, the concern here is not with legal moralism or the protection of some obscure legal good, like public health,[55] but with the banal question whether the indirect consequences of the consumption of certain drugs[56] suffice to justify its penalisation.[57] Since the affected interests are, as such, clearly identifiable as legal goods deserving of criminal law protection, the issue is not whether drug laws protect any goods deserving of legal protection, but rather

---

[50] Wohlers, *Deliktstypen*, above n 4 at 229ff; Wohlers, 'Verhaltensdelikte', above n 10 at 130; Wohlers and Went, 'Die Bedeutung der Straftheorie Hegels', above n 9 at 190.

[51] See on this point already Roxin, 'Zur neueren Entwicklung der Rechtsgutsdebatte', above n 22 at 583; Wohlers, *Deliktstypen*, above n 4 at 65ff; Wohlers and Went, 'Die Bedeutung der Straftheorie Hegels', above n 9 at 186, 191.

[52] See Wohlers, *Deliktstypen*, above n 9 at 70, 227–28.

[53] See further Jakobs, *Rechtsgüterschutz*, above n 9 at 23–24; Saliger, 'Was schützt der liberale Rechtsstaat?', above n 22 at 203–4; Wohlers, *Deliktstypen*, above n 4 at 264ff.

[54] W Wohlers and F Went, 'Die pseudo-paternalistische Legitimation strafrechtlicher Normen, dargestellt am Beispiel des Betäubungsmittelstrafrechts Deutschlands, der Schweiz und der Niederlande' in A von Hirsch, U Neumann and K Seelmann (eds), *Paternalismus im Strafrecht. Die Kriminalisierung von selbstschädigendem Verhalten* (Baden-Baden, Nomos, 2010) 303.

[55] See Jakobs, *Rechtsgüterschutz*, above n 9 at 34; Wohlers, *Deliktstypen*, above n 4 at 190ff.

[56] See Wohlers and Went, 'Die pseudo-paternalistische Legitimation strafrechtlicher Normen', above n 54 at 301 with further references.

[57] Critical Wohlers, *Deliktstypen*, above n 4 at 196ff; see also Jakobs, *Rechtsgüterschutz*, above n 9 at 34 (suggesting that the concern is 'to secure a minimum degree of social morality as a precondition for the continuation of society').

whether it is legitimate to use the criminal law to suppress conduct that will bring about such consequences only indirectly at most.[58]

Another example showing that the doctrine of legal goods fails to offer any answers to the crucial questions is the phenomenon of naked rambling. Its prohibition by criminal law would only be an instance of pure legal moralism if the objective was to prohibit naked rambling for its own sake. But, at least as far as I can see, this is not what anyone is seeking to do. If, for example, a Bavarian count with large landholdings felt tempted to wander around in his woods naked, we would perhaps consider such conduct eccentric; but in order for his conduct to raise any conceivable criminal law issue, the woods in question would have to be publicly accessible. It is only when the naked count wanders down a path used by other people that a conflict arises with the interests of other citizens who might be deterred (by the risk of encountering naked persons) from using this particular path. So long as the woodlands are owned by the naked rambler, one might allay one's concerns with the thought that, after all, nobody else needs to use precisely these woodlands for his or her recreational walks. But it is a different matter if, for instance, this particular path constitutes an unavoidable, and perhaps the only, route between two places, or when the naked rambler is visible from a public place. When this is the case, the issue concerns the demarcation of the spheres of freedom of different citizens, and we must ask whether a given type of conduct (say, naked rambling) may be prohibited for the reason that otherwise some fellow citizens would as a matter of fact be excluded from using certain public spaces.

Against this background it must be stressed that the importance of the doctrine of legal goods lies in its proper insistence that the basis on which given conduct is considered deserving of penalisation must be clearly brought to the fore. It is vital to establish which tangible or intangible legal good a criminal prohibition seeks to protect.[59] Whether this legal good really deserves criminal law protection is, however, not a question that the doctrine of legal goods can answer from within. Rather, this question must be decided according to criteria which are brought to the discussion from outside this doctrinal-theoretical framework.[60] Of decisive importance is, moreover, how remote the link between the conduct in question and the feared indirect consequences may legitimately be,[61] and how resilient or sensitive a person is expected to be when confronted with conduct of others that she finds disturbing or irritating.[62]

---

[58] On the question of 'remote harm', compare A von Hirsch and W Wohlers, 'Rechtsgutstheorie und Deliktsstruktur – zu den Kriterien fairer Zurechnung' in Hefendehl et al (eds), *Die Rechtsgutstheorie*, above n 22 at 196.

[59] See already Wohlers and Went, 'Die Bedeutung der Straftheorie Hegels', above n 9 at 192–93.

[60] See Wohlers, *Deliktstypen*, above n 4 at 229–30. On the question whether and how the doctrine of legal goods can be connected to doctrines of constitutional law, see further the references given in n 22 above.

[61] See on this point A von Hirsch, 'Extending the Harm Principle: "Remote" Harms and Fair Imputation' in AP Simester and ATH Smith (eds), *Harm and Culpability* (Oxford, Clarendon Press, 1996) 259; Wohlers, *Deliktstypen*, above n 4 at 281ff, esp 305ff; von Hirsch and Wohlers, 'Rechtsgutstheorie und Deliktsstruktur', above n 58 at 196.

[62] On the principle of tolerance which is raised by these issues, see esp A von Hirsch, 'Toleranz als Mediating principle' in von Hirsch et al (eds), *Mediating Principles*, above n 3 at 97; Simester and von Hirsch, *Crimes, Harms, and Wrongs*, above n 15 at 125ff.

B. The notion of behavioural crimes (*Verhaltensdelikte*)

From the starting point that the actual criminal law of practically every modern state unquestionably contains criminal prohibitions that cannot be justified in terms of the doctrine of legal goods, at least without excessive doctrinal contortions, Günter Stratenwerth[63] and Roland Hefendehl[64] have developed the concept of 'behavioural crimes'. 'Behavioural crimes' are defined as criminal offences which do not serve to protect a legal good (however defined), but respond to violations of 'deeply held cultural convictions',[65] or of a social norm 'whose recognition is so important to us as a community of shared values that we consider its violation to require recourse to penal law.'[66] Whereas for Hefendehl the category of behavioural crimes constitutes an exceptional category that stands alongside ordinary criminal law norms that protect legal goods, Stratenwerth argues that 'behavioural crimes' are in fact not the exception but the rule. For Stratenwerth, 'there are no crimes other than behavioural crimes, nor should there be any others.'[67] Their justification on the basis of mutual recognition and social consensus, is according to Stratenwerth 'no less suited' to the justification of criminal law norms generally 'than a justification which winds itself around five corners before it can somehow connect the norm to the protection of a personal legal good.'[68]

As I have argued elsewhere,[69] one cannot but agree with Stratenwerth's view as an analysis of the status quo. It cannot be denied that the legislator indeed acts as described by Stratenwerth, and his approach also correctly captures the responsiveness of the criminal law system to time and context.[70] These strengths of the theory are, however, also the sources of its main weaknesses, which become apparent when we turn from analysis to critique of criminal prohibitions. The reference to behavioural norms central to a society's identity as a 'community of values' leaves many questions unaddressed that are decisive in this context. Are 'behavioural norms'

---

[63] See Stratenwerth, 'Kriminalisierung bei Delikten gegen Kollektivrechtsgüter' in Hefendehl et al (eds), *Die Rechtsgutstheorie*, above n 22 at 255; Stratenwerth, 'Zur Legitimation von "Verhaltensdelikten"', above n 38 at 161.

[64] See R Hefendehl, *Kollektive Rechtsgüter im Strafrecht* (Cologne, Carl Heymanns, 2002) 52ff; R Hefendehl, 'Die Strafvorschriften im Naturschutzrecht – oder: Warum das Strafrecht für den Schutz der Natur nicht prädestiniert ist' (2001) 23 *Natur und Recht* 498, 504.

[65] Hefendehl, *Kollektive Rechtsgüter*, above n 64 at 56; Hefendehl, 'Die Strafvorschriften im Naturschutzrecht', above n 64 at 504; see further Joecks and Miebach, *Münchener Kommentar*, above n 35, Introduction, marginal note 34 (commentary by W Joecks); Wolter, *Systematischer Kommentar*, above n 1, Vor § 1 marginal note 11 (commentary by H-J Rudolphi). Against this line of argument, see K Amelung, *Rechtsgüterschutz und Schutz der Gesellschaft: Untersuchungen zum Inhalt und zum Anwendungsbereich eines Strafrechtsprinzips auf dogmengeschichtlicher Grundlage, zugleich ein Beitrag zur Lehre von der 'Sozialschädlichkeit' des Verbrechens* (Frankfurt, Athenäum, 1972) 346 and 393.

[66] Stratenwerth, 'Zur Legitimation von "Verhaltensdelikten"', above n 38 at 162.

[67] Stratenwerth, 'Kriminalisierung bei Delikten gegen Kollektivrechtsgüter', above n 63 at 257.

[68] Stratenwerth, 'Zur Legitimation von "Verhaltensdelikten"', above n 38 at 162.

[69] Wohlers, 'Verhaltensdelikte', above n 10 at 137–38; Wohlers, 'Die Tagung aus der Perspektive eines Rechtsgutsskeptikers' in Hefendehl et al (eds), *Die Rechtsgutstheorie*, above n 22, 281, 284; compare further Wohlers and Went, 'Die Bedeutung der Straftheorie Hegels', above n 9 at 196–97 and Bernhard, *Das Rechtsgüter-Trilemma*, above n 11 at 184.

[70] See the references in n 50 above.

worthy of protection simply because they exist? How can, and how should one determine which behavioural norms are so significant that they deserve protection through the criminal law? – and who decides whether this is the case? Does this approach leave open any possibility for criticising a legislative decision to criminalise certain conduct?[71]

In Swiss legal culture, which is shaped by particularly strong elements of direct democracy, one could perhaps still take the view that 'the people' qua sovereign can, after all, always by way of a referendum remove from the statute book a criminal law with which they disagree. The situation looks very different in countries where the population has no comparable means of influencing legislative outcomes. In these countries, one must then retreat to the fiction that the process of parliamentary debate and decision yields the convictions and values central for the identity of the society.[72] This might be a convincing theoretical conception from the vantage point of legal philosophy. If, however, one thinks of the real legislative processes in actual states one can subscribe to this approach only if one is prepared to admit that modern societies are nowhere near as rational as we generally like to think. If, on the other hand, we want to continue to demand that criminal legislation should be shaped by rational criteria, then we must insist that convictions and value judgements should not be considered deserving of protection through the criminal law simply because politicians have, in the course of some law-making procedure, reached an agreement that certain conduct should be penalised. The weakness of the conception of 'behavioural crimes' lies in the fact that its proponents have, thus far, failed to make clear how their theory would enable us to distinguish behavioural norms that merit criminal law protection from those that do not.

C. The offence principle

Having seen that neither the doctrine of legal goods nor the concept of 'behavioural crimes' can offer satisfactory answers to the questions posed by the penalisation of offensive conduct, we are now ready to turn to an Anglo-American approach which faces up to exactly these questions. The approach I refer to is one which – starting from the foundations laid by Joel Feinberg – has seen seminal contributions by Andreas von Hirsch, most recently in the book he co-authored with Andrew Simester on *Crimes, Harms, and Wrongs*.[73]

[71] Ulfrid Neumann thinks not: see U Neumann, 'Institution, Zweck und Funktion staatlicher Strafe' in M Pawlik and R Zaczyk (eds), *Festschrift für Günther Jakobs: zum 70. Geburtstag am 26. Juli 2007* (Cologne, Carl Heymanns, 2007) 435, 447; compare also Roxin, 'Zur neueren Entwicklung der Rechtsgutsdebatte', above n 22 at 592–93.

[72] According to Amelung, it is through the legislative process that norms are recognised as deserving of protection through penal sanctions; see Amelung, *Rechtsgüterschutz und Schutz der Gesellschaft*, above n 65 at 346.

[73] See Simester and von Hirsch, *Crimes, Harms, and Wrongs*, above n 15, chs 6–8. This publication builds on various earlier publications, including AP Simester and A von Hirsch, 'Rethinking the Offense Principle' (2002) 8 *Legal Theory* 269 and A von Hirsch, 'Belästigendes Verhalten: Gibt es ein strafrechtliches Belästigungsprinzip?' in his *Fairness, Verbrechen und Strafe: Strafrechtstheoretische Abhandlungen* (Berlin, Berliner Wissenschaftsverlag, 2005) 109.

Something like an 'offence principle' that could provide a standard for the legitimacy of criminal law norms is occasionally traced all the way back to the work of John Stuart Mill.[74] But the philosopher who developed the offence principle as a separate principle, against which the legislative decision to penalise conduct can be tested, is undoubtedly Joel Feinberg. In his four-volume study of *The Moral Limits of the Criminal Law*, published between 1984 and 1988, Feinberg certainly takes the 'harm principle' as the starting point and the core principle of criminalisation,[75] but he proposes supplementing it with a further principle better able to deal with incivilities. Feinberg defines this 'offence principle' as follows:[76]

> It is always a good reason in support of a proposed criminal prohibition that it would probably be an effective way of preventing serious offense (as opposed to injury or harm) to persons other than the actor, and that it is probably a necessary means to that end.

Feinberg elaborates upon the offence principle in the second volume of his study of the Moral Limits of the Criminal Law, which appeared in 1985 under the title *Offense to Others*. Offensive behaviour does not constitute, for Feinberg, a category of 'less serious harm'; it is to be distinguished from harmful behaviour in that its effects consist in the experience of negative reactive emotional states (disliked states of mind).[77] According to Feinberg, behaviour that causes such 'disliked states of mind' may be considered an appropriate candidate for criminalisation, if two further conditions are met: (1) The behaviour interferes with the rights of others and therefore amounts to wrongful, that is right-violating, conduct;[78] and (2) on balance, taking into account both the intensity, duration, and avoidance options of offended persons, and the strength of the personal interest and the social usefulness of the performance of the offending conduct, the interests of the offended outweigh the interests of the agent engaging in the offensive conduct.[79] Feinberg's discussion clearly foregrounds this second, balancing consideration. He explicitly rejects introducing considerations of the 'reasonableness' of the disliked states of mind,[80]

---

[74] So Saliger, 'Was schützt der liberale Rechtsstaat?', above n 22 at 197; see also J Tasioulas, 'Crimes of Offence' in von Hirsch and Simester (eds), *Incivilities*, above n 14, 149, 168; compare further G Seher, *Liberalismus und Strafe. Zur Strafrechtsphilosophie von Joel Feinberg* (Berlin, Duncker & Humblot, 2000) 106 fn 334; Wohlers, *Deliktstypen*, above n 4 at 254ff (arguing that Mill only accepted criminal laws based on the need to protect others against harm).

[75] See J Feinberg, *Harm to Others. The Moral Limits of the Criminal Law*, vol 1 (Oxford, Oxford University Press, 1984).

[76] J Feinberg, *Offense to Others. The Moral Limits of the Criminal Law*, vol 2 (Oxford, Oxford University Press, 1985) 1.

[77] Feinberg, ibid, 1–2. On the distinction between harm and offence, see further von Hirsch and Simester, 'Penalising Offensive Behaviour', above n 14 at 116ff; Seher, *Liberalismus*, above n 74 at 108f; for criticism, see KA Papageorgiou, *Schaden und Strafe: Auf dem Weg zu einer Theorie der strafrechtlichen Moralität* (Baden-Baden, Nomos, 1994) 263ff; Tasioulas, 'Crimes of Offence', above n 74 at 164ff.

[78] See Feinberg, *Offense*, above n 76 at 2, 68f, 94.

[79] On the issues that matter for the balancing test, see Feinberg, *Offense*, ibid, 25ff and 37ff, and Simester and von Hirsch, *Crimes, Harms, and Wrongs*, above n 15 at 93.

[80] For critical discussion, see RA Duff and SE Marshall, 'How Offensive Can You Get?' in von Hirsch and Simester, *Incivilities*, above n 14, 57, 62ff; P Roberts, 'Penal Offence in Question: Some Reference Points for Interdisciplinary Conversation' in von Hirsch and Simester (eds), *Incivilities*, above n 14, 1, 18; Tasioulas, 'Crimes of Offence', above n 74 at 154ff.

arguing that this would leave too much power to the legislator.[81] Moreover, it would often be impossible to say whether to experience, for example, the presence of a naked person as offensive was 'reasonable' or 'unreasonable'.[82] In fact, much, perhaps all, depends on the happenstance of existing cultural conventions – conventions that not only differ from place to place but which are also subject to constant shifts and changes, a point Feinberg illustrates with respect to beachwear over the decades.[83]

Feinberg vividly illustrates the kinds of behaviours he has in mind with the example of a very special ride on a public bus. What makes the ride so special is the behaviour of various other passengers during the trip. These passengers engage in diverse unappealing and disgusting behaviours, producing unusual sounds, smells, or messages. Some are naked, but otherwise do not draw attention to themselves; others engage in sexual activities ranging from kisses to mutual satisfaction and even sexual intercourse.[84]

According to Papageorgiou, the problem with Feinberg's argument is that his impressive example of the ride on the bus stands in no relation to the phenomena we are concerned with in real life.[85] In real life, Papageorgiou argues, we have a much wider range of responsive options at our disposal. These options include zoning decisions where certain behaviour is allowed in some areas but not in others, exhortations to respect rules created for the comfort of all, and possibly coercive mechanisms for ensuring compliance.[86] But the question remains what to do if exhortations remain without effect and if preventive coercion is not an option. When Papageorgiou suggests that the bus driver simply ought to reprimand the misbehaving passengers, and if all else fails insist that they get off the bus,[87] his scenario is no less unrealistic than the bus ride imagined by Feinberg.

The real problem with Feinberg's approach is that Feinberg initially provides a normative criterion – the conduct in question must wrongfully interfere with the rights of others – but then omits to further explore and deepen this criterion in his subsequent discussion, except to state that no wrong exists where the third party has consented to exposing herself to the offensive behaviour (volenti non fit injuria).[88] In the result, one therefore has to agree with Seher that, while Feinberg's position is not entirely clear, it seems most probable that he derives the wrongfulness of the conduct from the result of the balancing exercise of the competing interests.[89] But if

[81] Feinberg, *Offense*, above n 76 at 36f

[82] Feinberg, *Offense*, ibid, 35f; see further D Husak, 'Disgust: Metaphysical and Empirical Speculations' in von Hirsch and Simester (eds), *Incivilities*, above n 14, 91, 96ff (with respect to cases of disgust).

[83] Feinberg, *Offense*, ibid, 47.

[84] Compare Feinberg, *Offense*, ibid, 10ff.

[85] Feinberg himself points out that, as far examples of behaviour which disgusts practically everybody are concerned, criminal prohibitions are hardly needed, since practically no one will engage in the conduct in any event: Feinberg, *Offense*, ibid, 31.

[86] Papageorgiou, *Schaden und Strafe*, above n 77 at 267ff.

[87] Papageorgiou, ibid, 270.

[88] Feinberg, *Offense*, above n 76 at 32f and 45.

[89] Seher, *Liberalismus*, above n 74 at 120f; see also T Hörnle, 'Legal Regulation of Offence' in von Hirsch and Simester (eds), *Incivilities*, above n 14, 133, 137.

that is so, Feinberg's normative criterion loses its independent content, and the criticism which Simester and von Hirsch have directed against the consequentialist structure of Feinberg's model is revealed as well-founded.[90] If and because the central issues for Feinberg are the extent and intensity of the offended party's feelings, as well as the avoidability of the encounter,[91] there is a risk that in a generally intolerant social climate, Feinberg's approach would justify a rather extensive reach of the penal law;[92] as Simester and von Hirsch illustrate using the example of begging[93] and as is indeed acknowledged by Feinberg himself.[94]

In order to avoid these implications, Simester and von Hirsch contend that, in cases of offensive conduct (aligning it in this regard with the criteria for the application of the harm principle), a second normative element is required: offensive conduct must also be wrongful.[95] This additional normative element consists, according to Simester and von Hirsch, in the fact that the perpetrator fails to treat other persons 'with due consideration and respect', wherefore the offended party is not accorded 'full moral standing as a person'.[96] The conduct is wrongful when the offended person is treated in a manner 'that is grossly inconsiderate or disrespectful'.[97] Even so, according to Simester and von Hirsch, the mere causing of offence is not sufficient to warrant criminal punishment.[98] On their view, only such conduct as (indirectly) also leads to some kind of harm ought to be subject to penal law;[99] the offence principle thus picks up cases of indirectly harmful behaviour which the harm principle cannot be stretched to cover because the link between the conduct and the harm is too weak or indirect.[100]

A subcategory of offensive conduct consists, for Simester and von Hirsch, in behaviour involving uses of public space which, at the same time, excludes other members of society from using that space, or deters them factually from exercising

---

[90] See especially Simester and von Hirsch, *Crimes, Harms, and Wrongs*, above n 15 at 92ff; against the offence principle as a separate criminalisation principle: Papageorgiou, *Schaden und Strafe*, above n 77 at 263ff; see also Hörnle, 'Legal Regulation of Offence', above n 89 at 138ff.

[91] Compare Simester and von Hirsch, *Crimes, Harms, and Wrongs*, above n 15 at 123f, 128ff.

[92] Simester and von Hirsch, ibid, 94; von Hirsch, 'Belästigendes Verhalten', above n 73 at 115; von Hirsch and Simester, 'Penalising Offensive Behaviour', above n 14 at 119; compare also Hörnle, 'Legal Regulation of Offence', above n 89 at 137f.

[93] Simester and von Hirsch, *Crimes, Harms, and Wrongs*, above n 15 at 94, 107.

[94] Compare Feinberg, *Offense*, above n 76 at 66: the balancing-test cannot give a liberal all reassurance she might like to have.

[95] Simester and von Hirsch, *Crimes, Harms, and Wrongs*, above n 15 at 95ff; von Hirsch and Simester, 'Penalising Offensive Behaviour', above n 14 at 119ff; see also von Hirsch, 'Belästigendes Verhalten', above n 73 at 115 (that a behaviour is disliked by others does not make it wrongful); Wohlers, *Deliktstypen*, above n 4 at 269ff (that a behaviour upsets others or makes them angry, is as such not a good reason for penalising the behaviour).

[96] Simester and von Hirsch, *Crimes, Harms, and Wrongs*, above n 15 at 100.

[97] Simester and von Hirsch, ibid, 107; von Hirsch and Simester, 'Penalising Offensive Behaviour', above n 14 at 119f; see further von Hirsch, 'Belästigendes Verhalten', above n 73 at 115ff; and critically Hörnle, 'Legal Regulation of Offence', above n 89 at 139ff.

[98] Simester and von Hirsch, *Crimes, Harms, and Wrongs*, above n 15 at 118.

[99] See Simester and von Hirsch, ibid, 112ff.

[100] See Simester and von Hirsch, ibid, 115, 117, 119f, 127; see also von Hirsch, 'Belästigendes Verhalten', above n 73 at 113f.

their (theoretically unchallenged) right to use the space.[101] Again, the fact that such behaviour creates a situation where others experience the use of public space as less enjoyable is, by itself, not sufficient to justify criminalisation of the conduct in question.[102] In these kinds of cases (including indecent exposure[103]), the classification of the conduct as wrongful depends on the 'negotiated social conventions' of a society.[104] Those conventions are subject to certain restrictions (notably, human rights),[105] and to the consideration that in a pluralistic society a certain amount of social tolerance is essential;[106] all of which leads to the conclusion that only aggressive or intrusive, but not ordinary, peaceful begging is classified as offensive conduct that could be made subject to criminal law.[107] On the other hand, people do have a right not to be confronted in public with conduct that, according to accepted social convention, belongs in private spaces.[108] If one follows this conception, the presence of naked passengers on public transport can obviously not be equated with the negative or positive experiences one may have when crossing a nudist beach.[109] With regard to cases of naked rambling, this means that everything depends on where the naked rambling takes place. If and insofar as the wearing of clothes is the social norm in public space, nakedness will and ought to be considered as an imposition of something that, according to the negotiated social conventions, belongs in private spaces and/or designated physical areas.

The huge advantage of this conception lies in the fact that it is well equipped to respond to differences of time and place within and between societies. Whereas topless women are probably the norm on public beaches on the Cote d'Azur – which is why taking off her top on such a beach would not only not get a woman much attention there, but would also not be considered offensive conduct potentially subject to the criminal law – it could probably not be denied that the same behaviour on a beach in Alexandria (Egypt), or perhaps in Long Island, New York, would breach the local negotiated social conventions, with the result that it could, and probably also should, be considered offensive conduct there. This result will be uncomfortable for those who expect the criminal law to guarantee certain timeless and context-independent, basic requirements of human communal life. If one is, however, prepared to accept that any legal order – including the criminal law of such a legal order – cannot be thought of except as tied to a certain time and context,

---

[101] Simester and von Hirsch, *Crimes, Harms, and Wrongs*, above n 15 at 98f, 105f, 132ff.

[102] Simester and von Hirsch, ibid, 107.

[103] Simester and von Hirsch, ibid, 101; compare also Tasioulas, 'Crimes of Offence', above n 74 at 169.

[104] Simester and von Hirsch, *Crimes, Harms, and Wrongs*, above n 15 at 99, 101ff; compare also Husak, 'Disgust', above n 82 at 105; Roberts, 'Penal Offence', above n 80 at 19; Tasioulas, 'Crimes of Offence', above n 74 at 164.

[105] Simester and von Hirsch, *Crimes, Harms, and Wrongs*, above n 15 at 103f.

[106] Simester and von Hirsch, ibid, 125ff; see also von Hirsch, 'Belästigendes Verhalten', above n 73 at 119ff.

[107] Von Hirsch, ibid, 121.

[108] Von Hirsch and Simester, 'Penalising Offensive Behaviour', above n 14 at 122; Tasioulas, 'Crimes of Offence', above n 74 at 151.

[109] Simester and von Hirsch, *Crimes, Harms, and Wrongs*, above n 15 at 102, 129; von Hirsch, 'Belästigendes Verhalten', above n 73 at 122.

then one will have to accept as unavoidable that the same kind of conduct can count as offensive in some jurisdictions but not in others.

The real problem with Simester and von Hirsch's approach is, rather, that it is extremely difficult to determine concretely what the 'negotiated social conventions' of a particular society are. This can be illustrated with the expectation of tolerance. No one would deny that one can and must expect people who live in a pluralistic society to treat each other with a certain amount of tolerance. The question is, however, who must show what degree of tolerance for what kind of conduct. At this point it will always be necessary to make further efforts to determine and to concretise the relevant standards. And in this context, one cannot really avoid facing up to the question what weight should be given to brute social facts. Social conventions are lived conventions. The question then is whether, and (if the answer is yes) to what degree, the factually observable, lived social conventions can or should, in the process of determining the 'negotiated social conventions', be subject to normative corrections. And at this point one again meets the basic problem of who has the authority to decide, and according to which criteria, what constitutes a legitimate object of protection for the criminal law. To my mind, in any existing society this function would have to be performed by the legislator. The advantage of the approach developed by Simester and von Hirsch is that it attempts to provide the legislator with reasonably usable criteria, and this in turn allows us to demand from the legislator that he gives proper reasons for the decision to criminalise conduct. In other words, the legislator cannot simply stop at the creation of some fanciful new 'legal good' but must explain in concrete terms why a particular behaviour is considered a legitimate object for criminalisation.

II. Concluding Remarks

The discussion above has shown that German and Anglo-American criminal law scholars employ very different methodologies. Whereas the Anglo-American scholars work with examples which are considered evident or intuitively plausible – think of Feinberg's imagined 'ride on the bus' – German criminal law scholarship attempts to approach similar questions on a much more abstract plane. If one is prepared to accept that neither the doctrine of the legal good, nor the even more abstract conception of behavioural crimes (*Verhaltensdelikte*), is able to provide the legislator with sufficiently concrete guidance for decisions to criminalise conduct, this suggests that German criminal law doctrine would benefit greatly from a change of perspective to a more phenomenological approach, as exemplified in Andreas von Hirsch's writings.[110]

---

[110] See already Hörnle, 'Legal Regulation of Offence', above n 89 at 136; Wohlers and Went, 'Die Bedeutung der Straftheorie Hegels', above n 9 at 197f.

The objection sometimes raised in the German literature, that the offence principle is too vague[111] and that there is therefore a danger that it will simply be used to cloak what is in substance legal moralism,[112] is in light of the argument made here without foundation. In fact, the combined harm-and-offence principle offers standards that are much more concrete than the doctrine of legal goods which dominates German scholarship. The biggest obstacle to the change of perspective advocated here is probably the strong desire among German scholars to develop a comprehensive theoretical construct that, ideally, derives from one foundational principle.[113] In substance, however, it seems to me that the combined harm-and-offence principle offers the criteria that have so far been lacking from the conception of behavioural crimes, and which might – as Stratenwerth once demanded – enable us 'to provide a rational justification for criminal law norms'.[114]

---

[111] Saliger, 'Was schützt der liberale Rechtsstaat?', above n 22 at 205.

[112] Saliger, ibid.

[113] The suggestion made by Tatjana Hörnle (in her discussion of the conception developed by Simester and von Hirsch) that one should focus on the question whether behaviour violates the rights of others, might perhaps provide an answer in the search for a single foundational principle (see Hörnle, 'Legal Regulation of Offence', above n 89 at 140ff). In light of the argument I have developed here, Hörnle's conception can (contrary to the view taken by Simester and von Hirsch, *Crimes, Harms, and Wrongs*, above n 15 at 134ff) not be countered with the argument that it presupposes a society or legal order with an elaborated catalogue of constitutionally guaranteed fundamental freedoms. While freedoms worthy of criminal law protection may be derived from the constitution, this need not be so. It suffices if these freedoms are recognised by, or can be derived from, ordinary law. Whether other scholars will follow Hörnle's proposed change, from the question whether behaviour interferes with a protected legal good, to the question whether it violates another's rights, will depend on whether the notion of a rights violation can be made sufficiently operational. In this context, too, the questions raised in the text in respect of the offence principle, concerning the appropriate balancing criteria and the question what normative status (if any) should be accorded to brute social facts, will have to be faced.

[114] Stratenwerth, 'Zur Legitimation von "Verhaltensdelikten"', above n 38 at 165.

IV.

CRIMINAL JUSTICE IN A LIBERAL STATE

14

Can Punishment Be Just?

BERND SCHÜNEMANN

I. The Three Levels of Penal Justice

To reflect on the philosophical foundations of criminal justice in an essay dedicated to Andreas von Hirsch is as obvious as it is bold. This is so, first, because von Hirsch has for decades been the unchallenged master of this field, and has analysed deeply nearly every relevant aspect of it.[1] And it is so, secondly, because his unwavering pleasure in intellectual dispute really does tempt one to search for a new nuance. So I have decided to address in the first part of this chapter the age-old question whether the imposition of an evil on a human being who himself has before inflicted an evil on another is compatible with our fundamental notions of justice. Connected to this abstract question regarding the general justification of state punishment is, on a second and more concrete level, the question (which the honorand has equally thoroughly analysed) of how serious the wrongfulness of conduct has to be before it may legitimately be penalised. The upshot of this is that the definition and demarcation of conduct proscribed by the criminal law is not simply a task that falls within the legislator's discretion, but part of the justice of punishment in a properly constituted state; so that the answer given by penal theory acquires constitutional status. And the same is true, in my opinion, for a further level of concretisation, the rules of criminal procedure. It is impossible to call a particular act of punishment 'just' if its imposition does not result from a process so structured as to maximise the likelihood that the criteria for just punishment formulated at the abstract level, as well as those contained in the substantive criminal law, have in fact been satisfied. For this reason I want to answer the philosophical question regarding the justice of punishment in three separate stages, with each subsequent stage presupposing and taking further the results reached at the earlier stage(s). I will attempt, constraints of space notwithstanding, to advance substantive propositions at each stage of the analysis.

Provocatively one might say that the criminal law separates citizens from criminals, free men and women from those akin to creatures kept in a cage. In order to have any social effects at all, criminal law requires – and I will give reasons for this

---

[1] The relevant works are listed in the honorand's list of publications, included in this collection.

contention in a moment – a sort of 'overkill', a response which is in itself unjust if, like Aristotle, one saw punishment as an instance of corrective justice. This is the reason why the imposition of punishment is tied to particularly strict legitimation requirements that can only be fulfilled through compliance with an elaborated doctrinal scheme. At one time one could have taken German criminal law doctrine to provide such a set of criteria. However, with the Europeanisation of criminal law and criminal procedure which has been occurring with breath-taking speed over the last decade, doctrinal insights are increasingly belittled and are, even in Germany, becoming displaced by a simplistic, statute-focused positivistic attitude.[2] Yet the task of criminal law theory, which is to exercise – as a fourth constitutional power of sorts – a kind of non-coercive but nevertheless influential intellectual control over the state's use of penal force, is perhaps even more important in respect of the bureaucratically organised power structures of the European Union (EU)[3] than in respect of domestic law.[4] I therefore also want to try to make my subsequent arguments on penal justice fruitful for European criminal law. In this way I hope to pay my respects also to Andreas von Hirsch's second great lifetime achievement: to have built – perhaps one can even say: to embody – a bridge between Anglo-American criminal jurisprudence and German criminal law theory and doctrine.[5]

II. A Penal Theory fit for Contemporary European Culture

When the penal authority of the state was still viewed as an analogue to (or even as pre-empting) divine justice, retributive theory provided punishment with its obvious purpose and justification. Yahweh's orgies of retribution, the doomsday of Christianity, and Allah's judgment have left deep traces not only in the legal cultures imprinted by these religions but also in the philosophical edifices of Kant and Hegel, the titans of German idealism. Hegel's well-known arithmetic, that crime is the negation of Right and punishment the negation of that first negation,[6] is of

---

[2] See B Schünemann, 'Ein neues Bild des Strafrechtssystems?' (2014) 126 *Zeitschrift für die gesamte Strafrechtswissenschaft* 1.

[3] For elaboration, see W Streeck, *Gekaufte Zeit – Die vertagte Krise des demokratischen Kapitalismus* (Frankfurt, Suhrkamp, 2013).

[4] See B Schünemann, *Die Europäisierung der Strafrechtspflege als Demontage des demokratischen Rechtsstaats* (Berlin, Berliner Wissenschaftsverlag, 2014).

[5] This includes the honorand's contribution to B Schünemann (ed), *A Programme for European Criminal Justice* (Cologne, Carl Heymanns, 2006).

[6] In Hegel's own words, 'When an infringement of right as right occurs, it does have a *positive* external existence, but this existence *within itself* is null and void. The *manifestation* of its nullity is that the nullification of the infringement likewise comes into existence.' GWF Hegel, *Elements of the Philosophy of Right*, ed AW Wood, transl HB Nisbet (Cambridge, Cambridge University Press, 1991; orig 1820) § 97, at 123. The formulation quoted in the text is taken from Hotho's lecture notes, included ibid, § 97 (Addition (H)) 123.

course mathematically unsound, as the Kantian talionic principle[7] illustrates even more clearly: if A takes out B's eye, and is then made to lose one of his own eyes, the social result is that two people are now missing an eye; in other words, the harm has been doubled. The only inference one can draw directly from the principle of justice is therefore the duty to make restitution. The same is true for the secular version of retributivism which taps into the idea of commutative justice. We first encounter this variant of the retributive theory in Aristotle, later also in Nietzsche's work, and now it appears to enjoy a degree of popularity again in Anglo-American criminal law theory in form of the so-called 'unfair advantage theory' put forward by, inter alia, Morris[8] and Murphy.[9] But the violation of right demands the restoration of right, not some pointless infliction of injury on those who have inflicted injuries on others – this logically necessary conclusion is one that cannot be changed by any of the verbal acrobatics that, in the course of centuries, have been advanced in ever more curious forms.

Once we brush aside the veil of retributive rhetoric, we can see the true social character of punishment: as vengeance that has been taken out of the hands of the victim (and his or her clan) and which is now exercised by the state in substitution. It is certainly true that in archaic, pre-statal societies the blood feud fulfilled an important and useful social function, and it is also true that, given the destructive consequences that threatened when clans lacked a willingness to reconcile, the blood feud's replacement with state punishment constituted an enormous societal advance. Yet neither of these considerations legitimates state punishment norma-tively, since they are purely empirical arguments from which we cannot derive any normative conclusions without committing a naturalistic fallacy. The same may be said of the modern taming of the impulse of revenge, which was first considered by the kidnapping victim Jan Philipp Reemtsma and then found its way into modern penal theory in the notion that the victim needs reassurance that she, indeed, suf-fered a wrong, not merely bad luck or the misfortune of an unhappy fate.[10] Its logi-cal flaw, shared with other expressive theories of punishment,[11] resides in the fact that it renders plausible only the expression of disapproval, not the imposition of any connected hard treatment.[12] The argument that, in order to express the degree

[7] I Kant, *The Metaphysics of Morals* (1797) (Ak 6: 332) in *The Cambridge Edition of the Works of Immanuel Kant: Practical Philosophy*, transl M Gregor, introd A Wood (Cambridge, Cambridge University Press, 1996) 473.

[8] H Morris, *On Guilt and Innocence: Essays in Legal Philosophy and Moral Psychology* (Berkeley CA, University of California Press, 1976).

[9] JG Murphy, *Retribution, Justice, and Therapy: Essays in the Philosophy of Law* (Dordrecht, Springer, 1979). For discussion, see B Schünemann, 'Aporien der Straftheorie in Philosophie und Literatur: Gedanken zu Immanuel Kant und Heinrich von Kleist' in C Prittwitz et al (eds), *Festschrift für Klaus Lüderssen: zum 70. Geburtstag am 2. Mai 2002* (Baden-Baden, Nomos, 2002) 327ff, and T Hörnle, *Straftheorien* (Tübingen, Mohr Siebeck, 2011) 55.

[10] See Hörnle, ibid, 37ff. Compare C Roxin, in this volume, text at fn 86.

[11] On this point, see Hörnle, ibid, 29 ff.

[12] Moreover, European criminal legal systems lack the features that make a justification of punishment based on the needs of victims plausible in other systems, such as Islamic criminal law. The criminal law of European countries for instance does not consider that in cases of serious crimes, a victim's subsequent forgiveness could make punishment superfluous.

of disapproval adequately, 'the verbal message must be reinforced by actual hard treatment'[13] in my view turns the relationship between symbolic censure and real punishment on its head.

Despite all these modern attempts to domesticate revenge and retribution through purely linguistic means, it remains the case that the institution of criminal law can rationally only be justified through the purpose of crime prevention.[14] As a starting point I still find Feuerbach's model of 'deterrence-based general prevention' (*Androhungs-Generalprävention*) useful.[15] Unlike Bentham's conception of prevention,[16] which occupies a similarly important position in the Anglo-American world, Feuerbach's model reaches beyond a purely utilitarian justification to provide the necessary additional deontological justification vis-à-vis the affected individual.[17] The threat of punishment calls on the addressee of the prohibition not to commit the criminalised act, which necessarily presupposes the capacity of the addressee to be motivated by that appeal and accordingly to refrain from committing the crime. Punishment is imposed, in Feuerbach's words, so that the threat cannot be unmasked as an empty one,[18] which presupposes that the perpetrator could have avoided committing the crime, since a fully determined world would not contain any empty but only pointless threats.[19] And precisely herein lies the justification of the penal sanction imposed on the perpetrator: the commission of a criminal act that was both prohibited and avoidable by the perpetrator, justifies blaming the individual personally and thus a finding of guilt.[20]

This change in the role of the culpability principle, which is transformed from a principle that justifies punishment, with a retributive conception of the criminal law (where it is a necessary and sufficient condition of just punishment), into a

---

[13] Hörnle, *Straftheorien*, above n 9 at 42.

[14] See B Schünemann, 'Zum Stellenwert der positiven Generalprävention in einer dualistischen Straftheorie' in B Schünemann, A von Hirsch and N Jareborg (eds), *Positive Generalprävention. Kritische Analysen im deutsch-englischen Dialog* (Heidelberg, CF Müller, 1998) 109ff.

[15] Paul Johann Anselm Feuerbach (1775–1833) was a German criminal law scholar and reformist. His main work is the *Revision der Grundsätze und Grundbegriffe des positiven peinlichen Rechts* (1799; reprinted Aalen, Scienta Verlag, 1966).

[16] See J Bentham, *An Introduction to the Principles of Morals and Legislation*, ed W Harrison (Oxford, Basil Blackwell, 1960; orig 1789) ch 14.

[17] Feuerbach's approach is discussed by L Greco, *Lebendiges und Totes in Feuerbachs Straftheorie: Ein Beitrag zur gegenwärtigen strafrechtlichen Grundlagendiskussion* (Berlin, Duncker & Humblot, 2009). Greco argues that Feuerbach's notion of culpability manifesting itself in inconsiderateness contains a deontological element which cannot be derived from consequentialist considerations of deterrence and is connected to the idea that the perpetrator consents to his punishment (ibid, 484ff, esp at 505).

[18] PJA Feuerbach and CJA Mittermaier, *Lehrbuch des gemeinen in Deutschland gültigen peinlichen Rechts*, 14th edn (Gießen, Heyer, 1847) 39.

[19] I will discuss this further in the text in relation to the example of Xerxes. The counter-argument made by CF Hommel (*Über Belohnung und Strafe nach türkischen Gesetzen*, 2nd edn, ed H Holzhauer (Berlin, Erich Schmidt Verlag, 1970; orig 1772) 135), that one also punishes the dog for stealing a sausage, does not actually provide a challenge against the theory of negative general prevention. This is so because punishing a dog can only be done for training purposes, in other words, it can only be a measure of special prevention and, as such, it would never be imposed if there was no danger of recurrence.

[20] See further B Schünemann, 'Zum gegenwärtigen Stand der Lehre von der Strafrechtsschuld' in D Dölling (ed), *Jus humanum: Grundlagen des Rechts und Strafrecht. Festschrift für Ernst-Joachim Lampe zum 70. Geburtstag* (Berlin, Duncker & Humblot, 2003) 537ff.

limiting principle in a preventive conception of criminal law (where it is an additional necessary condition), simultaneously anchors criminal law firmly in the philosophy of freedom. If the perpetrator was unable to comply with a prohibition, say because it was impossible for him to know of its existence and content, there is, on the one hand, no basis for legitimating punishment through the attribution of blame. On the other hand, punishment is then also pointless because unavoidable human conduct cannot be guided by legal norms. To punish in such a situation would be to imitate the Persian ruler Xerxes who, according to Herodotus, in a storm sought to have the surging waves of the Hellespont disciplined with 300 lashes.

The foolishness of Xerxes may well cause mirth in London, and in Brussels too. But it is seldom noticed that English criminal law contains similar absurdities, and that the Europeanisation of criminal law threatens to extend some of these across the whole of Europe. Apart from the cases in which the burden of proof is reversed in violation of the culpability principle, which belongs to the third, procedural level of concretisation, I can mention as examples the refusal to recognise extreme intoxication as a ground of exculpation and to replace it with the much more differentiated construction of the *actio libera in causa*[21] which has been developed on the basis of the culpability principle; and the criminal punishment of (artificial) legal persons, which is presently spreading across Europe like a new religion.[22] The punishment of an individual because of a culpable violation of a norm protecting a legal good differs so fundamentally from a fine imposed on a company for some internal organisational shortcoming with respect to their content, purpose and legitimation, that it is a legitimatory sleight of hand, executed behind the smokescreen of obfuscatory language, to call the latter 'punishment'. Fining a legal person – the standard sanction of international market regulation – is in effect simply a

---

[21] The Common Law has traditionally viewed extreme intoxication not as grounds for excuse or mitigation but, to the contrary, as an aggravating factor of criminal liability, and this is in principle still the case under the *Majewski* rule. See D Ormerod, *Smith and Hogan's Criminal Law*, 11th edn (Oxford, Oxford University Press, 2005) 273ff. See further V Helmert, *Der Straftatbegriff in Europa: Eine rechtsvergleichende Untersuchung der allgemeinen Voraussetzungen der Strafbarkeit in Deutschland, England, Frankreich und Polen* (Berlin, Duncker & Humblot, 2011) 124ff and C Safferling, *Vorsatz und Schuld: Subjektive Täterelemente im deutschen und englischen Strafrecht* (Tübingen, Mohr Siebeck, 2008) 460ff. On the doctrinal construction of the '*actio libera in causa*', see (from a German perspective) C Roxin, 'Bemerkungen zur actio libera in causa' in W Küper, I Puppe and W Tenckhoff (eds), *Festschrift für Karl Lackner zum 70. Geburtstag* (Berlin, De Gruyter, 1987) 307, 314ff; G Jakobs, 'Die sogenannte actio libera in causa' in A Eser (ed), *Festschrift für Haruo Nishihara zum 70. Geburtstag* (Baden-Baden, Nomos, 1998) 105ff; D Dold, 'Die actio libera in causa als Sonderfall der mittelbaren Täterschaft' (2008) 155 *Goltdammer's Archiv für Strafrecht* 427; Schünemann, 'Zum gegenwärtigen Stand', above n 20 at 554ff. From an Anglo-American perspective, see S Dimock, 'Actio Libera in Causa' (2013) 7 *Criminal Law and Philosophy* 549.

[22] On the pressure coming from the EU in this regard, see A Schork and T Reichling, 'Neues Strafrecht aus Brüssel? – Europäische Kommission forciert Verschärfung des Kapitalmarktstrafrechts und Einführung eines Unternehmensstrafrechts' (2012) 17 *Strafverteidiger Forum* 125; J Vogel, 'Unrecht und Schuld in einem Unternehmensstrafrecht' (2012) 32 *Strafverteidiger* 427. On the criminal law imperialism of the UK Bribery Act, see J Kappel and O Lagodny, 'Der UK Bribery Act – Ein Strafgesetz erobert die Welt?' (2012) 32 *Strafverteidiger* 695; and G Trüg, 'Sozialkontrolle durch Strafrecht – Unternehmensstrafrecht' (2011) 16 *Strafverteidiger Forum* 471, as well as the contributions to E Kempf, K Lüderssen and K Volk (eds), *Unternehmensstrafrecht* (Berlin, De Gruyter, 2012).

reduction of corporate profits, the harsh consequences of which are felt only by shareholders, who typically lack influence, and by innocent company employees. Moreover, in practice it regularly results in an amelioration of the sanctions imposed on the responsible managers, which in fact undermines the preventive effect. The only sensible alternative model – one based on restrictive measures not conceptualised as penal sanctions – is beginning to gain ground in the German debate but remains a mere dream for the future in a world where legislation and court practice is firmly governed by the Anglo-American model of indiscriminate and thoughtless imposition of criminal fines.[23]

Only the link outlined above between threat-based general prevention and the culpability principle can, therefore, support punishment as a both useful and justifiable imposition of hard treatment. I therefore do not feel the need to argue further about the question whether, as Andreas von Hirsch believes, 'the element of censure remains central'[24] or whether, as I would say, the necessity of hard treatment is (especially in view of the concept of crime which I will address in the next sub-section) the fundamental element that in a just state could not be legitimated without the censure-generating culpability principle. For this reason one must also praise the German Constitutional Court for having, in its *Lisbon* judgment, placed the culpability principle among the unchangeable, Europe-proof, foundations of the German constitutional state.[25]

This specific combination of deterrence-based general prevention with the principle of culpability provides the only coherent legitimation for actual penal practice, from which traditional retributivist models remain far removed. As Immanuel Kant correctly observed,[26] retribution is limited by the talionic principle. If we do something worse to the perpetrator than he himself is responsible for, then this is precisely not retribution but vengeance. Actual criminal law enforcement, however, remains within the limit set by a talionic principle only in the case of homicide offences and very serious offences of bodily injury and mutilation; in all other cases the penal sanction in fact reaches far beyond the talionic limit. Someone who commits a crime against property, especially if he is a repeat offender, might find himself locked away in prison for years. And the same happens to sexual offenders, who

---

[23] Some decades ago I first suggested a form of guardianship over companies as a suitable measure, which would be similar in its effects to a court-ordered compliance system. This would be a far more effective measure than monetary fines for improving flaws in the company's internal organisation, which is often cited as the reason why sanctions should be imposed. See B Schünemann, 'Die großen wirtschaftsstrafrechtlichen Fragen der Zeit. Eine Vorschau auf die Zürcher Strafrechtslehrertagung' (2013) 160 *Goltdammer's Archiv für Strafrecht* 193, 199ff.

[24] See A von Hirsch, 'Die Existenz der Institution Strafe: Tadel und Prävention als Elemente einer Rechtfertigung' in his *Fairness, Verbrechen und Strafe: Strafrechtstheoretische Abhandlungen* (Berlin, Berliner Wissenschaftsverlag, 2005) 41, 57.

[25] BVerfGE 123, 267 (Judgment of 30 June 2009 – Lissabon-Vertrag) with an approving comment by B Schünemann, 'Spät kommt ihr, doch ihr kommt: Glosse eines Strafrechtlers zur Lissabon-Entscheidung des BVerfG' (2009) *Zeitschrift für internationale Strafrechtsdogmatik* 393ff; also (with a rejection of groundless criticisms of the Lisbon judgment) B Schünemann and B Roger, 'Die Karawane der Europäisierung des Strafrechts zieht weiter. Zur demokratischen und rechtsstaatlichen Bresthaftigkeit des EU-Geldsanktionengesetzes' (2010) 5 *Zeitschrift für internationale Strafrechtsdogmatik* 515.

[26] Kant, *Metaphysics*, above n 7 at Ak 6: 332, 473.

have undoubtedly done a terrible thing to the body and soul of their victim, but usually only for a very short period of time. This almost constant excess of the criminal sanction, this structural *overkill*, exposes the retributive theory as mere window dressing: only deterrence-based general prevention can make sense of our practice. Since only a small proportion of crimes actually results in the detection, conviction and sentencing of the perpetrator, the threat of punishment must be sufficiently serious to impress even those potential offenders who make the low likelihood of detection part of their calculation.

Not only the legitimation of state punishment, but also the main principle delimiting the criminal law's field of application – the *ultima ratio* principle – can be derived only from the understanding I am defending. This principle is a foreign body both within a retributive theory and within the theory of norm-affirmation developed by Jakobs.[27] It is precisely because of their overkill effect that penal sanctions may only be threatened and imposed when other means of discouraging conduct fail and may not be imposed at all when the violation is trivial. In contrast, according to a retributive theory even petty offences must be penalised, if only with a modest sanction, and possible non-punitive preventive measures must be ignored. Jakobs' theory of 'general prevention through norm-affirmation' (*geltungserhaltende Generalprävention*)[28] likewise appears to require that the validity of less significant norms must be reaffirmed through the imposition of sanctions for their breach.

III. Just Punishment Requires a Just Demarcation of Criminal Conduct

In this section I want to offer some observations regarding a question that has dominated the recent work of our honorand: whether and how a penal theory can develop principled limits for the substantive reach of the criminal law. We have seen that, in contrast to the obligation to make restitution, the imposition of a penal sanction is *not* a necessary consequence of the concept of right, or of the notion of a violation of right, because the sanction does not remove the damage but increases it. It follows from this that a criminal act must be something much worse than a mere rights-violation, and for this reason all the neo-Kantian and neo-Hegelian theories, which in the wake of Kant even today want to derive the criminal law from the violation of right as such,[29] start from a mistaken premise. It is not the formal

---

[27] See, eg, G Jakobs, *Norm, Person, Gesellschaft: Vorüberlegungen zu einer Rechtsphilosophie*, 3rd edn (Berlin, Duncker & Humblot, 2008) 114ff. For a discussion of Jakobs' theory, compare also C Roxin in this volume, text at fns 24–26.

[28] Most recently in G Jakobs, *System der strafrechtlichen Zurechnung* (Frankfurt, Klostermann, 2012) 14f.

[29] For a fuller discussion and critique of these theories, see Schünemann, 'Aporien der Straftheorie', above n 9 at 330ff.

violation of a right, but only the imperative to provide maximal protection to the goods and interests that are most important, valuable and essential for the social existence of individuals, that can justify the use of a tool as harmful – one could even say 'poisonous' – as the criminal law. About 250 years ago Cesare Beccaria[30] rooted this limitation of the criminal law in the idea of the social contract which grounds every state constitution, and introduced the notion of 'damage to the social fabric' (*Sozialschaden*) as what captures the specific wrong of crime. It is this notion of the *Sozialschaden* that has – in a way that I can only mention here but not retrace – found, through the work of Birnbaum[31] and Binding[32], its way into German doctrine by shaping the concept of the *Rechtsgutsverletzung* or violation of a 'legal good'.[33]

The necessity of a criminal law prohibition for the effective protection of a legal good is thus the condition for just punishment on (what I earlier called) the second level of concretisation. Recently quite a few scholars have, however, taken the view that, since the doctrine of legal goods is not mentioned in the text of the German constitution, it cannot generate any constitutional limits to the legislator's decision to criminalise conduct; the legislature, it is claimed, has a very broad discretion to choose which conduct to criminalise.[34] In its decision regarding the constitutionality of the criminal prohibition of incestuous relations between siblings, the German Constitutional Court sided, on the face of it, with these critics by denying constitutional status to the doctrine of the legal good.[35] In substance, however, the Constitutional Court addressed almost exclusively the question whether the legal goods protected by the crime of incest are indeed deserving of legal protection.[36]

---

[30] Cesare Beccaria (1738–94) was an Italian criminal law scholar and reformist, well known inter alia for his politically influential contractarian argument against capital punishment. His most influential work is *Dei delitti e delle pene* (1764). For an English edition, see C Beccaria, *On Crimes and Punishments*, transl GR Newman and P Marongiu (New Brunswick NJ, Transaction Publishers, 2009).

[31] Johann Michael Franz Birnbaum (1792–1877) was a German criminal law scholar, best known for his article 'Ueber das Erforderniß einer Rechtsverletzung zum Begriffe des Verbrechens, mit besonderer Rücksicht auf den Begriff der Ehrenkränkung', which appeared in 1834 in the second volume of the *Archiv des Criminalrechts – Neue Folge*.

[32] Karl Binding (1841–1920) was a leading German criminal law scholar, best known for his four-volume treatise on *Die Normen und ihre Übertretung* (published between 1872 and 1920).

[33] For a fuller argument, see B Schünemann, 'Das Rechtsgüterschutzprinzip als Fluchtpunkt der verfassungsrechtlichen Grenzen der Straftatbestände und ihrer Interpretation' in R Hefendehl, A von Hirsch and W Wohlers (eds), *Die Rechtsgutstheorie. Legitimationsbasis des Strafrechts oder dogmatisches Glasperlenspiel?* (Baden-Baden, Nomos, 2003) 133. The relationship between the doctrine of legal goods and the harm and offence principles analysed so fruitfully by the honorand would deserve a separate monograph. One discussion of the interaction between these ideas can be found in Hassemer's contribution to this volume.

[34] For references, see Schünemann, 'Das Rechtsgüterschutzprinzip', ibid, fn 1. On the most recent discussion, see S Swoboda, 'Die Lehre vom Rechtsgut und ihre Alternativen' in (2010) 122 *Zeitschrift für die gesamte Strafrechtswissenschaft* 24; C Roxin, 'Der gesetzgebungskritische Rechtsgutsbegriff auf dem Prüfstand' (2013) 160 *Goltdammer's Archiv für Strafrecht* 433.

[35] BVerfGE 120, 224 (241) (Judgment of 26 February 2008 – Geschwisterinzest) on the criminal offence of incestuous relations between adult siblings.

[36] T Hörnle, 'Das Verbot des Geschwisterinzests – Verfassungsgerichtliche Bestätigung und verfassungsrechtliche Kritik' (2008) 61 *Neue Juristische Wochenschrift* 2085; C Roxin, 'Zur Strafbarkeit des Geschwisterinzests – Zur verfassungsrechtlichen Überprüfung materiellrechtlicher Strafvorschriften' (2009) 29 *Strafverteidiger* 545; B Schünemann, 'Zur Garantenstellung beim unechten Unterlassungsdelikt'

Since the court has also, with increasing urgency, referred to the criminal law as *ultima ratio*,[37] and since one must always ask the question, '*ultima ratio*: to what end?', it is clear that the requirement that criminal prohibitions must protect legal goods remains the central doctrine in the area where the objective of prevention intersects with legitimation; and that it constitutes a precondition of just criminal punishment, whatever the chosen terminology may be.

Of course, principles formulated on this high level of abstraction do not come with exact rules for their application. Moreover, the catalogue of goods which are important for the lives of individuals keeps changing, as cultural and socio-economic conditions evolve. For this reason there will always be a broad range of debatable cases which will be subject to democratic deliberation and which will ultimately be decided by the legislator. But this is insufficient reason to leave the legislator free rein in cases where it is quite clear that the aim is not the protection of a legal good but merely the execution of some political agenda, that punishment is not necessary in order to protect a legal good, or that criminal punishment is simply out of proportion to the value of the good and/or the degree of the danger to which the good is exposed. Due to limitations of space I will merely give a few examples.

A. Political moralising

We now think it self-evidently true that criminal sanctions used to suppress homo-sexual behaviour are not concerned to protect any legal good but, rather, aim at the enforcement of a particular political ideal of sexual orientation; yet it took the German legislator until 1994 to recognise this point fully.[38] A current example of a flagrant violation by the legislator of the principle of the protection of legal goods can be found in the recently introduced criminal prohibition, in the context of in vitro fertilisation, of pre-implantation genetic testing for disability of an embryo created from the genetic material of non-disabled parents.[39] Since a woman can, of

---

in M Böse and D Sternberg-Lieben (eds), *Grundlagen des Straf- und Strafverfahrensrechts: Festschrift für Knut Amelung zum 70. Geburtstag* (Berlin, Duncker & Humblot, 2009) 303, 304 at fn 3; K Kühl, 'Besonders hohe Grenzen für den Strafgesetzgeber' in M Jahn, H Kudlich and F Streng (eds), *Strafrechtspraxis und Reform: Festschrift für Heinz Stöckel zum 70. Geburtstag* (Berlin, Duncker & Humblot, 2010) 117, 129.

[37] BVerfGE 126, 170 (195, 197) (Judgment of 23 June 2010 – *Untreuetatbestand*) regarding the degree of vagueness in the offence of abuse of an economic position of trust, § 266 StGB.

[38] The main steps towards the decriminalisation of homosexual relations between males were taken in the late 1960s and early 1970s and in 1973 led to decriminalisation of non-exploitative male homosexual relations between participants of at least 18 years of age. The remaining discrepancy between the age thresholds in Germany for lawful consensual male homosexual relations (minimum age of 18) and lawful consensual heterosexual relations (14) fell away in 1994 (29th Strafrechtsänderungsgesetz of 31 May 1994).

[39] In 2011, the *Embryonenschutzgesetz* (ESchG: Law Concerning the Protection of Embryos), which regulates and prohibits various techniques of medically assisted reproduction, was amended through the insertion of a new § 3a EschG. This provision prohibits any person from testing an embryo created in vitro for genetic abnormalities, unless at least one partner of the couple seeking the service carries a high risk of genetic abnormalities in offspring. For this ground of justification to apply, an ethics commission attached to the centre for medically assisted reproduction has to approve the testing.

course, not be forced to have any embryo implanted into her womb at all, the only purpose served by this threat of punishment is to enforce the political programme of certain religious and other groups who apparently want to force non-disabled women in particular to play the lottery when it comes to procreation, undeterred even by the resulting grotesque self-contradiction of German criminal law which, after all, during the first three months of pregnancy exposes all embryos already inside the womb to the possibility of being aborted at the request of the pregnant woman (§ 218a StGB[40]).

B. Pre-emptive endangerment offences

The criteria for regulating risks have been developed and concretised by criminal law doctrine over time. The classic notion of a crime as consisting of 'injurious conduct' (*Verletzungsdelikt*) was first expanded through the notion of a crime of 'concrete endangerment' (*konkretes Gefährdungsdelikt*), then by the idea of a crime of 'abstract-concrete endangerment' – which is also sometimes referred to as a 'crime of dangerous conduct' (*Gefährlichkeitsdelikt*) or as a 'crime of conduct in principle capable of creating danger' (*Eignungsdelikt*) – and, finally, by the notion of a 'crime of abstract endangerment' (*abstraktes Gefährdungsdelikt*). The latter category supposedly encompasses conduct which, on its own, does not create any appreciable danger for a legally protected interest but is, at most, statistically correlated to the violation of a legal good. Looked at both from the perspective of prevention and from the perspective of justice, such criminal prohibitions can only be legitimate if the law succeeds in capturing the 'collective switching point' at which prevention through the criminal law has to start, simply because beyond this point the source of the danger dissipates into the anonymous and becomes no longer controllable through later-stage intervention. For this reason also intervention can legitimately start here, because releasing a source of danger into an uncontrollable future can count as an irresponsible act for which an individual can justly be punished.[41]

Examples of legitimate criminal law prohibitions of this kind are the offences of capital investment fraud and market manipulation. An example of an *illegitimate* prohibition is provided by the crime of 'preparation of a serious act compromising state stability',[42] recently inserted into German criminal law in dutiful implementa-

---

[40] At least three days before seeking an abortion on non-medical grounds, the pregnant woman has to attend a counselling session at an approved counselling centre (see § 219 StGB). Even though the pregnant woman has to attend prior counselling, the choice whether or not to seek an abortion remains hers.

[41] See B Schünemann, 'Kritische Anmerkungen zur geistigen Situation der deutschen Strafrechtswissenschaft' (1995) 142 *Goltdammer's Archiv für Strafrecht* 201, 210ff; B Schünemann, 'Rechtsgüterschutz, ultima ratio und Viktimodogmatik – von den unverrückbaren Grenzen des Strafrechts in einem liberalen Rechtsstaat' in A von Hirsch, K Seelmann and W Wohlers, *Mediating Principles. Begrenzungsprinzipien bei der Strafbegründung* (Baden-Baden, Nomos, 2006) 18, 28ff.

[42] § 89a StGB (*Vorbereitung einer schweren staatsgefährdenden Gewalttat*). For trenchant criticism, see T Fischer, *Strafgesetzbuch (StGB): Kommentar*, 60th edn (Munich, CH Beck, 2013) § 89a, marginal note 3ff.

tion of the Council of Europe's Convention on the Prevention of Terrorism[43] and the EU Council of Ministers' Framework Decision on Combating Terrorism,[44] as there are forms of this offence that do not punish any potentially dangerous conduct, but only the personal character of an individual who is contemplating dangerous deeds.

C. Collective legal goods

Particularly difficult are the so-called collective legal goods, which are concerned with the systemic conditions on which individuals in society depend for positive social interaction.[45] An example is provided by corruption of public officials. It is one of the requirements of a functioning Rule of Law state that public officials restrict themselves to the implementation of the law, which means that any private advantage or benefit given to an official before he or she takes some official action compromises this system. Whether a benefit given to an official *after* he or she took the action in compliance with the legal rules should also be criminalised on the grounds that such gifts likewise endanger the systemic conditions of proper administration, is an open question falling within the legislator's discretion to resolve. Consequently different legal systems in the EU treat this issue differently.

I have only been able to give a few examples on the second level of penal justice. I hope these examples have nevertheless shown that there are quite a number of criteria of justice that concern and apply to the substantive criminal law. It is the task of criminal law theory to identify these criteria in order to impose limits on the legislature and the courts, and thereby to prevent arbitrariness in legislation as well as in the application of the law.

IV. The Requirements of Penal Justice Regarding the Structure of the Criminal Trial

On the third level of concretisation – the rules concerning the criminal trial – a number of standards binding the legislator can be derived from the requirement that punishment must be just.

This already starts with the requirement not to permit the trial judge any unfettered discretion, but to bind his 'terrible power' into a close-meshed net of rules which – as I see it – create some *procedural balance*. This does not exhaust itself in the formal guarantee of an accused's status as an active subject (and not a mere

---

[43] Council of Europe Convention on the Prevention of Terrorism, signed at Warsaw on 16 May 2005, CETS No 196.

[44] Council Framework Decision 2002/475/JHA of 13 June 2002 on combating terrorism, [2002] OJ L164/3.

[45] See R Hefendehl, *Kollektive Rechtsgüter im Strafrecht* (Cologne, Carl Heymanns, 2002).

object) of criminal procedure; it also entitles him to an effective defence and to an effective system of legal appeals against any judicial decision. This is so because power granted without control is arbitrary. This realisation has by now also found its way into international human rights instruments like the International Covenant on Civil and Political Rights (ICCPR). But that fact does not render superfluous its grounding in principles of penal justice and hence in the constitution of any state committed to the Rule of Law. For instance, the right to the review of every criminal conviction is not contained in the text of the European Convention on Human Rights (ECHR) as such, but only in Article 2 of Protocol 7, and neither Germany nor the United Kingdom has ratified this protocol to date.[46] The equivalent guarantee in Article 14(5) of the ICCPR only guarantees an accused 'the right to his conviction and sentence being reviewed by a higher tribunal according to law,' which leaves the shape and hence also the effectiveness of this review fully to the discretion of the national legislator. One way of exercising this discretion would be to create a criminal appeals system with the right to a full re-hearing of the case (including a re-taking of the evidence) by a higher court.[47] Penal justice may, however, be endangered rather than increased by such a system, especially since the reliability of witness evidence decreases across time. Moreover, one then faces the problem of how the risk of arbitrary decision-making by the second-instance judge may be controlled. Real control occurs, for this reason, not through a simple repetition but through a legal and logical checking of the three areas of activity of the first-instance judge: compliance with procedural law, assessment of evidence, and application of the substantive law to the facts thus found. The first- and last-mentioned areas can be subjected to full control, the second area only to a reasonableness test or a plausibility assessment. I am therefore of the view that the requirement of just punishment can generate binding criteria for the structure of criminal appeals. One can, on this basis, for instance conclude that the marginalisation, in the recent jurisprudence of the German Federal Court, of procedural violations as a ground of review[48] in criminal matters is incompatible with the principles of just punishment, and should really already have been brought to an end by the German Constitutional Court.

The impairment of penal justice by the weakening of appellate control in Germany is, however, far exceeded by developments at EU level. The principle of mutual recognition contained in the Treaty of Lisbon, and now found in Article 82 of the Treaty on the Functioning of the European Union (TFEU), has the effect that throughout the EU the most punitive national legal system applicable to an offence can investigate and prosecute that case, which seriously weakens the defence case

---

[46] Indeed, the United Kingdom has not even signed the Protocol yet. For an up-to-date chart of signatures and ratifications of Protocol 7, see: conventions.coe.int/Treaty/Commun/ChercheSig.asp?NT=117&CM=7&DF=16/11/2012&CL=ENG.

[47] In Germany, this type of appeal is called *Berufung*.

[48] For details, see C Roxin and B Schünemann, *Strafverfahrensrecht: Ein Studienbuch*, 27th edn (Munich, CH Beck, 2012) 472ff.

and gravely upsets the balance of procedural rights.[49] Some years ago the honorand and I participated in an expert working group financed by the EU. The group proposed to strengthen the role of the defence in European criminal trials, and thus to ameliorate such unbalancing effects, through the creation of a new procedural role, the *Eurodefensor*.[50] This proposal was completely ignored in Brussels, which surprised me as little as the recent judgments of the Court of Justice of the European Union (CJEU) in the cases of *Radu*[51] and *Melloni*.[52] In complete disregard of the most elemental principles of democracy, these judgments elevated Council Framework Decision 2002/584/JHA establishing the European Arrest Warrant above the guarantees contained in various Member States' constitutions, and failed even to pose questions regarding the procedural preconditions of penal justice. Both the European Council of Ministers and the European Court of Justice – as the latter's arbitrary pre-Lisbon recognition of implied ancillary criminal law competences at EU level showed[53] – view the criminal law as just another enforcement mechanism for legal norms, without any sensitivity for the questions of justice posed specifically by the use of criminal law.

A detailed study could derive further binding conclusions for criminal procedure from the principle of penal justice, especially as regards the procedure before the trial court. For any imposition of punishment to be just, it is necessary, first, that the procedure followed is capable of establishing the substantial truth regarding the events in respect of which punishment may be imposed. For this reason, one must view with grave concern the Common Law's traditional adversarial trial, which is spreading in Europe and has to the largest extent been introduced in Italy. The legitimating model of the Common Law trial is not the ideal of truth discovery but that of a fair contest. The latter is, as a justification for the imposition of punishment, nonsensical. The supposed contestants are the prosecution and the defence; the punished individual is the accused. Even though I also view a fair balance of procedural rights as indispensable for the process of establishing the truth, one must not close one's eyes to the fact that nearly equal power of the parties can only obtain in a civil case (and indeed civil procedure is where the roots of the Anglo-American criminal trial lie). But in criminal cases the enormous structural superiority of the prosecutorial authorities can never be fully compensated.[54]

[49] See B Schünemann, 'Ein Gespenst geht um in Europa – Brüsseler "Strafrechtspflege" intra muros' (2002) 149 *Goltdammer's Archiv für Strafrecht* 501; and B Schünemann, 'Von Lissabon über Karlsruhe nach Stockholm – Demokratisches Defizit, mangelnder Mindeststandard, Verlustliste der Verteidigung' (2011) 5 *StrafRechtsReport* 130 (with further references).

[50] See Schünemann, *Programme for European Criminal Justice*, above n 5 at 105, 166ff; C Nestler, 'Europäisches Strafprozessrecht' (2004) 116 *Zeitschrift für die gesamte Strafrechtswissenschaft* 332.

[51] Case C-396/11 *Radu* (Judgment of 29 January 2013) CJEU (GC).

[52] Case C-399/11 *Melloni* (Judgment of 26 February 2013) CJEU (GC).

[53] Case C-176/03 *Commission v Council* (Judgment of 13 September 2005) ECJ. For devastating criticism, see R Hefendehl, 'Der EuGH stellt die strafrechtliche Kompetenzordnung auf den Kopf – und wundert sich über die Kritik' in JC Joerden and AJ Szwarc (eds), *Europäisierung des Strafrechts in Polen und Deutschland – rechtsstaatliche Grundlagen* (Berlin, Duncker & Humblot, 2007) 41.

[54] See further B Schünemann, 'Zur Kritik des amerikanischen Strafprozessmodells' in E Weßlau and W Wohlers (eds), *Festschrift für Gerhard Fezer zum 70. Geburtstag am 29 Oktober 2008* (Berlin, De Gruyter, 2008) 555ff.

Even more catastrophic results for penal justice are generated by the recent European trend (of which recent reforms in German procedural law provide a particularly sorry example) to slap some form of plea-bargaining onto a reformed inquisitorial criminal procedure as followed by most Continental jurisdictions. This does not merely abandon the aim of establishing the truth during the trial. In the specific context of the Continental systems of criminal procedure, especially in Germany, it also further increases the already excessive power of the trial judge to the point where even the Olympian gods could not compete. This is so because one and the same judge (i) decides, after reading the file compiled by the prosecution, whether the case will be tried in court, already forming a view on the likelihood of conviction, which muddies his objectivity and creates a risk that the trial may turn into a self-fulfilling prophecy; (ii) conducts the trial; (iii) hears the evidence; (iv) assesses the evidence; (v) renders judgment regarding both guilt and sentence; and (vi) has for more than 30 years also usurped the right to influence or end the criminal trial proper in terms of an arrangement reached with the defence – and in such an arrangement, the accused's cooperation is bought with a promise of mild punishment behind which, of course, lurks the threat of a much harsher sanction following conviction after a full trial.[55] Five years ago the German legislator placed this until then completely extra-legal practice on a statutory footing (§ 257c StPO). In doing so, the legislator has replaced the procedural preconditions for the just imposition of punishment with the arbitrary power of a human being who happens to be wearing judicial robes.[56]

V. Concluding Remarks

Andreas von Hirsch has shown us that it is possible for the philosophy of criminal law to formulate criteria for penal justice that are also requirements for the proper exercise of power in a state committed to the Rule of Law, and hence binding upon the legislator. Modern criminal law theory in the United States and the United Kingdom, in Germany and in Scandinavia bears the imprint of his ideas, which set standards relevant everywhere. *Ad multos annos!*

---

[55] For criticism, see B Schünemann, *Absprachen im Strafverfahren? Grundlagen, Gegenstände und Grenzen. Gutachten B zum 58. Deutschen Juristentag* (Munich, Deutscher Juristentag, 1990). See also B Schünemann, 'Die Urteilsabsprachen im Strafprozess – ewige Wiederkunft des Gleichen?' in MA Zöller et al (eds), *Gesamte Strafrechtswissenschaft in internationaler Dimension. Festschrift für Jürgen Wolter zum 70. Geburtstag am 7. September 2013* (Berlin, Duncker & Humblot, 2013) 1107. A similar concern about American law is expressed by Tonry, in his contribution to this volume.

[56] Paradoxically, the German Constitutional Court has held that the legal provisions themselves are compatible with the Constitution, whereas the practice that evolved both before and after these provisions were introduced violates the Constitution to a significant extent. See BVerfG, judgment in cases 2 BvR 2628/10 and others of 19 March 2013 (*Verständigungsgesetz*) concerning trial-concluding arrangements made between the trial court, the prosecution and the accused in criminal cases.

15

Punishment and the Ends of Policing*

JOHN KLEINIG

I. Is Punishment Ever a Legitimate Police Function?

There are reasons to think that it could be. Consider the following. Social contract theorists such as John Locke argue that among the rights with which humans are endowed is a right to punish those who violate their rights (their own and others'). Locke writes that in the state of nature [pre-civil society] 'the execution of the law of nature [the moral law] is ... put into every man's hands, whereby everyone has a right to punish the transgressors of that law to such a degree as may hinder its violation.'[1] Such punishment, he considers, has both retributive and consequentialist determinants and limitations: the right to punish is a right 'only to retribute to [the wrongdoer], so far as calm reason and conscience dictates, what is proportionate to his transgression, which is so much as may serve for reparation and restraint.'[2]

Although everyone has that right in a state of nature, it is, as Locke is quick to point out, a precarious right, as indeed are the primary rights with which he believes humans are endowed [life, liberty and property]. It is one thing to possess a right – whether as an endowment of God or as a natural inference from one's status as a rational being. It is another to be in a position to exercise that right effectively. We cannot trust our fellow human beings, and they cannot trust us, accurately or disinterestedly to discern the law of nature and breaches thereof or to apply that law impartially, and even if they manage to do this, they are unlikely to be able to put such judgements into effect. Those who violate rights are usually disinclined to offer themselves up to the punitive judgement of others, who may in any case lack the means to enforce such judgement.

* An earlier version of this chapter was greatly improved as a result of comments from Antje du Bois-Pedain and Andrew Simester. I am also grateful to Tziporah Kasachkoff for many stylistic improvements.
[1] John Locke, *Second Treatise of Civil Government*, § 7, available generally at www.gutenberg.org/ebooks/7370/.
[2] Ibid, § 8. Many questions are raised by this account of the natural executive right but I shall, for the most part, bypass them in order to focus on the narrower topic I have set myself: whether punishment is ever a legitimate police function. For a good overview of the questions I am omitting, see AJ Simmons, 'Locke and the Right to Punish' (1991) 24 *Philosophy & Public Affairs* 311.

And so, Locke continues, rational creatures such as ourselves will see the wisdom of joining together in what we know as civil society, creating institutions that will enable us to exercise our rights to the fullest. In his account of civil society, Locke posits the formation of three institutional structures that are lacking in the state of nature but essential to the enjoyment of our rights. These are, first, a legislature to draw up and promulgate societally recognised rules or laws to which all will be subject, second, a judiciary administered by impartial judges who will interpret and apply what the legislature has mandated, and finally an 'executive' that will give practical effect to the laws by apprehending those who have violated them and ensuring that the punitive judgements associated with such breaches are put into effect.

Who comprise this executive? I have often used Locke's summary in the ninth chapter of the *Second Treatise* to draw attention to the integral role of police in civil society. We have empowered police to ensure that rights violators are 'brought to justice.' But it does not take too much thought to see that this is an oversimplification, even if, for some purposes, a useful one. Despite the argument's drift, we do not usually see it as the role of police to punish rights violators and are often indignant when they 'take the law into their own hands' and presume themselves to be the agents of societal punishment. In any case, what we now denominate as police did not have that modern institutional form when Locke was writing.[3] In Locke's time, the executive function in England was fragmented and disorganised. Many prosecutions were private and the execution of police powers was carried out by a mix of private agencies, constables (often local householders in rotation), those who deputised for them, nightwatchmen, and associational collectives, with some public assistance in the case of street crimes. Although prefigured, it was not until 1829 that democratic policing as we now understand it was instituted in London and spread from there.

And yet what we ask of police is an integral part of the 'executive' that Locke sees as lacking in the state of nature and the punishment that is visited on rights violators. As Locke makes clear, people who violate the rights of others 'will seldom fail, where they are able, by force to make good their injustice' and, particularly if they resist, can be dangerous to those who attempt to punish them. What we now refer to as police clearly have a role in meeting these social needs and expectations.

So, then, how should we see the role of police in executing the right to punish? How far may they go? Does a little 'street justice' constitute a proper police function or does it overreach what should be observed as clear boundaries?

In what follows, I shall explore in greater depth the role that police may have in society's punitive activity. I shall argue that although there is good reason within traditional contract theory to see police simply as gatekeepers to the criminal justice system and its punitive function, an expanded understanding of the police role may leave greater room for their playing a more substantive role in imposing societal punishment. It is, however, prone to abuse and one that, as a matter of social policy

---

[3] Having spent some time in France, Locke was probably familiar with the *Maréchaussée*. Because of its military links, however, it was not really a precursor to Sir Robert Peel's civilian force in London.

we may wish to minimise if not discourage. In section II below, I review the rationale for the traditional division of labour within the criminal justice system, one that effectively excludes police from having any punitive role. Section III will review that role, broadening it from gatekeeping to social peacekeeping. In section IV, I consider how, within a larger social peacekeeping conception, police may be considered to have a limited role as agents of societal punishment. I indicate what that limited area might be. I argue, however, that because police-administered punishments are so prone to abuse – in (so-called) 'contempt-of-cop arrests',[4] investigative paybacks, and anticipatory deposits – that we should be exceedingly cautious about formalising this role, lest it become a cloak for such abuses. To the extent that it finds expression it should be held to strict standards of accountability.

II. The Criminal Justice System

Although it is a bit grandiose to speak of a criminal justice *system* – given the somewhat piecemeal way in which its various elements have evolved and the uncoordinated way in which these elements actually operate – there is, nevertheless, a discernible rationale to the tripartite character of the contractualist depiction of civil society's essential institutions. Left to themselves, and given what we know about them, unregulated humans do not do a particularly good job of living with each other. And this is the case even if we assume – as it appears to be within the Lockean contractualist position – that a distinctive feature of human experience is the capacity for moral decision-making. Whether that amounts to a capacity to discern some externally validated law of nature or to make practical decisions based on judgements of appropriateness need not detain us at this point. What does seem to be a reasonable observation is that humans as we find them differ considerably in their determinations of what is to be done. Locke links some of those differences to deficiencies of reason, some to tunnel vision, some to corrupt judgement and evil intent, and some to weakness of will. Left to themselves individuals unconstrained by the norms and structures of civil society will ordinarily find it difficult to pursue the life goals that they formulate for themselves and that embody the values they see as appropriate to their status as rational moral agents.

To characterise those values Locke uses the language of rights-possession – in particular, the possession of rights to *life, liberty and property*. Others have opted or argued for the language of human flourishing or dignity.[5] However we wish to frame the language of our distinctiveness, the contractualist claim is that, absent certain institutional structures – those that define civil society – opportunities to live full human lives are likely to be seriously impoverished. There needs to be some suitably

---

[4] An unlawful arrest instigated by behaviour that is perceived to be disrespectful to a police officer rather than criminal.

[5] For an attempt to link these various conceptualisations, see J Kleinig and NG Evans, 'Human Flourishing, Human Dignity, and Human Rights' (2013) 32 *Law and Philosophy* 539.

broad framework of norms to which all see themselves conscientiously and effectively obligated, and these are conceptualised by Locke as the pronouncements of a consensually established legislature. There is, of course, a certain conceit to the idea of a social contract. It is a theoretical construct more than it is an historical event, although it manages to retain some of its persuasiveness through social gestures such as voting and its broadly accepted conformity to expectations about what reasonable people such as ourselves would choose to be fair. Such legislatures have a much wider brief than is encompassed by the criminal justice system, though the determination of what forms of conduct should fall within the latter's purview is an important one. Nevertheless, given the moral challenge that the practice of punishment involves, it is important that there is some broadly constituted source for deciding what behaviour is deserving of punishment and what should be regulated in other ways (if at all). If the imposition of punishment is to be distinguished from other impositions that humans may place on their fellow citizens, the process of criminalisation needs to be grounded in an institution that garners respect even if not love. The grounds for criminalisation must be amenable to some form of public reason.

Even so, a legislature is not sufficient for the needs of those for whom it is intended. Laws promulgated need to be interpreted and applied and, because of the way in which they function, legislatures may not be the most appropriate agents for that. As primarily political structures, legislatures are too beholden to majoritarian or other partisan interests. And so contractualists have argued for a judiciary that will interpret and apply laws impartially and fairly and, in the event that there are constitutional constraints, will ensure that those constraints are observed. Of course, the theory is better than the practice, even with a tiered judiciary that allows for appeals and reviews. The traditional judicial virtues of independence, impartiality, integrity, and competence have often been breached, victims of the same failings that supposedly drove people into the contract in the first place. Nevertheless, the institutional role offers some protection against the pervasive and more extreme expressions of human frailty and perversity.

The joint activities of legislature and judiciary go only to the establishment of fairly interpreted and adjudicated social norms. Their enforcement is left to an undifferentiated 'executive'. It is clear from Locke's account, however, that this executive, however institutionalised, is intended to sub-serve the work of the legislature and judiciary. This may be one of the ideological impulses behind the Anglo-Australian notion of the 'original authority' of the constable – the idea that police have an 'original' discretionary authority *under the law* and are not answerable first and foremost to their superiors.[6] Yet even if this frees exercises of police discretion from command authority, it does not give operational police a power to act independently of the legislature and courts. Police may be held accountable before the law for such exercises of executive authority.

---

[6] *Enever v R* (1906) 3 CLR 969; cf J Carabetta, 'The Employment Status of Police in Australia' (2003) 27 *Melbourne University Law Review* 1. Although police should be expected to have an expertise that is superior to the ordinary citizen, their moral authority is not superior to that possessed by humans in a state of nature.

The normal order of things, then, will be that police, as agents of civil authority, will keep their eyes and ears open for breaches of criminal law and will take necessary steps to investigate such breaches, apprehend violators, and ensure that they are brought before a prosecutor or court, along with whatever appropriately gathered evidence will bear on the question of guilt or innocence. (Or something like this, given that different criminal justice systems will have their own ways of making up the deficiencies of the state of nature.) This is not to suggest that the role of police is limited to such activity or that there is no more to the executive function than what police do. Moreover, once verdicts are rendered, police may have only a small role to play in the event that a person is found guilty and sentenced. And the social role that police have in contemporary liberal democracies encompasses a far broader range of activities than 'law enforcement'. As I shall suggest, a vaguer but better characterisation of their role is that of being social peacekeepers. This, we will later see, has some bearing on the issue of punishment, for a significant part of police work may consist in order maintenance. The maintenance of order should not be thought of in simple law enforcement terms but, more broadly, to include a range of interventions designed to prevent various forms of social disorder from significantly breaching a legal threshold and providing an occasion for arrest. It is at this level of social disorder that police may consider some form of informal punitive intervention to be justified.

III. The Police Role (or the Ends of Policing)

Some policing function seems to be integral to human social life. Leaving aside stories of an Eden-like past or a Utopian future, human sociality, critical as it is to our development as the persons we are, has always been a fraught arrangement. Whatever ancient documents we consult, the human condition has been marked by conflict and repair, infringement and punishment, and each social grouping has needed to develop its own policing function. The social contract is a latecomer to this human stage, mostly a seventeenth-century construct intended to articulate for declining monarchies and emerging democratic states a rationale for their strictures and coercive function.[7] It is at best old wine in new bottles, the wine constituted by the essential but nevertheless conflictive character of human sociality.

Although contractualists such as Locke appear to have had no clearly articulated structure of institutional policing in mind, the idea of a professionalised – in the sense of specialised and paid – executive was certainly in the air at the time, and Locke makes it clear that because of human frailty, the legislative and executive

---

[7] There are of course precursors. Marsilius of Padua was an early and influential proponent of conditional government in which authority is vested in the people, but one can also go back to the biblical idea of covenant for earlier expressions of civil mutuality – even where something closer to a theocracy was involved.

powers of government ought to be separated.[8] Of course, nothing strictly follows
from Locke's discussion of civil government to prevent the privatisation of some of
its functions and, at least so far as its executive functions are concerned, we have
in recent decades seen increasing pressures for their privatisation, especially in
the correctional and security areas, but also with respect to the state's military functions. An argument to the effect that most of a government's 'executive' functions
should be carried out by government agents really requires a different set of arguments from those we have been canvassing – arguments either to the effect that
what are termed 'essential governmental functions' will be more fairly or efficiently
provided through public than private agencies, or that there is something morally
problematic about 'delegating' the coercive powers of 'essential government functions' to private agencies.[9] We shall not attempt to review or rehearse such arguments here, even though it is recognised that an increasing number of policing and
other executive functions are now being outsourced to private contractors.[10] Here
we will think of police as publicly paid agents of societal law and order.[11]

Two brief preliminary comments on 'the ends of policing' are in order. The first
is that there may be no fixed ends. In its institutionalised forms, policing has served
a variety of ends – such as securing citizens against violations by others, the maintenance of societal or class divisions, and the protection of an existing regime against
its subjects – and those ends have evolved over time. Some ends we may consider
inappropriate. Secondly, and connectedly, to establish legitimate ends we probably
need to embed the discussion of ends within a larger socio-political framework.
Liberal democratic thought (with its frequent appeal to a social contract) is one
such framework, and the one that will be presupposed for the purposes of the present discussion.

Let us start with the formation of the London Metropolitan Police Force (the
Met) in 1829, generally considered the birth of contemporary liberal democratic
policing. In Lt Col Charles Rowan and Richard Mayne's original handbook,
Instructions to Police Officers, there is a simple statement of ends: 'the principal
object to be attained is "*the Prevention of Crime*".' [12] This is an admirable if somewhat truncated view of the police role, with its focus on pre-emptive deterrence
rather than catching crooks or punishing perpetrators. And it is made even more
admirable insofar as deterrence resides in the authority of the uniform as much as
in any threat it portends. A decade or so after the Met's formation, detective work
was added to the police function, as the Force took over the work of Henry Fielding's
eighteenth-century Bow Street Runners.

---

[8] Locke, *Second Treatise*, above n 1, § 144.
[9] See A Dorfman and A Harel, 'The Case Against Privatization' (2013) 41 *Philosophy & Public Affairs*
67.
[10] See A Stanger, *One Nation Under Contract: The Outsourcing of American Power and the Future of
Foreign Policy* (New Haven CT, Yale University Press, 2009).
[11] For a study of some of the issues introduced by private policing, see B Forst and PK Manning, *The
Privatization of Policing: Two Views* (Washington DC, Georgetown University Press, 1999).
[12] Metropolitan Police, *Instructions to Police Officers* (London, HMSO, 1829), 1.

If crime prevention was the immediate end of police work, its more distant end was, as Rowan and Mayne put it, 'security of person and property [and] the preservation of the public tranquility.' It is probably the 'preservation of the public tranquility' that has become the more controlling end of liberal democratic policing. Nowadays, we use police for crowd and traffic control, order maintenance and emergency response. Reviews of the work they actually do indicate that less than half their work is concerned with actual crime fighting.[13] This is not to downgrade their crime fighting role or to ignore the extent to which only they are equipped to perform that social function. Nevertheless, just as we have broadened our understanding of the role that government may play in regard to human flourishing, so too police have been accorded an expanded social role.

As noted earlier, my own preference here is to view police primarily as social peacekeepers. It reflects an evolution of the governmental role since Locke, from the limited negative one of rights protection to the inclusion of various welfare and maintenance of order provisions. Police authority is based first and foremost in the idea that they are competent to exercise the role of social peacekeepers, and not simply in their capacity to use force (though that is one of the means at their disposal). I think this view has at least three advantages – developed at greater length elsewhere[14] – and I review that position here in the light of criticisms to which it has been subject.

A. The 'King's Peace'

Historically, the social peacekeeping view resonates with an older conception of policing as securing the 'King's Peace' – a zone of tranquillity that the King's presence was intended to bring with it. So seen, policing is viewed in the context of a permanent need for some kind of public order and of the importance of that order for humans to flourish. Against this, it might be argued – as it is by Jeffrey Reiman – that[15]

[l]inking a modern-day conception of the police as peacekeepers to the notion of the 'king's peace' does little more than exploit a verbal similarity. It is not even clear that the king's peace should be thought of as historically continuous with present-day police forces, since the king's peace was a late-feudal development and today's police are a response to modern industrialization (large and mobile urban proletariats and so on). The king's peace was enforced by magistrates and sheriffs; it predates modern policing by hundreds of years. More importantly, the keepers of the king's peace did not engage in dispute resolution or emergency medical service. What they did was closer to the law enforcement, crime-fighting function that Kleinig wants to expand beyond – and that is the sympathetic interpretation of the king's peace. The critical interpretation is that the

---

[13] See VE Kappeler, 'So You Want to Be a Crime Fighter? Not so Fast' EKU Police Studies Online, available at www.plsonline.eku.edu/insidelook/so-you-want-be-crime-fighter-not-so-fast; and Kappeler, 'How Much Crime Fighting Do Crime Fighters Really Do?' available at: plsonline.eku.edu/insidelook/how-much-crime-fighting-do-%E2%80%98crime-fighters%E2%80%99-really-do.

[14] J Kleinig, *The Ethics of Policing* (Cambridge, Cambridge University Press, 1996) ch 1.

[15] J Reiman, 'The Scope and Limits of Police Ethics' (1997) 16 *Criminal Justice Ethics* 44, reviewing *The Ethics of Policing*.

work of the keepers of the king's peace was that of wresting criminal justice out of the hands of local communities and establishing on the ground the monopoly on coercion that defines the nation state in theory.

No doubt there are important differences between the King's Peace as originally intended and the notion of social peacekeeping that I am advancing. That was something I do not (and did not) deny. Yet the notion of the King's Peace does represent an important precursor in the way that the Magna Carta, also a feudal document (1215), is a precursor to the European Convention on Human Rights (1950+). We rarely discuss the development of human rights without going back to the Magna Carta. There is an important historical resonance and evolution that links one with the other. The same is true of the King's or Queen's Peace, which, in the British Commonwealth, is still recognised as a social order that the monarch is bound to provide for her subjects. In Commonwealth countries it has a practical residue in the offence of 'breaching the peace.'[16] Thus I do not find the distance that Reiman sees between the King's Peace and social peacekeeping to be as dramatic as he claims. Moreover, insofar as the focus of the King's Peace was the sovereign's commitment to the safety of subjects, I think the connections are quite substantive and not merely nominal.

B. The crime-fighting role

The view of police as social peacekeepers captures a range of police functions that do not have a tight connection with law enforcement – the maintenance of public order through crowd and traffic control, and responsiveness to various social emergencies, only some of which involve crime (and when they do, often low-level and nuisance crime). As I have already asserted, this does not belittle the crime-fighting role of police but embeds it in a larger social task to which police are now called.[17] Again, Reiman takes issue with this:[18]

---

[16] The language of breaching the peace is preserved in the US Constitution, art 1.

[17] In an influential statement of the police role, Herman Goldstein catalogued the police functions as follows:

- 'To prevent and control conduct widely recognized as threatening to life and property
- To aid individuals who are in danger of physical harm, such as the victims of violent attack
- To facilitate the movement of people and vehicles
- To assist those who cannot care for themselves, the intoxicated, the addicted, the mentally ill, the physically disabled, the old, and the young
- To resolve conflict, whether it be between individuals, groups or individuals, or individuals and their government
- To identify problems that have the potential for becoming more serious problems
- To create and maintain a feeling of security in communities.'

Policing a Free Society (NY, Ballinger, 1977) 35. See also the American Bar Association, *Standards Relating to the Urban Police Function*, § 1–2.2, available at: www.americanbar.org/publications/criminal_justice_section_archive/crimjust_standards_urbanpolice.html.

[18] Reiman, 'The Scope and Limits of Police Ethics', above n 15 at 44–45. Reiman's critique also reflects his largely Marxist account of contemporary liberal democratic societies. I can go only so far with that – it has some empirical basis but tends to be too monolithic.

It seems to me to attribute far more intentionality (not to mention good intention-ality) to the way in which the tasks that police do have actually fallen to them. The very fact that police are armed (and dressed in military-style uniforms) for law enforcement makes it just about irresistible that they will be used for crowd and traffic control. After all, if a small group of individuals is to keep a large, unpredictable and potentially dangerous group in line, it will certainly help if the small group is armed and in distinctive dress. Rather than alternatives to the crime-fighter role, it seems that crowd and traffic control are direct extensions of that role. As for the other jobs assigned to the police, it must be noted that these jobs are not normally performed by the police for the society as a whole. They are largely performed for the poor. Middle class and richer folks do not turn to the police for dispute resolution or assistance in medical emergencies. They call on lawyers and psychiatrists for the first and go to doctors and private hospitals (not to mention discrete and high-priced clinics) for the second. Far from us having decided to assign these helper roles to the police, I think they have fallen to the police due to the larger society's failure to provide for the poor the specialized services that are available for a price to the better off. Neglected in this way, the poor call on the police when there is trouble and understandably so. The police are always there, they make housecalls, and they do not charge. Practices that result from our neglectful treatment of the poor should hardly be lifted to normative status in the way that Kleinig in effect does by speaking of what 'we' have assigned to the police. Postmodernist critics, if they have accomplished anything, should certainly have made us all more hesitant about speaking of what society does in the first person plural, as if society were of one mind and spoke with a single voice. Only some have had the power to assign the police these extra jobs, and even those power-ful few seem more to have dumped the jobs on the police than thoughtfully to have assigned them.

A couple of points call for response. I do not wish to argue that the police role has evolved with any more deliberative intentionality than the role of academics or mayors. Social demands and tasks arise, and those who have to respond to them make decisions about how best or most conveniently to address them. Things that once did not 'fall' to police, academics, and mayors now do, and some things that once 'fell' to them have become the responsibility of others. As first and round-the-clock responders to social crises, criminal and non-criminal, police are likely to find themselves called upon to perform tasks that are not crime-related. For such tasks – whether delivering babies or administering CPR – police now frequently receive basic training. And, if individual front-line police officers do not, specialist police units are often created (for juveniles, the mentally disturbed, and other specialised groups) to provide the needed service. Additionally, for many traffic and crowd control purposes, the standard uniform and weaponry are hardly necessary.[19] What Reiman loses sight of, I believe, is – as noted earlier – that only a minor (albeit very important) portion of police work is now focused on crime-fighting activities, with a larger portion being given to social peacekeeping tasks.[20] And this, I believe, goes

---

[19] And may sometimes be counterproductive because less than clearly visible in fast-moving situations. So police now often wear reflective jackets over their uniforms. If needed, the uniform remains a sign of authority.

[20] It might be useful to reflect on the way in which, for most academics, their work has shifted from research to teaching (and administration).

hand in hand with changing conceptions of what we may reasonably expect government to provide – not merely protection against criminal threats to our lives,
liberties, and property, but also provision of some of the conditions necessary for
thriving lives.[21]

I should make it clear, however, that in arguing for broadening the focus of
policing to social peacekeeping I am not shifting it away from crime fighting. In
maintaining social order and keeping the peace, police are often helping to avert
situations that would likely result in an increase in criminal activity. Moreover,
crowd and traffic control, the emergency responses, and so forth, often help to create or maintain social environments that are less prone to criminal activity.[22]

The lack of intentionality behind the changing police role need not signal either
the randomness of that change or the fact that a powerful few have dumped certain
social tasks onto the police. Certainly Reiman is right to notice that there is no universal 'we' that decides what social roles will be, and that changes are susceptible to
shifts in social power. Within liberal democratic communities, however, police do
not usually comprise a minority with little power, and what they do and don't take
on is as much within *their* power to determine as it is within the power of others who
have effective standing within the community. For example, considerable debate
has focused on the role that police should have in anti-terrorism efforts or in the
detection of illegal immigrants, two tasks that might seem closer to their crime-
fighting role; tasks that may involve intelligence gathering and profiling as much as
enforcement. In relation to these police have often been quite vocal about their
participation *or* non-participation.

C. The use of force

The third reason for my wanting to view and cast the ends of policing more broadly
is that doing so deflects some attention from the use of force to which, because of
the concern with crime control, many accounts of policing make sole explicit reference. In an influential account of policing, Egon Bittner writes: 'the role of police is
to address all sorts of human problems when and insofar as the problems' solutions
may require the use of force at the point of their occurrence.'[23] There is no doubt
that the legal use of force is something that we largely confine to police. That is one
of the social contractualist sacrifices we make. To be sure, not all use of force is
ceded, but where protection is needed and police are available to provide it, we
generally consider it *their* prerogative to exercise it.[24] Indeed, we may take action

---

[21] This is reflected in much post-Rawlsian discussion concerning the distribution of 'primary goods'.
[22] Some of this police activity might be integrated into the larger framework of situational crime
prevention. See A von Hirsch, D Garland and A Wakefield (eds), *Ethical and Social Perspectives on
Situational Crime Prevention* (Oxford, Hart Publishing, 2004).
[23] E Bittner, 'The Capacity to Use Force as the Core of the Police Role' in FA Elliston and M Feldberg
(eds), *Moral Issues in Police Work* (Totowa NJ, Rowman & Allanheld, 1985) 21.
[24] Cf Indian Penal Code 1860, s 99: 'There is no right of private defence in cases in which there is time
to have recourse to protection of the public authorities.' I thank Andrew Simester for this reference.

against citizens who assert their erstwhile natural right where police are – presumably – able to exercise it more effectively and appropriately.[25] But the use of force, even in the case of police, is something that we grant as a second or last resort rather than a first one. This is easily lost sight of in the United States where, for the past 150 years and as a matter of course, police have been visibly armed and routinely handcuff those they arrest.[26] In contrast, in the United Kingdom, the authority to arrest, and its implementation, need not involve any use or display of coercive force, even if it usually involves some minor physical contact.[27] The performative, 'You're under arrest' or 'You'd better come with me' is an exercise of authority rather than coercion. An arresting police officer may not be armed, and the requirement of compliance need not be accompanied by handcuffing.[28] True, the performative phrase is backed up by force: the non-compliant arrestee is not 'free to leave'. And true, Bittner claims only that the problems dealt with by police '*may* require the use of force' rather than that they need to do so. But at least in arrest decisions that *may* has become a *must*, and a means has been assimilated to an end.

Once again, Reiman shows a degree of scepticism about deflection from the 'forceful' role of police. He writes:[29]

> The very fact that neither the police nor the community[30] ever seems to take very seriously the notion of the police as anything but law enforcers renders Kleinig's claims about the beneficial consequences of viewing the police as peacekeepers highly unlikely. Moreover, at least one of the promised benefits – reduced reliance on deadly force – has occurred in recent years, as a result of public outcry and legal decisions, during a period in which few police organizations have reconceived themselves as social peacekeepers.
>
> Most importantly, however, characterizing the police as peacekeepers has the tendency to cover over what is still the most salient fact about the police, the very thing that calls for special justification and for special accountability, namely, that the police have the authority to order us around and to use violence to back those orders up. No matter how hallowed you think your doctor is, you can still ignore his orders, and if he persists, just tell him to go to hell and walk away. Try that with a cop. It is, in my view, profoundly dangerous to freedom to let this unusual fact slip from view ... Missing from Kleinig's rejection of police claims to professional autonomy is recognition of the specialness of the authority of the police to use force, an authority which is the people's and only lent to the police and thus appropriately subject to evaluation by its rightful owners ... The police

[25] Not, of course, that they may use it without accountability. Police authority is viewed as a grant rather than an independent possession.

[26] Just as significantly, in the US, it is frequently argued, and now has Supreme Court backing, that the people have a residual right to bear arms. Whether this is a wise understanding of a residual right to use force is another matter.

[27] According to Halsbury's *Laws of England*, 'Arrest consists in the seizure or touching of a person's body with a view to his restraint; words may, however, amount to arrest if, in the circumstances of the case, they are calculated to bring, and do bring, to a person's notice that he is under compulsion and he thereafter submits to the compulsion.'

[28] More on that later. However, I am told that even in the UK and Australia, where handcuffing has always been discretionary, and requires a reason (beyond the decision to arrest), the handcuffing of arrestees has become more routine.

[29] Reiman, 'The Scope and Limits of Police Ethics', above n 15 at 45.

[30] I note that it is now Reiman's turn to generalise over 'the community'!

are rightly subject to outside review to an extent that the local power company is not, and the reason is the special authority and power the police have and the appropriately tense relation between that power, necessary as it is, and the free citizenry it both protects and threatens.

There is of course an important point to Reiman's concern. We should not lose sight of the distinctive and almost exclusive power that police have or of the fact that it is 'on loan' to them. And yes, insofar as force is a means and one that is frequently exploited *is* something for which the police should be held accountable. Nevertheless Reiman's resistance to my view that his (and others') focus on police use of force constitutes a confusion of means with ends strikes only a glancing blow. Reiman himself is comfortable interpreting the feudal idea of the King's Peace in terms that bespeak the forcible means available to the King. And as distinctive as police access to force is, we find repeated complaints about the ways that police allow that power to distance themselves from the communities they serve. Repeated and often unsuccessful attempts to encourage varying forms of community policing are a response to this and police forces themselves often support various charitable and youth initiatives as part of an effort to reintegrate with the community from which they come and to which they should be responsive. (Certainly the use of force brings with it significant ethical challenges, challenges often not well met, but so do other means arising from their role – for example, their use of deception and, more generally their discretion to arrest.[31]) Police department slogans, such as the NYPD's 'courtesy, professionalism, respect', also remind us of ethical requirements that attach more generally to their peacekeeping role.

With respect to the details of Reiman's criticism, I believe he oversteps the mark, at least so far as the contrast between police and doctors is concerned. Even if a person cannot ignore a police officer's order to stop or move, that person does not have to speak with the officer (the right to silence can be asserted, with the possible exception of providing one's name), that person may (under most circumstances) refuse to be searched, and may leave once s/he has ascertained that s/he is not under arrest. That, at least, is the law. Whether a particular police officer takes notice of it is, of course, another matter, and changes to police practice may need to be brought about collectively rather than individually.[32]

In sum, I do not believe that Reiman's criticisms refute my contention that police authority is to be thought of as grounded primarily in a competence to maintain social peace – a broader remit; although that authority may sometimes need to be

---

[31]   Reiman and I have already had an exchange over police discretion. See J Reiman, 'Is Police Discretion Justified in a Free Society?' in J Kleinig (ed), *Handled With Discretion: Ethical Issues in Police Decision Making* (Lanham MD, Rowman & Littlefield, 1996) 71; J Kleinig, 'Selective Enforcement and the Rule of Law' (1998) 29 *Journal of Social Philosophy* 117; J Reiman, 'Against Police Discretion: Reply to John Kleinig' (1998) 29 *Journal of Social Philosophy* 132.

[32]   See the ACLU document, 'Know Your Rights: What To Do If You're Stopped By Police, Immigration Agents or the FBI', available at www.aclu.org/drug-law-reform-immigrants-rights-racial-justice/know-your-rights-what-do-if-you. Much of the current debate about police stop-and-search practices in New York concerns what is seen as overreaching in this regard. See, especially, *Floyd, et al v City of New York, et al*, 08 Civ 1034 (SAS) (2013), available at www.nysd.uscourts.gov/cases/show.php?db=special&id=317.

backed up by force it often accomplishes its purposes as a result of the larger competence it expresses.

IV. Police and Punishment

Within this larger (than crime control) conception of policing, might there be a place for police-administered punishment? I will suggest that although a good case can be made for a limited disciplinary, 'retributive', or punitive police role within the larger framework of social peacekeeping, there are several significant practical and moral hazards that make it a very restricted discretion.

There is nothing in the concept of social peacekeeping that excludes a punitive police role. (The same of course might be said of a crime-fighting conception.) To get a better sense of how punishment stands to police work we would do well to look first at the moral division of labour advocated by traditional contractualist thinking. There, so long as we stay with a traditional conception, policing, as an executive function, operates under the purview of the legislature and courts. Police do not determine what a crime is. Neither do they decide who is a criminal. These are matters for the law and the courts to determine – at least in broad terms. That is a critical qualification, because even in their law-enforcement role, police are accorded considerable discretion. However, once we move from the generalities of legislative fiat to the particularities of the world in which the law is to be applied, we often find enormous situational complexity for which the generalities of the law are not well crafted.

Some of these complexities may be dealt with at a judicial level. A court may indicate some of the parameters within which a law has to be understood as well as make determinations with respect to individuals who have been brought before it.

But as well as being social agents ex post, operating within a framework of legislative determination and change and subsequent judicial interpretations, police must also operate ex ante, deciding whether and how to respond to concrete situations. Did individual *A* break law *B*, or otherwise disturb the peace, and if so how should that be dealt with? Discretion is called for. Discretion may informally operate at the level of the police agency (an understanding that, unless they are driving recklessly, drivers will not be apprehended if they are traveling less than 10 per cent over the speed limit) or at the level of individual officers. In the latter case, exercises of discretion are not merely exercises of personal judgement about particular situations, but exercises of *professional* judgement, in which officers draw upon their understanding of the purposes of their role and are (ideally) informed by considerations of 'best practice'. We thus think of police discretion as an authority they have under the law and within the domain of their public accountability.

May police exercises of discretion include a punitive function? That police sometimes do act punitively is clear enough, though in individual cases it may not always be clear whether a particular police imposition is genuinely punitive rather than retaliatory or vengeful. I take it that retaliation, like revenge, is a response to personal upset or hurt, that vengeance is a response to perceived (moral) wrongdoing, and punishment – at least in the case of police – is a response to what is perceived as the unjustified violation of an authoritative public norm.[33] Such complexities aside (for the moment), there is some reason to think that the task of social peacekeeping may not merely be consistent with a punitive police role but actually call for it.

Perhaps the most plausible context for the police exercise of punitive authority falls within their order-maintenance rather than their crime-fighting role. As noted earlier, a significant proportion of police work involves order-maintenance tasks, some merely regulative but others corrective, though not quite to the point of crime-fighting. Police intervention is desirable to prevent a situation from degenerating into one in which the machinery of criminal law is called for. Disorder in public bars or streets, neighbourhood disturbances, minor infractions (antisocial behaviour), drunkenness without driving, and so on, especially (though not exclusively) in poor or declining communities, may call for a heightened police presence and response. Arrest might be legitimately effected, but may set in motion a cumbersome and unnecessarily heavy-handed machinery. Or it may aggravate a situation that is better handled more decisively on the spot.[34] On the other hand, leaving a situation to play out on its own may be unwise. Gary Sykes has argued that, in communities that have been ravaged by economic and other changes, and have not been well served by other sources of social support so that they now teeter on the brink of disorder, street justice administered by police may respond to some of that disorder.[35] It is Sykes's view not only that may police think it appropriate that they respond in such informal but decisive ways, but also that such acts are often appreciated by those for whom other social welfare services are lacking.[36] In principle he supports such informal punishments. They can connect usefully with notions of police discretion, in which the complexity of social life makes it appropriate that police use their professional judgement about how situations should best be handled.[37] Some public order infractions may be seen as warranting a punitive societal

---

[33] These distinctions go back to some early work: J Kleinig, *Punishment and Desert* (The Hague, Martinus Nijhoff, 1973), though see more recently S Uniacke, 'What is Wrong with Revenge?' (2000) 34 *Journal of Value Inquiry* 361.

[34] Forcible removal from premises, confiscation of car keys, seizing drugs or alcohol, and on-the-spot fines are common practices. Even if these are sometimes justified, they can lend themselves to excess, especially the confiscation – 'civil forfeiture' – of valuable property that police then use for their own purposes. See, for example, S Stillman, 'Taken', *New Yorker*, 12 August 2013, available at www.newyorker.com/reporting/2013/08/12/130812fa_fact_stillman.

[35] GW Sykes, 'Street Justice: A Moral Defense of Order Maintenance Policing' (1986) 3 *Justice Quarterly* 497.

[36] As Sykes develops his case, such order maintenance and peacekeeping policing harks back to the conception of policing as 'community building', for which they have a 'moral mandate' (ibid, 501, 508). He believes that the 'professionalization' of policing, which severely regulates police discretion and restricts police to a gate-keeping role is inadequate to the needs of certain social communities.

[37] The kind of discretionary action contemplated here is probably to be distinguished from (though may sometimes be no less controversial than) the Anti-Social Behaviour Orders (ASBOs) introduced by the British Labour Government in 1998, and which often sought to ban unruly people from certain

response, though not one that requires the heavier (or unreliable) machinery of the criminal justice system.

There is, I suspect, more than a little to be said for this story, and although it would no doubt work better in some social contexts than others, I would not limit it to the underserved communities contemplated by Sykes. The complexities of social life do call for situational judgements, and mere warnings or a legalism that feeds every formal infraction (misdemeanour) into the hopper of the criminal justice system are likely to be inadequate or inappropriately heavy-handed. This is especially the case with loitering with intent, disorderly conduct, vagrancy, public drunkenness, and the like. There is also a range of ill-defined minor offences, especially involving young people, to which police may (but perhaps ought not to) appeal for purposes of making arrests. The police officer may confiscate contraband, seek to ban a person from a particular venue for a time, or impose some other social restriction or requirement when arrest and processing might not be called for. At certain times and places, that role for the beat officer was recognised and valued.

Theory is one thing, however, practice another, and in a short but perceptive critique of Sykes, Carl Klockars suggests that it inappropriately works from the top-down rather than bottom-up.[38] What Sykes theorises as an appropriate moral impulse for police officers to administer street justice does not mesh with the moral impulse that actually drives police to act punitively. What Sykes interprets as a community mandate for street justice is generally better understood as the moral interest that a police officer has in his or her own territory. Order maintenance is seen as maintenance of authority over *one's own* territory.

I think Klockars is onto something important here, and I shall seek to spell it out with what is, in effect, a bottom-up review of some typical contexts in which the punitive authority of police is or has been exercised – contempt-of-cop arrests, punishment for trouble and risk, guaranteeing justice, and the use of deadly force.

A. 'Contempt-of-cop' arrests

There is of course no offence denominated 'contempt of cop'; however, police who are aggrieved by the questioning of (what they perceive as) their non-negotiable social authority may punish those who show what they interpret as disrespect for it by arresting them, whereby the arrest and its (usually) unpleasant but nevertheless judicially non-punitive sequels constitute a form of (police) punishment.

---

associations and areas. The latter were generally sought by local councils and needed court approval. Although said to be non-punitive, it is likely that many of the orders issued also had a punitive function. For contrary views of ASBOs, see AP Simester and A von Hirsch, 'Regulating Offensive Conduct Through Two-Step Prohibitions' in von Hirsch and Simester (eds), *Incivilities: Regulating Offensive Behaviour* (Oxford, Hart Publishing, 2006) ch 7; and P Ramsay, *The Insecurity State: Vulnerable Autonomy and the Right to Security in the Criminal Law* (Oxford, Oxford University Press, 2012) ch 5.

[38] CB Klockars, 'Street Justice: Some Micro-moral Reservations: Comment on Sykes' (1986) 3 *Justice Quarterly* 513.

Because the actions that are constituted by 'contempt of cop' are – at least in the United States – generally protected by First Amendment free speech rights, police who wish to punish those they deem as disrespecting them usually formally arrest them for disorderly conduct, breach of the peace, obstruction, and so on. Legally speaking, only 'fighting words' serve to remove first amendment protections[39] but as a matter of police practice a much lower standard operates.

Police training often inculcates in officers and reinforces for them the importance of asserting their authority – manifested in 'coming on strong' to take control of a situation – of not backing down[40] and, more often than one would want, treating situations in which legitimate questioning of the use of that authority is interpreted as illegitimate interference with legitimate police activity.[41] As a result police often respond in thin-skinned ways to any sort of questioning or challenge. Sometimes people want to do no more than observe or document police action, and officers take umbrage at the fact that their conduct is being monitored. Refusal to leave or stop monitoring what is going on may lead to what is in effect a contempt-of-cop arrest.

For the most part, such 'contempt-of-cop' arrests, and the charges within which they are concealed, are not proceeded with by prosecutors or are later dismissed by judges. Nevertheless, miffed officers, or officers who have inadequate alternative grounds for expressing umbrage at having their social authority questioned, will be able to get some sort of what they see as punitive (more accurately, retaliatory) satisfaction from the fact that the person they arrested will have been 'taught a lesson' and will think twice on a future occasion.[42] Worse still, that person may come to be haunted by it when applying for a job or grant or other benefit that requires an answer to the question whether he or she has ever been arrested.[43]

Police 'punitive' action of this kind cuts at the heart of the US first amendment guarantee of free speech which, more than anything, is supposed to protect the right to criticise exercises of governmental authority.[44] Even if some questioning of police

---

[39] See *Gooding v Wilson* 405 US 518, 522 (1972) (quoting *Chaplinsky v New Hampshire* 315 US 568, 572 (1942); *Lewis v City of New Orleans* 415 US 130, 135 (1974, Powell J, concurring). Fighting words are those which by their 'very utterance inflict injury or tend to incite an immediate breach of the peace.' Moreover, as Justice Powell writes/repeats in *Lewis*, 'a properly trained officer may reasonably be expected to "exercise a higher degree of restraint" than the average citizen, and thus be less likely to respond belligerently to "fighting words"'. In the UK, *Harvey v Director of Public Prosecutions* [2011] EWHC B1 (Admin) seeks to moderate 'contempt-of-cop' arrests that come to be made under s 5 of the Public Order Act 1986.

[40] A 'corrective' police adage puts it: 'back off, not down'.

[41] For a review of cases, see CE Lopez, 'Disorderly (mis)Conduct: The Problem with 'Contempt of Cop' Arrests' Issue Brief, American Constitution Society (Washington DC, 2010), available at www.acslaw.org/sites/default/files/Lopez_Contempt_of_Cop.pdf; also M Wilson and S Moore, 'As Officers Face Heated Words, Their Tactics Vary', *New York Times*, 25 June 2009, available at www.nytimes.com/2009/07/25/us/25cop.html?hpw.

[42] Lopez reviews several videos that point to a discrepancy between officers' written reports of incidents in which disrespect was taken to be involved and the video records (ibid, 8–10).

[43] Sealing an arrest record is not always an easy matter.

[44] See *City of Houston v Hill* 482 US 451, 462–63 (1987): 'The freedom of individuals to verbally oppose or challenge police action without thereby risking arrest is one of the principal characteristics by which we distinguish a free nation from a police state.'

authority may be impertinent, such punitive arrests constitute a form of retaliatory overreaching by police. Even in jurisdictions without US First Amendment-style protections, we might consider that most of what may be categorised under 'contempt-of-cop' arrests represents overreaching by police.

B. Punishing for trouble and risk

Another frequent context for police administered informal punishment is occasioned by burdensome activities and investigations, in which the police may have to expend considerable resources and even be placed at some risk. Charges ultimately laid will relate to the offence but probably not the burdens or dangers associated with the activity or investigation, and police may wish to exact some punitive cost for those burdens or dangers. This is not quite the same as 'contempt-of-cop' punishment, though in certain cases it may reflect a related motivation. After a high-speed chase or an attempted avoidance of or escape from custody, police frequently feel deeply aggrieved by the effort and risk to which they have been put and believe that the 'perpetrator' should be made to pay for the trouble he has caused them. Not all such 'kicking ass' will be punitive – often police are simply dealing (inappropriately) with an adrenaline rush – but there is often a shared sense among police that, as long as the person was not already handcuffed and thus under control, they were justified in 'roughing up' their charge.[45]

The increasing use of tasers (and sprays) by police may also reflect 'punitive' tendencies – on the one hand for the failure to be responsive to police authority and, on the other, as a type of contempt-of-cop punishment. Even though tasers may represent a (mostly) welcome addition to the police arsenal, since they offer an alternative to the use of firearms, there has also been a tendency to use them to teach a lesson to those who show resistance to police authority; a 'punitive' reaction in situations where passive resistance should be dealt with in less painful or more patient ways.[46]

Although one can understand that police may believe a further offence was committed beyond the one for which the person has been charged, the idea that police should take it upon themselves to punish that offence represents a dangerous understanding of what they may do. When police accept their role, they also accept the burdens and risks associated with it, and that may – within limits – include the expenditure of significant effort and incurring of danger. These are not *additional*

---

[45] To this we might add the over-tightening of handcuffs. For a review of cases, see 'Civil Liability for the Use of Handcuffs: Part I – Handcuffs as Excessive Force' (2008) 10 *AELE Monthly Law Journal* 101, available at www.aele.org/law/2008LROCT/2008-10MLJ101.pdf; also MA Brave and JG Peters, 'Liability Constraints on Human Restraints', LAAW International Inc (1993), available at www.laaw.com/finalre2.htm.

[46] See J Kleinig, *The Ethics of Policing* (Cambridge, Cambridge University Press, 1996); J Kleinig, 'Ethical Constraints on Taser Use by Police' (2007) 1 *Policing: A Journal of Theory and Practice* 284. The moral temptation associated with tasers and sprays is that they can be used to punish without tell-tale damage.

costs for which punishment is due and which police can impose. At least, if they are costs for which punishment is due – say, the resisting of arrest or the injuring of an officer during the course of arrest – then they are probably already accommodated within legislation and are appropriately charged and pursued through the courts. Allowing the police to determine for themselves that a line has been overstepped that they can then respond to punitively takes us back into a situation for which the institution of policing was intended as a remedy.

C. Guaranteeing justice

A different kind of circumstance is one in which people are caught *in flagrante delicto*. In such cases, the police may feel they have 'no doubt' about the person's guilt, and so a heavy, punitive response, particularly if the crime was an egregious one, may be thought to constitute a 'down-payment' on what it is expected that the courts will (or at least should) eventually impose. Such victim-oriented responses may also constitute moral assertions of police authority – of, as they see it, their morally mandated social role, in which some punishments may be theirs to impose.

Such cases are sometimes prompted by scepticism concerning the functioning of the criminal justice system. Not every charge that is laid, however well-grounded in the eyes of the police, is followed through; not every case that comes to court will successfully meet the high standards of proof that are demanded; and not every plea-bargained result will satisfy police officers' sense of justice. Police may feel that the 'deposit' constitutes a guarantee that the person will not get away scot free or with a mere slap on the wrist. Often police think of themselves as the thin blue line between barbarism and civilisation, with the courts seen as unreliable supports of the latter.

Now there are some formally straightforward offences for which police might – within limits – impose social punishments such as fines for speeding or criminal trespass or other simple violations.[47] Normally, though, such fines may be appealed if the alleged offender chooses to go to court. I see no insuperable problems with these cases. But the possibilities for police dispensation are generally not limited to these. In many cases involving serious offences, and in which police have some obvious evidential basis for judging the person guilty and worthy of punishment, we might reasonably ask whether, because of the importance of getting the societal punishment right, it should be *for them* to engage in any sort of punitive response. When people are discovered *in flagrante delicto* for serious offences, it is reasonable to ask whether things are exactly as they seem – whether, for example, provocation or some other defence might be available. Even if the judgements of police are exactly correct, it is precisely because of human fallibility, the probability that police judgements will not be accurate, and the serious and condemnatory nature of the

---

[47]   These are offences in which liability tends to be strict – such as tailgating, lane-hogging, not wearing a seatbelt, and using a cellphone while driving – and for which police may be authorised to administer on-the-spot fines.

punitive response, that we have the structure of institutions we have in order to be reasonably assured of the accuracy of those judgements. As we are too often made aware, those judgements may later need to be reconsidered. Perhaps especially when people are caught *in flagrante delicto*, we may need to be wary of overly hasty judgements in which things turn out not to be as they seem.

Although this is only a contingent argument against police exacting punishments in these cases, it reflects a deeper concern we have about criminalisation and punishment. Those offences we characterise (or should characterise) as crimes are those for which society registers its condemnation, and such condemnation is riskily left in the hands of 'judges' who may bring their limited and often partial interests into their judgments. It is for this reason that for genuinely criminal violations we have chosen (even if not always utilised well) the elaborate structures of the criminal justice system.

D. Deadly force

A final context in which the police have often exercised a 'punitive' function can be found in their use of deadly force. Until the landmark US Supreme Court decision in *Tennessee v Garner*,[48] which collapsed a long-standing fleeing-felon rule into the 'defence-of-life' rule, police were permitted to use deadly force to prevent those about to be apprehended for felonies from escaping custody. Traditionally, such exercises of force were seen as proportionate to the offence, mainly because felonies were relatively few and viewed very seriously. Thus the court in *Petrie v Cartwright* had no difficulty in stating that 'it made little difference if the suspected felon was killed in the course of capture since, in the eyes of the law, he had already forfeited his life by committing the felony.'[49] As one commentator put it, the use of deadly force represented the 'premature execution of the inevitable judgment.'[50] That said, in theory – and to some extent in practice – *Garner* distinguished coercive police work from the punitive ends of the criminal law. Police could kill only in defence of life – punitive intentions, and even the desire to ensure 'capture', could not enter into their calculations.

Although the court in *Garner* recognised the substantially changed circumstances from those in which the fleeing-felon rule was formulated, and sought to limit the shooting of fleeing felons to situations in which some grave danger to others (including police) was posed, there is still a tendency among many police officers to view armed persons or those fleeing from the scene of a violent offence as retributively warranting a deadly response. In responding thus, they circumvent the judicial process and act as judges and executioners.[51] Although police

---

[48] *Tennessee v Garner* 471 US 1 (1985).
[49] *Petrie v Cartwright* 70 SW 297, 299 (Ky 1902).
[50] HL Boatright, 'Legalized Murder of a Fleeing Felon' (1929) 15 *Virginia Law Review* 583.
[51] To the extent that police are tempted to think that they may do this, the growing literature on extrajudicial killings in anti-terrorism efforts – some of which supports such killings – provides a salutary reminder of the limited circumstances under which such killings might be justified. See, eg,

commonly claim – and are usually given the benefit of the doubt in doing so – that the person in question appeared to be armed (in the event that they turn out not to be), or refused to lay down a weapon when ordered to do so, a review of police shootings suggests that in a good number of cases there was an implicit judgement not simply that the persons in question posed a threat, but that by virtue of that supposed threat the officers were justified in bringing the encounter to a deadly conclusion. In a revealing case study, Kenneth Winston shows how male and female officers, confronted by an armed person, might see their roles very differently – in the one case as being retributively warranted in shooting a resistant armed person and in the other as being under a superior obligation to take the person into custody unharmed. Winston refers to a case in which a female officer was upbraided by male colleagues for not shooting an armed suspect who was slow to drop his weapon. In their view, retributive proportionality justified her shooting the suspect; the suspect deserved to be shot. In her view, her task was to deliver the suspect up to the criminal justice system, and let the system determine what should be done with him.[52]

Police are of course justified in defending themselves (or others) and may use deadly force to do so if the person is carrying a deadly weapon. But there are too many instances of police shootings in which the judgement that a deadly weapon is in play has been hastily – and (from a moral point of view) inadequately – made, or in which firearms are deployed upon a simple refusal to drop a 'deadly weapon', or when the weapon has been wielded by someone who is obviously less than responsible and poses no immediate danger (withdrawal is possible pending the arrival of a specialised team). Some of these cases are more aptly characterised as 'serving them right' for not complying with police authority.

V. Conclusion

Although it has needed updating, one of the strengths of social contract theory has been that it seeks to minimise the short-sightedness of individual judgement, particularly in those cases in which judgement will result in impositions on others. Although humans as we encounter them are in need of social constraints, those constraints ought to be administered wisely and sparingly. The interactive structures of legislature, courts and police are best utilised when each is open to review by the other and by those upon whom social constraints are to be imposed. Although there is a grey area in which the formalised and somewhat cumbersome processes of criminal justice may be too heavy handed, and it might seem appropriate for police to adopt an informal punitive role, the moral hazards of endorsing such a

ML Gross, 'Assassination and Targeted Killing: Law Enforcement, Execution or Self-Defence?' (2006) 23 *Journal of Applied Philosophy* 323.

[52] KW Winston, 'Teaching with Cases' in J Kleinig and ML Smith (eds), *Teaching Criminal Justice Ethics: Strategic Issues* (Cincinnati OH, Anderson, 1997) 145.

position are too great to constitute the formal justification of a practice of police punishment. Perhaps for some minor violations (involving fines) police might be given limited and reviewable discretion. For more serious criminality, however, police ought to be trained in alternative dispute resolution techniques or non-punitive responses rather than given a power that is likely to be abused.

16

The Place of Criminal Law Theory in the Constitutional State

ANTJE DU BOIS-PEDAIN

Theories of punishment have long provided a focal point for reflection on a polity's authority structures and their normative appeal. For much of the history of political thought, penal laws and practices were taken to be central to what constitutes political community and political authority. With the rise of liberal political theory, however, punishment's centrality in understanding the nature and functions of political authority has been replaced with a focus on individual freedom and its protection and advancement through appropriate legal-political institutions. As one writer puts it, the legitimacy of the liberal constitutional state resides in the assumption that 'it – and it alone – can provide the conditions of freedom for all.'[1] This new conception of what is at the heart of political community – and political authority – has found shape and expression in written constitutional documents. These documents have, in the legal doctrine of many polities, been assigned a status superior to ordinary laws, setting (often judicially enforceable) limits to what legislatures, executives and courts may do without constitutional change. Polities without written constitutions have similarly come to evolve notions of fundamental 'constitutional' laws and principles that perform similar functions.[2]

This rise of constitutional law casts a shadow over the normative claims made by penal or criminal law theory.[3] Many constitutional lawyers struggle to see anything distinctive about penal practices – anything that could not be unpacked, and satisfactorily dealt with, under the twin constitutional lodestars of 'proportionate constraints' on 'constitutionally protected liberty rights'.[4] Few penal theorists

---

[1] M Thorburn, 'Constitutionalism and the Limits of the Criminal Law' in RA Duff et al (eds), *The Structures of Criminal Law* (Oxford, Oxford University Press, 2011) 86, 88. This formulation of the liberal state's authority grounds has a distinctive Kantian and Hegelian ring to it. It is also compatible with the basic authority accounts of contractarian political theory.

[2] Compare TRS Allan, *The Sovereignty of Law: Freedom, Constitution and Common Law* (Oxford, Oxford University Press, 2013). A legal system without a written constitution may also 'import' human rights codes contained in transnational or international documents as an internal standard of elevated hierarchical status, as was done in the UK through the Human Rights Act 1998.

[3] I use the terms 'penal theory' and 'criminal law theory' interchangeably in this chapter.

[4] For an example of such a view, see KF Gärditz, 'Strafbegründung und Demokratieprinzip' (2010) 49 *Der Staat* 331. Contra Gärditz, see R Zaczyk, 'Demokratieprinzip und Strafbegründung. Eine Erwiderung auf Klaus Ferdinand Gärditz' (2011) 50 *Der Staat* 295; and recently on this debate SP Hwang, 'Demokratische Willensbildung vor grundrechtlicher Rahmenordnung' (2012) 51 *Der Staat* 233.

would accept this proposition. But they struggle to place their theories and normative claims in relation to the theories and doctrines of constitutional law. Just how and why is state punishment different from other exercises of state power? Why do we have to account for it in penological terms, and how does this affect the legitimacy conditions of the practice?

In recent years, criminal law theorists in different jurisdictions have gone to great lengths to show that the existing doctrines of constitutional review fail to contain the reach of the criminal law, and the preconditions for imposing sanctions on individuals, in quite the way and to quite the extent called for by penal theory.[5] To my mind, this literature leaves little doubt that existing constitutional law and doctrine considerably undershoots the guarantees offered by an evolved penal theory. But that does not deflect all challenges posed by constitutional law to penal theory. It answers (only) the charge of penal theory's alleged practical irrelevance: if these writers' analyses are correct, the proper limits to state power, in the field of penal law, are not fully set by the kinds of constitutional guarantees typical of existing liberal constitutions.

Yet even after the independent significance of penal theory has thus been reasserted, we are left with the question of the normative force of its insights and claims. What kind of normativity pertains to the criteria for justified penal sanctions identified by criminal law theorists within an existing constitutional order? How are, and how can, penal theory's normative claims be related to the norms and functions of constitutional law?

Some penal theorists respond to this query by opting for a form of constitutional incorporation of the insights of penal theory. These scholars either recast their theoretical insights as progressive interpretations of existing constitutional standards, or they put them forward as propositions regarding the possible and desirable content of ideal liberal constitutions.[6] What penal theorists who employ these modes of argument share is an (explicit or implicit) preference for a strategy of constitutional recognition of penal theory's specific normative claims and solutions – a preference

---

[5] For Germany, see the extensive studies by O Lagodny, *Strafrecht vor den Schranken der Grundrechte: die Ermächtigung zum strafrechtlichen Vorwurf im Lichte der Grundrechtsdogmatik dargestellt am Beispiel der Vorfeldkriminalisierung* (Tübingen, Mohr Siebeck, 1996); I Appel, *Verfassung und Strafe. Zu den verfassungsrechtlichen Grenzen staatlichen Strafens* (Berlin, Duncker & Humblot, 1998). For Canada, see K Roach, 'Canada's Experience with Constitutionalism and Criminal Justice' (2013) 25 *Singapore Academy of Law Journal* 656; K Roach, 'The Primacy of Liberty and Proportionality and not Human Dignity When Subjecting Criminal Law to Constitutional Control' (2011) 44 *Israel Law Review* 91; and K Roach, 'The Charter versus the Government's Crime Agenda' (2012) 58 *Supreme Court Law Review* 211. For Israel, see A Barak, 'The Constitutionalization of the Israeli Legal System as a Result of the Basic Laws and Its Effect on Procedural and Substantive Criminal Law' (1997) 31 *Israel Law Review* 3.

[6] See, eg, RS Frase, 'What's "Different" (Enough) in Eighth Amendment Law?' (2013) 11 *Ohio State Journal of Criminal Law* 9 (supporting an expansive reading of recent US Supreme Court cases striking down excessive punishments for certain groups of offenders); D Baker, 'Constitutionalizing the Harm Principle' (2008) 27 *Criminal Justice Ethics* 3 (arguing that the US and Canadian constitutions only allow for imprisonment as a sanction when the criminal provision is justifiable in terms of the 'harm principle'); M Buchandler-Raphael, 'Drugs, Dignity, and Danger: Human Dignity as a Constitutional Constraint to Limit Overcriminalization' (2013) 80 *Tennessee Law Review* 291 (developing similar constitutional constraints based on human dignity).

that is likely to be based on an (open or tacit) assumption that, without such constitutional recognition, penal theory cannot claim to offer legitimacy conditions for penal practice. But not every penal theorist accepts that constitutional incorporation of the insights of penal theory is a desirable, or even a possible, avenue to pursue. More sceptical theorists believe that the relationship between constitutional law and penal theory must be structured differently, offering both political-pragmatic and theoretical reasons.[7]

In this chapter I want to make some headway in answering the question how penal theory can, and should, position itself in relation to constitutional law and doctrine. I first review the extent to which German constitutional law and doctrine allows for, and resists, the incorporation of penal theory's normative claims. This section depicts the uphill struggle of classic constitutional law doctrine to capture the specificity of penal law. It thus reminds us – if such a reminder is needed – that, contrary to the challenge of irrelevance, penal theory sets different and stricter standards for the exercise of state power through penal law than standard constitutional doctrines can provide. I then turn in section II to the question whether incorporation is, at least, a practically feasible solution. Here, I take up a suggestion made by Douglas Husak to recognise 'a right not to be punished' as a philosophically grounded right, and ask whether constitutional recognition of this philosophical right would successfully incorporate penal theory's normative claims into constitutional law. The result I reach is not an encouraging one. In all likelihood, a constitutional order that explicitly grants citizens a 'right not to be punished' would and could operate no differently from existing constitutional orders that do not. Full incorporation is not a realistic strategy because the transformation of penal theory's claims into constitutional standards brings with it constitutionally required impact limitations. The price demanded by the preservation of the constitutional balance of power between the different organs of state is the transformation of detailed and concrete guidance into a mere stop-gap against excessive misjudgement.

This, then, brings me to the question whether non-incorporation really leaves penal theory without a place within the law for its particular propositions and conclusions. Can penal theory, at best, offer constitutional states a set of standards for the ethical-political evaluation of state practice, including existing law – a kind of 'running commentary' on the ethical merits and the political wisdom of the present system – that constitutional lawyers and ordinary law-makers may safely ignore if they wish? Or is there a deeper reason why lawyers and law-makers should pay attention, in their daily practices, to the claims and insights of penal theory? In this final section III, I suggest that the deeper reason why lawyers should pay attention is the same reason why penal theory resists full incorporation into constitutional

---

[7] See, eg, CF Stuckenberg, 'The Constitutional Deficiencies of the German Rechtsgutslehre' (2013) 3 *Onati Socio-Legal Series* 31, 38f; D Sternberg-Lieben, 'Rechtsgut, Verhältnismäßigkeit und die Freiheit des Strafgesetzgebers' in R Hefendehl, A von Hirsch and W Wohlers (eds), *Die Rechtsgutstheorie. Legitimationsbasis des Strafrechts oder dogmatisches Glasperlenspiel?* (Baden-Baden, Nomos, 2003) 65, 78ff; and L Greco, 'Verfassungskonformes oder legitimes Strafrecht? Zu den Grenzen einer verfassungsrechtlichen Orientierung der Strafrechtswissenschaft' in B Brunhöber et al (eds), *Strafrecht und Verfassung* (Baden-Baden, Nomos, 2013) 13, 22ff.

law: like constitutional law, penal theory is grounded in an understanding of the nature of citizenship and of state authority that is fundamental to the justified imposition of constraints on an individual's freedom. That power over the individual is exercised in accordance with the constitution is just one condition of its justified exercise. If it is indeed the case that penal theory provides us with a set of conditions under which the exercise of penal power conforms with our understanding of the nature of citizenship, and of state authority, at a particular time, and if it is further true that these conditions cannot be cast in the mould of constitutional law, then the normative claim that penal theory makes is the claim that we only really live in a concrete order of freedom if we treat penal theory as providing legally relevant answers to the questions of why, and under what conditions, it is permissible for a constitutional state to subject a person to punishment.

These questions are not only important in their own right: they are also fitting ones to pursue in a volume dedicated to Andreas von Hirsch. Von Hirsch certainly understands his penal theory as one well suited to any liberal constitutional state. At the same time, he has reacted with scepticism to sustained efforts by other penal theorists to embed their understandings of the proper limits of penal authority directly in constitutional provisions and guarantees.[8] Against Tatjana Hörnle's strategy of grounding criminal law prohibitions of certain forms of offensive conduct in constitutional rights and values, he has stated two major reservations. The first is a general concern that penal theory may well be impoverished, and its normative claims watered down, if the theorist roots her arguments in the ultimately contingent constitutional liberty rights of a particular constitutional state.[9] The second concern relates to the specific use made of constitutional rights as grounds of criminalisation. For von Hirsch, this turns the constitutional guarantees of freedom on their head: from protections against the invasions of state power to limitations of individual freedom.[10] The functional transformation of liberty-rights into positive grounds for repressive state intervention is particularly problematic because it tends to overstate the case in support of particular criminal law prohibitions, and to make short shrift of limiting principles developed by criminalisation theory. If offensive conduct is viewed as an invasion of the constitutional rights of others, or as a challenge to constitutional values, there is less room for consideration of the extent to which others might be expected to tolerate provocative or unacceptable instances of self-expression.[11]

These arguments are directed against a particular proposal to merge philosophical propositions with constitutional standards. But von Hirsch has also engaged with the general question whether constitutional incorporation of penal theory's standards is a sensible strategy. In 'Should There Be Constitutional Constraints Against Grossly

---

[8] See A von Hirsch, 'Harm und Offence: Schädigungsprinzip und Belästigungsprinzip als Kriterien für die Kriminalisierung von Verhalten' in H Putzke et al (eds), *Strafrecht zwischen System und Telos: Festschrift für Rolf Dietrich Herzberg zum siebzigsten Geburtstag am 14. Februar 2008* (Tübingen, Mohr Siebeck, 2008) 915.

[9] Ibid, 926.

[10] Ibid, 927.

[11] Ibid, 929.

Disproportionate Punishments?',[12] he argues that the best way to make sense of the notion of 'grossly disproportionate punishments' is to see them as punishments that send a message *in terrorem*: they no longer address the legal subject as a moral agent capable of moral choice and deliberation, but try to frighten addressees into compliance. Understood in this way, a constitutional norm against grossly disproportionate punishments protects citizens against being treated by the state in a manner incompatible with their essential character as moral agents. Such a protection may be desirable as a reminder of the state's deep commitment to treating persons under its authority 'as responsible agents entitled to recognition of their dignity.'[13] At the same time, a tighter constitutional requirement – say, a constitutional guarantee of strict proportionality in punishment – would, according to von Hirsch, not be a desirable development. Deciding on the merits of sentencing theories should 'be within the province of the legislature.'[14] The legislature 'ordinarily should decide such basic principles of sentencing policy as the relative weight to be given to proportionality and to crime-preventive aims.'[15] It is only in 'special situations' that 'fairness-claims should be backed by constitutional safeguards: this should occur when their claims for protection are especially strong, and the potential adverse consequences to individuals particularly drastic.'[16] Taken together, these publications provide intriguing pointers to how our honorand views the function and value of penal theory in the constitutional state. I will return to them in the final section of this chapter.

We cannot begin our discussion without a working definition of what constitutes 'criminal law' and 'state punishment'. Given the focus of this chapter on the interrelationship between constitutional law and penal theory, I will adopt Husak's proposal of linking the criminal law with state punishment in the following way: a law counts as 'criminal law' if, and only if, the state is authorised to punish persons who have acted in breach of this law. Reciprocally, impositions of state power will not be classified as 'punishments' unless they are imposed on individuals after, and by reason of, a finding that this individual has breached a criminal law.[17] While some might argue that this definition holds us hostage to the happenstance of the actual content of the laws of particular states, this does not in my view give rise to serious difficulties. There is no problem, in the present context, with referring to and relying on contingent social practices to identify the content of both criminal law and state punishment. After all, as Feinberg correctly observed, what counts as 'punishment' is inescapably shaped and defined by social conventions.[18] What counts as

---

[12] A von Hirsch, 'Should There Be Constitutional Constraints Against Grossly Disproportionate Punishments?' in T Elholm et al (eds), *Ikke kun straf: Festskrift til Vagn Greve* (Uppsala, Iustus Förlag, 2008) 211. For a German treatment of this question, see A von Hirsch, 'Ein grundrechtliches Verbot exzessiver Strafen? Versuch einer Begründung' in F Herzog and U Neumann (eds), *Festschrift für Winfried Hassemer* (Heidelberg, CF Müller, 2010) 373.

[13] Von Hirsch, 'Should There Be Constitutional Constraints', above n 12 at 216–17.

[14] Ibid, 214.

[15] Ibid, 218.

[16] Ibid.

[17] D Husak, 'Why Criminal Law: A Question of Content?' (2008) 2 *Criminal Law & Philosophy* 99, 100.

[18] J Feinberg, 'The Expressive Function of Punishment' reprinted in RA Duff and D Garland, *A Reader on Punishment* (Oxford, Oxford University Press, 1994) 73, 86f.

legal punishment therefore depends on the conventions for the authoritative expression of censure instituted by the legal practices of particular jurisdictions. So long as our interest lies not in exploring the outer conceptual boundaries of the notion of state punishment but merely in having a workable sense of what area of law may be affected by penal theory's normative claims, we can live with the conceptual limitations of this definition.

I. Criminal Law Theory in German Constitutional Jurisprudence

Under established German constitutional doctrine, criminal prohibitions affect constitutionally protected liberty rights in three distinct ways.[19] First, the criminal prohibition affects whatever particular liberty right(s) that the prohibited conduct might be considered to exercise. For example, a criminal prohibition against saying certain things in court that applies to lawyers representing clients – say, a criminal prohibition against calling the opposing claimant 'a dishonest fool' – affects both the lawyer's freedom of expression[20] and her right to the free exercise of her profession.[21] Moreover, any prohibition[22] affects the residual constitutionally protected 'freedom to act as one pleases'.[23] Secondly, because a criminal prohibition declares that the conduct is wrong, and conviction marks the perpetrator out as a wrongdoer – someone upon whom the mark of official disapproval of his conduct is publicly placed – the prohibition, as well as any subsequent conviction, affects the constitutionally protected personality right (right to respect for and free development of one's personality[24]) of the person engaging in the conduct.[25] Thirdly, the

---

[19] This account draws heavily on Lagodny, *Strafrecht vor den Schranken der Grundrechte*, above n 5. For a concise summary, see O Lagodny, 'Das materielle Strafrecht als Prüfstein der Verfassungsdogmatik' in Hefendehl et al (eds), *Die Rechtsgutstheorie*, above n 7, 83.

[20] Guaranteed by Art 5(1) of the German Constitution (*Grundgesetz*).

[21] Guaranteed by Art 12(1) of the German Constitution (*Grundgesetz*).

[22] In the Israeli Supreme Court, disagreement has arisen as to whether *every* criminal prohibition that permits the imposition of imprisonment necessarily restricts the right to liberty, or whether the right to liberty should be interpreted restrictively so as not to include 'the right to ignore the criminal norms defined by law as offences which entail punishment of imprisonment' (for discussion of this case law, see M Gur-Arye and T Weigend, 'Constitutional Review of Criminal Prohibitions Affecting Human Dignity and Liberty: German and Israeli Perspectives' (2011) 44 *Israel Law Review* 63, 75ff). Under German constitutional law, the status of the prohibited behaviour as wrongful or otherwise is irrelevant to the question whether a constitutional liberty right is engaged by the prohibition, although the wrongfulness of the conduct – particularly, whether it violates the rights of others – may of course play a role in resolving the question whether prohibiting and penalising the behaviour is justified.

[23] 'Allgemeine Handlungsfreiheit', guaranteed by Art 2(1) of the German Constitution (*Grundgesetz*).

[24] 'Allgemeines Persönlichkeitsrecht', guaranteed by Art 2(1) read in conjunction with Art 1(1) of the German Constitution (*Grundgesetz*).

[25] This consideration generates what is in effect a right against 'unfair labelling' by the state. Since a criminal sanction, according to the Constitutional Court, always expresses a social judgement that the conduct is a public wrong (*sozialethisches Unwerturteil*), the individual subject's personality right is in play whenever a criminal sanction is threatened or imposed for conduct, even if the sanction itself is mild.

concrete penal sanction imposed affects yet other constitutionally protected rights – liberty in the case of imprisonment, property in the case of fines, and perhaps other rights depending on the type of sanction and the direct effects of its imposition upon the convicted offender.

This inevitably large cluster of affected constitutional rights notwithstanding, constitutional justification for such various rights-infringements is, for the most part, not difficult to provide. While some particular freedoms – say, freedom of expression – allow for restrictions only in the name of a narrow catalogue of listed interests, most liberty rights are open to restriction simply through ordinary legislation pursuing a legitimate state aim. Such legislation only needs to meet the general constitutional proportionality test: that the aim it pursues is an intelligible and non-prohibited state aim; and that the provision is rationally capable of furthering the achievement of that aim. Given the deference shown by the Constitutional Court to the legislature's choice of aims and to the legislature's view of the suitability, necessity and appropriateness of the legal means selected to further these aims, even laws that pursue problematic or insignificant objectives, or do so in a haphazard and incoherent way, are unlikely to fail the constitutional proportionality test if some basic sense can be made of them.[26] Under this kind of analysis, the criminal law – in Otto Lagodny's words – 'ingeniously escapes effective constitutional scrutiny.'[27]

Constitutional proportionality analysis generally does not reach the issues that German criminal law theorists consider to be of pressing normative importance. This is so whether these theorists support the doctrine of the legal good or prefer alternative models to determine the proper reach of criminal law.[28] In discussions of the purposes of criminal law, the Constitutional Court has always gone out of its way to avoid nailing its flag to any particular penal-theoretical mast.[29] Its agnosticism regarding particular penal theories[30] is exemplified in its judgment on the constitutional permissibility of the mandatory life sentence for murder:[31]

It is disputed whether already the sheer existence of the prohibition, or only a subsequent conviction, affects this right.

[26] See the analysis of the case law in T Weigend, 'Der Grundsatz der Verhältnismäßigkeit als Grenze staatlicher Strafgewalt' in T Weigend and G Küpper (eds), *Festschrift für Hans Joachim Hirsch zum 70. Geburtstag am 11. April 1999* (Berlin, de Gruyter, 1999) 917, 932ff. For a more theoretical discussion of the proportionality principle's usefulness as a constraining principle of criminal law, see W Hassemer, 'Der Grundsatz der Verhältnismäßigkeit als Grenze strafrechtlicher Eingriffe' in A von Hirsch, K Seelmann and W Wohlers (eds), *Mediating Principles. Begrenzungsprinzipien bei der Strafbegründung* (Baden-Baden, Nomos, 2006) 121; U Neumann, 'Das Verhältnismäßigkeitsprinzip als strafbegrenzendes Prinzip' in von Hirsch et al, ibid, 128.

[27] Lagodny, *Strafrecht vor den Schranken der Grundrechte*, above n 5 at 536.

[28] See, especially, the chapters by Hörnle, Hassemer and Wohlers in this volume.

[29] See BVerfGE 45, 187 (220) (Mandatory Sentence of Life Imprisonment for Murder): 'It cannot be the task of the Constitutional Court to decide, as a question of constitutional law, the debate among penal theorists regarding the justification of punishment.'

[30] Weigend, 'Der Grundsatz der Verhältnismäßigkeit', above n 26 at 927, calls this the Court's 'abstinence from the theoretical discussion of the purposes of punishment'.

[31] BVerfGE 45, 187 (220) (Mandatory Sentence of Life Imprisonment for Murder); see also BVerfG 109, 133 (172ff) (Continuing Detention of Dangerous Offenders).

The Constitutional Court . . . views the function of criminal law in general terms as the protection of the fundamental values of communal life. Commensurate deserts [*Schuldausgleich*], prevention, the resocialisation of offenders, atonement and retribution for past wrongs have all been recognised as elements of an appropriate penal sanction.

In other decisions, the Court has added that 'Notwithstanding its task to deter and to resocialise, [the criminal sanction is] retribution for past wrongdoing.'[32]

Only one central theoretical-doctrinal construct of German penal theory has received unqualified recognition as a constitutional standard by the Constitutional Court: the culpability principle, which is seen as rooted in, and required by, the constitutional commitment to human dignity and to the Rule of Law.[33] Here, recognition by the Constitutional Court has been accompanied by considerable deference to doctrinal understandings of what the culpability principle requires.[34] One reason for this deference is likely to be that the demands of the culpability principle are not (at present) seriously in dispute among criminal-law scholars.

However, none of the constitutional tests and standards for criminal-law prohibitions treat the criminal law as distinctly different or set it apart from other branches of law. While the negative ethical judgement communicated in a criminal conviction affects the personality right of the convicted individual, it is not only through the application of criminal prohibitions that state action can affect, and potentially violate, this right: official statements and declarations made in other contexts can equally affect it, as can other state conduct involving an intrusion into a core sphere of privacy or unwarranted exposure of a person's innermost self.[35]

Ironically, perhaps the closest the German Constitutional Court has come to recognising the specificity of criminal law has been in its first abortion law decision of 1975.[36] Here, a majority of the Court held that the German legislator was not free to fully decriminalise abortion in the first trimester. (The Court accepted a possible legislative compromise solution under which individuals would not be prosecuted for abortion if a prescribed counselling and medical assessment procedure was followed prior to performing the abortion.) What is of interest in the present context is the reason the Court gave for insisting that abortion, at least in the absence of serious risk that the pregnancy endangered the life or health of the pregnant woman,

---

[32] BVerfGE 21, 391 (404).

[33] See, eg, BVerfGE 20, 323 (331); BVerfGE 45, 187 (259f) (Mandatory Sentence of Life Imprisonment for Murder); BVerfGE 86, 288 (313) (Release on Parole of Offenders Sentenced to Life Imprisonment); BVerfGE 123, 267 (413) (Lisbon Treaty).

[34] As Heinrich Amadeus Wolff has pointed out, the Constitutional Court has found it unnecessary to develop the culpability principle on independent constitutional grounds and has instead simply lifted the approach of the German Federal Court (the highest ordinary court) to a constitutional level. See HA Wolff, *Ungeschriebenes Verfassungsrecht unter dem Grundgesetz* (Tübingen, Mohr Siebeck, 2000) 228f.

[35] See generally HD Jarass, 'Das allgemeine Persönlichkeitsrecht im Grundgesetz' (1989) 42 *Neue Juristische Wochenschrift* 857; HD Jarass and B Pieroth, *Grundgesetz für die Bundesrepublik Deutschland: Kommentar*, 12th edn (Munich, CH Beck, 2012) (Commentary to Art 2, marginal notes 28ff); and the case summary in T Kingreen and R Poscher, *Grundrechte: Staatsrecht II*, 29th edn (Heidelberg, CF Müller, 2013) 91ff.

[36] BVerfGE 39, 1 (First Abortion Law Decision; judgment of 25 February 1975).

remained at least in a formal sense a criminal act. This reason was that the constitutional duty to protect human life, including the life of the foetus, obliged the state to at least mark out abortion as a wrongful act (in the absence of serious risk to the pregnant woman). The idea here appears to be that it is only through criminalising an act that the state can express a social judgement that the conduct is a public wrong (*sozialethisches Unwerturteil*). It remains unclear to what extent this implies an importation of any particular theoretical understanding of the criminal law.

The 1975 abortion decision, in my view, illustrates the dangers inherent in a constitutional recognition of penal theory. First, it is not clear that penal theory will necessarily support the claim that only criminalisation can mark out an act as wrongful. Are only penal theories which defend that claim compatible with German constitutional law? A second problem is that the soundness of the contention that criminalisation and only criminalisation marks out an action as wrongful really depends on certain background conditions of social and legislative practice. Its truth depends on whether social agents really do hold the belief that, when an act is criminalised, this means that they should consider it seriously morally wrongful. Given the prevalence of criminal laws which do not prohibit conduct that is wrong in the morally rich sense implied by '*sozialethisches Unwerturteil*', one may well doubt the correctness of the assumption that criminalisation succeeds in communicating what the Court is so keen for the legislator to communicate.

And we have not even begun to challenge the third, and possibly most serious, objection to the use made here by the Constitutional Court of penal theory: that – against a backdrop of widespread disagreement among citizens about whether first-trimester abortions are seriously morally wrongful, only slightly morally wrong, or not morally wrong at all – the Court forces the legislator to, in effect, enter this debate with an authoritative 'communication' that it is hoped will *shape* the moral views of the population. This is hardly a use of the criminal law that any penal theorist would happily support – not even theorists attracted to versions of legal moralism. It was, perhaps, a lingering awareness of the sheer perversity of using *a coercive legal instrument* to influence social attitudes that led the Court, in its second abortion law decision in 1993, to allow for a form of 'moral counselling' (ie, counselling that confronts the abortion-seeking woman with arguments why abortion should be considered wrong) as an alternative to criminalisation.[37] It appears that, by then, the Court had come to believe that criminal prohibitions are not the only way in which the state can mark out an action as wrongful. This would suggest that constitutional law is back where it started: with no certain grasp of, and no way of reflecting in its own doctrines, the specificity of criminal law.

Perhaps, however, these are just the regrettable imperfections of German constitutional law and doctrine? Maybe a full incorporation of penal theory into constitutional law would lead to better results? This is the possibility I want to address next.

---

[37] BVerfGE 88, 203 (Second Abortion Law Decision; judgment of 28 May 1993). Interestingly, the Court did not reach the view that it would be in any way inappropriate for state authority to try and influence the moral views of the population. Its concern merely was that criminal law is hardly an appropriate policy tool for strategies of public moral education.

II. Shaping the Interface between Constitutional Law and Penal Theory through a Constitutional 'Right not to be Punished'? The Limited Potential of Constitutional Incorporation

A possible strategy for the incorporation of penal theory into constitutional law could be to postulate a constitutional right not to be subjected to unjustified punishment. Arguably, this would import penal theory '*tout court*' into constitutional doctrine.

In a recent paper, Husak has suggested that the best way of thinking about what the task of justifying state punishment involves is to think of people as having 'a right not to be punished'. Husak clarifies that his choice[38]

> to employ the language of rights to describe what is morally problematic about punishment is not designed to make punishments nearly impossible to justify. *All* rights – even our most valuable – are subject to infringements[39] . . . Expressing what is problematic about punishment in terms of rights helps to remind us that laws backed by penal sanctions are presumptively unjust. The burden of proof in justifying the infringement of rights is generally placed on those who would potentially violate them – in this case, on a state that enacts criminal legislation that makes persons eligible for penal sanctions.

Husak expects two major advantages to result from this perspective:[40]

> [E]xpressing what is problematic about punishment in terms of rights helps us to resist the tendency to accept some *kinds* of reason as sufficient to justify the enactment of a criminal offense and the punishment of those who breach it. A long tradition holds that rights protect persons from the application of policies supported by mere utilitarian considerations.

The reasons that will suffice to show that the right not to be punished is infringed rather than violated, Husak then goes on to suggest, are 'the very considerations that show a punishment to be justified.'[41] And because the justification 'overrides' rather than 'cancels' the right, the person whose right not to be punished is justifiably infringed is 'owed a rationale for the way she is treated.'[42] Moreover, Husak says:[43]

> If I am correct to suppose that punishments infringe a right, the right that is infringed is important . . . We all care very much about whether we are deliberately made to endure

---

[38] Husak, 'Why Criminal Law', above n 17 at 105–6.
[39] Husak uses the terms 'infringement' and 'violation' in the following way: Infringement means that a right is interfered with (or, in Husak's terminology, implicated), but that the interference is justified. Violation designates an unjustified interference with a right. See Husak, ibid, 105.
[40] Ibid, 106.
[41] Ibid.
[42] Ibid, 107.
[43] Ibid.

hard treatment and censure by our government. I assume that rational persons would allow infringements of the right not to be punished only under narrowly defined conditions. Among the conditions that must be satisfied is that the laws that subject us to punishment, must conform to a respectable theory of criminalization.

While Husak does not explicitly say so, it is not far-fetched to think that a suitable mode for implementing his approach would be to recognise a 'right not to be punished' as a constitutional right, either by way of constitutional interpretation or by way of constitutional amendment.[44] The question is whether such a step would indeed increase the level of protection individuals have against being unjustly penalised, to the point where the normative standards developed by penal theory would then be enforceable as constitutional law.

The first issue to address in this regard is whether constitutional recognition of a 'right not to be punished' could indeed effectively counteract the dangers of utilitarianism. In the present context, these are the dangers of consequentialist reasoning in connection with justifying rights-infringements. There is a deep affinity between consequentialist justifications for interferences with rights and utilitarian reasoning about public policy. Both suggest a perspective on individual rights which views them as interests that can be outweighed by other interests of sufficient importance. The kind of constitutional reasoning congenial to these modes of justification thus tempts us to view state punishment as just another means of implementing rationally-grounded public policy objectives. Of course, most penal theorists, including Husak, do not think of the criminal law as a mere policy tool of convenience; in fact, it is precisely for the reason that criminal law is somehow 'special' that Husak accepts both the wrongfulness constraint and a version of the ultima ratio principle.[45] Yet incorporating a 'right not to be punished' into the constitutional structure may invite, rather than counteract, a consequentialist approach to criminal legislation and a 'tool of governance' conception of criminal law.

To see how this might happen, let us consider the model of a liberal criminal law developed by Santiago Mir Puig on the basis of the constitutional proportionality principle.[46] Like Husak, Mir Puig assumes that the seriousness of the interference with citizens' rights through punishment requires a 'substantial state interest',[47]

---

[44] Indeed, scholars have already suggested variants of this. See, eg, D Baker, *The Right Not to Be Criminalized: Demarcating Criminal Law's Authority* (Farnham, Ashgate, 2011).

[45] See D Husak, *Overcriminalization: The Limits of the Criminal Law* (Oxford, Oxford University Press, 2008) 66ff (on the wrongfulness constraint); D Husak, 'The Criminal Law as Last Resort' (2004) 24 *Oxford Journal of Legal Studies* 207. In a recent paper, Husak explicitly draws attention to the fact that the main pressure point on his argument against over-criminalisation is his reliance on the claim that the criminal law is 'special': Husak, 'Reservations about Overcriminalization' (2011) 14 *New Criminal Law Review* 97.

[46] S Mir Puig, 'Der Verhältnismäßigkeitsgrundsatz als Verfassungsgrundlage der materiellen Grenzen des Strafrechts' in Herzog and Neumann (eds), *Festschrift für Hassemer*, above n 12 at 521.

[47] Husak, 'Why Criminal Law', above n 17 at 111; Mir Puig, 'Der Verhältnismäßigkeitsgrundsatz', above n 46 at 525. Mir Puig refers to these interests as legal goods of sufficient importance to allow protection through criminal law (*Strafrechtsgüter*), which he defines as encompassing only fundamental individual (direct) or collective (indirect) interests of citizens. This will at least have a very large overlap with the 'prevention of serious harms' criterion formulated by Husak for what counts as a 'substantial state interest'.

and that the criminal law must 'directly advance the government's purpose'[48] (that is, be suitable for the achievement of its objective) and 'no more extensive than necessary to achieve its objective'.[49] This standard effectively 'conforms to a utilitarian justification of the criminal law':[50]

> If criminal law was useless and unable to prevent any criminal conduct at all, it would not be legitimate, since the state may restrict the rights of its citizens only if this results in greater protection of their rights overall.

For that reason, Mir Puig argues, the utilitarian constitutional proportionality standard encompasses a number of traditional criminal law principles (subsidiarity, ultima ratio, fragmentary character of criminal law and criminal law minimalism).[51] Moreover, the overall justification for creating and maintaining a criminal justice system in a constitutional state committed to the principles of democracy and welfare must, according to Mir Puig, be the prevention of crime[52] – and this also affects the entities which must be compared in order to judge whether the criminal prohibition is backed by interests that outweigh the interference with rights. In order for a criminal law to meet the test of proportionality, the question to ask is not whether the threatened punishment is proportionate to the crime that has actually been committed, but whether it is proportionate in order to deter the kinds of crimes that the prohibition aims to prevent.[53]

Now, in his own analysis Husak is quite upfront about the fact that consequentialist considerations dominate when it comes to the justification of a criminal law to citizens qua taxpayers and members of the public. Husak identifies as reasons citizens have not to create a particular criminal law – indeed, not to create any criminal justice system at all – (1) the costs of enforcement through an apparatus of trained professionals in the prosecutorial, court and prison systems; (2) the risk any citizen faces of being accused and punished by mistake; and (3) the ineradicable possibility of abuse of power by the officials acting within the system.[54] Husak con-

---

[48] Husak, ibid, 108. Mir Puig, ibid, 526, uses the familiar constitutional terminology of 'suitability' (*Geeignetheit*).

[49] Husak, ibid, 108. Mir Puig, ibid, 526, employs the terms '*Erforderlichkeit*' (necessity) and '*Angemessenheit*' (proportionality in view of the weight of the values and interests at stake; the latter consideration is also referred to as 'proportionality in a narrower sense').

[50] Mir Puig, ibid.

[51] Ibid.

[52] Ibid, 523.

[53] Ibid, 528. Of course, if Schünemann (in this volume) is right that the punishment for crimes of lesser seriousness has an inevitable element of 'overkill' in it (an overkill effect that comes about because of the severe reputational consequences of criminal convictions, and – where imprisonment is the chosen sanction – because of the way in which imprisonment affects a punished person's life course), the justification of these penal consequences may still not be a matter of a simple application of the proportionality principle as the constitutional lawyer knows it. The German Constitutional Court has rejected an interpretation of the constitutional proportionality principle that would have allowed it to police 'excessive punishment' at the lower end of crime seriousness. In BVerfGE 50, 205 (*Bagatelldelikte*), the Court held that the legislator was free to criminalise theft of nearly valueless goods; the argument that *any* criminal conviction and punishment for the appropriation of such goods would violate the *constitutional* standard of proportionality, was rejected.

[54] Husak, 'Why Criminal Law', above n 17 at 109.

tends that 'consequentialist considerations . . . play an indispensable role' in overcoming these drawbacks of punishment: 'What is needed to justify the penal law to citizens is some additional value punishment can be expected to promote [above and beyond] the value of realizing retributive justice.'[55]

This, however, is not the end of the matter. To see how a 'right not to be punished' might nevertheless offer some resistance to curtailment based on utilitarian thinking, we have to attend to Husak's contention that 'an adequate justification of punishment' must justify our practices 'from two different perspectives: . . . the perspective of the society that creates an institution of criminal justice [and] the perspective of the individual who suffers its infliction.'[56]

The cost–benefit considerations summarised above are meant only to address the justification of punishment from the first perspective, the perspective of citizens concerned to avoid wasteful or disadvantageous institutional structures. When Husak formulates the criteria of a justified criminal law with the affected individual's perspective in mind, he lists them as follows: that the law is designed to prevent harm, prohibits conduct that is wrongful, and imposes a punishment that is deserved; that the governmental interest in enacting the law must be substantial, the law must directly advance the government's purpose, and the law must be no more extensive than necessary to achieve its objective.[57] Some of these criteria are evidently compatible with a utilitarian approach to their application: the last-named three are in fact identical to the criteria developed on the basis of the constitutional proportionality test. Less obviously, we could argue that 'harm prevention' and 'wrongfulness' should be approached as plausible elements in showing that the governmental interest is substantial. These criteria are also capable of being unpacked in a utilitarian fashion. Were that done, it would leave us with the requirement that the imposed punishment must be 'deserved' as the last line of defence against utilitarianism. Husak certainly understands the desert criterion as one where consequentialist considerations play no role.[58] But if this is so, 'desert' must be our bulwark against utilitarian justifications of the infringements of the proposed constitutional right. Since we cannot know what the desert requirement entails without drawing on some comprehensive theory of punishment's justification, we have reason to expect that recognising a 'right not to be punished' as a constitutional right would force law-makers and state officials to keep criminal punishment within the boundaries drawn by penal theory, and that this change would significantly restrict the possibility of criminalisation and punishment being done for purely utilitarian reasons; thereby increasing the protection of individual citizens against undeserved punishment beyond the degree of protection offered by existing constitutional guarantees.[59]

---

[55] Ibid, 111.
[56] Ibid, 108.
[57] Ibid, 108–9.
[58] Ibid, 109.
[59] Mir Puig, 'Der Verhältnismäßigkeitsgrundsatz', above n 46 at 528–29, accords a similar utilitarianism-constraining role to the culpability principle, which he bases on the constitutional commitment to human dignity. This might suggest that existing constitutional law already contains

Given the result of our discussion so far, the main advantage of constitutional recognition of a right not to be punished is that it reduces the risk that the standard justification of state action in a liberal-democratic state – that the curtailment of individual freedom pursues a legitimate state aim in a broadly proportionate manner – might be (mis-)taken to be all that is needed to justify specifically penal action. While this is certainly important, one must still ask how much constitutional punch penal theory thereby acquires.

Penal theorists offer different understandings of penal desert. These differences have their roots in different understandings of the legitimate functions of the state, and of the nature and functions of state punishment (particularly its distinctiveness or similarity compared to other restrictive state measures), as well as in different assumptions about the factual efficacy of prohibitions in discouraging behaviour. We cannot, and should not try to, give constitutional recognition to one particular penal theory. This is because the differences between different penal theories are grounded in different reasonable understandings of the penal functions and authority of a liberal state, and to choose between them at the level of constitutional law would suppress such reasonable disagreement. This, of course, is the very opposite of what a liberal constitution should do. The function of liberal constitutional law is to provide a polity with 'institutions and principles which can embody future democratic decision procedures and mechanisms of collective action,'[60] thus allowing the polity to organise its communal life despite the persistence of reasonable disagreement. The very reasonableness of such disagreement means, as Dworkin once put it, that:[61]

> It is part of our common political life . . . that any decision about the distribution of any good – wealth, welfare, honours, education, recognition, office – may be reopened, no matter how firm the traditions that are then challenged, that we may always ask of some settled institutional scheme whether it is fair.

The political process does not (because it cannot) dissolve the disagreement. Rather, it enables the polity to act in ways that are appropriate given the reasonableness of the disagreement and the need to act in the presence of it. Liberal constitutions are thus designed to acknowledge, manage and preserve 'the *place of reasonable*

---

a non-utilitarian bulwark against punishment in excess of what is 'deserved'. But, contrary to Mir Puig's belief, the culpability principle can only generate 'absolute' desert constraints that resist being 'outbalanced' by other interests and values if one derives it not only from human dignity but also from a penal-theoretical understanding of the specific nature of punishment. This is so because, if state punishment were just one of many kinds of restrictions that can be imposed on human freedom of action in the interests of other members of the polity, there would be no reason why the culpability principle could not be overcome by sufficiently important policy objectives (as is, indeed, amply demonstrated by the German Constitutional Court's case law establishing a constitutional justification for continuing preventive detention of certain types of dangerous offenders beyond the point in time where a deserved sentence for the criminal act the offender has committed has been served). Mir Puig, like Husak, needs to take the utilitarianism-trumping standard he seeks from penal theory and cannot generate fully from commitments already part of existing constitutional law.

[60] S Besson, *The Morality of Conflict: Reasonable Disagreement and the Law* (Oxford, Hart Publishing, 2005) 317.

[61] R Dworkin, *Law's Empire* (London, Fontana, 1986) 219.

conflict in the law . . . in our legal and political settlements.'[62] When a constitution provides recognition to 'essentially contestable concepts such as equality or free-dom of speech' – and the same may be said for a desert constraint in punishment – we cannot interpret this move as an attempt to *minimise* disagreement by setting a constitutional boundary.[63] This is so because the application of this type of pre-commitment will 'always be a matter of *judgement*, be it the legislature's or the judiciary's.'[64] We should embrace this fact, and recognise that the function of constitutional incorporation of 'abstract normative and contestable concepts' is 'precisely to create disagreement and prevent any conception from being settled once and for all.'[65]

In a constitutional order designed to ensure these practices and outcomes, con-stitutional law has to negotiate a balance between judicial control and legislative choice. Under any system of checks and balances likely to be chosen by a demo-cratic, liberal state, constitutional adjudication will therefore police an outer boundary of arbitrary state action rather than engage in the search for an ideal answer that is then imposed as judicial fiat. In turn, a constitutional approach has the potential to reshape the propositions of penal theory more thoroughly than its advocates expect. While liberal constitutions already constrain, in a very broad sense, the kind of penal theory that can govern the penal practices of such a polity (in that whatever penal theory we support also has to make room for the standard justification of state action in a liberal-democratic state), in practice the variability of penal theorists' approaches, combined with the general liberal-constitutional legitimation for exercises of state authority, will limit the effects of the constitu-tional recognition of penal theory to little more than what is currently done under the heading of a general proportionality review.

At the same time, constitutional incorporation may come at the price of diluting penal theory's more complex conceptual constructions and arguments. This is a danger stressed by Greco, who argues that a penal-theoretical concept necessarily loses much of its differentiation and richness of meaning through the process of being 'translated' into constitutional law.[66] This is so, he argues, because constitu-tional law merely – negatively – sets an absolute boundary to state action, whereas doctrinal and theoretical reasoning strives – positively – to provide nuanced and fully worked out answers to difficult questions.[67] As constitutional standards, the theoretical and doctrinal constructs of penal theory therefore lose the conceptual complexity which enables them to give positive concrete guidance, while introduc-ing a risk that an unthinking identification of 'what the constitution requires' with what a particular conception of a doctrinal concept entails might stifle theoretical debate and ossify further conceptual development.[68]

---

[62] Besson, *The Morality of Conflict*, above n 60 at 116.
[63] See Besson, ibid, 303.
[64] Ibid, 313–14.
[65] Ibid.
[66] See Greco, 'Verfassungskonformes oder legitimes Strafrecht?', above n 7 at 22–25, 30–35.
[67] Ibid, 24.
[68] Ibid, esp at 25 and 32.

The strategy of constitutionalisation gets penal theory's normative claims caught between the Scylla of a 'fading away' of the normative principles central to a fully developed criminal law theory, under the harsh and relentless glare of a constitutional proportionality test, and the Charybdis of 'import strategies' that vastly overstate the kinds of binding conclusions that can reasonably be drawn from criminal law theory in the constitutional setting. The price, in both cases, is that penal theory becomes dysfunctional: in the former case, because its claims get absorbed into constitutional principles and no longer provide rich and nuanced guidance on specific questions; in the latter, because criminal law theory cannot be frozen in time but must remain responsive to further doctrinal development and debate.

There is, thus, a sense in which penal theory is simply unsuited to constitutional incorporation and necessarily resists being constitutionalised. When carried across into liberal constitutions as specific standards of constitutional law, the concepts and insights penal theory offers can no longer operate in a way that fulfils penal theory's functions adequately. Even after incorporation, penal theory will therefore play its most important role *outside* constitutional law. To understand how and why this is the case, is the theme of the final section.

III. What Penal Theory has to Offer Law and Practice in a Constitutional State

If penal theory cannot *become* constitutional law, on what basis can it then be argued that penal theory should and must nevertheless be treated as providing *legally* relevant answers to the question when a person may be subjected to state punishment? To see what role penal theory should play in a constitutional state, we have to take a step back and reflect on the relationship that constitutional law and penal practice each have to the fundamental structure of political society, and to the foundational commitments made by participants in the social and political life of constitutional states.

A good starting point for such reflection is provided by Kremnitzer's observation that 'Common to constitutional and criminal law is the perception – based upon the autonomy of the self and human dignity – of the individual as the foundation of society and law, as an end in himself.'[69] To 'treat people as ends in matters of justice' in our collective political life is, as Besson explains, 'to conduct ourselves in ways that are publicly justifiable to their and our own common human reason, and . . . offering such justifications as the occasion demands.'[70] This captures precisely the terms in which citizens of a liberal constitutional state relate to each other through

---

[69] M Kremnitzer, 'Constitutional Principles and Criminal Law' (1993) 27 *Israel Law Review* 84, 85.
[70] Besson, *The Morality of Conflict*, above n 60 at 109.

their institutions of public authority. In Macedo's felicitous formulation, 'the moral lodestar of liberalism is the . . . project of public justification.'[71]

In the area of criminal law, the project of public justification is the *justification of the imposition of punishment by the state*. What does this involve? One important insight was implicit in our discussion in section II, of the drawbacks of punishment from a citizen's perspective that Husak has identified and of how these drawbacks might be overcome.[72] When social institutions of punishment are absorbed into state structures, punishment's justification qua state institution hinges on the general grounds for the justification of the existence and shape of *all* state institutions. In such a system,[73]

> all justification must ultimately refer back to the terms of social cooperation. There is nothing in these terms and the corresponding political duties *logically* to necessitate specific responses to violations of these duties . . . [T]he response to wrongdoing is justified . . . in terms of the response's *appropriateness* for achieving an aim, which must be in line with and serve the terms of social cooperation.

When we understand criminal law and punishment as a state function, we come to view[74]

> the criminal law not as a necessary institution and punishment not as a moral inevitability, but rather both as the continuation, rationalization, and humanization of historically contingent practices, which need either to be adjusted to serve the purposes of justice or to be jettisoned altogether.

This view of the criminal law and punishment is echoed by the German Constitutional Court, when it remarks that[75]

> the history of criminal justice clearly shows how extremely cruel sanctions have come to be replaced by increasingly milder ones . . . Any judgment about the kind of sanction that is compatible with the dignity of human beings can, therefore, only be taken to represent current insights and cannot claim to be timelessly valid.

Whereas the twin demands of political morality – that humans treat each other as bearers of rights, and that humans organised into a society grant each other authority over one another only to the limited extent that such curtailment of their

---

[71] S Macedo, *Liberal Virtues: Citizenship, Virtue and Community in Liberal Constitutionalism* (Oxford, Clarendon Press, 1991) 78.

[72] See text at nn 55 to 57 above.

[73] E Melissaris, 'Toward a Political Theory of Criminal Law: A Critical Rawlsian Account' (2012) 15 *New Criminal Law Review* 122, 138.

[74] Melissaris, ibid, 143. The point is made by Melissaris in his development of a Rawlsian theory of criminal law, but it holds good whether or not one adopts a Rawlsian version of liberalism. For instance, von Hirsch explicitly keeps open the possibility that criminal punishment as a state accountability mechanism could be *abolished* when it is no longer needed to serve any crime-preventive function. See A von Hirsch, *Censure and Sanctions* (Oxford, Oxford University Press, 1993).

[75] BVerfGE 45, 187 (229) (Mandatory Sentence of Life Imprisonment for Murder). ['Die Geschichte der Strafrechtspflege zeigt deutlich, dass an die Stelle grausamster Strafen immer mildere Strafen getreten sind . . . Das Urteil darüber, was der Würde des Menschen entspricht, kann daher nur auf dem jetzigen Stand der Erkenntnis beruhen und keinen Anspruch auf zeitlose Gültigkeit haben.']

freedom is fair and necessary for the achievement of valuable shared social ends –
are, arguably, timelessly valid,[76] the appropriate or desirable public-political
responses to wrongdoing are not in the same way timeless. All we can say about the
latter in general terms is that when state punishment is selected as the appropriate
response to certain violations of political duties, it has to be structured such that it
is recognisably *punishment*, as well as recognisably *just*. Hence the legislator must to
some extent live with pre-existing social notions of what punishment is, and for
what it is deserved.

We can now see another, deeper, reason why criminal law theory is not fully
'subsumable' into constitutional *law*. Since 'criminalisation and punishment are
contingent, historically qualified means of achieving stability and assurance,'[77] the
theoretical commitments and constructions that support any particular set of
responses cannot be formulated at the level of a political process that establishes the
'basic structure of society' through pre-commitments in the shape of constitutional
law. What role is played by the institutions of criminal law and state punishment in
a constitutional state is deeply contextual and sensitive to changes in the social
world. At the constitutional level, one can at most acknowledge their significance
and potential role in broad terms, but one cannot once and for all pin down their
reach and content. If penal theory's pronouncements on important sub-questions
were to be incorporated into the constitutional documents as particular guarantees, this would lead – over time – to distortions in the overall coherence of a state's
legal system, and amount to an impediment in that state's political system's ability
to respond appropriately to the social phenomena of wrongdoing – including
breaches by citizens of other citizens' fundamental political entitlements. Full 'constitutionalisation' of the limits to state power that a properly developed criminal
law theory can provide is *theoretically impossible*, because the concrete restrictions
and the concrete guarantees have to be continually worked out, and revisited, in
response to changing social and institutional facts over time.

What, then, is the role of criminal law theory in a constitutional state? The answer
starts with a better understanding of what criminal law theory *is* in such a state, an
answer that we are now ready to give. *The theory of the criminal law is the fully developed theory of the 'appropriate response to crime' of its time.* The role of criminal law
theory in political and legal discourse is to perform the *ongoing* task of institutions
of liberal-democratic states to develop criteria for the appropriateness of responses
to certain rights-violations in reaction to the social realities of the time. A good

---

[76] The twin demands of political morality noted in the text are those made and accepted by all classical
liberal writers. But the claim of timeless validity of the fundamental principles of political order is also
present in Hegel's work. Because Hegel develops his theory of the state out of the necessity for human
beings to recognise and relate to each other as humans in society, he takes himself to have demonstrated
conclusively that the liberal state is the only stable social arrangement in the long run. At the same
time, he thinks that questions such as what forms punishment should take cannot be resolved at the
general philosophical level but will be determined by variable circumstances and needs which shape the
diverse criminal justice practices of actual states. See GWF Hegel, *Elements of the Philosophy of Right*, ed
AW Wood, transl HB Nisbet (Cambridge, Cambridge University Press, 1991; orig 1820) §§ 257ff (on the
state); § 218 (Addition (H)) (on state punishment).

[77] Melissaris, 'Toward a Political Theory', above n 73 at 122.

criminal law theory offers a developed polity a way of thinking about, and of evaluating, the appropriateness of the use of penal sanctions, as well as the range and types of these sanctions. It helps rational and demystified penal practices along.

This kind of guidance is 'thicker' than the few pointers that constitutional rules and principles provide. But it originates from the same commitment to mutual recognition and meaningful human agency, and the same conception of the functions that the rules of the polity are intended to serve, on which the constitution is also based.[78] How guidance through penal theory is achieved, in practice, is well illustrated by Andreas von Hirsch's argument for a limited constitutional protection against grossly disproportionate punishment.[79] The constitutional protection against grossly disproportionate punishment – triggered, as von Hirsch explains, only by punishments which work *in terrorem* – belongs within the constitutional documents precisely because it is one of those fundamental and timeless commitments that flow from the recognition of basic humanity in one's fellow citizens that is the precondition for all legitimate public power. But note how much more restrained von Hirsch intends this constitutional protection to be than is the (also prescriptive) normative guidance offered by his fully-fledged theory of proportionate sentencing. Von Hirsch accepts that adoption of his fully-fledged penal theory remains, for courts and legislators, entirely voluntary, as these players in the criminal justice system cannot, and should not, be *constitutionally coerced* into administering any particular penal theory. But even though many of his theoretical arguments then remain at the level of a moral-political appeal, one that reaches binding force only through the ability of judges to 'fuse' such theoretical insights with the interpretation of the laws they apply, this guidance is, even for and within the legal system, more meaningful than the bare 'ultimate constitutional stop' of the constitutional guarantee against grossly disproportionate punishments. Von Hirsch's preference for a limited protection against 'grossly disproportionate' punishment, as opposed to a constitutional requirement of 'proportionate punishment', is based on a correct understanding of the type of guarantee that can be enshrined in a constitutional document, as well as on a clear realisation that under such a system, the much richer principled guidance offered by desert theory remains just as important to the project of providing a full public justification of punishment as it would be in a state without constitutional law.

Of course, this leaves us with the familiar disjunction: not everything that is done to a citizen by way of punishment, and which can be shown by penal theory to be

---

[78] It is because criminal law and constitutional law in the formal sense share this deeper political-philosophical basis that Kremnitzer can claim that 'the constitutional principles [enshrined in Israel's Basic Law] already existed prior to the enactment of the Basic Law.' (Kremnitzer, 'Constitutional Principles and Criminal Law', above n 69 at 84.) These principles existed in the sense that those who reflected on the sources of the authority of the state, whether they were active in government, in the courts or as legal scholars, had identified the foundations of legitimate government in these terms, and were therefore prepared to treat these principles as action-guiding and limit-setting long before their formal enactment as 'higher' (constitutional) law.

[79] See von Hirsch, 'Should There Be Constitutional Constraints', above n 12. His arguments are summarised in the text at nn 12 to 16 above.

unjustified, is also a breach of that citizen's constitutional rights and guarantees. But this is not so very different from the familiar disjunction of constitutional theory – not *all* 'ordinary unlawfulness' is a violation of constitutionally protected rights. The German Constitutional Court struggled with this puzzle for some considerable time. On the one hand, the Constitutional Court's jurisdiction is, when citizens bring a complaint, limited to cases where the citizen's constitutional rights have been violated by a public authority (which can be the legislature, an executive organ, or a court). On the other hand, if a judgment by an ordinary court is wrong in law, the judgment (in a civil or administrative case) is bound to negatively affect the citizen's constitutionally protected property right;[80] and a criminal conviction and sentence that is wrong in law affects an even wider range of constitutionally protected rights.[81] Does it not follow from this that every mistake in the application of law that has led to a negative judicial outcome for the citizen is ipso facto also a violation of the citizen's constitutional rights?[82] No, said the Court. If the complainant wants to challenge the application of ordinary law by the ordinary courts as a violation of her constitutional rights, she must show that the judge made no ordinary mistake when she misapplied the law. In order to fall within the jurisdiction of the Constitutional Court, the complainant must assert that the misapplication of ordinary law manifests a failure by the judge to understand the significance of the constitutional rights implicated in this case, or to grasp what value-orientation the constitution required of her in relation to the decision at hand.[83] This distinction between 'ordinary violations of the law' and 'specific violations of constitutional rights' means that many – though by no means all – complaints before the German Constitutional Court fail, simply because the complainant's complaint is taken to relate only to an 'ordinary' mistaken application of law. Many unjustified exercises of public authority through ordinary misapplications of the law remain unredressed because of the supposedly greater interest we have in retaining an effective distinction between ordinary legal review and constitutional appeals. Similarly, when we decline to treat any instance of the application of penal law that penal theory can show was unjustified as a violation of a constitutional right, this disjunction is something we may have to live with and accept if we want to retain a proper role for penal theory in constitutional as well as in ordinary legal discourse.

---

[80] This is so because if the losing party does not 'pay up', the judgment can and will be executed against the losing party's property. Of course, administrative and civil judgments can affect other constitutional rights too.

[81] See the discussion in Section I of this chapter.

[82] Some legal systems struggle so badly with this juridical brain-teaser that they abolish specifically 'constitutional' review and turn their constitutional court into a general court of appeal. This was, for instance, done in South Africa.

[83] In German constitutional law doctrine, this is referred to as a '*spezifische Grundrechtsverletzung*' – a violation specifically of constitutionally guaranteed fundamental rights.

IV. Concluding Remarks

This chapter has considered the question to what extent penal theory can, and should be, 'constitutionalised'. In the course of reviewing attempts made by penal theorists to 'harness' the normativity-claims of constitutional law to their pronouncements, I addressed the likely effects that recognition of a proposed constitutional 'right not to be punished' would have on the content and construction of penal theories, and on the content and scope of penal law in practice. I maintained that constitutional recognition of such a right would make only a small difference to the constitutionally enforceable protections of citizens against the penal powers of the liberal state. But, on reflection, this gives penal theorists less reason to worry than one might have thought. This is so because constitutional law – its non-incorporation of penal theory notwithstanding – cannot suppress the continuing normative significance of criminal law theory. Even in a constitutional state, criminal law theory has continuing normative importance. While it cannot be restated through or incorporated fully within the set of constitutional guarantees without losing much of its functionality as a comprehensive guidance system for the properly motivated liberal legislator, government official, and judge, it retains the normativity that resides in that function even after the constitutionalisation of the state.

17

Criminal Law Theory and
the Limits of Liberalism

PAUL ROBERTS*

I. Questioning the Liberal Consensus in
Contemporary Criminal Law Theory

Andreas von Hirsch is a preeminent exponent of liberal criminal law theory. His extensive and influential writings on sentencing, penal theory and criminalisation have been instrumental in establishing a distinctively liberal conception of deonto-logical political morality as the broadly received orthodoxy amongst contemporary Anglophone criminal law theorists. Whereas for the theoretical pioneers of the 1960s and 70s (prominently including the two transatlantic Herberts, Hart[1] and Packer[2]) some form of Bentham-inspired utilitarianism seemed like the natural default position for those in search of a justificatory theory of criminal law, varia-tions on 'neo-Kantian' deontology rule the contemporary theoretical roost and avowed consequentialists have become an endangered species. Von Hirsch led the original charge against consequentialism in penal theory and sentencing practice from the mid-1970s onwards,[3] and in later collaborative work with Andrews Ashworth and Simester has elucidated an increasingly nuanced and persuasive account of liberal criminal law.[4]

This chapter aims to provoke further critical reflection and debate concerning the specifically 'liberal' credentials of contemporary Anglo-American criminal law theory. Much contemporary theorising about criminal law is conducted against a

* I am most grateful to the editors for their (liberal) encouragement, patience and attention to detail.
[1] HLA Hart, *Punishment and Responsibility: Essays in the Philosophy of Law* (Oxford, Clarendon Press, 1968); HLA Hart, *Law, Liberty and Morality* (Oxford, Oxford University Press, 1962).
[2] HL Packer, *The Limits of the Criminal Sanction* (Palo Alto CA, Stanford University Press, 1969).
[3] A von Hirsch, *Censure and Sanctions* (Oxford, Clarendon Press, 1993); A von Hirsch, *Past or Future Crimes: Deservedness and Dangerous in the Sentencing of Criminals* (Manchester, Manchester University Press, 1985); A von Hirsch, *Doing Justice* (New York, Hill & Wang, 1976); A von Hirsch, 'Punishment Futures: The Desert-model Debate and the Importance of the Criminal Law Context' in M Tonry (ed), *Retributivism Has a Past: Has it a Future?* (New York, Oxford University Press, 2011).
[4] A von Hirsch and A Ashworth, *Proportionate Sentencing: Exploring the Principles* (Oxford, Oxford University Press, 2005); AP Simester and A von Hirsch, *Crimes, Harms and Wrongs: On the Principles of Criminalisation* (Oxford, Hart Publishing, 2011).

backdrop of liberal ideals, values and assumptions which are seldom fully articulated, much less systematically explored. Liberal philosophical commitments
often seem to operate, more or less unconsciously, as unexamined normative presuppositions. This is not necessarily problematic: there is nothing wrong in principle with a sensible division of theoretical labour between political philosophers
and criminal law theorists. It should also be said that some contemporary theorists
of the criminal law go out of their way to disown any association with liberalism, in
either its theoretical or normative registers.[5] In my experience, however, those concerned to distance themselves from liberalism rarely work with sympathetic or
well-articulated conceptions of liberal political morality. So even if we temporarily
'bracket' (ie beg) questions about the substantive merits of liberalism as normative
political philosophy, threshold (ontological or conceptual) issues of terminology
and classification still remain unaddressed. Just what is it that makes a justificatory
or normative theory of criminal law (as opposed, roughly speaking, to 'scientific'
empirical description of positive law and existing institutions) distinctively *liberal*?
Skating over debates *within* liberal theorising, this essay adopts an holistic, meta-
disciplinary perspective. Given that there appears to be something like a loose
liberal coalition uniting (most) contemporary criminal law theorists, what is the
nature and character of that 'liberalism' and what role does it play in the best
normative accounts of the criminal law?

It is necessary to begin by addressing some formative methodological issues. The
substantive parts of the inquiry will be greatly facilitated if we can first clarify the
nature of our questions, and thereby cultivate a more refined notion of what should
realistically be expected by way of answers. The enterprise of relating 'Criminal Law
Theory' to 'liberalism' naturally begins with the meaning ascribed to these two key
concepts, and I had therefore better be clear about my own field-defining conceptual presuppositions.[6] Conscious of the perils of trying to win any normative argument by definitional stipulation (ie by cheating), and also of the inherently
controversial nature of the exercise, I will adopt a paradigmatic or ideal-type
approach. So far as Criminal Law Theory is concerned, I will simply point to that
body of English language, predominantly Anglo-American scholarship on the theoretical and philosophical foundations of criminal law which has flourished over
the last 30 years or so,[7] and to which Andreas von Hirsch has been a pioneering

---

[5] See eg A Norrie, *Crime, Reason and History: A Critical Introduction to Criminal Law*, 2nd edn
(London, Butterworths, 2001) 31 ('we should put aside the continuing legal-liberal dream that [criminal
law] is potentially rational'), 233 ('the practical necessity and the intellectual impossibility of the
orthodox, liberal, positivist tradition in criminal law scholarship').

[6] For an entertaining (inadvertent) object lesson in the perils of definitional incontinence, see
J Goldberg, *Liberal Fascism* (London, Penguin, 2009). And cf S Fish, 'Liberalism Doesn't Exist' (1987) 36
Duke Law Journal 997.

[7] See eg RA Duff and SP Green (eds), *Philosophical Foundations of Criminal Law* (New York, Oxford
University Press, 2011); D Husak, *The Philosophy of Criminal Law* (Oxford, Oxford University Press,
2010); D Husak, *Overcriminalization: The Limits of the Criminal Law* (Oxford, Oxford University Press,
2008); J Gardner, *Offences and Defences* (Oxford, Oxford University Press, 2007); RA Duff, *Answering
for Crime: Responsibility and Liability in the Criminal Law* (Oxford, Hart Publishing, 2007); A Duff,
L Farmer, S Marshall and V Tadros, *The Trial on Trial Vol 3: Towards a Normative Theory of the Criminal*

contributor. Elucidating a serviceable ideal-typical conception of liberalism as a distinctive political morality presents a more formidable challenge, which is taken up in section II of this chapter. The aim will be to sketch, in miniature, an idealised model of liberal political theory which is tangible, comprehensible, recognisably attractive to liberals, adequately differentiated from theoretical rivals, and amenable to direct translation into institutionalised criminal law policies, principles, laws and practices.

Having mapped out the scope and nature of the inquiry and fixed basic concepts, the institutional or 'jurisprudential'[8] analysis developed in the remainder of the chapter has two parts, the first predominantly expository and the second more theoretically substantive. Section III fleshes out a liberal conception of criminal law. The only purpose of this exceedingly broad-brush sketch is to show that a great deal of what is familiar in modern Anglo-American criminal law is plausibly explicable, and potentially also justifiable, in terms of the version of liberal political morality presented in section II. Theorists have already made significant progress in employing the tools of analytical philosophy to reconsider contemporary criminal law doctrine and trace its normative foundations into (aspects of) liberal political morality. Section IV will suggest, however, that a liberal conception of criminal law inevitably encounters two methodological stumbling blocks, which seem to curtail liberalism's capacity for theorising criminal law. I will call these twin obstacles to liberal theorising the problem of incompleteness and the problem of under-determination. Taken together, they suggest that comprehensive normative justifications of penal law must draw on theoretical and normative resources that could only be found (if they can be found at all) by venturing beyond the confines of liberal political philosophy.

What follows from a new appreciation, or more acute perception, of liberalism's limitations as a source of normative theorising about criminal law? Liberals might be disappointed by the deflationary implications for liberal theorising. It is important to stress, however, that liberalism's theoretical limitations do not imply that a comprehensive normative rationalisation of criminal law must therefore be in tension with, much less dissent from or contradict, liberal political morality. A normative theory of criminal law incorporating non-liberal (as opposed to illiberal) theoretical resources should still be counted an authentically *liberal* theory, from a normative point of view, if it fully coheres with liberal political morality. Nor do its theoretical limitations imply that liberalism lacks tangible critical purchase on

Trial (Oxford, Hart Publishing, 2007); V Tadros, *Criminal Responsibility* (Oxford, Oxford University Press, 2005); S Shute and AP Simester (eds), *Criminal Law Theory: Doctrines of the General Part* (Oxford, Oxford University Press, 2002); RA Duff, *Punishment, Communication and Community* (Oxford, Oxford University Press, 2001); A Ashworth and M Wasik (eds), *Fundamentals of Sentencing Theory* (Oxford, Oxford University Press, 1998); GP Fletcher (ed), *New Voices in Criminal Theory* (1998) 1 *Buffalo Criminal Law Review* Special Issue; M Moore, *Placing Blame: A Theory of Criminal Law* (Oxford, Oxford University Press, 1997); AP Simester and ATH Smith, *Harm and Culpability* (Oxford, Oxford University Press, 1996); Michael Moore, *Act and Crime* (Oxford, Oxford University Press, 1993); S Shute, J Gardner and J Horder (eds), *Action and Value in Criminal Law* (Oxford, Oxford University Press, 1993); RA Duff, *Intention, Agency and Criminal Liability* (Oxford, Blackwell, 1990).

[8] By which I mean the discipline, process and methods of institutionalising political morality in concrete juridical formations, fusing, in practical reality, theory in law and law in theory.

contemporary criminal justice policy and practice, as this chapter will show. Non-liberals, meanwhile, should properly regard liberalism's limitations in theorising criminal law as a strength rather than a weakness of normative theorising in general. If, as I suggest, much of what liberals typically find attractive in modern criminal law doctrine and theory is (merely) consistent with, rather than being derived from, liberal political morality, the path is cleared for forging theoretical alliances with non-liberals and building a broader, more inclusive and stable 'overlapping theoretical consensus' around criminal law's foundational normative requirements. I will venture, in this chapter's concluding paragraphs, some brief ruminations on the implications of consensus-building in criminal law theory for sponsoring global penal justice in an era of international human rights law and cosmopolitan criminal jurisprudence.

II. Liberal Political Morality, in Miniature

Serious reflection on the notion of 'liberal criminal law' immediately encounters major conceptual and terminological difficulties. This chapter has already implicitly counter-posed 'liberal' to 'utilitarian' criminal law. Yet Bentham, and even more so Mill, must surely count as a 'liberal' on any historically respectable definition of liberalism. The movement in the history of philosophical ideas from Bentham to Kant, or in modern punishment theory from Hart to von Hirsch, is not well characterised as a shift *to* liberalism, but rather as a re-alignment within it: from a utilitarian liberalism to contemporary deontological liberalisms. This does not show that the liberal foundations of modern criminal law are uninteresting, or unproblematic, but it does underscore the methodological caveat that philosophical concepts and terminology derived from broader currents in the history of ideas may map onto exotic small islands in the stream, like criminal law theory, only imperfectly or obscurely, if at all.

Liberalism may be broad church, but there *is* a core liberal creed (to borrow Mill's revealing synecdoche) with articles of faith to which true believers must, and generally do, subscribe. Utilitarians like Bentham and Mill are inside the liberal big tent alongside Hobbes, Kant, Locke, Adam Smith, Rawls, Habermas, Rorty, Hart, Dworkin and their living secular co-religionists; just as assuredly Plato, Aristotle, Marcus Aurelius, Aquinas, Rousseau, Marx, Nietzsche, Heidegger, Roger Scruton, John Gray, and Alasdair MacIntyre – to say nothing of the likes of Carl Schmidt, Mao Tse Tung, or the Ayatollah Khommeini – represent those who would not be granted (and would never have requested) full admission. Lively debates about the liberal credentials of modern philosophers such as Charles Taylor, Michael Sandel and Joseph Raz indicate that the boundaries of liberalism may be blurry and productive of genuinely borderline cases. At least some contemporary theorists have thought it worthwhile to dispute the criteria for qualifying as a bona fide member of the liberal philosophical club. Such critical (self-)examinations hint at more than merely theoretical motivations for classifying philosophical theories as 'liberal' or otherwise – a possibility revisited in this chapter's concluding section V.

A *liberal* theory at its heart would have to be concerned with prioritising individuals' *liberty*.[9] Analytically, this means treating the individual as the primary unit of ethical concern. Liberalism is thereby immediately positioned as a secular philosophy. Political morality, on this view, is centrally concerned with the wellbeing and welfare of human beings rather than being orientated towards celebrating the glory of god(s), perfecting His Kingdom on Earth, or something of that order. This does not necessarily imply that liberal political morality is incompatible with or even mildly inhospitable towards religious conviction – of particular faiths or denominations, or in general – but it does mean that the problem of reconciling religious conviction with liberal political morality, assuming that such reconciliation may be possible and desirable (for particular religions, or at large), is already defined on this view as a problem for theology, not one for political philosophy. Religion is not a source of *theoretical* controversy for liberal theory, because liberalism is committed to rejecting all dogmatic arguments from religious faith or authority insofar as they purport to regulate the ordering of political relations in the public sphere. In this way, liberalism's thin militant secularism holds the ring for religious tolerance and pluralism. Freedom of religion, including the freedom to dissent or defect, is an important sphere of liberty with enormous historical resonance for liberals and – of course – undiminished contemporary significance for theists.[10] Those religions which conceive religious freedom primarily in terms of collective public worship, private conscience and everyday personal morality should not find liberal polities uncongenial or excessively burdensome, either spiritually or in practical life. Those religions which mandate theocracy, the uncompromising pursuit of one true path to enlightenment in all things, or preferential treatment in the public realm for believers over infidels and sinners, are, by contrast, set on a collision course with liberal political authority.

Liberal theory conceptualises individuals as the primary unit of ethical concern in the sense of Kant's fundamental injunction to treat human beings as ends in themselves, and not merely as a means to somebody else's ends – a thing of merely instrumental value that can legitimately be bent to another's will, used, abused and discarded like denatured chewing gum or an old worn-out pair of boots. Rawls' famous critique of utilitarianism as 'no respecter of persons' is drawn from the same liberal wellspring.[11] Dworkin's more juridified rendering, in terms of every

---

[9] I Berlin, *Liberty*, ed H Hardy (Oxford, Oxford University Press, 2002). And *per differentiam*, see H Arendt, *The Origins of Totalitarianism* (Orlando FL, Harcourt, 1976); V Grossman, *Life and Fate* (London, Vintage, 2006); J Chang and J Halliday, *Mao: The Unknown Story* (London, Vintage, 2007).

[10] MJ Perry, *The Political Morality of Liberal Democracy* (New York, Cambridge University Press, 2010).

[11] J Rawls, *A Theory of Justice* (Oxford, Oxford University Press, 1973) 29, 187 ('classical utilitarianism fails to take seriously the distinction between persons'). The 'no respecter' idiom is owed to HLA Hart, 'Natural Rights: Bentham and John Stuart Mill' in his *Essays on Bentham* (Oxford, Oxford University Press, 1982) 99.

person's fundamental right to 'equal concern and respect',[12] articulates the equality norm underpinning modern liberal legal systems and which is invoked directly in non-discrimination suits. Individuals are seen as separate in having their own personal interests (eg in continued survival, physical security, mental repose and stimulation, valuable opportunities, meaningful choices, etc) which could be advanced or harmed; *and* each individual's interests must be given equal consideration with everybody else's in public policy-making, legislation and law enforcement. The right is to equal *consideration*, not to formal equality of treatment or outcome – neither of which may be practically achievable given the diversity of individual needs, interests and desires, the tendency for interests to conflict in zero-sum configurations, finite resources and the brute unpredictability of happenstance. There are typically losers as well as winners in many if not most public policy choices, but at least everybody's interests are fairly (and in that sense *equally*) factored into the policy-making equation, irrespective of birth, colour, creed, class, gender, sexual orientation or other irrelevant personal characteristics.[13] That is the liberal polity's mutually constitutive promise to its citizens.

We should frankly concede that this line of argument has already narrowed the field of eligible theories to deontological variants of liberalism. So be it. In this instance, modest sacrifices of historical fidelity and theoretical inclusiveness are fair trade for the significant analytical and normative gains obtained by stiffening liberal theory's admissions criteria with some deontological fibre. For present purposes, we can safely set aside predominantly exegetical questions such as whether it is possible to reconcile Mill's liberal instincts with his official subscription to utilitarian dogma,[14] or how far Hart can square his avowedly utilitarian justification for punishment with his liberal preferences regarding the scope and detailed specification of substantive criminal laws.[15] Whether or not one is (also) persuaded by Bernard Williams' integrity-based objections to an unremittingly impartial utilitarian morality that denies any deep ethical significance to agent-relative reasons,[16] we should say, with Rawls,[17] that the utilitarian's professed egalitarianism is a sham equality in which all persons 'count' the same only because everybody ultimately counts for nothing under the tyranny of familiar monist consequentialisms. People

---

[12] R Dworkin, *Justice for Hedgehogs* (Cambridge MA, Harvard University Press, 2011) Part 5; R Dworkin, *Sovereign Virtue: The Theory and Practice of Equality* (Cambridge MA, Harvard University Press, 2002); R Dworkin, A Matter of Principle (Oxford, Oxford University Press, 1985) ch 9; R Dworkin, *Taking Rights Seriously*, rev edn (London, Duckworth, 1978).

[13] Birth, colour, creed etc are not *always* irrelevant characteristics for liberal public policy-makers, legislators or officials. I am speaking in broad terms.

[14] CL Ten (ed), *Mill's On Liberty: A Critical Guide* (Cambridge, Cambridge University Press, 2010); R Crisp, *Mill on Utilitarianism* (London, Routledge, 1997); CL Ten, *Mill On Liberty* (Oxford, Oxford University Press, 1980).

[15] Cf J Gardner, 'Introduction' to HLA Hart, *Punishment and Responsibility*, 2nd edn (Oxford, Oxford University Press, 2008) xxviii–xxxi; N Lacey, *State Punishment* (London, Routledge, 1986) 47–49, 187.

[16] B Williams, 'A Critique of Utilitarianism' in JJC Smart and B Williams (eds), *Utilitarianism: For and Against* (Cambridge, Cambridge University Press, 1973); B Williams, *Moral Luck* (Cambridge, Cambridge University Press, 1981).

[17] J Rawls, *A Theory of Justice* (Oxford, Oxford University Press, 1973) § 30.

are not merely experience machines whose value is exhausted by their utility as biological loci for welfare maximisation. Embodied individual *wellbeing*, rather than aggregated abstract welfare, should be government's ultimate ethical consideration; reflecting liberal deontology's insistence that human beings are intrinsically valuable, Kantian ends-in-themselves. Or if this conception of liberal theory is too rich for some tastes, we should at least say, borrowing Dworkin's methodological apparatus,[18] that the utilitarian conception of individual wellbeing is so far removed from our current institutional practices and the ideals and values which we take to vindicate them that it does not qualify, even at the threshold pre-interpretative level, as a plausible account of criminal law in modern liberal polities. Nor have the utilitarians yet provided us with good reason to think that our public institutions for proscribing criminal wrongs and censuring and punishing criminal wrongdoers should be systematically rethought and reformed[19] along utilitarian lines.

The primacy of individuals, and by extension of their interests, in liberal theory has generated many widespread misconceptions about liberalism, by no means only amongst theorists. Political theory since the 1980s has been the battleground for an increasingly stylised series of theoretical hostilities between 'liberals' and a loose collection of generally left-leaning 'communitarian' critics.[20] These debates were illuminating in their heyday, but much of their intensity seems to have dissipated. Several notable theorist-combatants have switched sides, or claimed to have been closet liberals all along.[21] One canard associated with the first rash of communitarian critiques was that liberal theory is committed to an abstract, a-contextual, dissociated, 'atomistic' conception of the self which is both completely unrealistic and ethically debased, in being estranged from its social environment and the fabric

---

[18] R Dworkin, *Justice for Hedgehogs* (Cambridge MA, Harvard University Press, 2011) Part 2; R Dworkin, *Law's Empire* (London, Fontana, 1986) ch 2.

[19] Utilitarians are not necessarily committed to endorsing utility maximisation as the direct goal of individual action or official policy-making. Various models of 'two-level' thinking might be invoked to try to explain why acting for ostensibly non-utilitarian reasons at the first-order level of human decision-making can be squared with a second-order theoretical utilitarian justification. (Less frequently, utilitarians argue the converse: that conventional moral practice should be brought into conformity with utilitarian theoretical reason.) Despite their ingenuity, utilitarians of this persuasion always seem to me to end up relying on inherently undisprovable empirical predictions (an argumentative gambit I call the 'empirical dodge') or disappearing up their own axiology. This is all a very long way from what Bentham promised the world when urging us to substitute his supposedly empirically-vindicated utilitarian science of morals for all that metaphysical hocus pocus of philosophical tradition.

[20] W Kymlicka, *Contemporary Political Philosophy: An Introduction*, 2nd edn (Oxford, Oxford University Press, 2002); S Mulhall and A Swift, *Liberals and Communitarians*, 2nd edn (Oxford, Blackwell, 1996).

[21] Michael Sandel, for example, notes that 'The "liberal-communitarian" debate that has raged among political philosophers in recent years describes a range of issues,' and confesses that 'I do not always find myself on the communitarian side': MJ Sandel, *Liberalism and the Limits of Justice*, 2nd edn (Cambridge, Cambridge University Press, 1998) ix. Also see A Etzioni, 'A Liberal Communitarian Paradigm for Counterterrorism' (2013) 49 *Stanford Journal of International Law* 330; R Rorty, *Objectivity, Relativism and Truth: Philosophical Papers vol 1* (Cambridge, Cambridge University Press, 1991); C Taylor, 'Cross Purposes: The Liberal-Communitarian Debate' in NL Rosenblum (ed), *Liberalism and the Moral Life* (Cambridge MA, Harvard University Press, 1989); P Selznick, 'The Idea of A Communitarian Morality' (1987) 75 *California Law Review* 445.

of interpersonal relations woven into and enriching real lives.[22] The primary target of these objections was Rawls' Original Position thought-experiment, in which disembodied pre-social 'selves' choose the basic constitution of society and its distribution of resources from behind a 'veil of ignorance'[23] – a supercharged, political theorists' reinterpretation of the prosaic wisdom that fair shares are best guaranteed if I cut the Mars Bar and you choose which 'half' you want. Yet the 'atomism' objection to liberal theory is baseless. In fact, liberalism as such does not need an articulated theory of the self, beyond the baseline proposition that there *are* individual selves and that these biologically embodied entities are of primary ethical concern. Liberals, that is to say, are entitled to adopt the best conception of individuated selves that can be reconstructed from critical introspection combined with cognitive science, social psychology, cultural anthropology, philosophy of mind or any cognate interdisciplinary inquiries – all of which, incidentally, are likely to be more instructive on the topic of 'selves' than conventional political theory. On any plausible conception, the liberal self would have to be embodied, socially situated, and framed within a network of projects and interpersonal relationships which in turn make liberty or 'personal autonomy' valuable; where that value is understood not in disembodied abstraction or as a goal of consequentialist maximising, but in terms of the constitutive role which liberty and personal autonomy play in enabling individual human beings to lead valuable and successful lives.[24]

Selfishness is another charge typically levelled at individualist philosophies, including liberalism. However, this familiar criticism confuses meta-ethical individualism with egotism. Liberals insist that individuals must be at liberty to prefer their own interests, preferences and projects over other people's competing interests, preferences and projects *sometimes* and *up to a point*. This is not just a question of preserving the freedom to be altruistic or, more generally, to *choose* to do good, willingly and wholeheartedly, rather than being forced into virtue.[25] The objection is far more basic, and comprehensive. One's life would not be authentically one's own if one were under a pervasive general duty to assist the needy or to sacrifice one's projects to the general good. That kind of political morality would reduce us all into permanent public servitude. Liberal self-preference, then, is not a doctrine of egotistical greed or vain self-regard. It is a logical implication and necessary political precondition of personal freedom to follow your own path in life, to make your own choices about what to do and to strive within the limits of natural endowment and social opportunity to become the person you want to be with the life you want

---

[22] C Taylor, 'Atomism' reprinted in *Philosophy and the Human Sciences: Philosophical Papers vol 2* (Cambridge, Cambridge University Press, 1985). Cf DJD Uyl and DB Rasmussen, 'The Myth of Atomism' (2006) 59 *Review of Metaphysics* 841.

[23] J Rawls, *A Theory of Justice* (Oxford, Oxford University Press, 1973) § 24.

[24] See further, J Raz, *Value, Respect, and Attachment* (Cambridge, Cambridge University Press, 2001).

[25] Assuming, *contra* Kant, that 'forced virtue' is not a conceptual oxymoron. There is no obvious abuse of language in saying that '*X* was forced to do the right thing,' and sometimes it is enough that a person acted in accordance with the dictates of public morality, irrespective of her subjective motivation.

to have, to form, revise and pursue your own personal conception of the good,[26] as an autonomous (but necessarily, inescapably socially-situated) self-author of your own life and fate.

A related objection to liberal political morality is that it fails fully to acknowledge the demands of social or distributive justice. Unlike the first two theoretical objections we have canvassed, which turn out on closer inspection to melt away into indistinct shadows, social justice remains a genuine bone of contention between liberals and their communitarian, socialist or communist critics. Moreover, liberalism's historical association with laissez faire free market economics and Lockean theories of property makes it fair game for these brickbats. Without purporting to resolve deep and enduring controversies in political theory, we should at least be clear that liberalism implies personal autonomy not merely in Kant's sense of having the intellectual faculties of the intelligent moral agent, but also in the practical sense emphasised by Raz[27] of having adequate social opportunities and material resources to make 'living your own life according to your own lights' a – normatively speaking – meaningful option. So long as what you want falls within the liberally acceptable parameters of pluralism and tolerance, and is compatible with like freedom for all (the equality constraint previously noted), the liberal polity should prima facie respect your choices and even try to provide you with material assistance and the wherewithal to succeed in your ambitions. How far one person's efforts should be taxed in order to provide social welfare assistance to those more in need (whether as a result of their own choices or otherwise) is, needless to say, a pre-eminent question for modern governments – and an ideological bellwether of the sort that used to differentiate mainstream political parties. For present purposes we need only note that questions of social justice are vigorously contested *within* liberalism, as well as between liberals and their critics. Rawls famously argued for a level of asset redistribution through tax-and-spend economic policies that many other liberals find implausible as a matter of *justice* rather than charity.[28] The idea of a 'social minimum' floor of welfare provision is more congenial to other liberal theorists.[29] All agree, however, that the 'liberty' to die on the street through starvation or in childbirth for want of basic medical provision, or to work 10-hour shifts down a coalmine until your lungs disintegrate and you drown in emphysema, is not what modern political liberalism stands for. Choosing the life you want for yourself implies both meaningful options *and* reasonably comfortable conditions of life and adequate material resources to have a fair chance of actually realising one's aspirations. Many governments, for reasons of internal incapacity or external pressures,

---

[26] Paraphrasing J Rawls, 'Kantian Constructivism in Moral Theory' (1980) 77 *Journal of Philosophy* 517, 525. Also see R Dworkin, 'Liberalism' in his *A Matter of Principle* (Oxford, Oxford University Press, 1985).

[27] J Raz, *The Morality of Freedom* (Oxford, Oxford University Press, 1986) Part V.

[28] J Rawls, *A Theory of Justice* (Oxford, Oxford University Press, 1973) §§ 11–17 (outlining the Difference Principle).

[29] J Waldron, 'John Rawls and the Social Minimum' (1986) 3 *Journal of Applied Philosophy* 21. Further down the track, those at the libertarian end of liberalism argue for minimalist conceptions of the social minimum, eg R Nozick, *Anarchy, State and Utopia* (Oxford, Blackwell, 1974).

are apparently simply incapable of creating or sustaining the social conditions in which their citizens could lead truly autonomous lives. But where governments *can* bring about the conditions in which personal autonomy flourishes, and where this might be achieved in fair equality, governments should generally[30] strive to do so because, say liberals, (social) justice demands it.

This broad-brush sketch of liberal political morality would be seriously incomplete without mention of one additional characteristic. The ease with which the phrase 'liberal democracy' trips off the tongue is an important clue to the intimate association between the liberal's promotion of individual freedom and a distinctively democratic model of political association. True, liberty-lovers are not necessarily democrats. It is certainly possible to imagine, in theory, a liberal constitutional monarchy or benign dictatorship of liberally-minded oligarchs in which equal liberty for all and the conditions of flourishing personal autonomy were maximally promoted and safeguarded, to the extent that prevailing social conditions might permit. Notwithstanding this theoretical possibility, modern liberals (and liberal institutions[31]) endorse democratic participation and accountability as another foundational article of faith. In a democracy, 'the people' make laws for themselves. In so doing, the *demos* ingeniously combines Hobbes' solution to the riddle of legitimate political authority (liberty, in a practical sense, is actually *increased* by coercive laws that guarantee security and make 'ordinary life' possible) with the salvageable elements of Rousseau's romantic dream of spontaneous collective self-government.

This is not the place to fret about the discontents of modern representative democracies and their evident institutional weaknesses and failings (worrying though they undoubtedly are). More interesting for present purposes is the official accountability strand of liberal democracy. Liberals are weaned on the wisdom that the price of liberty is eternal vigilance. Public power in all its forms must be subject to the rule of law – because (paraphrasing Locke) where law ends, there tyranny begins. The British version of liberal constitutionalism makes an exception for the legislature: the Queen in the Mother of Parliaments wields unlimited legislative power, or so the constitutional fable goes. Other versions of liberal democracy do not concede even that, extending constitutional judicial review to primary legislation.[32] The rule of law ideal implies a raft of further derivative principles of demo-

---

[30] In truly exigent circumstances, collective self-defence and public protection may sometimes legitimately take priority over the liberty of each individual rights-bearer (heeding Justice Robert Jackson's warning that if the logic of liberty is not tempered with 'a little practical wisdom, it will convert the constitutional Bill of Rights into a suicide pact': *Terminiello v City of Chicago* 337 US 1, 37; 69 S Ct 894, 911 (1949)).

[31] The European Court of Human Rights, for example, has improvised its own basic constitutional theory according to which, 'Human rights form an integrated system for the protection of human dignity; in that connection, democracy and the rule of law have a key role to play. Democracy requires that the people should be given a role . . . [T]he rule of law cannot be sustained over a long period if persons governed by the same laws do not have the last word on the subject of their content and implementation.' *Refah Partisi (Welfare Party) v Turkey* (2002) 35 EHRR 3, [43].

[32] For a recent review of different theories and approaches, see R Weill, 'The New Commonwealth Model of Constitutionalism Notwithstanding: On Judicial Review and Constitution-Making' (2014) 62 *American Journal of Comparative Law* 127. For theoretical critique of 'strong' judicial review, see J Waldron, 'The Core of the Case Against Judicial Review' (2006) 115 *Yale Law Journal* 1346.

cratic accountability including equality before the law for officials and private persons, unhindered access to law, natural justice in fair process, and even state assistance in making legal claims and, especially, in defending oneself against accusations of criminal wrongdoing. Individual liberty is protected by (positive) legal rights and (negative) legal proscriptions of others' potentially liberty-infringing conduct. Officials are supposed to respect and uphold these rights, but if they falter – possibly through corruption or incompetence – the citizen has direct access to the courts to force compliance and seek redress, sometimes from derelict officials as well as or instead of suing primary wrongdoers. The virtuous circle of liberal self-government is thereby completed. The liberal citizen who takes her case to court is enforcing the laws that *qua* member of the *demos* she issued to herself, in service of the collective interest in preserving liberty and promoting autonomous lives, an interest in which she has her own, very personal and indivisible stake in leading a self-authored life in accordance with her own authentic preferences, projects, values and commitments.

III. Liberal Criminal Law Theory for Liberals

We have seen that liberalism is a secular political morality which, in its currently dominant deontological strains, takes individual human beings as the primary units of ethical concern and is fundamentally orientated towards safeguarding individuals' liberty and promoting their personal autonomy. It does this without denying the socially-situated nature of the self, or neglecting (what it takes to be) the appropriate demands of distributive justice. As a public philosophy of government, liberalism is committed to equal liberty, non-discrimination, freedom of thought and conscience, toleration, pluralism, democratic accountability and the rule of law. The question now becomes: what, if anything, follows from this conception of liberal political morality for criminal law and criminal law theorising?

One is tempted to say, a great many things potentially follow. A reasonably comprehensive understanding of liberal political morality's implications for criminal law would doubtless require exhaustive particularistic analyses extending, both in length and profundity, far beyond the scope of this chapter. For example, there is likely to be a fairly direct connection between the liberal's scheme of fundamental values and the types of wrongs thought appropriate for ex ante restraint and ex post public condemnation by a liberal polity's criminal law. Being founded on equal liberty, liberal criminal law should be expected to target wrongs which typically erode or destroy liberty (eg homicide,[33] slavery, kidnapping, debilitating bodily injury, theft or criminal damage of major assets) or which tend to undermine

---

[33] Strictly speaking, one's interest in continuing to be alive is a precondition for liberty rather than part of its enjoyment. So to elucidate the point more fully, one should say that liberals will be likely to think that there are good prima facie reasons to criminalise both (i) wrongs that strike at the preconditions for liberty; and (ii) wrongful infringements of liberty.

personal security, freedom of movement, or an ontologically secure sense of self (eg rape, burglary, threats and intimidation, stalking, unreasonable risk-taking), as well as wrongs that strike at the fundamental equality norm (eg racially-motivated violence, misogynistic harassment or unfair discrimination). Conversely, the liberal's existential commitment to pluralism and tolerance in matters of faith, thought and conscience should generally preclude criminalisation of – amongst other things – apostasy, blasphemy, unorthodox lifestyle choices, scientific inquiry, the free circulation of ideas (including through art and literature), and any essentially self-regarding forms of personal self-expression, such as choice of dress, hairstyle or the name to which one answers. Extended jurisprudential analysis, to elucidate well-defined criminal prohibitions with compelling all-things-considered justifications and to formulate generic liberal principles of criminalisation, cannot profitably be pursued here. But a bit more can be said about liberal criminal law in general terms, without slipping into vacuity.

An important thought for liberals is that whilst effective political authority may be necessary to preserve and indeed enhance everybody's effective sphere of liberty, political authority itself poses many direct and more indirect threats to liberty – not least through one of its most obviously coercive regulatory techniques, the criminal law. So the state and its laws are simultaneously the guarantors of individual freedom and a constant source of – old and newly improvised – threats to liberty.[34] Applied to criminal law, this thought has inspired one of liberalism's greatest contributions to theories of legitimate government, Mill's Harm Principle:[35]

> [T]he sole end for which mankind are warranted, individually or collectively, in interfering with the liberty of action of any one of their number is self-protection ... [T]he only purpose for which power can be rightfully exercised over any member of a civilised community, against his will, is to prevent harm to others. His own good, either physical or moral, is not a sufficient warrant.

Sustained critical attention by subsequent generations of scholars has identified some basic difficulties and many incidental complexities in Mill's 'one very simple principle'. One obvious difficulty is that 'interferences with liberty of action' are pervasive in the modern regulatory state, and they are justified (when they are) on a variety of grounds including the correction of historic injustices, the pursuit of social justice in contemporary society, and promoting efficient administration. 'Self-protection' is patently not the exclusive rationale for clipping freedom's wings in modern liberal democracies. A second problem is that paternalistic interventions in freedom of action are fairly commonplace, and sometimes plausibly justifiable. Indeed, good faith paternalism, untainted by cynicism or hypocrisy (of the 'this is going to hurt me more than it hurts you' stripe), actually has much to recommend

---

[34] Cf J Shklar, 'The Liberalism of Fear' in NL Rosenblum (ed), *Liberalism and the Moral Life* (Cambridge MA, Harvard University Press, 1989). Shklar's stripped-down conception of liberalism's hard political core remains – justifiably – influential, though one might better ascribe a healthy suspicion of public power and its susceptibility to abuse (which is at least as old as Juvenal's timeless question, *quis custodiet ipsos custodes?*) to practical wisdom rather than fear.
[35] JS Mill, *On Liberty* (London, Penguin, 1985; orig 1859) 68.

it.[36] Far from being seen as reasons to reject the harm principle entirely, these and similar worries have only inspired contemporary liberals to attempt to improve upon Mill's original formulation. Suitably updated, the complementary principles – that penal regulation should be a last resort[37] owing to its corrosive impact on liberty whilst, conversely, liberty-harming (or liberty-threatening) conduct is likely to present the best candidates for justified penal proscriptions – continue to inspire liberal conceptions of the moral limits of the criminal law. There is no contradiction in limiting liberty-taking conduct – now seen in its true colours as mere licence to victimise – for the sake of expanding liberty;[38] the liberty of all those (including most offenders, most of the time) who live law-abiding lives under the aegis of the rule of law.

Liberals, then, are penal minimalists – a conviction that consequentialists like Bentham shared and advocated no less fervently than modern deontological liberals.[39] A commitment to penal minimalism does not end with treating criminal law as a weapon of last resort in the government's regulatory armoury. Minimalism is, for liberals, a genuine golden thread binding together disparate chapters and departments of criminal law into a coherent normative vision.[40] Penal minimalism supplies a flexible, unified normative standard for appraising the liberal credentials of, inter alia: offence definitions in substantive criminal law; general principles of criminal liability ('the General Part', as Glanville Williams taught common lawyers to think of it[41]); the law of criminal procedure (including criminal evidence); the law and practice of sentencing and punishment; *and* the practical implementation of criminal law through policing, criminal investigations, prosecutions, trials and penal treatment, whether administered in closed custodial institutions or imposed under supervision in the community.

Legislating, interpreting, applying and enforcing criminal laws presents officials with myriad choices, some of which are – often irreducibly and quite properly – matters for the exercise of professional discretion. A liberal commitment to penal

---

[36] J Feinberg, *The Moral Limits of the Criminal Law, Volume Three: Harm to Self* (Oxford, Oxford University Press, 1986); DN Husak, 'Paternalism and Autonomy' (1981) 10 *Philosophy and Public Affairs* 27.

[37] P Minkkinen, '"If Taken in Earnest": Criminal Law Doctrine and the Last Resort' (2006) 45 *Howard Journal of Criminal Justice* 521; cf D Husak, 'The Criminal Law as Last Resort' (2004) 24 *Oxford Journal of Legal Studies* 207.

[38] Thus, Kant's doctrine of right in vindication of his 'universal law of freedom': 'if a certain use of freedom is itself a hindrance to freedom in accordance with universal laws (ie, wrong), coercion that is opposed to this (as a *hindering of a hindrance to freedom*) is consistent with freedom in accordance with universal laws, that is, it is right. Hence there is connected with right by the principle of contradiction an authorization to coerce someone who infringes upon it': I Kant, *The Metaphysics of Morals*, ed M Gregor (Cambridge, Cambridge University Press, 1996; orig 1797) (Ak 6: 232) 25.

[39] Bentham favoured 'frugality' in punishment. See eg HA Bedau, 'Bentham's Utilitarian Critique of the Death Penalty' (1983) 74 *Journal of Criminal Law and Criminology* 1033.

[40] As opposed to English law's more dubious reception of the 'one golden thread' extolled by Viscount Sankey in *Woolmington v DPP* [1935] AC 462, 481–82 (HL). See P Roberts and A Zuckerman, *Criminal Evidence*, 2nd edn (Oxford, Oxford University Press, 2010) § 1.3 and ch 6.

[41] G Williams, *Criminal Law: The General Part*, 2nd edn (London, Stevens & Sons, 1961). And see J Gardner, 'On the General Part of the Criminal Law' in A Duff (ed), *Philosophy and the Criminal Law: Principle and Critique* (Cambridge, Cambridge University Press, 1998).

minimalism calls for restraint in the exercise of criminal law powers. Thus, investigative surveillance or other forms of 'proactive policing' should adopt the least intrusive, liberty-diminishing tactics consistent with operational effectiveness and the nature of the criminality being targeted. Police powers of stop, search, arrest and temporary custodial detention should not be invoked indiscriminately, but only on the basis of reasonable suspicion proportionate to the nature and extent of any given infringement on suspects' liberty. Momentary stops or fleeting street inspections of bags or pockets require less in the way of epistemically warranted suspicion than arrest and detention in a police station for several days, but liberals still insist that even minor interferences with liberty by state officials require *some* justification. It may be bad citizenship to refuse to help the police with their inquiries, but it should not be a crime.[42] Where criminal charges are warranted, prosecutors should pursue cases to trial only on the basis of solid evidence, and there should be procedural mechanisms for screening out evidentially weak cases before the accused is formally placed at peril of conviction. Nobody's liberty should be exposed on the precipice of criminal conviction unless the prosecutor has admissible evidence capable of making a jury sure of the accused's guilt.[43] Repeat prosecutions for the same, finally adjudicated, offence cannot be tolerated as routine policy.[44] Whilst allegations of criminal wrongdoing must be taken seriously, this does not mean pursuing suspected offenders until, one way or another, a conviction is secured, on the model of Kafka's nightmares or Vyshinsky's stage-managed show trials, both powerful cautionary tales for liberals. In terms of meting out punishments to offenders, it is difficult to see how multiple prosecutions for the same offence could ever be justifiable, at least not within the same jurisdiction.[45] Whatever punishment is thought to be deserved, it should be imposed in a single proceeding. More generally, liberal penal minimalism implies that both the quantitative amount of punishment imposed, and the particular forms and styles of hard treatment selected to implement it, should infringe liberty as little as possible, consistent with prevailing theories of proportionality in sentencing and advertised penal aims.

---

[42] *Rice v Connolly* [1966] 2 QB 414, 419 (Lord Parker CJ): 'though every citizen has a moral duty or, if you like, a social duty to assist the police, there is no legal duty to that effect . . . [T]he whole basis of the common law is the right of the individual to refuse to answer questions put to him by persons in authority.'

[43] Hence, cases lacking sufficient evidence to constitute a material 'case to answer' are halted by judicial intervention, without ever reaching the jury: *R v Galbraith* [1981] 1 WLR 1039 (CA). Generally, see AL-T Choo, *Abuse of Process and Judicial Stays of Criminal Proceedings*, 2nd edn (Oxford, Oxford University Press, 2008); Roberts and Zuckerman, *Criminal Evidence*, above n 40, § 2.5.

[44] Re-prosecution is *sometimes* warranted, as where the jury fails to agree a verdict or the accused tampers with the jury. Controversial exceptions to the common law double jeopardy prohibition were introduced in England and Wales by the Criminal Justice Act 2003, Part 10: see I Dennis, 'The Criminal Justice Act 2003: Prosecution Appeals and Retrial for Serious Offences' [2004] *Criminal Law Review* 619; D Hamer, 'The Expectation of Incorrect Acquittals and the "New and Compelling Evidence" Exception to Double Jeopardy' [2009] *Criminal Law Review* 63; cf P Roberts, 'Double Jeopardy Law Reform: A Criminal Justice Commentary' (2002) 65 *Modern Law Review* 393.

[45] Note that the objection to repeat prosecutions by different 'sovereigns' rests on the injustice of being punished (allegedly) in excess of one's just deserts. The liberty-based objection is distinctively political, and operates only *within* polities, not – or at least not necessarily or straightforwardly – *between* different legal jurisdictions.

It is worth underlining how the liberty-derived principle of penal minimalism has significant implications for each of these familiar divisions and phases of criminal law and the practical administration of criminal justice; not least because criminal law theorists have tended to lavish far more attention on substantive criminal law and theories of punishment than on questions of policing, enforcement, procedure or proof. In the heartlands of criminal law theorising, the priority of liberty is put to work across the spectrum of jurisprudential issues and puzzles comprising the General Part. Imposing criminal liability in circumstances where the accused could not realistically or reasonably comply with the law's requirements will always seem suspect to liberals. This is one general objection to many forms of vicarious, accessorial or conspiracy-based criminal liability: the accused is rightly held accountable for her own conduct, but cannot be expected to be her brother's keeper – or even her child's minder in relation to most forms of criminal liability. Mens rea standards satisfied by inadvertence are viewed as problematic on similar grounds. Even if negligence may sometimes be culpable enough to warrant penal censure,[46] creating extensive criminal law duties to take care would seriously burden liberty because citizens would have to be constantly 'looking over their shoulder' to ensure that they were not inadvertently committing criminal offences, distracting them from doing whatever it is that they would otherwise prefer to be concentrating on in leading their autonomous, (partly) self-authored lives. Where negligent wrongdoing would impose pronounced or obvious risks of very serious harm (as with those who carelessly throw broken electrical appliances off railway bridges or high-rise flats), or where additional duties of care are undertaken voluntarily (eg by motorists or those who run safari parks), liberals may be content to criminalise for the sake of safeguarding potential victims' liberty. But these would be regarded as exceptional cases requiring clear justification. Strict liability offences[47] are a fortiori problematic for liberals if they imply potentially oppressive duties of advertence and compliance-monitoring in order to guard against liability – or, horror of horrors, impose criminal liability on accused who literally could not have avoided criminal censure, as may be the case with some (more often cited than sighted) 'status offences'.[48] And if criminal liability for omissions truly is 'special' from a liberal perspective,[49] it is only in the contingent sense that positive duties to act are typically more comprehensively liberty-eroding than the negative duties to forbear normally imposed by criminal prohibitions. 'Do this!' nearly always imposes a more substantial tax on personal autonomy than 'Do whatever you like, so long as

---

[46] AP Simester, 'Can Negligence be Culpable?' in J Horder (ed), *Oxford Essays in Jurisprudence*, 4th Series (Oxford, Oxford University Press, 2000); K Huigens, 'Virtue and Criminal Negligence' (1998) 1 *Buffalo Criminal LR* 431.

[47] AP Simester (ed), *Appraising Strict Liability* (Oxford, Oxford University Press, 2005); J Horder, 'Strict Liability, Statutory Construction, and the Spirit of Liberty' (2002) 118 *Law Quarterly Review* 458.

[48] The jurisprudential cause célèbre is *R v Larsonneur* (1933) 149 LT 542, discussed eg by AP Simester et al, *Simester and Sullivan's Criminal Law: Theory and Doctrine*, 5th edn (Oxford, Hart Publishing, 2013) 79, 117–18.

[49] AP Simester, 'Why Omissions are Special' (1995) 1 *Legal Theory* 311; A Ashworth, 'The Scope of Criminal Liability for Omissions' (1989) 105 *Law Quarterly Review* 424.

you don't do that!' However, one should be wary of over-generalising such contingencies. Contrary to prevailing common law assumptions, using the criminal law to impose a (near) costless duty of easy rescue of those in mortal danger would seem on its face to be consistent with a strong liberal preference for liberty. Moreover, the extent to which positive legal duties in fact impinge on personal autonomy always to some extent turns on the values, goals and projects that particular individuals have chosen to weave into their lives. It is possible, given conceivable schemes of personal values and prevailing social mores in particular political communities, that criminalising certain omissions would actually *promote* rather than burden personal autonomy, at least for the majority of citizens.

The liberty-premiss arguably has further implications for criminal law defences. Radical capacity deficits pre-empting legal responsibility should exculpate, on this view, since the infant, the automaton and the legally insane all (in their different ways) could not 'have done otherwise', rendering directives to them to respect others' liberties both pointless and unreasonable.[50] Affirmative defences like duress, as well as circumstances affording partial defences (diminished responsibility, provocation, etc), are explicable in terms of requiring citizens to tailor their choices and conduct to avoid harming other people's interests (including victims' primary interests in liberty and personal autonomy) only to the extent that can reasonably be expected of ordinary human beings with their own lives to lead, as opposed to enforcing supererogatory self-sacrifice as the juridical norm – and punishing people for failing to live up to the standards of secular sainthood. Criminal law justifications as well as excuses can be seen to cohere with liberal political morality. Self-defence, in particular, answers to the compelling human imperative of self-preservation (recall Mill's specification of the Harm Principle) in exigent circumstances where formal guarantees of legal protection for one's vital interests offer too little, because their executive enforcement would come too late. Interventions to uphold the criminal law,[51] sometimes with fatal consequences, likewise find their justification in the desirability or, on more modest accounts, the permissibility of private citizens assuming the responsibilities of law enforcement – stepping into the shoes of a police officer, because there are no actual police officers around – in the agony of the moment or when fleeting opportunity adventitiously presents itself.

---

[50]   KJM Smith and W Wilson, 'Impaired Voluntariness and Criminal Responsibility: Reworking Hart's Theory of Excuses – The English Judicial Response' (1993) 13 *Oxford Journal of Legal Studies* 69. (Note that this elaboration of the liberty-premiss into a capacity-based rationale for criminal law defences rivals more familiar, desert-based accounts of exculpation in criminal law, predicated on *blameworthiness*. 'Moral involuntariness' – whatever that might actually entail – ostensibly undercuts moral and legal responsibility in a more comprehensive fashion than exculpatory contextual excuses. See further, A Simester, 'On Justifications and Excuses' in L Zedner and JV Roberts (eds), *Principles and Values in Criminal Law and Criminal Justice: Essays in Honour of Andrew Ashworth* (Oxford, Oxford University Press, 2012); J Gardner, 'The Gist of Excuses' (1998) 1 *Buffalo Criminal Law Review* 575).

[51]   Criminal Law Act 1967, s 3. English law requires only genuine (not necessarily reasonable) belief in the need for reasonable force to prevent crime, and the defence extends to property crimes as well as to offences against the person: see eg *R v Morris* [2013] EWCA Crim 436, [2014] 1 WLR 16.

It should be evident, even from this cursory survey, that an impressive amount of contemporary criminal law doctrine can be spun out of the liberty-premiss. Substantial convergence between liberal political theory and orthodox criminal law can be viewed, in broad methodological terms, as mutual corroboration of both theory and practice. The criminal law of a liberal polity would, *ex hypothesi,* exhibit a strong preference for liberty and personal autonomy, not only in its overarching penal minimalism but also in the institutional fabric of its principal liability doctrines, theories of attribution (as manifested, for example, in legal conceptions of causation and *novus actus interveniens*) and criminal law defences; and our data, in the form of Anglo-American criminal law theory extrapolating from common law penal traditions, broadly confirm the hypothesis. We are surely on the right track in supposing that liberal criminal law is centrally concerned with securing, enlarging and preserving individual liberty. Buoyed by this rather swift analytical success, it is tempting to imagine that parsimonious liberal premisses might be substantial enough to generate comprehensive explanatory accounts of penal law and penal institutions; that liberalism could explain *everything* about the normative foundations of criminal law needed to construct cogent justifications of what can, in fact, be justified in our existing penal practices, whilst exposing the remainder to more searching critical scrutiny and remedial attention. For example, one might follow Warren Quinn[52] in trying to argue that penal law is just an institutionalised collective form of self-defence. Or one might think that criminal law doctrine is an instrument – perhaps one amongst many – for maintaining social peace under the rule of law[53] or for maximising aggregate liberty in society.[54] There are countless variations on this theme.

My view is that no such attempt to reduce criminal law theory and/or the philosophy of punishment to liberal political morality is, or can be, entirely successful. Some variants of the argument are consequentialist, and hence fall prey to well-rehearsed objections to consequentialism in general; but my scepticism in this regard extends to deontological liberalisms as well. All reductive explanations of important social institutions should be approached with a healthy dose of scepticism, if only because it seems inherently unlikely that a set of social practices as historically embedded in institutionalised traditions, richly articulated in theory and practice, symbolically loaded, emotionally charged, and frequently controversial as modern criminal law will be satisfactorily explained by appealing to just one or two simple ideas or values. Of course, any useful theoretical model must necessarily be a lot simpler than the reality it represents. Simplification is inherent to *modelling.* However, good models or explanatory theories should emphasise key features and avoid distorting over-simplification. Liberal theory strikes me as

---

[52] W Quinn, 'The Right to Threaten and the Right to Punish' (1985) 14 *Philosophy & Public Affairs* 327.

[53] H Gross, *A Theory of Criminal Justice* (New York, Oxford University Press, 1979).

[54] J Braithwaite and P Pettit, *Not Just Deserts: A Republican Theory of Criminal Justice* (Oxford, Oxford University Press, 1990); A Sanders, R Young and M Burton, *Criminal Justice,* 4th edn (Oxford, Oxford University Press, 2010) 47–56.

suffering from two significant limitations in its efforts to rationalise criminal law. The first I call the problem of incompleteness; the second is the problem of indeterminacy.

IV. Two Theoretical Limitations: Incompleteness and Indeterminacy

Liberal theory, I suggest, is materially incomplete in its critical resources for understanding contemporary criminal law. Significant areas of theoretical incompleteness include the following three: liberal theory does not have its own distinctive or fully elucidated theory of moral agency; it offers no justificatory rationale for criminal prohibitions that are not concerned with protecting liberal values; and it cannot explain retributive justice as the ground of justified punishment for criminal wrongdoers.

Liberal theory is also materially indeterminate, in the sense that it seldom offers comprehensive or unequivocal guidance to policy-makers, legislators, judges, lawyers, or other criminal justice practitioners and officials who aspire to principled decision-making when confronted with difficult choices in their professional lives. Liberal political theory may address relevant practical issues (it is not *incomplete* in the first sense of theoretical omission) and supply a valuable intellectual framework for structuring normative reasoning, but its logic runs out, or becomes tangled or equivocal, before determinate solutions to practical problems can be ascertained. Assuming that the exhaustion of liberal theory does not coincide with the limits of normative rationality,[55] policy-makers and practitioners must then look beyond liberalism for practical normative guidance. The problem of indeterminacy is not supposed to represent a criticism of liberal theory per se, but rather draws attention to its pronounced limitations *as a resource for theorising criminal law*.

These are large theoretical claims, which I cannot even attempt to vindicate here. But the general tenor of each strand of argument can be drawn out far enough to indicate its potential significance for Criminal Law Theory and to provide some concrete illustrations of practical payoffs for criminal jurisprudence, policy-making and the practice of criminal law.

A. The problem of incompleteness

It is vital, first, to distinguish between *liberal theories* of agency and theories of agency that may well be compatible with liberalism. The liberal agent, we have seen,

---

[55] Ie the point where normative reasons run out entirely and decision-makers are entitled to indulge their own subjective preferences untrammelled by any institutional constraint. I surmise that criminal justice officials never have such complete discretion, or that it applies only to matters of complete normative indifference, like the prosecutor's favourite perfume or the judge's choice of socks.

is a concretely-situated autonomous self-author of his own life; or (as Marx almost said) an individual who makes his own life but not in material circumstances of his own choosing (and *ceteris paribus* people who live in liberal polities lead more autonomous lives than those who don't). Framed within the broader sweep of western thought, the model of the choosing self, endowed with free will and capable of making up its own mind about what to do and how to live, evidently predates liberalism by millennia. Liberalism is distinctive in propounding a normative conception of autonomy (one which would have been bewildering to the ancients), but this is projected onto a much older conception of human agency; a conception which (to my knowledge) has been shared by most non-liberals throughout history, and continues to represent the 'common sense view' embraced by modern criminal justice systems around the world. Thus, a theocratic polity might pass emphatically illiberal laws – eg designating apostasy or adultery as crimes punishable by death – but this does not necessarily imply a different conception of moral agency to that presupposed by liberals. The criminal law of this theocratic polity might well excuse infants and the insane from criminal liability on grounds of lack of capacity, prefer advertent standards of culpability to criminalising negligence, eschew strict liability, permit proportionate self-defence and exigent private law enforcement, and so forth, in much the same way *and for much the same reasons* as liberal states. The theocratic state passes illiberal criminal laws because it rejects the liberal's secular premiss: state criminal law must conform to its god's will, and crimes against god cannot be tempered by secular mercy – lest the souls of god's obedient servants in government should be damned alongside the abandoned souls of criminals. There is certainly a disagreement with liberalism here – but it is located exactly where one should expect to find it, in liberal *political theory* (or in *theology*, from the opposite perspective), rather than in rival conceptions of moral agency. Theories of agency, extending into theorising about criteria of attribution in criminal law, are pre-eminently topics for metaphysics and practical ethics. Most, if not all, of the analytical and normative work has already been done before we get to political theory in the strict sense. Given that the prevailing conception of moral agency in modern criminal law is not merely consistent with liberal political premisses, but in fact coheres with them perfectly (which still does not make it *a liberal theory* of moral agency), this traditional division of philosophical labour and its (implicit) translation into criminal jurisprudence should not disconcert liberals.

A second strand of incompleteness relates to ascertaining the justified moral limits of the criminal law. We have seen that the Millian move from liberty to Harm Principle is both slick – almost frictionless in its intellectual progress – and impressively fecund in accounting for a significant chunk of modern criminal law. It can hardly be doubted that a great many criminal law prohibitions, in liberal and non-liberal polities alike, target actual or threated harms *qua* set-backs to individuals' interests, including their primary interests in liberty and personal autonomy. Other familiar kinds of criminal prohibitions, including corrupting public officials and offences against the administration of justice, can be justified by extension, as necessary safeguards for the integrity of public institutions which are themselves necessary to protect individuals' primary interests. Theorists who have embarked upon systematic inquiries into the moral limits of the criminal law have discovered, however, that sooner or later the Harm Principle's bountiful theoretical well runs dry.[56] Particular prohibitions either defy rationalisation in distinctively liberal terms, or the intellectual contortions required to achieve theoretical reconciliation seem both extravagant and anyway ultimately fail to capture the essence of the prohibition under examination; not so much a successful explanation of puzzling phenomena, as a pyrrhic victory for changing the subject. You can say, for example, that the reason for criminalising cruelty to animals is that animal abusers have a habit of graduating to hurting humans; or that criminalising grave desecration retrospectively harms the deceased, or inflicts psychological harm on the living, or is really anyway a property crime harming the owner of the land. But a better explanation is probably that these actions are morally wrongful, and the wrong supplies a prima facie reason for criminalisation irrespective of any more or less tendentious connection to a living person's liberty interest.[57]

A variant of this argument, which overlaps with criminal law theorists' discussions of 'fair labelling',[58] extends to legislative strategies for individuating offences in positive criminal law. Why distinguish 'rape' from 'sexual assault', or 'grievous bodily harm' from 'actual bodily harm', or 'murder' from 'manslaughter', etc? Why not have a single offence of, say, 'physical assault' and mark gradations of seriousness and culpability through differential sentencing? Why not collapse the distinction between sexual and non-sexual assaults into a single category of unconsented bodily intrusion? This kind of proposal has recommended itself to those who insist that rape and other sexual assaults are more about violence than sex,[59] and that the

---

[56] Recall that Joel Feinberg's epic quadrilogy exploring *The Moral Limits of the Criminal Law* contains just one book on the Harm Principle (*Volume One: Harm to Others* (Oxford, Oxford University Press, 1984)), and three more exploring other candidate principles of criminalisation: *Volume Two: Offense to Others* (Oxford, Oxford University Press, 1985); *Volume Three: Harm to Self* (Oxford, Oxford University Press, 1986); and *Volume Four: Harmless Wrongdoing* (Oxford, Oxford University Press, 1988).

[57] The argument here, I should stress, is simply that a plausible rationale for criminalising wanton cruelty to animals cannot be derived from the liberal's liberty-premiss. The fact that there are special welfarist and humanitarian reasons for protecting non-human sentient life forms, which do not apply to inanimate objects or cultural artefacts, is beside the point. Many people – including many non-liberals, and some non-deontological liberals such as P Singer, *Animal Liberation*, 2nd edn (London, Pimlico, 1995) – share the strong intuitions that animals should not suffer needlessly, and that deliberately harming animals for no good reason is evil. However, nobody – to my knowledge – argues that non-human animals can and should lead autonomous lives in the Razian sense, nor that *this* supplies the justification for criminalising harm to animals. In short, the evil of wanton cruelty to animals is not explained by liberal political theory.

[58] J Chalmers and F Leverick, 'Fair Labelling in Criminal Law' (2008) 71 *Modern Law Review* 217; G Williams, 'Convictions and Fair Labelling' (1983) 42 *Cambridge Law Journal* 85; AJ Ashworth, 'The Elasticity of Mens Rea' in CFH Tapper (ed), *Crime, Proof and Punishment: Essays in Memory of Sir Rupert Cross* (London, Butterworths, 1981).

[59] On the politics of competing legislative programmes, see A Gruber, 'Rape, Feminism and the War on Crime' (2009) 84 *Washington Law Review* 581; SH Pillsbury, 'Crimes Against the Heart: Recognizing the Wrongs of Forced Sex' (2002) 35 *Loyola of Los Angeles Law Review* 845. And see J Gardner and S Shute, 'The Wrongness of Rape' in J Horder (ed), *Oxford Essays in Jurisprudence: 4th Series* (Oxford, Oxford University Press, 2000); N Lacey, 'Unspeakable Subjects, Impossible Rights: Sexuality, Integrity and Criminal Law' (1998) 11 *Canadian Journal of Law & Jurisprudence* 47.

criminal law should reflect and clearly signal that reality. Purely institutional reasons can be advanced to try to explain criminal law's traditional taxonomies of offences. For example, it might be said that different gradations of offence seriousness are needed to allocate proceedings to the appropriate level of trial venue – a particularly important consideration in common law jurisdictions, where the hallowed, but comparatively expensive, trial by jury is reserved for the most serious, 'indictable' offences. But again, the ingenuity of these rationalisations either runs out or fails, ultimately, to provide satisfactory explanations for institutionally embedded practices. It proves to be very difficult to dispense with the thought that a primary goal of criminal prohibitions is to track moral wrongs, or sometimes to create them.[60] Yet liberalism cannot claim any monopoly of wisdom across the panoramic vista of moral wrongdoing. Such light as can be shed on the problem of evil must be found in the entire canon of western philosophy, theology and literature, increasingly now in dialogue with global philosophical traditions. Liberals will naturally have their own distinctive 'take' on these intellectual resources; and the solace of philosophical modesty can be taken with no obvious political strings attached. Granted that (some) wrongs supply prima facie reasons for criminalisation, liberals will not accept all-things-considered arguments without running candidate prohibitions through liberal political filters, starting with the strong liberal commitment to penal minimalism and the presumption that criminal law should be the last resort. All that being said, liberal political morality contains no comprehensive institutional or principled objection to any and every conceivable non-liberal equality-derived criminal prohibition. If, plausibly, torturing animals for fun is evil and there is no good reason to do it; and if, again plausibly, there are no comprehensive institutional objections to criminalising (serious, intentional) harm to animals for sadistic pleasure, then liberal states a fortiori plausibly should criminalise sadistic cruelty to animals. Liberalism cannot authorise this conclusion without theoretical and normative reinforcements; which it is able to muster precisely because liberals' ethical theories of the good are richer, broader and in some sense[61] anterior to liberalism's theories of good government and legitimate political authority.

A third area of theoretical incompleteness concerns liberal conceptions of punishment; a problem located in 'penal theory' or the philosophy of punishment, whether conceived as a specialist department of Criminal Law Theory or possibly as a distinct, though obviously still very closely related, sub-specialism. To complain that liberalism lacks a convincing account of retributive justice will admittedly not cut any ice with theorists who regard retributivism as an antediluvian moral error

---

[60] Positive criminal law creates new, more particularistic moral wrongs by concretising general moral prohibitions. Thus, driving on the right hand side of the road is not immoral unless and until state law decrees that everybody must drive on the left.

[61] I am not propounding an excessively rigid, and consequently fallacious, distinction between personal ethics and collective morality. The two are patently merged or integrated in mature theories of political morality, including theories of liberal democracy. This does not imply that the entire sphere of personal ethics collapses into political morality – a normative proposition that liberals, in particular, emphatically deny.

or those who think that the long-running (and now rather stylised) dispute in penal theory between 'utilitarians' and 'retributivists' is either hopelessly stalemated or can be made to disappear with a bit of fancy philosophical prestidigitation.[62] My own view is that no theory of punishment can fully succeed, either as sociologically accurate description or as philosophically cogent normative justification, unless it engages with the ethics of retribution at the level of practical detail and psycho-social complexity that we find, for example, in Michael Moore's illuminating studies.[63]

Retribution, needless to say, is a much older idea than liberalism. It is shot through with theological resonance and associated, historically, with barbaric and inhumane forms of penal sanction, some of which make 'an eye for an eye' look positively genteel.[64] Many liberals instinctively and understandably want to dissociate themselves from this historical and theological legacy. It does not follow that objections to barbaric punishments are distinctively liberal. Enlightened despots as much as liberal democrats might strive to rid their criminal laws of wanton cruelty and inhumanity. English law dispensed with amputation, branding and disembowelment as punishments long before most people were democratically enfranchised. So – reprising a pattern of argumentation utilised before – the fact that liberals are committed to respecting human dignity should not be confused with the misapprehension that respect for human dignity is peculiar to liberal political morality. Most modern political philosophies claim to respect human dignity; issue is then joined over how exactly human dignity should be respected, and with what further institutional implications, in the arenas of political theory and policy debate. Liberals naturally put a liberal spin on protecting human dignity, prioritising individual liberty in ways and to an extent that non-liberals often find problematic. But those, say, who in good faith advocate criminal prohibitions on paternalistic grounds are not, generally speaking, fairly characterised as disparaging human dignity. The criminal law paternalist is more aptly described as somebody with a different, competing conception of human dignity; or a different understanding of the implications of human dignity for legitimate criminalisation.

Puncturing liberals' proprietorial pretensions regarding humane punishments is barely half the theoretical story. The central plotlines must attempt to reconcile

---

[62] See, eg, MN Berman, 'Two Kinds of Retributivism' in RA Duff and SP Green, *Philosophical Foundations of Criminal Law* (New York, Oxford University Press, 2011); PH Robinson, 'The Ongoing Revolution in Punishment Theory: Doing Justice as Controlling Crime' (2011) 42 *Arizona State Law Journal* 1089; G Binder, 'Punishment Theory: Moral or Political?' (2002) 5 *Buffalo Criminal Law Review* 321.

[63] MS Moore, 'The Moral Worth of Retribution' in F Schoeman (ed), *Responsibility, Character and the Emotions* (Cambridge, Cambridge University Press, 1987). Also see, eg, WI Miller, *Eye for an Eye* (New York, Cambridge University Press, 2006); JG Murphy, *Getting Even: Forgiveness and its Limits* (New York, Oxford University Press, 2003); JG Murphy and J Hampton, *Forgiveness and Mercy* (Cambridge, Cambridge University Press, 1988); KD Rutledge, 'Giving the Devil his Due: The Pursuit and Capture of Nazi War Criminals – A Call for Retributive Justice in International Criminal Law' (2005) 3 *Regent Journal of International Law* 27.

[64] M Foucault, *Discipline and Punish: The Birth of the Prison*, transl A Sheridan (London, Penguin, 1991) Part I. And see www.torturamuseum.com/index.html.

retributivism with liberal political morality – a philosophical tale which, I recognise, may require the suspension of widespread disbelief. This narrative is not entirely unknown to penal theory:[65] but concerted examination of the relationship between liberalism and retributivism has been isolated and infrequent relative to the oceans of ink devoted to theorising about punishment, and I do not think that anybody has yet made very substantial progress in producing a fully integrated theory of liberal retribution. If and when such a theory appears, it will be heavily indebted to a much older philosophical tradition that, for many centuries before and after the emergence of liberalism in modern western political thought, has been trying to explain when, why and how much punishment is deserved. The indispensability of these theoretical supplements reinforces the methodological limitations of liberal political theory for theorising penal law.

B. The problem of indeterminacy

The previous section identified areas of criminal law theory and the philosophy of punishment that liberal political theory does not reach. The problem of indeterminacy arises in relation to questions that liberal political theory *does* address but does not fully answer, in the sense of providing comprehensive normative guidance to policy-makers and practitioners. Liberal theory, in other words, *under-determines* criminal justice policy and practice. Indeterminacy of this kind is a general feature of the relationship between political theorising and practical action, and not something that should be regarded as a peculiar defect of liberalism. A parallel methodological stricture would constrain adherents of any other, non-liberal or illiberal political philosophy.

One kind of indeterminacy was hinted at previously, when it was noted that liberals' love of individual liberty goes hand-in-hand with tolerant pluralism in matters of freedom of thought, conscience and religion. Suppose, however, that a planned religious rally is expected to erupt into violence at the cost of many lives. Should the liberal state ban the rally to preserve the lives and liberties of potential victims, freedom of religion notwithstanding? Or should the lives that will be lost be regarded as regrettable but unavoidable collateral damage incidental to discharging the state's more pressing duty to vindicate a fundamental liberal right of religious expression? These kinds of practical tensions within the liberal scheme of fundamental values go right down to the root of Hobbes' ingenious solution to the paradox of legitimate liberal government. Leviathan enhances individual liberty by guaranteeing collective security. But if individual liberty for all but the most brutish and nasty would be exceedingly impoverished and short-lived once ever deprived of the state's security blanket, wouldn't just about any less-than-debilitating or more or less temporary sacrifice of liberty seem justified in order to keep that security blanket in place? Isn't the problem with pinning our hopes for liberty on

[65] P Butler, 'Retribution, For Liberals' (1999) 46 *UCLA Law Review* 1873; J Hampton, 'Retribution and the Liberal State' (1994) 5 *Journal of Contemporary Legal Issues* 117.

security just that security always wins out in a crisis; and that Leviathan could actually start behaving like a despot, even whilst wearing the mask of majoritarian democracy and adhering to its institutional forms and graces?

In rehearsing these deep theoretical tensions in political liberalism, I do not mean to imply that its critical resources are completely impotent, in criminal justice policy-making or in political debate more generally. On the contrary: liberal political theory has considerable normative purchase and rhetorical force in polities like the United Kingdom, which publicly subscribes to liberal political orthodoxies and likes to regard itself as a haven of liberal freedom and tolerance, but frequently appears to forget its official philosophical allegiances when it comes to legislating new criminal laws, developing penal policies, extending police powers of surveillance and investigation, or reforming criminal procedure to make it easier to convict more villains.[66] In the area of counter-terrorism, for example, 'security' has been trotted out as the all-purpose rationale for authorising extended periods of police custody and introducing post-charge questioning,[67] reliance on secret evidence in contested legal proceedings,[68] detention without trial, intrusive forms of surveillance and restrictions on liberty for terrorist suspects who have not been convicted of any offence,[69] and legislating new prophylactic criminal offences of extraordinary breadth and highly attenuated connections to anticipated harms.[70] None of this, however, reflects any deep tension in liberal political ideals, because the kind of terrorism at which these measures are aimed does not truly present any existential threat to collective security or 'the life of the nation'.[71] It is only the pro-

---

[66] See eg Ministry of Justice White Paper, *Swift and Sure Justice: The Government's Plans for Reform of the Criminal Justice System* (Cm 8388, 2012); Home Office Review, *Rebalancing the Criminal Justice System in Favour of the Law-Abiding Majority* (London, Home Office, 2006); Home Office, *Respect and Responsibility – Taking a Stand Against Anti-Social Behaviour* (Cm 5778, 2003); Criminal Justice System White Paper, *Justice for All* (Cm 5563, 2002). For critical (and overtly pessimistic) discussion, see M Tonry, *Punishment and Politics* (Cullompton, Willan Publishing, 2004); P Pettit, 'Is Criminal Justice Politically Feasible?' (2002) 5 *Buffalo Criminal Law Review* 427; D Garland, *The Culture of Control* (Oxford, Oxford University Press, 2001); A Ashworth, 'Is The Criminal Law A Lost Cause?' (2000) 116 *Law Quarterly Review* 225.

[67] Counter-Terrorism Act 2008, s 22; C Walker, 'Post-Charge Questioning of Suspects' [2008] *Criminal Law Review* 509.

[68] Justice and Security Act 2013, Part 2; *Tariq v Home Office* [2011] UKSC 35, [2012] 1 AC 452; *Al Rawi v Security Service* [2011] UKSC 34, [2012] 1 AC 531; *R (Roberts) v Parole Board* [2005] UKHL 45, [2005] 2 AC 738 (the applicant's position in *Roberts* being described by Lord Steyn, dissenting at [95]–[96], as 'Kafkaesque').

[69] Terrorism Prevention and Investigation Measures Act 2011 ('TPIMs'), superseding the Prevention of Terrorism Act 2005 (control orders), which in turn replaced the Anti-Terrorism, Crime and Security Act 2001, Part 4 (indefinite detention without trial). For discussion, see D Dyzenhaus, 'Preventive Justice and the Rule-of-Law Project' in A Ashworth, L Zedner and P Tomlin (eds), *Prevention and the Limits of the Criminal Law* (Oxford, Oxford University Press, 2013); L Zedner, 'Preventive Justice or Pre-Punishment? The Case of Control Orders' (2007) 60 *Current Legal Problems* 174.

[70] A Ashworth and L Zedner, 'Just Prevention: Preventive Rationales and the Limits of the Criminal Law' in RA Duff and SP Green (eds), *Philosophical Foundations of Criminal Law* (New York, Oxford University Press, 2011); J Hodgson and V Tadros, 'How to Make a Terrorist Out of Nothing' (2009) 72 *Modern Law Review* 984.

[71] Although a majority of their Lordships in *A v Home Secretary* [2005] 2 AC 68, [2004] UKHL 56 refused to second-guess the minister's judgement in this matter, Lord Hoffmann was surely right when he insisted, dissenting at [96], that 'Whether we would survive Hitler hung in the balance, but there is

saic case of governments, running scared before the twin-scourge of a volatile elec-
torate and the Murdoch press, choosing to sacrifice the liberty of a few for an illusion
of security for the many. The political calculation is all the easier when the few who
bear the brunt are foreigners (like the Belmarsh detainees) or numerically small
minority groups (predominantly non-white muslims) – even though discriminating against minorities in this way, albeit more careless than intentional, betrays
fundamental liberal values. Similarly pointed liberal critiques could be levelled
against recent legislation and operational policy in relation to the routine administration of criminal justice, including such dubious policing practices as indiscriminate public surveillance[72] and an over-extended National DNA Database,[73] not to
mention concerted efforts to re-brand criminality as 'anti-social behaviour' so that
it can be regulated more effectively (along with troublesome behaviour that is not
actually criminal) without having to comply with liberal principles of criminalisation or traditional due process guarantees.[74] Projected against this policy backcloth,
reassertion of orthodox liberal principles and criticism of government's illiberal
tendencies might appear almost radical.

   The indeterminacy of liberal political theory is exposed, not in cases of policy-
makers' ignorance, miscalculation or bad faith (involving institutional failings or
betrayals of liberal principles), but in practical situations where liberal commitments provide seemingly conflicted guidance or at least fail to indicate an unequivocally desirable course of action. Examples are legion: almost any randomly chosen
volume of the *Criminal Appeal Reports* would supply pertinent illustrations.
Consider this question of trial procedure which recently confronted the English
Crown Court:[75] should a defendant be permitted to wear the *niqab*, covering her
head and face except for her eyes, whilst standing trial for a criminal offence?
Muslim women are instructed by the Koran to dress modestly,[76] and some – by no

no doubt that we shall survive Al-Qaeda . . . Terrorist violence, serious as it is, does not threaten our
institutions of government or our existence as a civil community.' For general discussion of the liberty/
security nexus see J Waldron, *Torture, Terror and Trade-offs: Philosophy for the White House* (Oxford,
Oxford University Press, 2010).

   [72] B von Silva-Tarouca Larsen, *Setting the Watch: Privacy and the Ethics of CCTV Surveillance* (Oxford,
Hart Publishing, 2011); A von Hirsch, 'The Ethics of Public Television Surveillance' in A von Hirsch,
D Garland and A Wakefield (eds), *Ethical and Social Perspectives on Situational Crime Prevention* (Oxford,
Hart Publishing, 2000).

   [73] L Campbell, 'A Rights-based Analysis of DNA Retention: "Non-conviction" Databases and the
Liberal State' [2010] *Criminal Law Review* 889.

   [74] A von Hirsch and AP Simester (eds), *Incivilities: Regulating Offensive Behaviour* (Oxford, Hart
Publishing, 2006); A Ashworth, 'Social Control and "Anti-Social Behaviour": The Subversion of Human
Rights' (2004) 120 *Law Quarterly Review* 263.

   [75] *R v D (R)*, Transcript of Ruling by HHJ Peter Murphy at Blackfriars Crown Court, 16 September
2013 (*Judgment of HHJ Peter Murphy in Relation to Wearing of Niqaab by Defendant During Proceedings
in Crown Court.*) The Canadian Supreme Court in *R v NS* [2012] 3 SCR 726 had recently addressed the
related, but distinct, question of whether *witnesses* should be allowed to testify veiled in criminal trials.
Judge Murphy treated the question as a matter of first impression, with 'no authority directly on point
in our domestic law' (at [9]).

   [76] The *hijab* (concealing, covering up), Koran 24:31 (transl Yusuf Ali) ('And say to the believing
women that they should lower their gaze and guard their modesty; that they should not display their
beauty and ornaments except what (must ordinarily) appear thereof; that they should draw their veils
over their bosoms and not display their beauty except to their husbands.')

means all – versions of Islam interpret this injunction as requiring women to appear veiled in public. To the extent that wearing a veil is treated as a requirement of religious observance, the liberal's foundational commitment to pluralism and tolerance most especially in matters of religious freedom speaks strongly in favour of allowing the *niqab* to be worn in legal proceedings. Moreover, Muslim women often say that wearing the veil and dressing 'modestly' makes them feel safer and more secure in their person, enhancing their liberty and personal autonomy. This consideration takes on an important additional dimension in the context of defending a criminal charge, since requiring the accused to remove the *niqab* in court might conceivably inhibit her ability to mount an effective defence. She might, for example, be too embarrassed or intimidated to testify properly in her own defence, or to testify at all. Finally, liberals supposedly celebrate personal choice and self-expression, especially in relation to those choices that have a significant bearing on personal identity and 'the presentation of self in everyday life',[77] at least so long as these choices do not interfere with anybody else's rights. If a defendant wants to wear the *niqab* in court, or anywhere else in public, why should she be denied her right to present herself to the world as she sees fit?

One response is that we do not, in fact, have an unqualified right to present ourselves to the world as we see fit. Dangerous or offensive clothing may in general be proscribed, and a fortiori wearing such items in a courtroom. The defendant who turns up to court in a t-shirt bearing an offensive slogan will be told to take it off; the naturist who finds clothing inhibiting and prefers to appear au naturel will nonetheless be instructed to cover up in the dock. Forms of (un)dress conventionally regarded as offensive or disturbing are not tolerated, partly because of their reciprocal adverse effects on unwilling[78] viewers' personal autonomy, partly because they do not comport with the solemnity of the occasion. But does the *niqab* offend? Plainly, it does offend some people; but not, I think, on grounds that should trouble conscientious liberals. Some people are offended because they confuse Islamic dress with anti-western feeling, threats to traditional western institutions or ways of life, unwanted immigration or even terrorism. Since these associations are tenuous, contingent and – often – merely imagined, creatures of ignorance and suspicion, they pose no serious philosophical challenge to liberal tolerance and pluralism. It might be said that overt displays of religious affiliation implying 'foreign' allegiances, especially those which are highly visible because they depart from locally prevailing conventions of suitable habiliment, have no place in the public life of a secular democracy. It is for something like this reason that the French have 'banned the *burqa*'.[79] Notice, however, that the French ban arises from a republican sense of unity

---

[77] Cf E Goffman, *The Presentation of Self in Everyday Life* (London, Penguin, 1990; orig 1959).

[78] Recall that witnesses and jurors appear in court under compulsion, whilst judges and lawyers are only doing their job and can reasonably expect safe and wholesome working conditions.

[79] A Chrisafis, 'French Veil Ban: First Woman Fined for Wearing Niqab', *The Guardian*, 12 April 2011; *R (B) v Home Secretary* [2013] EWHC 2281 (Admin). Cf the position in Turkey, where restrictions on wearing religious dress in public have been regarded as logical outgrowths of the founding principles of Kemalist secular nationhood. Fear of foreigners does not come into it. Also see *Şahin v Turkey* (2007) 44 EHRR 5, ECtHR (GC).

in social solidarity, and as such reflects – if not, strictly, an illiberal impulse – then at least a corporatist or communitarian strain inflecting the French conception of liberalism. Neither inflection nor ban are themselves products of liberalism, which should be expected to prioritise pluralistic religious freedom – at least up to the point at which religious dissent poses an existential threat to the preservation of social peace or the life of the nation. But nobody is arguing that allowing female Muslims to wear the *niqab* in court might bring the British state to its knees or precipitate bloody revolution.

Another reason for objecting to the *niqab* might be that it is a visible symbol of patriarchy which celebrates women's oppression and demeans their subjectivity, thereby striking at the root of the liberal equality norm. Permitting defendants to appear so attired in a key, highly visible public institution like the criminal trial, it might be argued, amounts to state collusion in women's oppression, just as if the accused were permitted to come to court sporting a t-shirt bearing an offensive misogynist slogan. Liberals would have no difficulty denouncing, and intervening to prevent, *coerced* religious dress. However, the Koran specifically prohibits forced compliance with any aspect of *hijab*,[80] and the vast majority of Muslim women who take the veil (including western converts) insist that doing so is their own voluntary choice. This inconvenient empirical truth lands liberals on the horns of a dilemma. The first horn is labelled 'false consciousness': Muslim women may *say* they freely choose the veil, but this only goes to demonstrate the comprehensiveness of their disempowerment and oppression. These women have so completely internalised the oppressor's values that they now speak in the self-negating voice of patriarchy! The problem with all false-consciousness arguments is that they invariably prove far too much. In philosophical debate, 'false consciousness' tends to degenerate into 'anything I do not agree with'; in political practice, false consciousness leads to places liberals should never want to go. So it is tempting to veer towards the second horn of the dilemma, labelled *pour décourager les autres*. Granted now that *niqab* wearers really do freely choose the veil, won't the image of females appearing in court covered up in black from head to toe send out very bad messages about women's bondage and inferiority to other citizens, including non-Muslims and those far less sophisticated in their interpretation of curial imagery than the *niqab* wearers themselves? Isn't regulation demure clothing leaving only the wearer's eyes visible to the world all of a piece with the litany of historical and contemporary ways in which women and girls have been silenced, effaced, deformed and oppressed, denied full citizenship and excluded from political power – the relatively mild end of all-too-familiar practices extending to domestic violence, foot-binding, genital mutilation, suttee and all the rest?[81] Perhaps it will; perhaps it is. The problem for

[80] 'Let there be no compulsion in religion' (Koran 2: 256). The Muslim Council of Britain interprets this injunction to imply that 'although *Hijab* is certainly an integral part of the overall Islamic dress code, it is not for anyone to force it upon another human being' (as quoted in *R v D (R)*, above n 75, [19]).
[81] N Walter, *Living Dolls: The Return of Sexism* (London, Virago, 2010); M Hester, L Kelly and Jill Radford (eds), *Women, Violence and Male Power* (Buckingham, Open University Press, 1996); J Radford and DEH Russell, *Femicide: The Politics of Woman Killing* (Buckingham, Open University Press, 1992); N Wolf, *The Beauty Myth* (London, Vintage, 1991); CA MacKinnon, *Feminism Unmodified: Discourses on*

liberals is that many similar personal choices plausibly carry analogous risks. If we are to be prevented from exercising our choices in predominantly self-regarding matters of personal taste and preference, not because of any harm or risk that we ourselves pose but simply because careless observers might get the wrong idea, then individual liberty would always be hostage to the censure of – possibly ignorant or bigoted – public opinion. This is not a road that liberals have been inclined to travel, since Mill clearly signalled its propensity to become a liberty-eroding slippery slope.[82]

To this point, liberal political theory has seemingly generated rich and powerful critical resources for addressing the problem of the *niqab* wearing defendant. Potential arguments for demanding that criminal accused appear in court unveiled were smartly refuted by authentically liberal rejoinders. Even if certain objections plausibly gain more traction in liberal political morality (eg modest variants of the 'false consciousness' or 'bad example' arguments might fly if they could be adequately constrained by competing principles), it is difficult to see how such considerations could be sufficiently weighty to trump the liberal's foundational commitment to religious tolerance and pluralism. That liberal principles have taken us this far confirms that the *niqab*-wearing defendant does not present a problem of theoretical incompleteness of the kind identified in the previous section. Rather, we have reached the point of theoretical exhaustion where the indeterminacy of liberal theory is revealed in practice.

Suppose that a defendant wanted to wear a full-face crash helmet in court, which, with the visor up, would leave exactly the same strip of face and eyes visible to the observer as the *niqab*. The helmet itself is completely plain black and un-offensive (like the *niqab*), the defendant has a sincere and strong desire to wear it in court (she is not faking or playing for time),[83] and the motivation for her desire is not per se institutionally problematic in the sense of being incompatible with the nature and solemnity of the proceedings, eg she is not wearing the crash helmet in order to express her rejection of the court's authority or as ironic commentary on the state's – metaphorical or literal – predilection for bashing people over the head. Let us also assume that the accused's identity can be verified in a mutually acceptable fashion.[84] Of course, a trial court would not hesitate: this defendant would simply be ordered to remove the crash helmet without a moment's concern for her liberal freedom to choose what to wear; and this even though she would be perfectly at liberty to appear in court (albeit doubtless against defence counsel's advice) with green hair, or a nose ring, or in the costume of a Jedi knight (having surrendered her lightsaber

---

Life and Law (Cambridge MA, Harvard University Press, 1988).

[82] For a modern restatement, see A von Hirsch, 'Extending the Harm Principle: "Remote" Harms and Fair Imputation' in AP Simester and ATH Smith (eds), *Harm and Culpability* (Oxford, Oxford University Press, 1996).

[83] Perhaps the accused is suffering from some kind of delusion or phobia (which would have to be consistent with legal fitness to plead).

[84] This was achieved in *R v D (R)*, above n 75, by having a female police officer confirm the accused's identity in private during a short adjournment.

to security). The discriminating factor is that *we expect to see people's faces in court.*
More specifically, it is the firm expectation of our legal trial process that the faces of
all of the courtroom participants – judge, jurors, lawyers and witnesses, as well as
the accused – will be visible, both to the court (including the fact-finder) and to the
public.

If we inquire further why it is that our inherited trial procedures place such great
store beside face-to-face encounters we would doubtless find that the story is long,
complicated and in several chapters obscure and contested. We would certainly
discover that it cannot be told only within the confines and restricted to the intellectual resources of liberal political theory. Some of the reasons why 'face' is so
important in criminal trials relate to broader social conventions and cultural styles
supplying readymade 'scripts' for meaningful human interaction. Not for nothing
do we unselfconsciously refer to 'saving face' or 'losing face', extol the virtues of
dealing face-to-face, summon the courage to face our demons, or rail at faceless
wonders. These commonplace expressions are symptomatic of deeply held convictions about how we should assess the character and behaviour of other people, how
we should present ourselves to the world so that favourable impressions of us may
be formed, and how social bonds of mutual trust can be cultivated as a basis for ongoing cooperation in myriad spheres, dealings and relationships across all walks of
life. Human (self-) recognition in the 'face' of the Other has been characterised as
the generative precondition of all ethical conduct.[85] If that seems extravagant as a
metaethical claim, few in the West would deny the importance of 'showing your
face' if you want your interests to count, or of showing *by* your face that you mean
business and should be taken seriously. Face up, and face facts: the human face, in
our culture, is a loquacious site of personal expression and social communication
(and those who are incapable of reading faces consequently incur the penalties of
being socially maladroit).

Overlaid on these deeply embedded psycho-social conventions are additional
institutional investments peculiar to criminal proceedings. An intriguing feature of
these supervening institutional practices and expectations is that they tend to be
quite specific and even idiosyncratic to particular legal cultures and procedural traditions. Over time, working legal systems have improvised their own distinctive
variations on the shared western cultural investment in facial recognition.
Moreover, these concretised institutional forms typically become freighted and
infused with further layers of meaning, so that they end up standing for more – possibly, a great deal more – than their instrumental function or formal institutional
history might suggest to the uninitiated. Consider Magna Carta's impact on the
development of English criminal adjudication. One cannot begin to grasp its contemporary significance either from the (arcane) wording of the document itself or
even from detailed historical knowledge of its political origins or formal juridical

[85] A thought attributed to Emmanuel Lévinas by Z Bauman, *Postmodern Ethics* (Oxford, Blackwell,
1993) 73–75, who elucidates: 'Confronting the Other not as a person (*persona*: the mask worn to signify
the role played . . .), but as the *face*, is already the act of transcendence . . . Responsibility conjures up the
Face I face, but it also creates me as moral self . . . the only foundation morality can have.'

status.[86] Invocations of 'Magna Carta' today operate as legal-cultural shorthand for a richly-articulated common law narrative. This ramified juridical tradition encodes a set of institutional values that are grasped by insiders at a pre-theoretical, semi-conscious, partly affective level which often seems to pre-empt any need for further (self-) explanation, let alone elaborated normative rationalisations. The institutional work performed by such legal-cultural signifiers might be character-ised as chiefly 'symbolic' or the deployment of 'legal fictions', though neither term really does justice to the complexity, subtlety or importance of their contribution to the practical administration of criminal justice. Their significance is all the greater because the circulation of legal-cultural signifiers is not confined within profes-sional legal circles. Many of these cultural narratives also exert powerful holds on the popular imagination, and thereby come to play a pivotal role in maintaining social trust and popular respect for law, which are in turn vital sociological ingredi-ents in the practical efficacy of law and law enforcement and the sheet anchor of their normative legitimacy.

Magna Carta is anything but a garden variety piece of English legal history: but the methodological lesson is, I suggest, broadly generalisable. English criminal pro-cedure law encompasses a host of these legal-cultural signifiers, and some of them have been enormously influential in generating and sustaining our procedural tra-ditions. Elaborated 'thick description' of criminal adjudication cannot be attempted here. However, the significance of observing a defendant's face during a criminal trial is likely to be informed by some or all of the following 10 institutional variables (over and above the broader considerations of political morality that have already been discussed):

(i)   local conceptions of 'public trial' and its implications for public 'accessibility' (of various kinds) to the accused's person, image and identity;
(ii)   the extent to which[87] demeanour in general, and facial expression in particu-lar, is regarded as indicative of reliability and/or veracity, both by legal profes-sionals and by the community at large;
(iii) the extent to which oral evidence at trial is regarded as a primary evidential source, or merely as an incidental supplement to documentary proofs of one kind or another;

---

[86] Also see Lord Irvine of Lairg, 'The Spirit of Magna Carta Continues to Resonate in Modern Law' (2003) 119 *Law Quarterly Review* 227. Strictly speaking, most provisions of Magna Carta have been repealed: see *City of London Corporation v Samede* [2012] EWCA Civ 160, [30]. It is nonetheless regularly invoked in legal judgments as a source of fundamental legal principle, traditional institutional values and judicial cultural authority. Recently, see eg *R (Lumba) v Home Secretary* [2012] 1 AC 245, [2011] UKSC 12, [219] (Lord Collins JSC, quoting 'no free man shall be seized, or imprisoned . . . except . . . by the law of the land'); *R (AA) v Home Secretary* [2012] EWCA Civ 1383, [21] ('The importance attributed to personal freedom can be traced back at least to *Magna Carta*'); *R (McAuley) v Crown Court at Coventry* [2012] 1 WLR 2766, [2012] EWHC 860 (Admin), [25] ('a principle of the common law as old as Magna Carta that justice delayed is justice denied'); *Frank Cook v Telegraph Media Group* [2011] EWHC 763 (QB), [98] (quoting Blackstone's invocation of Magna Carta as the basis for jury trial).
[87] Here and following, 'if at all' should be taken as read.

(iv) the extent to which the accused is regarded as an eligible (and important) source of relevant evidential information, and the terms on which the accused is permitted – or required[88] – to furnish information, in the form of sworn testimony or otherwise, at trial;

(v) the extent to which the accused's reactions and demeanour throughout the trial process are regarded as a legitimate (and important) source of evidential information to which fact-finders should have access (in most cases);

(vi) the extent to which effective cross-examination may be hampered if the accused's face cannot be seen, coupled with prevailing institutional understandings of the significance of cross-examination in a criminal trial;

(vii) the relationship of party cross-examination to other institutional means of verifying or testing evidential information in criminal trial proceedings, which in turn is partly a function of;

(viii) the extent to which a trial, or criminal prosecutions viewed in their entirety, are 'adversarial' rather than 'inquisitorial';

(ix) the composition of the fact-finder – individual or collegiate? lay, professional or mixed panel? – coupled with prevailing institutional beliefs about the chosen fact-finder's abilities, and limitations, in accessing or processing particular kinds of evidential information; and

(x) local conceptions of procedural fairness, and the relationship between procedural fairness and accurate fact-finding in comprehensive normative (more or less fully jurisprudentially articulated and legally institutionalised) conceptions of legitimate criminal adjudication.

This roster of considerations bearing on the institutional significance of 'face' in criminal trials may not be exhaustive. In fact, it would probably prove impossible to produce any definitive list of such factors for many prominent features of legal institutional practices precisely because choices about what to include on the list, as well as their classification and relative priority, themselves reflect distinctive aspects of procedural tradition on which modern legal systems diverge, sometimes radically, and not merely in incidental matters of local colour and custom such as judicial costume or architectural preferences in courthouse decoration. I hope, nonetheless, to have said enough to vindicate the methodological conclusion that urgent and highly consequential choices in the design and operation of criminal trial proceedings cannot be settled merely by appealing to 'liberal political morality'. This does not imply any failure of liberal theorising on its own terms. Whilst liberal states should certainly strive to ensure that key public institutions such as criminal adjudication function in a manner consistent with fundamental liberal

---

[88] Of course, the accused is not literally compelled to testify in modern legal proceedings. However, even legal systems which proclaim full adherence to the privilege against self-incrimination may place considerable social and moral pressure on the accused to speak (as continental legal systems are said to do), or alternatively treat silence as a partial admission by conduct in some situations (as English law does, pursuant to the Criminal Justice and Public Order Act 1994, ss 34–38). See AL-T Choo, *The Privilege Against Self-Incrimination and Criminal Justice* (Oxford, Hart Publishing, 2013); Roberts and Zuckerman, *Criminal Evidence*, ch 13.

principles, aspects of criminal law's institutional architecture and practical implementation can be fully understood, and some difficult operational questions satisfactorily answered, only in the light of detailed knowledge of local procedural history and its contemporary reception and status in modern legal cultures. Liberal states might well give different answers to important procedural questions without necessarily jeopardising their liberal credentials, and for reasons that liberal political morality, unsupplemented, cannot supply or arbitrate.

V. From Liberal Criminal Law Theory to Cosmopolitan Criminal Jurisprudence

This chapter set out to encourage more sustained reflection and provoke further debate on the liberal presuppositions of contemporary Anglo-American Criminal Law Theory. Liberal theorists, prominently including Andreas von Hirsch, have conceptualised and elucidated criminal law doctrine in ways which, avowedly or implicitly, closely cohere with liberal political morality. Section III of this chapter endeavoured to show how great swathes of contemporary Anglo-American criminal law (including legislative principles of criminalisation, taxonomies of criminal offences and defences, principles of attribution, and theories of culpability) might be reconstructed as institutional derivations of a plausible conception of liberal political morality, such as the miniaturised bonsai model of liberalism presented in section II. But coherence is not isomorphic with normative justification. Section IV went on to suggest that liberal political theory does not explain or justify as much of modern criminal law as might commonly be supposed. Two kinds of methodological limitation were identified: *incompleteness*, where liberal theorising does not reach foundational questions of (for example) agency, criminal wrongdoing or retributive justice; and *indeterminacy*, where intensely practical issues, such as whether female Muslim defendants should be permitted to appear veiled in court, are addressed but ultimately left unresolved by appeals to liberal political morality. When they find themselves in these uncharted or dimly-lit theoretical waters, criminal law theorists – and criminal justice policy-makers and practitioners as well – must seek further and better illumination from normative supplements to liberal political theory.

Liberals, I have been at pains to stress, should not be demoralised by this argument's deflationary implications for liberal political theory. The need for liberal criminal law theorists to draw on non-liberal intellectual resources hardly commits them to *illiberal* laws, policies or practices. Nor is liberal theory neutered as a source of critical commentary on contemporary criminal justice policy, especially when senior officials and policy-makers often betray an uneven commitment to (or tenuous grasp of) liberal traditions in criminal law.

The implications of the argument for non-liberals seem especially significant, however, since the condition of legality in our time is increasingly cosmopolitan.

Modern law is simultaneously international, supra-national and transnational, as well as regional, domestic and local: it travels around the globe and pings across the internet, freely crossing national borders and bestriding traditional jurisdictional boundaries;[89] it is moulded into novel juridical institutions, normative configurations, regimes of governance and styles of regulation. Cosmopolitan law is a creature of multi-layered comparative jurisprudence and many-sided transnational judicial conversations.[90] Its penal dimensions have been fostered by a phalanx of interlocking institutional innovations, notably including the post-1945 framework of international human rights (prominently featuring the right to a fair trial), the burgeoning field of International Criminal Law, an emergent EU criminal law and policy, and the historic creation of a permanent International Criminal Court.[91] Although law has always to some extent crossed jurisdictional boundaries and produced institutional hybrids, contemporary cosmopolitan criminal jurisprudence is distinguished by the frequency, pace, intensity, complexity and global reach of its activities, ambitions and effects. Mirroring the broader processes of globalisation of which it forms an integral part, the novelty of legal cosmopolitanism lies in our distinctively twenty-first-century experiences of it.

To characterise a law or policy as 'liberal' is not necessarily to recommend it to the global constituency of state and non-state actors today engaged in the co-construction of cosmopolitan criminal jurisprudence. Whilst liberals are primed to find liberal criminal laws and policies congenial, there are many other significant elements within the international community, including numerous non-democratic and some theocratic polities, for whom liberalism is associated (fairly or not) with western bias and aggression, capitalist greed, social injustice, neo-colonialism, racism, militant Christianity, Islamophobia or moral degeneracy. Liberal criminal law would be a 'hard sell' to these hardboiled sceptics, some of whom (the BRICs, Turkey, Egypt, Israel, Pakistan, Nigeria, Indonesia, Iran, the Arab League ...) are, or could be, important strategic partners in the cosmopolitan development of criminal law. Of course, merely trying to conceal or sugar-coat the liberal foundations of criminal law as an exercise in salesmanship or propaganda would be self-defeating from a normative point of view (even on the unlikely supposition that sceptical audiences could actually be fooled). If the argument advanced in this chapter is broadly correct, however, there is no need for bad faith or self-deception. The criminal laws endorsed by liberals are not necessarily *liberal criminal laws*, in the sense of finding their direct or exclusive normative grounding in liberal political

---

[89] N Boister, *An Introduction to Transnational Criminal Law* (Oxford, Oxford University Press, 2012); W Twining, *Globalisation and Legal Scholarship* (Nijmegen, Wolf Legal Publishers, 2011); A Halpin and V Roeben (eds), *Theorising the Global Legal Order* (Oxford, Hart Publishing, 2009).

[90] A-M Slaughter, 'A Global Community of Courts' (2003) 44 *Harvard International Law Journal* 191; C McCrudden, 'A Common Law of Human Rights? Transnational Judicial Conversations on Constitutional Rights' (2000) 20 *Oxford Journal of Legal Studies* 499; P Roberts, 'Normative Evolution in Evidentiary Exclusion: Coercion, Deception and the Right to a Fair Trial' in P Roberts and J Hunter (eds), *Criminal Evidence and Human Rights* (Oxford, Hart Publishing, 2012).

[91] A Cassese, P Gaeta et al, *Cassese's International Criminal Law*, 3rd edn (Oxford, Oxford University Press, 2013); R Cryer, H Friman, D Robinson and E Wilmshurst, *An Introduction to International Criminal Law and Procedure*, 2nd edn (Cambridge, Cambridge University Press, 2010).

morality. Comprehensive justificatory theories of criminal law are obliged to fill in the gaps in (liberal, or any other) political theory by drawing on supplementary normative resources and incorporating significant features of local institutional architecture, legal culture and procedural tradition.

The benefits of reorganising ideas and correctly classifying arguments are not merely theoretical. There are also instrumental payoffs. Clarifying the philosophical pedigree of penal law and practice might spur the development of a robust and ethically substantial[92] overlapping consensus fixing the core requirements of cosmopolitan criminal law. It should also reinforce the normative and epistemological basis for recognising[93] criminal injustices wherever they occur in the world and whoever might be responsible. These are amongst the urgent tasks for an emerging cosmopolitan criminal jurisprudence whose rich intellectual resources assuredly encompass, but are not confined by, liberal criminal law theory.

---

[92] Ie substantively thicker moral agreement than the merely political (albeit principled) overlapping consensus envisaged by Rawls as applying to global justice generally: J Rawls, *The Law of Peoples*, rev edn (Cambridge MA, Harvard University Press, 2001); J Rawls, *Political Liberalism* (New York, Columbia University Press, 1993), Lecture IV. Whereas Rawls' account of global political justice is a *general* normative theory of international relations, ethically substantive overlapping consensus in criminal law could be particularistic, piecemeal and (partly) motivated by pragmatism.

[93] Recognition being a necessary precursor to criticism or remedial intervention. Whether in any given scenario the one should lead to either of the others is, of course, a complicated and contentious matter.

LIST OF PUBLICATIONS

Prof Dr Dr hc ANDREAS VON HIRSCH

Authored and co-authored books

(with AP Simester) *Crimes, Harms and Wrongs: On the Principles of Criminalisation* (Oxford, Hart Publishing, 2011).

(with Andrew Ashworth) *Proportionate Sentencing: Exploring the Principles* (Oxford, Oxford University Press, 2005).

Fairness, Verbrechen und Strafe: Strafrechtstheoretische Abhandlungen (Berlin, Berliner Wissenschaftsverlag, 2005) [a collection of previously published essays].

Proportionalitet och Strafbestämning (Uppsala, Iustus Förlag, 2001).

(with Anthony Bottoms, Elizabeth Burney and Per-Olof Wikström) *Criminal Deterrence and Sentencing Severity: An Analysis of Recent Research* (Oxford, Hart Publishing, 1999).

Censure and Sanctions (Oxford, Oxford University Press, 1993).

(with Nils Jareborg) *Strafmaß und Strafgerechtigkeit: Die deutsche Strafzumessungslehre und das Prinzip der Tatproportionalität* (Bonn, Forum Verlag, 1991).

(with Kay Knapp and Michael Tonry) *The Sentencing Commission and its Guidelines* (Boston MA, Northeastern University Press, 1987).

Past or Future Crimes: Deservedness and Dangerousness in the Sentencing of Criminals (New Brunswick NJ, Rutgers University Press, 1985; Manchester, Manchester University Press, 1986).

(with Kathleen Hahrahan) *The Question of Parole: Retention, Reform, or Abolition?* (Cambridge MA, Ballinger Publishing, 1979).

Doing Justice: The Choice of Punishments (New York, Hill and Wang, 1976; reprinted edn, Boston MA, Northeastern University Press, 1986).

Edited books

(with Ulfrid Neumann and Kurt Seelmann) *Solidarität im Strafrecht: Zur Funktion und Legitimation strafrechtlicher Solidaritätspflichten* (Baden-Baden, Nomos, 2013).

(with Ulfrid Neumann and Kurt Seelmann) *Strafe – Warum? Gegenwärtige Strafbegründungen im Lichte von Hegels Straftheorie* (Baden-Baden, Nomos, 2011).

(with Julian Roberts) *Previous Convictions at Sentencing: Theoretical and Applied Perspectives* (Oxford, Hart Publishing, 2010).

(with Ulfrid Neumann and Kurt Seelmann) *Paternalismus im Strafrecht: Die Kriminalisierung von selbstschädigendem Verhalten* (Baden-Baden, Nomos, 2010).

(with AP Simester) *Incivilities: Regulating Offensive Behaviour* (Oxford, Hart Publishing, 2006).

(with Kurt Seelmann and Wolfgang Wohlers) *Mediating Principles: Begrenzungsprinzipien bei der Strafbegründung* (Baden-Baden, Nomos, 2006).

(with Roland Hefendehl and Wolfgang Wohlers) *Die Rechtsgutstheorie: Legitimationsbasis des Strafrechts oder dogmatisches Glasperlenspiel?* (Baden-Baden, Nomos, 2003).

(with Wolfgang Frisch and Hans-Jörg Albrecht) *Tatproportionalität: Normative und empirische Aspekte einer tatproportionalen Strafzumessung* (Heidelberg, CF Müller, 2003).

(with Julian Roberts, Anthony E Bottoms, et al) *Restorative Justice and Criminal Justice: Competing or Reconcilable Paradigms?* (Oxford, Hart Publishing, 2003).

(with David Garland and Alison Wakefield) *Ethical and Social Perspectives on Situational Crime Prevention* (Oxford, Hart Publishing, 2000).

(with Bernd Schünemann and Nils Jareborg) *Positive Generalprävention: Kritische Analysen im deutsch-englischen Dialog* (Heidelberg, CF Müller, 1998).

For student readers:

(with Andrew Ashworth and Julian Roberts) *Principled Sentencing: Readings in Theory and Policy,* 3rd edn (Oxford, Hart Publishing, 2009).

(with Hyman Gross) *Sentencing* (Oxford, Oxford University Press, 1981).

Book chapters (selection)

(with Vivian C Schorscher) 'Die Kriminalisierung der unterlassenen Hilfeleistung: Eine Frage von "Solidarität" oder Altruismus?' in A von Hirsch et al (eds), *Solidarität im Strafrecht: Zur Funktion und Legitimation strafrechtlicher Solidaritätspflichten* (Baden-Baden, Nomos, 2013) 77–92.

'Punishment Futures: The Desert-model Debate and the Importance of the Criminal Law Context' in Michael Tonry (ed), *Retributivism has a Past. Has it a Future?* (Oxford, Oxford University Press, 2012) 256–74.

(with Vivian C Schorscher) 'A System of International Criminal Justice for Human Rights Violations: What is the General Justification for its Existence?' in Lucia Zedner and Julian V Roberts (eds), *Principles and Values in Criminal Law and Criminal Justice: Essays in Honour of Andrew Ashworth* (Oxford, Oxford University Press, 2012) 209–22.

'Proportionality of Sentence and the Role of Previous Convictions' in Lorenz Schulz et al (eds), *Festschrift für Imme Roxin* (Heidelberg, CF Müller, 2012) 149–63.

'Criminalizing Failure to Rescue: A Matter of "Solidarity" or Altruism?' in Rowan Cruft, Matthew H Kramer and Mark R Reiff (eds), *Crime, Punishment, and Responsibility: The Jurisprudence of Antony Duff* (Oxford, Oxford University Press, 2011) 241–53.

'Warum soll die Strafsanktion existieren? Tadel und Prävention als Elemente einer Rechtfertigung' in Andreas von Hirsch et al (eds), *Strafe – Warum? Gegenwärtige Strafbegründungen im Lichte von Hegels Straftheorie* (Baden-Baden, Nomos, 2011) 43–68.

'Proportionality and the Progressive Loss of Mitigation: Some Further Reflections' in Andreas von Hirsch and Julian V Roberts (eds), *Previous Convictions at Sentencing: Theoretical and Applied Perspectives* (Oxford, Hart Publishing, 2010) 1–16.

(with AE Bottoms) 'The Crime-Preventive Impact of Penal Sanctions' in P Cane and HM Kritzer (eds), *The Oxford Handbook of Empirical Legal Studies* (Oxford, Oxford University Press, 2010) 96–124.

'Ein grundrechtliches Verbot exzessiver Strafen? Versuch einer Begründung' in Felix Herzog and Ulfrid Neumann (eds), *Festschrift für Winfried Hassemer* (Heidelberg, CF Müller, 2010) 373–82.

(with Ulfrid Neumann) ' "Indirekter" Paternalismus im Strafrecht am Beispiel der Tötung auf Verlangen (§ 216 StGB)' in Andreas von Hirsch et al (eds), *Paternalismus im Strafrecht:*

Die Kriminalisierung von selbstschädigendem Verhalten (Baden-Baden, Nomos, 2010) 71–98 [reprinted from (2007) 154 *Goltdammer's Archiv für Strafrecht* 671–94].

(with Ulfrid Neumann) 'Indirekter Paternalismus und § 216 StGB: Weitere Bemerkungen zur Bedeutung und Reichweite des Paternalismus-Begriffs' in Andreas von Hirsch et al (eds), *Paternalismus im Strafrecht: Die Kriminalisierung von selbstschädigendem Verhalten* (Baden-Baden, Nomos, 2010) 99–110.

(with Vivian C Schorscher) 'Nachwort: Indirekter Paternalismus und die normative Basis des Tötung-auf-Verlangen-Verbots' in Andreas von Hirsch et al (eds), *Paternalismus im Strafrecht: Die Kriminalisierung von selbstschädigendem Verhalten* (Baden-Baden, Nomos, 2010) 333–38.

'Harm und Offence: Schädigungsprinzip und Belästigungsprinzip als Kriterien für die Kriminalisierung von Verhalten' in Holm Putzke et al (eds), *Strafrecht zwischen System und Telos: Festschrift für Rolf Dietrich Herzberg zum siebzigsten Geburtstag am 14. Februar 2008* (Tübingen, Mohr Siebeck, 2008) 915–30.

'Should there be constitutional constraints against grossly disproportionate punishments?' in Thomas Elholm et al (eds), *Ikke kun straf: Festskrift til Vagn Greve* (Uppsala, Iustus Förlag, 2008) 211–19.

(with AP Simester) 'Penalising Offensive Behaviour: Constitutive and Mediating Principles' in Andrew von Hirsch and AP Simester (eds), *Incivilities: Regulating Offensive Behaviour* (Oxford, Hart Publishing, 2006) 115–31.

(with AP Simester) 'Regulating Offensive Conduct Through Two-Step Prohibitions' in Andrew von Hirsch and AP Simester (eds), *Incivilities: Regulating Offensive Behaviour* (Oxford, Hart Publishing, 2006) 173–94.

'Toleranz als Mediating Principle' in Andrew von Hirsch et al (eds), *Mediating Principles: Begrenzungsprinzipien bei der Strafbegründung* (Baden-Baden, Nomos, 2006) 97–108.

(with Petter Asp and Dan Frände) 'Grundsätzliche Überlegungen zum Prinzip der beiderseitigen Strafbarkeit' in Bernd Schünemann (ed), *Ein Gesamtkonzept für die europäische Strafrechtspflege* (Cologne, Carl Heymanns, 2006) 240–50 [partially reprinted from Asp/ von Hirsch/Frände, in [2006] *ZIS* 512–20].

'Direkter Paternalismus: Sollten Selbstschädigungen bestraft werden?' in M Anderheiden et al (eds), *Paternalismus und Recht* (Tübingen, Mohr Siebeck, 2006) 235–48. [Reprinted in Andreas von Hirsch et al (eds), *Paternalismus im Strafrecht: Die Kriminalisierung von selbstschädigendem Verhalten* (Baden-Baden, Nomos, 2010) 57–70].

'Belästigendes Verhalten: Gibt es ein strafrechtliches Belästigungsprinzip?' in Jörg Arnold et al (eds), *Menschengerechtes Strafrecht. Festschrift für Albin Eser zum 70. Geburtstag* (Munich, CH Beck, 2005) 189–205.

'Tatproportionalität und Sanktionshärte: Führt ein tatproportionalistisches Strafzumessungsmodell zu strengeren Sanktionen?' in Christian Grafl and Ursula Medigovic (eds), *Festschrift für Manfred Burgstaller zum 65. Geburtstag* (Vienna, NW Verlag, 2004) 59–74.

'Der Rechtsgutsbegriff und das "Harm Principle"' in Andrew von Hirsch et al (eds), *Die Rechtsgutstheorie: Legitimationsbasis des Strafrechts oder dogmatisches Glasperlenspiel?* (Baden-Baden, Nomos, 2003) 13–25 [reprinted from (2002) 149 *Goltdammer's Archiv für Strafrecht* 2–14].

(with Wolfgang Wohlers) 'Rechtsgutstheorie und Deliktsstruktur – zu den Kriterien fairer Zurechnung' in Andrew von Hirsch et al (eds), *Die Rechtsgutstheorie: Legitimationsbasis des Strafrechts oder dogmatisches Glasperlenspiel?* (Baden-Baden, Nomos, 2003) 196–214.

'Begründung und Bestimmung tatproportionaler Strafen' in Andrew von Hirsch et al (eds), *Tatproportionalität: Normative und empirische Aspekte einer tatproportionalen Strafzumessung* (Heidelberg, CF Müller Wissenschaft, 2003) 47–82.

(with Andrew Ashworth and Clifford Shearing) 'Specifying Aims and Limits for Restorative Justice: A "Making Amends" Model?' in Andrew von Hirsch et al (eds), *Restorative Justice and Criminal Justice: Competing or Reconcilable Paradigms?* (Oxford, Hart Publishing, 2003) 21–42.

'Punishment, Penance and the State: A Reply to Duff' in D Matravers and J Pike (eds), *Debates in Contemporary Political Philosophy: An Anthology* (London, Open University Press, 2002) 408–22.

'Proportionale Strafen für Jugendliche – Welche Unterschiede gibt es im Vergleich zu Strafen für Erwachsene?' in Bernd Schünemann et al (eds), *Festschrift für Claus Roxin zum 70. Geburtstag am 15. Mai 2001* (Berlin, De Gruyter, 2001) 1077–94.

'The Project of Sentencing Reform' in Michael Tonry and Richard Frase (eds), *Sentencing and Sanctions in Western Countries* (New York, Oxford University Press, 2001) 405–20.

(with Clifford Shearing) 'Exclusion from Public Space' in Andrew von Hirsch et al (eds), *Ethical and Social Perspectives on Situational Crime Prevention* (Oxford, Hart Publishing, 2000) 77–96.

'The Ethics of Public Television Surveillance' in Andrew von Hirsch et al (eds), *Ethical and Social Perspectives on Situational Crime Prevention* (Oxford, Hart Publishing, 2000) 59–76.

'Proportionate Punishment and Social Deprivation' in Petter Asp et al (eds), *Flores Juris et Legum: Festskrift till Nils Jareborg* (Uppsala, Iustus Förlag, 2000) 319–32.

'Punishment, penance and the state: a reply to Duff' in Matt Matravers (ed), *Punishment and Political Theory* (Oxford, Hart Publishing, 1999) 69–82.

'Tadel und Prävention: Die Übelszufügung als Element der Strafe' in Bernd Schünemann et al (eds), *Positive Generalprävention* (Heidelberg, CF Müller, 1998) 101–07.

(with Tatjana Hörnle) 'Positive Generalprävention und Tadel' in Bernd Schünemann et al (eds), *Positive Generalprävention* (Heidelberg, CF Müller, 1998) 83–100 [reprinted from (1995) 142 *Goltdammer's Archiv für Strafrecht* 261–82].

'Extending the Harm Principle: "Remote" Harms and Fair Imputation' in AP Simester and ATH Smith (eds), *Harm and Culpability* (Oxford, Clarendon Press, 1996) 259–76.

'Proportionality and parsimony in American sentencing guidelines: The Minnesota and Oregon standards' in CMV Clarkson and R Morgan (eds), *The Politics of Sentencing Reform* (Oxford, Oxford University Press 1995) 149–98.

(with Douglas Husak) 'Culpability and Mistake of Law' in Stephen Shute et al (eds), *Action and Value in the Criminal Law* (Oxford, Oxford University Press, 1993) 157–74.

(with Nils Jareborg) 'Provocation and Culpability' in Ferdinand Schoeman (ed), *Responsibility, Character, and the Emotions: New Essays in Moral Psychology* (Cambridge, Cambridge University Press, 1987) 241–55.

'Guidance by numbers or words? Numerical versus narrative guidelines for sentencing' in Ken Pease and Martin Wasik (eds), *Sentencing Reform: Guidance or Guidelines?* (Manchester, Manchester University Press, 1987) 46–69.

(with Nils Jareborg) '"Neoklassizismus" in der skandinavischen Kriminalpolitik: sein Einfluss, seine Grundprinzipen und Kriterien' in A Eser and K Cornils (eds), *Neuere Tendenzen der Kriminalpolitik: Beiträge zu einem deutsch-skandinavischen Strafrechtskolloquium* (Freiburg, Max-Planck-Institut Eigenverlag, 1987).

Articles in peer-reviewed journals (selection)

'Harm and wrongdoing in criminalisation theory' (2014) 8 *Criminal Law & Philosophy* 245–56.

(with AP Simester) 'Remote Harms and Non-Constitutive Crimes' (2009) 28 *Criminal Justice Ethics* 89–107.

'Direct Paternalism: Criminalizing Self-Injurious Conduct' (2008) 27 *Criminal Justice Ethics* 25–33.

'Direct Paternalism: Punishing the Perpetrators of Self-Harm' (2008) 5 *Intellectum* 7–25.

(with Ulfrid Neumann) '"Indirekter" Paternalismus im Strafrecht – am Beispiel der Tötung auf Verlangen (§ 216 StGB)' (2007) 154 *Goltdammer's Archiv für Strafrecht* 671–94.

(with Petter Asp and Dan Frände) 'Double Criminality and Transnational Investigative Measures in EU Criminal Proceedings: Some Issues of Principle' [2006] *Zeitschrift für Internationale Strafrechtsdogmatik* 512–20.

(with Julian V Roberts) 'Legislating Sentencing Principles: The Provisions of the Criminal Justice Act 2003 relating to Sentencing Purposes and the Role of Prior Convictions' [2004] *Criminal Law Review* 639–52.

'Record-enhanced Sentencing in England and Wales' (2002) 4 *Punishment and Society* 443–57.

'Der Rechtsgutsbegriff und das "Harm Principle"' (2002) 149 *Goltdammer's Archiv für Strafrecht* 2–14.

(with AP Simester) 'Rethinking the Offense Principle' (2002) 8 *Legal Theory* 269–95.

'Proportionate Sentencing for Juveniles: How Different than for Adults?' (2001) 3 *Punishment and Society* 221–36.

'The Offence Principle in Criminal Law: Affront to Sensibility or Wrongdoing?' (2000) 11 *King's College Law Journal* 78–89.

'Offensive Conduct in Criminal Law' (2000) 83 *Kritische Vierteljahresschrift für Gesetzgebung und Rechtswissenschaft* 65–80.

(with Sue Rex) 'Community Orders and the Assessment of Punishment Severity' (1998) 10 *Federal Sentencing Reporter* 278–82.

(with Antony Duff) 'Responsibility, Retribution and the Voluntary: A Response to Williams' (1997) 56 *Cambridge Law Journal* 103–13.

(with Martin Wasik) 'Civil Disqualifications Attending Conviction: A Suggested Conceptual Framework' (1997) 56 *Cambridge Law Journal* 599–626.

(with Andrew Ashworth) 'Recognising Elephants: The Problem of the Custody Threshold' [1997] *Criminal Law Review* 187–200.

(with Uma Narayan) 'Three Conceptions of Provocation' (1996) 15 *Criminal Justice Ethics* 15–24.

(with Tatjana Hörnle) 'Positive Generalprävention und Tadel' (1995) 142 *Goltdammer's Archiv für Strafrecht* 261–82.

(with Julian V Roberts) 'Statutory Sentencing Reform: The Purpose and Principles of Sentencing' (1995) 37 *Criminal Law Quarterly* 220–42.

'Sentencing Guidelines and Penal Aims in Minnesota' (1994) 13 *Criminal Justice Ethics* 39–49.

(with Judith Greene) 'When Should Reformers Support Creation of Sentencing Guidelines?' (1993) 28 *Wake Forest Law Review* 329–44.

(with Andrew Ashworth) 'Desert and the Three Rs' (1993) 5 *Current Issues in Criminal Justice* 9–12.

'Proportionality in the Philosophy of Punishment' (1992) 16 *Crime and Justice: A Review of Research* 55–98.

(with Lisa Maher) 'Should Penal Rehabilitationism Be Revived?' (1992) 11 *Criminal Justice Ethics* 25–30.

(with Andrew Ashworth) 'Not Not Just Deserts: A Response to Braithwaite and Pettit' (1992) 12 *Oxford Journal of Legal Studies* 83–98.

(with Julian V Roberts) 'Sentencing Reform in Canada: Recent Developments' (1992) 23 *Revue Generale de Droit* 319–56.

(with Nils Jareborg) 'Gauging criminal harm: A living standard analysis' (1991) 11 *Oxford Journal of Legal Studies* 1–38.

'Criminal Record Rides Again' (1991) 10 *Criminal Justice Ethics* 2–56.

'The Politics of Just Deserts' (1990) 32 *Canadian Journal of Criminology* 397–414.

'Why Have Proportionate Sentences? A Reply to Professor Gabor' (1990) 32 *Canadian Journal of Criminology* 547–50.

'Proportionality in the Philosophy of Punishment: From "Why Punish" to "How Much?"' (1990) 1 *Criminal Law Forum* 259–90. [Also published in (1991) 25 *Israel Law Review* 549–80.]

'Federal Sentencing Guidelines: Do They Provide Principled Guidance?' (1989) 27 *American Criminal Law Review* 367–90.

(with Martin Wasik and Judith Greene) 'Punishments in the Community and the Principles of Desert' (1989) 20 *Rutgers Law Journal* 595–618.

'Selective Incapacitation Re-examined: The National Academy of Sciences' Report on Criminal Careers and Career Criminals' (1988) 7 *Criminal Justice Ethics* 19–34.

(with Martin Wasik) 'Non-custodial Penalties and the Principles of Desert' [1988] *Criminal Law Review* 555–72.

'Principles for Choosing Sanctions: Sweden's Proposed Sentencing Statute' (1987) 13 *New England Journal on Criminal and Civil Confinement* 171–96.

'Equality, "Anisonomy", and Justice: A Review of *Madness and the Criminal Law*' (1984) 82 *Michigan Law Review* 1093–112.

(with Julia M Mueller) 'California's Determinate Sentencing Law: An Analysis of its Structure' (1984) 10 *New England Journal on Criminal and Civil Confinement* 253–300.

'Commensurability and Crime Prevention: Evaluating Formal Sentencing Structures and Their Rationale' (1983) 74 *Journal of Criminal Law and Criminology* 209–48.

'"Neoclassicism", Proportionality, and the Rationale for Punishment: Thoughts on the Scandinavian Debate' (1983) 29 *Crime and Delinquency* 52–70.

'Recent Trends in American Criminal Sentencing Theory' (1983) 42 *Maryland Law Review* 6–36.

(with Don F Gottfredson) 'Selective Incapacitation: Some Queries about Research Design and Equity' (1983–84) 12 *New York University Review of Law and Social Change* 11–52.

'Constructing Guidelines for Sentencing the Critical Choices for the Minnesota Sentencing Guidelines Commission' (1982) 5 *Hamline Law Review* 164–216.

'Desert and White-Collar Criminality: A Response to Dr Braithwaite' (1982) 73 *Journal of Criminal Law and Criminology* 1164–75.

'Utilitarian Sentencing Resuscitated: The American Bar Association's Second Report on Criminal Sentencing' (1981) 33 *Rutgers Law Review* 772–89.

'Desert and Previous Convictions in Sentencing' (1981) 65 *Minnesota Law Review* 591–634.

'Prediction of Criminal Conduct and Preventive Confinement of Convicted Persons' (1972) 21 *Buffalo Law Review* 717–58.

INDEX